T0137825

# Lecture Notes in Computer Science 12792

More information about this subseries at http://www.springer.com/series/7409

Robert A. Sottilare · Jessica Schwarz (Eds.)

# Adaptive Instructional Systems

## Design and Evaluation

Third International Conference, AIS 2021
Held as Part of the 23rd HCI International Conference, HCII 2021
Virtual Event, July 24–29, 2021
Proceedings, Part I

 Springer

*Editors*
Robert A. Sottilare
Soar Technology, Inc.
Orlando, FL, USA

Jessica Schwarz
Fraunhofer FKIE
Wachtberg, Germany

ISSN 0302-9743 ISSN 1611-3349 (electronic)
Lecture Notes in Computer Science
ISBN 978-3-030-77856-9 ISBN 978-3-030-77857-6 (eBook)
https://doi.org/10.1007/978-3-030-77857-6

LNCS Sublibrary: SL3 – Information Systems and Applications, incl. Internet/Web, and HCI

This Springer imprint is published by the registered company Springer Nature Switzerland AG
The registered company address is: Gewerbestrasse 11, 6330 Cham, Switzerland

# Foreword

Human-Computer Interaction (HCI) is acquiring an ever-increasing scientific and industrial importance, and having more impact on people's everyday life, as an ever-growing number of human activities are progressively moving from the physical to the digital world. This process, which has been ongoing for some time now, has been dramatically accelerated by the COVID-19 pandemic. The HCI International (HCII) conference series, held yearly, aims to respond to the compelling need to advance the exchange of knowledge and research and development efforts on the human aspects of design and use of computing systems.

The 23rd International Conference on Human-Computer Interaction, HCI International 2021 (HCII 2021), was planned to be held at the Washington Hilton Hotel, Washington DC, USA, during July 24–29, 2021. Due to the COVID-19 pandemic and with everyone's health and safety in mind, HCII 2021 was organized and run as a virtual conference. It incorporated the 21 thematic areas and affiliated conferences listed on the following page.

A total of 5222 individuals from academia, research institutes, industry, and governmental agencies from 81 countries submitted contributions, and 1276 papers and 241 posters were included in the proceedings to appear just before the start of the conference. The contributions thoroughly cover the entire field of HCI, addressing major advances in knowledge and effective use of computers in a variety of application areas. These papers provide academics, researchers, engineers, scientists, practitioners, and students with state-of-the-art information on the most recent advances in HCI. The volumes constituting the set of proceedings to appear before the start of the conference are listed in the following pages.

The HCI International (HCII) conference also offers the option of 'Late Breaking Work' which applies both for papers and posters, and the corresponding volume(s) of the proceedings will appear after the conference. Full papers will be included in the 'HCII 2021 - Late Breaking Papers' volumes of the proceedings to be published in the Springer LNCS series, while 'Poster Extended Abstracts' will be included as short research papers in the 'HCII 2021 - Late Breaking Posters' volumes to be published in the Springer CCIS series.

The present volume contains papers submitted and presented in the context of the 3rd International Conference on Adaptive Instructional Systems (AIS 2021) affiliated conference to HCII 2021. I would like to thank the Co-chairs, Robert A. Sottilare and Jessica Schwarz, for their invaluable contribution in its organization and the preparation of the Proceedings, as well as the members of the program board for their contributions and support. This year, the AIS affiliated conference has focused on topics related to conceptual models and instructional approaches, design, development and evaluation of AIS systems, learner modelling and state assessment, as well as adaptation strategies and methods.

I would also like to thank the Program Board Chairs and the members of the Program Boards of all thematic areas and affiliated conferences for their contribution towards the highest scientific quality and overall success of the HCI International 2021 conference.

This conference would not have been possible without the continuous and unwavering support and advice of Gavriel Salvendy, founder, General Chair Emeritus, and Scientific Advisor. For his outstanding efforts, I would like to express my appreciation to Abbas Moallem, Communications Chair and Editor of HCI International News.

July 2021                                    Constantine Stephanidis

# HCI International 2021 Thematic Areas and Affiliated Conferences

**Thematic Areas**

- HCI: Human-Computer Interaction
- HIMI: Human Interface and the Management of Information

**Affiliated Conferences**

- EPCE: 18th International Conference on Engineering Psychology and Cognitive Ergonomics
- UAHCI: 15th International Conference on Universal Access in Human-Computer Interaction
- VAMR: 13th International Conference on Virtual, Augmented and Mixed Reality
- CCD: 13th International Conference on Cross-Cultural Design
- SCSM: 13th International Conference on Social Computing and Social Media
- AC: 15th International Conference on Augmented Cognition
- DHM: 12th International Conference on Digital Human Modeling and Applications in Health, Safety, Ergonomics and Risk Management
- DUXU: 10th International Conference on Design, User Experience, and Usability
- DAPI: 9th International Conference on Distributed, Ambient and Pervasive Interactions
- HCIBGO: 8th International Conference on HCI in Business, Government and Organizations
- LCT: 8th International Conference on Learning and Collaboration Technologies
- ITAP: 7th International Conference on Human Aspects of IT for the Aged Population
- HCI-CPT: 3rd International Conference on HCI for Cybersecurity, Privacy and Trust
- HCI-Games: 3rd International Conference on HCI in Games
- MobiTAS: 3rd International Conference on HCI in Mobility, Transport and Automotive Systems
- AIS: 3rd International Conference on Adaptive Instructional Systems
- C&C: 9th International Conference on Culture and Computing
- MOBILE: 2nd International Conference on Design, Operation and Evaluation of Mobile Communications
- AI-HCI: 2nd International Conference on Artificial Intelligence in HCI

# List of Conference Proceedings Volumes Appearing Before the Conference

1. LNCS 12762, Human-Computer Interaction: Theory, Methods and Tools (Part I), edited by Masaaki Kurosu
2. LNCS 12763, Human-Computer Interaction: Interaction Techniques and Novel Applications (Part II), edited by Masaaki Kurosu
3. LNCS 12764, Human-Computer Interaction: Design and User Experience Case Studies (Part III), edited by Masaaki Kurosu
4. LNCS 12765, Human Interface and the Management of Information: Information Presentation and Visualization (Part I), edited by Sakae Yamamoto and Hirohiko Mori
5. LNCS 12766, Human Interface and the Management of Information: Information-rich and Intelligent Environments (Part II), edited by Sakae Yamamoto and Hirohiko Mori
6. LNAI 12767, Engineering Psychology and Cognitive Ergonomics, edited by Don Harris and Wen-Chin Li
7. LNCS 12768, Universal Access in Human-Computer Interaction: Design Methods and User Experience (Part I), edited by Margherita Antona and Constantine Stephanidis
8. LNCS 12769, Universal Access in Human-Computer Interaction: Access to Media, Learning and Assistive Environments (Part II), edited by Margherita Antona and Constantine Stephanidis
9. LNCS 12770, Virtual, Augmented and Mixed Reality, edited by Jessie Y. C. Chen and Gino Fragomeni
10. LNCS 12771, Cross-Cultural Design: Experience and Product Design Across Cultures (Part I), edited by P. L. Patrick Rau
11. LNCS 12772, Cross-Cultural Design: Applications in Arts, Learning, Well-being, and Social Development (Part II), edited by P. L. Patrick Rau
12. LNCS 12773, Cross-Cultural Design: Applications in Cultural Heritage, Tourism, Autonomous Vehicles, and Intelligent Agents (Part III), edited by P. L. Patrick Rau
13. LNCS 12774, Social Computing and Social Media: Experience Design and Social Network Analysis (Part I), edited by Gabriele Meiselwitz
14. LNCS 12775, Social Computing and Social Media: Applications in Marketing, Learning, and Health (Part II), edited by Gabriele Meiselwitz
15. LNAI 12776, Augmented Cognition, edited by Dylan D. Schmorrow and Cali M. Fidopiastis
16. LNCS 12777, Digital Human Modeling and Applications in Health, Safety, Ergonomics and Risk Management: Human Body, Motion and Behavior (Part I), edited by Vincent G. Duffy
17. LNCS 12778, Digital Human Modeling and Applications in Health, Safety, Ergonomics and Risk Management: AI, Product and Service (Part II), edited by Vincent G. Duffy

18. LNCS 12779, Design, User Experience, and Usability: UX Research and Design (Part I), edited by Marcelo Soares, Elizabeth Rosenzweig, and Aaron Marcus
19. LNCS 12780, Design, User Experience, and Usability: Design for Diversity, Well-being, and Social Development (Part II), edited by Marcelo M. Soares, Elizabeth Rosenzweig, and Aaron Marcus
20. LNCS 12781, Design, User Experience, and Usability: Design for Contemporary Technological Environments (Part III), edited by Marcelo M. Soares, Elizabeth Rosenzweig, and Aaron Marcus
21. LNCS 12782, Distributed, Ambient and Pervasive Interactions, edited by Norbert Streitz and Shin'ichi Konomi
22. LNCS 12783, HCI in Business, Government and Organizations, edited by Fiona Fui-Hoon Nah and Keng Siau
23. LNCS 12784, Learning and Collaboration Technologies: New Challenges and Learning Experiences (Part I), edited by Panayiotis Zaphiris and Andri Ioannou
24. LNCS 12785, Learning and Collaboration Technologies: Games and Virtual Environments for Learning (Part II), edited by Panayiotis Zaphiris and Andri Ioannou
25. LNCS 12786, Human Aspects of IT for the Aged Population: Technology Design and Acceptance (Part I), edited by Qin Gao and Jia Zhou
26. LNCS 12787, Human Aspects of IT for the Aged Population: Supporting Everyday Life Activities (Part II), edited by Qin Gao and Jia Zhou
27. LNCS 12788, HCI for Cybersecurity, Privacy and Trust, edited by Abbas Moallem
28. LNCS 12789, HCI in Games: Experience Design and Game Mechanics (Part I), edited by Xiaowen Fang
29. LNCS 12790, HCI in Games: Serious and Immersive Games (Part II), edited by Xiaowen Fang
30. LNCS 12791, HCI in Mobility, Transport and Automotive Systems, edited by Heidi Krömker
31. LNCS 12792, Adaptive Instructional Systems: Design and Evaluation (Part I), edited by Robert A. Sottilare and Jessica Schwarz
32. LNCS 12793, Adaptive Instructional Systems: Adaptation Strategies and Methods (Part II), edited by Robert A. Sottilare and Jessica Schwarz
33. LNCS 12794, Culture and Computing: Interactive Cultural Heritage and Arts (Part I), edited by Matthias Rauterberg
34. LNCS 12795, Culture and Computing: Design Thinking and Cultural Computing (Part II), edited by Matthias Rauterberg
35. LNCS 12796, Design, Operation and Evaluation of Mobile Communications, edited by Gavriel Salvendy and June Wei
36. LNAI 12797, Artificial Intelligence in HCI, edited by Helmut Degen and Stavroula Ntoa
37. CCIS 1419, HCI International 2021 Posters - Part I, edited by Constantine Stephanidis, Margherita Antona, and Stavroula Ntoa

38. CCIS 1420, HCI International 2021 Posters - Part II, edited by Constantine Stephanidis, Margherita Antona, and Stavroula Ntoa
39. CCIS 1421, HCI International 2021 Posters - Part III, edited by Constantine Stephanidis, Margherita Antona, and Stavroula Ntoa

**http://2021.hci.international/proceedings**

# 3rd International Conference on Adaptive Instructional Systems (AIS 2021)

Program Board Chairs: **Robert A. Sottilare**, *Soar Technology, Inc., USA*, **and Jessica Schwarz**, *Fraunhofer FKIE, Germany*

- Roger Azevedo, USA
- Brenda Bannan, USA
- Avron Barr, USA
- Michelle D. Barrett, USA
- Benjamin Bell, USA
- Shelly Blake-Plock, USA
- Barbara Buck, USA
- Jody Cockroft, USA
- Jeanine Defalco, USA
- Jim Goodell, USA
- Ani Grubisic, Croatia
- Andrew Hampton, USA
- Xiangen Hu, USA
- Cheryl Johnson, USA
- Benny Johnson, USA
- Mercedes T. Rodrigo, Philippines
- Vasile Rus, USA
- Jordan Richard Schoenherr, Canada
- K. P. Thai, USA
- Richard Tong, USA
- Rachel Van Campenhout, USA
- Joost Van Oijen, Netherlands
- Elizabeth Veinott, USA
- Elizabeth Whitaker, USA
- Thomas E. F. Witte, Germany

The full list with the Program Board Chairs and the members of the Program Boards of all thematic areas and affiliated conferences is available online at:

**http://www.hci.international/board-members-2021.php**

# HCI International 2022

The 24th International Conference on Human-Computer Interaction, HCI International 2022, will be held jointly with the affiliated conferences at the Gothia Towers Hotel and Swedish Exhibition & Congress Centre, Gothenburg, Sweden, June 26 – July 1, 2022. It will cover a broad spectrum of themes related to Human-Computer Interaction, including theoretical issues, methods, tools, processes, and case studies in HCI design, as well as novel interaction techniques, interfaces, and applications. The proceedings will be published by Springer. More information will be available on the conference website: http://2022.hci.international/:

General Chair
Prof. Constantine Stephanidis
University of Crete and ICS-FORTH
Heraklion, Crete, Greece
Email: general_chair@hcii2022.org

**http://2022.hci.international/**

# Contents – Part I

## Evaluation of AIS

## Adaptation Strategies and Methods in AIS

# Contents – Part II

# Conceptual Models and Instructional Approaches for AIS

# A Conceptual Model for Hybrid Adaptive Instructional and Assessment Systems

Michelle D. Barrett$^{(\boxtimes)}$ 📵

Edmentum, Bloomington, MN 55437, USA
michelle.barrett@edmentum.com
https://www.edmentum.com

**Abstract.** Adaptive instructional systems (AIS) hold great promise for increasing the effectiveness and efficiency of educational systems due to their ability to tailor instruction to the specific needs of learners. In addition, because AIS necessarily elicit evidence of learning from students to drive adaptive decisions, there has long been interest in mining data from these systems for broader assessment purposes such as program evaluation and policy making. Recently, this desire was accelerated by the novel Coronavirus pandemic. It became difficult and in some cases impossible to bring groups of students together to take standardized assessments capable of providing comparable data points suitable for aggregation at district and state levels. Simultaneously, online AIS became a part of daily instruction for many students. This paper examines theories of change that have been proposed for AIS and theories of change commonly associated with assessment and accountability in K-12 education in the United States. It then proposes a conceptual model for hybrid adaptive instructional and assessment systems (AIAS) with the unique contribution of explicitly representing the role of the AIS within the broader assessment eco-system. Finally, the paper reflects on research that will be necessary to realize the benefits of the hybrid AIAS.

**Keywords:** Adaptive instructional system · Summative assessment · Interim assessment · Formative assessment · Elementary education · Secondary education

## 1 Introduction

Adaptive instructional systems (AIS) hold great promise for increasing the effectiveness and efficiency of educational systems due to their ability to tailor instruction to the specific needs of learners. In addition, because AIS necessarily elicit evidence of learning from students to drive adaptive decisions, there has long been interest in mining data from these systems for broader assessment purposes such as program evaluation and policy making. In a 2001 report from the National Research Council on the science and design of educational assessment, it was proposed that technology-based assessment embedded in instructional

© Springer Nature Switzerland AG 2021
R. A. Sottilare and J. Schwarz (Eds.): HCII 2021, LNCS 12792, pp. 3–13, 2021.
https://doi.org/10.1007/978-3-030-77857-6_1

settings would make it more feasible to build a coordinated and coherent assessment system [1]. Recently, this desire was accelerated by the novel Coronavirus pandemic. It became difficult and in some cases impossible to bring groups of students together to take standardized assessments capable of providing comparable data points suitable for aggregation at district and state levels. Simultaneously, online AIS became a part of daily instruction for many students. Yet, to date, the role of the AIS as a contributor to assessment systems has not been thoroughly explicated nor examined.

This paper examines theories of change that have been proposed for AIS and theories of change commonly associated with assessment and accountability in K-12 education in the United States. It then proposes a conceptual model for hybrid adaptive instructional and assessment systems with the unique contribution of explicitly representing the role of the AIS within the broader assessment ecosystem. Finally, the paper reflects on research that will be necessary to realize the benefits of the hybrid system.

## 2 Adaptive Instructional Systems

AIS are defined as

> ... artificially-intelligent, computer-based systems that guide learning experiences by tailoring instruction and recommendations based on the goals, needs, and preferences of each individual learner or team in the context of domain learning objectives [2].

According to the IEEE Learning and Training Standards Committee (LTSC) Adaptive Instructional Systems working group, there are four primary models which comprise the overall AIS conceptual model. These include a domain model, a learner model, an interface model, and an adaptive model. The domain model includes the knowledge model, learning objectives, content, feedback, question banks that will allow for input from the learner, and other information that is relevant to the subject or topical area for which the AIS is providing instruction. The learner model includes states and traits that describe attitudes, behaviors, and cognition of the learner. The interface model includes the technology that supports the learner's interaction with the other AIS components. Finally, the adaptive model assesses the states and traits of the learner in the context of the domain in order to select content, generate feedback, or generate tailored recommendations [3]. In K-12 education, the value proposition of the AIS is that by individualizing instruction using an approach similar to human tutoring, learners will experience substantial gains in learning outcomes on measures external to the AIS [4]. Well known studies of mastery learning and human tutoring by Bloom and his students [5–9] found effect sizes around 2.0 for these practices. More recent meta-analysis finds effect sizes just above 0.75 for both human tutoring and step-based AIS when compared to no tutoring [10]. The reader is referred to [11] for an overview of the literature resulting in the theory of change for such a system as shown in Fig. 1.

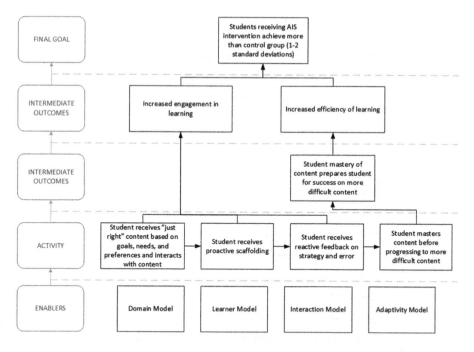

**Fig. 1.** AIS theory of change

## 3   Balanced Assessment Systems

Educational assessments are intended to gather evidence of learning and achievement to make specific inferences. Balanced systems of assessments [1] are systems of multiple assessments in which individual assessments belonging to the system are coherently linked through specifications of learning targets while allowed to serve different purposes for various stakeholders. These balanced systems therefore are theorized to allow inference at different levels of the educational eco-system and across different time points, providing multiple robust sources of evidence to support educational decision-making. Three tiers of assessment are typically represented in these systems, including summative assessment, interim assessment, and formative assessment. The tiers differ on dimensions of frequency of assessment and scope and duration of assessment cycle [12–15]. To date, the tiers also differ substantially in level of standardization of conditions under which learners provide evidence of their learning. As defined by the AERA/APA/NCME Standards for Educational and Psychological Testing, an assessment is standardized when the "directions, testing conditions, and scoring follow the same detailed procedures for all test takers." [16] As further outlined in these standards, standardization is implemented to increase accuracy and comparability, ensure all test takers have the same opportunity to demonstrate competency, and to remove unfair advantages, e.g., due to test security breaches.

Standardization is meant to allow comparability both within and across test administrations.

Figure 2 illustrates a common representation of a balanced assessment system.

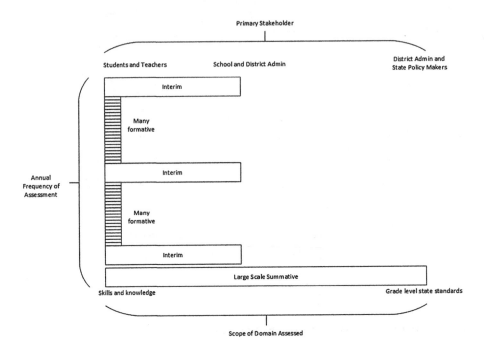

**Fig. 2.** Balanced assessment system

Summative assessment is often referred to as "assessment of learning". The notion behind summative assessment is that evidence is collected following instruction, examined, and then used to reflect a learning outcome. While the term is sometimes used to represent quizzes, tests, and papers that impact final grades in an instructional course (or the final grade itself) [17], it is more often used to reflect a test with high-stakes for an individual in education or workplace settings (e.g., post-secondary or other admissions decisions, hiring, promotion, or firing decisions) or the educational setting itself (e.g., accountability for schools, districts, or other educational entities). In the context of the K-12 balanced assessment systems, and in the context of this paper, large scale summative assessment refers to annual assessments used for policy making and accountability for schools, districts, or other educational entities. These assessments are optimized to measure on-grade student achievement and are sometimes used as promotion or graduation requirements for individual students. They are highly standardized in administration, directly controlling the context in which learners submit evidence of learning and achievement.

The middle layer of assessment in representations of balanced assessment systems typically includes assessments that may be called interim, benchmark, or predictive assessments. In some cases, diagnostic assessments also belong in this tier. Assessments in this layer are standardized assessments that occur at multiple time points (often 3–4 times) throughout the year. Purported purposes of these assessments are many [13]: (1) to provide district and school leaders with insights about student achievement across the district in relation to state standards and sometimes predictive of the large scale summative assessment, (2) to provide district and school leaders with longitudinal data with which they can evaluate programs they implement, (3) to measure student growth across multiple time points during the year, and (4) to identify opportunities students should have for remediation or acceleration, including off-grade needs, and (5) to change teacher behavior in serving those needs. Note that in this layer, assessments are standardized to allow for aggregation of data from individual students to classroom, school, and district levels. Standardization also allows for normative interpretations, and many commercially available interim assessments include national norms. Assessments such as these are currently widely used in practice for the first three purposes outlined above. However, with regards to the latter two purported purposes, the relationship between receipt of interim assessment results and subsequent action taken in the classroom remains less clear, with mixed research results from attempts to validate this portion of the theory of change for interim assessment [18].

The lowest layer of assessment in the balanced assessment is typically referred to as formative assessment and is often referred to as "assessment for learning". There are many available definitions for formative assessment [19], and a substantial literature base includes both the assessment domain and pedagogy/instruction domain. Therefore, a thorough review of the literature on formative assessment is outside the scope of this paper, although the reader is referred to [20] for a reasonably extensive overview. The notion behind formative assessment is that evidence is collected, examined to identify learning needs, and then used to adjust curriculum or pedagogy to improve learning outcomes for one or more students, creating a feedback loop of continuous improvement.

Note that this working definition has less to do with a specific format (e.g., quiz, test, paper) than it has to do with the intended use of the assessment results. One definition, proposed by the National Council of English Teachers [21], includes several statements of what formative assessments do: highlight the needs of each student, provide immediately useful feedback to students and teachers, occur as a planned and intentional part of learning in a classroom, focus on progress or growth, rely on teacher expertise and interpretation, inform immediate next steps, and allow teachers to better understand the learning process in general and the learning process of their current students in particular. Importantly, a distinction emerged from the work of Black and Wiliam [22] as they placed formative assessment within pedagogical theory. They clarify that not only a teacher, but a peer or even the student can be an agent in formative assessment. In addition, Black and Wiliam describe the formative assessment process as one that can be synchronous - teachers making real-time adjustments during one-on-one or whole classroom instruction - or asynchronous, for example via graded homework. It has also been proposed that the time-scale for this feedback loop (e.g., within a lesson, between lessons, or in between units) and the individual implementing the feedback loop (e.g., teacher, curriculum advisor) are not distinguishing factors when determining whether an assessment is formative [23]. In a balanced assessment system, it is presumed that formative assessment allows for the continuous documentation of student progress over time, and as such, occurs any time instruction and learning is happening.

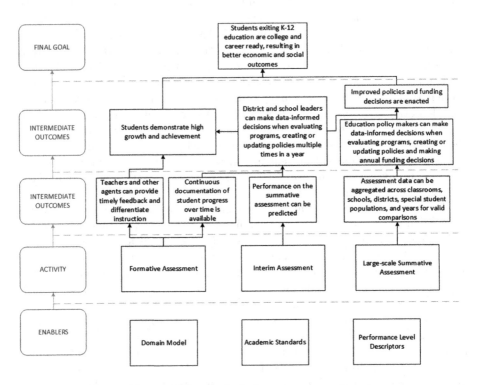

**Fig. 3.** Theory of change for balanced assessment system

A theory of change, which represents logic and conceptual relationships typically described in the literature for balanced assessment systems, is included in Fig. 3.

While these layered and balanced assessment systems have been proposed, exemplars of such systems in practice are scarce [24]. To work well, a balanced assessment system requires vertical coherence across tiers, ensuring assessments in the three different tiers are measuring the same domain constructs albeit at different granularity; horizontal coherence within tiers, ensuring the domain model and assessments align; and developmental coherence, that which allows that the location of assessment within time aligns with what is developmentally appropriate for learners [25]. In addition, difficult system design decisions must be made with regards to tightly coupling or loosely coupling components of a balanced assessment system, with benefits and drawbacks of each approach [24]. Tightly coupled systems may guarantee better coherence, yet may leave less flexibility in choice of assessments for school and district administrators and prevent program evaluation uses. Loosely coupled systems may allow for more flexibility in choice of assessments, which is important in the U.S. where local leaders govern the operation of public schools. They allow for checks and balances in the system. Yet, they may struggle to achieve coherence, as assessment alignment issues can invalidate inferences made from assessment. Loosely coupled systems also introduce the need for data and interoperability standards that govern the exchange of data among components of the system. Finally, as these systems evolve, it has become evident that it is tempting for vendors of assessments to blend solutions across tiers - for example, some may describe interim assessments as formative, while others would see interim assessment as too distal from instruction and learning, and too constrained by the need for standardized methods, to be considered formative assessment. This can cause confusion among consumers of assessments and may even challenge validity claims as assessment results are stretched for uses beyond their design.

These challenges aside, or perhaps particularly because of these challenges, the components of the proposed balanced assessment system provide a useful framework for considering the role of AIS in the context of assessment such that AIS can become a hybrid adaptive instructional and assessment system (AIAS), the focus of the next section of this paper.

## 4   AIAS Conceptual Model

The conceptual model for the AIAS integrates theories of change for both the AIS and the balanced assessment system. Figure 4 may be used as reference in the discussion of the conceptual model.

First, note that the conceptual model acknowledges that the core value proposition of the balanced assessment system is about enabling stakeholders at different levels of the educational ecosystem to make data-driven decisions that will improve student outcomes. This results in a tremendously dynamic system because an adaptive decision in one tier impacts all other tiers. Each of the adaptive loops is explicitly represented in this conceptual model. The AIS literature often refers to inner and outer loops in the adaptive decision making of these systems. The AIAS conceptual model draws attention to the fact that there may need to be an extended nomenclature for describing the multiple layers of adaptive loops at play in this eco-system.

The AIS conceptual model is included in the lower left hand quadrant of the model. Incorporated are the domain model, the interface model, and the learner model, with the adaptive model represented in the connector between formative assessment/evidence of learning and instruction and learning. A learning progression, a component of the domain model, is explicitly noted as it is useful for illustrating the concept of developmental coherence in the model. We extend the AIS to be an AIAS, which thus becomes an agent of formative assessment.

The model represents the AIAS and the human teacher working in tandem, and both the teacher and the AIAS are represented as agents of formative assessment. To date, in K-12 classrooms, AIS tend to be relegated to the role of supplementary instruction. This may be due to incongruity in goals of the AIS and goals of the teacher and the broader educational ecosystem [11]. Developing and testing theories related to how human teacher and AIS agents together interact and adapt instruction and the impact of those choices on learner outcomes has been a blind spot in the development of AIS to date; researchers in the domains of pedagogy, blended learning and AIS will need to come together to evolve understanding of optimal adaptive decision making loops at the instruction and learning levels.

The model presumes that evidence of learning from the AIS will be able to be aggregated to classroom levels (many do this today). In dashed lines - relationships yet to be established - it is also presumed that with additional research in psychometrics and with improved ability and desire to gather contextual information from the AIAS and teacher, evidence of learning will also be able to contribute to aggregate school, district, and state evidence. While interruption to instructional time in the service of measurement is a problem to be solved and a promise of AIAS, a lack of attention to contextual variables that may compromise the validity of aggregate inferences and using this data for accountability purposes could have serious and negative unintended consequences. Therefore, a number of considerations related to fairness, privacy, and security have to be addressed by design [26]. For example, it has been made clear during the pandemic that the notion of aggregating documentation of student progress from formative assessments is challenging due to lack of standardization of the context in which students participate in formative assessment. Imposing standardization on the formative interactions between teachers and students in the service of data collection would be inappropriate. In this situation, rather than controlling context of assessment administration directly via standardization, psychometric models would need to control for context based on contextual data available in the system. In addition, there may be valuable lessons to be learned from performance assessment methods seeking comparability, e.g., [27, 28].

The activities of interim and state assessment are represented as distal from the learner model, instruction, and learning. It has been well established that teachers find the results of these assessments difficult to use due to timing and dissonance between granularity of the feedback and instructional decisions. Therefore, the model does not rely on those activities to inform decision making at the AIAS or teacher levels, while not precluding it. In addition, these assessments play important roles in program evaluation that may require separation from lower level adaptive loops. However, it may become possible to greatly reduce the overall testing burden, for example by using sampling methods, as the research described above allowing greater aggregation of formative assessment data progresses, allowing for continuous monitoring of student growth.

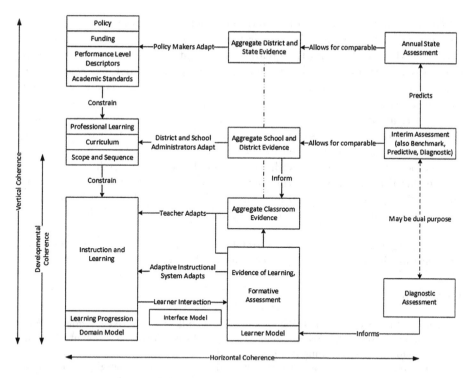

**Fig. 4.** Hybrid AIAS conceptual model

Lastly, note that the need for vertical, horizontal, and developmental coherence across all components remains a substantial element of this conceptual model. Research in the areas of alignment must continue to realize this model in practice.

# 5   Conclusion

Adaptive instructional systems (AIS) hold great promise for increasing the effectiveness and efficiency of educational systems due to their ability to tailor instruction to the specific needs of learners. In addition, because AIS necessarily elicit evidence of learning from students to drive adaptive decisions, there has long been interest in mining data from these systems for broader assessment purposes such as program evaluation and policy making.

This paper examined theories of change that have been proposed for AIS and theories of change commonly associated with assessment and accountability in K-12 education in the United States. It then proposed a novel conceptual model for hybrid adaptive instructional and assessment systems (AIAS) with the unique contribution of explicitly representing the role of the AIS within the broader assessment eco-system.

By systematically examining and representing the role of the AIAS, it becomes clear that two areas of research are necessary to advance toward using data from the AIAS within the greater assessment eco-system as envisioned by the National Research Council at the turn of the century. First, the roles of both teacher and AIAS as formative assessment agents, and the ways in which they can optimally interact to improve learner outcomes, should be examined. Second, it is of critical importance that we learn not only to control contextual variables through standardized assessment but to control for contextual variables in our aggregation of non-standardized formative assessment results.

The benefit of proceeding with such a model may include reduced standardized testing time, improved learner outcomes by harnessing the power of teacher and AIAS together, and the ability for stakeholders at additional layers of the balanced assessment system to monitor growth throughout the school year.

**Acknowledgements.** The author is grateful to Dr. Jinah Choi and Dr. Ziwei Zhou for their thoughtful review and comments during the preparation of this paper.

# References

1. National Research Council, Pellegrino, J.W., Chudowsky, N. (ed.): Knowing What Students Know: The Science and Design of Educational Assessment. National Academies Press, Washington, D.C. (2001)
2. Sottilare, R.: A comprehensive review of design goals and emerging solutions for adaptive instructional systems. Technol. Instr. Cogn. Learn. **11**, 5–38 (2018)
3. Brawner, K.: Bridging conceptual models and architectural interchange for adaptive instructional systems. In: Sottilare, R.A., Schwarz, J. (eds.) HCII 2020. LNCS, vol. 12214, pp. 34–44. Springer, Cham (2020). https://doi.org/10.1007/978-3-030-50788-6_3
4. Aleven, V., McLaughlin, E.A., Glenn, R.A., Koedinger, K.R.: Instruction based on adaptive learning technologies. In: Handbook of Research on Learning and Instruction, 2nd edn, pp. 552–560. Routledge, New York (2017)
5. Bloom, B.S.: Learning for mastery. Instruction and curriculum. Regional education laboratory for the carolinas and virginia, topical papers and reprints, number 1. Eval. Comment **1**(2), n2 (1968)
6. Bloom, B.S.: The 2 sigma problem: the search for methods of group instruction as effective as one-to-one tutoring. Educ. Res. **13**, 4–16 (1984)
7. Anania, J.: The effects of quality of instruction on the cognitive and affective learning of students. Ph.D. thesis, University of Chicago (1982)
8. Anania, J.: The influence of instructional conditions on student learning and achievement. Eval. Educ. Int. Rev. Ser. **7**, 1–92 (1984)
9. Burke, A.: Students' potential for learning contrasted under tutorial and group approaches to instruction. Ph.D. thesis, University of Chicago (1982)
10. VanLehn, K.: The relative effectiveness of human tutoring, intelligent tutoring systems, and other tutoring systems. Educ. Psychol. **46**, 197–221 (2011). https://doi.org/10.1080/00461520.2011.611369
11. Morgenthaler, L., Barrett, M.D: Core to the learning day: the adaptive instructional system as an integrated component of brick-and-mortar, blended, and online learning. In: Sottilare, R.A., et al. (eds.) HCII 2021. LNCS, vol. 12792, pp. 370–381. Springer, Cham (2021)

12. Stiggins, R.: Balanced assessment systems: redefining excellence in assessment (2006)
13. Perie, M., Marion, S., Gong, B., Wurtzel, J.: The role of interim assessments in a comprehensive assessment system (2007). https://www.achieve.org/files/TheRoleofInterimAssessments.pdf
14. Marion, S., Thompson, J., Evans, C., Martineau, J., Dadey, N.: A tricky balance: the challenges and opportunities of balanced systems of assessment. Center for Assessment. Systems of Assessment. NCME 3(13/19), 1 (2019)
15. Conley, D.T., Darling-Hammond, L.: Creating Systems of Assessment for Deeper Learning. Stanford Center for Opportunity in Public Education (nd). https://edpolicy.stanford.edu/sites/default/files/publications/creating-systems-assessment-deeper-learning.pdf
16. American Educational Research Association: American Psychological Association and National Council of Measurement in Education: Standards for Educational and Psychological Testing. American Educational Research Association, Washington, D.C. (2014)
17. Walcutt, J., Schatz, S. (eds.): Modernizing Learning: Building the Future Learning Ecosystem. Government Publishing Office, Washington, D.C. (2019)
18. Cordray, D., Pion, G., Brandt, C., Molefe, A., Toby, M.: The Impact of the Measures of Academic Progress (MAP) Program on Student Reading Achievement. Final report. NCEE 2013-4000. National Center for Education Evaluation and Regional Assistance (2012). https://eric.ed.gov/?id=ED537982
19. Bennett, R., Org, R.: Formative assessment: a critical review. Assess. Educ. Princ. Policy Pract. 18, 5–25 (2011). https://doi.org/10.1080/0969594X.2010.513678
20. Wiliam, D.: An integrative summary of the research literature and implications for a new theory of formative assessment. In: Handbook of Formative Assessment, pp. 18–40. Routledge, New York (2010)
21. National Council of Teachers of English: NCTE Position Statement: Formative Assessment that Truly Informs Instruction (2013). https://cdn.ncte.org/nctefiles/resources/positions/formative-assessment_single.pdf
22. Black, P., Wiliam, D.: Developing the theory of formative assessment. Educ. Assess. Eval. Account. 21, 5–31 (2009). https://doi.org/10.1007/s11092-008-9068-5
23. William, D.: Formative assessment: getting the focus right. Educ. Assess. 11, 283–289 (2006)
24. Marion, S., Thompson, J., Evans, C., Martineau, J., Dadey, N.: A tricky balance: the challenges and opportunities of balanced systems of assessment (2019). https://files.eric.ed.gov/fulltext/ED598421.pdf
25. Jin, H., Mikeska, J.N., Hokayem, H., Mavronikolas, E.: Toward coherence in curriculum, instruction, and assessment: a review of learning progression literature. Sci. Educ. 103(5), 1206–1234 (2019). https://doi.org/10.1002/sce.21525
26. Barrett, M.D.: The evolving assessment landscape and adaptive instructional systems - moving beyond good intentions. In: Sottilare, R.A., Schwarz, J. (eds.) HCII 2020. LNCS, vol. 12214, pp. 435–446. Springer, Cham (2020). https://doi.org/10.1007/978-3-030-50788-6_32
27. Eckes, T.: Introduction to Many-Facet Rasch Measurement: Analyzing and Evaluating Rater-Mediated Assessments. Peter Lang AG (2015)
28. Evans, C.M., Lyons, S.: Comparability in balanced assessment systems for state accountability. Educ. Meas. Issues Pract. 36, 24–34 (2017). https://doi.org/10.1111/emip.12152

# Designing Adaptive Blended Learning Experiences for Military Formal School Courses

Jody Barto[⊠] and Tarah Daly[⊠]

Cognitive Performance Group, Independence, OH, USA
{jody,tarah}@cognitiveperformancegroup.com

**Abstract.** The United States Marine Corps Training Command is responsible for preparing Marines to succeed in their Military Occupational Specialty (MOS) but faces increasing challenges including limited number of instructors, instructor time in billet, and classroom time available. Additionally, an institution-wide shift is taking place to better prepare Marines for tomorrow's increasingly uncertain, complex, and decentralized operating environment, by transitioning from passive, instructor-focused training towards an active, student-centered, adult learning model [1]. Making this shift requires efficiencies in how students learn the foundations of their MOS in order to increase time spent on problem solving and practical application exercises in the classroom. The purpose of the Adaptive Blended Learning Experience (ABLE) effort was to assess the outcomes of self-paced, adaptive online learning blended with classroom instruction, and develop a model to facilitate learning of MOS training concepts in a self-paced, adaptive format that enhances student learning and creates efficiencies for instructor time. This paper describes the development, implementation, and findings from an experimental study that compared the outcomes of an adaptive blended learning design to those of traditional classroom teaching practices. The results of this effort inform recommendations for best practices in implementing adaptive, blended learning designs throughout Training Command.

**Keywords:** Adaptive learning · Adaptive training · Blended learning · Marine corps · Moodle

## 1 Introduction

The United States Marine Corps Training Command, comprised of 87 formal learning centers, trains large numbers of Marines with limited instructors and time available. Instructors need strategies and tools to support and enhance the student learning experience while optimizing their use of time and resources. Additionally, formal school instructors are facing a greater need to develop Marines who are critical thinkers and self-directed, life-long learners [2] who can make decisions in increasingly uncertain, complex, and decentralized operating environments. An active, student-centered learning approach is taking shape in the Marine Corps where students are no longer passive receivers—they are challenged as adult learners to tackle problems in groups to

© Springer Nature Switzerland AG 2021
R. A. Sottilare and J. Schwarz (Eds.): HCII 2021, LNCS 12792, pp. 14–28, 2021.
https://doi.org/10.1007/978-3-030-77857-6_2

learn by doing and from each other [1]. To address these needs, courses need to be engaging, interactive, personalized, and an efficient use of instructor time. The Adaptive Blended Learning Experience (ABLE) project addressed these challenges and extended the research and development for the areas of adaptive learning and blended learning designs.

The objective of the ABLE effort was to develop a model to facilitate learning of Military Occupational Specialty (MOS) training concepts in a self-paced, adaptive format that enhanced student learning and created efficiencies for instructor time. Two Marine Corps Intelligence Schools (MCIS) courses teaching Center of Gravity (COG) analysis were selected as the testbeds for this study: Tactical Intelligence Officer Course (TIOC), a fully resident course, and MAGTF Intelligence Analyst Course (MIAC), which consists of resident and non-resident phases. An adaptive lesson was created in Moodle (a Learning Management System) to enable self-paced learning and personalized remediation of COG analysis basic concepts so subsequent instructor-led classroom time could be reserved for practical application exercises. An experimental study design was applied to measure learning effectiveness and time efficiency associated with the ABLE intervention of the COG analysis module in comparison to current teaching practice. The results of this effort contribute to developing a framework for effective, adaptive, blended learning course designs throughout Training Command that will be generalizable to other training and educational settings.

## 1.1 Adaptive Blended Learning Environments

Adaptive learning is an educational method that uses computer algorithms to deliver customized learning experiences addressing the unique needs of each learner. Adaptations can be based on learner preference for how to receive information, their incoming proficiency or experience, mastery of the concepts as they go through the lesson, and so forth [3]. Adaptive learning has been found to improve the effectiveness and efficiency of learning programs in comparison to non-adaptive teaching approaches [4, 5]. Garrison and Kanuka define blended learning as "the thoughtful integration of classroom face-to-face learning experiences with online learning experiences" [6]. Blended learning programs are also capable of producing higher learning gains than face-to-face classroom learning environments [7, 8]. Studies on the blending of an adaptive learning tool into a course have only collected subjective student reaction data [9, 10] as a way to validate the efficacy of the approach, as opposed to collecting objective data on learning effectiveness (e.g., test scores), or efficiency (e.g., LMS time logs). This literature gap presented an opportunity to study the integration of a self-paced, adaptive learning tool into courses to enhance and create efficiencies for the learning experience in the classroom and beyond. By implementing an adaptive blended learning intervention in Marine Corps formal school courses, it was expected that students would successfully learn COG foundational concepts in less time to place more focus on higher order learning (i.e., concept application, problem solving, and decision making) in the classroom [11].

## 2   The Adaptive Blended Learning Experience

An experimental study design was applied to test courses to measure learning effectiveness and time efficiency associated with the ABLE intervention of the COG analysis module in comparison to current teaching practices.

### 2.1   Testing in Resident and Non-resident Courses

The ABLE study selected the TIOC course for testing. TIOC is a required eight-week, fully resident course of instructor-led classroom instruction for Lieutenants (O-1) through Captains (O-3). Center of Gravity (COG) analysis is taught in TIOC as a module. A COG is "a source of power that provides moral or physical strength, freedom of action, or will to act" [12]. A COG analysis is conducted in military operations to identify an adversary's COG and devise a plan to attack it. The objective of the COG analysis module is for students to learn the Marine Corps' COG analysis process and apply it effectively to a historical scenario in a practical exercise three days later, which is evaluated using a Performance Evaluation Check List (PECL).

Traditionally, the COG analysis module has been taught by providing students with pre-work on their Moodle LMS course site one day prior to attending an 8-h classroom session. During the class session, foundations of COG analysis and the analysis process are taught in an informal lecture format, with the remainder of time spent on instructor-led practical application exercises where students gather in peer groups to apply the COG analysis process to a selection of historical scenarios. Groups then brief the class on their analyses for feedback from the instructor and their peers. While each group applies the same process, they may come to different conclusions on the same case. Instructors look for the reasoning behind the conclusion to assess the viability of the group's solution and whether students understand the process and how to apply it.

COG analysis was selected as an ideal topic to implement adaptive learning as students often struggle with it and MCIS instructors have sought more classroom time to remediate. Given more time with students, instructors would facilitate a deeper dive into more practical application scenarios during class to secure student comprehension and ability to apply the concepts. These MCIS objectives presented an opportunity to introduce an adaptive blended learning intervention that would tailor learning experiences to individual needs, by offering personalized remediation support for foundational concepts and procedures as preparation for interactive participation in problem solving and application exercises while in class.

### 2.2   The Center of Gravity Analysis Adaptive Moodle Lesson

An adaptive, self-paced Moodle lesson (an activity type) replaced the COG analysis foundations lecture for TIOC in the experimental condition. All participants individually completed the lesson on their laptops prior to participating in a blended learning exercise designed to integrate the independent adaptive learning experience with the subsequent classroom experience of working in small groups on practical application exercises.

The development of the Moodle lesson was a collaborative and iterative process between the design team and MCIS academic staff. The design team studied MCIS's

COG analysis readings assigned for pre-work and PowerPoint files used in class to develop an adaptive Moodle lesson that delivered the same foundational content from the lecture portion of the class. The team also added two historical practical application exercises to give participants practice applying the COG analysis process as preparation for class. By transitioning from lecture, a more passive teaching method, to a self-paced, adaptive lesson the student learning experience became more active, enhancing their motivation to learn [13]. As part of the development process, the team steered away from "data dumping," by focusing on retaining the content most critical to the course objectives and enhancing opportunities to learn and practice the application of those concepts. The resulting Moodle lesson structure involved the following sections: Sects. 1–5, which focused on teaching COG foundational concepts including definitions, history, process, frequently asked questions, and resources; and Sects. 6 and 7, which presented two historical practical application scenarios: the Falklands War and Battle of Britain. The lesson included content pages and question pages that required the participant to respond to learning check questions before proceeding. This structure enabled the team to examine the impact of self-paced, adaptive learning for different knowledge types—declarative, procedural, and application.

In efforts to enhance student motivation to learn, the adaptive Moodle lesson was self-paced, enabling participants to choose how they would navigate much of the material [13]. The lesson employed a micro-adaptive learning approach based on participant performance on learning check questions. Participants received targeted hints and remedial content based on their responses, followed by an opportunity to apply their new learning by responding to another similar question. Figure 1 depicts a remedial content page based on an incorrect participant response for the Battle of Britain practical application section. By increasing participant control over the learning experience and providing practice and remedial support to participants who have not securely grasped the concepts, we expected to demonstrate learning effectiveness and efficiencies for instructor time.

### 2.3 Blended Learning Strategy

A blended learning strategy was designed for the experimental course to help the instructor assess participant learning from the lesson, clarify gaps in understanding, and prepare participants to apply their learning to the upcoming practical application exercises. At the beginning of TIOC class time, the instructor facilitated a Chalk Talk exercise [14]. On a whiteboard, the instructor wrote the question, "What is still unclear for you on Center of Gravity analysis?" with a circle around it. Participants added their responses with dry erase markers in the space surrounding the circle at their own pace, and, along with the instructor, drew hard or dotted lines between responses where they saw connections. Once participants seemed satisfied with what was on the board, the instructor facilitated discussion on participants' responses.

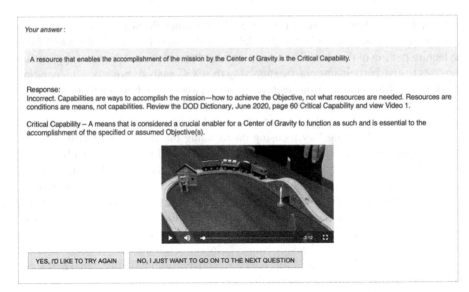

*Your answer:*

A resource that enables the accomplishment of the mission by the Center of Gravity is the Critical Capability.

Response:
Incorrect. Capabilities are ways to accomplish the mission—how to achieve the Objective, not what resources are needed. Resources are conditions are means, not capabilities. Review the DOD Dictionary, June 2020, page 60 Critical Capability and view Video 1.

Critical Capability – A means that is considered a crucial enabler for a Center of Gravity to function as such and is essential to the accomplishment of the specified or assumed Objective(s).

YES, I'D LIKE TO TRY AGAIN     NO, I JUST WANT TO GO ON TO THE NEXT QUESTION

**Fig. 1.** Remedial content page from battle of Britain practical application section

## 3 Method

An experimental study was conducted with TIOC students to measure learning effectiveness and time efficiency related to blending the adaptive Moodle lesson into formal school courses.

### 3.1 Participants

Table 1 describes participant demographics for this study.

**Table 1.** Participant demographics

|  | Experimental | Control |
|---|---|---|
| *n* | 17 | 28 |
| Mean age | 25.77 (3.29) | 26.18 (3.95) |
| Mean time spent in current MOS (years) | 0.15 (0.24) | 0.12 (0.19) |
| Mean time spent in Service (years) | 2.44 (2.39) | 4.38 (4.93) |
| Mean time spent on formal instruction in COG analysis (hrs) | 5.12 (9.54) | 2.89 (3.25) |
| Mean time spent using COG analysis in the Fleet or a similar non-educational setting (hrs) | 4.53 (12.06) | 1.71 (3.94) |

*Note. SD* in parenthesis.

The instructor who taught COG for these courses can be considered an expert instructor. He is a retired Marine Corps Lieutenant Colonel with over 30 years of military instruction experience. Prior to participating in our study, he taught the COG analysis topic at MCIS 12 times. In his self-described teaching philosophy, the instructor characterized himself as a learner-centered instructor and dedicated life-long learner.

## 3.2 Materials

The materials used for this study included the following:

**Informed Consent.** The participants signed an informed consent form describing the purpose of the study, stating participation was voluntary, their inputs were confidential, and they could discontinue participation at any time.

**Demographic Form.** The demographic form collected information on time in service, time in Intelligence MOS, age, number of hours receiving prior training on COG analysis, and number of hours applying COG analysis in the Fleet or similar non-educational setting.

**Knowledge Test.** The knowledge test (KT) is a 25-item test that assessed COG analysis foundational knowledge including terms, key concepts, and the process required to conduct COG analysis but not applied to a problem set. Question types included multiple choice and true/false. The same test was administered at four separate intervals. Participants did not receive feedback on their responses.

**Application Test.** The application tests (AT) were three different scenario-based tests, each using MCIS standard, well-established historic cases. Each application test required students to respond to nine multiple choice questions to effectively apply each step of the COG analysis process to the case. Among the multiple options provided, only one option correctly demonstrated the best way to apply that step in the process. Participants did not receive feedback on their responses.

**Student Reaction Form.** The student reaction form obtained Kirkpatrick Level 1 feedback and subjective usability and experience feedback [15].

**Instructor Evaluation Form.** The instructor evaluation form asked the instructor to respond to items assessing time spent on definitions and terms, the COG analysis process, historical and current practical application exercises, and the overall proficiency of the student group during class.

**Student Feedback Form.** The student feedback form obtained feedback on subjective learning from the lesson and the entire blended learning experience [15].

**PECL.** At the conclusion of the course module that the COG analysis lesson is a component, students were graded on the percentage of PECL items receiving a "yes" rating from instructors during the culminating exercise.

***COG Analysis Adaptive Lesson.*** The COG adaptive lesson is an adaptive lesson developed in Moodle, leveraging multi-media assets to deliver an interactive and adaptive COG analysis learning experience.

## 3.3 Procedure

The general procedure for the control and experimental groups is illustrated in Fig. 2. The experimental group, depicted by the orange cells, completed the informed consent form and the demographic questionnaire, took the knowledge pre-test, entered the COG adaptive lesson, took the knowledge post-test and then application test, responded to the student reaction form, and then participated in the instructor-led classroom portion of the course. Following the remainder of the COG resident instruction, students repeated the knowledge post-test and an application test, and completed the student feedback form. Three days later, students were graded on the PECL, and repeated the knowledge post-test and an application test. The control group followed a similar procedure but did not receive the COG adaptive lesson. The control group participated in the current, traditional COG course as is, then completed knowledge and application post-tests after the lecture portion of instruction, at the end of their class time, and again three days later.

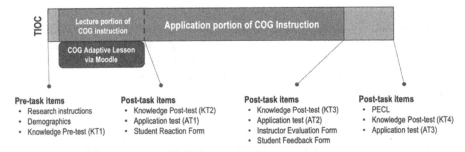

**Fig. 2.** Schedule of events and measures taken during TIOC

## 4   Analysis

### 4.1   Instructor-Led Classroom Efficiency

Time spent on different aspects of the COG analysis course within the classroom was recorded by the instructor via the Instructor Evaluation Form. Table 2 provides these time differences between TIOC experimental and control groups.

Experimental group participants spent no time in lecture while their control counterparts received 90 min of lecture. The instructor spent 10% more time facilitating practical application exercises in the experimental group. Student discussion time for the experimental group was utilized by the Chalk Talk blended learning exercise (60 min). The instructor reported that student discussion during the Chalk Talk was engaging and that the exercise lasted longer than originally planned, "Questions were insightful, which meant that the students had fully engaged with the on-line modules prior to class". Participant exposure to COG definitions, processes, and practical application exercises in the COG adaptive lesson, prior to class time, afforded the instructor time efficiencies in these areas and more time to facilitate active, learner-centered facilitation methods, such as discussions and practical application exercises. Total class time differences were due

**Table 2.** Instructor-led class time structure

| Description | Time (minutes) | |
|---|---|---|
| | Experimental | Control |
| Time Lecturing/Presenting (COG definitions, examples, process, and use of template) | 0 (0%) | 90 (27%) |
| Time Leading Student Discussion (COG definitions, examples, process, and use of template) | 60 (16.7%) | 0 (0%) |
| Time Facilitating Practical Applications (historical or current, real-world) | 300 (83.3%) | 245 (73%) |
| Totals | 360 | 335 |

*Note.* Percent of total class time in parenthesis.

to increased time spent on five practical application exercises in the experimental course versus four in the control course.

### 4.2 Knowledge Test Performance Scores

Knowledge tests (KTs) were administered at four intervals (see Fig. 2). Independent samples $t$-tests of experimental and control group KT1 scores revealed that all participants were not significantly different in their baseline knowledge of COG analysis concepts and processes, $t(43) = 0.94$, $p > .05$, prior to receiving COG instruction. Figure 3 illustrates control and experimental group KT scores and learning gains between test intervals.

The TIOC experimental group significantly improved their scores from KT1 to KT2, $t(16) = -5.10$, $p < .001$ as a result of adaptive learning. The participants also improved significantly as a result of class time with the instructor, from KT2 to KT3, $t(16) = -4.82$, $p < .001$. They retained their knowledge when tested again three days later, KT3 to KT4, $t(16) = 0.44$, $p > .05$. The control group, which experienced all their instruction via classroom time, improved significantly from KT1 to KT2, as a result of the instructor's lecture, $t(30) = -10.66$, $p < .001$, however, the participants in this group saw no further significant improvements in test scores on subsequent tests. TIOC control learning gains from KT1 to KT2 ($M = 44.62\%$, $SD = 21.82\%$) were significantly larger than the experimental group learning gains from KT1 to KT2 ($M = 24.94\%$, $SD = 20.98\%$), $t(43) = 2.98$, $p = .005$. However, between KT2 and KT3, learning gains (effect size between pre- and post- tests) in the experimental group were significantly larger ($M = 24.20\%$, $SD = 21.60\%$) than those in the control group ($M = 2.89\%$, $SD = 29.59\%$), $t(43) = -2.58$, $p = .013$. The aggregate learning gain from KT1 to KT3 in the experimental group ($M = 49.14\%$) vice aggregate learning gain in the control group ($M = 47.51\%$) suggest that exposure to foundational concepts and practical application exercises in the COG adaptive lesson along with a blended learning exercise, prior to participation in practical application exercises, produced maximal benefits to student learning despite the lack of statistically significant differences between the control and experimental groups, $t(43) = -0.18$, $p > .05$.

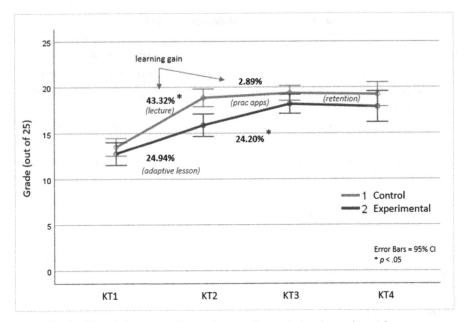

**Fig. 3.** Knowledge test performance scores for control and experimental groups

### 4.3 Application Test

The 9-item application test (AT) was administered at three intervals (see Fig. 2). Neither the experimental, $t(16) = -1.65$, $p > .05$, nor the control group, $t(27) = -0.56$, $p > .05$, improved their scores from AT1 to AT2, after exposure to either the COG adaptive lesson (experimental) or the in-class lecture portion (control) of the course. While the experimental group retained this level of performance for subsequent tests, the control group showed significant improvements from AT2 to AT3, $t(27) = -2.60$, $p = .015$, after practical application exercises in class. Control group improvements led to significantly better performance on AT3 compared to the experimental group, $t(43) = 2.62$, $p = .012$. Table 3 illustrates application test performance scores.

**Table 3.** Application test performance scores

| Item | Control group | | | Experimental group | | |
|------|---------------|------|------|---------------------|------|------|
| | *n* | *M* | *SD* | *n* | *M* | *SD* |
| Application Test 1 | 28 | 6.93 | 1.96 | 17 | 6.18 | 1.59 |
| Application Test 2 | 28 | 7.17 | 1.30 | 17 | 6.88 | 1.50 |
| Application Test 3 | 28 | 7.79 | 1.17 | 17 | 6.47 | 2.21 |

### 4.4 COG Adaptive Lesson Student Activity

The COG adaptive lesson experienced by experimental group participants contained 82 unique content pages and 29 total learning check questions using adaptive branching based on participant response. The activity log captured participant metrics associated with their interactions in the lesson, including time spent in the lesson in minutes ($M = 57.00$, $SD = 14.91$). The minimum time spent in the lesson was 32 min and the longest time spent in the lesson was 80 min. Time count started when a participant landed on the homepage of the lesson and ended when the participant clicked the "End Lesson" button after viewing the last page of the lesson content. Experimental group participants spent 36.7% less time in the COG adaptive lesson compared to the lecture portion of class in the control group (90 min).

Learning check questions were scored based on percent correct first time responses. The score for learning check questions was $M = 72.82\%$, $SD = 10.08\%$. The minimum score was 52.38% and the maximum score was 86.36%. Correlations among participant time, score, performance on both knowledge and application tests, and participant subjective ratings were calculated. Neither time in the lesson nor lesson score correlated significantly with other performance measures (i.e., KT or AT). However, participant time in the lesson appeared to correlate positively with subjective confidence ratings after exposure to the lesson and their overall subjective usability. This suggests that the longer a participant spends in the lesson, the higher their confidence in being able to apply COG concepts to historical applications, and the higher their favorability toward the COG adaptive lesson.

### 4.5 Student Subjective Responses

Subjective feedback was collected from experimental participants regarding their experiences via a reaction form (post-adaptive lesson) and a feedback form (post entire blended learning experience). Eleven questions addressing subjective usability on a 5-point Likert scale prompted participants to rate lesson clarity, quality, and logical arrangement of content. A summative score across the 11 items (55 total possible points) was translated into a percentage score. Average ratings ($M = 80.75\%$, $SD = 8.91\%$) point to positive subjective feedback. The most highly rated items were clarity ($M = 4.24$), consistency ($M = 4.47$), and how well the content explained COG analysis concepts ($M = 4.29$). Subjective effectiveness for learning was rated across five 5-point Likert items (25 total possible points) addressing various lesson components and was translated into a percentage score. Average ratings ($M = 72.47\%$, $SD = 11.39\%$) suggested participants thought the lesson was effective, as usability and effectiveness benchmarks from similar studies average 68% [16, 17].

A thematic analysis was conducted across experimental group qualitative responses. Participants in the experimental group provided 537 comments between the reaction form and the feedback form. From the total comments, 412 of those comments were grouped into 16 thematic categories (e.g., easy to use, improved understanding, engaging, did not like, confusing, not useful, etc.). Of these, 249 (60.4%) comments were positive, 37 (9%) were neutral, and 126 (30.6%) were negative. Many of the positive comments (62%) were made about the usefulness and improved understanding garnered from the adaptive blended learning experience. Participants shared that the Chalk Talk was useful to mitigate areas of confusion from the lesson prior to participation in practical application exercises. However, some indicated they felt confident in their understanding of COG analysis concepts post-adaptive lesson and would have more actively participated in the exercise if asked a broader question beyond areas that lacked clarity. Of the negative comments, 65% addressed how certain aspects of the experience were not engaging, not useful, or were confusing. Comments about the multimedia being not useful or confusing were, by and large, due to technical difficulties. Eight participants (47%) reported that long load times or their computer's lack of audio playback capability caused disengagement and frustration. Additionally, three participants were unable to complete the COG adaptive lesson and subsequent instruments due to network issues and were removed from all analyses.

The control group responded to similar reaction questions regarding the lecture's clarity, quality, and logical arrangement of content, with the addition of ratings on instructor effectiveness for addressing concepts, use of questioning to help in understanding of COG analysis, and how well the feedback and guidance supported participant learning. A summative score across eight 5-point Likert items (40 total possible points) was translated into a percentage score. Average ratings ($M = 94.64\%$, $SD = 6.76\%$) reflected a very effective and positive classroom lecture experience by the control group participants. The same thematic analysis procedures were applied to qualitative responses from control group participants regarding their reactions and feedback related to their classroom experience, however, some participants also commented on their experience with taking the test instruments in Moodle. They responded with 348 comments, of which 313 were categorized. There were 220 (70.3%) positive comments, 46 (14.7%) neutral comments, and 47 (15%) negative comments. Most of the positive comments (60.9%) addressed how participants enjoyed the examples provided in class. The majority of negative comments (42.5%) related to a lack of engagement and usefulness specifically associated with the use of PowerPoint slides and a lack of pre-work to orient them to the material prior to class. These comments provide support for the implementation of an adaptive lesson to learn COG foundational concepts and provide interactive opportunities for self-paced practice prior to class time.

Qualitative analyses also revealed broad themes and similarities within participant subjective responses. For both groups, participants shared positive reports of the instructor's facilitation of practical application exercises. They reported that the instructor was well-informed on the subject matter, engaging, clearly communicated, and used thought-provoking questions to facilitate deeper learning. These findings are not surprising and align with the instructor's learner-centric philosophy and background as a highly skilled instructor with thirty years of experience.

## 5  Discussion

This experimental study revealed that the results of the ABLE intervention were not statistically different in terms of learning effectiveness and demonstrated greater time efficiencies than the lecture for the control group. Taken together these findings support the development and implementation of an adaptive blended learning model to facilitate learning of MOS training concepts for learning effectiveness and efficiency in formal school courses.

We expected that experimental participants would show marked improvements over the control if this study was conducted with a typical Marine instructor. The adaptive lesson facilitated learning commensurate with a learner-centered expert instructor with 30 years of teaching experience. While Marine instructors are increasingly developed to employ learner-centered approaches, they typically hold 1–3 years of teaching experience. In a study on the baseline state of Marine instructor proficiency, 88% of the 93-person sample had 3 years or less of instructor experience [18]. Learning effectiveness of the ABLE intervention was demonstrated by improvements from pre to post test and through similar learning gains as the control. Even after the three-day interval from KT3 to KT4, participants showed evidence of knowledge retention based on their KT 4 performance scores, which did not significantly differ from KT3.

Experimental group participants completed the COG adaptive lesson in 36.7% less time than the lecture portion for the control group who relied on an in-person instructor, pointing to support of improved class time efficiencies. The adaptive lesson included COG foundational concepts typically included in a lecture, however, the lesson also enabled participants to apply their declarative knowledge to two practical application exercises, all in less time than the lecture on COG foundational concepts. Results from the KT performance scores across time also suggest that content efficiencies and condensed time allocation afforded by the COG adaptive lesson did not negatively impact participant learning or retention. For application tests, control and experimental groups performed similarly on AT1 and AT2. It was only at AT3, after the retention period, that the control group saw significantly higher test scores compared to the experimental group, which is a similar finding for KT performance, where our COG adaptive lesson did not negatively impact student learning. These findings may be explained by the additional exposure to historical scenarios received by participants during the lecture portion within the control group, according to instructor reporting. Additionally, during the period between AT2 and AT3, however, activity differences that may have potentially contributed to barriers for learning retention among control and experimental groups are not known. Retention of application knowledge gained from adaptive blended learning requires further study.

The use of an adaptive lesson in Moodle contributed to meeting TECOM's goal for creating learner-centered environments. As revealed by individual differences in the student interaction data, the adaptive lesson enabled learner control over the pace and navigation of the lesson, which was reported as a positive feature by learners. Providing participants with targeted hints and remediation based on individual responses are learner-centered practices for which participants indicated positive subjective feedback. Even after the entire blended learning experience, participants expressed positive feedback regarding use of class time to apply concepts learned from the COG adaptive lesson to practical application exercises. These participant responses provide further support for the decision to incorporate self-paced, adaptive Moodle lessons into formal school instruction.

This study also revealed the importance of how adaptive learning is blended into a course. Participants gave positive subjective feedback on the usefulness of the Chalk Talk exercise to prepare for practical application exercises. Many also reported that they did not experience areas of confusion post adaptive lesson and therefore, participation in this blended learning exercise would have been even more active and fruitful if the discussion question was of broader scope. Based on this finding, our team recommends implementing learner-centric blended learning exercises that address a similar scope of questions as the non-resident course experimental design, including both key learning takeaways and areas that are unclear. In a resident course this can be accomplished by a Chalk Talk exercise, for example, with two different whiteboards posing different questions.

While the potential benefits for learning effectiveness and efficiencies are apparent, there are realistic barriers to implementing adaptive blended learning interventions in formal school courses. The Moodle LMS provides an institutionally supported and inexpensive means for instructors and designers to develop adaptive lessons. However, technical issues such as excessive page load times were commonly experienced throughout this study. A lack of proper bandwidth or hardware can disengage students and create barriers to learning and achieving time efficiencies [19].

### 5.1 Future Directions for Adaptive Blended Learning Designs

Overall, the study's findings provide support for implementation of adaptive blended learning designs in formal schools. Based on our findings and lessons learned, the team offers four recommendations for faculty/trainers, designers, and staff in designing and implementing adaptive blended learning designs. First, it was apparent that the instructor in this study employed active, learner-centered approaches in his classroom facilitation. Student subjective data indicated that even his lecture, typically a more teacher-centric approach, was engaging and interactive. Not every instructor comes with this mindset and skillset. It is important to support and develop faculty to embrace adopting more learner-centered facilitation approaches (i.e., interactive exercises and discussions) to engage high levels of active participation and as a result, peer-to-peer learning for blending and practical application exercises [2]. Formal faculty development initiatives are ideal for this endeavor, although implementing a Chalk Talk exercise followed by soliciting qualitative student feedback on perceived engagement, learning, and ways to improve the exercise, can be a good first start.

Second, when designing an adaptive lesson, less is more. Limit and tailor your content to what is absolutely essential, putting more emphasis on developing useful learning check questions and adaptations for remediation. The concise content design and implementation within the COG analysis adaptive lesson supported participant navigation and interaction such that time efficiencies were gained without negatively impacting learning, user experience, or usability. Third, we recommend a micro-adaptive approach for a lesson that uses targeted feedback, additional content delivered in other modalities (e.g., videos, diagrams), and opportunities to respond to other similar questions. Adaptive remedial content provided through multiple means enabled participants to receive the types of learning support they needed, without the need for an instructor. Fourth, an organization's intent on integrating adaptive learning into their current learning model must decide to invest in the IT infrastructure that will support high levels of traffic across subordinate commands or institutions. Ensure students have the proper hardware and network bandwidth to effectively utilize adaptive learning tools. Adaptive, blended learning interventions can also be employed to enhance learning and create efficiencies in a variety of adult learning settings beyond military training. Both higher education and professional development in the for-profit and non-profit sectors are ripe opportunities for implementation.

**Acknowledgements.** This work was supported by the Office of Naval Research and the Marine Corps Training Command. The authors wish to thank the entire Adaptive Blended Learning Experience project team, Amy LaFleur, Natalie Steinhauser, Peter Squire, Col William T. Wilburn, Jr., Mr. John Bullock, LtCol Brendan McBreen, USMC (Ret.), and the instructors and staff from MCIS for their support of this research.

*The views of the author expressed herein do not necessarily represent those of the U.S. Marine Corps, U.S. Navy or Department of Defense (DoD). Presentation of this material does not constitute or imply its endorsement, recommendation, or favoring by the DoD.*

# References

1. United States Marine Corps. MCDP 7 (2020). https://www.marines.mil/News/Publications/MCPEL/Electronic-Library-Display/Article/2129863/mcdp-7/. Accessed 23 Dec 2020
2. Weimer, M.: Learner-Centered Teaching: Five Key Changes to Practice, 2nd edn. Wiley, Hoboken (2013)
3. Landsberg, C.R., Astwood, R.S., Jr., Van Buskirk, W.L., Townsend, L.N., Steinhauser, N.B., Mercado, A.D.: Review of adaptive training system techniques. Mil. Psychol. 24(2), 96–113 (2012)
4. Bond, A.J.H., Phillips, J.K., Steinhauser, N.B., Stensrud, B.: Revolutionizing formal school learning with adaptive training. In: Proceedings of the Interservice/Industry Training, Simulation, and Education Conference. National Training Systems Association, Orlando (2019)
5. Despotović-Zrakić, M., Marković, A., Bogdanović, Z., Barać, D., Krčo, S.: Providing adaptivity in moodle LMS courses. Educ. Technol. Soc. 15(1), 326–338 (2012)
6. Garrison, D.R., Kanuka, H.: Blended learning: uncovering its transformative potential in higher education. Internet High. Educ. 7(2), 95–105 (2004)
7. Bernard, R.M., Borokhovski, E., Schmid, R.F., Tamim, R.M., Abrami, P.C.: A meta-analysis of blended learning and technology use in higher education: from the general to the applied. J. Comput. High. Educ. 26(1), 87–122 (2014)
8. González-Gómez, D., Jeong, J.S., Rodríguez, D.A.: Performance and perception in the flipped learning model: an initial approach to evaluate the effectiveness of a new teaching methodology in a general science classroom. J. Sci. Educ. Technol. 25(3), 450–459 (2016)
9. Johnson, W.L., Lindsay, B., Naber, A., Carlin, A., Freeman, J.: Initial evaluations of adaptive training technology for language and culture. In: Proceedings of the Interservice/Industry Training, Simulation, and Education Conference. National Training Systems Association, Orlando (2018)
10. Sampaio, P.N., Teixeira, J.M., Camacho, M.F., de Freitas Gouveia, R.H.: Blended peer-assisted learning platform: improving learning outcomes with a collaborative environment. J. Educ. Technol. Syst. 39(4), 371–395 (2011)
11. Anderson, L.W., Krathwohl, D.R.: A Taxonomy for Learning, Teaching and Assessing: A Revision of Bloom's Taxonomy of Educational Objectives. Longman (2001)
12. DOD dictionary of military and associated terms. Joint Chiefs of Staff, Washington, D.C. (2020). https://www.jcs.mil/Portals/36/Documents/Doctrine/pubs/dictionary.pdf

13. Wlodkowski, R.J., Ginsberg, M.B.: Enhancing Adult Motivation to Learn: A Comprehensive Guide for Teaching all Adults. Wiley, Hoboken (2017)
14. Smith, H.: The foxfire approach to student and community interaction. In: Shumow, L. (ed.) Promising Practices for Family and Community Involvement During High School, pp. 89–103. Information Age Publishing, Charlotte (2009)
15. Kirkpatrick, D., Kirkpatrick, J.: Evaluating Training Programs: The Four Levels. Berrett-Koehler Publishers, San Francisco (2006)
16. Brooke, J.: SUS - a quick and dirty usability scale. In: Jordan, P., Thomas, B., McClelland, I.L., Weerdmeester, B. (eds.) Usability Evaluation in Industry, pp. 189–194, Taylor & Francis, London (2014)
17. System Usability Scale. Usability.gov. https://www.usability.gov/how-to-and-tools/methods/system-usability-scale.html. Accessed 13 Jan 2021 (2021)
18. Phillips, J., Ross, K., Hancock, H.: A customized model for accelerating military instructor skills based on the dreyfus and dreyfus stage model. In: Mangiate, E.S., Peno, K., Northup, J. (eds.) Skill Development from Novice to Expert: Voices from Different Fields. Information Age Publishing, Charlotte (in press)
19. Cross, K.P.: Adults as Learners. Jossey-Bass, San Francisco (1981)

# Personalized Mastery Learning Ecosystems: Using Bloom's Four Objects of Change to Drive Learning in Adaptive Instructional Systems

Anastasia Betts[1,2]([✉]), Khanh-Phuong Thai[1], and Sunil Gunderia[1]

[1] Age of Learning, Inc., Glendale, CA, USA
abetts@buffalo.edu
[2] University at Buffalo SUNY, Buffalo, NY, USA

**Abstract.** Adaptive instructional systems (AISs) hold tremendous promise for addressing learner variability at scale. Many AISs are grounded in Benjamin Bloom's (1971) Mastery Learning approach, which delivers differentiated instruction, appropriate scaffolding, and feedback to ensure each child masters each concept or skill before moving on. (Bloom's 1984) framework for learning went beyond the immediate interactions of learners and the AIS. He described "four objects of the change process" that must be addressed to significantly improve student learning: the *learner,* the *materials,* the *teacher,* and the learner's *environment,* where parents/caretakers are a critical component, especially for young children. This paper describes a learning engineering approach to craft a Personalized Mastery-Based Learning Ecosystem (PMLE) that uses all people, processes, data, and networked connections to create new capabilities, richer experiences, and unprecedented educational opportunities for children and their families. This ecosystem treats all individuals within the system as learners (child, parent, teacher, etc.) whose knowledge and expertise can be enhanced to benefit the child's learning. The PMLE enables parents and teachers to become empowered "agents" of change by providing them with knowledge, tools, and evidence-based strategies to support meaningful and effective interactions with the child, all driven by real-time data about the readiness of the child. This paper presents a vision of how AISs can move beyond working solely with the child to become more robust ecosystems that empower all agents of change to optimize personalization and ensure long-term success of all children at scale.

**Keywords:** Personalized learning · Mastery learning · Adaptive instructional system · Learning engineering · Learning ecosystem

## 1 Introduction

Holding all students to high standards is critical, but as reforms based on standardization have continued to experience little appreciable success, it is important that we ask ourselves if we are pursuing the right solutions. In the United States, stakeholders have argued that we must share a commitment to high quality, standardized learning expectations for all children. However, attempts to standardize education, or provide the same

---

The original version of this chapter was revised: chapter was previously published non-open access. The correction to this chapter is available at https://doi.org/10.1007/978-3-030-77857-6_46

R. A. Sottilare and J. Schwarz (Eds.): HCII 2021, LNCS 12792, pp. 29–52, 2021.
https://doi.org/10.1007/978-3-030-77857-6_3

education (i.e., the same content, at the same time, for the same duration, etc.) to all students is likely to create challenges, no matter how high the expectations are. A key factor driving these challenges is that students vary in their needs for instruction, support, and enrichment (Pape 2018). And while some students move quickly through content and require enrichment to keep from growing bored, others need to be taught in multiple ways, require plenty of time to practice and ask questions, need more scaffolding, and more support in general to reach learning goals (George 2005). In other words, perhaps it is not standardization that should be pursued, but rather ways to address learner variability.

The United States is an incredibly diverse country, with a rich tapestry of individuals from all walks of life, cultures, and creeds. This diversity has always been key to our success, as diversity is known to lead to more creativity, innovation, persistence, and better problem-solving in general (Phillips 2014). Research indicates that the variability present in the U.S. student population is due largely to the naturally differentiated development of young children (NAEYC & NCTM 2002), as well as children's background factors, including socio-economic status (SES), ethnicity, mother's education level, gender, adverse experiences, level of social support, and physical health (e.g., Abedi et al. 2006; Entwisle and Alexander 1990; Siegler 2009; McKown and Weinstein 2003; Pfefferbaum et al. 2016; Kalil 2013; Kim and Cicchetti 2010). For example, children's differences in motor skills and executive functioning development (attention, inhibition, working memory) impact how they process information, interact with digital media, and learn early math skills (e.g., Dulaney et al. 2015; Stipek and Valentino 2015; Andersson 2008; Yeniad et al. 2013; Blair and Razza 2007).

In other cases, differences in the home learning environments of children, such as the work habits of the family (e.g., routines, stability), academic guidance and support provided by parents, cognitive stimulation (e.g., cultivating curiosity, etc.), language development (e.g., frequency and quality of parent-child conversation), and the academic expectations parents have for their children, contribute to this diversity (Bloom 1984). As a result, there is extraordinary learner diversity and learner variability present in the student population of the United States, in the form of different cultural, socioeconomic and linguistic backgrounds, learner prior knowledge, skills, and aptitudes (Rose et al. 2013; Rose 2016), as well as other differences related to learning difficulties and giftedness (Pape 2018). This learner variability presents both challenges and opportunities.

## 1.1 The Challenge

Unaddressed learner variability may be the biggest factor in students' underachievement, from the onset of schooling in preschool, and throughout the K-12 years (Digital Promise 2016), as many children are not achieving the established minimum proficiency standards for mathematics and reading, as well as other content areas (de Brey et al. 2019; Schleicher 2019). This is of particular concern in the United States, which currently ranks 13th internationally in reading achievement, and 37th in mathematics achievement (Schleicher 2019). A closer examination of the performance of students from the United States reveals a more dire problem, with nearly two out of every three 4th grade students not proficient in their grade level standards in mathematics and reading – a number that grows to three out of four in mathematics by 12th grade (de Brey et al. 2019). Furthermore, when the data is disaggregated by socio-economic status, ethnicity, cultural background, home language and more, students from historically disadvantaged groups perform much worse than their more advantaged peers (de Brey et al. 2019). More concerning is the fact that the achievement of students has not significantly improved over the past two decades, despite numerous education reforms aimed at solving the problem (Keieleber 2019; Rebarber 2020).

The problem of underachievement often begins before children start formal schooling. Many children begin school with gaps in their learning foundation – gaps that only widen as children move on to successive grades (Duncan et al. 2007). These gaps are thought to form as the result of early experiences in the home. While some children may spend their early years in an enriching home learning environment filled with a wide array of literacy and numeracy experiences, other children may receive very little (if any) exposure prior to beginning kindergarten (Booth and Crouter 2008; Hart and Risley 1995). This creates a *learning opportunity gap* (Cameron 2018), as those children who have had early exposure to math and literacy enter school better prepared to learn, while those who have not benefitted from such exposure enter school unready to take advantage of the learning school has to offer (Betts et al. 2020).

Learning opportunity gaps mean that some children have more advantages, and other less, when it comes to learning. Not all children have equal opportunity to learn, because not all children are *ready* to learn the same content at the same time. To mediate the problem of learning readiness, teachers are asked to differentiate their instruction to meet each individual student's needs, but the task is herculean. At the elementary school level alone, teachers may be working with thirty or more students, all with vastly different skills and prior knowledge; at the secondary level teachers may be responsible for a hundred or more students. In any given classroom, a teacher may be required to provide instruction at three or four different grade levels, sometimes more. Consider that the average third grade teacher may have precocious students reading at a 5th grade level or higher, even while other students are struggling to master basic sound-symbol correspondences typically learned in 1st grade. It is nearly impossible for teachers to identify all of students' individual needs, must less address them—even for highly skilled teachers putting forth tremendous effort.

The goal of a one-size-fits all approach to education that standardizes the curriculum and learning expectations by grade level is to deliver instructional content that the typical or *average* student can learn within a school year. The problem is that there is, in fact, no such thing as an *average* student. In his book, "The End of Average," Rose (2016) debunks more than a century of thinking devoted to design of products and processes for the average human being. Whether you're designing a cockpit for the average pilot, or an educational system to serve millions of students, designing for the average is useless, or "worse than useless, in fact, because it creates the illusion of knowledge" (Rose 2016, p. 11). Rose points out that "individuals behave, learn, and develop in distinctive ways, showing patterns of variability that are not captured by models based on statistical averages" (Rose et al. 2013, p. 152). In other words, a system that standardizes approaches and processes to meet the needs of average students is likely to fail. Because no average student exists, processes designed to meet the needs of an average student end up serving, at best, the needs of the very few, or at worst, the needs of no one. It would seem that decades of data on the underachievement of students would support this notion.

## 1.2  The Opportunity

Unprecedented learner variability within the U.S. student population is a known challenge (Pape 2018), which may be why the one-size-fits-all approach of standardization has not proven effective in increasing student achievement. Learner variability is also not a new challenge. When considering the diverse learning needs of individual students, Bloom (1984) advocated for a mastery-based personalized learning approach that sought to ensure progression for all students regardless of learner variability. In a landmark study comparing three separate learning conditions—(1) one-to-one personalized Mastery Learning, (2) whole-group Mastery Learning, and (3) conventional classroom instruction. Unsurprisingly, students in the one-to-one Mastery Learning condition achieved at rates of two standard deviations above those in the conventional classroom (also known as the *2 sigma problem*). However, Bloom's experiment also showed that students in the whole-group Mastery Learning condition achieved one standard deviation above conventional classroom instruction, indicating that the Mastery Learning model could significantly improve student learning over conventional classroom instruction.

Mastery Learning works because it requires the accumulation of knowledge and the mastery of new skills before moving onto successive ones. To ensure that all students master content, learner variability must be accounted for. Mastery Leaning accounts for learning variability by personalizing the instruction through appropriately individualized scaffolds, feedback, and enrichments. The biggest challenge in Bloom's model, however, is meeting the varied needs of so many students simultaneously. Recent advancements in technology, data science, and adaptive instructional systems (AISs) may provide the solution for learner variability at scale (Ma et al. 2014; Steenbergen-Hu and Cooper 2014; U.S. Department of Education, Institute of Education Sciences, What Works Clearinghouse 2009; VanLehn 2011; Kulik and Fletcher 2016). For example, the work of VanLehn (2011) has shown that when adaptive learning systems are designed to emulate human tutors, recognizing the needs of their tutees and pacing the presentation of new materials accordingly, AISs can come moderately close to Bloom's level of success with one-to-one tutors.

However, learning variability factors that contribute to learning outcomes are not limited to the learning content alone. These factors also include each child's cognitive development, social and emotional development, their family background and physical development (Digital Promise 2021; Booth and Crouter 2008; Hart and Risley 1995; Pape 2018). In attempting to develop solutions to the 2-sigma problem, Bloom proposed that targeted modifications to four objects of change: the *learner,* the *instructional materials, teacher* quality and methodology, the learner's *environment* (at home, school, and socially). Modifications or enhancements to these four objects have the potential to increase student achievement (see Fig. 1). Yet, Bloom showed that making changes to one object was most likely insufficient to substantially increase student achievement, stating "two variables involving different objects of the change process may, in some instances, be additive, whereas two variables involving the same object of the change process are less likely to be additive" (Bloom 1984, p. 6). Meaning, working through only one of these areas, such as teacher quality or the quality of instructional materials is likely not enough to affect change—a more systematic multi-pronged approach is necessary.

The question is, how might we combine what is changeable with personalized Mastery Learning to produce additive learning impact? As technology and internet connectivity have increased in both homes and in schools, it is possible to expand the reach of AISs to more students than ever before. Our ability to use technology to connect home and school in new ways also provides additional opportunities, for learner variability is context specific (Rose 2016; Immordino-Yang 2016). Effective approaches addressing learner variability must take these differences into account, recognizing and leveraging opportunities inherent in the learner's ecosystem of resources (Betts et al. 2020). We believe the answer can be found in a learning engineering approach toward building of a Personalized Mastery Learning *Ecosystem.*

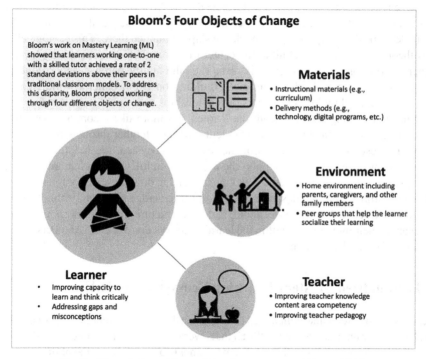

**Fig. 1.** Bloom's four objects of the change process (Bloom 1984)

## 1.3 Understanding Learning Ecosystems

In the biological sciences, the term ecosystem refers to the complex relationships and interactions between living things and their environment, usually toward the goal of ensuring survival (Merriam Webster 2021). Biological ecosystems are interconnected, interdependent, and context specific. Learning *ecosystems* are similar in that they include the "dynamic human interactions between people and their environment, relationships, resources and occurring processes" (Väljataga et al. 2020, p. 48). In biological ecosystems, adaptation and responsiveness are key components; everything in the system is impacted by everything else in the system, and failure to adapt is often a recipe for failure. In learning ecosystems, the same is also true. To succeed, the components of a learning ecosystem must adapt to the needs of the learner to effectively foster learning.

Thinking of the learning process as an ecosystem is not a new idea, even if the use of the metaphor is. The interconnectedness and interdependency of learners with their environment has been described or alluded to in the work of many educational theorists, including Lev Vygotsky (1896–1934), Benjamin Bloom (1913–1999), Urie Bronfrenner (1917–2005), and others. Vygotsky (1986) wrote extensively about the importance of "more knowledgeable others" in the child's learning environment, including parents and other family members, as well as teachers. As previously mentioned, Bloom (1984) described relationships between four objects of change (i.e., child, materials/curriculum, teacher, environment) which could be leveraged to increase the learner's ability to learn. Bronfrenner's (1986, 1992, 1999) created more expanded models of the learning ecosystem to describe the complexity of the relationships contained there. This ecological systems theory positioned the child at the center of a complex, ever-expanding layers of influence, from proximal to extremely distal (i.e., the family, parent-teacher, education policy, societal views on education, etc.). Building on Bronfrenner's work, Neal and Neal (2013) argued that these systems of relationships were less like successive levels of influence radiating outward from the learner, and more like a complex network of influences impacting the learner and interacting with each other through the learner.

While these conceptualizations of the learning ecosystem are helpful, it remains elusive how we can practically support the necessary multileveled and interdependence among systems to foster individual development, and to do so at scale for many learners at the same time. Here we describe our attempt to leverage research, technology, and data to construct such a social-technological infrastructure that empowers individuals and enables their interactions within the learning ecosystem. We call it the Personalized Mastery Learning Ecosystem.

## 2    Personalized Mastery Learning Ecosystem (PMLE)

Recent work by Betts and colleagues (2020) described an Ambient and Pervasive Personalized Learning Ecosystem (APPLE) that leverages the "people, processes, data, and networked connections" in a learner's environment to create "new capabilities, richer experiences, and unprecedented educational opportunities" (p. 23). APPLE described a future system where all "smart" things were connected such that data could be shared systematically across networked connections and with the humans in the system, for the benefit of the learner. For example, data on student performance in My Reading Academy, a program designed to help young learners master early literacy skills (Fabienke et al. 2021), could be shared with other programs such as Kindle or Audible to automatically generate "just-right" collections of books targeted and dynamically adapted based on real-time data about the child's current reading or listening comprehension levels (Betts et al. 2020). Though APPLE describes a possible future for adaptive learning that may yet be years away in terms of development, there are aspects of APPLE that are within reach, even today.

For the past several years, the learning engineering team at EdTech developer Age of Learning, Inc., has been developing and iterating on an AIS called Personalized Mastery Learning System (PMLS; Dohring et al. 2019). AISs are computer-based system that guide learning experiences by tailoring instructions and recommendations based on the learners' goals, needs, or preferences in the context of the learning domain (Sottilare and Brawner 2018). Similarly, the job of the PMLS is to assess in real-time what the learner already knows or has mastered, what the learner doesn't yet know, what the learner is most ready to learn next, and deliver appropriate instruction and scaffolding at a granular skill level.

This aligns closely with Bloom's (1984) Mastery Learning and the work of Vygotsky (1986), who described the learning process in terms of three areas of development: the zone of actual development (ZAD), the zone of proximal development (ZPD), and the zone of insurmountable difficulty (ZID) (see Fig. 2). Comparing the PMLS to Vygotsky's model, the process of learning is characterized by what the learner already knows and is capable of doing independently (ZAD), what the learner doesn't yet know and is incapable of doing or understanding (ZID) on their own, and the critical area in between that represents what the learner can do or understand with the help of a more knowledgeable other (ZPD).

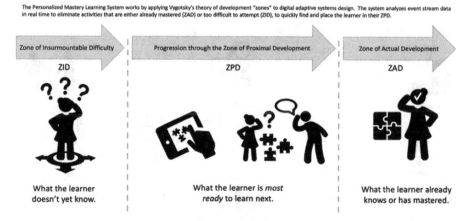

**The Personalized Mastery Learning System (PMLS)**

The Personalized Mastery Learning System works by applying Vygotsky's theory of development "zones" to digital adaptive systems design. The system analyzes event stream data in real time to eliminate activities that are either already mastered (ZAD) or too difficult to attempt (ZID), to quickly find and place the learner in their ZPD.

| Zone of Insurmountable Difficulty | Progression through the Zone of Proximal Development | Zone of Actual Development |
| --- | --- | --- |
| ZID | ZPD | ZAD |
| What the learner doesn't yet know. | What the learner is *most ready* to learn next. | What the learner already knows or has mastered. |

**Fig. 2.** How the PMLS aligns with Vygotsky's (1986) zones of development

## 2.1   From PMLS to PMLE

It is important to differentiate between the PMLS and PMLE. The Personalized Mastery Learning System is a digital, adaptive instructional system that includes the instructional design, data collection, analytics, and information delivery mechanisms (i.e., through dashboards, etc.). The Personalized Mastery Learning Ecosystem is the PMLS plus all components that exist outside of PMLS, including all the people (e.g., the child, peers, teachers, parents, caregivers, etc.), and offline materials (e.g., worksheets, projects, teacher-led lessons, parent-child math talks, etc.). In other words, the PMLS is one component (albeit a critically large one) of the broader, more inclusive, PMLE.

Just as an ecosystem describes the complex interactions between all the living and non-living parts of an environment, the Personalized Mastery Learning Ecosystem places the learner at the center and describes the complex interactions among the learner, all people, processes, data, and networked connections in the learner's environment (see Fig. 3). Through these interactions, the automated mechanisms of the system adapt to learners' individual needs and moves them through an iterative cycle of instruction and application, promoting the mastery of new concepts and skills. The people, processes, data, and networked connections include, in particular, Bloom's four objects of change: the child (learner), the instructional materials (through the evolving and adaptive PMLS), the teacher, and the environment (parents, caregivers, families, etc.). By connecting all in a systematic way, they are no longer objects of change to be acted upon, but rather agents of change that may be acted through.

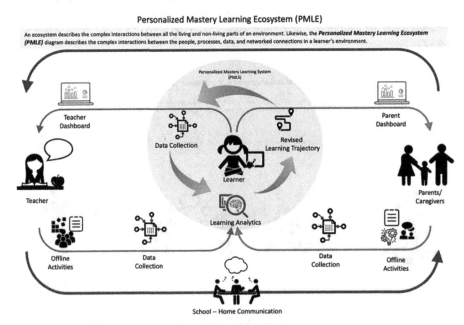

**Fig. 3.** Personalized mastery learning ecosystem.

## 2.2  The PMLE Places the Learner at the Center

In considering the diagram of the Personalized Learning Ecosystem (see Fig. 3), the *Learner* is positioned at the center, interacting directly with the PMLS for the purposes of ongoing assessment, dynamically adapting the learning *Materials* to the learner's individual needs, and providing actionable insights to the other humans in the system (e.g., teachers, parents, caregivers, families, etc.). As learners interact with the PMLS, the system captures key event-stream data as a means of evaluating the learners' needs in any given moment and dynamically adjusts their learning trajectories (Simon 1995). For example, during an interactive learning activity, the system evaluates everything the learner touches, determines the level of needed to scaffold the learner to success, and so on. In other words, the system evaluates where in the ZPD the learner is by assessing and providing only the scaffolds that are needed to ensure progress from instruction and practice to application. This approach moves the learner efficiently toward independence, or what Vygotsky (1986) called the zone of actual development. As learners' competencies are assessed during learning activities, the system adjusts the learning path of future activities. The system accomplishes this by determining whether the learner should stay in the current activity for more practice on the present learning objective, move forward to a new activity with a successive learning objective, or revisit a previous activity designed to strengthen and review prior competencies. In this manner, the system creates and adapts individualized learning trajectories through the learning content for each learner.

## 2.3   The PMLE Describes the Complex Interactions Among the Learner, All People, Processes, Data, and Networked Connections in the learner's Environment

As seen in Fig. 3, data collected from the PMLS are not only analyzed for the purposes of dynamically adjusting learning trajectories. Data are also analyzed to provide actionable insights and individualized activity recommendations to the *Teacher*. These recommendations range from small group instruction ideas, to printable individualized offline activities, to targeted whole group lessons, or tailored enrichment projects – all designed expressly for the purposes of teaching the learner in their ZPD. In this manner, the role of the PMLS in the broader PMLE is to act as a vigilant, automated, teaching assistant with its eye constantly evaluating the progress of learners, while providing both detail and evidence of that learning to teachers. This intelligent assistant pays attention to everything each student does, down to the last keystroke, and provides teachers with a comprehensive picture of where each and all students are with respect to their individual levels of understanding. The reporting features empower teachers with critical information that allows for more immediate, tailored, data-driven instruction—no matter how many students are in the classroom. The PMLS provides automatic formative and summative assessments, delivers customized adjustments and interventions, and immediate identification of students who may need special attention or intervention –all while freeing teachers' time to remediate, challenge, and motivate students to learn more.

In the home Environment, parents, caregivers, and families too receive direct, actionable, communications from the PMLS. Recommendations, based on the learner's ZPD, including such activities as parent-child math talks, "how-to-help" ideas, and hands-on projects. These activities are dynamically generated at the "just-right" level based on the learner's performance in the system. Moreover, the system also delivers parent education activities in the form of informational articles, tips, and educational videos on topics timed to coincide with their child's learning. For example, the system has the ability to detect learners who may be experiencing productive struggle while playing the learning games; in recognizing this, the system might then make the decision to suggest a video to parents about growth mindset (Boaler 2016; Dweck 2008). Educating the parent about key topics and concepts at critical moments in the child's development not only builds awareness but allows for parents to more readily leverage these "teachable moments," and to capitalize parents' role in helping to ripen the child's learning (Vygotsky 1986).

The PMLS is a powerful system that monitors the learners' progress in real-time, adapting their needs in every moment. But it is not complete. The PMLS only knows what the learners' actions reveal as they engage with the system. On its own, the PMLS does not know what the learner may be learning or accomplishing outside of the system. This is one of the reasons that a PMLE approach is more desirable and efficient. For example, if the learner has been away from the PMLS for a while (i.e., not engaging with the app or the games), the PMLS alone would have no way of knowing the progress the learner has made outside the system, say for example, during classroom instruction. By evolving toward an ecosystem and developing mechanisms to collect data on activities and experiences that occur outside of the core system, the PMLS is able to incorporate and leverage additional data to more readily adapt to the learner's needs.

For the PMLE to be effective, data must flow back into the PMLE from the offline activities that occur between the learner and the other humans in the system. For example, parent and teacher engagement data are collected based interactions in the respective parent and teacher dashboards. Parents and teachers may also enter data into the system (e.g., from offline activities), which is then incorporated into each child's learning analytics data profile. These complex interactions create "new capabilities, richer experiences, and unprecedented educational opportunities" (Betts et al. 2020, p. 23) by understanding the learners' ZPD at any given moment and delivering content and activity suggestions that are at the learners' "just-right" level.

The research literature has shown that parents lack confidence in supporting the early literacy and numeracy development of their children (Betts 2021; Sonnenschein et al. 2005), and that they look to the child's teacher for guidance. However, the research also shows that early childhood teachers also often have limited expertise in developing these early competencies, especially when it comes to early mathematics (Clements and Sarama 2014; Early et al. 2010; Li 2020). Given this finding, parents are often not receiving the appropriate guidance for the ways in which they can best support the early learning of their children. As such, the PMLE works to empower those individuals who are most well positioned to directly impact the learning and growth of the child, by providing them with learning and growth opportunities of their own.

Building the knowledge and competencies of both teachers and parents is a critical aim of the PMLE, as doing so ensures that the adults in the child's environment are able to provide the appropriate support at the moment it is needed. The data collected by the PMLE on student interactions with the system are used to drive these educational experiences for the adults. For example, the PMLS may conclude from the child's data that the child is engaged in productive struggle in one or more activities – meaning that while the child might appear to be "stuck," the adaptive algorithms of the PMLS recognize this particular kind of "stuckness" as productive (i.e., moving the child forward and building the child's persistence). In such a moment, the system recognizes that the parent may benefit from receiving information on growth mindset (Dweck 2008), and recommendations for how best to encourage and support their child's development of persistence. In response to this, the PMLE triggers the delivery of a short video to the parent that teaches them about productive struggle, persistence, the development of growth mindset, and provides actionable strategies for the parent to use to support their child in developing these positive learner characteristics. The PMLE then is able to digitally track whether or not the parent watched the video. Over many thousands of learners and parents, the PMLE uses data to determine whether there are relationships between parents who did or did not watch the video, and the impact on the child's performance. Based on this data, new algorithms are developed to anticipate the type of impact this might have on the child and learning trajectories can be adapted based on this added information. Similar opportunities for just-in-time learning and professional development are provided to teachers as well.

In sum, the PMLE empowers the adults in the child's environment to support the child through their ZPD, with the confidence that their efforts are the best match for what the child needs at that moment. This approach has the potential to not only address the unique needs of an individual learner, but for all learners at scale.

## 2.4 PMLE Requires Learning Engineering

Given many factors contributing to learner variability and variability in the agents of change, how do we build an effective PMLE that works for all learners?

There are decades of research on learning and instruction (e.g. Clark and Mayer 2003; Bransford et al. 2000; Bransford et al. 2005) and on distilling guidelines for practice and design (Bjork and Yan 2014; Pashler et al. 2007). While useful, when it comes to the design of specific instructional experiences, designers often deal with enormous complexities, trade-offs, and uncertainties associated with learning in real-world contexts. As a result, these guidelines alone prove to be insufficient (Koedinger et al. 2013). Particular complexities exist when designing for young children, where it is critical that learning experiences are appropriate to their developmental stages and cognitive growth (Gelman 2014; Fisher 2014). Existing literature does not yet provide comprehensive and detailed guidance on how to design learning experiences that address the needs of young children engaging with real learning in real contexts.

This issue is magnified with scale, not just with issues of learner variability, but also in the variability of time and space for learning opportunities, in the resulting rich data about learner engagement and performance, in the mass personalization (Schuwer and Kusters 2014) of learners and learner groups, and in the ways in which our pedagogy must adapt to these needs (Roll et al. 2018). All this must be accounted for as we think about how to combine technologies, pedagogies, research and analyses, and theories of learning and teaching to design effective learning interactions and experiences.

Growing efforts on *learning engineering* are beginning to shed light on processes that help define what works, why it works, and how to scale what works. "Learning engineering," a concept originally introduced by Herbert Simon (1967), has been formalized recently as "a process and practice that applies the learning sciences using human-centered engineering design methodologies and data-informed decision making to support learners and their development" (ICICLE 2019). Learning engineering applies the *learning sciences* – informed by cognitive psychology, neuroscience, and education research (Wilcox et al. 2016) – and engineering principles to create and iteratively improve learning experiences for learners. It leverages *human-centered design* to guide design choices that promote robust student learning, but also emphasizes the *use of data to inform iterative design*, development and the improvement process. The Knowledge-Learning Instruction (KLI) Framework (Koedinger et al. 2010) and similar efforts such as ASSISTments as an open platform for research (Heffernan and Heffernan 2014) are excellent examples of learning engineering in practice. They bundle the platform, the instructor role, and the content, in which affordances match content and enable them to provide rich and relevant interactions. Like the PMLS, these focus on the student-facing instructional system. However, the creation of a PMLE must also incorporate the home environment and the school-home connection in a child's learning.

The learning engineering approach for PMLE development must continue to leverage advances from different fields including learning sciences, design research, curriculum research, game design, data sciences, and computer science. It requires deep integration of research and practices across these different fields in the implementation of research-based and data-informed design cycles, all while being quick and lean enough to be sustainable in a resource-limited industry production environment. This often calls for agile development methodologies (Rubin 2012) to allow teams to nimbly iterate to explore concepts, test prototypes, and validate design decisions. The result is a social-technical infrastructure to support iterative learning engineering for scaling learning sciences through design research, deep content analytics, and iterative product improvements (more on this in Sect. 3.2). In this next section, we describe how Age of Learning applies this learning engineering approach toward a PMLE called *My Math Academy*.

## 3   *My Math Academy* PMLE: A Learning Engineering Approach

### 3.1   *My Math Academy* and Bloom's Four Objects of Change

*My Math Academy* targets three complimentary avenues for child learning: self-directed learning supported by adaptive algorithms using child performance data, parent-supported learning, and teacher-supported learning. All three avenues work together, leading to increases in children's math skills and knowledge, as well as their motivation, confidence, and persistence in learning math.

At the time of writing, we have a fully functional version of the child-facing *My Math Academy* games with over 2 million users. The child-facing app features 98 games consisting of 300+ activities, covering number sense and operations concepts and skills for pre-kindergarten through second grade. The parent-facing and teacher-facing dashboards and resources are publicly available, with improvements currently in progress. The PMLE of *My Math Academy* is actualized through a framework that accounts for Bloom's four objects of change: the child (learner) and the learning materials, the teachers, and the parents or caregivers in the home environment.

**The Child and the Learning Materials.** The PMLE places the child (learner) at the center of the system. It is through the child's interactions with the digital learning materials that data is collected, analyzed, and used to determine the child's learning needs at any given moment. The learning materials for *My Math Academy* are delivered primarily through a digital child-facing app, as well as targeted offline activities that designed to extend the child's learning from the app to the real world. Both the digital and offline materials contained in *My Math Academy* cover number sense and operations concepts and skills for pre-kindergarten through second grade. Specific skills covered range from counting to 10, to adding and subtracting three-digit numbers using the standard algorithm, skills that are foundational for later mathematical skill development. These activities were developed based on extensive research into early numeracy development, intervention programs, and state, national, and international standards frameworks, and are aligned with Bloom's Mastery Learning theory. This research helped us define granular, measurable learning objectives toward number sense development and build an extensive knowledge map representing the precursor, successor, and parallel relationships between those objectives.

In each game, learners progress through a narrative world, playing and interacting with "Shapeys," which serve as both characters and manipulatives in the game (see Fig. 4). Consistent with game-based assessment practices (e.g., Shute and Kim 2014), every game in *My Math Academy* is associated with a clear learning objective, learning tasks, and evidence of learning. Moreover, each learning objective is supported by an interactive instruction level that introduces skills, along with several layers of scaffolding and learning-specific feedback. Based on each learner's performance, the adaptive system decides what games to recommend and at which level of difficulty, using a predetermined network map of learning objectives and their prerequisite relationships (i.e., a knowledge map, where each node is a discrete learning objective). For each individual game, adaptivity functions provide scaffolding within each skill level, connect games to adjust to difficulty needs, and guide learners through a customized pathway between performance-based skills. Game-based pretests and final assessment tasks serve as embedded assessments that check for understanding at a granular skill level.

**The Teacher.** The PMLE empowers the teacher to be an agent of change in the child's learning, by providing key information, actionable insights, and recommendations for personalizing the learning for each student in the system. These data and recommendations are delivered to the teach via a *teacher dashboard* that provides real-time data about children's usage and progress within the app. It provides an overview of the entire class which can be filtered into teacher-created groups. It also contains activity recommendations for each child according to their level of mastery.

Figure 5 provides a sample teacher dashboard, in which children's' progress is color-coded for each granular learning objective. Blue denotes regular or quick progression (i.e., ready to learn). Yellow indicates a child is engaged in productive struggle, a relatively slower but continued progress that can benefit from review or teacher reinforcement (i.e., need for review or reinforcement; Hiebert and Grouws 2007). Red indicates a child who is stuck, having made no progress after multiple attempts at the same activity level; such a child requires teacher support (i.e., intervention). Finally, gray indicates that the child has not yet reached that learning objective. In this example, the "Grab and Count 11–15" activity is suggested for two specific children who are stuck and/or have not reached the Count 11–15 learning objective. In sum, the dashboard provides

**Fig. 4.** A snapshot of four different games within the *My Math Academy* system

teachers with objective data about children's current proficiency and learning trajectories and aims to help them better tailor classroom instruction to accelerate learning (Gersten et al. 2009).

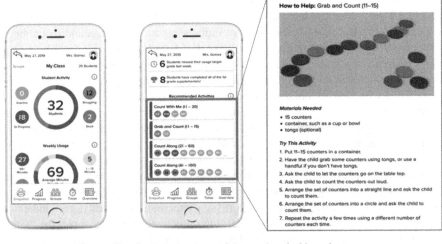

**Fig. 5.** Sample views of the teacher dashboard.

We have taken a phased approach to the development of the *My Math Academy* PMLE. Previous efforts have focused on developing features of the system that deliver information, insights, and actionable recommendations to the teacher. In other words, the information has flowed in one direction, outward from the PMLS to the teach via the teacher dashboard. Present efforts focus on developing ways for information to flow from the external environment (i.e., the broader PMLE) back into the PMLS. A range of possibilities is being explored, from more indirect methods of evaluating clickstream data collected through teachers' interactions directly with the digital dashboard (e.g., what tools, features, downloads, the teacher clicks on), to more direct methods of data collection such as data entered into the system by the teacher. Examples include the teacher entering the child's score in an offline activity, or indicating that specific students participated in teacher-led intervention lessons, etc. In this manner, information about each child can flow both in and out of the system, allowing for a fuller examination of the child's learning activities related to their progress through the digital learning materials.

**Parents and/or Caregivers in the Home Environment.** Parents and caregivers are often a child's first teacher, and as such Bloom considered them an essential object of change impacting a child's learning. While the child is the central user of *My Math Academy*, we consider the impact of parents (including caregivers), educators, and instructional materials as important variables in an effective system for learning (Bloom 1984). Children tend to do better in school and enjoy learning more when schools, families, and community groups work together to support learning (e.g., Henderson and Mapp 2002). As product developers, we have a responsibility to educators, parents, and families to model appropriate, effective uses of technology, social media, and methods of communication that are safe, healthy, acceptable, responsible, and ethical (Fred Rogers Center 2012). Moreover, well-designed technology can be used effectively for learning and for strengthening parent-child interactions and home-school connections. Effective technology tools connect on- and off-screen activities with an emphasis on co-participation between adults and children and children and their peers (Stevens and Penuel 2010; Takeuchi 2011; Takeuchi and Stevens 2011).

In line with this thinking, the PMLE provides information and recommendations directly to parents and families through the parent dashboard as means of encouraging and enhancing learning interactions between the child and the important adults in the home. The parent dashboard (Fig. 6) offers ideas for activities that families can engage in to provide additional learning opportunities for the child, based on his or her progress in the app. This is essential because the home learning environment and parental engagement are critical for children's development of early math skills (Epstein and Sanders 2002; Fantuzzo et al. 2004). Home-based family engagement practices also encourage family members to communicate high expectations for their child's learning, which is important for academic success (Thompson et al. 2014).

**Fig. 6.** Sample views of the parent dashboard. From left to right: (a) child usage overview, (b) math talk prompts & instructions, (c) offline enrichment activity, (d) parent education video.

### 3.2   Applying Learning Engineering to *My Math Academy* PMLE

The learning engineering team at Age of Learning is interdisciplinary, consisting of curriculum experts, learning scientists, data scientists, design researchers, efficacy researchers, and professional game developers. Together, this team produced the game-based learning solution called *My Math Academy*. It was built upon rigorous academic curriculum, developed with an emphasis on engagement, and grounded in theoretical foundations of learning sciences. The team also paid special attention to data, ensuring quality data for later applications of quantitative methods to inform ongoing improvements. True to the definition of learning engineering (ICICLE 2019) - "a process and practice that applies the *learning sciences* using *human-centered engineering design* methodologies and *data-informed decision making* to support learners and their development" - key to our learning engineering approach (Goodell and Thai 2020) are:

**Learning Sciences Research.** Applications of learning sciences research informs the initial design of *My Math Academy*, including applications of mastery-based learning (Bloom 1971; Guskey 1997), mathematics learning trajectories (Clements and Sarama 2014; Simon 1995), game-based learning and engagement (Barab et al. 2005; Bransford et al. 2000; Gee 2003; Shute 2008; Rupp et al. 2010), design strategies for long-term learning and transfer (Bjork 1994; Roediger and Karpicke 2006; Taylor and Rohrer 2010; Bransford and Schwartz 1999; Kellman and Massey 2013; Anderson et al. 1996), and game-based assessment and structured data for evidence (Mislevy et al. 2003; Owen et al. 2012; Shute and Kim 2014).

**Human-Centered Design Methodologies.** Human-centered design starts with understanding the challenge from the learners' perspective (IDEO 2015). Goodell and Thai (2020) proposed an AIS model that considers the learner as a key component at the heart of a distributed learning (eco)system in which the learner, along with other adults and peers, interact with technology components in varying environmental conditions. Such an AIS model requires the learning engineering team to be grounded in empathy (IDEO 2015), beginning with the needs and perspectives of the people we are designing for. This includes who they are, what they need to learn, how they learn, when and where they learn, why they want to learn, etc. In understanding how and why people behave the way they do, we can design for meaningful interactions and uncover opportunities for new innovation.

To do so, the *My Math Academy* team regularly recruit learners, parents, and teachers to playtest early production prototypes. This process is critical in understanding how children make sense of and solve problems through our proposed playful interactions, and how teachers and parents can be best supported in helping their children learn and grow. Data from such design testing sessions drive concrete interactions, user interface, and user experience design for each learning interactions, that are sensitive to children's developmental stages and parents' and teachers' needs and perspectives.

**Data-Informed Decision Making.** Beyond data from design testing sessions, *My Math Academy* was designed with a game-based learning data framework for event-stream data collection (Owen and Hughes 2019). This captures event-stream interactions from the child (e.g., keystrokes, clicks, taps, drags) within the context of learning mechanics and game progress. As players move through the system, *My Math Academy* games react to player performance on core game mechanics (i.e., basic actions that players perform), translating main game interactions into learning performance data. This this approach, we can generate quality in-game learning evidence because we took into account early in the design process what learning goals are to be assessed, how they will be assessed through game interaction design, and what evidence these designed interactions will provide. Such data captures a context-rich data stream of player interactions while enabling learning analytics and educational data mining investigations into emergent patterns in learner behaviors and performance (Baker and Yacef 2009; Siemens 2010; Romero and Ventura 2010; Ferguson 2012). Such data can also be interpreted in combination with other interactions and features, such as event-stream interactions and manual inputs from offline activities from teachers and parents.

All of this wide variety of collected data – and copious amounts of it, collected from the increasing number of learners and all agents of change engaging in the ecosystem – allow us to better calibrate and adapt our AIS and to develop new and better adaptive technology. Fundamentally this not only changes how content is delivered, but also change how learning materials are created and improved over time.

Figure 7 illustrates Age of Learning's learning engineering framework. Learning sciences research informed our initial design for learning and engagement. The *My Math Academy* learning engineering team iteratively released new content, which meant that curriculum research and design, game design, design research, production, learning analytics, and efficacy research were often taking place simultaneously. With the initial design, prototypes were built and tested with learners (children, parents, teachers), and data were collected (via design research sessions with prototypes, or via interaction logs and efficacy studies from live games) to draw insights into how well the games were engaging players in learning. Over time, and across approaches to research design and analysis, findings were layered and triangulated for deeper insights to inform further improvements and for contribution to a corpus of institutional knowledge as well as the knowledge base at large.

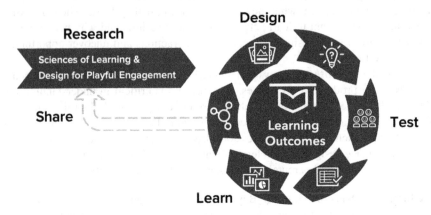

**Fig. 7.** Age of learning, Inc.'s learning engineering framework

**Agile Development Process.** For this learning engineering approach to work in an industry setting, we have found that the agile development process acts as a practical manifestation of this learning engineering framework. At Age of Learning, we formalized the learning engineering tenets into tools and processes embedded throughout the Scrum agile development process (Rubin 2012). Agile methodologies allow us to nimbly and quickly iterate to explore concepts, test prototypes, and validate design decisions.

By collaborating closely throughout this process, the learning engineering team strengthened our understanding of how learning works within the learning ecosystem and used those insights to improve the design of effective learning experiences. In effect, the learning engineering team members are learners too, acting as a fifth "agent" of the change process toward building effective education at scale.

## 4   Conclusion

Given the enormity of the student underachievement problem, the need for solutions that account for and address learner variability has never been more critical. As the population of the United States grows more diverse, resulting in even more learner variability, we can no longer rely on traditional methods of educating our children. And while efforts at personalization are encouraging and ongoing in many arenas, the ability to truly personalize for learners at scale has yet to be achieved. However, evolving technologies, processes, and approaches provide new opportunities and potential solutions. The evolution of the PMLE is just one such potential solution that leverages Bloom's four agents of change as part of a broader ecosystem of learner support.

The PMLE is an example of how AISs can move beyond working solely with the child to create more fully formed ecosystems that account for all of the "agents of change" that influence a child's learning, including the learners themselves, parents and caregivers, teachers, and the learning engineering teams. As all of the "learners" in the ecosystem increase their knowledge and understanding, and as the AIS ecosystem captures the outcomes of this learning, we are better able to optimize personalization for and ensure the long-term development and success of all children at scale.

# References

Abedi, J., Courtney, M., Leon, S., Kao, J., Azzam, T.: English language learners and math achievement: a study of opportunity to learn and language accommodation. Technical report 702. National Center for Research on Evaluation, Standards, and Student Testing (CRESST) (2006)

Anderson, J.R., Reder, L.M., Simon, H.A.: Situated learning and education. Educ. Res. **25**(4), 5–11 (1996)

Andersson, U.: Working memory as a predictor of written arithmetical skills in children: the importance of central executive functions. Br. J. Educ. Psychol. **78**(2), 181–203 (2008)

Baker, R.S., Yacef, K.: The state of educational data mining in 2009: a review and future visions. J. Educ. Data Mining **1**(1), 3–17 (2009)

Barab, S., Thomas, M., Dodge, T., Carteaux, R., Tuzun, H.: Making learning fun: quest atlantis, a game without guns. Educ. Tech. Res. Dev. **53**(1), 86–107 (2005)

Betts, A.: The RESET framework: examining critical factors in parent-child math participation. In: The IAFOR International Conference on Education – Hawaii 2021 Official Conference Proceedings. Paper presented at the IAFOR International Conference on Education, Hawaii (pp TBD). The International Academic Forum, Japan (2021)

Betts, A.: Mastery learning in early childhood mathematics through adaptive technologies. In: The IAFOR International Conference on Education–Hawaii 2019 Official Conference Proceedings. Paper Presented at the IAFOR International Conference on Education: Independence and Interdependence, Hawaii, pp. 51–63 (2019)

Betts, A., Thai, K.-P., Gunderia, S., Hidalgo, P., Rothschild, M., Hughes, D.: An ambient and pervasive personalized learning ecosystem: "smart learning" in the age of the internet of things. In: Sottilare, R.A., Schwarz, J. (eds.) HCII 2020. LNCS, vol. 12214, pp. 15–33. Springer, Cham (2020). https://doi.org/10.1007/978-3-030-50788-6_2

Blair, C., Razza, R.P.: Relating effortful control, executive function, and false belief understanding to emerging math and literacy ability in kindergarten. Child Dev. **78**(2), 647–663 (2007)

Bloom, B.S.: Mastery learning. In: Block, J.H. (ed.) Mastery Learning: Theory and Practice. Holt, Rinehart & Winston, New York (1971)

Bloom, B.S.: The 2 sigma problem: the search for methods of group instruction as effective as one-to-one tutoring. Educ. Res. **13**(6), 4–16 (1984)

Boaler, J.: Mathematical Mindsets: Unleashing Students' Potential Through Creative Math, Inspiring Messages and Innovative Teaching. Jossey-Bass, San Francisco (2016)

Booth, A., Crouter, A.C. (eds.): Disparities in School Readiness: How Families Contribute to Transitions Into School. Psychology Press, London (2008)

Bjork, R.A.: Memory and metamemory considerations in the training of human beings. In: Metcalfe, J., Shimamura, A.P. (eds.) Metacognition: Knowing About Knowing. MIT Press, Cambridge (1994)

Bjork, R.A., Yan, V.X.: The increasing importance of learning how to learn. In: Mcdaniel, M.A., Frey, R.F., Fitzpatrick, S.M., Roediger, H.L. (eds.) Integrating Cognitive Science with Innovative Teaching in STEM Disciplines, pp. 15–36. Washington University in St. Louis Libraries, Saint Louis (2014). https://doi.org/10.7936/K7qn64nr

Bransford, J.D., Brown, A.L., Cocking, R.R. (eds.): How People Learn: Brain, Mind, Experience, and School. National Academy Press, Washington, D.C. (1999)

Bransford, J.D., Schwartz, D.: Rethinking transfer: a simple proposal with multiple implications. Rev. Res. Educ. **24**, 61–100 (1999)

Bransford, J.D., Vye, N.J., Stevens, R., Kuhl, P., Schwartz, D., Bell, P., et al.: Learning theories and education: toward a decade of synergy. In: Alexander, P., Winne, P. (eds.) Handbook of educational psychology, vol. 2, pp. 209–244. Erlbaum, Mahwah (2005)

Bronfenbrenner, U.: Ecology of the family as a context for human development. Dev. Psychol. **22**(6), 723–742 (1986)

Bronfenbrenner, U.: Environments in developmental perspective: theoretical and operational models. In: Friedman, S.L., Wachs, T.D. (eds.) Measuring Environment Across the Life Span: Emerging Methods and Concepts. American Psychological Association, Washington, D.C. (1999)

Bronfenbrenner, U.: Ecological systems theory (1992). In: Bronfenbrenner, U. (ed.) Making Human Beings Human: Bioecological Perspectives on Human Development, pp. 106–173. Sage Publications Ltd (2005)

Cameron, C.E.: Hands on, Minds on: How Executive Function, Motor, and Spatial Skills Foster School Readiness. Teachers College Press, Chicago (2018)

Clark, R.C., Mayer, R.E.: E-learning and the Science of Instruction. Jossey-Bass, San Francisco (2003)

Clements, D.H., Sarama, J.: Learning and Teaching Early Math: The Learning Trajectories Approach. Routledge, London (2014)

Common Core State Standards Initiative: Development process (2021). http://www.corestandards.org/about-the-standards/development-process/

de Brey, C., et al.: Status and Trends in the Education of Racial and Ethnic Groups 2018. NCES 2019-038. National Center for Education Statistics (2019)

Digital Promise: Making learning personal for all: The growing diversity in today's classroom. Report (2016). https://digitalpromise.org/wp-content/uploads/2016/09/lps-growing_diversity_FINAL-1.pdf

Dohring, D., et al.: Personalized mastery learning platforms, systems, media, and methods: US Patent 10 490092B2 (2019). https://patents.google.com/patent/US10490092B2/en

Dulaney, A., Vasilyeva, M., O'Dwyer, L.: Individual differences in cognitive resources and elementary school mathematics achievement: Examining the roles of storage and attention. Learn. Individ. Differ. **37**, 55–63 (2015)

Duncan, G.J., et al.: School readiness and later achievement. Dev. Psychol. **43**(6), 1428 (2007)

Dweck, C.S.: Mindset: The new psychology of success. Random House Digital, Inc (2008)

Early, D.M., et al.: How do pre-kindergarteners spend their time? Gender, ethnicity, and income as predictors of experiences in pre-kindergarten classrooms. Early Child. Res. Q. **25**(2), 177–193 (2010)

Entwisle, D.R., Alexander, K.L.: Beginning school math competence: minority and majority comparisons. Child Dev. **61**(2), 454–471 (1990)

Epstein, J.L., Sanders, M.G.: Family, school, and community partnerships. In: Handbook of Parenting: Volume 5. Practical Issues in Parenting, pp. 407–437 (2002)

Fantuzzo, J., McWayne, C., Perry, M.A., Childs, S.: Multiple dimensions of family involvement and their relations to behavioral and learning competencies for urban, low- income children. Sch. Psychol. Rev. **33**(4), 467–480 (2004)

Ferguson, R.: Learning analytics: drivers, developments and challenges. Int. J. Technol. Enhanced Learn. **4**(5–6), 304–317 (2012)

Fisher, C.: Designing Games for Children: Developmental, Usability, and Design Considerations for Making Games for Kids. CRC Press, Boca Raton (2014)

Fred Rogers Center for Early Learning and Children's Media. A framework for quality in digital media for young children: Considerations for parents, educators, and media creators (2012). http://cmhd.northwestern.edu/wp-content/uploads/2015/10/Framework_Statement_2-April_2012-Full_Doc-Exec_Summary-1.pdf

Gee, J.P.: What Video Games Have to Teach Us About Learning and Literacy. Palgrave Macmillan, New York (2003)

Gelman, D.L.: Design for Kids: Digital Products for Playing and Learning. Rosenfeld Media (2014).

Gersten, R., et al.: Assisting students struggling with mathematics: response to intervention (RtI) for elementary and middle schools. NCEE 2009-4060. What Works Clearinghouse (2009)

George, P.P.: A rationale for differentiating instruction in the regular classroom. Theory Pract. **44**(3), 185–193 (2005)

Goodell, J., Thai, K.-P.: A learning engineering model for learner-centered adaptive systems. In: Stephanidis, C., et al. (eds.) HCII 2020. LNCS, vol. 12425, pp. 557–573. Springer, Cham (2020). https://doi.org/10.1007/978-3-030-60128-7_41

Guskey, T.R.: Implementing Mastery Learning. Wadsworth, Belmont (1997)

Hart, B., Risley, T.R.: Meaningful Differences in the Everyday Experience of Young American Children. Paul H Brookes Publishing (1995)

Heffernan, N.T., Heffernan, C.L.: The ASSISTments ecosystem: building a platform that brings scientists and teachers together for minimally invasive research on human learning and teaching. Int. J. Artif. Intell. Educ. **24**(4), 470–497 (2014)

Henderson, A.T., Mapp, K.L.: A new wave of evidence: the impact of school, family, and community connections on student achievement. Southwest Educational Development Laboratory, Austin, TX (2002)

Hiebert, J., Grouws, D.A.: The effects of classroom mathematics teaching on students' learning. In: Second Handbook of Research on Mathematics Teaching and Learning, vol. 1, pp. 371–404 (2007)

IDEO: The Field Guide to Human-centered Design: Design Kit. IDEO (2015)

IEEE Industry Connection Industry Consortium on Learning Engineering (ICICLE), December 2019. https://www.ieeeicicle.org

Immordino-Yang, M.H.: Emotions, Learning, and the Brain: Exploring the Educational Implications of Affective Neuroscience, p. 17. W.W. Norton & Company, New York (2016)

International Society of the Learning Sciences (ISLS). https://isls.org/Apr-2019. Accessed Dec 2019

Kalil, A.: Effects of the great recession on child development. Ann. Am. Acad. Pol. Soc. Sci. **650**(1), 232–250 (2013)

Kellman, P.J., Massey, C.M.: Perceptual learning, cognition, and expertise. In: Psychology of Learning and Motivation, vol. 58, pp. 117–165. Academic Press (2013)

Keieleber, M.: U.S. students' scores stagnant on international exam, with widening achievement gaps in math and reading, 3 December 2019. https://www.the74million.org/u-s-students-scores-stagnant-on-international-exam-with-widening-achievement-gaps-in-math-and-reading/

Koedinger, K.R., Booth, J.L., Klahr, D.: Instructional complexity and the science to constrain it. Science **342**(6161), 935–937 (2013)

Koedinger, K.R., Corbett, A.T., Perfetti, C.: The knowledge-learning-instruction (KLI) framework: toward bridging the science-practice chasm to enhance robust student learning. Cogn. Sci. (2010)

Kim, J., Cicchetti, D.: Longitudinal pathways linking child maltreatment, emotion regulation, peer relations, and psychopathology. J. Child Psychol. Psychiatry **51**(6), 706–716 (2010)

Kulik, J.A., Fletcher, J.D.: Effectiveness of intelligent tutoring systems: a meta-analytic review. Rev. Educ. Res. **86**(1), 42–78 (2016)

Li, X.: Investigating US preschool teachers' math teaching knowledge in counting and numbers. Early Educ. Dev. 1–19 (2020)

Ma, W., Adesope, O.O., Nesbit, J.C., Liu, Q.: Intelligent tutoring systems and learning outcomes: A meta-analysis. J. Educ. Psychol. **106**, 901 (2014)

Merriam     Webster.     https://www.merriam-webster.com/dictionary/ecosystem#learn-more. Accesses 23 Feb 2021

McKown, C., Weinstein, R.S.: The development and consequences of stereotype consciousness in middle childhood. Child Dev. **74**(2), 498–515 (2003)

National Association for the Education of Young Children: Early childhood mathematics: Promoting good beginnings. Position statement (2002)

National Center for Educational Statistics (NCES): List of current digest tables. https://nces.ed.gov/programs/digest/current_tables.asp. Accessed 20 Jan 2019

Neal, J.W., Neal, Z.P.: Nested or networked? Future directions for ecological systems theory. Soc. Dev. **22**(4), 722–737 (2013). https://doi.org/10.1111/sode.12018

Owen, V.E., Hughes, D.: Bridging two worlds: Principled game-based assessment in industry for playful learning at scale. In: Ifenthaler, D., Kim, Y.J. (eds.) Game-Based Assessment Revisited. AGL, pp. 229–256. Springer, Cham (2019). https://doi.org/10.1007/978-3-030-15569-8_12

Pape, B.: Learning variability is the rule, not the exception. Digital Promise (2018). https://digitalpromise.org/wp-content/uploads/2018/06/Learner-Variability-Is-The-Rule.pdf

Pashler, H., et al.: Organizing Instruction and Study to Improve Student Learning. IES Practice Guide. NCER 2007-2004. National Center for Education Research (2007)

Pfefferbaum, B., Noffsinger, M.A., Jacobs, A.K., Varma, V.: Children's cognitive functioning in disasters and terrorism. Curr. Psychiatry Rep. **18**(5), 48 (2016)

Phillips, K.W.: How diversity makes us smarter. Sci. Am. **311**(4), 43–47 (2014). https://www.scientificamerican.com/article/how-diversity-makes-us-smarter/

Rebarber, T.: The Common Core Debacle: Results from 2019 NAEP and Other Sources. White Paper No. 205. Pioneer Institute for Public Policy Research (2020)

Roediger, H.L., III., Karpicke, J.D.: Test-enhanced learning: taking memory tests improves long-term retention. Psychol. Sci. **17**(3), 249–255 (2006)

Roll, I., Russell, D.M., Gašević, D.: Learning at scale. Int. J. Artif. Intell. Educ. **28**(4), 471–477 (2018)

Romero, C., Ventura, S.: Educational data mining: a review of the state of the art. IEEE Trans. Syst. Man Cybern. Part C (Appl. Rev.) **40**(6), 601–618 (2010)

Rose, L.T., Rouhani, P., Fischer, K.W.: The science of the individual. Mind Brain Educ. **7**(3), 152–158 (2013)

Rose, T.: The End of Average: How to Succeed in a World that Values Sameness. HarperOne, San Francisco (2016)

Roser, M., Ortiz-Ospina, E.: Global education. Our World in Data (2016). https://ourworldindata.org/global-education

Rubin, K.S.: Essential Scrum: A Practical Guide to the Most Popular Agile Process. Addison-Wesley, Boston (2012)

Rupp, A.A., Gushta, M., Mislevy, R.J., Shaffer, D.W.: Evidence-centered design of epistemic games: measurement principles for complex learning environments. J. Technol. Learn. Assess. **8**(4) (2010). http://www.jtla.org

Schleicher, A.: PISA 2018: Insights and Interpretations. OECD Publishing (2019)

Schuwer, R., Kusters, R.: Mass customization of education by an institution of HE: what can we learn from industry? Int. Rev. Res. Open Distrib. Learn. **15**(2), 1–25 (2014)

Shute, V.J.: Focus on formative feedback. Rev. Educ. Res. **78**(1), 153–189 (2008). https://doi.org/10.3102/0034654307313795

Shute, V.J., Kim, Y.J.: Formative and stealth assessment. In: Spector, J.M., Merrill, M.D., Elen, J., Bishop, M.J. (eds.) Handbook of Research on Educational Communications and Technology, pp. 311–321. Springer, New York (2014). https://doi.org/10.1007/978-1-4614-3185-5_25

Siegler, R.S.: Improving the numerical understanding of children from low-income families. Child Dev. Perspect. **3**(2), 118–124 (2009)

Siemens, G.: What Are Learning Analytics? (2010). http://www.elearnspace.org/blog/2010/08/25/what-are-learning-analytics/

Simon, H.A.: Motivational and emotional controls of cognition. Psychol. Rev. **74**(1), 29 (1967)

Simon, M.: Reconstructing mathematics pedagogy from a constructivist perspective. J. Res. Math. Educ. **26**(2), 114–145 (1995)

Sonnenschein, S., Baker, L., Moyer, A., LeFevre, S.: Parental beliefs about children's reading and math development and relations with subsequent achievement. Paper presented at the Society for Research in Child Development, Atlanta, GA (2005)

Sottilare, R., Brawner, K.: Exploring standardization opportunities by examining interaction between common adaptive instructional system components. In: Proceedings of the First Adaptive Instructional Systems (AIS) Standards Workshop, Orlando, Florida, March 2018. ISBN 978-0-9977257-3-5

Steenbergen-Hu, S., Cooper, H.: A meta-analysis of the effectiveness of intelligent tutoring systems on college students' academic learning. J. Educ. Psychol. **106**, 331–347 (2014). https://doi.org/10.1037/a0034752

Stevens, R., Penuel, W.R.: Studying and fostering learning through joint media engagement. Paper presented at the Principal Investigators Meeting of the National Science Foundation's Science of Learning Centers, Arlington, VA (2010)

Stipek, D., Valentino, R.A.: Early childhood memory and attention as predictors of academic growth trajectories. J. Educ. Psychol. **107**(3), 771 (2015)

Stotsky, S.: Education reform: does anything work? Acad. Quest. **31**(4), 501–505 (2018)

Takeuchi, L.: Families matter: designing media for a digital age. In: The Joan Ganz Cooney Center at Sesame Workshop, New York (2011)

Takeuchi, L., Stevens, R.: The new coviewing: designing for learning through joint media engagement. In: The Joan Ganz Cooney Center at Sesame Workshop, New York (2011)

Taylor, K., Rohrer, D.: The effects of interleaved practice. Appl. Cogn. Psychol. **24**(6), 837–848 (2010)

The Nation's Report Card: NAEP Report Card: 2019 NAEP Mathematics Assessment (2019a). https://www.nationsreportcard.gov/highlights/mathematics/2019/g12/

The Nation's Report Card: NAEP Report Card: 2019 NAEP Reading Assessment (2019b). https://www.nationsreportcard.gov/highlights/reading/2019/g12/

Thompson, K.M., Gillis, T.J., Fairman, J., Mason, C.A.: Effective Strategies for Engaging Parents in Students' Learning to Support Achievement. Maine Education Policy Research Institute (2014)

UNESCO: 6 out of 10 children and adolescents are not learning a minimum in reading and math (2017). http://uis.unesco.org/en/news/6-out-10-children-and-adolescents-are-not-learning-minimum-reading-and-math

U.S. Department of Education, Institute of Education Sciences, What Works Clearinghouse: Middle school math intervention report; Cognitive Tutor Algebra I, July 2009. http://ies.ed.gov/ncee/wwc/interventionreport.aspx?sid=87

Väljataga, T., Poom-Valickis, K., Rumma, K., Aus, K.: Transforming higher education learning ecosystem: teachers' perspective. Interact. Des. Archit. J. **46**, 47–69 (2020)

VanLehn, K.: The relative effectiveness of human tutoring, intelligent tutoring systems, and other tutoring systems. Educ. Psychol. **46**, 197–221 (2011). https://doi.org/10.1080/00461520.2011.611369

Vygotsky, L.: Thought and language: newly revised and edited. A. Kozulin (ed.). The Massachusetts Institute of Technology, Cambridge (1986)

Willcox, K.E., Sarma, S., Lippel, P.H.: Online Education: A Catalyst for Higher Education Reforms. MIT, Cambridge (2016)

Yeniad, N., Malda, M., Mesman, J., Van IJzendoorn, M.H., Pieper, S.: Shifting ability predicts math and reading performance in children: a meta-analytical study. Learn. Individ. Differ. **23**, 1–9 (2013)

# Towards a Unified Model of Gamification and Motivation

Ian T. Dykens⬤, Angelique Wetzel, Stephen L. Dorton^(⊠) ⬤, and Eric Batchelor

Sonalysts, Inc., Waterford, CT 06385, USA
{idykens,hail}@sonalysts.com

**Abstract.** Since the advent of gamification, organizations have begun transitioning away from a "learning by listening" approach towards training programs that incorporate game-like elements with the hope that by doing so improvements in user performance, engagement, and motivation would be immediately realized. However, these outcomes are difficult to achieve in practice. Part of the difficulty encountered when designing and implementing a gamified training program can be traced back to the unknown relationships between game elements, user psychology, and pedagogical theory. This difficulty is encountered because the cause and effect relationships between the implemented game elements and the desired training outcomes remain unknown. Prior efforts have been made to construct best-practice guides to support the researchers and developers of gamified training programs; however, these guides rarely outline the relationship between specific game elements and student psychology. As a result, several models and definitions of gamification have been developed in concurrent isolation. Doing so has caused confusion within the domain of pedagogical gamification research. In an effort to reconcile the relationships between specific game elements, user performance, engagement, and motivation within Gamified Training Programs (GTP), we have made an initial step towards a model that unifies the extant understanding of gamification and its relationship with motivational psychology through the development of the Unified Gamification and Motivation (UGM) Model.

**Keywords:** Gamification · Training · Motivation · Engagement

## 1 Introduction

Gamification methods have become increasingly popular in recent years as organizations evaluate and refine their approaches to user training. Gamification has been defined as the use of game design elements within non-game contexts [14]. Gamified Training Programs (GTP) are beginning to replace the antiquated "learning by listening" approach through the incorporation of game-like elements that encourage free interaction with, and exploration within, prescribed training materials [16]. Gamification promises to enable organizations to achieve their goals of user behavior modification, skill development, and skill sustainment. However, the development of effective GTP has proven to be a formidable challenge for many organizations due to the unknown relationships

© Springer Nature Switzerland AG 2021
R. A. Sottilare and J. Schwarz (Eds.): HCII 2021, LNCS 12792, pp. 53–70, 2021.
https://doi.org/10.1007/978-3-030-77857-6_4

between game elements, user motivation, and pedagogical theory; as well as the unknown relationship between utilized game elements and desired training outcomes [29, 32, 45].

One of the primary concerns within gamification research is the lack of consensus regarding the effect of even the simplest game elements such as points, badges, and leaderboards (PBL) [15]. For example, prior research has attempted to identify improvements in user engagement through the implementation of PBL elements only to find that results were either a product of novelty or could not be identified as having originated from any single specific element [45]. Additionally, the theories and frameworks that constitute the user's psychology (i.e., motivation) within GTP remain widely undefined and reflect a similar lack of consensus as seen within literature examining game elements [15, 45].

Prior efforts have been made to construct heuristics and 'best-practice' guides for use in the development of GTPs [24, 27]. However, these guides rarely outline the relationship between game elements and user psychology. As a result, several models and definitions of gamification have been developed in concurrent isolation, which has caused confusion within the field of instructional gamification research. For example, Kiili's [25] model of experiential gaming aimed to incorporate Kolb's [17] 1984 cycle of experiential learning and Csikszentmihalyi's [12] flow state within an iterative development model. Although Kiili's model illustrated the relationship between flow and Garris et al.'s [16] game cycle, neither model addressed the underlying psychology of user motivation or engagement. Even within current research calling for the promotion of user autonomy through the use of informative feedback, a holistic representation of motivation's role within the gaming cycle appears to remain a nonentity [32].

Generally speaking, the field of gamification research is divided into two distinct markets: That of academia and that of commercial practitioners. Academic gamification research, such as that of de Freitas & Jarvis [13], aim to develop models of gamification through pedagogical research and science-based hypothesis testing. Conversely, the commercial sector adopts a more 'popular-science' approach, opting instead to apply rapid prototypes and mass-market distribution while relying on the real-world knowledge of designers and engineers. An example of such an approach is exemplified by Chou's Actionable Gamification Manual [10]. Likewise, the works of Burke [8] and Paharia [35] focus on providing a technician's guide by presenting examples of commercial successes and failures of applied gamification. Regardless of the criticisms of either approach, neither is wholly correct nor complete. The strength provided by the grounded theories established via the scientific approach is contrasted by the realized economic success of commercial gamification.

For that reason, the aim of this paper is to present research that was conducted to tie these approaches, constructs, and models together so that system developers would be able to trace specific game elements to specific impacts upon user performance. The resultant Unified Gamification and Motivation (UGM) Model illustrates the theorized relationships between specific game elements, sources of internal and external motivation, and the relationship between user engagement and performance. It is desired that the UGM Model will be used to guide future approaches within gamification research, with the ultimate goal of validating or refuting the relationships identified in the model using real-world data from GTPs across one or more enterprises. Employing this model as the metadata construct within a GTP will not only enable a personalized and empirical assessment of user motivation and training effectiveness, but could also support the continued advancement of GTPs that are instructional, enjoyable, and successful.

## 1.1 Advances Within the Field of Gamification Research.

The task of unifying game elements with motivational affordances is not a novel concept. Before modern gamification was defined by Deterding, Dixon, Khaled, and Nacke [14], others approached game design from a pedagogical standpoint. Garris, Ahlers, and Driskell [16] considered the breadth of prior research regarding education and user motivation to construct the Input-Process-Outcome Game Model. This model functionally represented an algorithmic approach that could be used to gamify a non-game task (i.e., user training). Within the model, both game characteristics and instructional content were shown feeding into a cyclical model of user action, system-generated feedback, and user cognition of the presented feedback. Within this cycle, motivational mechanisms that composed the user's psychology were believed to encourage their intrinsic desire to continue interacting with instructional content. The model ends by debriefing the user via the administration of an evaluation to gauge their retention of the desired training outcomes. In addition to their algorithmically-pedagogical approach to gamified training, Garris et al. [16] summarized two decades of prior game research in order to define six dimensions of game design: Fantasy, rules/goals, sensory stimuli, challenge, mystery, and control. Likewise, four characteristics of user cognition were defined: Interest, enjoyment, task involvement, and confidence. These four characteristics are some of the most supported aspects of motivation in the field of gamification, and have become the theoretical foundation of a multitude of gamification studies.

De Freitas & Jarvis [13] later utilized the prior work of Garris et al. [16] to develop the 4D-Framework of game based learning. The evolution of the 4D-Framework can be tracked through the following years as it was subsequently adapted to illustrate academia's emergent understanding of gamification. As such, the 4D-Framework began unifying models of user psychology and gamified training to classify 25 specific game elements [42] from which van Staalduinen & de Freitas [43] then developed the Game-Based Learning Framework (GBL Framework). The GBL Framework was developed as an attempt to create a unified model that illustrated the relationship between pedagogical theory, the 4D-Framework, Garris et al.'s [16] Game Model, Csikszentmihalyi's flow theory [12], and user motivation.

The GBL Framework clearly defined a three-phase pedagogic sequence (learning, instruction, and assessment), as well as a cyclic model of learning, experimentation, feedback, and continued user engagement. The GBL Framework provided a unified model that could be referenced by researchers to appreciate the process of establishing a GTP. However, despite its successes, the GBL Framework did not define what specific game elements support continued user motivation. Although van Staalduinen and de Freitas [43] acknowledge the relationship between user motivation and increased engagement, the relationship between increased engagement and improved performance has not been affirmed.

Determining the nature of the relationship between user engagement and performance is complicated by two principal factors. First, performance is a metric that can be defined by a multitude of criteria that are specific to each domain, user population, and training program. In one instance where increased test scores could be considered an improvement in performance, other agencies could put very little value on test scores and place more value on the time it takes for the user to complete a task, or the relative amount of deviation from a specified set of instructions. At face value it is impossible to know the impact that PBL style gamification mechanics could have on any or all of these metrics. As such, without having a reference guide that specifies how each individual gamification element could support, or deter the user's ability to display improved performance, it is understandably overwhelming. As a result, the developers of learning management systems are not able to guarantee that the introduction of PBL mechanics will lead to an observable improvement in the user's performance.

Second, achieving improved user engagement does not guarantee improved performance. Curriculum and system developers may hope to achieve higher levels of user performance using gamification techniques to bolster user engagement. However, performance improvements can only be realized if the core of the training materials are effective. Therefore, improved engagement with good training materials would likely benefit user performance, whereas improved engagement with ineffective training materials would not realize the same success.

## 1.2  Reviewing Prior Gamification Research

62 studies pertaining to gamification were reviewed and synthesized to facilitate a comparison of gamification approaches and reported outcomes. Additional support was provided by Dichev & Dicheva [15], which was a highly influential source due to its detailed analysis of game element research. Within the reviewed studies, 135 instances of game

**Table 1.**  Game dimensions and elements enumerated from the literature

| Dimension | | | | | | | | | |
|---|---|---|---|---|---|---|---|---|---|
| Purpose | 11 | Feedback | 98 | Ownership | 16 | Challenge | 6 | Reward | 4 |
| Element* | | | | | | | | | |
| Goals | 2 | Points | 24 | Choice | 2 | Health | 1 | Virtual Currency | 1 |
| Narrative | 3 | Badges | 27 | Avatar | 7 | Time Limit | 1 | Gift | 1 |
| Hero | 1 | Leaderboards | 24 | Customization | 1 | Competition | 4 | Random Reward (Digital) | 2 |
| Luck | 2 | Levels | 8 | Chatrooms | 1 | | | | |
| Other | 3 | Progress Tracking | 4 | Voting | 2 | | | | |
| | | Unlocks | 1 | Fame | 3 | | | | |
| | | Other | 10 | | | | | | |

**Note.** Each number represents the amount of times a dimension or element was enumerated in a sample of 46 articles. A total of 135 elements were enumerated. *Elements are refinements of their high-level dimensions element utilization were outlined (Table 1). In total, 52 positive outcomes of gamification were specified, some of which were reported in conjunction with similar outcomes (Table 2).

The performance measures reported within the reviewed literature varied widely in application; however, 12 of the 14 studies that reported an increase in performance used PBL mechanics. Despite this finding, it remains inappropriate to map the use of PBL mechanics to the reported increase in user performance because very few empirical measures were used to evaluate the impact of individual game elements [32]. In nearly all of the reviewed studies, game elements were presented in combination, making the process of isolating the individual effect of any single game element difficult. Mapping specific outcomes to any single game element will require the collection of large sums of data within a controlled longitudinal experiment [21]. Only then could the impact of specific game elements on user motivation be scientifically validated. In the meantime, it is possible to identify theoretical mappings between game elements and motivational affordances by reviewing prior literature within gamification research. The goal of the resultant model was to provide guidance for future empirical studies.

**Table 2.** Reported outcomes of gamified training programs from the literature

| Outcome | n | % |
|---|---|---|
| Increased Performance | 14 | 27 |
| Increased Participation | 5 | 10 |
| Improved Motivation | 5 | 10 |
| Improved Satisfaction | 5 | 10 |
| Increased Communication | 3 | 6 |
| Increased Playfulness | 3 | 6 |
| Increased use of Learning Environment | 2 | 3[†] |
| Increased Engagement | 2 | 3[†] |
| Improved Retention Period | 2 | 3[†] |
| Increased Time-on-Task | 1 | 2 |
| Satisfied Competence Need | 1 | 2 |
| Increased Effort | 1 | 2 |
| Reduced Attrition | 1 | 2 |
| Reduced Undesirable Behaviors | 1 | 2 |
| Other* | 6 | 12 |

**Note.** A total of 52 observed outcomes were reported from a sample of 46 studies. *'Other' refers to more unique outcomes such as reducing the amount of 'guess and check' behavior or improving student punctuality and attendance (which are slightly different than participation). [†] Values rounded down

## 2 Gamification Typology

In order to develop the UGM Model, it was necessary to deconstruct and reorganize the current understanding of how GTPs are structured. By doing so, it is possible to illustrate how different gamification methods can be mapped to specific motivational affordances, and in turn, how those affordances may support increased performance and other positive outcomes when applied within a GTP. A gamification typology was developed to illustrate these relationships between gamification dimensions and specific game elements (Fig. 1). This typology is not a how-to guide for gamification; rather, it is a summary of how gamification has been used and is currently defined by Deterding et al.'s [14] definition: the use of game design elements in non-game contexts.

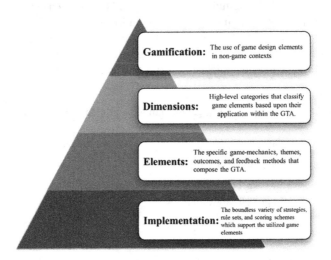

**Fig. 1.** Gamification typology.

### 2.1 The 5 Dimensions of Gamification

The elements used within a GTP can be categorized into five dimensions: Purpose, Feedback, Ownership, Challenge, and Reward. These dimensions were derived from the work of Garris et al. [16], de Freitas & Jarvis [13], and Wilson et al. [45], and have been broadened to simplify the classification of the game elements. Each of the five dimensions represents a general category of game elements based upon their application within a GTP.

- **Purpose:** The purpose dimension contains any and every game element that aims to instill a sense of meaning (valence), provide context (narrative), and establish clear and concise criteria for the successful completion of training objectives (e.g., quests, goals, etc.).
- **Feedback:** The feedback dimension represents the immense array of strategies that convey information regarding the user's performance within the GTP.

- **Ownership:** The ownership dimension represents the characteristics of a GTP which provide the user with avenues for customizing their training experience by providing methods of personal expression and opportunities to exercise free will.
- **Challenge:** Challenge represents the strategies which present opportunities for users to apply physical & cognitive effort towards the successful completion of solution identification and problem solving activities.
- **Reward:** The reward dimension represents potential strategies for acknowledging the user's applied efforts and achievements within a GTP.

### 2.2 Game Elements

Game elements are the specific mechanisms that make the GTP 'gamified'. Potential game elements range from PBL to boss fights, avatars, and competitions. There is no limit to the creation of new game elements, which is the reason for the continuous success found within the videogame industry. A selection of game elements are presented within Table 3 and are accompanied by a brief definition, and some sources that exemplify their application. Likewise, game elements featured within the developed UGM Model are those which were popular within the reviewed literature.

### 2.3 Implementation

The Implementation level of the gamification typology is intentionally vague to reflect the adaptable nature of gamification, and the near infinite number of strategies in which game elements could be implemented within a GTP. Examples of potential implementations can be seen in the utilization of PBL mechanics. Points can be weighted to incentivize the completion of particular training objectives, badges can be designed to reward specific behaviors, and leaderboards can be constructed in a multitude of configurations to reward high achievers. In order to detail the infinite potential implementations of game elements within the GTP, it would be essential to consider game design heuristics and even develop and validate a set of heuristics for each application of a GTP.

Moving forward, it will be essential that GTP developers design implementation strategies that complement the strengths of simultaneously utilized elements while avoiding the mediating factors of improper game design. The implemented rules, strategies, and values placed upon the utilized game elements should be selected based upon their theorized impact on user motivation while heeding the warnings and 'lessons learned' presented within technical literature. The successful gamification of a training program will require the vigilant consideration of game elements and their theorized impact on user motivation. Failure to adequately consider the impact of utilized game elements may result in the failure of a GTP (in terms of effectiveness) and may even result in a GTP being rejected by the users [28]. Herein lies the root of the gamification problem: How can training programs be effectively gamified so that the user's intrinsic motivation is supported while also encouraging users to complete specific training materials?

## 3  Motivation

The field of user training has seen a recent shift from a traditional, didactic model of instruction to a user-centered model which emphasizes a more active user role. It is

**Table 3.** Game elements within the UGM Model

| Game element | Definition | Exemplifying Sources |
|---|---|---|
| Competition | Competition represents any event which uses peer-vs-peer challenges with the aim of identifying the superior performer | [19, 39] |
| Quests | Quests (i.e., goals, objectives, missions, etc.) are tasks that are supported by clearly defined victory and failure states | [7, 39, 41] |
| Narrative | Narrative establishes the theme, history, and context of a GTP | [4, 6] |
| Avatar | An Avatar is the virtual construct that acts as a vessel for the user's personal identity within the GTP (e.g., the soldier in a FPS, Pac Man, Mario, etc.) | [1, 23, 39] |
| Player Generated Content | Player generated content generally defines any source of player customization within the GTP (e.g., player handles, emblems, sprays, etc.) | [3] |
| Voting | Voting is the process of soliciting user feedback to guide the development or progression of a GTP | [26, 40] |
| Social Comparison | Social Comparison is the phenomenon in which users consciously or unconsciously compare their progress or experiences within the GTP to those of their peers | [3, 38] |
| Leaderboard | Leaderboards visually represent empirical measurements of user performance in comparison to that of their peers. Traditionally, leaderboards use a ranked order diagram. Leaderboards are the most common application of points within gamified training programs | [29] |

(*continued*)

**Table 3.** (*continued*)

| Game element | Definition | Exemplifying Sources |
|---|---|---|
| Progress Trackers | Progress trackers are graphical representations of user achievement. Progress trackers can illustrate the completion of a procedure or the growth/decline of skill currency | [5] |
| Badges | Badges are virtual constructs that represent the completion of a particular objective. Badges are akin to awards and progress trackers, yet are universally available to users within a GTP and feature the clearly established victory states established by quests | [19, 34] |
| Gift | A gift is a reward that acknowledges user performance by presenting a financial/material gain (e.g., where the Nobel Prize is the award, the million dollar 'prize' is the gift) | [21, 37] |
| Award | Awards are rewards that are presented as acknowledgements of user performance and do not represent a financial/material gain (e.g., Medal of Honor, Purple Heart, etc.) | [9] |
| Solution Identification & Application | Solution Identification & Application is accomplished by designing a problem or a puzzle which is to be solved by users. The successful completion of a solution identification & application will require the application of taught declarative/procedural knowledge in unison with applied skill-based behaviors | [45] |
| Task Complexity | Task complexity reflects the level of difficulty which is designed into the solution identification & application strategies. The diffic0ulty of prescribed task are adapted to match user ability and to encourage continued personal development | [45] |

common practice within many modern learning management systems to motivate users through the use of numerous game elements. Their principal aim is to enhance the user's engagement with prescribed training materials. By designing learning environments with user motivation in mind, it is theorized that an increase in the duration and quality of the interaction will be realized, and as a result, organizations would be more likely to achieve their training objectives. A literature review was conducted to identify the motivational dimensions that could be leveraged to enhance a GTP in order to identify how increased interaction with a thoughtfully constructed GTP may impact, or be impacted by, a user's unique motivational affordances. Following the literature review, a number of theories were identified and analyzed in relation to one-another within the field of motivation. A thematic analysis was then conducted to determine the most recurring and relevant motivational elements that could then be applied within a GTP.

### 3.1 User Motivation Thematic Analysis

The thematic analysis resulted in the development of five primary dimensions of motivation based upon their frequent appearance within the literature regarding motivational theories. These five dimensions include Feedback, Valence, Goal-Setting, Autonomy, and Mastery (see Table 4).

- **Feedback:**Feedback (also called knowledge of results and progress in relation to goals) was found to have a positive influence upon a user's motivation across several of the reviewed theories [16, 18, 22, 30, 33, 35].
- **Valence:** Valence refers to the user's beliefs regarding the desirability of outcomes that are obtained by successfully completing their training. This factor is also referred to as "experienced meaningfulness" within the literature. As a rule-of-thumb, the more a user believes that the outcome of their training is meaningful, the more motivated they are to participate in the training in order to obtain the results [11, 16, 18, 31, 33, 36].
- **Goal-Setting:** Goal-setting was found to influence the user's motivation [16, 30, 33]. In particular, specific and challenging goals were found to be the most effective approaches to increased user motivation.
- **Autonomy:** Autonomy is a user's feeling of personal responsibility. Feelings of autonomy are related to high internal work motivation [18].
- **Mastery:** Mastery is experienced when a user achieves an expert level of competency at a particular task. Mastery is considered to be an important factor that can positively influence user motivation [2, 22, 36].

A number of personal characteristics that could influence a user's motivation to complete their training and potentially impact their level of performance within a GTP were identified. These personal characteristics include self-efficacy, achievement motivation, expectations for success, locus of control, and conscientiousness [11, 30, 36, 44]. Within Table 5, these five personal characteristics can be seen acting as moderators that have the potential to influence the relationship between game elements and user motivation. Table 6 outlines the relationships between the reviewed motivation theories and which of the five motivational elements and five moderators each theory is linked to. These relationships are represented within the UGM Model.

**Table 4.** The five primary dimensions of motivation

| Dimension | Description | Exemplifying Source(s) |
|---|---|---|
| Feedback | Also called knowledge of results, summary feedback (progress in relation to goals), feedback of performance | [16, 22, 30, 31, 33] |
| Valence | A user's beliefs regarding the desirability of outcomes obtained from training, also called experienced meaningfulness. In one theory, this comes from skill variety, task identity, and task significance | [11, 16, 30, 36] |
| Challenging Goals | Goals that challenge the user in respect to their ability | [16, 30, 33] |
| Autonomy | The degree of control a user has over their experience within the GTP | [18] |
| Mastery | Also called mastery goal orientation, the level of expertise and competence of the user | [2, 22, 36] |

**Table 5.** Common performance and motivation moderators

| Moderators | Description | Exemplifying Source(s) |
|---|---|---|
| Self-Efficacy | Belief in one's capabilities to organize and execute the courses of action required to produce given attainments | [11, 36] |
| Achievement | An individual's need to meet realistic goals and experience a sense of accomplishment | [11, 33, 44] |
| Expectancy for Success | An individual's perception of their competence at a certain activity in the future | [11] |
| Locus of Control | Those with an internal locus of control attribute their success to their own efforts and abilities | [11] |
| Conscientiousness | A personality trait characterized by organization, purposeful action, self-discipline and a drive to achieve | [11] |

**Table 6.** Links between the theories of motivation, motivational elements, and moderators

| Motivation Theory | Motivational Dimensions | | | | | Moderators | | | | |
|---|---|---|---|---|---|---|---|---|---|---|
| | Feedback | Valence | Goals | Autonomy | Mastery | Self-Efficacy | Achievement Motivation | Expectancy for Success | Locus of Control | Conscientiousness |
| Job Characteristics Model | X | X | | X | | | | | | |
| Goal-Setting Theory | X | X | X | | | X | | | | |
| Motivation-Hygiene Theory | X | | | | X | | | | | |
| Expectancy Value Theory | | X | | | | | X | X | | |
| Achievement Motivation Theory | X | | X | | | | X | | | |
| Model of Games and Learning | X | X | X | | | | | | | |
| Integrative Theory of Training Motivation | | X | | | | X | X | | X | X |
| Heuristic Model of Motivation | X | X | | | | | | X | | |

## 4 The Unified Gamification and Motivation (UGM) Model

The UGM Model (Fig. 2) was developed using the results of the two conducted literature reviews. The corresponding affiliations (as previously indicated in Table 6) were then added to illustrate the relationships between the dimensions of gamification, user motivation, and their moderating factors. The gamification typology is shown cascading from the top of the model towards the center, branching out incrementally to illustrate the theoretical breakdown from gamification dimensions into specific game elements. Below the gamification typology, a selection of motivational affordances are shown feeding into their respective theoretical models. These models are then shown supporting the user's sense of motivation as well as their interaction with the identified moderating factors.

At the base of the UGM Model, motivation is affiliated with engagement - a direct finding from the reviewed literature. Engagement is often confused with motivation when considering the impact of game elements on user training. In actuality, game elements are only believed to impact user motivation (as illustrated within the UGM Model). The degree and quality of the user's motivation will then either lead to sustained engagement or disengagement when the user's level of motivation is no longer adequate. Therefore, engagement is the physical and observable product of user motivation. As such, it can be assumed that an increase in user motivation leads to an increase in user engagement [45]. However, the relationship between user engagement and performance remains less clear. We can infer, based upon the reviewed literature that if an increase in motivation was found, and an increase in performance was reported, then it is likely that the increase in performance was due, at least in part, to the unreported increase in user engagement with either the prescribed training material or a GTP in general.

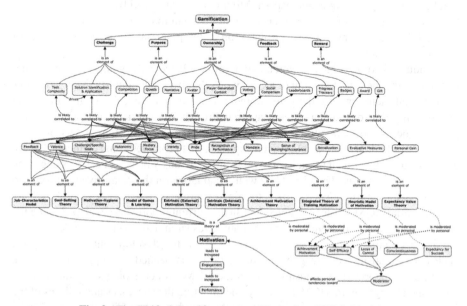

**Fig. 2.** The Unified Gamification and Motivation (UGM) Model.

The affiliations drawn between the gamification typology and the motivational theories and affordances were justified by the reported findings within the reviewed literature. However, affiliations between the gamification elements and motivational affordances were drawn based upon a combination of outcomes presented within the reviewed literature, as well as respectable conjecture from the authors' own perspectives. A reference chart of the drawn affiliations within the UGM Model is shown in Table 7.

## 5    Discussion

The UGM Model illustrates the affiliations between game elements and motivational affordances that should guide the development of a GTP. Arguably, the most important takeaway from the UGM Model is the complexity of the relationships between game elements and motivational affordances. Not only do single game elements affiliate with multiple motivational affordances, but the motivational affordances themselves relate to multiple theoretical approaches of user motivation. The complexity found within the breakdown of user motivation readily illustrates the degree of difficulty that is encountered when attempting to classifying any single theoretical foundation of motivation as the predominate contributor to user motivation within a GTP.

In complement to the presented motivational theories within the UGM Model, a breakdown of moderating factors was provided to illustrate how unique personality characteristics that are specific to each user could impact the relative effectiveness of specific game elements. It is likely that preexisting user-specific characteristics such as self-efficacy and conscientiousness, as well as prior dispositions towards mandated and gamified training, could derail a GTP once implemented [28]. This is identical to what many training professionals face on a daily basis: A student with a negative attitude will be difficult to motivate and instruct. Moving forward, it will be necessary to ensure the thoughtful design of game elements and implementation strategies that support user motivation while giving careful consideration to the potentially moderating effects of user predisposition.

Conducting knowledge elicitation to determine what specific game elements should be used during the initial fielding of a GTP would likely help to identify the general user motivational factors within the given domain. Once established, the ideal GTP would then use empirical data that had been captured through user interactions to identify what game elements most effectively promote desired behaviors in different sets of users. The GTP could then adopt a data-driven approach that promotes game elements that are engaging and educational to each user while simultaneously phasing back less engaging and effective elements. The ideal GTP would capitalize on the data-driven approach to provide each user with a personalized training experience.

The initial UGM Model presented within the current report was developed using the findings and theories presented within academic research. However, the model remains highly speculative and must be validated. As such, the development of an effective GTP is essential in order to generate the data that is needed to empirically validate or refute the theorized relationships within the UGM Model. Doing so would serve to refine and strengthen the UGM Model by documenting the successes and failures of the implemented game elements. When used as the foundation of a GTP, the UGM Model

**Table 7.** The UGM Model reference chart

| Motivational Elements | Challenge | | | Purpose | | Ownership | | | | Feedback | | | Reward | |
|---|---|---|---|---|---|---|---|---|---|---|---|---|---|---|
| | Task Complexity | Solution Identification & Application | Competition | Quests | Narrative | Avatar | Player Generate Content | Voting | Social Comparison | Leaderboards | Progress Trackers | Badges | Award | Gift |
| Feedback | | | | | | | | | | X | X | X | | |
| Valence | | X | X | X | X | | | | | | | X | | |
| Challenge | | X | X | X | | | | | | X | | | | |
| Autonomy | | | | X | | | | X | | | X | X | | |
| Mastery Focus | X | X | X | X | | | | | | X | | | | |
| Variety | | | X | X | X | | | | X | | | | | |
| Pride | | X | X | | | X | X | | X | X | | X | X | |
| Recognition of Performance | | | X | | | | | | X | X | | X | X | |
| Mandate | | | | X | | | | | | | | | | |
| Sense of Belonging | | | | | | X | X | | X | X | | | | |
| Socialization | | | X | X | | X | X | | X | X | | | | |
| Evaluative Measures | | | | | | | | | | | X | | | |
| Personal Gain | | | | | | | | | | | | | | X |

**Note.** The element 'quests' is shared by three dimensions: Challenge, Purpose, & Ownership would enable curriculum administrators to update the underlying theoretical relationships between utilized game elements and user motivation to reflect future advancements within the field of gamification. Any finding produced after the implementation of a GTP, in regards to user motivation, would likely draw considerable attention and interest from both commercial and academic institutions alike. Regardless, employing the UGM Model as the metadata construct within future GTPs will not only provide the foundation to personalized and empirical assessments of user motivation and training effectiveness, but could also support the continued advancement of gamified training programs that are instructional, enjoyable, and successful.

**Acknowledgements.** This material is based upon work supported by PEO IWS 5.0 under Contract No. N00178-17-C-1333. Any opinions, findings, and conclusions or recommendations expressed in this material are those of the authors, and do not necessarily reflect the views of PEO IWS 5.0. This document was approved for release with unlimited distribution (#2021-0032).

# References

1. Alcivar, I., Abad, A.G.: Design and evaluation of a gamified system for ERP training. Comput. Hum. Behav. **58**, 109–118 (2016)
2. Ames, C., Archer, J.: Achievement goals in the classroom: students' learning strategies and motivation processes. J. Educ. Psychol. **80**, 260–267 (1988)
3. Amriani, A., Aji, A., Utomo, A.Y., Wahidah, F., Junus, K.: Gamified E-learning model based on community of inquiry. Presented at the 2014 IEEE International Conference on Advanced Computer Science and Information Systems, Jakarta, Indonesia, pp. 474–480 (2014)
4. Armstrong, M.B., Landers, R.N.: An evaluation of gamified training: using narrative to improve reactions and learning. Simul. Gaming **48**(4), 513–538 (2017)
5. Bernik, A., Bubaš, G., Radošević, D.: A pilot study of the influence of gamification on the effectiveness of an e-learning course. Presented at the 26th Central European Conference on Information and Intelligent Systems (CECIIS 2015), pp. 73–79 (2015)
6. Bonde, M.T., et al.: Improving biotech education through gamified laboratory simulations. Nat. Biotechnol. **32**(7), 694–697 (2014)
7. Boskic, N., Hu, S.: Gamification in higher education: how we changed roles. Presented at the European Conference on Games Based Learning, Reading, United Kingdom, pp. 741–748 (2015)
8. Burke, B.: Gamify: How Gamification Motivates People to do Extraordinary Things. Bibliomotion Inc., New York (2014)
9. Çakıroglu, Ü., Basibüyük, B., Güler, M., Atabay, M., Memis, B.Y.: Gamifying an ICT course: Influences on engagement and academic performance. Comput. Hum. Behav. **69**, 98–107 (2017)
10. Chou, Y.: Actionable Gamification: Beyond Points, Badges, and Leaderboards. Octalysis Media, Freemont (2014)
11. Colquitt, J.A., LePine, J.A., Noe, R.A.: Toward an integrative theory of training motivation: a meta-analytic path analysis of 20 years of research. J. Appl. Psychol. **85**, 678–707 (2000)
12. Csikszentmihalyi, M.: Flow: The Psychology of Optimal Experience. HarperCollins, New York (1991)
13. de Freitas, S., Jarvis, S.: A framework for developing serious games to meet learner needs. Paper presented at the 2006 Interservice/Industry Training, Simulation, and Education Conference, Orlando, Florida, pp. 1–11 (2006)

14. Deterding, S., Dixon, D., Khaled, R., Nacke, L.: From game design elements to gamefulness: defining "gamification". Paper presented at the 2011 MindTrek conference, Tampere, Finland, pp. 1–15 (2011)

15. Dichev, C., Dicheva, D.: Gamifying education: what is known, what is believed and what remains uncertain: a critical review. Int. J. Educ. Technol. High. Educ. **14**(9), 1–36 (2017)

16. Garris, R., Ahlers, R., Driskell, J.E.: Games, motivation, and learning: a research and practice model. Simul. Gaming **33**, 441–467 (2002)

17. Gros, B.: Digital games in education: the design of game-based learning environments. ResearchGate, pp. 1–21 (2006)

18. Hackman, J.R., Oldham, G.R.: Motivation through the design of work: test of a theory. Organ. Behav. Hum. Perform. **16**, 250–279 (1976)

19. Hakulinen, L., Auvinen, T., Korhonen, A.: The effect of achievement badges on students' behavior: an empirical study in a university-level computer science course. Int. J. Emerg. Technol. Learn. **10**(1), 18–29 (2015)

20. Hamari, J., Koivisto, J.: "Working out for likes": an empirical study on social influence in exercise gamification. Comput. Hum. Behav. **50**, 333–347 (2017)

21. Hanus, M.D., Fox, J.: Assessing the effects of gamification in the classroom: a longitudinal study on intrinsic motivation, social comparison, satisfaction, effort, and academic performance. Comput. Educ. **80**, 152–161 (2015)

22. Herzberg, F.: One more time: how do you motivate employees? Harvard Business Review (1968)

23. Jang, J., Park, J., Yi, M.Y.: Gamification of online learning. Presented at the 17th International Conference on Artificial Intelligence in Education, Switzerland, pp. 646–649 (2015)

24. Karagiorgas, D.N., Niemann, S.: Gamification and game-based learning. J. Educ. Technol. Syst. **45**(4), 499–519 (2017)

25. Kiili, K.: Digital game-based learning: towards an experiential gaming model. Internet High. Educ. **8**(1), 13–24 (2005)

26. Knutas, A., Ikonen J., Nikula, U., Porras, J.: Increasing collaborative communications in a programming course with gamification: a case study. Presented at the 15th International Conference on Computer Systems and Technologies (CompSysTech 2014), New York, pp. 370–377 (2014)

27. Kuntas, A., van Roy, R., Hynninen, T., Granato, M., Kasurinen, J., Ikonen, J.: Profile-based algorithm for personalized gamification in computer-supported collaborative learning environments. Proceedings of GHITALY17 the 1st Workshop on Games-Human Interaction, Cagliari, Italy, pp. 1–6, April 2017

28. Landers, R.N., Armstrong, M.B.: Enhancing instructional outcomes with gamification: an empirical test of the technology-enhanced training effectiveness model. Comput. Hum. Behav. **71**, 499–507 (2017)

29. Landers, R.N., Landers, A.K.: An empirical test of the theory of gamified learning: the effect of leaderboards on time-on-task and academic performance. Simul. Gaming **45**(6), 769–785 (2014)

30. Locke, E.A., Latham, G.P.: Building a practically useful theory of goal setting and task motivation. Am. Psychol. **57**, 705–717 (2002)

31. McMillan, J.H., Forsyth, D.R.: What theories of motivation say about why learners learn. New Dir. Teach. Learn. **45**, 39–52 (1991)

32. Mekler, E.D., Bruhlmann, F., Tuch, A.N., Opwis, K.: Towards understanding the effects of individual gamification elements on intrinsic motivation and performance. Comput. Hum. Behav. **71**, 525–534 (2017)

33. Miner, J.B.: Organizational Behavior 1: Essential Theories of Motivation and Leadership. Routledge, New York (2015)

34. O'Byrne, W.I., Schenke, K., Willis, J.E., III., Hickey, D.T.: Digital badges: recognizing, assessing, and motivating learners in and out of school contexts. J. Adolesc. Health. **58**(6), 451–454 (2015)
35. Paharia, R.: Loyalty 3.0. McGraw Hill (2013)
36. Pintrich, P.R.: The role of motivation in promoting and sustaining self-regulated learning. Int. J. Educ. Res. **31**, 459–470 (1999)
37. Pettit, R.K., McCoy, L., Kinney, M., Schwartz, F.N.: Student perceptions of gamified audience response system interactions in large group lectures and via lecture capture technology: approaches to teaching and learning. BMC Med. Educ. **15**(92), 1–15 (2015)
38. Shi, L., Cristea, A.I., Hadzidedic, S., Dervishalidovic, N.: Contextual gamification of social interaction: towards increasing motivation in social e-learning. Presented at the 13th International Conference on Web-based Learning (ICWL 2014), Tallinn, Estonia, pp. 116–122 (2014)
39. Sillaots, M.: Gamification of higher education by the example of course of research methods. In: Popescu, E., Lau, R.W.H., Pata, K., Leung, H., Laanpere, M. (eds.) ICWL 2014. LNCS, vol. 8613, pp. 106–115. Springer, Cham (2014). https://doi.org/10.1007/978-3-319-09635-3_11
40. Smith, E., Herbert, J., Kavanagh, L., Reidsema, C.: The effects of gamification on student learning through the use of reputation and rewards within community moderated discussion boards. Presented at the 24th Annual Conference of the Australasian Association for Engineering Education, Australia (2014)
41. Su, C.H., Cheng, C.H.: A mobile gamification learning system for improving the learning motivation and achievements. J. Comput. Assist. Learn. **31**(3), 268–286 (2015)
42. van Staalduinen, J.P.: A first step towards integrating educational theory and game design. In: Felicia, P. (ed.) Improving Learning and Motivation Through Educational Games: Multidisciplinary approaches. IGI Global, Hershey (2010)
43. van Staalduinen, J.P., de Freitas, S.: A game-based learning framework: linking game design and learning. In: Learning to Play: Exploring the Future of Education with Videogames, pp. 1–37 (2011)
44. Wigfield, A., Eccles, J.S.: Expectancy-value theory of achievement motivation. Contemp. Educ. Psychol. **25**, 68–81 (2000)
45. Wilson, K.A., et al.: Relationships between game attributes and learning outcomes. Simul. Gaming **40**(2), 217–266 (2009)

# Designing Learning Experiences to Encourage Development of Critical Thinking Skills

Lauren Massey[1], Roger Smith[1] (ID), Elizabeth T. Whitaker[2], and Robert Wray[1](✉) (ID)

[1] Soar Technology, Inc, Ann Arbor, MI 48105, USA
wray@soartech.com

[2] Georgia Tech Research Institute, 400 10th St NW, Atlanta, GA, USA

**Abstract.** Today, various actors are exploiting and misusing online social media to spread disinformation and to create false narratives. This paper summarizes an education and training approach targeted to help people think more critically about potential disinformation. The approach we outline emphasizes the development and maturation of general critical-thinking skills, in contrast to technical skills (e.g., social network analysis). However, it also offers opportunity to apply these skills in a scaffolded, adaptive environment that supports the learner in putting concepts into use. The approach draws on the situated-learning paradigm to support skill development and reflects empirically-based best practices for pedagogy for critical thinking. This analysis and review provides context to inform the design of a learning environment to enable targeted practice of critical thinking skills. The paper outlines the high-level design, describes several specific "experiential lessons" and overviews a few technical challenges that remain to be overcome to make the training feasible for wide-scale use.

**Keywords:** Critical thinking · Instructional design · Adaptive training

## 1 Introduction

Today, various actors are exploiting and misusing online social media to spread disinformation and to create false narratives. These disinformation campaigns can be directed as locally as an individual or as broadly as a nation-state. Individual users of social media would benefit from improved awareness, understanding, and recognition of such disinformation campaigns. Further, organizations (corporations, governments, etc.) are increasingly subject to both deliberate disinformation and "organic" misinformation that can drastically impact the organization [1]. These organizations are increasingly looking to engage subject matter experts who can readily identify disinformation activities, assess impacts, and recommend counter maneuvers that can mitigate the effects of these campaigns.

Professional training for social-network analysts typically emphasizes concepts, tools and methods that can help an analyst understand the contours and dynamics of the information environment. Examples include technical training in social-network

© Springer Nature Switzerland AG 2021
R. A. Sottilare and J. Schwarz (Eds.): HCII 2021, LNCS 12792, pp. 71–87, 2021.
https://doi.org/10.1007/978-3-030-77857-6_5

analysis and topic analysis. These skills are critical for the development of effective analysts. However, we contend that in addition to the technical domain knowledge, critical thinking skills are also relevant and essential, both for detailed analysis by professionals, as well as improved overall awareness amongst users of online social networks.

Of course, individuals would benefit from looking at information objectively and dispassionately, aware of their own preferences and preconceptions and cognitive biases and how these factors can influence their own conclusions. A more practical issue is to define paths for learning and skill development that may result in this goal. The understanding of the impact of biases on human decision making broadly, and various kinds of analysis more specifically, has led to various theories and approaches that seek to limit the impact of biases. These methods include automated decision aids [2], attempts to "crowd source" perspectives from many individuals [3, 4], and improved educational and training methods [5–7].

This paper focuses on relevant and practical educational and training methods. How are critical thinking skills best learned and developed? We review a number of past and recent approaches, emphasizing approaches that focus on developing learner skills that deepen analysis and mitigate cognitive biases in practice. That is, we are particularly interested in methods and approaches that change behavior, rather than simply impart knowledge. We also focus especially on the use of simulation for skill-based training. Simulation allows a learner to repeatedly practice a skill in an environment that (when well designed) delivers timely and constructive feedback on the developing skill.

The remainder of the paper outlines a preliminary design for an experience-based learning environment focused on analyzing the structure of a narrative or argument, evaluating the sources and reliability of statements within those narratives, and identifying hypotheses and alternatives based on analysis. We also discuss design considerations in making such a learning environment feasible, including 1) the capture of learner activity and delivery of timely feedback and 2) the need for synthesis of learning content to support scalability and cost requirements.

## 2    Critical Thinking Skills

Understanding what is happening on social media and distinguishing between genuine and "fake" activity and information is a significant challenge, even for well-educated adults [8]. Online social network (OSN) activity introduces a number of factors that make interpretation of activities and sensemaking difficult. First, the scale of activity one encounters in online social networks is difficult to comprehend. For some topic or thread, 100s or even 1,000s of actors may contribute, react, and respond. Second, the nature of online social network activity is abstract and ephemeral compared to real-world social interaction. Online activity lacks many cues that can be used in interpersonal interaction that convey affect and establish trustworthiness. Finally, there is typically greater ambiguity in online interactions [9]. It can be difficult to know if some source is trustworthy or not. Actors may not always be who they present themselves to be but that lack of genuineness is easier to mask and harder to detect in online interactions [10].

These factors stress the fundamental limitations of human reasoning, resulting in so-called "cognitive biases," and may lead to distortions of understanding and conclusions

[11]. Examples include anchoring bias [12] – being overly influenced by a starting point in terms of estimating an outcome – and confirmation bias [13] – seeking and using only information that tends to confirm one's preconceptions. Although it is argued that various cognitive biases observed in human decision making were adaptive in the evolutionary frame of human cognitive development [14], human cognition does not appear well-adapted to the scale, abstraction, and ambiguities of online social media activity. The result is that a more deliberate and structured process of understanding and evaluating online social network activity is needed.

"Critical thinking" is the term often used and applied to situations that require a thorough analysis and evaluation of a situation. We assert that the encouragement and support of the development of critical thinking skills is a foundational tool to improve sensemaking for online social network activity. We adopt Dwyer's definition of critical thinking [15, 16]:

*"Critical thinking is a metacognitive process that, through purposeful, self-regulatory reflective judgment, consists of a number of sub-skills and dispositions that, when used appropriately, increases the chances of producing a logical solution to a problem or a valid conclusion to an argument."*

A key feature of this definition is that critical thinking is viewed as a metacognitive process with various components that can be brought to bear in a deliberate (or "purposeful") way to reach a valid conclusion. This process- and skill-based view of critical thinking skills (CTS) suggests that there should be ways to improve critical thinking abilities thru training and the deliberate development of skills. Going even further, the notion that there are specific sub-skills at least suggests that it may be possible to develop individual component skills via "part task" instruction and experience [17], allowing potential analysts of online social network activity to develop and to mature individual aspects of their critical-thinking skills as overall CTS ability develops.

Dwyer [15] surveys current approaches to assessment and instruction of CTS. Clear empirical outcomes are clouded by varying and inconsistent assessment measures and how they map to the specific CTS framework that is taught. However, Dwyer's review does identify two outcomes important for the work we are undertaking. First, CTS instruction is most effective when skills are introduced explicitly (a clear learning objective, rather than the by-product of learning something else) and separately from other material and then "infused" with specific domain content. Second, via a number of examples but in particular a carefully controlled experiment [18], computer-based instruction has been shown to have a marked impact on CTS (as measured by common survey instruments). This observation is important because one encounters recurring skepticism that computer-based instruction is conducive to the development of high-level cognitive skills like CTS, even when there is evidence that outcomes from classroom and computer-based instruction are comparable [19]. Dwyer's extensive review of the literature makes clear that computer-based instruction can be effective for this domain.

Finally, based on his extensive review of empirical outcomes in instruction and assessment of CTS, Dwyer offers four major desiderata for the design of CTS instruction. They are:

1. Active learning: Enabling learning by doing, including both guided practice and pedagogical scaffolding [20].
2. Computer-based instruction ("E-learning"): Using computer-based delivery of instructional content (including multimedia content) for learning.
3. Collaborative learning: Enabling learners to dialogue and discuss their work, including the informal construction of arguments, which is a core aspect of CTS.
4. Argument mapping: A technique that results in a visual representation of an argument or case.

Our instructional design for the development of CTS takes all of these factors into account, which we discuss further in the next section.

## 3   Instructional Approach to CTS

How might we approach a computer-based (or at least computer-mediated) approach to CTS training in the context of online social network sensemaking? Figure 1 illustrates the high-level approach we are taking. Existing domain and tool training are already available to train a potential analyst in both the specifics of domain concepts (e.g., social network analysis) and the introduction of various CTS concepts, such as logical fallacies in arguments and metacognitive monitoring for cognitive biases. Traditional CTS education and domain-technical training provide the "foundations" (grey, dashed lines) for our approach.

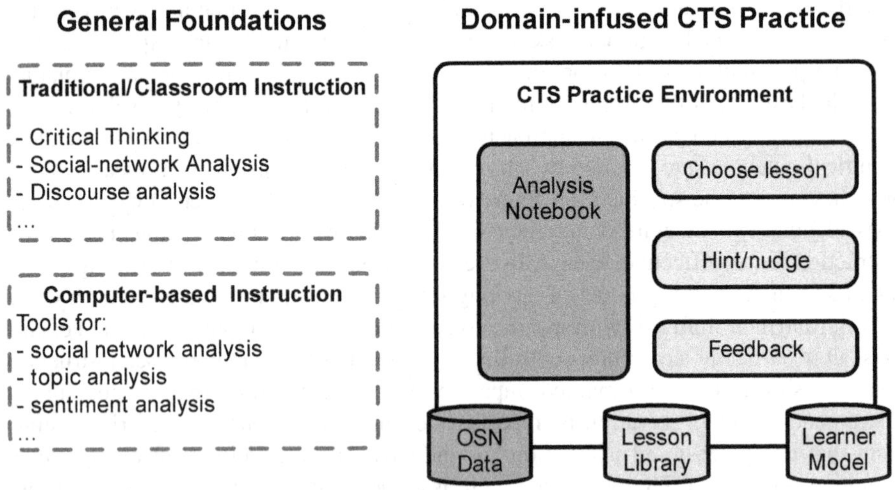

**Fig. 1.** The instructional approach to CTS supplements traditional instruction in critical thinking and methods of social-media analysis with a practice environment that allows learners to use skills and apply concepts in the context of social-media analysis.

In accordance with the "best practices" for CTS pedagogy as outlined in the previous section, we seek to complement these foundational training and learning methods and tools with a practice-/game-environment that will allow the learner to gain experience and receive feedback in using and applying CTS skills. Practice exercises are situated within the context of sensemaking about social media activity (topic analysis, social network analysis, etc.). Overall, this design provides the "mix" of overt CTS instruction, domain instruction, and "infused" examples and practice that Dwyer identifies as the most effective for the development of CTS [15].

As illustrated in the figure, the practice environment includes domain-centric components (pink) and learner-centric components (yellow). The primary domain component is a task-aware software notebook that both presents and captures notes from an analysis. The following section describes how we are using this notebook for some specific lessons. The system also includes a repository of online social network data (e.g., Twitter posts) that can be used along with the notebook. Currently, we are planning to use pre-processed data for the lessons so that the learner can focus on higher-level analysis tasks rather than needing to know how to use specific social-network analysis tools for CTS-focused practice.

**Table 1.** Mapping desired pedagogical features to practice environment capabilities.

| Pedagogical feature | Capabilities and approach |
| --- | --- |
| Active learning | The practice environment gives the learner autonomy to make decisions and explore alternatives. It guides focus toward well-defined analysis goals and questions (scaffolding), but in the context of a realistic analysis challenge |
| E-learning | The practice environment is a software environment. It supports the major advantages of computer-based instruction, including repeatability, anytime availability, and the ability to narrow problem scope to match abilities and reduce learner cognitive load |
| Collaborative learning | The practice environment as designed can be used by small teams of co-located learners working together. Longer-term, the practice environment may also support a similar form of collaboration, as well as more formal collaborative exercises (e.g., checking one another's work on a joint problem) |
| Argument mapping | The notebook design will include an ability to construct argument maps. Longer-term, we envision a tool that could partially construct argument maps (for a well-defined lesson) automatically, which will support both learner scaffolding as well as enable more targeted and tailored feedback |

The yellow components are designed to support improved learning and fulfill the desiderata for CTS learning environments introduced in the previous section. The strategy is summarized in Table 1. The learning components are founded on prior work in developing experiential learning environments that dynamically adapt to learner needs, providing targeted feedback [21, 22], coaching and hinting [23], and adaptive selection of learning experiences appropriate for the learner's current need [24, 25]. Adaptive interventions are enabled by on-going assessment and a learner model that estimates learner abilities and needs [26].

The learning environment includes a library of lessons that can be chosen based on the learner's progress and the system's assessment of learner needs. We have developed methods for defining experiential lessons (or "scenarios") so that they can be easily authored by instructional designers but that also embed meta-data to support adaptive selection and encode sufficient "hooks" to support alternative paths and dynamic assessment [27, 28].

Having introduced the high-level approach and outlined the technical foundations to realizing that approach, we now turn to describing some specific examples of lessons in the CTS practice environment.

## 4   Experiential Development of Critical Thinking Skills

In this section, we describe a number of examples to illustrate concretely the design of the CTS learning environment introduced above. The lessons are structured in accordance with a common framework of CTS used in higher education, as codified in a 1990 Delphi Report [29]. Table 2 summarizes this Delphi Report framework as we are applying it in lesson designs for our system. There are multiple CTS frameworks on which to found and center this design [15] and it may be that other frameworks are apt for future lessons. However, the framework does provide context and focus for the three primary skills targeted in the lessons described in the following subsections.

**Table 2.** The Delphi Report's framework for core critical thinking skills and sub-skills [28].

| Critical thinking skill | Definition (from Delphi Report) | Subskills |
|---|---|---|
| Analysis | "...*identify the intended and actual inferential relationships among statements, questions, concepts, descriptions or other forms of representation intended express beliefs, judgments, experiences, reasons, information, or opinions*" | Examining ideas Identifying arguments Analyzing arguments |
| Evaluation | "...*assessment of propositions and claims in terms of their credibility, relevance, logical strength (i.e. with respect to their relationship with other propositions) and the potential for omissions, bias and imbalance in the argument, thus deciding the overall strength or weakness of an argument*" | Assessing claims Assessing arguments |
| Inference | "... 'gathering' of credible, relevant and logical evidence based on the previous analysis and evaluation of available evidence, for the purposes of 'drawing a reasonable conclusion'" | Querying evidence Conjecturing alternatives Drawing conclusions |

We next outline lessons based on the CTS framework presented in Table 2. The specific lessons are summarized according the subskills and core critical-thinking skill of the framework in Table 3. Although the lessons are presented here in a temporal progression through an analysis, each lesson targets specific skills in a stand-alone fashion, rather than assuming and relying on a pre-defined, fixed, sequential progression thru the lessons. This approach allows flexibility, so that various lessons can be presented or chosen according to specific subskills for which a learner may benefit from further practice. Such dynamic, adaptive environment presentation of content is consistent with the goal of presenting real but achievable challenges as a learner progresses [30, 31].

Finally, to "infuse" with domain examples with CTS practice, all of the lessons are situated within the context of social media analysis. The lessons chosen for this training are centered around a relevant social-media topics, the response to coronavirus in the United Kingdom. (The lesson examples are inspired by actual OSN activity but are wholly synthetic; no real data or account information is used in the examples presented in the paper.)

In the example lessons, learners are presented with the task of reviewing the analysis of a "colleague." The trainee is told that their colleague's task was to review a provided given dataset and assess if there is a need for an intervention because of a growing number of protests. The prior analysis (or sub-sections of it) is provided to the learner and the learner is given a specific task, corresponding to one of the CTS sub-skills enumerated in Table 2. Although the learner is informed the work they are reviewing is from a colleague analyst's assessment, it is actually an instructor-authored argument focused on the sub-skills the learner needs to practice.

Table 3. Mapping individual lessons to CTS sub-skills.

| Lesson | Learning objective (practice a sub-skill) | CTS |
|--------|------------------------------------------|-----|
| 1 | Identify the argument | Analysis |
| 2 | Create an argument map | Analysis |
| 3 | Assess credibility of claims | Evaluation |
| 4 | Assess relevance | Evaluation |
| 5 | Recognize logical fallacies | Evaluation |
| 6 | Draw conclusions | Inference |

### 4.1 Example Lesson: Analysis

Analysis lessons are focused on identification and understanding of arguments. The learner is provided a summary analysis. The specific task for this lesson is to identify arguments leading to a summary recommendation. Specifically, this lesson directs the learner to 1) identify the analyst's recommendation, 2) identify the argument(s) that support the recommendation, and 3) characterize how each the individual arguments relates to the recommendation (e.g., does the argument support or oppose the final recommendation?). These three tasks directly map to the three sub-skills of the CTS analysis described in Table 2.

An example of a "completed" analysis and resulting recommendation is shown in Fig. 2. The figure enumerates a series of statements that comprise the "prior analysis" that the learner has been asked to review in the Analyst Notebook. In this lesson, the existing analysis focuses on the activities of a specific OSN account (@decaf30) and various statements that the prior analyst has observed about the activities of this account and related accounts. The statements in the analysis may or may not relate to the resulting recommendation, which is to "ban account @decaf30 from platform", as shown on line 25.

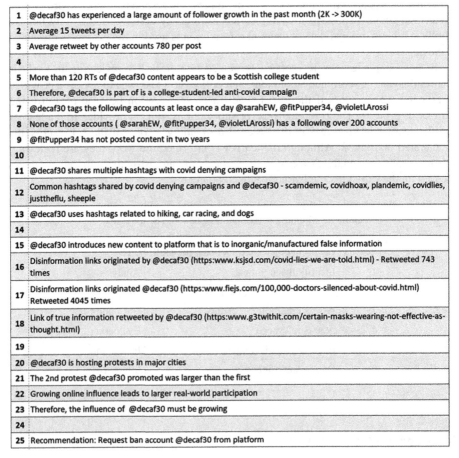

| 1 | @decaf30 has experienced a large amount of follower growth in the past month (2K -> 300K) |
| 2 | Average 15 tweets per day |
| 3 | Average retweet by other accounts 780 per post |
| 4 | |
| 5 | More than 120 RTs of @decaf30 content appears to be a Scottish college student |
| 6 | Therefore, @decaf30 is part of is a college-student-led anti-covid campaign |
| 7 | @decaf30 tags the following accounts at least once a day @sarahEW, @fitPupper34, @violetLArossi |
| 8 | None of those accounts ( @sarahEW, @fitPupper34, @violetLArossi) has a following over 200 accounts |
| 9 | @fitPupper34 has not posted content in two years |
| 10 | |
| 11 | @decaf30 shares multiple hashtags with covid denying campaigns |
| 12 | Common hashtags shared by covid denying campaigns and @decaf30 - scamdemic, covidhoax, plandemic, covidlies, justtheflu, sheeple |
| 13 | @decaf30 uses hashtags related to hiking, car racing, and dogs |
| 14 | |
| 15 | @decaf30 introduces new content to platform that is to inorganic/manufactured false information |
| 16 | Disinformation links originated by @decaf30 (https:www.ksjsd.com/covid-lies-we-are-told.html) - Retweeted 743 times |
| 17 | Disinformation links originated @decaf30 (https:www.fiejs.com/100,000-doctors-silenced-about-covid.html) Retweeted 4045 times |
| 18 | Link of true information retweeted by @decaf30 (https:www.g3twithit.com/certain-masks-wearing-not-effective-as-thought.html) |
| 19 | |
| 20 | @decaf30 is hosting protests in major cities |
| 21 | The 2nd protest @decaf30 promoted was larger than the first |
| 22 | Growing online influence leads to larger real-world participation |
| 23 | Therefore, the influence of  @decaf30 must be growing |
| 24 | |
| 25 | Recommendation: Request ban account @decaf30 from platform |

**Fig. 2.** A lesson presents a "colleague's" prior work in the Analyst Notebook and asks the learner to perform specific steps.

The learner must identify which arguments in the text are related to that recommendation by highlighting the text, as shown in Fig. 3. For example, line 15 states the account @decaf30 is spreading disinformation by posting false articles and line 16 and 17 supports this statement by indicating specific links to the "fake news" articles.

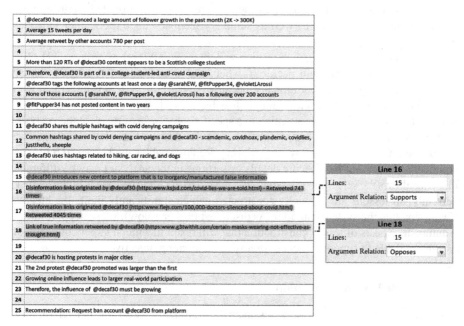

| 1 | @decaf30 has experienced a large amount of follower growth in the past month (2K -> 300K) |
| 2 | Average 15 tweets per day |
| 3 | Average retweet by other accounts 780 per post |
| 4 | |
| 5 | More than 120 RTs of @decaf30 content appears to be a Scottish college student |
| 6 | Therefore, @decaf30 is part of is a college-student-led anti-covid campaign |
| 7 | @decaf30 tags the following accounts at least once a day @sarahEW, @fitPupper34, @violetLArossi |
| 8 | None of those accounts ( @sarahEW, @fitPupper34, @violetLArossi) has a following over 200 accounts |
| 9 | @fitPupper34 has not posted content in two years |
| 10 | |
| 11 | @decaf30 shares multiple hashtags with covid denying campaigns |
| 12 | Common hashtags shared by covid denying campaigns and @decaf30 - scamdemic, covidhoax, plandemic, covidlies, justtheflu, sheeple |
| 13 | @decaf30 uses hashtags related to hiking, car racing, and dogs |
| 14 | |
| 15 | @decaf30 introduces new content to platform that is to inorganic/manufactured false information |
| 16 | Disinformation links originated by @decaf30 (https:www.ksjsd.com/covid-lies-we-are-told.html) - Retweeted 743 times |
| 17 | Disinformation links originated @decaf30 (https:www.fiejs.com/100,000-doctors-silenced-about-covid.html) Retweeted 4045 times |
| 18 | Link of true information retweeted by @decaf30 (https:www.g3twithit.com/certain-masks-wearing-not-effective-as-thought.html) |
| 19 | |
| 20 | @decaf30 is hosting protests in major cities |
| 21 | The 2nd protest @decaf30 promoted was larger than the first |
| 22 | Growing online influence leads to larger real-world participation |
| 23 | Therefore, the influence of @decaf30 must be growing |
| 24 | |
| 25 | Recommendation: Request ban account @decaf30 from platform |

| Line 16 | |
| --- | --- |
| Lines: | 15 |
| Argument Relation: | Supports ▼ |

| Line 18 | |
| --- | --- |
| Lines: | 15 |
| Argument Relation: | Opposes ▼ |

**Fig. 3.** Illustration of learner engagement with an analysis lesson.

After the learner selects specific lines, a pop-up box appears near the selected text and request input related to the line, as depicted in Fig. 3. The learner provides information about

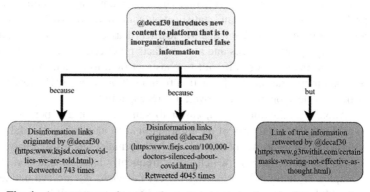

**Fig. 4.** Argument map based on learner statement categorization actions for lines 15–18 of provided analysis.

specific lines in the analysis, such as marking lines that support or oppose assertions in other lines. In the example, the learner has indicated that line 16 supports line 15 while line 18 offers opposes line 16.

The information captured in this analysis can be used to create an argument map to visually present the learner's interpretation of the analysis. The argument map representation of the learner's inputs in Fig. 3 is shown in Fig. 4. We are exploring ways to allow the learner to view an argument map based on the classifications they have made, as well as to allow learners to create such argument maps themselves within the Analyst Notebook.

The system monitors the learner as they progress and can provided feedback both as specific actions are taken as well as summary feedback once the learner indicates that they have completed the specified analysis task. Based on prior work in tailoring feedback to both a learner's specific action and their overall level of progress [21, 32], we envision a system that will decide if, when, and what kinds of "nudges", "hints" and "feedback" to provide. Additionally, because the learning system is integrated with the notebook, more explicit scaffolding is feasible as well, such as using visualization methods to direct the learner's attention to a specific subset of assertions in the analysis.

Variation is another important dimension of the design. Variation via alternative lessons would enable both replay and tailoring. Replay enables the learner to repeat an experiential lesson but the specific details (assertions in the analysis) may be different. Tailoring allows the selection of lessons customized to the observed needs of the learner. Currently, all lessons are manually constructed, which significantly limits the breadth of variation that the system can offer. As discussed further below), we see opportunities to automate aspects of lesson construction that will result in a much larger collection of lessons available to support practice for a specific learning objective.

### 4.2   Example Lesson: Evaluation

Evaluation lessons focus on the assessment of arguments based on their credibility, relevance, and logical strength. Assessment of credibility refers to ensuring that the evidence for an argument is reliable. There are many ways a credible source could pose problems (e.g., a "significant" statistical outcome may not provide a complete story). We are developing lessons that will allow learners to assess foundational claims via reference to underlying data sources and also artifacts produced from specialized analysis tools. These lessons are more difficult to construct (and to sketch in a paper) because they depend on integration of information from multiple sources. However, such lessons are critical for development of an overall CTS capability.

Another evaluation lesson, easier to summarize in a paper, focuses on the need to evaluate the soundness of an argument and to identify logical fallacies in unsound arguments. There are many examples of both formal (logically inconsistent) and informal logical fallacies, many of which occur frequently in argumentation. Table 4 lists five examples of commonly occurring logical fallacies. We are evaluating which specific logical fallacies are most important to include in the overall learning system, but these examples illustrate the kinds of fallacies that may occur in arguments for which the system will allow the learner to practice.

As in the analysis lesson, an argument evaluation lesson presents the learner with a series of assertions, premises and conclusions, within the notebook tool. Figure 5 presents an example of a conclusion and the premises contributing to that conclusion. For this lesson, the learner is asked to assess the soundness of the analyst's argument and is directed to assume direct evidence (e.g., the number of protesters at actual events that have occurred) is correct/has been previously verified.

The evidence that the analyst "cites" does support the conclusion that the account's followers are growing quickly and that real-world protests based on the account's activity are also growing. However, the argument then extrapolates from follower growth and protest size to conclude that the real-world participation growth will continue to grow at the same rates going forward. This is an example of a "slippery slope" argument (as defined in the table) and fails to consider other factors, such as network growth dynamics (growth tends to slow as group size gets bigger) and the practical limitations that will arise as real-world protests increase in size.

**Table 4.** Examples of logical fallacies that can be introduced in evaluation-focused lessons.

| Logical fallacy | Description |
| --- | --- |
| Affirming the consequent | Inferring the converse of a true conditional statement (also known as converse error, fallacy of the converse) |
| Affirming a Disjunct | When there is an "or" relationship in some premise and one of the factors is shown to be true, then the other factors is assumed to be false (inverse error, fallacy of the inverse) |
| Generalization | A mistake in which examples are presented from a class in which some property holds is taken as meaning all examples of the class hold that property |
| Slippery Slope | An argument that consists of a series of events in which one outcome leads to another outcome without (apparent) consideration of counter-arguments and possibilities |
| Post hoc ergo propter hoc | A conclusion based solely on the order of events, which does not consider other factors potentially responsible for the result that might rule out the connection |

Learning support for this kind of lesson is largely limited to providing feedback on the learner's conclusion. However, it can be differentiated and customized based not only on the straightforward "correct" or "incorrect" results but also the kind of mistake the learner makes. For this example, if the learner chose the "post hoc" fallacy instead of "slippery slope," feedback could be presented that further distinguishes between these cases, such as highlighting the "past tense" focus of the "post hoc" fallacy and the "future tense" framing of "slippery slope".

Finally, similar to the analysis lessons, as the learner progresses through evaluation lessons, the system can adapt to provide more examples depending on the needs of the learner and their performance assessing credibility, relevance, and logical fallacies. If the learner is struggling to identify specific fallacies then the presented lessons can be focused toward more examples of that fallacy.

### 4.3 Example Lesson: Inference

Inference lessons concentrate on drawing conclusions. This process moves the learner focus from analyzing and evaluating existing information (the "colleague's" analysis)

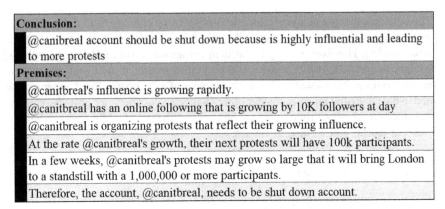

**Fig. 5.** Illustration of a fallacious argument in an evaluation lesson.

toward producing new information. The lesson is similar to the evaluation lesson (Fig. 6). A number of premises are provided but the conclusion is omitted. The learner must evaluate the premises and then draw a conclusion. Currently, the approach to these lessons is to allow the learner to choose from a pre-authored list but, as the system develops, we expect to enable a user to enter their suggested argument as free-text.

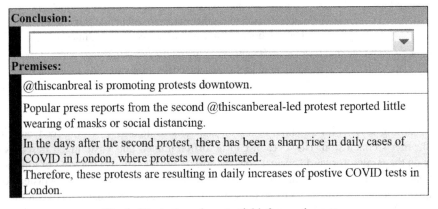

**Fig. 6.** Illustration of a potential inference lesson.

The premises provided may include distracting/irrelevant information, logical fallacies, or premises not supported by evidence. The learner must be able to examine the evidence given through noise to arrive at a valid conclusion. For example, we anticipate pairing these lessons with evaluation lessons focused on identification of fallacies, where the inference lessons are focused on producing a better conclusion/sound argument in comparison to the fallacious ones.Once the learner has provided a conclusion, the response should be assessed. Assessing a response chosen from a pre-defined list is obviously simple; reliable assessment of free-text responses will be much more challenging. Feedback can address not only correctness, but also indicate or highlight potential gaps in their consideration of the solution (e.g., overlooking some claim or accepting a claim uncritically) if they drew the wrong conclusion, overlooked evidence given, or suffered from a logical fallacy. Outcomes of the feedback is recorded and used to inform future training attempts.

## 5  Practical Requirements for Feasibility and Effectiveness

The practice lessons we have described are responsive to best practices for the development of critical thinking skills and provide an opportunity to develop and to exercise specific components of these skills in the context of real domain examples. We are currently developing software prototypes that will enable demonstration, pilot testing and further refinement of the approach. However, in order to provide a customized and tailored learning experience that is also practical for routine delivery of effective lessons, two additional functional requirements must be addressed: learner instrumentation and content generation.

In order to provide a customized, adaptive learner experience, the system needs to understand what the learner is thinking, or at least what actions that they may be taking in response to those thoughts. The Analyst Notebook is central to our instrumentation strategy, as it provides a mechanism for capturing fine-grained user actions (clicks, selections, etc.) and provides a common interface for user interaction. Although full instrumentation of all the tools that an analyst might use would be beneficial, that path is not feasible given the proprietary characteristics of the tools. This constraint, while at first seemingly limiting, has allowed the design and user experience to focus much more centrally on CTS, rather than technical details of analysis. That is, in reference to Dwyer's recommendations, the resulting lessons are "infused" with social-network domain examples, but remain focused on argumentation and critical thinking rather than technical domain expertise.

We capture and package learner data in a consistent format that allows integration across various sources of instrumentation [33] and that includes components that can measure and assess responses during the lesson, rather than just at the end. In previous work, we have also instrumented to enable passive detection of behavioral cues, such as mouse movements [34]. Such passive cues can be used to estimate confidence in a learner's choice [35, 36] and may be a relevant consideration as the prototype develops.

The other key challenge, perhaps more difficult to overcome, is the need for effective but inexpensive content generation. There are two primary needs for content generation: lesson authoring and tailored feedback. Currently, both the lessons and the feedback are manually authored. This approach is acceptable for demonstration but will not scale to allow learners the varied and tailored practice that is likely needed to support highly developed CTS. We are currently exploring the use of text generation via various transformer-based, generative-language models [37, 38] to provide examples of source data to provide evidence (including disconfirming evidence) for a premise. For example, Line 13 in Fig. 2 asserts that @decaf30 posts about a range of everyday topics, which is indirectly an argument that @decaf30 is not a "bot" or "troll" account. We are using text generation to produce text examples that supports (or counters) such claims in the arguments of lessons. This text-generation capability will make it vastly easier to create lessons that allow the learner to assess the credibility of a claim without needing intensive, manual authoring.

## 6 Conclusions

There is an acute need for skilled operators who understand both the propagation and dynamics of online social information and can think critically about the narratives, actors, and groups thru which those dynamics occur. In this paper, we have outlined a prototype practice environment designed to enable practice and development of critical thinking skills within the context of these social-network effects. The practice environment is under development and is being coordinated with the development of a CTS curriculum and technical training in OSN analysis tools. In addition to the challenge of developing a learning environment, we are also developing learner instrumentation and content generation methods designed to support the delivery of effective learning while also being scalable, cost-effective, and accessible.

As we develop and pilot further, we will be able to investigate and evaluate questions that cannot be readily addressed until there is a more fully functional system. These questions include:

- How much investment of time from a learner is needed before meaningful differences in overall performance come about? Because the domain itself is already complex, fast-changing, and not fully understood, the methods used to develop critical thinking skills must be highly efficient. It is unlikely that the targeted learners will be able to invest time comparable to a college course on CTS. Thus, a core question is to identify an approximate meaningful but minimal time investment. This need also motivates the desire to use tailoring and adaptation to attempt to provide each individual learner a targeted and time-efficient experience.
- What specific learning objectives and lesson elements should be prioritized? Are there specific skills that should be emphasized or specific biases that should be a particular focus within the CTS framework? These questions pertain to both how much is known about how to improve performance in specific ways and also identifying specific skills and de-biasing strategies with larger potential impact in the online social media domain. The lessons we presented here, based on a relatively mature CTS educational framework, are a good start, but it is an open question how to best design and structure CTS practice experiences to ensure effective learn.

**Acknowledgements.** This work was supported by the Office of Naval Research via contracts N68335-18-C-0724, N68335-20-C-0085, and N68335-20-C0952. The views and conclusions contained in this document are those of the authors and should not be interpreted as representing the official policies, either expressed or implied, of the Department of Defense or Office of Naval Research. The U.S. Government is authorized to reproduce and distribute reprints for Government purposes notwithstanding any copyright notation hereon.

# References

1. Singer, P.W., Brooking, E.T.: LikeWar: The Weaponization of Social Media. Eamon Dolan Books (2018)
2. Phillips-Wren, G., Power, D.J., Mora, M.: Cognitive bias, decision styles, and risk attitudes in decision making and DSS. J. Decis. Syst. **28**, 63–66 (2019)
3. Saab, F., Elhajj, I.H., Kayssi, A., Chehab, A.: Modelling cognitive bias in crowdsourcing systems. Cogn. Syst. Res. **58**, 1–18 (2019)
4. Tetlock, P.E., Gardner, D.: Superforecasting: The Art and Science of Prediction. Crown Publishers, New York (2015)
5. Fay, R.G., Montague, N.R.: Witnessing your own cognitive bias: a compendium of classroom exercises. Issues Account. Educ. **30**, 13–34 (2014)
6. Dunbar, N.E., et al.: Implicit and explicit training in the mitigation of cognitive bias through the use of a serious game. Comput. Hum. Behav. **37**, 307–318 (2014)
7. Sellier, A.-L., Scopelliti, I., Morewedge, C.K.: Debiasing training improves decision making in the field. Psychol. Sci. **30**, 1371–1379 (2019)
8. Greifeneder, R., Jaffé, M.E., Newman, E.J., Schwarz, N. (eds.): The Psychology of Fake News: Accepting, Sharing, and Correcting Misinformation. Routledge, Milton Park (2020)
9. Marín-López, I., Zych, I., Monks, C.P., Ortega-Ruiz, R.: Empathy, morality and social and emotional competencies in interpersonal interactions online. In: Coetzee, M. (ed.) Thriving in Digital Workspaces, pp. 217–233. Springer, Cham (2019). https://doi.org/10.1007/978-3-030-24463-7_11
10. Beskow, D.M., Carley, K.M.: Bot-hunter: A Tiered Approach to Detecting & Characterizing Automated Activity on Twitter. SBP-BRiMS (2018)
11. Kahneman, D.: Thinking, Fast and Slow. Doubleday, New York (2011)
12. Tversky, A., Kahneman, D.: Judgment under uncertainty: hueristics and biases. Science **185**, 1124–1131 (1981)
13. Nickerson, R.S.: Confirmation bias: a ubiquitous phenomenon in many guises. Rev. Gen. Psychol. **2**, 175–220 (1998)
14. Haselton, M.G., Nettle, D., Andrews, P.W.: The evolution of cognitive bias. In: Buss, D. (ed.) The Handbook of Evolutionary Psychology. Wiley, Hoboken (2005)
15. Dwyer, C.P.: Critical Thinking: Conceptual Perspectives and Practical Guidelines. Cambridge University Press/Sheridan Books, Cambridge (2017)
16. Dwyer, C.P., Hogan, M.J., Stewart, I.: An integrated critical thinking framework for the 21st century. Think. Skills Creativity **12**, 43–52 (2014)
17. Adams, J.A.: Part trainers. In: Finch, G. (ed.) Educational and Training Media: A Symposium. National Academy of the Sciences, Washington, D.C. (1960)
18. Hitchcock, D.: The effectiveness of computer-assisted instruction in critical thinking. Informal Logic **24**, 183–218 (2004)
19. Astleitner, H.: Teaching critical thinking online. J. Instr. Psychol. **29**, 53–76 (2002)
20. Pea, R.D.: The social and technological dimensions of scaffolding and related theoretical concepts for learning, education, and human activity. J. Learn. Sci. **13**, 423–451 (2004)
21. Wray, R.E., Woods, A., Priest, H.A.: Applying Gaming Principles to Support Evidence-based Instructional Design. In: I/ITSEC 2012, Orlando (2012)
22. Schatz, S., Wray, R., Folsom-Kovarik, J.T., Nicholson, D.: Adaptive perceptual training in a virtual environment. In: Human Factors and Ergonomic Systems (HFES-2012), Boston (2012)
23. Wray, R.E., Lane, H.C., Stensrud, B., Core, M., Hamel, L., Forbell, E.: Pedagogical experience manipulation for cultural learning. In: Workshop on Culturally-Aware Tutoring Systems at the AI in Education Conference Brighton, England (2009)

24. Folsom-Kovarik, J.T., Wray, R.E., Hamel, L.: Adaptive assessment in an instructor-mediated system. In: Lane, H.C., Yacef, K., Mostow, J., Pavlik, P. (eds.) AIED 2013. LNCS (LNAI), vol. 7926, pp. 571–574. Springer, Heidelberg (2013). https://doi.org/10.1007/978-3-642-39112-5_61

25. Gress, A., Folsom-Kovarik, J.T., Davidson, I.: Transfer learning in intelligent tutoring systems: results, challenges, and new directions. In: FLAIRS 2017. AAAI Press (2017)

26. Folsom-Kovarik, J.T., Newton, C., Haley, J., Wray, R.E.: Modeling proficiency in a tailored, situated training environment. In: Behavior Representation in Modeling and Simulation (BRIMS) Conference, Washington, D.C. (2014)

27. Folsom-Kovarik, J.T., Woods, A., Wray, R.E.: Designing an authorable scenario representation for instructor control over computationally tailored narrative in training. In: Proceedings of the 29th International FLAIRS Conference. AAAI Press, Key Largo (2016)

28. Wray, R.E., Woods, A., Haley, J., Folsom-Kovarik, J.T.: Evaluating instructor configurability for adaptive training. In: Proceedings of the 7th International Conference on Applied Human Factors and Ergonomics, Orlando (AHFE 2016). Springer, Heidelberg (2016)

29. Facione, P.A.: The Delphi report: Committee on Pre-college Philosophy. California Academic Press, Millbrae (1990)

30. Vygotsky, L.S.: Mind and Society: The Development of Higher Psychological Processes. Harvard University Press, Cambridge (1978)

31. Durlach, P.J., Lesgold, A.M. (eds.): Adaptive Technologies for Training and Education. Cambridge, New York (2012)

32. Wray, R.E., Woods, A.: A cognitive systems approach to tailoring learner practice. In: Proceedings of the 2013 Advances in Cognitive Systems Conference, Baltimore, MD (2013)

33. Wray, R.E., Bridgman, R., Haley, J., Hamel, L., Woods, A.: Event-based keyframing: transforming observation data into compact and meaningful form. In: Proceedings of the 22nd International Conference on Artificial Intelligence, Las Vegas. Springer, Cham (2020)

34. Wearne, A., Wray, R.E.: Exploration of behavioral markers to support adaptive learning. In: Kurosu, M. (ed.) HCI 2018. LNCS, vol. 10903, pp. 355–365. Springer, Cham (2018). https://doi.org/10.1007/978-3-319-91250-9_28

35. Stowers, K., Brady, L., Huh, Y., Wray, R.E.: Assessing the role of behavioral markers in adaptive learning for emergency medical services. In: Nazir, S., Teperi, A.-M., Polak-Sopińska, A. (eds.) AHFE 2018. AISC, vol. 785, pp. 184–193. Springer, Cham (2019). https://doi.org/10.1007/978-3-319-93882-0_19

36. Hehman, E., Stolier, R.M., Freeman, J.B.: Advanced mouse-tracking analytic techniques for enhancing psychological science. Group Process. Intergroup Relat. **18**, 384–401 (2015)
37. Microsoft.   https://www.microsoft.com/en-us/research/blog/turing-nlg-a-17-billion-parameter-language-model-by-microsoft/
38. Radford, A., Wu, J., Child, R., Luan, D., Amodei, D., Sutskever, I.: Language Models are Unsupervised Multitask Learners. Open AI (2019)

# Learning the Cognitive Skill of Topographic Map Reading Through Adaptive, High-Repetition Training

Paul J. Reber[✉] [iD], Evan Grandoit, Kevin D. Schmidt, Thomas C. Dixon, and Caelie P. McRobert

Northwestern University, Evanston, IL 60208, USA
preber@northwestern.edu

**Abstract.** The Cognitive Expertise through Repetition-Enhanced Simulation (CERES) project is aimed to provide a novel approach to accelerating the development of expertise in topographic map reading skill. Practice at this complex cognitive skill is accomplished through rapid-paced, simulation-based training events with a large procedurally generated database of training content items to provide continuing novel challenges. On each short training event, participants are presented with simultaneous views of a novel topographic map and a video render of first-person perspective movement through the terrain. The trainee goal is to identify what position on the map is reflected by the movement clip. Trainee performance level was continually assessed during training and the difficulty of training content was adjusted adaptively to enhance learning and maintain engagement and motivation with the training task. Data are reported from a sample of naïve online participants (n = 37, 169 h of total training) who acquired topographic map reading skill based on their experience with the CERES protocol. Participants without any prior topographic map reading training or experience nevertheless exhibited improved performance over training. In addition, a substantial subgroup also demonstrated very high levels of engagement and motivation with the training protocol. We conclude that the approach of rapid-paced training to induce practice with a complex cognitive skill can be administered in an individualized adaptive manner to accelerate the development of skilled expertise.

**Keywords:** Cognitive skill learning · Adaptive training · Topographic map reading

## 1 Introduction

The Cognitive Expertise through Repetition-Enhanced Simulation (CERES) project is founded on research aiming to accelerate the development of expertise in topographic map reading through a novel method of adaptively delivering large amounts of task practice to trainees. By structuring training into many short, individual training events, the protocol provides drill-training for complex cognitive skills while adaptively adjusting the content to maximize training effectiveness. Each individual practice event engages

© Springer Nature Switzerland AG 2021
R. A. Sottilare and J. Schwarz (Eds.): HCII 2021, LNCS 12792, pp. 88–104, 2021.
https://doi.org/10.1007/978-3-030-77857-6_6

the trainee with a novel version of the training simulation and performance is used for ongoing assessments of the current level of skill development. Training events are adjusted adaptively to keep training at an appropriate level of difficulty based on the current ability of the trainee. This leads to increasing the level of challenge as trainees build their skill, which is hypothesized to accelerate the learning process and also maintain a high level of motivation and engagement with training.

Topographic maps provide various details about terrains, such as elevation, vegetation density, and feature location. These maps offer unique information about an area, which can support navigation. However, the widespread use of these maps presents challenges. Reading topographic maps requires spatial processing skills needed to match 2D map details to 3D terrain features, visualize various routes based on map features, mentally rotate terrain feature positions based on visualized route, and make purposeful route decisions [1, 2]. Novices are known to be more likely to make navigation errors when reading topographic maps compared to those with more experience [3, 4]. Practice to facilitate expertise could decrease these incidences of error in beginners [5].

The experiment reported here describes training with an online version of the CERES topographic map reading protocol. Performance gains are exhibited through a population recruited through the Amazon Mechanical Turk marketplace. These participants have no prior experience with reading topographic maps, nor any intrinsic motivation to build this cognitive skill (other than to be compensated for performance). Participants were provided with very minimal instruction before attempting the task and, thus, performance improvements reflect the efficacy of a "learn by doing" approach based on providing many novel repetitions of practice with this complex cognitive skill.

## 1.1 Theoretical Foundations

Improving skills through practice is an intuitive idea for which a clear framework was articulated over 50 years ago [6]. Modern theories of the mechanisms of learning through practice have come to incorporate the understanding of multiple memory types in the brain, including both implicit and explicit memory [7]. Our research approach is grounded in the cognitive neuroscience of memory systems including both types of memory together with how these kinds of memory are affected by the neuroscience of reward during learning. Explicit knowledge is typically acquired in instructional contexts and reflects one component of developing expertise in a complex cognitive skill. Implicit learning is acquired through practice and contributes to developing expertise throughout the learning process, playing roles early in learning [8], throughout the process of building on knowledge representations via practice [9], and supporting eventual fast, automatic, effortless performance that emerges with skilled expertise [10–12].

Both implicit and explicit learning can be enhanced by adaptive approaches to training that reflect processes to enhance acquisition of task knowledge specific to the type of learning. Prior research on adaptive training approaches have generally focused on methods to elicit? explicit memorization. Metzler-Baddeley and Baddeley [13] compared learning in a computer-based adaptive spacing condition, in which participants were given more time to practice Spanish vocabulary words they had more trouble remembering, to participants who studied the same list of Spanish vocabulary words but at a random frequency. Those in the adaptive spacing condition scored higher on both immediate and delayed recall tests than those in the random spacing condition. Similarly, Sampayo-Vargas, Cope, He, and Byrne [14] tested the effect of adaptive difficulty based on individualized performance during language learning. Participants were assigned to either an adaptive or non-adaptive difficulty computer game condition. In the adaptive difficulty condition, the amount of learning assistance was changed based on a specific number of consecutive responses. Those in the adaptive difficulty game condition showed higher rates of learning than participants in the other conditions. These studies provide evidence that continuous assessment and modification of practice sessions to adjust to participant performance is effective for computer-based trainings and produces improved learning outcomes over non-adaptive trainings protocols.

Salden, Aleven, Schwonke, and Renkl [15] used an adaptive difficulty training approach based on gradually reducing learning supports described as "fading," defined as decreasing the amount of learning support gradually based on individual success. These researchers compared secondary school students in three different types of math tutoring groups: static fading, fixed fading, and adaptive fading. Students in the adaptive fading group demonstrated greater math scores on both immediate and delayed posttest scores when compared to the other two groups. This approach to adaptive training by increasing difficulty as trainees acquire skill is similar to the approach used here of gradually reducing the availability of visual features (attack points) that can be used to connect the surrounding environment to a topographic map.

Implicit learning generally depends critically on feedback provided during learning and therefore reward associated with correct responses [7]. The current training protocol is based on creating large numbers of training events for each trainee with feedback after each response. Neuroscience-based theories of how reward affects learning highlight the importance of dopaminergic function expressed through *reward-prediction error* (RPE), an increasingly important component of reinforcement learning [16, 17]. The contribution of RPE is the observation that reward is maximized not solely by success and positive feedback, but that the experience of reward is magnified by surprise at success, that is, if the prediction of success was low, subsequent reward is potentiated by large "prediction error." This simple idea implies that learning may be accelerated by adaptively managing expectations of reward during training. Here, an experiment attempted to accomplish this through adaptively adjusting the difficulty level of the training task. By providing trainees with the most difficult training task that they are likely to be able to solve, the protocol aims to increase the frequency of the highly rewarding experience of subjective surprise at an accurate response. This approach is also likely an efficient use of training time as less time is spent on well-learned (too easy) content or on content that is beyond the trainee's current level of ability. In addition to potentially accelerating the learning process, increased experience of reward may also lead to increased motivation, engagement, and drive to accumulate training 'sets and reps.'

Maximizing reward this way is well-represented in research on 'gamification' of training or education [18]. Gamification, the use of game features for non-entertainment purposes, has been used to improve motivation and engagement in various learning contexts [19–21]. Sailer et al. [20] report that specific game elements, such as points, are associated with increased motivation. They posit the reason is because points are direct indicators of performance and can fulfill the need for competence, which is a factor of greater motivation. Papp [22] studied the effects of gamification on student learning and motivation of mathematics and business communication for grade school and college students, respectively. Students reported feeling rewarded by the gamified course, with 66% of the students reporting spending time outside of the classroom to meet up together and go over the course material, indicating increased motivation. These studies provide evidence that using game elements in a learning environment can facilitate increased motivation to learn. This increased motivation and engagement could facilitate more voluntarily completed 'sets and reps,' which could then lead to expertise development.

## 1.2 Repetition Training for Topographic Map Reading

We have previously described our ongoing development of a protocol for training topographic map reading through high-repetition training [23, 24]. An important goal of this approach is to capture implicit learning from practice from field exercises without the time, cost and risk of extended practice in the field. To decrease these expenses and risks, utilizing simulation-based training can be an effective alternative. The use of simulation-based training can provide the numerous occasions for practice that is vital for expertise development.

The core element of this approach is to create a training protocol in which participants learn this complex cognitive skill through intense, repeated and rapid practice on the task. We constructed the training protocol around short simulation-based training events, in which participants are provided with a novel topographic map and a short video clip showing a simulated movement through the terrain associated with the map. Participants indicate where on the map they believe the video would be taken from and are immediately provided with feedback about the accuracy of their response. The view, response and feedback processes take typically around 20–30 s in total so that the process can be repeated many times over hours of training. Critically, we have prepared a very large database of training stimuli so that trainees repeat the skill through their practice, not by repeating the same items in practice (which would lead to simple rote memorization rather than skill building). The demands on content creation were met by using procedural content development to algorithmically create the terrains and simulation-based video clips of movement.

To adaptively manage difficulty dynamically during training, it is necessary to (a) organize training content in order to flexibly select training items based on current needs and (b) to continually assess trainee ability level to identify those current needs. Here we describe research implementing an adaptive, gamified approach to high-repetition simulation-based training. Participants completed multiple hours of this training protocol through an online interface to improve their navigation skill using topographic maps. We hypothesize that participants in a topographic map reading training protocol with adaptive learning features and gamified elements will show increased engagement and improved topographic map-based navigation.

## 2    Technical Approach

To evaluate the learning effectiveness of our high-repetition protocol and assess the influence of our adaptive difficulty adjustments on the learning process, we recruited participants online (remotely) to complete the CERES training protocol. Participants had no known prior topographic map reading experience, nor any noted motivation to acquire this skill, aside from complying with task instructions to be compensated for participating. To perform the training task, participants were simultaneously presented with a scale rendering topographic map, a short video clip reflecting simulated movement at a particular location on the map, and a lensatic compass image showing the direction of movement. Participants were expected to primarily learn through feedback on the accuracy of their responses and complete several training events each minute on the task. To provide strong signaling about their current success, we used a system of earning points, with more points rewarded for more accurate responses. This point system was also used to set training goals for online participants. These training goals included instructions stating that they needed to earn 1000 points to be compensated for participation. This 1000-point threshold also reflects a level of minimum compliance with task instructions and some attempt to make accurate responses. A secondary goal stated that participants who reached 2000 points would be eligible (if they chose) for additional compensated 30-min training sessions.

Throughout participants' training, task difficulty was adaptively adjusted based on the participants' accuracy on past trials. One way in which difficulty was adapted was through selecting content from terrain regions designed to be either more or less challenging based on the number of reference features. In addition, the designated search area within which participants were asked to identify the video's location was increased as participant accuracy increased. By increasing task difficulty to a level appropriate to each participant, we aimed to accelerate learning and maintain motivation and interest in the training task. Selecting stimuli appropriate to the participant's ability level was made possible by continual data-driven assessment of the trainee's current level of map reading ability from the large number of training events completed. Increasingly accurate performance signaled an improvement in skill and was used to guide content selection toward more difficult stimuli. Participants were consistently exposed to the most challenging content at which they were expected to succeed, maximizing the participants' subjective sense of reward and therefore increasing motivation and accelerating learning.

Task performance was measured by the accuracy of participants' responses indicating both the direction of movement reflected in the video and the specific location on the map from which the video was drawn. In addition, measures of increasing task difficulty and effort invested in answering (e.g., response time, number of user interface events) measured the context in which these responses were provided.

### 2.1    Participants

A total of 67 participants were recruited from the Amazon Mechanical Turk marketplace to complete an initial 30 min training session for compensation of $6. Participants were provided informed consent (Northwestern University IRB, STU213554) before their first session and were at least 18 years of age. Prior topographic map experience was not required or expected. Of the initial recruitment group, 33 met the performance criteria required to be invited to participate in additional training sessions at the same rate of compensation. These participants completed an additional 268 training sessions (range 0–44 sessions), producing a total of 15,777 trials of map training performance data.

## 2.2 Materials

For training, a stimulus database of 800 first-person perspective videos was created. Each video clip included 10 s of movement and was selected from one of 8 different simulated, procedurally generated terrains. The videos were rendered within a Unity game engine. Procedural generation of novel terrains for navigation was developed in collaboration with Charles River Analytics (PI: James Niehaus, Ph.D.) and is described in detail in [24].

Each novel terrain is a 5-kilometer (km) × 5 km region containing elevation changes (hills, valleys, etc.), water, and simulated vegetation elements to create geotypical biomes based on flora descriptions from US National Park websites. These open-access flora types were imported and included from the Unity asset store. Additional simulated man-made structures were added to the terrains, rendered as colored pylons, to provide reference features to guide orientation within the simulated terrains. As noted below, these features were placed strategically to control the difficulty of the training task. Simulated topographic maps were rendered for each of the simulated terrains, including contour lines marking elevation, extent of water, density of vegetation, and location of simulated structures.

Video clips of movement through the terrain were rendered by selecting a pseudo-random location and compass facing (constrained to not be placed in water). The video clips simulated a forward walking movement for 5 s followed by a 5 s, 360-degree spin to show surroundings. All movement videos were rendered under clear weather conditions and a consistent time of day (mid-afternoon).

## 2.3 Training Procedure

Prior to starting the training protocol, participants read a short description of the task and provided informed consent. They were then shown a 3 min instructional video that provided a general overview of the training task and the user interface controls, as well as a brief explanation of navigation based on a topographic map. Because participants were recruited online through a general marketplace for workers performing short cognitive tasks for pay, we had no expectation of them having any prior experience with topographic map reading. To maximize time use with these participants, we adopted a "learn by doing" approach, using minimal initial instruction. Additionally, the interface included a few adaptive instruction elements that were presented based on performance. If participants made three or more significant errors in indicating their facing, an additional 1 min video explaining how to read the lensatic compass dial image was presented. If participants made three or more significant location errors, an additional 1 min video was presented that explained the user interface elements designed to help determine location. It was expected that the main source of learning within the task would be

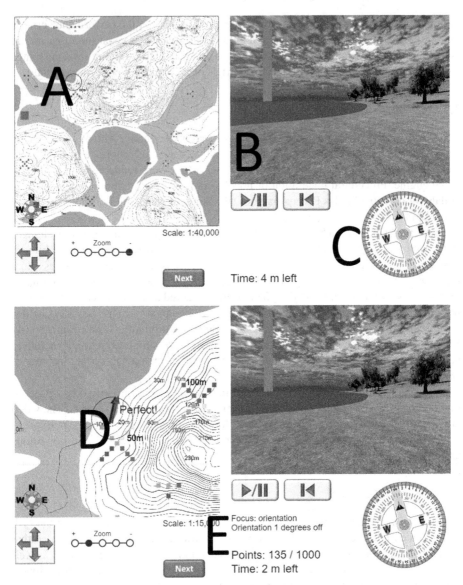

**Fig. 1.** The CERES user interface. (A) The task objective was to accurately mark the video location and direction of travel within the blue circle. (B) The first-person video simulated walking forward 5 m from somewhere within the blue circle and spinning clockwise. (C) The initial position of this compass showed the direction of travel (NNE). (D) The participant responded by clicking to mark the location and dragging the blue arrow in the direction of travel. The green arrow appeared to show the correct response. (E) Feedback appeared as error in degrees or meters and total points accumulated.

through the feedback about the accuracy of their performance, which was provided after each response.

Once instructed, participants began the main part of the training program, which consisted of a series of rapid simulation-based training events, termed 'trials.' In each trial, participants were presented with a display that simultaneously showed the topographic map of the current terrain, the 10 s video clip of movement through that terrain, and a lensatic compass image that indicated the direction of movement (see Fig. 1). The goal was to identify the location and direction of movement reflected in the video. The direction of movement could be determined strictly from the lensatic compass heading (although participants were not necessarily familiar with the use of such a compass before participating). The location of the video on the map could be determined from visible features (elevation changes, water, vegetation, structures) and was assisted by providing a 'search circle' that contained the correct answer. The size of this search circle was adaptively adjusted (see below) to created greater or less difficulty in the task. To aid participants in making their response, they were given the option to zoom in on the topographic map and pause or repeat the video clip. Responses were made in two parts: First, by clicking the computer mouse on the map at the location thought to be reflected in the video, which caused a blue arrow to appear. Then, while holding down the mouse button, participants indicated the direction of movement in the video by dragging the mouse (and thus the arrow) in the direction shown by the lensatic compass heading.

After completing their response, participants were provided with feedback about their accuracy. A green arrow indicating the correct location and direction was overlaid on the map along with a semantic indication of performance ("Perfect!", "Excellent", "Very good", "Ok"). In addition, the specific amount of error was provided in either degrees of orientation from the true facing or meters from the correct location. At the beginning of training, feedback was directed specifically at improving the orientation aspect of the participant's responses to draw attention to learning to use the compass. After three consecutive responses within 15 degrees of error, feedback switched to focus on location.

In addition, participants were provided with performance feedback through a point scoring system that rewarded their performance based on both direction and location accuracy. Participants could earn up to a maximum of 260 points per response. Typical early performance produced scores of around 40 points per response (see Results below) and increased with practice.

The point system was used to provide overall performance feedback to participants and to set training goals. Participants were instructed that they needed to earn at least 1000 points over the 30 min session to show that they were complying with task instructions. This set a performance criterion to eliminate participants who appeared to be making no attempt to accurately perform or learn the task. Participants who earned 2000 or more points received a 'qualification' through the Amazon Mechanical Turk marketplace that enabled access to repeat the training protocol if they elected to continue training. Compensation for these additional sessions was set at the same rate of $6 per 30 min session.

## 2.4 Adaptive Training Elements

The design goal of using adaptive training in CERES was to give trainees (participants) the most difficult training problems they would be likely to succeed at by continually and individually adjusting the difficulty of training. There were two mechanisms used for this adaptation over the course of the training protocol: adjusting the size of the search region and selecting training stimuli from terrain regions designed to be more or less difficult.

**Search Region.** On each trial, a blue circle was superimposed over the topographic map, indicating an area in which the movement video was located. Initially, this region was a circle with a 200 m radius. If the participant's response was selected from within this region as intended, the magnitude of their error was limited to within twice the circle's radius. Location performance was assessed after every trial, and if the participant's response was within 150 m of accurate on 3 consecutive trials, the search circle radius was increased by 50 m. If their response was more than 300 m from accurate for 3 consecutive trials, the radius was decreased by 50 m. This simple heuristic capitalizes on the ability to do continual performance assessments within a high-repetition protocol and to make adjustments to difficulty personalized to the individual trainee's current performance level.

**Terrain Difficulty.** The ability to accurately determine map location from the movement video depends on the ability to identify features within the video that can be connected to the topographic map. The available features are: elevation changes, water features, vegetation density and simulated structures. We first attempted to create terrains with overall differences in difficulty level by manipulating the degree and number of these features through the procedural content generation tools. We then placed different patterns of simulated man-made structures rendered as pylons within the video and corresponding-colored squares on the topographic maps. Both the density and distinctiveness of the pylon placement were controlled within regions (quadrants) of the whole terrain to create areas with easily available attack points to guide navigation and areas where location needed to be determined from subtler topographic features.

Examples of how the simulated structure pylons were used to create easier and more difficult regions can be seen by contrasting Fig. 1, which was drawn from an 'easy' region, and Fig. 2, which shows more difficult trials. In Fig. 1, the large teal pylon provides a very distinctive attack point to connect the video view to the topographic map. In more difficult regions, pylons were smaller and generally less distinctive.

Across all regions and maps, the pylons tended to be placed in small pattern-based groups (squares, crosses, X-shapes, etc.). For regions intended to be easier, the pylons were rendered as 40 m tall with distinctive color patterns. For more difficult regions, pylons were rendered as only 30 m tall and were all the same color.

For the easiest regions, provided to participants early in training, we additionally placed a few distinctive 200 m tall pylons at strategic points to be particularly useful as navigation attack points. These distinctive pylons were not placed on the more difficult terrains that would be encountered later in training. On these later terrains, the pylon clusters tended to follow simple grid patterns rather than being strategically placed.

As with the search region size, terrain difficulty was individually adapted for each participant based on performance. Performance was continually assessed and when 4 highly accurate responses (<100 m location error) were made in a set of 5 training events, participants would be advanced to the next, more difficult region within a terrain.

The training stimulus databased contained 25 videos within each region, and if all were completed by a participant, they advanced to the next region even if the performance criterion was not met. When all regions in a particular terrain were completed, participants were then moved to the next, more difficult terrain.

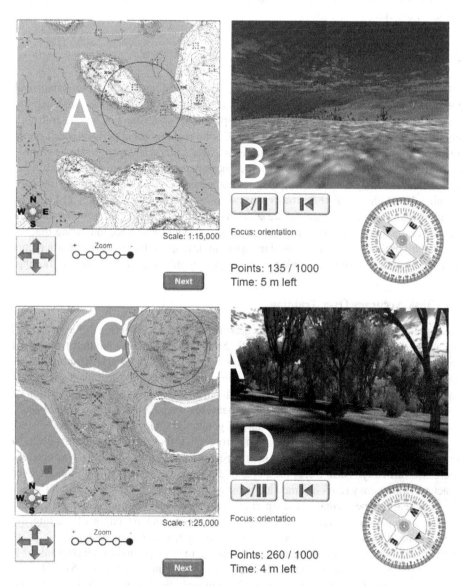

**Fig. 2.** Examples of more difficult training trials. (A, C) Examples of much larger search regions within which to locate the video source. (B) Terrain with fewer topographical navigation features and smaller, less distinctive pylon patterns. (D) Densely forested terrain posed challenges to identifying reference features for navigation.

The approach to controlling difficulty through the placement of distinctive features reflects a novel approach to training navigation that is enabled by the use of simulation-based training. The implementation details reflect our hypothesis that structure placement would affect performance during learning to allow the training protocol to be effectively adaptive. Establishing that performance varied with our predictions about difficulty was a goal of the current experiment.

## 3 Results

Of the 67 participants recruited to participate, 20 exhibited low levels of performance in the initial session indicating either a lack of understanding of task instructions, inability to understand core concepts behind topographic map understanding or general non-compliance with the task procedure. Of the 47 who met the initial performance criteria (earning 1000 points), 32 also met the more advanced criteria and qualified to be eligible to continue to additional training sessions. These participants completed an additional 271 30-min training sessions at the same compensation rate for a total of 169 h of training data with the CERES protocol over 15,777 trials in total (range 17–2143 across participants). Participants meeting the advanced criteria showed a general understanding of the compass and how to identify location on a topographic map, indicating that we had at least preliminary success training topographic map reading in 48% of participants recruited from an online marketplace with no prior map reading experience or training.

### 3.1 Task Accuracy Over Training

Task performance was measured with six dependent variables reflecting different aspects of task performance. Initial performance is shown in Fig. 3 across the first two terrain region areas designed to be of relatively easier difficulty (up to 50 trials). Response accuracy was measured by both the direction of travel indicated by the participant's response (orientation, degrees) and how close their indicated location was to the true location of the video render (location, meters). These measures were combined into a point score that provides an overall summary measure of general accuracy in performance.

A challenge posed by adaptive training protocols is that performance is expected to improve with training, but direct measures of performance are also affected by adaptively increased difficulty. Thus, direct measures of performance accuracy may improve over practice, or they may remain somewhat constant in the face of increasing difficulty. For the early learning performance data, participants can be seen to improve in the accuracy of their orientation responses, reflecting an improving understanding of reading the compass heading and video direction, $F(1, 35) = 5.65$, $p < .05$ (including participants with at least 50 trials in these regions), also leading to more points earned per trial, $F(1, 35) = 5.68$, $p < .05$. Participants also improved in response time, $F(1, 35) = 9.33$, $p < .01$. While the location accuracy does not improve directly, it should be noted that the size of the search region provided to participants was steadily increasing, making accuracy of this element of the response more difficult.

The tension between improving performance and increasing difficulty is visible in Fig. 4, which shows performance over up to 500 trials of training after those presented in

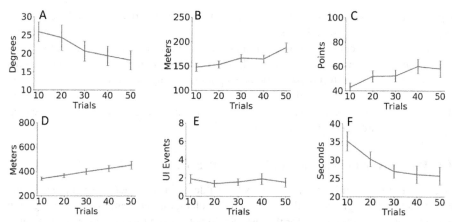

**Fig. 3.** Early learning performance by participants on the first two (easy) terrain regions over the first 50 trials of performance (shown in blocks of 10). (A) Accuracy in indicating the direction of movement based on the video and compass heading, shown as degrees of error from accurate (better performance is lower). (B) Accuracy in the location of the response made by participants in meters (better performance is lower). (C) Points awarded per response (better is higher). (D) Size of the search circle region, which increases based on successful performance and creates more difficult trials. (E) Average number of actions using the user interface options to support their responses. (F) Response time (seconds) for each trial (lower is more rapid responses).

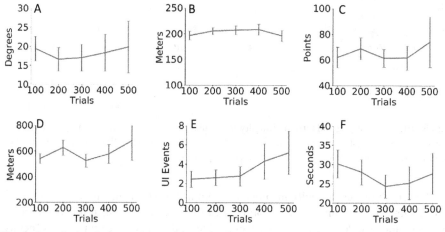

**Fig. 4.** Learning performance by participants during trials after the early phase for qualified (n = 32) participants. (A) Accuracy in indicating the direction of movement based on the video/compass (better performance is lower). (B) Accuracy in the location of the response remained relatively constant despite the increasing difficulty of the task. (C) Points awarded per response maintained or increased throughout the extended training. (D) Size of the search circle region was relatively large and increasing in size over training, reflecting the adaptive increases in difficulty as participants trained. (E) Average number of actions using the user interface options to support their responses increased with task difficulty, reflecting increased effort to maintain performance. (F) Response time (seconds) for each trial (lower is more rapid responses).

100    P. J. Reber et al.

Fig. 3. Over the course of these trials, participants were required to identify their location over increasingly large search regions and on terrains with many fewer easily identifiable features (Fig. 2). Accuracy measures remained relatively constant at an effective level throughout these increases in difficulty. The rise in the use of more user interface features (Fig. 4E) reflects the effort these participants put into trying to figure out the location on the map associated with the video. These user interface events were frequently replaying the videos with many pause/resume actions as well as zooming in and exploring the map to look for features to connect to the video.

### 3.2 Difficulty of the Training Task Across Regions

One of the goals of this experiment was to evaluate our approach to manipulating the task difficulty through the available methods for changing the availability of navigation features (attack points) to use for the task. We hypothesized that procedurally generated terrains with fewer topographic and water features would be more difficult. We also hypothesized that the number and distinctiveness of the simulated structures (pylons) would influence task difficulty. These were separately manipulated by using different methods of placing pylons across quadrant regions within different overall terrains.

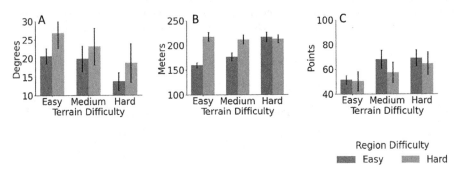

**Fig. 5.** Effects of region and terrain difficulty manipulation on performance. (A) Error in estimation of the direction of movement (orientation, degrees). (B) Error in location on the map (meters). (C) Performance measured by points earned per responses.

The effect of our difficulty manipulations on task performance is shown in Fig. 5, which shows performance by orientation, location and the combined points measures across regions we designated as easy/hard and terrains across three intended difficulty levels. A three-way repeated measures ANOVA of terrain difficulty and region difficulty on location error revealed a main effect of terrain difficulty on location accuracy, $F(2, 41) = 5.23, p < .01$, and a main effect of region difficulty, $F(1, 32) = 52.34, p < .001$. These effects indicate that our attempt to increase difficulty by changing the availability of topographical features, water features, biome familiarity and structure placement were generally effective. Additionally, there was an interaction between difficulty types reflecting the smaller region effect on the hard terrains, $F(2, 37) = 3.63, p < .05$. However, the adaptive approach to training meant that participants experienced the terrains intended to be more difficult later in training when they had acquired more expertise.

The lack of terrain difficulty on orientation direction responses is likely due to these being mainly dependent on the compass reading and not on terrain features.

### 3.3   Engagement and Effort

A goal of our adaptive training approach that focused on increasing the difficulty of each trial as participants improved was to maintain engagement with the training under the hypothesis that succeeding at hard tasks is more intrinsically rewarding. An anecdotal measure of this effect is reflected in the fact that we were able to collect data at an accelerated pace through the Amazon Mechanical Turk marketplace. Even when access to training sessions was restricted to participants qualified based on prior experience, participants signed up for and completed sessions as fast as we could make them available. Five of the most active participants completed more than 20 sessions (range 24–44) and even reached out to us to ask for more training opportunities, reporting the task as enjoyable.

As a quantitative measure of engagement of the task, we observed that many participants greatly exceeded the stated performance requirements that we provided them. Participants had to earn more than 2000 points to be eligible for additional paid training sessions. A sizeable subset of participants exhibited consistent performance far in excess of this criterion. We identified 22 participants whose enthusiasm for the task apparently inspired them to continue training performance consistently past the 2000-point criterion. These participants earned an average of 3900 points per session, completing an average of 23.2 additional trials even after passing the 2000-point mark.

There was no benefit or reward to these participants for completing these additional trials. If anything, they could have shifted their attention to other tasks being completed for pay. Some participants (n = 25) did exhibit this approach to the task, doing the minimum and simply stopping performance once the criteria were met.

We hypothesize that for these 22 highly engaged participants (33% of the recruited sample), the fact that the training protocol provided a continually increasing level of challenge motivated them to continue the task beyond the instructed requirement. While we do not have a comparison group asked to perform the training in a non-adaptive protocol to compare engagement levels, in our experience with learning and memory research, it is quite unusual to see a substantial subgroup of participants motivated to overperform this way.

## 4   Discussion

Using the CERES training protocol to provide high-repetition practice on the cognitive skill of topographic map reading, we were able to train participants with no prior map experience to be able to locate their position on a simulated map. Participants exhibited relatively accurate responding early in training and maintained their accuracy even as the task difficulty was increased adaptively. The effectiveness of the basic training task suggests the value of practice in building complex cognitive skills, even in the case of minimal prior experience and no provided classroom-like instruction.

The training protocol used several adaptive elements as part of the training experience. Participants were provided with a search region indicator to constrain their responses, which grew substantially as they improved their ability to do the task. In addition, we explored several methods of manipulating difficulty in the training stimuli by decreasing the availability of environmental features to guide orientation. In general, fewer visible, distinctive simulated structures or map features made localization within the map more challenging. Participants were given increasingly challenging task stimuli as they progressed through training.

A consequence of the adaptive training approach is that individually adaptive difficulty leads to challenges in quantifying task improvement through performance even though it is being continually assessed. Participants' learning would typically lead to clearly increasing accuracy but this effect is balanced by the increasing difficulty of the task. In some instances, this leads to quantitative elements of learning being more visible in measures of task difficulty than in task performance. This effect could be addressed by using pre-prepared skill assessments, which are not structured to use adaptive difficulty but are given at selected points early and late in training. We did not use that approach here, but it should be considered as a regular feature of adaptive training for skilled performance.

Adaptive training may lead to a more positive trainee experience by focusing training examples on challenging problems, which may tend to appear more subjectively interesting. Working on a hard problem that can be successfully solved is intuitively rewarding, and this phenomenon is also a clear prediction of theories of human reward processing and reinforcement learning. Our approach to adaptive training aimed to provide trainees with the hardest current version of the task that they were expected to be able to answer successfully. Providing this successfully is technically challenging because it requires an accurate assessment of current ability and a sufficient understanding of task difficulty to select the correct next problem. In the current study, evidence that the implementation of this approach was successful was provided by the substantial number of participants who appeared to be enthusiastically and fully engaged with performing the task. Approximately a third of our recruited population returned frequently to continue their training and consistently completed more training than was required of them. The excess effort invested in learning a task of no particular relevance to them suggests we achieved a highly effective level of engagement through the adaptive elements of the CERES training approach.

The experiment reported here provides additional strong evidence in favor of the CERES training approach to building topographic map reading skill. Expertise is built through repetitive use of a complex skill in a simulation-based environment. Large numbers of trial-unique stimuli keep the training focus on the skill and not on rote memorization of specific examples. The ability to continually assess trainee's current skill level in recent responses allows for a range of individually adaptive adjustments to the training plan that are aimed to both accelerate learning and maintain high levels of motivation and engagement. Detailed analysis of the performance data from participants will be used to guide further improvements in the implementation of the topographic map reading training protocol. Effective training techniques identified in the current training task are also expected to be able to be generalized to similar approaches to rapidly training other complex cognitive skills in the same repetition-based manner.

# References

1. Taylor, H.A., Brunye, T.T., Taylor, S.T.: Spatial mental representation: implications for navigation system design. Rev. Hum. Factors Ergon. **4**(40), 1–40 (2008). https://doi.org/10.1518/155723408X342835
2. Rapp, D.N., van den Broek, P., McMaster, K.L., Kendeou, P., Espin, C.A.: Higher-order comprehension processes in struggling readers: a perspective for research and intervention. Sci. Stud. Read. **11**(4), 289–312 (2007). https://doi.org/10.1080/10888430701530417
3. Hickox, J.C., Wickens, C.D.: Effects of elevation angle disparity, complexity, and feature type on relating out-of-cockpit field of view to an electronic cartographic map. J. Exp. Psychol. Appl. **5**(3), 284–301 (1999). https://doi.org/10.1037/1076-898X.5.3.284
4. Aretz, A.J., Wickens, C.D.: The mental rotation of map displays. Hum. Perform. **5**(4), 303–328 (2009). https://doi.org/10.1207/s15327043hup0504_3
5. Ericsson, K.A.: Deliberate practice and acquisition of expert performance: a general overview. Acad. Emerg. Med. **15**(11), 988–994 (2008). https://doi.org/10.1111/j.1553-2712.2008.00227.x
6. Fitts, P.M., Posner, M.I.: Human Performance. Brooks/Cole, Monterey (1967)
7. Reber, P.J.: The neural basis of implicit learning and memory: a review of neuropsychological and neuroimaging research. Neuropsychologia **51**(10), 2026–2042 (2013). https://doi.org/10.1016/j.neuropsychologia.2013.06.019
8. Sun, R., Merrill, E., Peterson, T.: From implicit skills to explicit knowledge: a bottom-up model of skill learning. Cogn. Sci. **25**(2), 203–244 (2001). https://doi.org/10.1207/s15516709cog2502_2
9. Anderson, J.R.: Acquisition of cognitive skill. Psychol. Rev. **89**(4), 369 (1982). https://doi.org/10.1037/0033-295X.89.4.369
10. Anderson, J.R.: The adaptive nature of human categorization. Psychol. Rev. **98**(3), 409 (1991). https://doi.org/10.1037/0033-295x.98.3.409
11. Fisk, A.D., Ackerman, P.L., Schneider, W.: Automatic and controlled processing theory and its applications to human factor problems. Adv. Psychol. **47**, 159–197 (1987). https://doi.org/10.1016/S0166-4115(08)62309-2
12. Schneider, W.: Training high-performance skills: fallacies and guidelines. Hum. Factors **27**, 285–300 (1985). https://doi.org/10.1177/001872088502700305
13. Metzler-Baddeley, C., Baddeley, R.J.: Does adaptive training work? Appl. Cogn. Psychol. Official J. Soc. Appl. Res. Mem. Cogn. **23**(2), 254–266 (2008). https://doi.org/10.1002/acp.1454
14. Sampayo-Vargas, S., Cope, C.J., He, Z., Byrne, G.J.: The effectiveness of adaptive difficulty adjustments on students' motivation and learning in an educational computer game. Comput. Educ. **69**, 452–462 (2013). https://doi.org/10.1016/j.compedu.2013.07.004
15. Salden, R.J.C.M., Aleven, V., Schwonke, R., Renkl, A.: The expertise reversal effect and worked examples in tutored problem solving. Instr. Sci. **38**, 289–307 (2010). https://doi.org/10.1007/s11251-009-9107-8
16. Berridge, K.C.: From prediction error to incentive salience: mesolimbic computation of reward motivation. Eur. J. Neurosci. **35**(7), 1124–1143 (2012). https://doi.org/10.1111/j.1460-9568.2012.07990.x
17. Schultz, W.: Dopamine reward prediction-error signalling: a two-component response. Nat. Rev. Neurosci. **17**(3), 183 (2016). https://doi.org/10.31887/DCNS.2016.18.1/wschultz

18. Landers, R.N., Callan, R.C.: Casual social games as serious games: the psychology of gamification in undergraduate education and employee training. In: Ma, M., Oikonomou, A., Jain, L.C. (eds.) Serious Games and Edutainment Applications, pp. 399–423. Springer, London (2011). https://doi.org/10.1007/978-1-4471-2161-9_20

19. Cronk, M.: Using gamification to increase student engagement and participant in class discussion. In: World Conference on Educational Multimedia, Hypermedia and Telecommunications, vol. 2012, no. 1, pp. 311–315 (2012)

20. Sailer, M., Hense, J.U., Mayr, S.K., Mandl, H.: How gamification motivates: an experimental study of the effects of specific game design elements on psychological need satisfaction. Comput. Hum. Behav. **69**, 371–380 (2017). https://doi.org/10.1016/j.chb.2016.12.033

21. Stansbury, J.A., Earnest, D.R.: Meaningful gamification in an industrial/organizational psychology course. Teach. Psychol. **44**(1), 38–45 (2017). https://doi.org/10.1177/0098628316677645

22. Papp, T.A.: Gamification effects on motivation and learning: application to primary and college students. Int. J. Cross-Discip. Subj. Educ. **8**(3), 3199–3201 (2017)

23. Schmidt, K., Feinstein, B., Grabowecky, M., Reber, P.J.: Cognitive expertise through repetition enhanced simulation (CERES): topographic map reading. In: Interservice/Industry Training, Simulation, and Education Conference (I/ITSEC) (2019)

24. Grandoit, E., Schmidt, K., Grabowecky, M., Reber, P.J.: Cognitive expertise through repetition enhanced simulation (CERES): training to understand topographic maps. In: Interservice/Industry Training, Simulation, and Education Conference (I/ITSEC) (2020)

# Learning Engineering as an Ethical Framework

## A Case Study of Adaptive Courseware Development

Rachel Van Campenhout[✉]

Duquesne University, Pittsburgh, PA, USA
vancampenhoutr@duq.edu

**Abstract.** The advances in technology continually push at the boundary of what is possible in online learning environments. Digital learning generates data at scale that can be analyzed to gain new insights into the learning process, which in turn sparks further changes in technology. Adaptive instructional systems have been growing in type and complexity, which also increases the scope of the technology and the teams who work to develop them. In this time of intense exploration and innovation in learning science and technology, it is also imperative to put in place a system of ethics to center this innovative spirit on the intended user: the learner. I propose that learning engineering provides a purpose to advocate for the best interests of the learner as the Learning Engineering Process is carried out. This practitioner purpose can help the learning engineer develop an ethical voice and engage in a dialogic ethic as new technology is being developed. I use a case study on the development and improvement of adaptive activities to illustrate both the Learning Engineering Process as well as how this process supports an ethical practice. In this paper I situate learning engineering in an ethical framework and provide a contextual example to spark discussion on the role of ethics in an increasingly complex learning ecosystem.

**Keywords:** Learning engineering · Learning engineering process · Ethics · Adaptive courseware

## 1 Learning Engineering

### 1.1 An Introduction to Learning Engineering

This paper will explore both the role and process of learning engineering as defined by the IEEE IC Industry Consortium for Learning Engineering (ICICLE), and as I experienced firsthand as a learning engineer developing adaptive courseware for Acrobatiq[1]. As a professional organization, ICICLE works to define and provide standards for learning engineering as a profession and academic discipline. Through collective work, learning engineering is defined as "a process and practice that applies the learning sciences using human-centered engineering design methodologies and data-informed decision making

---

[1] Acrobatiq originated as a start-up from Carnegie Mellon University's Open Learning Initiative in 2013. Acrobatiq was acquired by VitalSource Technologies in 2018.

© Springer Nature Switzerland AG 2021
R. A. Sottilare and J. Schwarz (Eds.): HCII 2021, LNCS 12792, pp. 105–119, 2021.
https://doi.org/10.1007/978-3-030-77857-6_7

to support learners and their development" [1]. Learning engineering can be valuable in a variety of contexts for the interdisciplinary nature of the role and expertise it applies to learning. While the skills needed for the role and how it is differentiated from related fields [2–4] will not be discussed in detail in this paper, Goodell and Thai [5] outline key research and disciplines incorporated into learning engineering:

The learning engineering process enables data-informed decision-making through development cycles that include learning sciences, design-based research, and learning analytics/educational data mining. It leverages advances from different fields including learning sciences, design research, curriculum research, game design, data sciences, and computer science. It thus provides a social-technical infrastructure to support iterative learning engineering and practice-relevant theory for scaling learning sciences through design research, deep content analytics, and iterative product improvements.

The ICICLE community's design special interest group, led by Aaron Kessler, has also worked to develop a model of how learning engineering is done: the Learning Engineering Process (LEP) [6]. Within a specific context, a learning engineer or learning engineering team will define the problem to be solved, design the solution including instrumentation to gather data, implement the learning environment/solution, analyze data and review results, and identify areas needed for iterative improvement [6]. While the LEP as shown here did not exist in this format at the time that the adaptive activity case study outlined in this paper took place (2015–2017), it was the commonalities of learning engineering practices in various settings (such as this one) which helped to shape the model. The fit of the LEP for this case study is itself an example of the applicability of the model in varied environments—from universities to private companies and from the design of single course learning experiences to entire adaptive technology systems (Fig. 1).

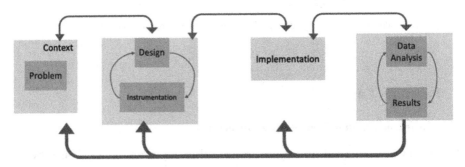

**Fig. 1.** The learning engineering process as developed by Kessler et al. [6].

The LEP provides a model for how individuals or teams can engage in learning engineering [6], but learning engineering will look different depending on the context in which it is used. As noted by Goodell et al. [7], there are three types of roles a learning engineer can serve in an organization. First, a learning engineer could serve as a consultant to help or advise on the creation of learning resources. Second, a learning engineer could be a single role on a diverse, interdisciplinary team working toward the development of a learning environment. Third, a diverse team could serve as a learning engineering unit in which every member contributes specialized knowledge (instead of a single dedicated role) to accomplish a goal. At various points in the LEP, the learning engineer may also engage in knowledge domain modeling, root cause analysis, learner modeling, or activity modeling. Through instrumentation the learning engineer gains insights from student behaviors, teaching practices, product efficacy, etc. and is able to interpret that information for meaningful data-driven feedback loops [7].

Herbert Simon, Nobel Laureate at Carnegie Mellon University, first proposed the role of the learning engineer to be individuals who are professionals of creating learning environments at universities and to assist faculty in developing a professional approach to increase student learning [8]. Carnegie Mellon University provided leadership in the development and spread of the learning engineering role [9], and the role was carried over to Acrobatiq when it formed from the Open Learning Initiative (OLI) in 2013. While there are many scenarios in which a learning engineer could be working, this paper will use the specific context of learning engineering as it was enacted in the initial start-up years of Acrobatiq. Jerome [3] moved from OLI to Acrobatiq and wrote of the role: "A learning engineer works both pedagogically and technologically to improve, create and make a whole experience and then evaluate the effectiveness of it with data." Within this context, the Learning Engineering Process was put in place to utilize the learning science research from OLI to develop courseware on a cutting-edge, data-driven platform, and the role of the learning engineer was to manage the LEP in order to develop this courseware product. The learning engineer was a role on a diverse team which also included product managers, project managers, software engineers, data scientists, marketing, and also by extension included external stakeholders (partners and customers).

This case study will also serve to illustrate how learning engineering provides an ethical model to advocate for learners, and in that way create the best possible learning environment. As our diverse team worked to develop this courseware product, the student—who would be the end user—was not in the room as a decision maker. The learning engineer was the person who maintained the higher-order student learning goals and evaluated input and work from the team to ensure it served this goal. To be an advocate for the student and what is best for their learning requires constantly questioning decisions to ensure the best interests of the student have not gotten lost in complex team dynamics and development processes.

## 1.2 A Learning Engineering Case Study: Adaptive Activities

**Context.** The Learning Engineering Process will provide a model for the case study: the creation, implementation, and redesign of adaptive activities in courseware. For this case study, I will refer to the Acrobatiq environment in which we were developing content for courseware as well as the delivery platform and authoring environment. The development of the adaptive activities was part of the Bill and Melinda Gates Foundation Next Generation Courseware Challenge [10]. As a learning engineer, I was responsible for updating six introductory higher ed courses which originated at OLI with new content, multimedia, adaptive activities, and assessments. The student's context was also a component of this LEP process [11]. These courses would serve students as their primary learning resource in a variety of contexts at different institutions—completely independent asynchronous online to instructor-led blended models. Because of the wide range of students and the situations in which they would be learning, it was important that the courseware was based on principles that would serve all learning contexts. I worked with product and engineering to test and review the platform interface as it was developed; prepared updates for marketing to deliver to the Gates Foundation; trained and managed nearly 30 subject matter experts, reviewing and revising content as necessary; and managed the implementation team who moved content into the authoring platform, reviewing and testing once complete. Even when working with a diverse team developing both technology and content, the goal was always the same for everyone: produce the best possible learning experience for students.

**Define the Problem/Project.** The first step of the LEP is to define the problem to be solved. The problem in this case study was actually a project goal: to create adaptive activities for courseware. The purpose of these activities was to provide additional formative practice, tailored to each individual student. The adaptive activity had sets of scaffolding questions from easy to difficult for each learning objective in the module. When a student entered the activity, the platform would determine what level of scaffolding the student needed based on a predictive learning estimate generated for the module's learning objectives. The design of the activity was intended to produce a streamlined experience for students who had done well in the content, and provide scaffolded support for those who struggled in order to better prepare them for a summative assessment. The intended learners were college and university students at different partner institutions across the country (Fig. 2).

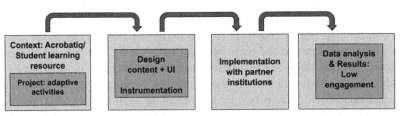

**Fig. 2.** The initial LEP stages of design, development, implementation, and data analysis of the adaptive activities.

**Research.** Before any design or instrumentation could begin, the learning engineers had to have a clear understanding of the research which would impact the design and development of these activities. The relevant research for the adaptive activities ranged from Cognitive Load Theory [12], to formative practice and feedback [13, 14], to learning curves [15]. The research on scenario-based learning and scaffolding was also consulted and shaped the content decisions [16, 17]. Understanding the relevant literature must be the first step to ensure the product or project being developed takes advantage of what is already known to be successful or unsuccessful. As Ertmer and Newby [18] state, the research and theories on human learning shape the selection, implementation, and prediction of how successful an instructional strategy might be. Knowing the relevant research shaped the design and instrumentation phase.

**Design.** The design phase accounted for two separate but intertwined objectives: the design of the adaptive activities as a platform feature and student interface, and the design of the content from a pedagogical perspective. The design of the feature itself went through a typical development process for most software applications. The requirements were gathered, wireframes were developed, discussed, revised. The feature was coded and reviewed by the team periodically for changes and the final version was validated.

The design of the content was guided by the research with the goal of providing students of different abilities an experience that would fit their needs. The activity was designed to cover each learning objective from the module, with a series of questions for each objective written to increasing levels of difficulty. Students who had high learning estimates on the objectives in the module would only see the questions which most closely mirrored those they might see in the assessment. Students who struggled on learning objectives would get those questions, plus additional questions before each that would help scaffold a knowledge gap. The design of the activities was outlined by the learning engineers and then each subject matter expert was trained on the concept of the activity and specific requirements for the content. The completed activities were reviewed in design documents by the learning engineer to ensure it adhered to the objective of the activity.

The design phase itself consists of several iterative improvement cycles. Neither the platform feature nor the content for the adaptive activities was completed without review and revision. However, these cycles were completed by internal review and not though live student engagement in a natural setting. The purpose of these cycles was to produce the best possible learning activity for students using as much information as possible during the design and development phase.

**Instrumentation.** Once the adaptive activities were ready from both the software and content side, the content was put into the courseware by the implementation team using the authoring interface. The authoring interface allowed each question to be tagged with the learning objective, skill, and difficulty level (this mirrored the design documents where the content was written). These tags allowed the platform to gather data on each question as students answered them. This information would feed into the analytics engine to update the student learning estimates in order to adapt the adaptive activities as well as to populate instructor dashboards. The raw data would also be stored in a database for future analysis.

**Implementation.** Once complete, each of the courses were implemented at a variety of institutions where students used the courseware as a part of their credit-bearing courses. For this project, I had minimal involvement with the implementation once the courseware itself was complete. The next step was to analyze the data from student use.

**Data Analysis.** After the first semester was completed with the courseware, the team began looking into the data generated through student use. The wealth of data ranged from the number and length of login times, to question difficulty and discrimination, to predictive learning estimates. There were natural questions that came to mind when we talked about analyzing the data. One of those questions was, how did students engage with the courseware over time? Essentially, we wanted to see how many students in the class did all of the different components of the courseware as the course progressed. To answer this, our data scientist developed engagement graphs. These data visualizations plotted the number of students who read, completed formative practice, adaptive activities, and summative assessments for the entire course (Fig. 3).

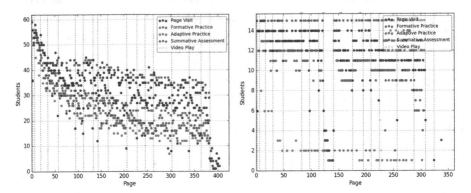

**Fig. 3.** Engagement graphs from two different courses showing low student adaptive activity engagement (pink) (used with permission). (Color figure online)

These engagement graphs showed a very informative view of all student activity. It was not surprising to see that students began to engage less with the courseware over time (mirroring typical retention trends), but the graph showed that in a clear way. We noticed that many graphs had a vertical gap between the reading dots and the doing dots, indicating that there were students who read the page but did not engage in the practice. We refer to this as the reading-doing gap. We noticed that the assessment dots were the highest of all, indicating some students only entered the courseware to complete the required quizzes or tests.

When I was looking at the engagement graph for one course, I noted how low the dots were for the adaptive activities. This was certainly not ideal—the adaptive activities would not be helpful if they were not used. While one explanation was that the activities weren't required or even recommended in the course, this seemed unlikely. I asked to look at engagement graphs for the same course at other institutions and saw similar results. We then looked at other courses and confirmed this was a trend globally.

Investigating the data helped to narrow the likely causes; it was not a problem local-ized to a single instructor's implementation, or even to a specific course. This led me to look at their placement and design in the courseware itself. The activities were located on the module summary page. The page began with a summary of the content, then had a metacognitive survey evaluation for students to fill out about the learning objectives, then the adaptive activity, then the quiz. The adaptive activity and quiz were both links which opened an assessment interface. The links had titles and icons, but I suspected that the title "quiz" was much clearer in its purpose simply through the familiar name. With all the other content types on the page, I hypothesized that the location and description of the activity was causing low engagement (Fig. 4).

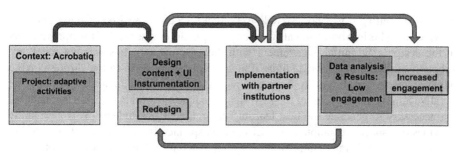

**Fig. 4.** The complete LEP cycle for the adaptive activity development.

**Iterative Improvement: Redesign.** The solution I decided upon to remediate the low engagement we were seeing in the data for the adaptive activities was a design solution. New lesson pages were added between the content pages and the summary page, the adaptive activities were moved to this new page, and I added content to explain the purpose of the activity for the learner. I hoped that this new placement in the flow of the student experience and the new language would help the students see it, understand the purpose of it, and complete it.

**Iterative Improvement: Implementation, Data Analysis, and Results.** The updated courses were provided to the institutional partners for the following semester. After students completed the semester, the engagement graphs were created for analysis. The graphs showed that engagement was up significantly. Students were engaging with the adaptive activities at the same level as the other content (Fig. 5).

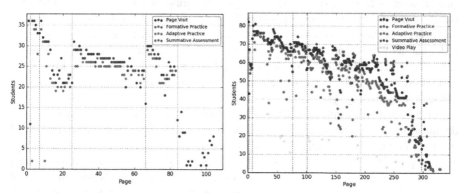

**Fig. 5.** Engagement graphs for different courses showing increased student engagement with the adaptive activities (pink) after the redesign (used with permission). (Color figure online)

These results showed that the design of the user interface impacted how students engaged with the features of the courseware. A change in the design changed the results. The team, including myself, designed the courseware using as much research and data-driven decision making as possible, however, until the courseware was used by students in a natural setting it was not possible to predict the outcome with certainty. The data provided insights into how students were engaging in the course that led to improvements in the design. The initial engagement with the adaptive activities was not ideal, but subpar results would only be a failure if no attempts are made to follow through on the iterative improvement cycle to diagnose, redesign, and reimplement the solution. The iterative improvement cycles of the LEP are not unique to learning engineering, but they are necessary to generate the best learning environment for students. This case study provides one specific example of the LEP which spanned from the research and design phase through the iterative improvement cycle, which took over two years in total.

## 2   Ethics in Education

The ethical considerations in education come from a variety of different approaches depending on how one is situated in the community—as a student, a teacher, an instructional designer, a technologist, or a developer of educational technology products. This section will not provide an exhaustive review of the many ways ethics has been discussed and researched in the domain of education, but rather provide key frameworks and views to enlighten the way learning engineering can embody an ethical approach to supporting learners.

Ethical standards are incorporated into professional organizations such as the Association for Educational Communication and Technology (AECT) which help guide students, educators, and professionals in the field [19]. When AECT was called the Development of Audio-Visual Instruction, James Finn developed a set of characteristics for the profession, stressing the need for ethics [20]. He wrote that the field should have "a well defined code of ethics" and that professionals "are hired or licensed with an obligation on the part of each professional to the ethics and standards of his profession." The ethics standards included in the AECT standards provide a guide to align professional actions, but there are more specific ethical issues facing professionals in the field. A study of professional technologists uncovered a set of ethical issues that concerned them: copyright, learner privacy, accessibility, diversity, conflicts of interest, and professionalism [21]. This research identified specific legal and professional issues to be tackled in the current professional field, and while it is vital to address these specific topics, they do not serve as a guiding system of ethics.

In 2007 the Definitions and Terminology Committee of the AECT put forth a new definition of educational technology: "Educational technology is the study and ethical practice of facilitating learning and improving performance by creating, using, and managing appropriate technological processes and resources" [22]. The inclusion of ethical practice in this definition is an indicator of the importance of developing educational technology with an ethical framework. Implementing ethics in the development of new technology is not only a top-down system enacted by professional organizations or administrators, but also an increasingly demanded component of company culture from practitioners concerned about the uses of emerging technology [23]. By understanding how learning engineering supports an ethical framework, practitioners can embody ethics in their daily work and incorporate this into the culture of an organization.

In the broader educational context, the purpose of learning is certainly clear to those who are directly involved in the learning process—teachers. Within the context of teacher-student relationships, the "ethic of caring" emerged from Noddings [24, 25] and continued in subsequent research [26, 27]. In an exploratory study, Rose and Tingley [28] interviewed science and math teachers to investigate their perspectives and practice of instructional design, and found caring to be central to their instructional design practice. The ethic of caring seems natural when the relationship between teachers and students is direct, especially in primary and secondary education, but instructional design is often done by those in the profession who work outside the classroom [29]. Researchers focused on the profession of instructional design have worked to develop models that support ethics through design, where the instructional designer acts out of concern for the students who receive the instruction, and believes that a caring and ethical design will be more effective than one which is solely focused on learning outcomes [29].

Specific ethical issues do not provide enough generalizability for an ethical framework, and while an ethic of caring provides a broad sense of moral responsibility, it is perhaps too broad to guide the actions of individuals or groups. Let us look at how researchers in the instructional design field (a related field, and a necessary background in learning engineering) ascribe value to purpose and an ethical voice. Identifying specific ethical issues can help to establish an ethical code, which when used by professionals, adds an ethical voice into the discourse of an organization [21]. This ethical voice stems from a place of purpose. Schwier [30] states that instructional designers should not only understand how they practice their profession, but have a clear understanding of why they practice, that instructional designers can help to shape a discourse on the purpose and form of learning. "But collectively, shared purpose or vision shapes our professional identities by providing a metaphorical vessel to contain the disparate roles we play in our daily lives. Larger purpose provides perspective and the lynchpins of a professional community." The development of an ethical voice can serve as a way to guide professionals when making specific decisions as well as maintain a higher-order understanding of purpose in the field. An ethical voice helps professionals hold themselves and organizations to a higher standard than simply meeting legal or economic requirements [21]. While the professional community of learning engineers covers a very broad range of contexts, it can be seen in the developing definitions and standards that a general purpose of the profession is to apply learning science, data-driven decision making, and iterative improvement for the betterment of the end user, the learner.

In this specific case study—and likely in many technology development environments—we did not work directly with students to develop the adaptive activities and courseware. Is an ethical voice stemming from a professional purpose enough? How do we practice an ethic of caring? The answer may be in how we conceptualize students, the very people on whom our professional purpose is focused. In instructional design or engineering design systems, the learner/user is considered to be part of the system [6]. However, for an ethical framework, we should consider the learner as an entity in relationship to ourselves, in addition to understanding their role in a development system. Philosophers have long worked on this idea of conceptualizing other people, and how we relate to them through communication, and while this paper certainly won't delve into an overview of the philosophical constructs of the self and other, I will select a basic concept and how it was used in a related field. Martin Buber develops an ethic of dialogue through his analysis of I-to-you and I-to-it relationships in *I and Thou* [32].

When one treats another person as a means to an end, that person becomes an object; when one treats another as a human, one enters an ethical dialogic relationship with that person. Salvo [31] puts forth that it is the ethical responsibility of usability designers to maintain a dialogic relationship between the producers and consumers of technology using participatory design, and although it is not always possible to engage in a dialogic relationship, it is an ethical act to strive toward this end. Kelly [33] identified communication as a virtue for participatory design, supporting a set of ethical principles for the field. The application of dialogic ethics to participatory design may be specific to the design context, but this philosophy of dialogic ethics can be incorporated into a system of ethics in a broader educational development context, and specifically in cases where the learner is not directly present. The value of dialogue is clear for both the ability to maintain an ethical relationship with the learner as a full and complex person, as well as a means of engaging in a professional practice with others.

## 3   Learning Engineering as an Ethical Framework

Learning engineering provides a professional purpose, which helps to develop an ethical voice. Yet an ethical voice alone could still potentially advocate for the learner abstractly as an *it*, and not as a *person*. The learning engineer should strive to maintain a conceptual understanding of the learner, and through that engage in a dialogic ethic, using an ethical voice. When the learning engineer engages in the LEP with a team, the shared purpose facilitates a dialogic ethic between team members at various stages in the cycle. As the learning engineer and team move through the LEP—focused on the learner as a person and driven by purpose—the team and process are both working in an ethic of caring (Fig. 6).

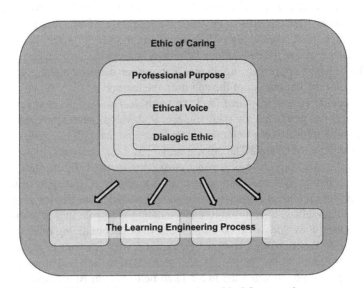

**Fig. 6.** A learning engineering ethical framework.

Using this learning engineering case study, we can map the ethical constructs discussed here using this example. The first point to consider is how learning engineering itself provides an ethical approach to developing learning environments for students. Learning engineering is a practice and process that supports learners and their development. The purpose of learning engineering is to support the learner—and by working in service to the learner—we work within this purpose and this shapes an ethical voice for the learning engineer. This ethical voice strives to maintain the student-not-present in the development of courseware as a person, and not an *it*, and therefore keep them in the dialogue. In the development of the adaptive activities, this ethical voice helped me to maintain focus on the learner. I would often imagine different students with complex histories, motivations, and goals and consider how my work would benefit each. This conceptualization helped me to keep the student from becoming an abstraction. Much like in the design use-case [30], engaging in dialogic ethics helps the learning engineer be a better user-advocate and keep the student central in the technical development process.

My professional purpose was to serve learners by developing effective, researched-based learning activities and I worked to create this shared goal with my team. I trained subject matter experts to consider the student as the center of their goal: how to scaffold content to help students at different levels of mastery. This ethical voice made it easier for me to analyze or question decisions in the development of the activities to ensure the interface was going to best serve the students, as indicated through the relevant research for this project. While an ethical voice facilitated the actions I took or questions I asked as I worked on the adaptive activities, it should be noted that these questions or objections were made to other members of the team, some of whom were my superiors. Using an ethical voice in this way did not cause friction within the team because the team shared the same purpose. A clear central purpose not only helped me as a learning engineer to cultivate and use an ethical voice, but it also served to maintain a dialogic ethic between team members. Open and honest communication can be difficult between team members, but we must strive to cross this communication divide [31]. Kelly [33] even notes it is a virtue of courage when a practitioner needs to push back within an organization. Collaboration and a shared understanding is key for a successful learning engineering team [7]. When discussing ideas or requests that were not in line with research principles, the shared purpose of serving students provided our team a common goal to communicate around, and this shared understanding helped this diverse team work together through a dialogic ethic.

While the role of learning engineer provided an ethical voice, the Learning Engineering Process can also maintain ethical purpose through engaging in the process itself. Dialogic ethic provides a way to design ethically and not simply for expediency; it "creates a background for understanding usability as an ethical design praxis rather than an efficient mode of technological design and manufacturing" [31]. Developing adaptive courseware is a more complex process than the usability context, but the dialogic ethic similarly provided the team with a way to ground the courseware development in the ethical praxis of serving the learner. Salvo [31] also notes that a clear link between dialogic ethics and usability saves the usability process from simply being a step in a development process that doesn't address identified issues, but yet is still used as an assurance to the end user that the product has been tested for "usability." An ethical practice derived from purpose can save the technological product from being developed without sincerity. In this case, the steps of the LEP were meaningfully carried out through ethical purpose and dialogue. When we identified potential problems in either the content or the environment for the courseware, changes and improvements were made so that the implementation of the courseware would be shared with students in good faith. The initial design placement of the adaptive activities was not ideal for engagement, but the original design was created based on research sincerest efforts to serve the learner, and was improved by completing the LEP faithfully.

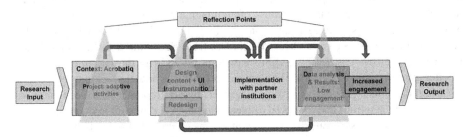

**Fig. 7.** Key research and reflection points in the LEP for the adaptive activity development.

The LEP model is also itself an ethical tool due to the metacognitive reflection points the process enables. There are several critical points in the LEP that facilitate an active awareness of the learning engineering purpose in that context, highlighted in Fig. 7. First, and most naturally, is the context and definition of the problem, which includes research. The central purpose shapes the goal of the project or problem. Consulting the relevant research helps to design and develop the learning environment responsibly, as the body of literature can steer you towards effective methods and away from problematic ones. Second, within the design process are many iterative cycles where the ethical voice can be used to reflect upon the design and evaluate it against the research. During the design of the adaptive activities, this phase allowed me to ask questions of the design and content. Was this content well scaffolded? Would this design cause extraneous cognitive load? Third, data analysis is an active reflective act; the LEP does not end when the learning environment is complete and students begin their learning process. As an iterative improvement model, reflection on the performance of the learning environment is a critical component of the cycle. This step is where I identified the unexpected engagement in adaptive activities and this reflection point helped me compare the data with my expectations and search for possible causes. Finally, we return to the reflection points earlier in the LEP as we make changes, whether that requires change in the design, implementation, etc. In the redesign of the adaptive activities, I once again evaluated how a change might better align with learning science and design research, and engaged in the same reflection of expectations in the next data analysis step.

Learning engineering uses a practical application of learning science and cognitive science research as a means of achieving goals or solving problems. Research is critical at the start of the LEP, but also at the end of the process as an artifact or output of the LEP. The relevant literature for the context of the project should be consulted to ensure methods are being used which are proven to be effective for learning. At the end of the process, the data and findings should also be shared back to the community to provide information for other researchers and to maintain transparency and accountability to the learner. For these adaptive activities, the relevant research was consulted and used to measure the development against, and the findings were shared after the LEP had been cycled through [34]. Reporting research findings is a way to maintain accountability to the end user—the students—while also engaging in a reflection point of the LEP. Salvo [31] notes that it is imperative for the researcher to locate themselves in the research, and in this case, the learning engineer to identify themselves as the active participant in the LEP as well as the research it generates. Nodding [24] expressed that researchers who work to better understand teaching become "part of an educational enterprise that supports a caring community," which I believe can now be expanded to both the developers and researchers of educational technology who do so with an ethical framework.

# 4   Conclusion

Both the role of learning engineer and the Learning Engineering Process provide ethical tools with which to work. Learning engineering provides a context and purpose for creating learning environments—in service of the learner. This purpose helps to shape an ethical voice as well as maintain the learner as a full conceptual person at the heart of this purpose and voice, which can be used in a dialogic ethic during the development of the learning engineering project or goal. The Learning Engineering Process provides clear points to reflect on the project and evaluate its progress against the original goal and research to ensure the purpose of the project is being carried out in good faith for the learner, an ethical accountability which is further extended by sharing research back to the professional community. Even in contexts where the learner is not directly present, this learning engineering ethical framework can help the learning engineering team maintain the learner at the heart of the process and therefore become part of an extended educational community of caring.

    While I worked as a learning engineer within a specific context that may be different from many others, this case study on adaptive activities in courseware can serve as an example of the benefits of the Learning Engineering Process. My hope is that the ethical framework I proposed serves as a point of conversation and reference for the growing field of learning engineering, and can be refined and revised over time. Additional learning engineering case studies and ethical applications from diverse contexts could lead to a set of ethical principles common to the field, similar to how ethical standards have been identified in related design fields [21, 33, 35]. The ethical dimensions of learning engineering are well worth teasing out. As Campbell et al. [35] asked, "What could we achieve if we were thoughtful, deliberate, and unapologetic in aligning design projects with the ethical knowledge of designers? If we developed a community in which the moral dimensions of practice were explicitly developed through reflexive dialogue?" The sharing of ethical experiences within the community can begin a dialogue which centers ethics in practice. The valuable work of the IEEE ICICLE community to develop standards for learning engineering can guide the emerging field, and the continued development of a learning engineering ethical framework could help guide new practitioners as they begin to engage in the profession and practice.

**Acknowledgements.** I would like to thank Erin Czerwinski for her mentorship in learning engineering when I began in the role, Bill Jerome and Benny Johnson for their continued enthusiasm for learning engineering, and Jim Goodell and Aaron Kessler for their feedback on the idea for this paper. I would also express my gratitude to the ICICLE group for providing a community of practice and for the continued development of the field.

# References

1. IEEE ICICLE: What is Learning Engineering? (2020). https://sagroups.ieee.org/icicle/. Accessed 01 Nov 2021
2. Goodell, J., Kessler, A., Kurzweil, D., Koldner, J.: Competencies of learning engineering teams and team members. In: IEEE ICICLE proceedings of the 2019 Conference on Learning Engineering, Arlington, VA, May 2019 (2020)
3. Jerome, B.: The need for learning engineers (and learning engineering). Eliterate (2013). https://eliterate.us/learning-engineers/. Accessed Jan 2021
4. Hobson, L., Kessler, A.: Dr. Aaron Kessler - The Learning Engineering Process. The Dr. Luke Hobson Podcast (2020). https://drlukehobson.com/podcast-episodes/ep-15-dr-aaron-kessler. Accessed 01 Nov 2021
5. Goodell, J., Thai, K.-P.: A learning engineering model for learner-centered adaptive systems. In: Stephanidis, C., et al. (eds.) HCII 2020. LNCS, vol. 12425, pp. 557–573. Springer, Cham (2020). https://doi.org/10.1007/978-3-030-60128-7_41
6. Kessler, A., Design SIG Colleagues. Learning Engineering Process Strong Person (2020). https://sagroups.ieee.org/icicle/learning-engineering-process/. Accessed 01 Nov 2021
7. Goodell, J., Lee, M., Lis, J.: What we discovered at the roots of learning engineering. In: Proceedings of the 2019 Conference on Learning Engineering. In IEEE ICICLE proceedings of the 2019 Conference on Learning Engineering, Arlington, VA, May 2019 (2020)
8. Simon, H.A.: The job of a college president. Educ. Rec. **48**, 68–78 (1967)
9. Lieberman, M.: Learning Engineers Inch Toward the Spotlight. Inside Higher Ed (2018). https://www.insidehighered.com/digital-learning/article/2018/09/26/learning-engineers-pose-challenges-and-opportunities-improving. Accessed 01 Nov 2021
10. House, A., Means, B., Peters Hinton, V., Boyce, J., Wetzel, T., Wang, S.: Next Generation Courseware Challenge Evaluation. SRI International, Menlo Park (2018). https://www.sri.com/wp-content/uploads/pdf/next_generation_courseware_challenge_evaluation_final_report_dec_2018.pdf. Accessed 01 Nov 2021
11. Goodell, J., et al.: Learning Engineering Toolkit (2021)
12. Sweller, J.: Cognitive load theory and educational technology. Educ. Tech. Res. Dev. **68**(1), 1–16 (2019). https://doi.org/10.1007/s11423-019-09701-3
13. Dunlosky, J., Rawson, K., Marsh, E., Nathan, M., Willingham, D.: Improving students' learning with effective learning techniques: promising directions from cognitive and educational psychology. Psychol. Sci. Public Interest **14**(1), 4–58 (2013). https://doi.org/10.1177/152910 0612453266
14. Huang, K., Chen, C.H., Wu, W.S., Chen, W.Y.: Interactivity of question prompts and feedback on secondary students' science knowledge acquisition and cognitive load. Educ. Technol. Soc. **18**(4), 159–171 (2015)
15. Koedinger, K.R., Mathan, S.: Distinguishing qualitatively different kinds of learning using log files and learning curves. In: ITS 2004 Log Analysis Workshop, pp. 39–46 (2004)
16. Blayney, P., Kalyuga, S., Sweller, J.: Using cognitive load theory to tailor instruction to levels of accounting students' expertise. Educ. Technol. Soc. **18**(4), 199–210 (2015)

17. Sanders, D., Welk, D.: Strategies to scaffold student learning: applying Vygotsky's zone of proximal development. Nurse Educ. **30**(5), 203–204 (2005)
18. Ertmer, P., Newby, T.: Behaviorism, cognitivism, constructivism: comparing critical features from an instructional design perspective. Perform. Improv. Q. **6**(4), 50–72 (1993). https://doi.org/10.1111/j.1937-8327.1993.tb00605.x
19. AECT: Association for Educational Communications and Technology, AECT Standards (2012). https://www.aect.org/docs/AECTstandards2012.pdf. Accessed 01 Nov 2021
20. Finn, J.D.: Professionalizing the audio-visual field. Audio-Visual Commun. Rev. **1**(1), 6–18 (1952)
21. Lin, H.: The ethics of instructional technology: issues and coping strategies experienced by professional technologists in design and training situations in higher education. Educ. Tech. Res. Dev. **55**(5), 411–437 (2007). https://doi.org/10.1007/s11423-006-9029-y
22. Januszewski, A., Molenda, M.: Educational Technology: A Definition with Commentary. Erlbaum, Mahwah (2008)
23. Neubert, M.J., Montañez, G.D.: Virtue as a framework for the design and use of artificial intelligence. Bus. Horiz. **63**(2), 195–204 (2020). https://doi.org/10.1016/j.bushor.2019.11.001
24. Noddings, N.: An ethic of caring and its implications for instructional arrangements. Am. J. Educ. **96**(2), 215–230 (1988). https://doi.org/10.1086/443894
25. Noddings, N.: The Challenge to Care in Schools: An Alternative Approach to Education. Teachers College Press, New York (1992)
26. Nias, J.: Primary teaching as a culture of care. In: Prosser, J. (ed.) School Culture, pp. 66–81. SAGE Publications Ltd (1999). https://doi.org/10.4135/9781446219362.n5
27. Vogt, F.: A caring teacher: explorations into primary school teachers' professional identity and ethic of care. Gend. Educ. **14**(3), 251–264 (2002). https://doi.org/10.1080/0954025022000001071
28. Rose, E., Tingley, K.: Science and math teachers as Instructional designers: linking ID to the ethic of caring. Can. J. Learn. Technol./La Revue Canadienne de l'apprentissage et de La Technologie **34**(1) (2008). https://doi.org/10.21432/t2hc73
29. Osguthorpe, R.T., Osguthorpe, R.D., Jacob, W.J., Davies, R.: The moral dimensions of instructional design. Educ. Technol. **2**, 1–8 (2003)
30. Schwier, R.A.: A grand purpose for ID? In: Association of Educational Communication and Technology Conference, Chicago, Illinois (2004)
31. Salvo, M.J.: Ethics of engagement: user-centered design and rhetorical methodology. Tech. Commun. Q. **10**(3), 273–290 (2001). https://doi.org/10.1207/s15427625tcq1003_3
32. Buber, M.: I and Thou. Charles Scribner's Sons, New York (1970)
33. Kelly, J.: Towards ethical principles for participatory design practice. CoDesign **15**(4), 329–344 (2019). https://doi.org/10.1080/15710882.2018.1502324
34. Van Campenhout, R., Jerome, B., Johnson, B.G.: The impact of adaptive activities in acrobatiq courseware - investigating the efficacy of formative adaptive activities on learning estimates and summative assessment scores. In: Sottilare, R.A., Schwarz, J. (eds.) HCII 2020. LNCS, vol. 12214, pp. 543–554. Springer, Cham (2020). https://doi.org/10.1007/978-3-030-50788-6_40
35. Campbell, K., Schwier, R.A., Kenny, R.F.: Agency of the instructional designer: moral coherence and transformative social practice. Australas. J. Educ. Technol. **21**(2), 242–262 (2005). https://doi.org/10.14742/ajet.1337

# Teaching Reinforcement Learning Agents with Adaptive Instructional Systems

Joost van Oijen$^{(\boxtimes)}$, Armon Toubman, and Olivier Claessen

Royal Netherlands Aerospace Centre, Amsterdam, The Netherlands
{Joost.van.Oijen,Armon.Toubman,Olivier.Claessen}@nlr.nl

**Abstract.** Traditionally, adaptive instructional systems (AISs) are built to instruct human students. However, they are not the only students that might benefit from an AIS. The field of reinforcement learning (RL), a subfield of machine learning, studies the instruction of synthetic students called agents, by means of various algorithms. In this paper, we advocate the use of an AIS as a conceptual framework to design and teach RL agents. We form our argument by deconstructing what it means to build and use an AIS for a human student, and discuss how the various concepts and relationships may apply to RL agents. We illustrate our findings by means of examples from the reinforcement learning literature and show a domain implementation of an AIS for RL agents.

**Keywords:** Adaptive instructional systems · Machine learning · Reinforcement learning · Training

## 1 Introduction

A proposed definition of adaptive instructional systems (AISs) is as follows: "computer-based systems that guide learning experiences by tailoring instruction and recommendations based on the goals, needs, and preferences of each learner in the context of domain learning objectives." [1]. The purpose of an AIS is to optimize learning for a learner (or team of learners), based on some learning objective. This can be mastering a skill, gaining a competency or learning to achieve a task. Traditionally, AISs are built to instruct human students. However, they are not the only students that might benefit from an AIS. In this paper we explore AISs for training computational learners.

Reinforcement learning (RL) is a class of machine learning techniques that enables intelligent (virtual) agents to learn behaviors through interaction with an environment [2, 3]. Rather than being explicitly taught, a RL agent learns from its experiences through trial-and-error. In the last decade, due to algorithmic innovations and the increased availability of computational power, many advances have been made in the field that allow agents to solve increasingly complex problems in intricate environments [4]. As a consequence, RL algorithms are beginning to find their way in the applied research domain where agents can be employed for applications such as simulation-based training or analysis to take on the role as intelligent role-players or entities.

© Springer Nature Switzerland AG 2021
R. A. Sottilare and J. Schwarz (Eds.): HCII 2021, LNCS 12792, pp. 120–136, 2021.
https://doi.org/10.1007/978-3-030-77857-6_8

Meanwhile, there is no one-size-fits-all solution and it remains a challenge to exploit new RL algorithms and develop agents capable of learning and performing specific tasks in a target application domain. While a RL agent may have the learning capability (i.e., the algorithm) to learn complex tasks, it still needs to be trained and made fit-for-purpose for the target domain. Such operationalization of RL agents involves for instance: (1) setting up a training goal by the design of tasks for the teaching of skills and knowledge; (2) forming an instructional strategy, viz. a training design or curriculum to train the learner on those tasks; and (3) providing a learning environment that is representative for the target operational environment. Although there is a wealth of literature that addresses algorithmic improvements for the learning mechanisms, providing experimental results in various (often low-fidelity, toy-like) domains, there is less guidance available on general design strategies for exploiting, training, and integrating RL agents in target domains.

In this paper, we advocate the use of an adaptive instructional system (AIS) as a conceptual framework to design and teach RL agents. We will show that, although AISs were originally intended to optimize human training, many analogies can be drawn between (1) the functions provided by an AIS and (2) the functions required to train RL agents. In the mapping between the functions of an AIS and RL, we abstract away from the specific algorithmic technology (cf. the learner) and focus on the training design and instructional process, namely teaching a learner to operate in a task domain. Similar to how the fields of cognitive and neuroscience have inspired and continue to influence RL research (leading to improved learning algorithms), instructional sciences may inspire and influence training methods for RL agents (leading to optimized learning through instruction). The aim of this paper is thus to promote synergies and exchange lessons learned between practitioners of AIS research and practitioners of RL research.

We begin this paper by presenting our motivation (Sect. 2). Next, we compare and analyze the training concepts relating to a human learner and an agent learner using examples from RL literature (Sect. 3). We continue by zooming into the central concept, namely a training system by means of an AIS, where the actual learning takes place (Sect. 0). Here, we discuss how an AIS may be applied to teach a RL agent. Following this discussion, we illustrate the views presented in Sect. 3 and 4 by outlining a system that operationalizes learning agents within a concrete target domain, namely a military training simulation system in the air combat domain (Sect. 5). We conclude the paper with a general discussion of our analysis and opportunities for future directions (Sect. 6).

## 2  Motivation

In this paper we advocate the use of AIS theory as an instrument to operationalize RL agents. Here, operationalize means the process of employing a general-purpose (untrained) RL algorithm, and training it such that it can operate and perform in a desired target or task environment. It addresses the question of how to make a RL agent 'fit-for-purpose'. Our four motivations for applying AIS theory to RL agents are the following.

1. **Reaching a conceptual development framework for RL.** An AIS provides a conceptual framework for computer-based teaching of learners. It offers a structured

method for addressing key design questions, such as how to define the task, skills or knowledge to teach; how to define the expected standard of performance; how to measure and evaluate the learner against this standard; and what instructional strategies to apply. Where RL research usually has a prime focus on improving learning algorithms, an AIS focuses on optimizing the learning process through training in a specific task domain. The latter receives less attention in RL research but is a crucial step to successfully integrate RL technology in industrial applications. AIS theory can be used to fill this gap, both from a theoretical and a technical viewpoint.

2. **Technology abstraction for RL research.** The concept of an AIS provides a clear separation between the algorithmic learning technology, in other words a learner, and the task domain and environment it is applied to. By abstracting the learner from the training process and the environment using an AIS, the application domain can be designed independently, regardless of the underlying learning technology. New RL algorithms can then more easily be integrated or exchanged, with less impact on the system as a whole. Although specific technical solutions exist for common interfaces between RL algorithms and environments (such as OpenAI Gym [5]), we aim for a more holistic view on this abstraction.

3. **Working towards a mixed-learner AIS.** In a shared human-agent training environment, an AIS has the potential to fulfil multiple purposes. For instance, consider a simulation-based training environment where an AIS is used to train humans operating in teams. A common approach is to employ agents as simulated role players that can replace human roles. In such an environment, a similar AIS for training humans can potentially also be used for training agent role players. From an implementation perspective, there are many commonalities for developing such an AIS, in terms of a domain model, training needs and goals, performance measurements and evaluations, and a learning environment.

4. **Identifying cross-field research opportunities.** The concept of AISs can promote research synergies between machine learning and instructional science, similar to the bi-directional synergy between machine learning and cognitive and neuroscience [6]. On the one hand, theories on instructional strategies can be used to optimize computational learners (e.g. consider transfer learning techniques [7]). On the other hand, simulations of instructional strategies applied to computational learners can lead to insights on optimization techniques for human learning (an example for part-task training is described in [8]). In this context, an AIS for RL agents can act as an experimentation testbed to explore, test and validate instructional strategies for humans. A key challenge here is the construction of a computational learner that can act as a representative model for human learning.

## 3 Comparative Analysis of Training Concepts

To support the idea of applying concepts originating from human instructional systems to agent learners, a broad context of training is required. In this section we provide a comparative analysis of training concepts using a basic model of a training process, as shown in Fig. 1. The model focuses on teaching a learner (human or agent) some task using a training system, hereby 'updating' the learner such that it can be deployed to an operational environment.

In the remainder of this section we describe different concepts from Fig. 1 using analogies between human and agent learning and training, based on literature on machine learning. Section 3.1 presents the learner as the subject of training. Section 3.2 discusses the need analysis by which tasks can be defined that form the training objective for the training system. Section 3.3 describes the training system in terms of instructional strategies. Finally Sect. 3.4 addresses how the learner, post-training, can be deployed to the operational environment.

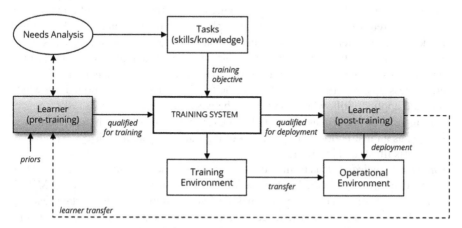

**Fig. 1.** Basic model of a training process

### 3.1  The Learner, Its Learning Mechanism and Priors

The learner is the subject that undergoes training. In the remainder of this paper, the term agent learner or human learner is used when a distinction is called for; otherwise the term learner is used.

In order to be qualified for training, a learner must meet two requirements. First, it must embody a *learning mechanism* that is capable of learning the task. Second, a training can demand a minimum set of *priors* (previously obtained skills and knowledge) from the learner. We discuss the learning mechanism and the priors below.

**Learning Mechanism.** For a human learner, the learning mechanism is the human brain (i.e. the 'hardware'). In contrast, agents and their learning mechanisms (i.e. algorithms) are invented and engineered. Thus when the goal is to build specific task-capable agents, choosing or developing the learning algorithm becomes part of the design process. Current mainstream machine learning algorithms are limited to *narrow AI*, implying they are limited to learn a specific task in a scoped context (the task domain). There is no one size fits all and different types of algorithms are specialized for different types of capabilities. Therefore it is essential to align the learner's algorithm with the nature of the task to learn. This requirement is discussed further in Sect. 3.2.

**Priors.** For a human learner, the priors are basic abilities, skills and knowledge acquired through earlier life experiences or prior education and training (i.e., the 'software'). Two types of priors can be distinguished in agent learners, namely pre-trained models and encoded knowledge (discussed below). They differ in how they are established, either implicitly obtained from an earlier training, or explicitly encoded by a designer:

- *Pre-trained models.* These are the result of a previous training or learning experience on a different but related task. The use of such models for a new training process is known as transfer learning. This can significantly increase training efficiency for a target task, requiring less data (training samples) and computational time. Pre-trained models are used extensively for deep learning on vision tasks [9] or language tasks [10]. Widespread use in those domains is possible because of their general nature (dealing with images or language). In contrast, pre-trained models for behavioral (RL) tasks are far less common because of the specificity of the tasks and the domain in which they are applied. Still, when transferring between highly comparable tasks, transfer learning can be applied successfully [7]. Developing priors through pre-training can be seen as an instructional strategy, part of the training system. This cycle of learner transfer is illustrated in Fig. 1.
- *Encoded knowledge.* This form of explicit priors represents symbolic knowledge that is encoded directly into the learner, for instance by a subject matter expert (SME). It can represent inference or decision-making rules, beliefs or goals. Certain learning algorithms depend on the existence of encoded knowledge, prior to any training. For instance in h-DQN [12], a hierarchical deep reinforcement learning algorithm, a human specifies a set of goals that represent sub-tasks in complex task domains. Consequently, an agent learns how to achieve individual goals and when to pursue them to achieve a higher-level goal; or in dynamic scripting [11], a rule-based machine learning algorithm, a human must author a rule base of possible if-then rules, after which the learning algorithm optimizes behaviour rules scripts determined through trial-and-error.

### 3.2 Needs Analysis and Training Objective

In the design of a training system, a needs analysis is performed to define the training objective. In human training, methods such as a job, task or competency analyses are performed to gain insight into the task activities and required knowledge, skills and abilities (KSA). Such analysis is typically part of the first phase of the Analyze, Design, Develop, Implement, and Evaluate (ADDIE) process for instructional design [13].

In RL, a needs analysis is also important to gain insight into the requirements for the learner in terms of cognitive abilities. These abilities must be aligned with the capabilities of its learning mechanism. In other words, can it be expected that the learner will be capable of learning the task; does it have the required 'hardware'? If basic required abilities are lacking, the learner is not suited for the training in question.

A classic example from literature is the *deep Q-network* (DQN) algorithm which has shown impressive results on many task domains, but fails on tasks that require the ability of simple planning of sequential tasks [4]. Different algorithms are equipped with different architectural features to support certain abilities, as seen for instance for capabilities of visual-spatial processing [14], long-term planning [2] or short [15] or long-term memory [16]. It can be difficult to quantify and relate human-like cognitive abilities to abilities that can be expressed by machine learning algorithms. Sometimes, abilities are not always known and limitations may only be found through experimentation. Still, an analysis is crucial to be confident that a specific algorithm is capable, or to use as guidance to select or dismiss candidate algorithms.

### 3.3 Training System

The training system offers the learner a training environment in which it can learn the task. Instructional strategies are designed and implemented with the goal to optimize the learning process within the learner regarding task performance. Below three methods are described: adaptive instruction, curriculum learning and social learning.

**Adaptive Instruction.** For human learning, adaptive instruction can be used to keep the learner within the 'zone of proximal development' by balancing the task challenge and the competence level of the learner [17]. To keep the learner engaged, the task should not be too easy or too complicated, leading to possible boredom or anxiety consequently. For agent learners a similar balance is required, though not for the purpose of keeping learners motivated, but for functional reasons of learning efficiency [18].

Adaptive instruction generally centers around two instructional strategies: (1) guiding the level of support or (2) change the nature of the content [1]. The former is an explicit form of aiding by a tutor (scaffolding), such as giving hints or advice. The latter is an implicit form of aiding through adaptation of the task environment, such as changing the difficulty level. These two strategies are described next for agent learners:.

1. *Scaffolding.* Scaffolding in RL can be associated with *reward shaping* as a technique to guide the learning process using feedback signals (rewards), indicating positive or negative trends towards the training objective [19]. It is an indirect approach to incorporate task knowledge into the learner through inference. For sub-symbolic algorithms (e.g. neural networks) that do not allow prior encoding of task knowledge, feedback signals are the only medium for an agent infer any knowledge on the task. When any prior task knowledge (the 'rules of the game') cannot be communicated to the learner, this generally leads to slow and 'sample-inefficient' learning.

2. *Environment adaptation.* Adaptation of the learning environment or scenario can be used to change the difficulty level of the task to optimize learning [20]. Part of adaptive design is to identify so-called complexity factors to be used as control dials for adaptations. During training, such adaptations can guide the learner from simple to more complex environments. In RL, there is another purpose for environment adaptation, namely to optimize the coverage of the possible observational input of the learner, without specifically changing complexity. This allows the learner to generalize a learned behavior to all possible contexts. Through smart and fast scenario adaption, this can significantly increase learning efficiency. This feature is less relevant for human learners as they are more proficient in this cognitive ability.

**Curriculum Learning.** Curriculum learning is a method of training based on the idea of gradually increasing task complexity. The idea of curriculum learning for machines dates back to 1993 [21] and is currently a well-researched area in RL [22]. In curriculum learning the goal is to strategically decompose a task (a whole-task) into so-called part-tasks. Such decomposition could be based on e.g. different sub-tasks, certain skill-sets or options for scaling the complexity of the environment.

By presenting part-tasks to a learner in a well-designed curriculum can significantly speed-up learning. However a bad designed curriculum can also lead to worse performance, compared to solely training on the whole-task. Depending on the implementation, curriculum learning can be seen as form of adaptive instruction when used within a single training session, or as consecutive trainings with different task objectives (indicated by the learner loop from Fig. 1).

**Social Learning.** Social learning is a form of learning where new knowledge and skills can be acquired by imitating or observing others. In RL, comparable techniques have been used successfully. In imitation learning, an agent learns to imitate behavior based on demonstrations given by another agent [23]. In observational learning, an agent learns from observing another agent performing a task in a shared environment [24]. The difference is subtle. In the former, an agent purely imitates behavior, regardless of the correctness of the demonstrated behavior with respect to the task. In the latter an agent learns the underlying task by observing the actions of the teacher and its effects on the environment, i.e., it learns both good and bad behavior in achieving the task.

Both approaches can be performed in an online or offline fashion. In an online setting, the teacher is present together with the learner in a shared training environment (e.g. human or other agent). In an offline setting, learning is based on existing/recorded datasets where no interactive environment is available. This is also termed as offline RL [25] or data-driven RL [26]. Offline learning can be seen as building priors before training and is a favored approach for bootstrapping the learning process of learner.

### 3.4 Operational Deployment

After successful training, the learner is qualified for deployment in the operational environment. Relevant aspects that come into play are the validation of the learner, the transfer from the learning to the operational environment, and continuous learning.

**Validation of the Learner.** A validation process judges the performance of the learner on the task in the operational environment. In human learners validation can take the form of e.g. qualification assessments, tests or examinations. Several validation approaches exist that can also be applied to agent learners:

1. *Benchmarking.* In benchmarking, the performance of a learner is compared to some reference point. This method can be used when clear metrics can be defined and measured to score a learner on task performance. It is used extensively for RL agents in games, since scoring mechanisms are commonly available and performance can easily be compared against human-based reference points [4]. Benchmarking is

also a popular technique to compare different learning algorithms on the same task environments.

2. *Test scenarios.* This method is borrowed from traditional supervised learning and is based on dividing predefined scenarios into sets of training and test scenarios. This approach is used to prevent overfitting of the task performance in situations experienced during training and be able to generalize to situations occurring during operation. Test scenarios can be used after training to judge this ability of the learner.

3. *Human judgement.* This approach assesses learners' behaviors based on subjective human opinions such as from SMEs. As a human-in-the-loop approach, it is commonly not favorable as it is a resource intensive process. However, quantitative metrics cannot always be defined to fully cover all facets of a learner's performance. For instance, consider measuring aspects such as realism or human-likeness when agents require to simulate the role of human players. An example of a validation procedure for agents as human role players for air combat training is seen in [27].

**Transfer of Training Environment.** This is the ability of the learner to apply the task learned in the training environment to the operational environment. For the scope of this paper we assume that for RL, final training in the operational environment is always required. Therefore this type of transfer is also represented in Fig. 1 by the learner transfer loop towards a follow-up training with the same task but different environment.

**Continuous Learning.** Human learners inherently continue learning after training and can become more proficient in task performance due to experience on-the-job. Certain professions require learners to initiate recurrent or refresher training, as skill-decay can occur over time. For agent learners, continuous learning is a design choice.

An advantage of online learning is that the learner can continuously adapt to evolving environments, beyond the scope that may have been taken into account during training. However compared to a training environment, agents in operational environments may not be permitted to make critical mistakes and may require adherence to safety constraints. Techniques such as safe reinforcement learning addresses this issue [28].

A possible downside is that validated performance cannot be guaranteed any longer. For instance, continuous optimization on certain aspects of a task could lead to decreased performance on other aspects. This is known as the stability-plasticity problem in learning algorithms where plasticity is required to integrate new skills, but also stability to retain existing skills [29]. Similar to human learners, recurrent training and validation can be used to ensure the retention of skills.

## 4   Adaptive Instructional System for Learner Agents

In this section we zoom in on the training system that is central to Fig. 1 and present it as an adaptive instructional system (AIS). For professional training of human learners, AISs are becoming more in demand, due to the availability of high fidelity simulation-based training environments and the trend towards more personalized training to suit the needs of individual learners. In this section we explore the application of the AIS concept to agent (cf. computational) learners, as opposed to human learners. First, we present the definitions for the components of an AIS that we use in this section.

## 4.1 Defining the Components of an AIS

Adaptive instructional systems are often characterized by four functional components [30]. Although the exact division of functions and responsibilities of these components and their interactions varies from system to system, we use the following descriptions:

1. **Domain Model**: defines the task objectives and the domain (expert) knowledge on the task to be learned, such as the skills, knowledge or problem-solving strategies. Besides information on *what* has to be learned, it provides a performance standard: metrics or indicators that can be used to judge the learner's performance and progress with respect to the task.
2. **Learner Model:** based on the task objectives and performance standard, the learner model measures and evaluates the learner's progress towards this standard. Additionally it maintains the learner's evolving states (e.g. cognitive, affective, motivational or physiological states) that can be used to adapt the training and optimize the learning process.
3. **Instructional Model:** based on the current learner's evaluation and mental states, the instructional model implements the system's instructional strategies. It plans, coordinates and applies teaching activities through direct interventions (such as providing feedback to the learner) or indirect interventions (such as adapting the learning content or environment).
4. **Interface Model:** provides a user interface for the instructional system to interact with the learner and learning environment.

## 4.2 Reinforcement Learning by an AIS

When an AIS is considered for training an agent learner, the functions of an AIS resemble the typical functions of a learning algorithm. Below, we illustrate this using a basic description of RL.

RL algorithms are based on the concept that an agent learns sequences of decisions (called a policy) by experiences obtained through interaction with an environment. An agent continuously takes actions based on its current policy and observes a new state of the environment. In parallel, the agent receives feedback signals (called rewards) from an external critic, to indicate positive or negative trends towards some goal. The learning process revolves around correlating these signals with the agent's own actions and the resulting changes in the environment in order to update its policy, with the goal to maximize future accumulative rewards.

Different aspects of a RL algorithm can be mapped to the functions of an AIS, as defined in Sect. 4.1. Figure 2 illustrates this mapping. The Domain Model contains the training goal of the RL algorithm, such as winning a game, defeating an enemy or accomplishing a task. In a RL algorithm, the goal is often not explicitly stated but rather kept in the head of the designer. The Learner Model judges the current policy of the agent by measuring its behavior, either directly or indirectly through environment observations (the latter is not shown in the illustration). The Instructional Model determines what feedback to give to the agent and when. This is commonly implemented by a reward function. Finally, the Interface Model defines the actions and observations for the agent's

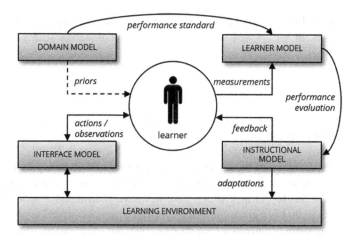

**Fig. 2.** AIS for an agent learner

interface with the environment. In addition to the AIS functions, Fig. 2 shows two concepts: (1) the ability to bootstrap the agent with priors, such as starting with pre-trained models or encoding domain knowledge (cf. Sect. 3.1), and (2) the ability of indirect intervention through environment adaptation (cf. Sect. 3.3).

In the mapping presented in Fig. 2, a basic RL algorithm is essentially dissected into its individual functions, each one addressing a key question for a designer of a training system:

- How to define the task and its performance metrics?
- What behaviors to measure from the learner to evaluated its performance?
- What instructional strategies to apply?
- What sensors and actuators does the learner require to perform its task?

Although RL algorithms come in many different forms and flavors, these core questions apply to all when applying them to a task domain.

## 4.3 Advantages of an AIS

The main advantage of mapping the training process of RL agents in the framework of an AIS becomes apparent when agents are considered for operation within a broader application scope, rather than a mere demonstration of learning abilities in a 'toy-problem' environment. In such a broader scope, designers of RL agents may be bound to external system constraints such as available simulation environments, or be dependent on SMEs to provide task objectives, task analysis and performance standards.

In this respect, the "AIS view" of a RL agent provides a separation of the *learning,* focusing on the agent's cognitive abilities and treated as a black box, from *training,* focusing on applying these abilities to teach concrete tasks relevant for some target application domain. This enhances the abstraction from the specific algorithmic learning technology that is applied and makes it easier to consider and integrate alternative or improved algorithms as they become available, with limited impact on the instructional components. In Sect. 5 we illustrate the embedding of learner agents in a broader application scope.

### 4.4 Dependencies on the Learner's Capabilities

An AIS forces a view that separates internal learning processes within the agent from external instruction. These two parallel processes could potentially lead to conflicts. This is best described by the exploration-exploitation dilemma in RL [3]. Exploration is the intentional deviation of the agent from its currently known policy by performing (semi-) random actions, with the goal to explore its task domain and potentially find new optimal solutions to the task which may not have been found if it would solely pursue its current policy in a greedy fashion. From an external instruction point of view, this behavior may seem erroneous where an AIS could have the tendency to correct this intentional behaviour.

Exploration strategies belong to the category of RL challenges that deal with optimizations for agents to learn faster in understanding the scope of task domain and the role they play in it. Other well researched internal learning strategies are *intrinsic motivation* (developmental learning) [31] and *meta-learning* (learning to learn) [32]. In human learners, analogous internal learning processes are present. However, these tend to be more stable and predictable during adulthood. When initiating training, one can have the prior assumption that humans are equipped with 'startup software' acquired during childhood, and that they have the ability to generalize and apply previously learned problem-solving strategies to new situations. This lacking ability of agents is currently one of the biggest challenges in machine learning [6]. The consequence is that RL agents often need to be trained 'from scratch'. This should be taken into account when designing an AIS. For instance, for humans, one wouldn't use the same AIS designed to train professional skills for a child as for an adult.

## 5   Towards a Domain Implementation

In this section we show an example of how agent learners can be made fit-for-purpose for a concrete application domain, using an AIS and combining the insights from Sect. 3 and 0. The example domain that is used is that of a military (training) simulation system in the air combat domain where agents adopt the role of simulated fighter pilots. This use of agents in this domain has been well researched, both for RL algorithms [33–35] and simulation systems for human training [36, 37].

A high-level design for the training system implementation is shown in Fig. 4. It provides the infrastructure for (1) an air combat training simulation environment with aircraft models, (2) pilot agents with a learning algorithm and acting and sensing capabilities (for the aircraft's navigation, sensor and weapon systems in the environment), and (3) an instructional component to form an AIS (see subscript of Fig. 4).

The role of the AIS is to teach individual tasks that can be stored in a Task Library and reused by scenario developers to 'compose' pilot behaviors for a desired scenario. A task could represent defending a section of air space; a tactical engagement with an opponent; or individual tactical maneuvers such as formation flying or performing an evasive maneuver. Task compositionality offers the freedom of choosing different suitable learning algorithms for different task types and has been proposed in this application domain before [38, 39]. In the remainder, the AIS process of teaching tasks is described for two concrete examples, each handled by a different learning algorithm.

## 5.1  Task Learning

We have implemented two learning algorithms for different tasks. The first one is a neural network-based RL algorithm that is used for low-level aircraft maneuvering tasks. The second is a rule-based RL algorithm that is used for tactical-level tasks. The latter allows for the encoding of task knowledge from SMEs, for instance to constrain behaviors to specific tactics and procedures.

Figure 3 shows a scenario that combines the use of these task types. The scenario is a 2v2 encounter between blue and red forces in three phases: the ingress, engagement and egress phase. A formation flying task has been defined for the ingress and egress phases; and a complete 1v1 engagement task covers the engagement phase. The training of these two tasks with their selected learning algorithms is described below.

**Fig. 3.** An air-to-air encounter in a 2v2 scenario. During ingress (left), blues fly in formation towards red; following, individual 1v1 engagement take place between blue and red (middle); during egress (right), blue forces regroup and exit in formation after successful engagements. (Color figure online)

## Task: Formation Flying

In this task the agent is taught a maneuver to keep relative position and attitude relative to another aircraft (i.e. keeping a formation). The learning algorithm used is a neural network-based RL algorithm (DQN). To teach this maneuver, the AIS generates suitable training scenarios. During a scenario, the tutor continuously evaluates the agent's performance and provides feedback to the learning algorithm. The agent will learn to control the navigation systems of the aircraft, including heading and speed.

To speed-up learning, smart scenario adaptation is used to optimize the learning experiences and thereby the learning speed of the agent. This involves (1) preparing new scenarios with (semi)-randomized initial positions and bearings between the learning agent and the reference agent, and (2) terminating and starting a new scenario when either a set amount of time has passed or when the distance between the two agents becomes too large.

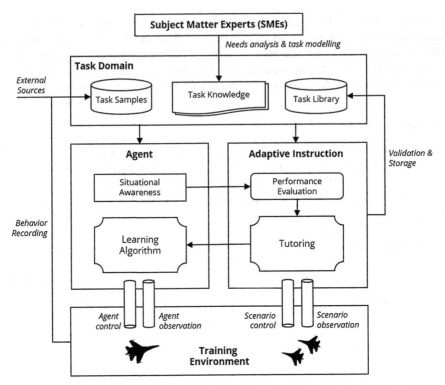

**Fig. 4.** Training system for an agent learner. From the AIS point of view, the *learner* is the Agent (middle left); the *Domain Model* is represented by the Task Domain (top); the *Learner Model* and *Instructional Model* are embedded in Adaptive Instruction (middle right); and the *Interface model* is represented by the control and observation interfaces of the agent and tutor.

The task can be parameterized with distance and bearing configurations. These parameters become additional inputs to the learning algorithm and are varied between training scenarios. The algorithm thus learns many task variations in the same training. The resulting task model can then be used by scenario developers for all sorts of formation configurations in 3D-space with any number of aircrafts. The task is used for both the ingress (approach) and egress (regrouping) phase in the scenario in Fig. 3.

**Task: Engagement**
In this task the agent is taught to perform a 1v1 engagement with an enemy aircraft. The learning algorithm that is used dynamic scripting which has been demonstrated in the air combat domain before [34, 40]. In contrast to the previous task, this algorithm uses priors defined by an SME. This is a rule database from which the learning algorithm can select and tryout a subset of rules with the goal to learn optimal combinations.

In contrast to the previous task, the AIS only provides feedback to the learning algorithm once at the end of a scenario (i.e. an engagement). Based on performance metrics such as a win or loss, missile usage or time, an evaluation is made to determine the success of the currently used rules. Based on this evaluation, the agent selects a new subset of rules for a new scenario. Over time, successful (combination of) rules are enforced and unsuccessful ones will fade. Similar smart scenario adaptation is used to speed-up learning: e.g. a new scenario is started when either one of the agents is killed, no more missiles are left, or some maximum scenario time has been reached.

## 5.2 Data-Driven Task Learning

One aspects from Fig. 4 that has not yet been discussed (and has not been implemented) is the Task Samples shown in the Task Domain. These represent datasets that could be obtained from simulator recordings (e.g. human demonstrations) or external sources (e.g. live recordings) that relate to the task to be learned. Such datasets could be used for offline training to bootstrap the learning process of the agent. For instance, a pre-trained model for the task could be learned by means of offline imitation or observational learning (see social learning in Sect. 3.3), and then be used as a prior for the online training. An approach for such data-driven learning in the domain of military simulation is described in [41] and termed data-driven behavior modelling (DDMB).

## 5.3 Concluding

The training system that was described attempts to touch upon all design aspects described in Sect. 3 and 4 and should be considered for training an agent. Summarized, these concern the need to perform a needs analysis to define the task and choose a suitable learning mechanism; the option or requirement to implement priors (pre-trained models or encoded knowledge); the implementation of the actual adaptive instruction through AIS components; and possible validation strategies to apply.

Although the use of different learning algorithms require different strategies for the AIS, many processes and components can be shared. The installment of reusable AIS components enhances abstraction from the learning algorithm and limits the impact on the system as a whole when new algorithms are introduced.

# 6    Discussion and Future Directions

In this paper we argued the use of AISs to operationalize RL agents for fit-for-purpose application domains. The key role of an AIS is to introduce a training system that bridges the gap between having an agent with a general-purpose learning algorithm and training that agent to operate in some task domain.

As AISs have their foundation in human instruction, we analyzed the process of training by drawing comparisons between human and agent learning and training in Sect. 3. We found that many concepts from RL research can be mapped to concepts from human instruction and vice-versa. Of course there remain fundamental differences between human and agent learners: e.g. machines don't get tired or bored, and machine learning algorithms have yet to parallel the ability of human learners to generalize problem-solving and learn from few experiences. As a consequence, different instructional approaches are deemed necessary, tailored to the different characteristics of the learners. The same is true also between two RL algorithms with different mechanisms for learning. Still, the overall goal of instruction is the same, which is to optimize training for learners in a task domain. Having a shared high-level framework for training and adaptive instruction as presented in Sect. 3 and 4 helps to place the various requirements, processes and strategies for teaching RL agents into perspective.

From an implementation perspective, the AIS concept seems to be a good fit for teaching agents. It abstracts away from the algorithmic learning technology, allowing system designers to focuses on the design of the instructional components around it. This is demonstrated in Sect. 5 by an implemented training system where the task domain can be shared by both agents and humans.

In this paper, a first step is taken towards applying AIS theory to teaching agents. For future directions, this line of thought can be continued. For instance, exploring the potential alignment with standardization and interoperability efforts of AISs [42, 43]. Similar approaches can benefit the development of training systems for agent learners. As learning algorithms will continue to become more advanced and are expected to be equipped with capabilities parallel towards human learning, the more likely it will be that instructional strategies between humans and agents become more comparable. This will encourage further cross-field synergy between RL and instructional science that can be explored using AISs.

# References

1. Sottilare, R., Brawner, K.: Exploring standardization opportunities by examining interaction between common adaptive instructional system components. In: Proceedings of the First Adaptive Instructional Systems (AIS) Standards Workshop, Orlando, Florida (2018)
2. Berner, C., et al.: Dota 2 with large scale deep reinforcement learning. arXiv preprint arXiv: 1912.06680 (2019)
3. Sutton, R.S., Barto, A.G.: Reinforcement Learning: An Introduction. MIT Press, Cambridge (2018)
4. Mnih, V., et al.: Human-level control through deep reinforcement learning. Nature **518**, 529–533 (2015)
5. Brockman, G., et al.: OpenAI Gym (2016)
6. Lake, B.M., Ullman, T.D., Tenenbaum, J.B., Gershman, S.J.: Building machines that learn and think like people. Behav. Brain Sci. **40** (2017)
7. Taylor, M.E., Stone, P.: Transfer learning for reinforcement learning domains: a survey. J. Mach. Learn. Res. **10** (2009)
8. van Oijen, J., Roessingh, J.J., Poppinga, G., García, V.: Learning analytics of playing space fortress with reinforcement learning. In: International Conference on Human-Computer Interaction. pp. 363–378. Springer (2019). https://doi.org/10.1007/978-3-030-22341-0_29
9. Oquab, M., Bottou, L., Laptev, I., Sivic, J.: Learning and transferring mid-level image representations using convolutional neural networks. In: Proceedings of the IEEE Conference on Computer Vision and Pattern Recognition, pp. 1717–1724 (2014)
10. Brown, T.B., et al.: Language models are few-shot learners. arXiv preprint arXiv:2005.14165 (2020)
11. M Spronck, P.H., Ponsen, M.J.V., Sprinkhuizen-Kuyper, I.G., Postma, E.O.: Adaptive game AI with dynamic scripting. Mach. Learn. **63**, 217–248 (2006)

12. Kulkarni, T.D., Narasimhan, K., Saeedi, A., Tenenbaum, J.: Hierarchical deep reinforcement learning: Integrating temporal abstraction and intrinsic motivation. Adv. Neural. Inf. Process. Syst. **29**, 3675–3683 (2016)
13. Branch, R.M.: Instructional Design: The ADDIE Approach. Springer, Boston (2009). https://doi.org/10.1007/978-0-387-09506-6
14. Albawi, S., Mohammed, T.A., Al-Zawi, S.: Understanding of a convolutional neural network. In: 2017 International Conference on Engineering and Technology (ICET), pp. 1–6. IEEE (2017)
15. Bakker, B.: Reinforcement learning with long short-term memory. In: NIPS, pp. 1475–1482 (2001)
16. Rae, J.W., Potapenko, A., Jayakumar, S.M., Lillicrap, T.P.: Compressive transformers for long-range sequence modelling. arXiv preprint arXiv:1911.05507 (2019)
17. Hedegaard, M.: The zone of proximal development as basis for instruction. In: Moll, L.C.E. (ed.) Vygotsky and Education: Instructional Implications and Applications of Sociohistorical Psychology, pp. 349–371. Cambridge University Press (1990)
18. Fleer, S.: Scaffolding for learning from reinforcement: Improving interaction learning (2020)
19. Laud, A.D.: Theory and application of reward shaping in reinforcement learning (2004)
20. Niehaus, J., Riedl, M.O.: Scenario adaptation: An approach to customizing computer-based training games and simulations. In: Proceedings of the AIED 2009 Workshop on intelligent Educational Games, pp. 89–98 (2009)
21. Elman, J.L.: Learning and development in neural networks: the importance of starting small. Cognition **48**, 71–99 (1993)
22. Narvekar, S., Peng, B., Leonetti, M., Sinapov, J., Taylor, M.E., Stone, P.: Curriculum learning for reinforcement learning domains: a framework and survey. J. Mach. Learn. Res. **21**, 1–50 (2020)
23. Hussein, A., Gaber, M.M., Elyan, E., Jayne, C.: Imitation learning: a survey of learning methods. ACM Comput. Surv. (CSUR) **50**, 1–35 (2017)
24. Borsa, D., Piot, B., Munos, R., Pietquin, O.: Observational learning by reinforcement learning. arXiv preprint arXiv:1706.06617 (2017)
25. Levine, S., Kumar, A., Tucker, G., Fu, J.: Offline reinforcement learning: Tutorial, review, and perspectives on open problems. arXiv preprint arXiv:2005.01643 (2020)
26. Fu, J., Kumar, A., Nachum, O., Tucker, G., Levine, S.: D4rl: datasets for deep data-driven reinforcement learning. arXiv preprint arXiv:2004.07219 (2020)
27. Toubman, A.: Validating air combat behaviour models for adaptive training of teams. In: Sottilare, R.A., Schwarz, J. (eds.) HCII 2019. LNCS, vol. 11597, pp. 557–571. Springer, Cham (2019). https://doi.org/10.1007/978-3-030-22341-0_44
28. Garcıa, J., Fernández, F.: A comprehensive survey on safe reinforcement learning. J. Mach. Learn. Res. **16**, 1437–1480 (2015)
29. Mondesire, S.C., Wiegand, R.P.: A demonstration of stability-plasticity imbalance in multi-agent, decomposition-based learning. In: 2015 IEEE 14th International Conference on Machine Learning and Applications (ICMLA), pp. 1070–1075. IEEE (2015)
30. Sottilare, R.: Understanding the AIS problem space. In: Proceedings of the 2nd Adaptive Instructional Systems (AIS) Standards Workshop (2019)
31. Aubret, A., Matignon, L., Hassas, S.: A survey on intrinsic motivation in reinforcement learning. arXiv preprint arXiv:1908.06976 (2019)
32. Gupta, A., Eysenbach, B., Finn, C., Levine, S.: Unsupervised meta-learning for reinforcement learning. arXiv preprint arXiv:1806.04640 (2018)
33. Karli, M., Efe, M.Ö., Sever, H.: Air combat learning from F-16 flight information. In: 2017 IEEE International Conference on Fuzzy Systems (FUZZ-IEEE), pp. 1–6. IEEE (2017)
34. Toubman, A.: Calculated moves: Generating air combat behaviour. Ph.D. dissertation (2020)

35. Zhang, X., Liu, G., Yang, C., Wu, J.: Research on air confrontation maneuver decision-making method based on reinforcement learning. Electronics **7**, 279 (2018)

36. Doyle, M.J., Portrey, A.M.: Rapid adaptive realistic behavior modeling is viable for use in training. In: Proceedings of the 23rd Conference on Behavior Representation in Modeling and Simulation (BRIMS), pp. 73–80 (2014)

37. Freeman, J., Watz, E., Bennett, W.: Adaptive agents for adaptive tactical training: the state of the art and emerging requirements. In: Sottilare, R.A., Schwarz, J. (eds.) HCII 2019. LNCS, vol. 11597, pp. 493–504. Springer, Cham (2019). https://doi.org/10.1007/978-3-030-22341-0_39

38. van Oijen, J., Toubman, A., Poppinga, G.: Effective behaviour modelling for computer generated forces. In: Interservice/Industry Training, Simulation and Education Conference (I/ITSEC). I/ITSEC (2019)

39. Warwick, W., Rodgers, S.: Wrong in the right way: balancing realism against other constraints in simulation-based training. In: Sottilare, R., Schwarz, J. (eds.) Adaptive Instructional Systems. HCII 2019. LNCS, vol 11597, pp. 379–388. Springer (2019). https://doi.org/10.1007/978-3-030-22341-0_30

40. Ludwig, J., Presnell, B.: Developing an adaptive opponent for tactical training. In: Sottilare, R., Schwarz, J. (eds.) Adaptive Instructional Systems. HCII 2019. LNCS, vol 11597. pp. 532–541. Springer (2019). https://doi.org/10.1007/978-3-030-22341-0_42

41. Luotsinen, L.J., Løvlid, R.A.: Data-driven behavior modeling for computer generated forces. In: NATO Modelling and Simulation Group Symposium M&S Support to Operational Tasks Including War Gaming, Logistics, Cyber Defence (MSG-133), pp. 1–13 (2015)

42. Sottilare, R.: Exploring methods to promote interoperability in adaptive instructional systems. In: Sottilare, R.A., Schwarz, J. (eds.) HCII 2019. LNCS, vol. 11597, pp. 227–238. Springer, Cham (2019). https://doi.org/10.1007/978-3-030-22341-0_19

43. Brawner, K.: Bridging conceptual models and architectural interchange for adaptive instructional systems. In: Sottilare, R.A., Schwarz, J. (eds.) HCII 2020. LNCS, vol. 12214, pp. 34–44. Springer, Cham (2020). https://doi.org/10.1007/978-3-030-50788-6_3

# Designing and Developing AIS

# SQLearn: A Browser Based Adaptive SQL Learning Environment

Pushkar Bhuse[1], Jash Jain[1], Abheet Shaju[1], Varun John[2], Abhijit Joshi[1], and Ramkumar Rajendran[2(✉)]

[1] Dwarkadas J. Sanghvi College of Engineering, Mumbai, India
abhijit.joshi@djsce.ac.in
[2] Indian Institute of Technology Bombay, Mumbai, India
{write2john,ramkumar.rajendran}@iitb.ac.in

**Abstract.** The advent of E-learning has allowed students to have access to a massive group of educators and learning resources. However, the concept of online learning still lacks a quality that deems it inferior to classroom education and that is the ability to understand the needs of individual students. With reference to online learning, the complexity of different online resources plays a crucial role in determining the usefulness of that resource for a given user. As a result, students get intimidated by these divergences in explanations, making the effectiveness of e-learning subject to a user's psychology and self-motivation. Thus, there is a need to understand the dynamics of a student's learning behavior before suggesting resources. In order to address this need, in this research paper, we present an Adaptive Educational Hypermedia System (AEHS) called SQLearn which assesses the performance of students with an assessment as they study a topic and consequently assists their learning experience. SQLearn consists of two main components, the Testing Platform, and the Web Browser Extension which works in unison to understand students learning behavior. After analyzing a student's learning behavior, the designed system is capable of suggesting them online resources to help them grasp concepts they is weak at. The system is also capable of making inferences based on the students answering behavior to help them maintain an optimum learning and answering speed. In order to test the efficacy of the designed system, a pilot study was conducted with 11 undergraduate students. This study helped bolster claims regarding the usefulness of the system while also motivating the creation of a more accurate system.

**Keywords:** Recommendation systems · SQL · Web-based personalisation · E-learning · Knowledge-based systems · Adaptive Educational Hypermedia System

## 1 Introduction

The popularity and ease of use granted by online learning allows users to learn new topics anywhere and at anytime. This is due to the numerous learning resources that are published online every day resulting in an explosion of content and knowledge. However,

© Springer Nature Switzerland AG 2021
R. A. Sottilare and J. Schwarz (Eds.): HCII 2021, LNCS 12792, pp. 139–152, 2021.
https://doi.org/10.1007/978-3-030-77857-6_9

this abundance of learning materials creates a difficulty for learners to find resources that suit their needs, capability, and requirements the most [1]. Under these circumstances, information overload intensifies gradually, which results in an increasingly prominent learning loss. This problem can be effectively addressed through a personalized system that can help learners find the resources that satisfy their own unique needs [2].

Through Adaptive Educational Hypermedia Systems, an ITS could modify its tutoring experience to match the way a student learns. Consequently, a considerable effort has been put into generating more accurate learning resource recommendations based on varying parameters, for example, collaborative filtering, knowledge-based recommendations, content-based recommendations, etc. [3]. However, these efforts have only been focused within the boundaries of the system's own LMS. By exploring the influence of the internet's heterogeneity and the role it plays in students learning process, a student can be directed to resources most apt for him/her. To do so on a more generalized level, there is an imminent need to build a system that can perform the above-mentioned tasks while catering to the specific behavior of an individual user. In this paper we propose such a system to learn SQL - SQLearn.

SQLearn consists of two main components, which is the testing platform and the browser extension. The testing platform has been designed to teach and assess the learners performance and consequently provide recommendations based on his performance and interaction behavior with the system. In order to observe and analyze the interaction behavior of the user, a browser extension has been developed which works in unison with the above-mentioned testing platform. The subtopics on which questions are asked are arranged in a carefully designed curriculum that begins with relatively easy concepts to complex ones. On each subtopic MCQ's are asked. While using the testing platform, the learner is given the liberty to browse the internet in order to gain conceptual clarity. As a user answers questions while simultaneously browsing the internet in search of conceptual clarity, the browser extension records the learners browsing behavior. By doing so, the system can understand the methodology followed by the learner to in turn provide personalised and adaptive hints and suggestions to aid his/her learning process. In order to test the efficacy of the proposed system, a pilot study was conducted on 11 undergraduate students majoring in Information Technology and Computer Engineering. This study helped bolster claims made while designing the system while laying the groundwork for a more advanced and sophisticated learning mechanism.

The rest of this paper is arranged as follows. Section 2 covers the existing work that served as an impetus to this research. Section 3 discusses the scope of this research and also explains the design of SQLearn. Section 4 deals with the working of SQLearn with reference to the various system prompts to personalize the user experience. Lastly, Sects. 5 and 6 explain the Pilot Study which was conducted to test the effectiveness of the proposed systems and the inferences that were generated from them.

## 2   Related Works

The difference in complexities of various online learning resources makes the effectiveness of e-learning subject to factors other than the learner's knowledge, for example, their motivation towards the subjects or even the rate at which they grasps concepts [4]. Thus, there was a need to understand the dynamics of a student's learning behavior before suggesting resources [5]. This need gave rise to Adaptive Educational Hypermedia Systems (AEHS) [6]. AEHS combines the ontology of a topic along with personalization strategies of Adaptive systems to dynamically align with a learner's needs [7]. Moreover, the vastness of online resources highlighted the need for multimedia learning resource recommendation systems. These systems work precisely to suggest relevant resources to learners based on their interests or relevance to the topic being studied. Over the years, various methods of multimedia recommendations have been explored. In [8], J. Shu et al. proposed a content-based multimedia recommendation system aimed at harnessing textual information of the resources with the help of Convolutional Neural Networks to generate content-based recommendations. Mihai G in [9] proposed a recommender system based on association rules for the distributed learning management system by employing distributed data mining algorithms and data obtained from Learning Management Systems (LMS). In [10], C.J. Butz emphasized the use of the Bayesian Network to classify a topic as "known", "ready to learn" or "not known" based on the probability distribution. The decision-making process conducted in this intelligent system was guided by Bayesian networks.

However, these systems did not harness a user's test performances in their recommendation mechanism. To counter this, Ryan Baker in [4] presents an automated detector to predict a student's performance on a paper test of preparation for future learning by using feature engineering and linear regression which is cross-validated at the student level. In order to granulate a topic, Yu Yan presents the idea of a Syntax Knowledge Point (An SKP is a Syntax Knowledge Point which basically is the smallest unit of learning when it comes to studying a new topic) in [11] to divide topics into specific subdomains making the recommendation process more focused. However, current research in AEHS has not taken into account a learner's actual learning behavior when they are introduced to a novel topic. The way a person grasps a topic speaks volumes about what resource will suit him/her and thus there is a need to explore this avenue. With respect to SQL, the SQL tutor in [12] employed Constraint-Based Modelling to suggest corrective measures to rectify SQL queries. However, it did not analyze the shortcomings of a learner in a specific subtopic and only suggested corrections to the query at hand.

## 3   Scope of Work

Students learning a new topic online are generally overwhelmed by the quantity of online learning resources. This leads to difficulties in finding an appropriate starting point and also finding the right content to progress positively. SQLearn aims to create a straightforward and hassle-free solution to online learning by attempting to eliminate problems related to cold-starting and early forfeit. SQLearn focuses on providing learners with content that is best suited for them based on their websites of choice as well as those curated by domain experts without them having to research by themselves and scrape the internet. This curation and recommendation occurs on the basis of a few parameters.

The above mentioned parameters are based on the learner's profile including their bias towards a particular domain of websites which allows the learner to maintain their level of comfort while learning something new. Along with profiling, SQLearn also tracks the user's interaction behaviour.

The system tracks how the user interacts with the platform while taking an assessment. This helps in collecting various parameters that contribute towards tweaking the system's response to enable a personalized and intuitive learning experience. Monitoring the learner's interaction helps in spotting and analyzing anomalous behavior such as spending too much time on a particular question or answering a question in a split second and thus enables the system to send appropriate responses to learners to help them avoid such mistakes in the future. The subsequent sections of the paper explain the system design and the functioning of its components.

### 3.1  System Design

The system consists mainly of two components, the online testing platform to regulate learnings and the browser extension to monitor user behavior while studying from online sources.

The idea on which SQLearn is built dictates that students' learning ability and how well they grasp a topic can be inferred by the way they access learning resources. In this system, a user is analyzed with regards to the way he/she accesses various metrics attached to it. This includes the following:

1.  Time spent on a given online source and the frequency at which it is accessed
2.  The author of the source or the domain name of website (e.g. www.wikipedia.com)
3.  The total number of learning resources accessed
4.  The type of hypermedia (text, video, audio) and also a change in students' performance (positive or negative) as can be observed by assessments.

Based on these parameters and expert knowledge in the domain of SQL, an algorithm can be devised that can suggest which online resource would be apt for a student who wishes to learn a given concept. In order to achieve this with reference to SQL, we created a unique and generalized knowledge map of SQL. The questions asked during a testing session harnesses the created SQL Knowledge Graph to ensure a learning experience that proceeds in gradation in accordance to SQL concepts in increasing level of difficulty. The SQL Knowledge Graph (Fig. 1), is used by the proposed system to curate an orderly flow of questions, beginning with the most independent and relatively easy concepts moving on to the most complex and interdependent ones. As shown in Fig. 1, each node depicts a subtopic of SQL and the solid arrows indicate the logical links between these subtopics. The dotted lines are used to depict the logical flow followed by the system to progress from one subtopic to another unrelated subtopic.

### 3.2  Testing Platform

The assessment platform is a web page which is the primary form of interaction that the learner has with SQLearn. The learner is taught a total of ten subtopics in SQL as mentioned above, through a series of tests. Each test has ten questions. Each test presents the learner with an array of questions that he/she has to answer. Every question asked is followed by four options. The questions may be either theoretical or query-based. Consequently, the questions may also carry additional pictorial data in the form of tables to support the queries being asked.

The assessment platform works in tandem with the Chrome extension (explained in the later sections of the paper) and collects user data. The assessment platform collects two types of data.

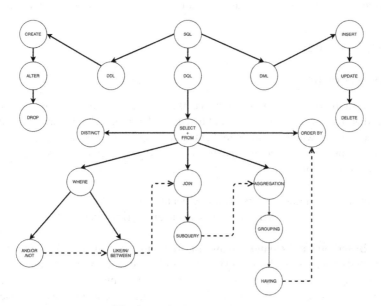

**Fig. 1.** Topic dependency graph

1. Learner Metadata (Personal Information)
2. Learner Response

**Learner Metadata** is information about the learner such as his age, his educational background, known proficiency in SQL along with his field of study. This data is collected by the platform when the learner first signs up to use the system.

**Learner Response** is data entailing the learner's response to the question and time taken to answer the questions. This data is collected while the learner is taking the test.

The amalgamation of these data helps in profiling the learner and helps in fine-tuning their recommendations. The recommendations are provided to the learner in the form of popups to enhance the level of interactivity provided. The learner is taught a total of ten subtopics in SQL as mentioned above, through a series of tests. Each test has ten questions.

### 3.3 Web Browser Extension

The browser extension is the most crucial element to capture the data used to personalize the learning experience for the user. The browsing behavior of a user on learning resources, while the user is giving a test on the platform is logged into the database. The raw data which is logged about these learning resources is the URL of the learning resource and the timestamps during which a user was accessing the said learning resource. Accessing a learning resource is the time during which the resource was open on the screen of a user. A user can switch between multiple learning resources. Hence a user accesses a single learning resource in different intervals. The timestamps of these intervals are logged which is the basis of features that are used as the system prompts.

## 4 Adaptive Logic

### 4.1 System Prompts

To create a personalized learning experience, the testing platform and browser extension mentioned above work in unison to adapt to a user's learning behavior and consequently adapt to their needs which would help them answer questions on various subtopics with ease. With regards to the type of behavior the learning environment captures, SQLearn generates two types of prompts:

1. Prompts based on the learners browsing behaviour
2. Prompts based on a learners behaviour while answering questions

**Prompts Based on the Learners Browsing Behavior.** To generate these prompts, the data collected about a user's browsing behaviour is harnessed (by employing the browser extension). Depending on the user's progress in a given subtopic with reference to how many online resources they have needed to access, the system suggests them steps for a more fruitful online browsing experience. It is important to note that these prompts are generated by the system in only those cases where a user fails to answer a question correctly. As shown in Fig. 2, the system takes a series of sequential decisions in order to determine which response would be most apt for a user depending on his current browsing behaviour. In order to do so, it uses certain constants set by the system as shown in Table 1 to help make decisions. The possible prompts that can be generated by the system are the following:

1. If a user has not made an effort to refer to any online resources before attempting a question, the system prompts the user to browse the internet.
2. Depending on a user's browsing behavior while answering earlier questions, the system generates the websites most favourable to him. In context of this system, if a user has spent a predominant amount of time browsing through resources of a particular website (For the current system design, 35% of his browsing time), then the system suggests urls of pages created by his most accessed websites and also relevant to the subtopic they are stuck at. For example, if a user spends most of his time on content posted by "www.wikipedia.com", then the system suggests resources created by www.wikipedia.com which are relevant to the subtopic they needs help in.

3. In order to help a user expand his horizon and visit different platforms, the system randomly suggests 3 urls of web resources relevant to the subtopic being studied by the user.
4. If the system detects that no more new recommendations can be made to aid the user, the user is given a choice to go back to answering questions on subtopics that are predecessors of the subtopic at hand as per the SQL Knowledge Graph. By doing so, a user can take a step back in an orderly manner to strengthen his concepts.

**Table 1.** Constants and Variables involved in System Prompts based on learners browsing behavior.

| Name | Type | Description |
|---|---|---|
| recommendation_repository[s] | Constant | List of website URLs on subtopic "s" stored in the system for recommendation |
| minimum_browsing_distribution | Constant | Minimum Distribution value required to consider a website domain "frequently browsed" {current value = = 0.35}. The function "Distribution" is defined in Table 2 |
| T-critical | Constant | Minimum time required to be spent on a website to consider it's browsing experience worthwhile {current value = = 5 s} |
| browsed_website_domain_names | Variable | List of the domain names of the websites accessed by the learner throughout his/her learning experience |

**Table 2.** Functions harnessed by the system to generate prompts based on learners browsing behaviour.

| Function | Input | Output |
|---|---|---|
| Distribution(d) | Domain name "d" whose distribution value needs to be calculated | Fraction of the amount of time spent on websites of domain name "d" throughout the whole browsing experience |

**Prompts Based on a Learners Behavior While Answering Questions.** To generate these prompts, the data collected about a user's browsing As opposed to the learners browsing behavior, how he/she answers questions can provide us with more direct indications regarding their learning behavior. In case a learner tends to answer questions too fast or too slow, it would be beneficial to prompt them regarding their actions to bring them back on track. To generate these prompts, the data collected about a user's behavior while answering questions is harnessed (by employing the testing platform. For these

**Fig. 2.** System responses to learners browsing behavior. The decisions taken by the system to generate prompts based on a user's browsing behavior are determined by the information collected by the Web Browser Extension mentioned in Sect. 3.3. In order to make binary decisions, the system relies on predetermined constants (shown in Table 1) and functions (shown in Table 2). Along with these, the system maintains dynamically updated variables which have been explained in detail in Table 1.

prompts, the system tries to infer if the rate at which a student answers questions presented to them are plausible are not. Essentially, through this system, an attempt is made to tackle the problem of answering questions too fast (flukes) or answering questions too slow. The decision made regarding which prompt would be most apt to the user is shown in Fig. 3. As shown in the figure, the system considers n consecutive questions to draw an inference regarding a user's answering behavior (n being equal to 3 in the proposed system). By analyzing each passage of n consecutive attempts, the following possible prompts can be generated:

1. If users takes less than 5 s or less than half of the average time taken to answer a given question (whichever is lower) for n consecutive attempts, the system indicates that they are going unusually fast and may be randomly choosing his answers. Such a prompt could curb users from continuing this answering behaviour and spend more time on questions.
2. If users takes more than 3 times the average time taken to answer a question for n consecutive questions, the system indicates that they are going much slower than usual. Such a prompt could help users get more involved, focused and active in their attempts.

To begin with a seed value, a small scale study was conducted to generate the average time that could be taken to answer each question individually which were backed by professionals. In order to generate the seed value, students proficient in SQL were asked to answer the questions asked on the testing platform and an average of their answering time was taken. Additionally, professors of SQL in university in which the pilot study was conducted were asked to verify the plausibility of these seed values. Also, as users answer a given question, its average time is continuously updated by the system. By doing so, an inaccurate seed value can be corrected for future use.

**Table 3.** Constants and Variables involved in System Prompts based on learners answering behavior.

| Name | Type | Description |
|---|---|---|
| T-min-answer | Constant | The minimum time expected to be spent on a question while answering it {T-min-answer = 10 s} |
| consecutive_questions | Constant | The number of consecutive questions considered {consec = 3} |
| answer_avg_time[q] | Variable | average time taken to answer question q (correctly or incorrectly) |
| answer_time[k] | Variable | Time taken to answer the kth question |
| violation_level[k] | Variable | The violation level committed by a learner while answering the kth question |
| attempts[q] | Variable | The number of times question q has been attempted |

**Table 4.** Functions harnessed by the system to generate prompts based on learners answering behaviour.

| Function | Input | Output | Description |
|---|---|---|---|
| consecutive_violations(n, c) | n = question number from which violation level needs to be checked<br><br>c = Number of previous consecutive violation levels that need to be considered | The action number that needs to be taken {possible values are 1, 2, 3} | This function sees the last c violation levels of answered questions, ie.: n, n−1, n−2....., n-c-1<br>if last "c" violations are either 1 or 2, the returned value is 1<br>if last "c" violation levels are 3, the returned value is 2<br>else, the returned value is 3 |

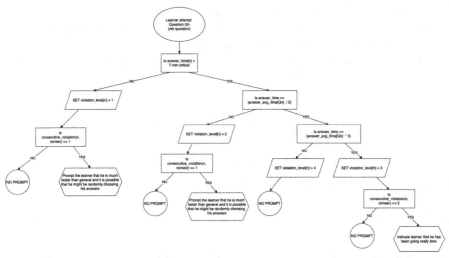

**Fig. 3.** System responses to learners browsing behavior. The decisions taken by SQLearn to generate prompts based on a user's answering behaviour are determined by the information collected by the Testing Platform itself (mentioned in Sect. 3.2). In order to make binary decisions, the system relies on predetermined constants (shown in Table 3) and functions (shown in Table 4). Along with these, the system maintains dynamically updated variables which have been explained in detail in Table 3.

## 5   Pilot Study

In order to test the efficacy of SQLearn, a pilot study was conducted on the students of an Engineering college in Mumbai, India. The aim behind the study was to test the working of the designed system along with analyzing the integrity of database logs.

This study was conducted on a total of 11 students with the male: female ratio being 7:4. The average proficiency of students in SQL (self-reported value) was 3 out of 5. Since all students were of the age of 19 and in their Sophomore of an Engineering Undergraduate Program (IT and Computer Engineering), each of them could be expected to be well-versed with the concept of online learning and the usage of the internet in learning.

The browser extension was uploaded and made available on the chrome store after review (Available in Appendix-A). The testing platform was set up on a Microsoft Azure server. A pool of 19 students was willing to participate in the pilot study out of which 11 students were available to participate on the designated date. A communication channel was set up to have an initial conversation about the system and the study. On the day of the study an initial short interactive demonstration of the system (Available in Appendix-A) was held to run through how a student is supposed to take a test. The students then took the test simultaneously during which their responses and other metadata were logged in the database. To limit the time of the study, only a subset of the subtopics shown in the SQL Knowledge Graph in Fig. 1 was chosen which is shown in Table 5. Questions were asked only on these subtopics of SQL. On completion of the study, the participants were asked to fill a Study Completion Form (Available in Appendix-A) containing questions on their experience while using the designed system, their suggestions to improve the learning experience and objective questions to understand if the users found the system useful.

The study was conducted as a preliminary level of validating the parameter assumptions taken by the system and exploring the adaptation possibilities using student browning behavior.

## 6 Discussions

The Pilot Study presented several inferences that will be useful in improving the performance and accuracy of SQLearn. As shown in Table 5, students generally spent more time on more complex subtopics as compared to the easier ones. Corroborated by the fact that 58.3% of the participating students reported that the difficulty of questions was 3 on a scale of 1 to 5 (Available in Appendix-A), the systems performance could be increased by improving the quality and complexity of questions asked on the Testing Platform. Thus, by increasing the complexity of questions, students can be challenged on a more appropriate level, thus allowing them to use the system's functionalities to the fullest.

The Pilot Study saw a varied distribution in the browsing behavior of students. As shown in Fig. 4 and Fig. 5 collectively, students with various learning natures can be seen through this Pilot Study.

Students like Student #1, who prefer spending more time on one resource as opposed to students who prefer hopping from one website to another in quick successions (like Student #9) could be seen. Thus, there exists a possibility that the personalization of the system could be improved by comprehending these types of browsing behaviors.

Lastly, based on the feedback received by participating students, it could be noted that 58.3% of the students felt that suggestions based on browsing behavior was a useful

**Table 5.** Average time distribution of students when answering questions on a given subtopic.

| Subtopic | Average time spent (in minutes) |
| --- | --- |
| SELECT - FROM | 0.5 |
| WHERE | 2.87 |
| DISTINCT | 1.31 |
| SET OPERATORS | 3.43 |
| PREDICATES | 1.21 |
| JOINS | 2.49 |
| SUBQUERY | 2.43 |
| AGGREGATION | 2.22 |
| GROUP BY | 1.86 |
| HAVING | 2.03 |

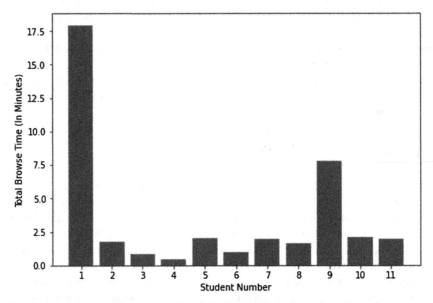

**Fig. 4.** Number of websites accessed by individual students throughout the testing process

learning tool, 41.7% of the students felt that Randomly suggesting resources was a useful learning tool and 16.7% of the students felt that System Prompts based on Answering Speeds was a useful learning tool.

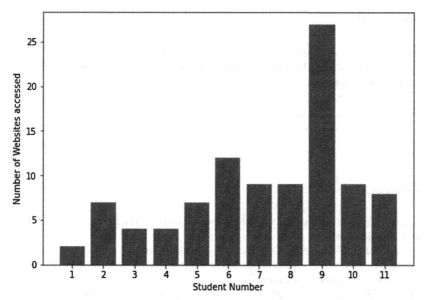

**Fig. 5.** Amount of time spent by an individual student browsing the internet during the test

## 7 Conclusion

In this research, we developed an AEHS which harnesses a learners browsing behaviour to adapt and recommend online resources to aid in the process of learning SQL. Through this system, learners can effectively understand concepts of SQL without having to manually browse through the internet to search for resources most appropriate for them. Even though the system attempts to solve a problem of a significant problem, it does however, suffer from a few shortcomings and thus a scope for improvement.

The entire system is based on collecting and analysing the browsing behaviour of the users to further recommend them reading material, but this might lead to concerns regarding the privacy of the users and could therefore affect the popularity of the system in a negative manner. From the Testing Platform's end, the current version of the system only has one type of question ie. Multiple Choice Questions. Thus, there is limit on the variety of questions being asked to the student. Lastly, The sample of students on which the pilot study was conducted was small. Bigger sample size could ensure a more steady pattern amongst user responses and could lead to a more precise inference process.

In order to encourage further research on the conceptualization of this system, various modifications can be explored. The system responses could be made real-time using state of the art Machine Learning techniques. This could be supplemented with the use of an Adaptive Questionnaire wherein the difficulty of the questions varies as per the answering pattern of the user. New types of questions including Match the Following or Multiple Answer Questions can be added to make the system more versatile in terms of the questions being asked to the user. A positive system response can be added to keep the user engaged and motivated while taking the test.

## Appendix - A

1. SQL Recommendation System - Google Chrome Extension : https://chrome.google.com/webstore/detail/sql-recommender-system/pkdlcabmd mmjdjpaflaphjehabkglgpk
2. SQL Recommendation System - Testing Platform: https://sqlrecommender.southe astasia.cloudapp.azure.com/
3. Study Completion Form: https://forms.gle/bnYj6seGpzbEBCzw6.

## References

1. Tavangarian, D., et al.: Is e-Learning the Solution for Individual Learning? Electron. J. E-learn. **2**(2), 273–280 (2004)
2. Baker, R.S.J.D., Gowda, S.M.: Automatically detecting student's preparation for future learning: help use is key. In: Proceedings of the 4th International Conference on Educational Data Mining, Eindhoven, The Netherlands
3. Khanal, S.S., et al.: A systematic review: machine learning based recommendation systems for e-learning. Educ. Inf. Technol. 1–30 (2019)
4. Clark, D.: Psychological myths in e-learning. Med. Teach. **24**(6), 598–604 (2002)
5. Tsai, M.-J.: The model of strategic e-learning: understanding and evaluating student e-learning from metacognitive perspectives. Educ. Technol. Soc. **12**, 34–48 (2009)
6. Mulwa, C., et al.: Adaptive educational hypermedia systems in technology enhanced learning: a literature review. In: Proceedings of the 2010 ACM Conference on Information Technology Education (2010)
7. Souhaib, A., Mohamed, K., Eddine, E.K.K., Ahmed, I.: Adaptive hypermedia systems for e-learning. Int. J. Emer. Technol. Learn. (iJET), 5(SI3), 47–51 (2010). Web. 17 Nov. 2020
8. Shu, J., Shen, X., Liu, H., Yi, B., Zhang, Z.: A content-based recommendation algorithm for learning resources. Multimedia Syst. **24**(2), 163–173 (2017). https://doi.org/10.1007/s00530-017-0539-8
9. Mihai, G.: Recommendation system based on association rules for distributed e-learning management systems. ACTA Universitatis Cibiniensis **67**(1), 99–104 (2015)
10. Butz, C.J., Hua, S., Brien Maguire, R.: A web-based intelligent tutoring system for computer programming. In: IEEE/WIC/ACM International Conference on Web Intelligence (WI 2004). IEEE (2004)
11. Yan, Y., Hara, K., Kazuma, T., He, A.: A Method for Personalized C Programming Learning Contents Recommendation to Enhance Traditional Instruction. https://doi.org/10.1109/AINA.2017.13
12. Mitrovic, A.: An intelligent SQL tutor on the web. Int. J. Artif. Intell. Educ. **13**(2–4), 173–197 (2003)

# Towards the Design of an Adaptive Presence Card and Trust Rating System for Online Classes

Jonathan D. L. Casano$^{(\boxtimes)}$ and Jenilyn L. Agapito

Ateneo de Manila University, 1108 Quezon City, Metro Manila, Philippines
jcasano@ateneo.edu.com

**Abstract.** This paper presents the initial design and mechanics of two proposed trackers – the Presence Card (PC) and the Trust Rating (TR) – to define an alternative way of checking attendance, and to challenge the spread of formal and informal outsourced work in the conduct of online classes. The PC and TR mechanics were implemented in various undergraduate and graduate classes to demonstrate how it may be used and to collect insights from the students about such an intervention. Using the metrics we have identified during testing together with an analysis of the survey results, we conclude the paper with directions and ideas towards adaptive versions of the PC and TR mechanics.

**Keywords:** Trust rating · Presence rating · Cheating · Attendance · Online learning

## 1 Introduction

In light of the COVID-19 pandemic, schools around the world were forced to shift to online learning to provide academic continuity. Online learning refers to learning that occurs partially or entirely over the Internet [1]. Two aspects of the learning transaction challenged in an online learning environment are that of attendance and integrity of student submissions.

Research done on the relationship between attendance, cheating, and student outcomes show a pattern of good attendance being tied to good and honest performance i.e. high scores in assessments and high authenticity scores as rated by both teacher and peers [2]. However, the traditional definition of attendance as physically going to class does not apply in online learning environments. In an online setting, students may "attend" class by interacting with the learning materials instead [3]. It is then important to redefine how attendance is tracked by understanding the ways students access and participate in online classes.

Because of the absence of face-to-face rituals and limitations in connectivity infrastructure in developing countries like the Philippines, teachers often imply attendance from student submissions. Alternatively, teachers check attendance based on who attends synchronous sessions. While decent, these strategies may be sub-optimal as it fails to

© Springer Nature Switzerland AG 2021
R. A. Sottilare and J. Schwarz (Eds.): HCII 2021, LNCS 12792, pp. 153–166, 2021.
https://doi.org/10.1007/978-3-030-77857-6_10

capture the student's ability to show up or make his presence known even during moments of no evident progress.

This study aims to find directions on how an adaptive system for tracking student attendance and perceived submission authenticity may be designed. This paper particularly focuses on the initial design and mechanics of two proposed trackers – the Presence Card (PC) and Trust Rating (TR) – to explore an alternative way to check attendance and to challenge the spread of formal and informal outsourced work. The PC and TR mechanics were implemented in various undergraduate and graduate classes to demonstrate how it may be used and to collect insights from the students about such an intervention in their online classes. The results of a qualitative survey are then used to inform directions for designing an adaptive PC and TR system.

## 2  Review of Related Literature

The shift to online learning posed greater challenges to two aspects of the teaching and learning process – attendance and academic integrity.

Even before this shift, the problem of good performance in instructional activities (e.g. exercises, laboratory work) not translating to good performance in assessments (e.g. quizzes, examinations, practical demos) is already perennial [4].

This problem seems to persist even when there is effort to align the instructional activities to the assessments [5]. In some cases, teachers would include exercise questions verbatim in the next quiz, and there would still be students who will get perfect scores in the exercises but will get less than acceptable scores in the corresponding quizzes [6].

Teacher-researchers corroborate that this pattern might be indicative of cheating. For instance, a recent study by Amigud and Lancaster [7] investigated factors that drive students to engage in contract cheating – the process of outsourcing one's work, sometimes for a fee. Their analysis of 5,000 student Twitter messages uncovered the observation that students have a subjective threshold, which may vary across students and circumstances. This means students participate in learning activities and perform needed academic work until they reach a threshold at which they become unwilling to continue. The refusal to suffer the consequences of academic failure may be enough to drive them into outsourcing their work either formally (i.e. paying for contract cheating services) or informally (e.g. asking for a more-than-acceptable level of help from peers). Outsourcing is sought as the means to quit the task without losing their personal sense of honesty and participation (i.e. "I did part of the work, right?") [7]. It is then entirely possible that students may decide to do honest academic work only up to their subjective thresholds and outsource the rest.

For a while, Honor Codes were being used as a means to address this problem. However, the shift to online learning made it exponentially difficult to address this issue using honor codes alone [8].

Research done on the relationship between attendance, cheating, and student outcomes show a pattern of good attendance being tied to good and honest performance (i.e. high scores in assessments and high submission integrity scores as rated by both teacher and peers) [2].

The definition of attendance adopted by most universities refers to the student's physical presence in classes [9]. However, this definition is not transferable to an online learning environment. Student interaction in an online learning setup can occur asynchronously (e.g. discussion forums, email consultations) and/or synchronously (e.g. presence in live lectures, synchronous online messaging consultations) [10]. Without the usual face-to-face class rituals and given the infrastructure limitations (e.g., internet connectivity issues, environment restrictions), instructors potentially opt to imply attendance based on whether students make submissions or not. Presence in synchronous sessions is likewise a common metric used. But as mentioned, infrastructure limitations especially in developing countries make this a rather suboptimal measure. These approaches also fail to capture the student's ability to make their engagement with the course known even when there are no tangible indicators of progress. It is possible for students to interact with course materials asynchronously but are unable to promptly complete tasks because they might be incubating [11] or are stuck in the plateau of latent potential [12]. They may be quiet but they are *pounding the rock* [13] and eventually may give results.

It is then important to understand the different ways students participate in online learning environments. It is also equally important for teachers to provide opportunities for them to make their presence or engagement with the course known.

## 3    The Presence Card (PC) and Trust Rating (TR)

The Presence Card (PC) resembles a loyalty card kept within the student's record (accessible only to each student either via an LMS (Moodle/Canvas or via a simple access-managed spreadsheet) that records indicators of how much the teacher felt the presence of the student during the week. Figure 1 shows a paper and spreadsheet prototype of a PC.

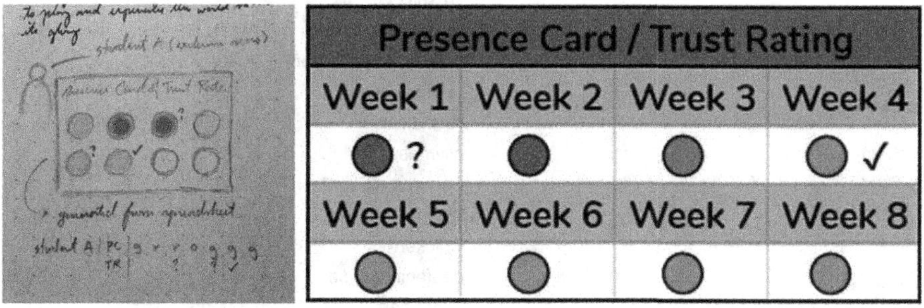

**Fig. 1.** Paper prototype and spreadsheet prototype of the Presence Card.

The hollow circles (paper) or cells (spreadsheet) symbolize the number of weeks in the semester/term. At the end of each week, the teacher updates the cells depending on how much he/she was able to feel the presence of the student during that week – green for adequately felt, orange for weekly felt, or red for not felt at all (or some variation of this gradation).

Implementation of this metric requires teachers to provide opportunities for students to make their presence felt– assessments (quizzes, homework), discussion forums, online consultations, and submission of weekly summaries, to name a few.

The Trust Rating (TR) was conceptualized as a formal response to student-submitted Honor Codes. As mentioned previously, Honor Codes are typically used as a mechanism for students to indicate that they are submitting honest work. It is a way for students to say *"Please trust my submission. I did this work on my own or I asked for help in a way that did not undermine my learning process."* But there is currently no official way for teachers to respond to this. The lack of literature on this especially in the Philippine context implies that there might have been no attempts to implement a document that teachers could fill out and return to the students to say *"Yes, I trust you. Excellent work."* or *"No, sorry, I am not yet certain your work is authentic.".* Consequently, students are not given the opportunity to improve this implicit rating of trust.

What normally happens as an attempt to respond to the Honor Code is to include perceived authenticity/originality as a criteria for grading (easy, less-time-consuming way) or invite the student for consultation to verify authenticity/originality when in doubt (difficult, more-time-consuming way).

The Trust Rating (TR) mechanic seeks to provide a more formal, structured way of communicating to students the teacher's perceived legitimacy of their submitted work.

In 2016–2018, we implemented this mechanic in the Introductory Computer Programming classes we handled. In this implementation, the Trust Ratings we represented as arrows that reflected high trust (upward pointing arrow ▲), neutral trust (black box ■), and low trust (downward pointing arrow ▼). Figure 2 shows a sample record of students with their corresponding TRs.

| Username | | Final Trust Rating | Final Grade | Magis Points | | Class Username | EG | TR | PE | ME |
|---|---|---|---|---|---|---|---|---|---|---|
| kurinchan | B+ | ▲ | A★ | 5 | | crushingcrackers | A | ▲ | A | A |
| Katoari | A- | ▼▲ 3 19 TUE | B+ | | | ickyorange | B | ▼ | A | B |
| | | | | | | unwelcomechowder | B | ▲ | A | B |
| unfinishedcracke | A- | ▲ | B+ | | | tamesausage | B | ▼ | A | B |
| repentantpie | A- | ▲ | B+ | | | jitterytacos | C+ | ▼ | A | B |
| unfoldedpolenta | A | ▲ | A★ | 5 | | oilymuesli | | | | |
| equatorialrice | B+ | ▼▲ 3.20.19 | B | | | EphemeralEunoia | A | ▲ | A | B+ |
| | | | | | | leanpie | | ▼ | A | B |
| Talepang | A | ▲ | A | | | Chicken | A | ▲ | A | A |
| iamdaynedayne | A | ▲ | A | | | deafeningcordial | | ▲ | B+ | B |
| MiaTaurus | B+ | ▲ | A | | | heartyhart | B or up | ▲ | A | B |

**Fig. 2.** A record of students in two Introductory Computer Programing classes with their corresponding Trust Ratings.

The Trust Ratings were updated every two weeks or whenever a major course requirement has been checked. Students who received neutral or low trust ratings were encouraged to schedule a 15-min consultation at their convenience so they may show knowledge of concepts we wanted them to understand or demonstrate command of a skill we wanted them to learn. We tried to be as diplomatic and as student-centered as possible in the conduct of these defenses as we recognized there might be added pressure in these one-on-one interactions. Students were permitted to choose the questions/problems they were most comfortable conducting the defense around. The hope was to reinforce a feeling of control in the student.

We recognize that the previously implemented symbols ($\blacktriangledown$, $\blacksquare$, $\blacktriangle$) might have been an inaccurate way to visualize what we were trying to convey. Ultimately, it is important for teachers to be able acknowledge whether students are submitting honest work or not. The symbols were then changed to question marks (**?**) and check marks ($\checkmark$) to indicate "*I am not yet sure of the legitimacy of your submissions so far*" and "*At this point, I trust your submissions are legitimate.*", respectively. The question mark is also a non-derogatory symbol since it represents uncertainty rather than a negative connotation of not trusting the student's work, which could have been a message depicted by the downward arrow used in the previous implementation ($\blacktriangledown$). Figure 1 also shows how the TR was represented along with the PC.

# 4  Testing Methods

A prototype of the Presence Card and Trust Rating was implemented in two undergraduate courses and one graduate course handled by one of the authors of this paper who is an instructor from Ateneo de Manila University, Philippines. These were classes taken by Computer Science students during the First Semester of School Year 2020–2021. These were CSCI 20 – Introduction to Computing (undergraduate), CSCI 30 – Data Structures and Algorithms (undergraduate), and CSCI 201 – Advanced Data Structures and Algorithms (graduate). As a response to the shift to online learning, Ateneo divided a school year into quarters. Hence, the First Semester consisted of Quarters 1 and 2. Each quarter ran for 7–8 weeks.

The goal was to execute and test the mechanics of the PC and TR. Additionally, qualitative insights of the students regarding the two systems were collected through a short online survey. The results of this implementation will then be used to inform the design of an adaptive mechanism for the Presence Card and Trust Rating.

The prototype comes in the form of a Google spreadsheet created for each of the students in the class. This is to simulate giving them a "profile" that basically shows them their presence and trust ratings for that particular course. A student's sheet is restricted to him/her; that is, other students cannot view their classmate's sheet. It contains the student's name, his/her photo, and the Presence Card. Figure 3 shows an example of how a student's sheet looked like.

The teacher updates a student's card for the class based on the metrics discussed below. This was done for the duration of the quarter. At the end of the said quarter, students were asked to complete a short survey that asked the following questions:

- Were you checking the course tracker?
- Did you feel that the Trust Rating you received (after a few weeks) was accurate?
- Would you say that the Trust Rating was a motivator for you to not outsource work (i.e. look for a more-than-acceptable-level of help)?
- Did you feel that the Presence Rating you received per week was accurate?

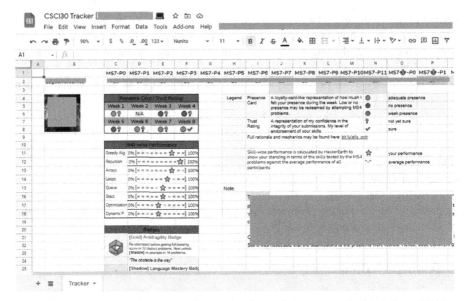

**Fig. 3.** A sample student *profile* (spreadsheet) showing their Presence and Trust ratings. All identifiable information was covered in aqua. 'N/A' record for Week 2 is due to classes being cancelled for the whole week as a response to the Covid-19 situation.

- Would you say that the Presence Rating was a motivator for you to engage with the asynchronous learning materials on a weekly basis? (instead of cramming everything towards the end)

### 4.1    Metrics Used for the PC and TR Prototype Testing

To provide context regarding the metrics used in determining the weekly PC and TR ratings for each student, we first describe the approach used to deliver the three classes from which our respondents were taken.

Following a station-rotation model [14], the classes were designed to have three learning stations namely, (1) a station for synchronous lectures and discussion via Zoom once a week, (2) a station for asynchronous learning videos and programming exercises uploaded on Wednesdays and accessible by students through a LMS, and (3) a station for interactive problem solving using an online judge where new problems are added every Friday.

Taking into account the learning stations described above as well as the behaviors we anticipated students to exhibit as they rotate through the stations, we designed a few straightforward rules that allowed us to determine the PC and TR ratings for each student per week. These rules are presented in Table 1.

**Table 1.** Metrics used to determine the Presence and Trust Ratings of a student per week.

| Rating | Symbol and Interpretation | Learning Stations Considered | Metrics |
|---|---|---|---|
| Presence | Adequate Presence | 1, 2 and 3 | The student is able to attend a synchronous session for the week, is able to interact with the asynchronous learning materials, and is able to submit an attempt at solving a programming problem. |
| | | 2 and 3 | The student did not attend the synchronous session for the week but is able to interact with the asynchronous learning materials and submit an attempt at solving a programming problem. |
| | | 2 | The student did not attend the synchronous session for the week and did not attempt to solve any of the programming problems but interacted with the asynchronous learning material. |
| | | 3 | The student did not attend the synchronous session nor interacted with the asynchronous learning materials but attempted to solve programming problems in the online judge. |
| | Weak Presence | 1 | The student attended the synchronous session for the week but did not interact with both the asynchronous learning resources or the online programming problems. |
| | No Presence | 1, 2 and 3 | The student did not attend the synchronous session for the week and did not register any interaction with both the asynchronous learning resources or the online programming problems. |

*(continued)*

**Table 1.** (*continued*)

| Trust | ? Uncertain | 3 | The student's submitted code does not contain comments that explain the logic. |
|---|---|---|---|
| | | 3 | The student is able to solve a programming problem of higher complexity but struggles with solving a programming problem of lower complexity. |
| | | 3 | The student is able to solve a difficult problem during the first try when there is a record of the *faster* students solving the same problem but requiring multiple attempts. |
| | | 3 | The student submits solutions to the difficult programming problems in bulk (within a few minutes between each other) and most of them correct on the first try. |
| | | 2 and 3 | The student is able to solve the programming problem in the online judge but is not able to solve the corresponding practice problem given as an asynchronous exercise. |
| | ✔ Certain | 2 and 3 | The student is able to solve both the practice exercise and the problem corresponding to the practice exercise. |
| | | 3 | The student had multiple incorrect attempts in solving the problems before arriving at a correct answer. |
| | | 3 | The student is using print statements in code to check the values of the variables at certain parts of the code execution. |
| | | Note: | At the end of the quarter, if the student appeals that the TR rating received was inaccurate, the student is asked to prepare and submit a screencast of themselves teaching a particular topic discussed in class. A comprehensive discussion would merit a *Certain* Trust Rating |

# 5   Results and Discussion

## 5.1   Survey Results

A total of 43 students responded to the survey. The distribution among the three courses mentioned earlier is shown in Fig. 4.

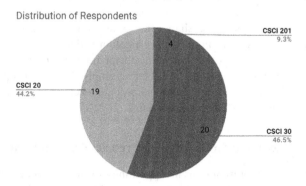

**Fig. 4.** Distribution of students who completed the survey.

**Table 2.** Summary of student responses in the survey.

| Checked the tracker | PR was accurate | PR was a motivator | TR was accurate | TR was a motivator |
|---|---|---|---|---|
| 35 | 35 | 26 | 29 | 31 |

Table 2 presents a summary of the students' responses. Out of the 43 respondents, 35 (81%) said they did check their course tracker and felt that the presence rating they received each week was accurate. Twenty-six out of the 35 respondents (74%) said the Presence Rating was a motivator for them to engage with the asynchronous learning materials on a weekly basis. However, one of the respondents pointed out it can also be daunting for some students especially those who may be struggling with mental health issues who tend to avoid doing work at certain times as a coping mechanism. The student posits that having such a tracker might be more stressful rather than helpful for these learners. There was one student who had neutral feelings about it and five said it was not necessarily a motivator for them. Though they did not elaborate on why that is the case.

Twenty-nine of the 35 respondents (82%) who checked their trackers felt that the Trust Rating they received was accurate. One respondent said for some weeks he/she felt it was accurate while for some he/she felt it was not as accurate. Two others did not particularly pay attention to it. Thirty-one respondents (88%) said the Trust Rating served as a motivator for them not to outsource their work. One respondent expressed how he/she generally does not like outsourcing his/her work because it makes him/her feel bad. Hence, he/she would not outsource his/her work with or without the tracker. This poses an evident limitation to the evaluation collected from the students. It is unclear whether the other students shared the same sentiment regarding the idea of outsourcing their work. A more in depth investigation is definitely necessary to make any generalizable claims about the motivating factor for both the Presence Card and Trust Rating. Nonetheless, the results of the survey imply that students potentially see the value of having a concrete representation of how their teacher perceives their presence in a course and the integrity of their submissions.

## 5.2 Design Considerations for an Adaptive Presence Card and Trust Rating

The results of the survey present to us an opportunity to further explore the mechanics behind the Presence Card and Trust Rating systems. One of the goals of implementing the prototype and asking students to evaluate their perception of its value was to be able to determine directions for designing an adaptive system capable of tracking student presence and academic integrity. We discuss in this section what might be some design considerations for realizing that as brought about by the prototype testing.

Most of the respondents signified that they felt the presence rating they received was accurate. Hence, the adaptive system should be able to record student interactions with asynchronous learning materials similar to those manually tracked in the prototype testing (videos and learning materials posted on the course LMS, online judge submission). These asynchronous materials may vary per course depending on what the teacher provides the students. Additionally, the teacher may be given the ability to indicate additional presence metrics that cannot be automatically tracked by the system (e.g. attendance to synchronous session, virtual consultation, email communication). Using these, the system can then propose engagement opportunities for the students depending on what the system determined to be their presence rating. Some ideas are shown in Table 3.

**Table 3.** Proposed adaptivity mechanics for Presence Rating.

| Sample Scenario | Adaptivity Mechanics |
|---|---|
| System gives a student an Adequate Presence rating (◐) | At the start of the course, the teacher can include some challenge problems or supplementary materials that can only be unlocked if they interact with the required learning materials. A student with an adequate presence rating is indicative of such. Hence, the system can point him/her to these supplementary materials to keep him/her engaged with the course. |
| System gives a student Weak Presence rating (◕) | The system shows a watered down version of the learning materials for the week. This includes versions of learning activities with lesser difficulty. Additionally, the teacher may receive a prompt to conduct consultation with this student. |
| System gives a student a No Presence rating (●) | The inability to interact with asynchronous materials and participate in synchronous activities may potentially be due to the absence of access to the Internet. Hence, for this case, the idea is that the system would send one multiple-choice type question to the student via SMS similar to the work of Herras et al. [15]. If a student does not respond, the teacher receives a prompt to conduct consultation with the student or report the student's absence to the proper offices. |

Majority of the respondents likewise indicated they felt that the trust ratings they received were accurate. Hence, the system should be adaptive enough to ask additional redeeming exercises/requirements from students whose work is flagged to be possibly inauthentic. On the other hand, the system may also consider leveraging the good-standing members of the class as potential helpers to keeping the culture of authenticity. We expound on these ideas further in Table 4.

**Table 4.** Adaptivity mechanics for Trust Rating.

| Sample Scenario | Adaptivity Mechanics |
| --- | --- |
| The teacher is not sure whether a submitted work is authentic (pending Uncertain rating ❓) | Once the teacher flags a submission as possibly inauthentic, the system will automatically identify 3 random students who will blindly critique the work and also rate it as authentic or inauthentic. After the critique, the teacher will decide based on the additional authenticity checks done by the three random students if the submission would earn a Certain or Uncertain Trust Rating. While this is going on the system would take note of the elements in a submission that make it more susceptible to being flagged as inauthentic (plagiarism score within class or compared to code found online, similar code comments with other students in class etc.) This would repeatedly be done towards making the Trust Rater smart enough to not need the intervention of the 3 random student raters. |
| System gives a student an Uncertain Trust Rating (❓) | The students would be shown an additional activity to complete asking him/her to submit a screencast explaining the topics within the week where an Uncertain trust rating was received. |
| System gives a student a Certain Presence Rating (✔) | Similar to community review initiatives such as Overwatch (DoTA2) and Birdwatch (Twitter), the system would allow good-standing members of the class access to a widget that allows them to verify the validity of possibly inauthentic student submissions. These students are also prioritized to have a higher chance of being included in the 3 random student raters needed in the first scenario described. |

# 6 Conclusions and Future Work

This work presents the Presence Card and Trust Rating system implemented as a response to the challenge of student attendance and academic honesty in online learning environments. Mechanics and metrics for PC and TR tracking were discussed. A prototype of the said system was implemented in undergraduate and graduate classes to test its design as well as to collect feedback about its use in an online classroom. Directions for an adaptive implementation are then presented based on the results of the prototype testing.

The survey responses from the students showed that the majority of them were checking their "profiles" and felt that the presence and trust ratings they received were accurate. This may imply that the metrics used to manually score them were realistic and may be used as the basis for designing an adaptive PR and TR system.

Proposed adaptivity mechanics were presented based on the PR and TR prototype that was tested. The hope is to be able to build a system that can automatically track indicators of presence and submission integrity as well as provide ways for teachers and students to manually indicate additional metrics. The system then makes relevant recommendations or adjustments depending on the presence and/or trust rating earned by a student.

**Acknowledgements.** We thank the students who generously participated in the surveys we conducted and the Department of Information Systems and Computer Science for allowing us the use of the Moodle LMS to store our asynchronous learning materials. We would likewise want to thank the Ateneo de Manila University Loyola Schools for giving us access to the Zoom accounts we used to conduct the synchronous online lecture sessions for class.

# References

1. Means, B., Toyama, Y., Murphy, R., Bakia, M., Jones, K.: Evaluation of evidence-based practices in online learning: a meta-analysis and review of online learning studies (2009)
2. D'Souza, K.A., Siegfeldt, D.V.: A conceptual framework for detecting cheating in online and take-home exams. Dec. Sci. J. Innovat. Educ. **15**(4), 370–391 (2017)
3. Butner, B.K., Smith, A.B., Murray, J.: Distance technology: a national study of graduate higher education programs. Online J. Dist. Learn. Adm. **2**(3), 1–7 (1999)
4. Wiliam, D.: Assessment: the bridge between teaching and learning. Voices Middle **21**(2), 15 (2013)
5. Abrams, L., Varier, D., Jackson, L.: Unpacking instructional alignment: the influence of teachers' use of assessment data on instruction. Perspect. Educ. **34**(4), 15–28 (2016)
6. Reeves, T.C.: How do you know they are learning? The importance of alignment in higher education. Int. J. Learn. Technol. **2**(4), 294–309 (2006)
7. Amigud, A., Lancaster, T.: 246 reasons to cheat: an analysis of students' reasons for seeking to outsource academic work. Comput. Educ. **134**, 98–107 (2019)
8. Mason, T., Gavrilovska, A., Joyner, D.A.: Collaboration versus cheating: reducing code plagiarism in an online MS computer science program. In: Proceedings of the 50th ACM Technical Symposium on Computer Science Education, pp. 1004–1010, February 2019
9. Nieuwoudt, J.E.: Investigating synchronous and asynchronous class attendance as predictors of academic success in online education. Aust. J. Educ. Technol. **36**(3), 15–25 (2020)

10. Delahunty, J., Jones, P., Verenikina, I.: Movers and shapers: teaching in online environments. Linguist. Educ. **28**, 54–78 (2014)
11. Talandron, M.M.P., Rodrigo, M.M.T., Beck, J.E.: Modeling the incubation effect among students playing an educational game for physics. In: André, E., Baker, R., Hu, X., Rodrigo, M., du Boulay, B. (eds.) Artificial Intelligence in Education. AIED 2017. Lecture Notes in Computer Science, vol 10331, pp. 371–380. Springer, Cham (2017). https://doi.org/10.1007/978-3-319-61425-0_31
12. Plateau of Latent Potential. https://www.samuelthomasdavies.com/book-summaries/self-help/atomic-habits/#:~:text=It%20is%20often%20because%20you,to%20continue%20playing%20the%20game. Accessed 07 Sept 2020
13. Pounding the Rock https://www.poundingtherock.com/2011/12/27/2103117/jacob-riis-biography-pounding-the-rock-stonecutter-credo
14. Horn, M.B., Staker, H.: Blended: Using Disruptive Innovation to Improve Schools. Wiley, New York (2017)
15. Herras, I.Y., Abanes, D.R.N., Del Rosario, N.B., Casano, J.D.: Designing Pre-test Questions as Phone Notifications: Studying the Effects of a Mobile Learning Intervention (2019)

# Education, Ethical Dilemmas and AI: From Ethical Design to Artificial Morality

Joan Casas-Roma$^{(\boxtimes)}$, Jordi Conesa, and Santi Caballé

SmartLearn Research Group, Universitat Oberta de Catalunya, Barcelona, Spain
{jcasasrom,jconesac,scaballe}@uoc.edu
http://smartlearn.uoc.edu

**Abstract.** Ethical dilemmas are complex scenarios involving a decision between conflicting choices related to ethical principles. While considering a case of an ethical dilemma in education presented in [17], it can be seen how, in these situations, it might be needed to take into consideration the student's needs, preferences, and potentially conflicting goals, as well as their personal and social contexts. Due to this, planning and foreseeing ethically challenging situations in advance, which would be how ethical design is normally used in technological artifacts, is not enough. As AI systems become more autonomous, the amount of possible situations, choices and effects their actions can have grow exponentially. In this paper, we bring together the analysis of ethical dilemmas in education and the need to incorporate moral reasoning into the AI systems' decision procedures. We argue how ethical design, although necessary, is not sufficient for that task and that artificial morality, or equivalent tools, are needed in order to integrate some sort of "ethical sensor" into autonomous systems taking a deeper role in an educational settings in order to enable them to, if not resolve, at least identify new ethically-relevant scenarios they are faced with.

**Keywords:** AI Ethics · Online learning · Artificial morality · Ethical sensors

## 1 Introduction and Motivations

The new disciplinary approach of learning engineering as the merge of breakthrough educational methodologies and technologies based on internet, data science and artificial intelligence (AI) have completely changed the landscape of online education over the last years by creating accessible, reliable and affordable data-rich powerful learning environments [12]. Particularly, AI-driven technologies have managed to automate pedagogical behaviours that we would deem as "intelligent" within an online education setting.

This work has been supported by the project colMOOC "Integrating Conversational Agents and Learning Analytics in MOOCs", co-funded by the European Commission (ref. 588438-EPP-1-2017-1-EL-EPPKA2-KA), and by a UOC postdoctoral stay.

R. A. Sottilare and J. Schwarz (Eds.): HCII 2021, LNCS 12792, pp. 167–182, 2021.
https://doi.org/10.1007/978-3-030-77857-6_11

However, as reported in more mature sectors where AI-driven technologies have already been developed and deployed, automatic decision-making processes many times bear unexpected outcomes. For instance, machine learning (ML) based systems have been reported to discriminate certain social communities in the context of law courts, job applications or bank loans due to the use of biased datasets to feed the ML models [4,13,25]. Different studies conclude that, in order to avoid unforeseen outcomes in their integration, the ethical dimension of deploying AI in different settings must be taken into account. This becomes particularly important when thinking about the effects that applying AI systems to education could have to current and future generations of students. Due to this, special care needs to be taken when considering how AI systems could deal with ethical dilemmas that can appear in an educational setting.

In order to provide a starting point and guide our discussion throughout this paper, let us consider the following case of an ethical dilemma in the context of education, as it appears in [17]. An eight-grade student's marks are not enough to pass to ninth-grade, and her teachers agree that she is unprepared for the next grade. Should the student be allowed to pass? Given the standard norms, the automatic answer might be "no". However, we have some more information available about the student; we know she is likely to drop out entirely if she is not allowed to pass, and her teachers also note that she has put a lot of effort that resulted into improving her grades, until she recently grew discouraged. Given these new bits of information, should the student be allowed to pass? We still have some more details about this case, though: she has lived in three foster homes for the past years, and her brother died from a gunshot. Furthermore, a potential alternative school for struggling students is a well-known "school-to-prison" pipeline. Again, should the student be allowed to pass?

Although this is an example of a quite extreme case, it shows how, in order to evaluate and make a decision about a situation with clear ethical effects in their outcomes, one needs to consider a broad picture of the scenario. In this particular case, and even though the dilemma takes place in an educational setting, the elements that need to be considered step "beyond the classroom"; namely, the situation starts being shaped as a dilemma as soon as we start considering not just the student's information that we would normally find represented within the educational system (marks, grade pass, etc.), but also the student's personal and contextual situation. In this sense, what makes this situation particularly challenging goes beyond the usual norms that one would apply in the educational system and step right into the student's own case. As it is pointed out in [9], ethical dilemmas are often about the exception, rather than the norm, and they usually involve solutions with potentially conflicting goals that cannot all be fully satisfied at the same time. As such, ethical dilemmas do not usually have a clearly "good" outcome, as one solution favoring one dimension will often disregard another one.

After having introduced the guiding case study, we introduce the notion of the layered approach to ethical dilemmas in Sect. 1.1. We explore distinct considerations related to the integration of ethical behaviors in technological tools in Sect. 2. With this considerations at hand, we discuss the challenges that each layer of our guiding case study would pose in Sect. 3. Having identified the complexities behind this kind of dilemmas, we introduce the notion of *ethical sensors* in Sect. 4. Finally, we provide some conclusions and directions of future work in Sect. 5.

## 1.1 Ethical Dilemmas in Education: A Layered Approach

The previous dilemma allows us to distinguish three different layers that should be taken into account when considering the ethical dimension of a conflicting situation like the one depicted in the case study: the *Educational* layer, the *Personal* layer, and the *Social* layer. In a nutshell, those layers (see Fig. 1) distinguish three contexts that, although being all potentially important in an ethically-relevant scenario, belong to different spheres of the student's learning context.

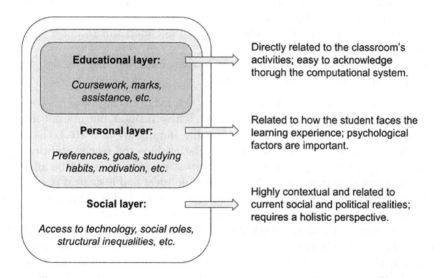

**Fig. 1.** The different ethically-relevant layers of a student's learning experience.

The Educational layer refers to those elements that belong to, and are explicitly accounted for, the educational context –namely, anything that would normally take place within the classroom. Course contents, classroom activities, evaluations, homework, etc. These elements are already part of the student's *persona* within the educational environment, and they aim to measure their knowledge, progress and skills within the learning process. They are the most readily-available elements for an educational institution to look at, as they naturally fall within the scope of what the students do in their learning process and within the standard course of events of their learning. In the case study presented in the previous section, those elements would correspond to:

- The student's final marks.
- The norm requiring students to achieve a certain mark in order to pass to next grade.
- The student's marks record.

The Personal layer refers to those elements related to the student's way of being, their goals, preferences and motivations, the way the student faces learning challenges, etc. –namely, they are part of what makes each and every individual person be the way they are. Even though these elements are not explicitly taken into account within the educational system, they have a direct effect in the way the student approaches their learning process. Even though not being explicitly represented in the educational environment, they clearly bear a direct relationship with the student's learning journey, and are often known and taken into account by human actors involved in the learning process. In the previous case study, those elements would correspond to:

- The student's intention to drop out from the educational system if she is not allowed to pass to ninth grade.
- The student's effort (and success) in raising her marks in the past through more dedication.
- The student's discouragement after having improved her marks, which resulted in her results worsening again.

The Social Layer refers to those elements belonging to the student's context, but which are external to their way of being. These include, but are not limited to, the people with whom they share their life (family, friends, etc.), the place where they live (home, geographical area), relationships and responsibilities they may have towards other people, past and current events that might be affecting the student's life significantly, as well as socio-political and historical particularities of the student's social context (which might be related to ethnicity, gender roles, etc.). These contextual elements can have a big effect on the student's life and, consequently, on the student's learning process. Aside from potentially affecting the student's access to educational resources, they can have an effect on the way the student behaves, the way the student devotes their time to learning, and can even frame the student in specific roles related to different social communities and contexts. In the previous case study, those elements would be (among others, but focusing on the ones that are being explicitly mentioned):

- The student having lived in three different foster homes for the past years, which indicates an unusual and potentially troublesome family structure for the student.
- The student's brother having died from a gunshot. This not only highlights an important personal loss for the student that can have profound emotional consequences, but might also suggest troublesome living conditions for the student and her family.

Even though this classification is not meant to be exhaustive, it is enough to show how these three different layers play a quite important role when considering an ethical dilemma such as the one presented in the case study. Furthermore, this classification allows us to see how each further layer is harder to explicitly account for by using the tools of the educational system itself, but, at the same time, each further layer might point to deeper factors related to the student's situation that need to be considered in the dilemma. How, if possible at all, can all this be acknowledged in order to be used as part of a semi-autonomous decision-making system within a learning environment?

# 2 Beyond Tools: AI and Ethical Behavior

Before trying to answer that question, we first need to examine what the relation between technology and ethical[1] challenges has been. The use of AI in decision-making was seen, years ago, as the most reliable way of eliminating human bias and unfair decisions [8]; it was thought that data was objective and that computational systems were neutral with regards to interests and prejudices, and thus it was believed that those systems would be able to make neutral and fair decisions much more easily that any human would. Nevertheless, researchers soon realized that this was not the case. The way data was gathered, represented, selected and used, the way algorithms were encoded, the rules governing automated decision systems, all those pieces of the mechanism could easily encapsulate personal, social and historical biases in a wide variety of ways [8,13,18]. The question, then, arose: how could AI systems be made in such a way to prevent unintentional harm from being done?

Even though computers are clearly technological tools, the way computational artifacts have evolved in the recent decades sets them apart from other technological creations [14]. There currently is a strong distinction between a computer program and the traditional notion of a tool, such as a screwdriver, a jackhammer, or even a hand calculator. Perhaps the most evident distinction is that, while a traditional tool waits for someone to use it, AI programs can act somewhat autonomously react to, and affect their environment. Due to this, the ethical considerations traditionally applied to the design and use of technology (safety mechanisms, emergency buttons, etc.) no longer fill the needs behind AI systems. As a tool gets more autonomous, the responsibility for its ethical use gets farther away from its intended user and needs to consider a broader set of scenarios.

The study of the ethical dimension of artificial agents has led to some different classifications of both what constitutes and ethical agents, and what kinds of ethical agents there might exist. Moor distinguishes in [19] between four kinds of (non-exclusive) ethical agents:

- *Ethical impact agents*: Those agents whose actions have ethical consequences, regardless of whether these are intended, or not.

---

[1] Although the terms "ethics" and "morality" have slightly different definitions (one being a more reflective discipline, while the other one being more about prescription of behavior), we use them interchangeably in this work to refer to behaviors that are both in accordance to certain ethical principles, as well as considered to bear "good", or "right" outcomes.

- *Implicit ethical agents*: Those agents that have ethical considerations (normally, safety, or security considerations) built into their design.
- *Explicit ethical agents*: Those agents that can identify and process ethical information, as well as use it to make sensitive decisions on what should be done.
- *Full ethical agents*: Those agents who, aside from being able to identify and process ethical information, have those metaphysical features that are usually attributed to human agents; namely, consciousness, intentionality and free will.

Similarly, Wallach and Allen [23] define three layers of moral agency based on the two properties of *autonomy* (the degree in which an agent can act independently) and *sensitivity* (the degree in which the agent can identify and factor ethical information into their decision system):

- *Operational morality*: Agents with both low autonomy and low sensitivity, but which have some ethical considerations engineered in their design.
- *Functional morality*: Agents that either have high autonomy and low sensitivity, or the other way around (i.e.: low autonomy and high sensitivity).
- *Full moral agency*: Agents with high degrees of both autonomy and sensitivity, capable of acting as "trustworthy moral agents" [23, p. 26].

Wallach and Allen explicitly refer to Moor's categorization and, although they agree with Moor's aim and approach towards explicit ethical agents, they also point out how Moor does not provide instructions regarding how this direction should be pursued. In this sense, the authors defend how their account of the development of technology based on an interaction between autonomy and sensitivity provides good directions. As increased autonomy is an already ongoing trend in technological advancement, the question behind artificial moral agency requires an increase in ethical sensitivity.

The challenge behind the design of artificial ethical agents has usually been tackled through *ethical design*. Nevertheless, as soon as we recognize that the next steps behind that challenge lie in increasing ethical sensitivity, ethical design may be faced with certain limitations requiring us to divert our attention to a more explicit approach to ethical reasoning: the creation of *artificial morality*.

## 2.1   Ethics by Design: Forewarned is Forearmed

Ethical design faces the ethical challenges behind technology through anticipation [18]. When designing a new technological artifact, considering what this new artifact can do, who might use it, how it may be used, and what outcomes their uses can bring about helps understand situations in which the artifact can have an ethically-relevant effect. Once this combination of internal (the artifact's allowances) and external factors (its users, potential contexts, etc.) is considered, the designers can anticipate risks and dangers and integrate those into the design of the artifact itself.

One can find ethical design in technology way before complex AI-driven systems, and it can easily be found in almost any kind of technological tool [14,23]; emergency buttons on tools that, if they were to get out of control, could cause severe damage (like jackhammers, kitchen blenders, motorbikes), manual safety blocks and latches in firearms to prevent unintended firing, etc. However, the more autonomous technological artifacts become, the more complex their "safety mechanisms" must become. For instance, internet search engines are equipped with automated filtering tools to prevent showing inappropriate content to unintended audiences; a search engine *could* show these results, but its potential searches are limited beforehand due to ethical reasons. Similarly, a plane's autopilot system has a constrained range of manoeuvres it can perform, with limited speeds, turning, and ascend/descend angles; beyond what is mechanically and physically possible, these limitations are imposed in order to avoid discomfort to the passengers. More complex systems, such as an ML-based algorithm programmed to decide whether an applicant can get a bank loan, have been known to show biases and unfair behaviors [13]; among other options, ethical design can be applied in order to pre-process the data to filter those fields that should not play a role in the decision-making.

When considering the categories introduced in the Sect. 2, ethical design would likely lead to what Moor classifies as ethical impact agents and implicit ethical agents, and to what Wallach and Allen call operational morality. Even in the case of fairly complex systems (such as ML-based automated decision systems), ethical concerns are explored *beforehand*, planned and dealt with in advance. Although this does not mean that the system cannot be checked, revised and improved over time, aside from the ethically-relevant situations that have been foreseen in its design, the system does not adapt. Furthermore, there is no explicit representation of the ethical weight of the system's actions. As such, ethical design leads to systems that, regardless of their degree of autonomy, lack ethical sensitivity (following Wallach and Allen's terminology).

In order to leap this gap and reach some sort of explicit ethical sensitivity, which would be necessary for artifacts exhibiting functional morality, we need to define and embed morality as part of the system's decision procedures. In order to do this, ethical design is not enough: we must take a step forward and venture into the realm of artificial morality.

## 2.2 Artificial Morality: Towards Encoding Moral Value

Even though certain behaviors can be encouraged or limited through rules, norms and patterns, ethical behavior usually requires some sort of awareness of what is at stake in a situation. Take, for instance, a famous case in the fiction literature of ethical autonomous systems: Isaac Asimov's *I, robot* [5]. Although being a fictional work, Asimov's rules of robotics have been thoroughly considered and discussed as a potential starting point for ethical machines [3,11]; needless to say, this set of rules has been shown to lead to paradoxes that would make them insufficient to guide artificial ethical behavior. Nevertheless, even if we hypothetically accept that those rules are good enough to guide ethical robots, the robots would still need to be *aware* of what constitutes an ethically-relevant fact. Take, for instance, the first rule governing the ethical behavior of robots:

> A robot may not injure a human being or, through inaction, allow a human being to come to harm.

In order for a robot to act according to this rule, it must be able to understand what "harm" means to a human, and what situations could possibly lead to a human coming to harm. In fact, a different understanding of what counts as "harm" could lead to many different interpretations to guide the robot's behavior[2]. Even being just a fictional example, this helps to highlight how, in order to exhibit ethical behavior and adapt to potentially unforeseen situations involving multiple agents, interests and contexts, an explicit awareness of what counts as "moral" is needed.

This requirement for explicitness, which would be needed in order to achieve explicit moral agents and functional morality (as well as beyond that), makes artificial morality a more promising avenue than ethical design, which is based on *a priori* anticipation to ensure that behavior is constrained *according* to certain ethical principles. Instead, artificial morality is rooted in the notion of "agent" and "agency"; automated decision-making systems here are not considered mere tools, but they are implicitly considered to be autonomous over certain decisions. As such, this approach is based on integrating moral reasoning into the decision system itself. The agent is given agency to identify, evaluate and potentially make autonomous decisions over potentially new ethically-relevant situations –just as we humans do.

The overall idea behind the engineering of these systems is simple: the "morality" of a decision should be identified, weighted and brought into the picture, just as it is already done with other notions (such as "utility", "performance", "benefit", etc.) that are factored into the decision procedure. Intuitively speaking, this sounds quite natural to what we humans do when we reason about a situation; sometimes, our decision is entirely based on the benefit we would receive from acting in a certain way; other times, we become aware of the moral weight involved in such decision and choose to act in a different way, even if it not as beneficial to us as it could be. Beyond this intuition, however, identifying, capturing and weighing morality in a computational way suddenly becomes a huge conceptual challenge where, for every answer, we are faced with a plethora of both theoretical and technical questions. As identified by [24], this challenge can be looked at from three main design perspectives:

1. *Top-down approaches* are based on understanding and defining beforehand all those situations that could be relevant in order to distill a set of rules to guide the behavior of the artificial moral agent (some examples are [6,7,21]).
2. *Bottom-up approaches* are inspired by trial-and-error learning which, in fact, we humans use while developing our moral character. Machine learning and

---

[2] In the story "Liar!" [5, ch. 6], precisely, a robot continuously lies to the characters in order to avoid hurting their feelings, which is an unintended understanding of the term "harm" that was not planned in the design of that robot.

evolutionary algorithms are some of the underlying mechanisms that could be used under this approach (see [1,15]).

3. *Hybrid approaches* combine both previous approaches in order to dynamically learn from relevant cases, while sticking to a certain set of rules that might constrain or guide the way those cases are processed. Hybrid approaches have the advantage of being more flexible than pure top-down approaches, while being less unpredictable than purely bottom-up ones (see [2,22]).

Despite the clear challenge behind the computational representation of something as contextual as "morality", several prototypes have been designed and implemented in order to explore this uncharted territory [10]; this sheds some light into this and provide some first steps that can be followed to enhance this kind of explicit ethical systems[3].

# 3 Exploring the Challenges Behind the Case Study

Although it is true that ethical dilemmas in the context of education need not be as deeply nuanced as the one we present in this paper, that case is useful to understand the multiple layers that may be involved in those scenarios. Needless to say, a case like that, where not even human teachers can agree on (different professionals propose very different approaches to it in [17]), would be extremely challenging to solve computationally. However, we can tentatively venture into exploring some of the many challenges that each layer of that case would need to be faced by autonomous ethical agents. Far from trying to provide a solution to that problem, this exploration can help us understand the challenges that a computational approach to it will face, thus guiding future steps in this line.

## 3.1 The Educational Layer

As it has been explained in Sect. 1.1, the Educational layer represents the most direct representation of the student's activities as part of the expected learning process. The information contained in this layer encapsulates the standard norm and conditions required to pass grade, as well as the student's actual results; furthermore, and through the student's record, one can get a picture of the student's performance in the past, and might allow to spot performance trends and unusual variances that could be used to support making a decision.

If we are to focus, for now, only on the Educational layer, the ethical dilemma depicted in the case study somewhat vanishes –or, at the very least, gets strongly diluted. Because this layer is driven by a clear rule (the required mark to pass

---

[3] It is worth mentioning that these two approaches to ethical systems, ethical design and artificial morality, are not mutually exclusive. In fact, Moor points out in his work how the categories he defines in [19] are not exclusive either –an explicit ethical agent can easily be an ethical impact agent and an implicit ethical agent as well. Following this, furnishing an agent with some artificial morality mechanisms does not imply having to ditch ethical design approaches beforehand.

grade) and a fact (the mark scored by the student), there is not much to consider at this point... unless we bring the student's record into the picture. A student whose marks are good enough, but which have shown improvement in the past (even if with ups and downs), might be able to keep the pace with the next grade; conversely, a student whose marks have been consistently low would not probably be able to cope with the next grade any better than with the current one.

This task at hand could be approached through ethical design by a set of rules, without the need to furnish the agent with any sort of explicit moral reasoning. Because the rule and the data are clear, the only thing that could be taken into account in this decision is the tendency depicted in the student's records. One can easily imagine an automated system that, provided the students' records follow a certain specified tendency, is more prone to either rounding up a slightly low mark[4] to allow a grade pass, or, at least, bring a human-in-the-loop to make a decision on a "fringe case".

## 3.2    The Personal Layer

The Personal layer poses some computational challenges with respect to the Educational layer. Namely, as the Personal layer is directly related to the student's beliefs, goals, intentions, etc., which are way harder to capture from "within" the computational setting that an artificial agent, such as a personal tutoring system, would have access to. This layer would normally be grasped and understood, in a traditional learning context, by the student's teachers[5].

This layer presents severe conceptual representation challenges. Because we are focusing on the personal attitude of the student towards the situation, we are faced with notions such as the student's *intention, effort, dedication* and *discouragement*, among others. While it can be argued that, in an online learning environment, dedication could be somewhat acknowledged (through maybe hours connected on campus, activities and exercises solved, etc.), the other three belong to the internal mental state of the student and are hard to account for through the usual environment in online learning. An even trickier part of this layer lies in the fact that this decision is all about potential future outcomes. This decision is no longer about what the normal rule about grade passing and

---

[4] This would then open up the Sorites question about "how low is low enough" for the system to make this decision, but this question falls outside the scope of this paper.

[5] It is worth recalling a recent case that occurred during 2020 in the UK in which, due to students being unable to attend an A-level exam due to the Covid-19 pandemic, an automated system was implemented in order to predict the student's grades [16]. It turned out that the predictions made by the students' teachers and the ones made by the automated system were quite different (being way lower in the automated prediction), which resulted in several protests that led to the UK government disregarding the automated predictions and following the human teachers' predicted grades. This ties up directly with the fact that human teachers had access to this Personal layer of their students that the automated system, which was fed only on data of what we call the Educational layer, lacked.

the student's grades are, but rather it is about how the future scenario could be, after a decision has been made, and how this may affect the student's possibilities.

In this sense, the student's success in raising her grades (which can be acknowledged by the system through her records) is key in considering whether the student should be given this chance; a student whose grades have been invariably low would not probably be able to cope with the next grade –or, at least, there is no evidence supporting that. However, and because this not guarantee, in any way, that the student will be able to keep the pace, this might require some sort of vote of confidence where a teacher might agree to allow the student to pass grade, but only if the student promises to make an effort to keep the pace with it; this agreement might work, or it might not, but it is something that only time will tell.

Automatizing this to some degree becomes challenging, as it risks turning the exception into a norm. In the case that occupies us, the fact that the student has shown that she can keep up with the workload, given enough effort and dedication, should be key in deciding whether the exception should be considered. An automated system, therefore, should be able to look up for signs in the student's record showing that they could, indeed, face the challenge a new grade would present[6].

## 3.3  The Social Layer

The Social layer requires an understanding that goes beyond the students and that deals with the context they are living in. This context has an influence over the student and their behavior, as well as over potential opportunities and limitations the student might have. Among other factors, family, social roles, historical and geographical inequalities can have a strong impact on the student and their learning process. Understanding how those factors can influence the student is a challenge for both human teachers and automated systems. Although demographic data of the students might be available, inferring information automatically from that data in order to understand the social context of the students can potentially lead to biases, profiling and discriminatory segmentation of the students, as it has been seen in other areas where ML technologies have been used on demographic data [13]. This layer, therefore, presents a particularly deep challenge: whereas the social context is indeed relevant and can provide important information regarding the students' living conditions, it is also mainly based on generalizations that can lead to unfair decisions based on social profiling.

Whereas the Personal layer had to do with the student's particular case and, therefore, was hard to generalize into an "exceptional norm", the Social layer deals with generalizations and, as such, is hard to apply to the particular case. Even though social circumstances can lead to systematic profiling and

---

[6] Learning analytics could help understand the student's performance and dedication and provide some grounds for a more informed decision.

discrimination, in our case study the Social layer is meant to highlight how, because of the inherent problems the student faces in her social environment, further care could be placed in her case in order to make an exception to the usual norm. In this case, therefore, the Social layer should be meant to play a "positive discriminatory" effect, rather than a negative one. Understanding how the student's environment might constrain her performance, her dedication and her emotional well-being can be a reason to provide an additional margin of tolerance to that student's case in order to make up for that.

However, and just as it happened in the aforementioned sectors where AI has systematically been discriminatory because of social considerations, the same thing could happen if the trend was inverted. Because social differences reflect *general* patterns, those patterns might not apply to the particular cases of people belonging to those social groups. Belonging to a particular social circle might indicate a propensity, or a major probability, towards being affected by some of the characteristics (positive, or negative) that are considered "common" of that social group. Nevertheless, transforming a general tendency, depicted by statistical patterns, into particular cases, always bear the risk to unfairly misrepresent those particulars. The characteristics that are more prone to occur in that social group could not, however, be systematically taken for granted, but they could rather be open for consideration.

The fact that the social environment is highly contextual and usually requires a holistic understanding of the social reality of the moment could suggest that a human-in-the-loop should be needed in order to understand each particular case. The role of a pedagogical agent in this case would be not to make a decision on its own, but rather to identify the case as potentially relevant and bring a human-in-the-loop in order to make a supported decision. This collaborative role that technology can have in ethical decision-making, where an automated system may be able to identify cases that require more careful human-in-the-loop supervision, leads us to the identification of the need for ethical sensors in this kind of systems, which we explain in the next section.

## 4    Awaking Awareness: From Physical to Ethical Sensors

Even with just a brief analysis of the guiding case study, it is enough to show the complexity that ethical dilemmas carry with them. Our reflections around this case lead us to realize that, before even attempting to imagine a computational system able to provide a satisfactory decision to a situation as complex as that, the system would need to raise an *awareness* of the ethical dimension behind that decision. As we have previously mentioned, the Educational layer in itself had almost no hint of an ethical dilemma at all. Nevertheless, by directing our attention to the Personal and Social layers of that particular student, the ethical dimension behind such decision arose. Only once we become aware of such dimension we start wondering whether following the standard norm would be the right thing to do, or whether we need to carefully consider other factors bearing an ethical weight before making a decision. Following this line, we recognize that our autonomous ethical agents need something else, before they can even consider how to make an acceptable decision as part of ethical dilemmas: they need to be able to *recognize* them.

The notion of a "sensor" is quite common in computational technology. Physical sensors allow computers to take parts of the physical worlds as input and react to them accordingly: light, temperature, movement, writing, faces, etc. Physical sensors allow to leap the existing gap between certain non-digital parts of the world and digitalize them in order to be used in a computational environment. The sensory organs in the human body, in fact, do pretty much the same: our senses capture the "raw" information we perceive in the world (light, sound, touch, etc.) and send it to our brains so that we can make a model and interpret them. We can follow this analogy further on and go beyond the physical sensors in our body. Aside from being able to gather and interpret physical information about the world, we are also able to extract and infer other kinds of information from a perceived situation, such as psychological, emotional and ethical information. Just as we can perceive and "mindread" someone else's thoughts, worries and feelings, we can also intuitively perceive when a decision carries out an ethical weight with it. The ethical relevance of the situation is not clearly signaled by any physical, or mental signal; instead, when we put together our mental model of a situation we are faced with, we can (often) recognize whether it carries out an ethical component in it. What makes a particular situation qualify as ethically-relevant, however, greatly varies depending on the context. Regardless of the particularities behind each situation, the important thing is that, just as we have sensory inputs directed towards sensing the physical world, we are also able to "sense" the ethical dimension of a scenario. Following this analogy, then, it is only natural to ask ourselves the question: could artificial agents be equipped with a similar sort of *ethical sensors*, just like how they already are equipped with physical sensors?

We believe that, in order to design artificial moral agents able to recognize and deal with the ethical dimension of situations they may face, they should be equipped with some sort of ethical sensors. Although the parallelism with physical sensors is useful, ethical sensors would need to be, in fact, an internal procedure within the artificial agent, rather than an input hardware component. In other words, ethical sensors would need to interact not with the "outer world", but rather with the "inner model" of the outer world already created within the agent's representation system. These sensors should allow the agent to raise awareness about decisions that could have a profound ethical impact. Unlike physical sensors, which gather "actual" data about the world and construct a picture of the current scenario, ethical sensors would need to consider "potential" outcomes that could follow a decision and understand how these would shape future scenarios.

In this sense, we claim that artificial morality is key. Whereas ethical design allows to encapsulate and foresee specific situations that may arise in certain domains, it is not grounded on the compositional evaluation of the different "pieces" that form the situation, but rather on the consideration of the situation as a whole. Conversely, artificial morality can take a more granular approach to ethically-relevant scenarios that might *arise*, or *emerge*. For instance, [1,2] provide hybrid and bottom-up prototypes of artificial moral agents that learn, via examples, how to deal with new morally-relevant scenarios. Even though these prototypes focus on solving moral dilemmas by following other examples and, therefore, by capturing their patterns, one can conceive these agents as being able to "distill" the ethical relevance of the different elements forming the distinct cases that are used to train them; in other words, the agents could grow an awareness about which elements can potentially bear ethical weight within them. This would be a first step towards being able to recognize when a certain scenario, even if brand new in the set of examples used to train the agent, might bear ethical relevance.

It is worth noting that the path between recognizing ethical dilemmas and solving them is far from direct. Nevertheless, if artificial agents are to be more and more integrated in our educational environments, then it we need to ensure that they can, at the very least, *recognize* when a decision can potentially have an ethical impact on students, or teachers. Furthermore, ethical dilemmas in education can be quite complex to evaluate and solve, and it might be challenging, or even impossible, the find the "right" choice –even among human teachers. In those cases, artificial agents deployed in an online learning environment (personal tutoring systems, pedagogical conversational agents, etc.) could, if equipped with ethical sensors, recognize when a decision could qualify as an ethical dilemma and bring a human-in-the-loop to supervise and consider how to deal with that particular case.

## 5    Conclusions and Future Work

Ethical dilemmas usually bear a huge degree of complexity with them and it is often not even clear whether a "right choice" exists. Making a decision usually involves adhering to certain principles while disregarding others, and this may bring severe detrimental consequences to some of the parties involved in the situation. In this sense, ethical dilemmas in education are no different. As artificial agents gain more autonomy and become more integrated in the educational system, one must consider how these artificial systems could be equipped to handle ethically-relevant situations that arise in online learning environments. In this work we have briefly compared two main approaches to ethical artificial agents: ethical design and artificial morality. Each one have their strengths and weaknesses and can, therefore, tackle different parts of the problem at hand.

Far from aiming to provide a general solution to the automated solving of ethical dilemmas, in this work we direct our attention to a challenge that would come prior to solving an ethical dilemma: recognizing that there is one. While ethical design preemptively constrains certain behaviors and functionalities that fit a pre-specified pattern, existing prototypes of systems equipped with some sort of artificial morality behave as "ethical problem solvers": their inputs are decisions *known* to be ethically-relevant, and so they are designed to munch those scenarios and spit out an ethically-acceptable solution. Although this is something that ethical autonomous agents will need to do eventually, these agents would firstly need to be able to recognize ethically-relevant scenarios, prior to using their moral reasoning mechanisms to understand what the best choice would be –and, in case there is no clear answer, bring a human professional into the decision process. In this line, we introduce the notion of *ethical sensors* as mechanisms aimed not at solving ethical problems, but rather at identifying what can make a decision qualify as "ethically-relevant". Being better suited to the design of explicit ethical agents, we believe that artificial morality provides a better starting point towards the design of ethical sensors. The need to find a balance between ethical sensitivity and privacy remains open and needs further discussion, however, as in order to achieve more ethical sensitivity the system would probably need to have more data available.

As part of our future work, we want to study how artificial morality proto-types shaped in either a hybrid or a bottom-up fashion, such as [1, 2, 20], could be used as a starting point to the design of ethical sensors. Intuitively, the pat-terns learned by those systems could be used to identify what makes a morally-relevant situation be considered so. Once those elements have been identified, we could start prototyping ethical sensors that, given situations that are not preemptively identified as being morally-relevant, could identify whether those situations could carry moral relevance by following a compositional, or emergent analysis of the elements that form such situations. Although designing artificial pedagogical agents that are able to solve ethical dilemmas is, indeed, our ulti-mate goal, we first need to ensure that those agents will be able to recognize them.

# References

1. Anderson, M., Anderson, S.: Geneth: a general ethical dilemma analyzer. In: Pro-ceedings of the AAAI Conference on Artificial Intelligence, vol. 28 (2014)
2. Anderson, M., Anderson, S.L., Armen, C.: Medethex: a prototype medical ethics advisor. In: AAAI, pp. 1759–1765 (2006)
3. Anderson, S.L.: Asimov's "three laws of robotics" and machine metaethics. Ai Soc. **22**(4), 477–493 (2008)
4. Angwin, J., Larson, J., Mattu, S., Kirchner, L.: Machine bias. ProPublica, 23 May 2016 (2016)
5. Asimov, I.: I, robot. HarperCollins Publishers (2013)
6. Blass, J.: Interactive learning and analogical chaining for moral and commonsense reasoning. In: Proceedings of the AAAI Conference on Artificial Intelligence, vol. 30 (2016)
7. Blass, J., Forbus, K.: Moral decision-making by analogy: Generalizations versus exemplars. In: Proceedings of the AAAI Conference on Artificial Intelligence, vol. 29 (2015)
8. Caliskan, A., Bryson, J.J., Narayanan, A.: Semantics derived automatically from language corpora contain human-like biases. Science **356**(6334), 183–186 (2017)
9. Casas-Roma, J., Conesa, J.: Towards the design of ethically-aware pedagogical conversational agents. In: Barolli, L., Takizawa, M., Yoshihisa, T., Amato, F., Ikeda, M. (eds.) 3PGCIC 2020. LNNS, vol. 158, pp. 188–198. Springer, Cham (2021). https://doi.org/10.1007/978-3-030-61105-7_19

10. Cervantes, J.A., López, S., Rodríguez, L.F., Cervantes, S., Cervantes, F., Ramos, F.: Artificial moral agents: a survey of the current status. Sci. Eng. Ethics **26**(2), 501–532 (2020)
11. Clarke, R.: Asimov's laws of robotics: implications for information technology. Mach. Ethics 254–284 (2011)
12. Dede, C., Richards, J., Saxberg, B.: Learning Engineering for Online Education: Theoretical Contexts and Design-Based Examples. Routledge (2018)
13. Favaretto, M., De Clercq, E., Elger, B.S.: Big data and discrimination: perils, promises and solutions. A systematic review. J. Big Data **6**(1), 1–27 (2019)
14. Gunkel, D.J.: The Machine Question: Critical Perspectives on AI, Robots, and Ethics. MIT Press, Cambridge (2012)
15. Honarvar, A.R., Ghasem-Aghaee, N.: An artificial neural network approach for creating an ethical artificial agent. In: 2009 IEEE International Symposium on Computational Intelligence in Robotics and Automation-(CIRA), pp. 290–295. IEEE (2009)
16. Kolkman, D.: "f**k the algorithm"?: What the world can learn from the UK's a-level grading fiasco, August 2020. https://blogs.lse.ac.uk/impactofsocialsciences/2020/08/26/fk-the-algorithm-what-the-world-can-learn-from-the-uks-a-level-grading-fiasco/. Accessed 10 Feb 2021
17. Levinson, M., Fay, J.: Dilemmas of educational ethics: Cases and commentaries. Harvard Education Press (2019)
18. Mittelstadt, B.D., Allo, P., Taddeo, M., Wachter, S., Floridi, L.: The ethics of algorithms: mapping the debate. Big Data Soc. **3**(2) (2016)
19. Moor, J.: Four kinds of ethical robots. Philosophy Now **72**, 12–14 (2009)
20. Muntean, I., Howard, D.: Artificial moral agents: creative, autonomous, social. An approach based on evolutionary computation. In: Seibt, J., Hakli, R., Norskov, M. (eds.) Sociable Robots and the Future of Social Relations: Proceedings of Robo-Philosophy 2014, pp. 217–230. IOS Press (2014)
21. Vanderelst, D., Winfield, A.: An architecture for ethical robots inspired by the simulation theory of cognition. Cogn. Syst. Res. **48**, 56–66 (2018)
22. Wallach, W., Franklin, S., Allen, C.: A conceptual and computational model of moral decision making in human and artificial agents. Top. Cognit. Sci. **2**(3), 454–485 (2010)
23. Wallach, W., Allen, C.: Moral Machines: Teaching Robots Right from Wrong. Oxford University Press, Oxford (2008)
24. Wallach, W., Allen, C., Smit, I.: Machine morality: bottom-up and top-down approaches for modelling human moral faculties. AI Soc. **22**(4), 565–582 (2008)
25. Yapo, A., Weiss, J.: Ethical implications of bias in machine learning. In: Proceedings of the 51st Hawaii International Conference on System Sciences (2018)

# Formal Methods in Human-Computer Interaction and Adaptive Instructional Systems

Bruno Emond$^{(\boxtimes)}$ (iD)

National Research Council Canada, Ottawa, Canada
bruno.emond@nrc-cnrc.gc.ca
http://www.nrc-cnrc.gc.ca

**Abstract.** Building reliable interactive systems has been identified as an important and difficult task from the late '60s. One approach to augment the reliability of interactive systems is to use formal models during system development. Formal methods have received attention for the design and analysis of human-computer interaction (HCI) for thirty years. The field of adaptive instructional systems (AIS) in general, and intelligent tutoring systems in particulars, have been mostly relying on empirical methods for training systems validation (the system supports learning), rather than formal methods for verification (the system meets its specifications). Empirical methods focus on the validity of pedagogical interventions at the individual task and problem sequence levels, using learning analytic methods such as Bayesian knowledge tracing, additive factors models, or machine learning models of human performance. The purpose of the paper is to explore some parallel and the applicability of HCI formal models to AIS. The paper: a) presents key concepts related to HCI formal models using semi-formal representations (workflow graphs), b) gives examples of formal properties to be verified, c) discuss briefly formal notations, and d) defines adaptive human-computer interaction. The last section of the paper discuss the similarity between HCI formal models and AIS standard modules, and identifies some area of applicability of HCI formal models to AIS design, recognizing the central value of AIS empirical methods at the foundation of AIS iterative design.

**Keywords:** Formal methods · Human-computer interaction · Adaptive instructional systems

## 1 Introduction

Building reliable interactive systems has been identified as an important and difficult task from the late '60s [38]. One approach to augment the reliability of interactive systems is to use formal models during system development. Such models provide the means to assess the logical consistency of interactive systems design, and simulate their execution over time. Formal models have been applied

© National Research Council of Canada 2021
R. A. Sottilare and J. Schwarz (Eds.): HCII 2021, LNCS 12792, pp. 183–198, 2021.
https://doi.org/10.1007/978-3-030-77857-6_12

to a variety of Human-Computer Interaction (HCI) contexts [22,49], and can be used in an iterative refinement system development methodology from informal to formal system specifications and implementation [6]. Formal methods such as Z, Lotos, modal logic, labelled transition systems, or Petri nets have received attention for the design and analysis of human-computer interaction for thirty years [51]. Formal methods can be used to specify design principles such as reachability, visibility, task completion, and reliability [5]. Formal methods utility has been shown in the verification of human computer interactions in safety-critical systems, such as nuclear plans, health-care devices, and in the modelling of human-in-the-loop complex systems [51].

The field of adaptive instructional systems (AIS) in general, and intelligent tutoring systems in particulars, have been mostly relying on empirical methods for training systems validation (the system supports learning), rather than formal methods for verification (the system meets its specifications). Empirical methods focus on the validity of pedagogical interventions at the individual task and problem sequence levels, using learning analytic methods such as Bayesian knowledge tracing, additive factors models, or machine learning models of human performance.

The purpose of the paper is to explore the applicability of human-computer interaction formal models to adaptive instructional systems. The motivation is rooted in engineering practice to ensure system quality by applying formal methods to verify system specification properties at the system design phase. The paper is divided in two main sections followed by a conclusion. Section 2 presents key concepts related to formal methods in human-computer interaction. The section situates the use of formal methods in relationship to other methods for usability evaluation (Sect. 2.1). Then a generic HCI workflow is presented for characterizing the relevant entities than need to be modelled in formal models (Sect. 2.2). The remaining subsections outlines important interaction properties to verify (Sect. 2.3), and formal notations (Sect. 2.4). Section 2.5 defines the concept of adaptive HCI. Section 3 presents core adaptive instructional system modules and situates them in the context of HCI formal methods. In spite of the technical aspect of the paper topics, the material is presented in a semi-formal manner using graphical representations to convey the analysis.

# 2    Formal Methods in Human-Computer Interaction

## 2.1    Usability and Formal Methods

Usability is an essential characteristic of product quality and reliable interactive systems [25]. However, there is no simple definition of what constitutes usability. Every definition refers to other characteristics contributing to the overall usability of a product. The result of a systematic literature review of usability measures used to assess mobile application [48] shows that 75 attributes were distinguished in the body of 790 indexed documents. In line with ISO [25], the most frequent are efficiency (70%), satisfaction (66%) and effectiveness (58%) but other properties are also used such as learnability (45%), memorability (23%), cognitive load (19%) and errors (17%). The foremost attribute, efficiency is the ability of a user to complete a task with speed and accuracy. Efficiency is measured in a number of ways, such as the duration spent on each screen, the duration to complete a given task, and a user's error rate [48].

Usability can be assessed by inspection, empirical, or formal methods. Each method has its benefits and costs. In spite of their measurements variability [23], inspection methods such as cognitive walk-through, heuristic evaluation, and thinking-aloud study can be applied at different phases of system development using usability guidelines. Empirical methods which collect user performance measures within an experimental design can allow statistical comparisons of effectiveness, efficiency and satisfaction measures. Empirical methods are the ultimate source of information to determine the usability of a product for a given user population sample. However, empirical methods can be costly to run and need to be performed with near-complete product, or being inserted as a method for continuous evaluation of a product.

Inspection and empirical methods focus on the validation of software features. The issue being addressed by these methods is if a product meets its intended usage. Formal methods, on the other hand, focus on the verification of software features. The issue being addressed is if the product meets its specifications. As a distinction well understood in the area of modelling and simulation, verification and validation are complementary. The objective of formal methods is to determine the presence or absence of properties through a formal analysis of formal specifications of a system to allow a designer to check the conformity of the system to the intended design. Formal methods are essentially applicable to verify the usability of a human-computer interface through its intended effectiveness and efficiency.

Formal methods such as Petri nets, labelled transition systems, modal temporal logic, Z, Lotos have received attention for the design and analysis of human-computer interaction for thirty years [51]. In can even be traced back to the work of Parnas in the early 1960s on transition diagrams for interactive systems design [40]. Formal methods can be used to specify design principles such as reachability, visibility, task completion, and reliability, and can play an important role in the verification and validation of interactive systems.

## 2.2   Workflow

Dix's PIE (Program-Interpretation-Effect) model is the simplest workflow or a human-computer interaction system. Figure 1 shows its elements. The model describes an interactive system in terms of possible inputs, and the observable effect they have. The PIE model considers inputs as a sequence of user-initiated commands (programs). The relation between inputs and outputs is described with an interpretation function. The device executing the function is a black box.

Figure 2 presents an adapted representation of the workflow between a user and a computing artifact from Abowd's thesis [1]. The figure is split between an artifact and a user focus. On the left-hand side, the interface is linked to a model-view-controller entity through control and presentation commands. On

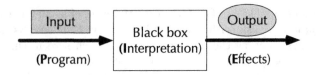

**Fig. 1.** The simplest black-box model [13] - **Programs-Interpretations-Effects**.

the right-hand side, the user is linked to the interface by articulating gestures on the interface and observing their effects. The programs and effects of Fig. 1 are replaced by articulations and observations in Fig. 2. The artifact is no longer a black box. The task element is independent of both the artifact and the user. The figure contains the main elements that need to be taken into account for human-computer interface models: the machine behaviour, the operational goals and task specifications, the model of the machine behaviour by the user, and the interface through which a user acts on the machine and obtains information about the machine states [12]. The artifact behaviour is composed of many internal states and events. However, the interface is an abstraction of the underlying machine behaviour [24]. From this perspective an important aspect of user interface design involves selecting only the relevant machine states information to support a user task execution [24, 26].

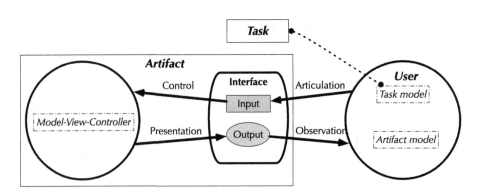

**Fig. 2.** Basic human-computer interaction workflows.

The MVC (Model–View–Controller) paradigm grew out of the Smalltalk programming environment [29]. The MVC model component corresponds to the data processed by the artifact, the view displays data to the user, and the controller converts the user's actions on the interface to commands for the data model or the view [29]. More recently, the classical MVC paradigm has been extended with the Formal Interaction Logic Language (FILL) [50] which adds an interaction layer between the physical representation of the interface (view and controller) and the system interface (system model). The basic architecture of a user interface model assumes a difference between the physical presentation (interaction elements with which the user directly interacts) and the interaction logic of the artifact (data processing between the physical representation and the system to be controlled) [49].

The user entity is composed of a task model, and a model of the artifact. The model of the artifact corresponds to the user understanding of the artifact behaviour. As it will be presented later in the paper, formal HCI models of users do not necessarily have cognitive properties. The task model is meant to capture the implicit and intended model of operations according to the system designer [10]. There is a large body of literature and user interface design methods that are based and require some form of task analysis. The Goals-Methods-Operators-Selection rules (GOMS) [8] for example has had an important impact on formal models of human computer interface. From a design and modelling point of view, it allows to bind task goals to possible methods to attain these goals by using available interface operators. Other task-analytic modelling notations include ConcurTaskTrees [41], and the Enhanced Operator Function Model (EOFM) [3]. Some of the task-oriented methods are concerned with the capture of observable manifestation of human behaviour (task models), while others are concerned with describing the cognitive process that drives the observable human behaviour (cognitive models). An early example of the latter is Norman's seven-stage cycle of interaction: Establish a goal, form the intention, specify the action sequence, execute the action, perceive the system state, interpret the system state, evaluate the system state with respect to the goals and intentions [36].

## 2.3   Interaction Properties

The basic idea behind formal methods is to ignore the hidden states of users (cognitive states) and artifacts (computational states not visible from the interface) and analyze a formal notation that describes the relations between inputs and outputs, as a means to assess the presence or absence of some properties, as the system specifications determine projected paths and transitions between observable effects of user actions [13]. Figure 3 presents an abstract representation of a network of user actions/articulations and perceived observable effects that could be part of a system's user interface specification.

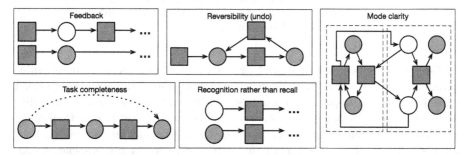

**Fig. 3.** Abstract representation of properties for simple networks of connected user inputs (square blue) - observable effects (red circle) - non-observable state (white circle). (Color figure online)

In Fig. 3, it is possible to see how a formal analysis of specifications of connected articulations and effects could be used to determine if interaction properties are present or not. For example, a system providing:

- *feedback* shall produce an observable state before other user actions are performed;
- *reversibility (undo)* shall allow to go back to a previous state with a sequence of actions;
- *task completeness* shall support attaining a desired observable state (goal) by a sequence of actions from an initial state;
- *recognition* shall give observable cues for facilitating input selection;
- *mode clarity* shall have observable correlates to system internal mode states.

**Table 1.** Examples of formal properties. List built from [5] and [38].

| Reachability | **A state can be reached by performing user actions from an initial state** |
| --- | --- |
| | Total reachability; Strong reachability; Weak reachability; Simple reachability; State avoidability; State inevitability; Accessibility; Availability; Event constraint; Rule set connectedness; Exclusion of commands; Unavoidable interactor |
| Visibility | **Each action is associated with a perceivable effect** |
| | Continuous feedback; Eventual feedback; Existence of messages explaining user errors; Feedback; Reactivity; Visibility; Visibility of system status |
| Task completion | **An action sequence will allow to achieve a goal from an initial state** |
| | Reinitiability; Recoverability; Restartability; Result commutativity; Strong task completeness; Weak task completeness; Succession of commands; Undo within N steps; Undoability; Reversibility |
| Reliability | **From a state, a user can determine that some future states will occur** |
| | Behavioural consistency; Behavioural properties; Consistency of actions; Feature assurance; Determinism; Completeness; Deadlock freedom; Minimum memory load on user; Predictability; Recognition rather than recall; Reliability; Conformity; Robustness; Honesty |

Table 1 presents a list of formal properties that have been used to evaluate human computer interfaces [5, 38]. The formal properties have been grouped under four generic properties: reachability, visibility, task completion, and reliability. Reachability is a generic property of a connected network of articulations and observations where a state can be reached by performing user actions from an initial state. Visibility is the generic property that each action is associated with a perceivable effect. The important user interface guideline to always provide some feedback following a user action falls under this category. Task completion is a generic property of a connected network of articulations and observations where an action sequence will allow to achieve a goal from an initial state. The capability of a system to support reversing the effects of an action (undo) is also an important property of usable human-computer interface. Finally, reliability is the generic property that from a state, a user can determine that some future states will occur. All the properties listed in the table can be determined to hold or not from a formal specification of a human-computer interface as a set of connected user actions and perceivable effects.

## 2.4    Formal Notations

Formal methods use symbolic or graphical notations with well-defined syntax (notation) and semantics (interpretation). Examples of formal specification languages include algebraic data types, process calculi, Petri nets, coloured Petri nets [27], linear logic [18,28], and other formal representation systems [38]. The main interest in formal methods is to be able to determine if some desired system properties are present or not in the specifications without having to run the system [52]. Three main formal methods approaches can be found in HCI: 1) theorem proving, 2) model checking, which verifies if a system model satisfies or not some properties, and 3) equivalence checking which consists of formally proving if two representations of the system exhibit exactly the same behaviour or not [38].

Formal models in HCI are based on a set of states and transitions between states. Human-computer interaction can be formalized as a sequence of state transitions triggered by mixed initiatives from system users or the computer. Petri nets is one formalism that has both a symbolic and a graphical representation [45]. Formal methods in HCI are based on a similar semantics than process mining [45], which is a sequence of timestamps or sequenced events. However, formal methods intend to determine if a sequence model has or not some properties, while process mining is concerned with the relations with system observations either to evaluate the conformance of a model, discover a model, or enhance a model. Human behaviour is not explicitly modelled in any of these techniques, they can only be used to find system conditions theorized to be preconditions to system failures [5]. These models can be expressed in a temporal logic, where the verification of a property consists of exhaustively searching the state spaces to determine if the proposition expressing the property holds [5].

Table 2 presents a set of frequently user temporal logic operator, when applied to a network of connected states and transitions [5]. In this network of states and transitions, time sequence does not need to be represented explicitly because the information is implicit in the state sequence. Another notation that is used in formal HCI models include Labelled Transition Systems for Human–Machine Interactions, which assumes that a command in a mental model of a user corresponds exactly to the same command on the system [31]. The Enhanced Operator Function Model (EOFM) is another possibility where the formalism captures the behaviour of individual humans or, with the EOFM with communications (EOFMC) extension, teams of humans as a collection of tasks, each composed representing a hierarchy of activities and actions [4].

Table 2. Frequently used temporal logic operators [5].

| Operator type | Name | Usage | Interpretation |
|---|---|---|---|
| Path Quantifier | All | **A** $\psi$ | Starting from the current state, all future paths satisfy $\psi$ |
| | Exists | **E** $\psi$ | Starting from the current state, there is at least one path that satisfies $\psi$ |
| Temporal Operator | NeXt | **X** $\psi$ | $\psi$ is true in the next state of a given path |
| | Future | **F** $\psi$ | $\psi$ is eventually true in some future state of a given path |
| | Global | **G** $\psi$ | $\psi$ will always be true in a given path |
| | Until | $\phi$ **U** $\psi$ | $\phi$ will be true until $\psi$ is true for a given path |

## 2.5  Adaptive Human-Computer Interaction

The concept of adaptation is a key concept in many scientific domains such as life and human sciences. The concept has emerged in computer science as a means to address the growing complexity of computer systems. In particular, the insertion of machine learning components in computer systems requires a new approach to adaptive testing for rigorous software engineering, especially on the issue of quality assurance based on adaptation [17]. All fundamental building blocks in human–computer interaction have a control loop component [34]. Looking at the user interface as a form of stimulus-response interaction with the user does not capture the closed-loop dynamic behaviour or human-computer interaction. As the user's skill level increases, or the computer interface changes, the user behaviour will also change [34]. Interactive behaviour for any given artifact-task combination arises from the limits, mutual constraints, and interactions between and among each member of the cognition-artifact-task triad [16,20].

Control loops are also essential for computer program execution, but they are not necessarily adaptive. Many computer programs can appear adaptive on the surface. However, it seems to stretch the concept if any conditional statement in a computer program can be considered adaptive. Bruni et al. provides a simple criterion to identify adaptable and non-adaptable computer systems [7]. The criterion is based on the possibility to identify control data that can affect the system behaviour at run-time. From this perspective, adaptation is defined as the run-time modification of behaviour control data. If no run-time control data can be identified or changed at run time, then the system is not adaptable. Such a distinction should be able to separate the activities relevant for adaptation (those that affect the control data) from those relevant for the application logic only (that should not modify the control data) [7]. From the perspective of human-computer interaction, a possible criterion to qualify for adaptation would be that different users would have a different experience depending on the sequence of actions that they had with a system, and that this experience is a function of a user model being updated in real time. The reference to a user model is key because a random user interface would be different for every user, but it would not be adapting.

According to Murray-Smith [34], an adaptive, and computational interaction should involve at least one of the following characteristics: 1) some means to update a model with observed data from users, 2) an algorithmic element that, using the user model, can directly synthesize or adapt the user interface design; 3) a way of automating and instrumenting the modelling and user interface design process; and 4) the ability to simulate or synthesize elements of the expected user-system behaviour.

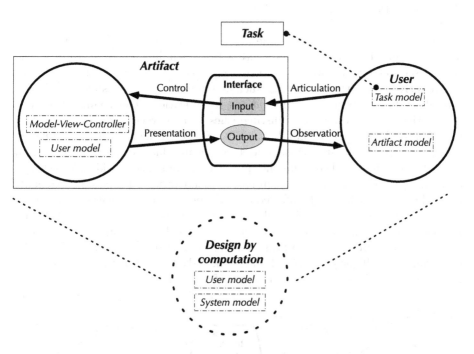

**Fig. 4.** Adaptive human-computer interaction workflows, adding user models to the artifact, and computational optimization of user interface design using human-computer system model.

Figure 4 intends to capture these adaptive characteristics by adding them to the basic HCI workflow of Fig. 2. Two elements are introduced, a model of the user held by the artifact so that elements of the interface can change in real time as a function of user model states. The user model inserted in the artifact is taking care of points #1 and #2 above. The second element is a set of instruments that provide support for the automatic generation of interface designs through combinatorial optimization [39] or simulations using human-interface system models. The "Design by computation" element is taking care of points #3 and #4 listed by Murray-Smith [34].

Design by computation can take the form of mathematical transformation of reconfigurable formal user interface models [49], or be used to propose for example an initial layout of visual elements, which could be optimized by computing an object function such as Fitts' law, and visual perception models, and task performance based on keystroke-level task performance [39]. Cognitive architecture such as ACT-R can be used to explain observed user behaviour given a specific design, and then run as a simulation to explore alternative options [16], or explore the cognitive consequences of different instructional materials [15].

## 3   Adaptive Instructional Systems

The previous sections outlined some key concepts related to the application of formal methods in human-computer interaction, including adaptive systems. The current section aims to situate adaptive instructional system in this context.

Adaptive instructional systems, such as Intelligent Tutor systems (ITS), are typical artificial intelligence applications in education. The common analysis of adaptive instruction systems distinguishes four interacting components: 1) a model of the knowledge or skill domain, 2) a model of the learner(s), 3) a model for the pedagogical interventions, and 4) a user interface to the training system [43]. The domain model contains the specifications of the set of skills, knowledge, and strategies of the topic being tutored; the student model consists of elements of the domain model that are inferred from the performance of learners; the pedagogical model takes the domain and student models as input and selects tutoring strategies, steps, and actions to optimize students' learning, and tutor-student interface model presents and capture student interactions [42]. In addition, if the Generalized Intelligent Tutoring Framework (GIFT) architecture is taken as a reference model for the main components of an adaptive instructional system.

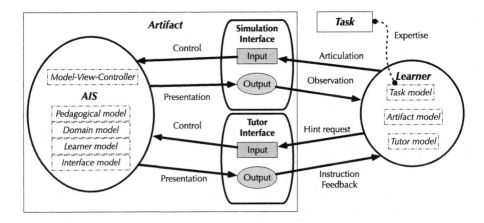

**Fig. 5.** Adaptive instructional system workflows.

Figure 5 presents a workflow view between an adaptive instructional system and a learner. The figure assumes that the instructional system is decoupled from a training simulation. The AIS is composed of the main standard modules. An AIS also provides two interfaces, one for the training simulation and one for the tutor. In this respect, the user is also having a tutor model to represent the tutor communication behaviour. The tutor model is a typical element to consider with intelligent tutoring because of the known strategy of some learners to try to game the system by focusing on the tutor behaviour rather than on learning a task model. As with the HCI work flow, the artifact model corresponds to the operational understanding on how to use the interface.

As with HCI properties presented in Sect. 2.3, there are a number of properties related to sequences of interface articulations or hint requests and observations or instructions that are subject of verification from formal specifications. Table 3 presents a number of properties that could be verified from their presence or not from the formal specification of an instructional system. The property types and examples were taken from Cockburn et al. [9]. The AIS interface model which controls the communication with the learner, being through a graphical interface or using advanced natural language dialogues [37] are both subject to be modelled as a state transition network. Domain models, conceived as leaning scenarios and sequenced material could also be subject to formal analysis to verify is the sequence conforms to the instructional designer intention. HCI formal models could certainly be applied for the validation of systematic design and learning hierarchies which are a commonly advocated tool for designing instructional sequences [32], or for verifying the structural properties that are desirable for a learning flow [47].

**Table 3.** Properties related to pedagogical sequences. From Cockburn et al. [9].

| Property types | Examples |
|---|---|
| Temporal | Feedback is provided either concurrently, immediately after, or delayed from a learner action |
| Aggregation | Feedback is provided independently for each discrete action or accumulated or a sequence of actions (after action review) |
| Modality | Instructions and feedback can be presented as text, speech synthesis, video, or statistics in tabular format |
| Performance | Feedback is provided in terms of deviation to an ideal sequence with no reference to its outcome or results |
| Results | Feedback is provided about the outcome of the action such as success or failure in relation to a desired outcome |

Learner models in adaptive instructional systems address different cognitive properties than user models in HCI. User models in HCI are based on cognitive behaviour related to objective measures of perception and motor behaviour such as Fitts' law, and visual searching, and task performance based on a keystroke-level task performance [39]. Other high levels of cognition related to human-computer interface such as memory and problem-solving strategies can also be addressed with cognitive models. Like objective measures of perception and motor behaviour, cognitive models apply to specific problem condition and tasks.

However, user models in adaptive instructional systems have a larger scope and aim at capturing skills and competencies at a more abstract level. AIS user models include overlay models such as rule space methods, model tracing, and constraint-based models [42]. Overlay models decompose the domain knowledge in small units and provide a programmed path through these units. A user is modelled as a function of the level of mastery achieved in traversing the path. Another of learner model is based on knowledge space theory. In this case the learner models is not based on cognitive structures pre-established like in overlay models but on problem types that are or are not mastered [42]. A student's competence is reflected in the student model as a probabilistic estimate of the types of problems that the student is capable of solving in the domain [42].

Establishing support for links between knowledge components models, learning tasks, learning sequences, and learner's performance can be associated to an instructional system design loop [2]. This loop requires data analysis methods like Bayesian knowledge tracing [11] or additive factor models [30] which rely on assumptions about knowledge components learning curves [19]. When looking at adaptive instructional systems, it is commonly recognized, at least for intelligent tutoring systems, that there are two other loop types [46]: 1) the step loop which provides a response to a learner action within an instructional task mostly in the form of a performance feedback or a hint, and 2) the task loop which provides a learner with a change of task, either to increase or reduce task difficulty depending on the task mastery assessment.

A key principle is that assessment is always a process of reasoning from evidence, with the purpose to assist learning, measure individual and collective achievement, and to evaluate training sequences [35]. This model is articulated with more details in the Evidence Centred Design conceptual assessment framework [33]. The conceptual assessment framework specifies the information needed to perform measurement and assessments. The framework includes a model of learner proficiency, measurement and evaluation models, and a task model linking learners' productions to targeted proficiency [21]. The association between knowledge components and learning tasks is often referred to as a Q-matrix [44], and is particularly important for the evaluation of knowledge components models, and is central to the iterative design of adaptive instructional systems [14]. This level of analysis to determining item difficulty, and learner competencies are key methods for iterative design, at the curriculum level.

## 4    Conclusion

Building reliable interactive systems has been identified as an important and difficult task from the late '60s. One approach to augment the reliability of interactive systems is to use formal models during system development. Formal methods have received attention for the design and analysis of human-computer interaction (HCI) for thirty years. The field of adaptive instructional systems (AIS) in general, and intelligent tutoring systems in particulars, have been mostly relying on empirical methods for training systems validation (the system supports learning), rather than formal methods for verification (the system meets its specifications). Empirical methods focus on the validity of pedagogical interventions at the individual task and problem sequence levels, using learning analytic methods such as Bayesian knowledge tracing, additive factors models, or machine learning models of human performance.

The paper explored some parallel and the applicability of HCI formal models to AIS. Through a series of sections, key concepts related to HCI formal models using semi-formal representations (workflow graphs) were presented. Some properties that could be verified from a network of connected states and transitions were also presented. The paper briefly discussed formal notations, and provided a definition of adaptive human-computer interaction. The last section outlined the similarity between HCI formal models and AIS standard modules, and identified some area of applicability of HCI formal models to AIS design. Human-computer interaction can be formalized as a sequence of state transitions triggered by mixed initiatives from system users or the computer. The conceptual analysis indicated that HCI models have the potential of being applied to AIS models when the underlined structure can be characterized as a network of state transitions. The formal analysis using the HCI methods could be performed early in the design phase to validate steps and tasks loops [46], while another set of learning analytics and machine learning methods support an iterative design.

The purpose of the paper was to explore the applicability of human-computer interaction formal models to adaptive instructional systems, but the exploration remained essentially conceptual and semi-formal, and further investigation is required on specific use cases. Current research activities are seeking to apply HCI formal models to the verification of virtual reality training scenarios.

# References

1. Abowd, G.D.: Formal Aspects of Human-Computer Interaction. University of Oxford, Oxford (1991)
2. Aleven, V., McLaughlin, E.A., Glenn, R.A., Koedinger, K.R.: Instruction based on adaptive learning technologies. In: Mayer, R.E., Alexander, P.A., (eds.) Handbook of Research on Learning and Instruction, Chap. 24, pages 538–576. Routledge, October 2016
3. Bolton, M.L., Siminiceanu, R.I., Bass, E.J.: A systematic approach to model checking human-automation interaction using task analytic models. IEEE Trans. Syst. Man Cybernet. Part A: Syst. Hum. **41**, 961–976 (2011)
4. Bolton, M.L., Bass, E.J.: Enhanced Operator Function Model (EOFM): a task analytic modeling formalism for including human behavior in the verification of complex systems. In: Weyers, B., Bowen, J., Dix, A., Palanque, P. (eds.) The Handbook of Formal Methods in Human-Computer Interaction. HIS, pp. 343–377. Springer, Cham (2017). https://doi.org/10.1007/978-3-319-51838-1_13

5. Bolton, M.L., Bass, E.J., Siminiceanu, R.I.: Using formal verification to evaluate human-automation interaction: a review. IEEE Trans. Syst. Man Cybernet. Syst. **43**(3), 488–503 (2013)
6. Bowen, J., Reeves, S.: Formal models for informal GUI designs. Electron. Not. Theor. Comput. Sci. **183**, 57–72 (2007)
7. Bruni, R., Corradini, A., Gadducci, F., Lluch Lafuente, A., Vandin, A.: A conceptual framework for adaptation. In: de Lara, J., Zisman, A. (eds.) FASE 2012. LNCS, vol. 7212, pp. 240–254. Springer, Heidelberg (2012). https://doi.org/10.1007/978-3-642-28872-2_17
8. Card, S., Moran, T.P., Newell, A.: The Psychology of Human Computer Interaction. Lawrence Erlbaum Associates (1983)
9. Cockburn, A., Gutwin, C., Scarr, J., Malacria, S.: Supporting novice to expert transitions in user interfaces. ACM Comput. Surv. **47**(2), 1–36 (2015)
10. Combefis, S., Giannakopoulou, D., Pecheur, C., Feary, M.: A formal framework for design and analysis of human-machine interaction. In: 2011 IEEE International Conference on Systems, Man, and Cybernetics, pp. 1801–1808. IEEE, October 2011
11. Corbett, A.T., Anderson, J.R.: Knowledge tracing: modeling the acquisition of procedural knowledge. User Modell. User-Adapted Interact. **4**(4), 253–278 (1995)
12. Degani, A., Heymann, M.: Formal verification of human-automation interaction. Hum. Fact. J. Hum. Factors Ergon. Soc. **44**(1), 28–43 (2002)
13. Dix, A.: Formal Methods for Interactive Systems. Academic Press, London (1991)
14. Emond, B.: Learning traces, measurement and assessment templates for AIS interoperability. In: Sottilare, R.A., Schwarz, J. (eds.) HCII 2020. LNCS, vol. 12214, pp. 71–87. Springer, Cham (2020). https://doi.org/10.1007/978-3-030-50788-6_6
15. Emond, B., Comeau, G.: Cognitive modelling of early music reading skill acquisition for piano: a comparison of the Middle-C and Intervallic methods. Cogn. Syst. Res. **24**, 26–34 (2013)
16. Emond, B., West, R.: Cyberpsychology: a human-interaction perspective based on cognitive modeling. Cyberpsychol. Behavi. **6**(5), 527–536 (2003)
17. Gabor, T., et al.: The scenario coevolution paradigm: adaptive quality assurance for adaptive systems. Int. J. Software Tools Technol. Transf. **22**(4), 457–476 (2020)
18. Girard, J.-Y.: Linear logic. Theoret. Comput. Sci. **50**(1), 1–101 (1987)
19. Goldin, I., Pavlik, P.I. , Ritter, S.: Discovering domain models in learning curve data. In: Sottilare, R.A., Graesser, A.C., Hu, X., Olney, A.M., Nye, B.D., Sinatra, A.M. (eds.), Design Recommendations for Intelligent Tutoring Systems: Volume 4 Domain Modeling, pp. 115–126. US Army Research Laboratory, Orlando, FL (2016)
20. Gray, W.D., Altmann, E.M.: Cognitive modeling and human-computer interaction. In: Karwowski, W. (ed.) International Encyclopedia of Ergonomics and Human Factors, pp. 387–391. Taylor & Francis Ltd, New York (2001)
21. Hao, J., Mislevy, R.J.: The evidence trace file: a data structure for virtual performance assessments informed by data analytics and evidence-centered design. Technical report 1, Education Testing Services, December 2018
22. Harrison, M.D., Masci, P., Campos, J.C.: Formal modelling as a component of user centred design. In: Mazzara, M., Ober, I., Salaün, G. (eds.) STAF 2018. LNCS, vol. 11176, pp. 274–289. Springer, Cham (2018). https://doi.org/10.1007/978-3-030-04771-9_21
23. Hertzum, M., Jacobsen, N.E.: The evaluator effect: a chilling fact about usability evaluation methods. Int. J. Hum. Comput. Interact. **15**(1), 183–204 (2003)

24. Heymann, M., Degani, A.: Formal analysis and automatic generation of user interfaces: approach, methodology, and an algorithm. Hum. Fact. J. Hum. Fact. Ergon. Soc 49(2), 311–330 (2007)
25. ISO/IEC 25010: Systems and software engineering - Systems and software Quality Requirements and Evaluation (SQuaRE) - System and software quality models (2011)
26. Janlert, L.-E., Stolterman, E.: Things That Keep Us Busy. The MIT Press, Cambridge (2017)
27. Jensen, K., Kristensen, L.M.: Coloured Petri Nets. Springer, Heidelberg (2009). https://doi.org/10.1007/b95112
28. Kanovich, M.I.: Petri nets, Horn programs, Linear Logic and vector games. Ann. Pure Appl. Logic 75(1–2), 107–135 (1995)
29. Krasner, G.E., Pope, S.T.: A description of the model-view-controller user interface paradigm in the smalltalk-80 system. J. Object-Orient. Program. 1(3), 26–49 (1988)
30. Martin, B., Mitrovic, A., Koedinger, K.R., Mathan, S.: Evaluating and improving adaptive educational systems with learning curves. User Model. User-Adapt. Interact. 21(3), 249–283 (2011)
31. Maudoux, G., Pecheur, C., Combéfis, S.: Learning safe interactions and full-control. In: Weyers, B., Bowen, J., Dix, A., Palanque, P. (eds.) The Handbook of Formal Methods in Human-Computer Interaction. HIS, pp. 297–317. Springer, Cham (2017). https://doi.org/10.1007/978-3-319-51838-1_11
32. McEneaney, J.E.: Simulation-based evaluation of learning sequences for instructional technologies. Instruct. Sci. 44(1), 87–106 (2016)
33. Mislevy, R.J., Steinberg, L.S., Almond, R.G.: On the structure of educational assessments. Measur. Inter-disciplinary Res. Perspect. 1, 3–67 (2003)
34. Murray-Smith, R.: Control theory, dynamics, and continuous interaction. In: Oulasvirta, A., Kristensson, P.O., Bi, X., Howes, A. (eds.) Computational Interaction, Chap. 1, pp. 17–41. Oxford University Press (2018)
35. National Research Council: Knowing What Students Know: The Science and Design of Educational Assessment. National Academy Press, Washington, DC (2001)
36. Norman, D.A.: Cognitive engineering. In: Norman, D.A., Draper, S.W. (eds.) User centered system design: New perspectives on human-computer interaction, page 32–65. Lawrence Erlbaum, Mahwah (1986)
37. Nye, B.D., Graesser, A.C., Xiangen, H.: AutoTutor and family: a review of 17 years of natural language tutoring. Int. J. Artif. Intell. Educ. 24(4), 427–469 (2014)
38. Oliveira, R., Palanque, P., Weyers, B., Bowen, J., Dix, A.: State of the art on formal methods for interactive systems. In: Weyers, B., Bowen, J., Dix, A., Palanque, P. (eds.) The Handbook of Formal Methods in Human-Computer Interaction. HIS, pp. 3–55. Springer, Cham (2017). https://doi.org/10.1007/978-3-319-51838-1_1
39. Oulasvirta, A., Dayama, N.R., Shiripour, M., John, M., Karrenbauer, A.: Combinatorial optimization of graphical user interface designs. Proc. IEEE 108(3), 434–464 (2020)
40. Parnas, D.L.: On the use of transition diagrams in the design of a user interface for an interactive computer system. In: Proceedings of the 1969 24th National Conference on -, New York, New York, USA, 1969, pp. 379–385. ACM Press (1969)
41. Paterno, F., Mancini, C., Meniconi, S.: ConcurTaskTrees: a diagrammatic notation for specifying task models. In: International Conference Human-Computer Interaction, pp. 362–369 (1997)

42. Pavlik, P.I., Brawner, K.W., Olney, A., Mitrovic, A.: A review of learner models used in intelligent tutoring systems. In: Sottilare, R.A., Graesser, A., Hu, X., Holden, H. (eds.) Design Recommendations for Intelligent Tutoring Systems. Volume 1: Learner Modeling, vol. 1, pages 39–68. US Army Research Laboratory (2013)

43. Sottilare., R.A.: Developing standards for adaptive instructional systems: 2018 update. In: Proceedings of the 6th Annual GIFT Users Symposium, Orlando, FL, 2018, pp. 1–5. U.S. Army Research Laboratory (2018)

44. Tatsuoka, K.K.: Rule space: an approach for dealing with misconceptions based on item response theory. J. Educ. Measur. **20**(4), 345–354 (1983)

45. van der Aalst, W.M.P.: Process Mining: Discovery, Conformance and Enhancement of Business Processes. Springer-Verlag, Heidelberg (2011). https://doi.org/10.1007/978-3-642-19345-3

46. Vanlehn, K.: The behavior of tutoring systems. Int. J. Artif. Intell. Ed. **16**(3), 227–265 (2006)

47. Vidal, J.C., Lama, M., Bugarín, A.: Petri net-based engine for adaptive learning. Expert Syst. Appl. **39**(17), 12799–12813 (2012)

48. Weichbroth, P.: Usability of mobile applications: a systematic literature study. IEEE Access **8**, 55563–55577 (2020)

49. Weyers, B.: Formal description of adaptable interactive systems based on reconfigurable user interface models. In: Weyers, B., Bowen, J., Dix, A., Palanque, P. (eds.) The Handbook of Formal Methods in Human-Computer Interaction. HIS, pp. 273–294. Springer, Cham (2017). https://doi.org/10.1007/978-3-319-51838-1_10

50. Weyers, B.: Visual and formal modeling of modularized and executable user interface models. In: Weyers, B., Bowen, J., Dix, A., Palanque, P. (eds.) The Handbook of Formal Methods in Human-Computer Interaction. HIS, pp. 125–160. Springer, Cham (2017). https://doi.org/10.1007/978-3-319-51838-1_5

51. Weyers, B., Bowen, J., Dix, A., Palanque, P. (eds.): The Handbook of Formal Methods in Human-Computer Interaction. HIS, Springer, Cham (2017). https://doi.org/10.1007/978-3-319-51838-1

52. Wing, J.M.: A specifier's introduction to formal methods. Computer **23**(9), 8–22 (1990)

# Automating Team Competency Assessment in Support of Adaptive Dynamic Simulations

Jeremiah Folsom-Kovarik[1]([✉]), Anne M. Sinatra[2], and Robert A. Sottilare[1] [ID]

[1] Soar Technology, Inc., Orlando, FL, USA
{jeremiah,bob.sottilare}@soartech.com
[2] US Army Combat Capabilities Development Command Soldier Center (DEVCOM-SC),
Simulation and Training Technology Center (STTC), Orlando, FL, USA

**Abstract.** Team training in online, simulated environments can improve teamwork skills and task performance skills in a team setting. Teamwork assessment often relies on human observers. Instructors, team leaders, or other observers typically assess complex team competencies using checklists of observed behavior markers to infer performance. Automation can reduce training bottlenecks, provide evidence for objective assessment, and increase the impact of team training. A software capability is being developed to automate team assessments in dynamic online simulations. The simulations are dynamic to the extent that team actions and performance can change the progression of simulation events, assessment context, and the expected behavior of individuals contributing to team performance. A goal of automation design is to enhance usability for non-technical personnel to select, configure, reuse, and interpret team assessments in dynamic simulations. As a result of the reusable design, the assessments can generalize across different simulation software, settings, and scenarios. This paper describes work in progress on the research and development of an automated team assessment capability for the US Army's Generalized Intelligent Framework for Tutoring (GIFT), an open source adaptive instructional architecture.

**Keywords:** Adaptive instruction · Automated assessment · Team training

## 1 Introduction

The U.S. Army's Generalized Intelligent Framework for Tutoring (GIFT) is an adaptive instructional software architecture [1] that can be used to monitor behaviors and provide feedback based on the real-time performance of teams. While GIFT is primarily used in military training domains, it has also can be highly versatile in supporting education and training in a variety of domains (e.g., simulation based team tasks, problem solving or psychomotor tasks). GIFT is in a category of learning technologies called adaptive instructional systems (AISs), "computer-based systems that guide learning experiences by tailoring instruction and recommendations based on the goals, needs, and preferences of each learner [or team] in the context of domain learning objectives" [2].

GIFT is also compatible or interoperable with team training environments including simulations and serious games, such as Virtual Battle Space 3 (VBS3). VBS3 is one

© Springer Nature Switzerland AG 2021
R. A. Sottilare and J. Schwarz (Eds.): HCII 2021, LNCS 12792, pp. 199–214, 2021.
https://doi.org/10.1007/978-3-030-77857-6_13

simulation in which teams train together in a shared synthetic environment that represents a geographic area or terrain archetype (e.g., jungle, mountains, desert). With GIFT and VBS3, Soldiers can practice infantry maneuvers and tactics while their performance is continuously assessed against a set of Intelligent Tutoring System (ITS) author defined team performance objectives.

The GIFT team functional resilience (TFR) project aims to research and develop usable methods and technology enhancements that support automated team assessments within GIFT where GIFT is coupled with a team training simulation or serious game. Team functional resilience is a complex team cognition precursor for teams whose members provide heterogeneous individual functions interdependently to achieve team performance goals [3]. The ability to continue the mission in the face of missing functionality, such as when one team member underperforms or is otherwise compromised, can be described as functional resilience. Automating assessment of team functional resilience will enable GIFT to give teams immediate, objective, and adaptive feedback.

GIFT includes a tool, GameMaster, that lets human observers view real-time performance of a team of learners as they train within the VBS3 world [4]. GameMaster shows the state of automated assessments, and also prompts observers to determine and record learner progress toward defined, non-automated competencies.

In addition to human observation with GameMaster, GIFT provides a framework for conditions that can be authored, and automate assessment by monitoring activity within VBS3 on a second-by-second basis and interpreting behavior observations according to configurable conditions and rules. Adding automation to simulation-based training systems can enhance assessment by providing objective evidence to support assessments, weighting and prioritizing findings, and lightening the load on observers when critical events happen quickly or in different parts of the simulation. Automated assessments in GIFT can initiate real-time adaptive interventions (e.g., feedback or changes to scenario difficulty) or structure feedback for team-focused after-action review (AAR).

To automate assessment for TFR in a training simulation, we identified three primary research and development objectives:

- Research and develop a methodology to measure and assess individual contributions to overall team performance, identifying functional compromise and recovery
- Research and develop a scalable, reusable model of team performance that can be used in various contexts and for individuals of varying competencies
- Research and develop a methodology to support dynamic assignment of team roles and responsibilities as the simulation state changes during training execution

As a result of automating team assessments with reusable definitions, data structures, and dynamic roles, GIFT can enhance human observations in team training. In the current state of development, automated assessments generate an adaptive AAR document. The document structures observed performance markers in relation to team skills so that instructors or team leaders can lead concrete, comprehensive discussions with learners. In the future, automated assessments in GIFT can also drive immediate feedback such as adaptive simulation changes. Additionally, if authored, simulation events and character behaviors can be adjusted in real time to adapt the challenge of the training and to target specific team members or relationships. The contributions described will make these adaptations more applicable in adaptive dynamic training simulations. Next, we describe the GIFT architecture and how GIFT can stimulate low-adaptive simulations and serious games like VBS3 to provide more adaptive instructional interventions. Low adaptive systems only accommodate differences in the learner's in-situ performance during training and do not consider the impact of other factors (e.g., motions, prior knowledge, goal-orientation, or motivation) that influence learning. Subsequent sections of this paper describe team assessment in theory and in practice, the research and development contributions of the GIFT TFR project to automated assessment capabilities, and recommended next steps for assessment of teams in adaptive instructional contexts. The implications of this research are focused on GIFT but are far reaching in their influence on the design of all instructional systems, adaptive or not. There is a growing focus on collaborative learning in pre-K, K-12, adult learning and in military organizations. Collaborative learning is an instructional approach "in which two or more people learn or attempt to learn something together" [5]. This is an important approach, not just because of its effectiveness, but also because of its alignment with how people tend to work together in teams. Team-based tutoring systems should be easily deployed and used to reflect how prevalent teams are in the workplace.

## 2   Overview of GIFT

As noted above, GIFT is an adaptive instructional architecture that supports authoring, real-time instructional management and experimentation processes. GIFT's authoring capabilities include a drag-and-drop interface that uses configurable course objects (e.g., media, adaptive courseflow, conversation trees, authored branches and practice environments) [6]. Practice environments are ready-made interfaces to simulations like VBS, unity-based environments, and compatible learning management systems (e.g., Blackboard, Canvas, edX). Courses built using GIFT can also be used to guide and support experimentation experiences, but the key functions of GIFT exist in its real-time instructional management processes which are governed by a modular architecture (Fig. 1). GIFT's tools allow for content from different domains to be authored, which allows for GIFT to support the creation of tutors that are not tied to one specific topic.

GIFT uses data from sensors and other learner interactions to infer the states (e.g., learning, performance, emotions) of individual learners and teams. These learner states are used by the pedagogical module to select strategies and recommendations which are passed to the domain module where they are evaluated in context to determine the next actions by the tutor [8]. Context is the set of defined conditions under which the team performs their assigned tasks and includes the state of the environment and the team at any given time. It is important to note that the relevance of any AIS interventions is context-dependent. For example, feedback provided under one set of conditions may not be as relevant under another set of conditions. Artificial Intelligence (AI) plays a critical role in determining optimal interventions. Since it would be tedious to explicitly author an intervention for every possible condition of the team and the mission environment, AI is often used to weigh and infer the best available alternatives.

The gateway module provides a standard interface to facilitate the exchange of data with external simulations. This is of importance when the basis of automated assessment

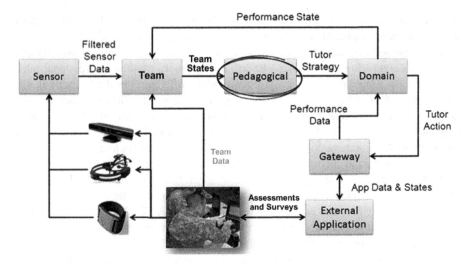

**Fig. 1.** GIFT Real-time Instructional Architecture [7]

is interaction data of team members within an external simulation (e.g., VBS3). Next, we discuss details of sourcing measures of assessment and producing recommended interventions in both low-adaptive systems and AISs.

## 3  Overview of Team Dimensional Training

GIFT is being enhanced with experimental software to operationalize team assessment using Team Dimensional Training (TDT). First introduced to structure military team assessment and feedback, TDT provides a model of team process and performance that enables assessing teams or identifying the ways expert teams differ from less expert teams [9, 10]. A contribution of the work described herein is to show how TDT dimensions can be defined and assessed in a general manner within a software system. Operationalizing TDT enables GIFT to automate team assessments and provide feedback in the form of a more detailed structured AAR.

A full description of TDT is available in the above references. In summary, the TDT model describes antecedents of teamwork, such as team processes and attitudes that fall within four dimensions. The four dimensions derived from Salas' 7 Cs [11] are:

- Communication, or the clarity and form of delivering information
- Information exchange, or choosing what information to share, when, and to whom
- Supporting behavior, or helping another accomplish a task
- Leadership, or the initiative of any team member to provide guidance to the team

In context of GIFT, the work to describe how each TDT dimension is expressed in a particular team task or domain typically requires subject matter expertise. However, connecting domain-specific assessments to TDT dimensions enables finding trends in team processing and identifying opportunities to improve underlying, process-level team function. Assessment that focuses only on specific observed behaviors might be hard for the team to generalize beyond the task at hand, but using those behaviors as input to assess the TDT dimensions gives the team a way to improve that can impact all team tasks.

Within TDT, team functional resilience may be considered to draw on all four dimensions. A critical dimension in team resilience is the supporting behavior of the tutor [12]. Individuals can make the team resilient to functional loss by preventing or reducing a loss, such as helping a person when their function becomes compromised, or by correcting the loss and taking over a function from a teammate. Furthermore, proper communication and information exchange help the team to recognize a threat to performance. Leadership is involved when individuals take steps before a compromise to avoid it, like appropriately dividing tasks or reminding each other of procedure.

Defining how to assess TDT dimensions is associated with a structured approach to observing and measuring trainee responses that is intended to increase inter-rater reliability for human instructors or observers of training. Targeted Acceptable Responses to Generated Events or Tasks (TARGETs) are a checklist of correct and possible incorrect trainee responses created with a task analysis in advance of training [13]. However, TARGETs require authoring effort to define, and effort during training execution to collect data [14]. Therefore, an opportunity exists to automate assessments with AI methods that build on TARGETs.

## 4   Team Assessment in Practice

In this section, we discuss the general role of analysis, evaluation and assessment in adaptive instruction. We also describe operational concepts for both manual and automated adaptive team assessments to compare and contrast the current state of practice for training with our proposed and emerging state of practice. This provides both an understanding of the training process and highlights the importance of team assessment in the training process.

### 4.1   Analysis, Evaluation and Assessment in Adaptive Instruction

At this point, we review the role of *analysis* and *evaluation* in the training development, reuse, and sustainment process and the role of assessment in the real-time instruction process. Often the terms analysis, evaluation and assessment are used interchangeably, but they have different roles in the team instructional process. The ADDIE process model [15] describes five stages (analysis, design, development, implementation and evaluation) in the development and continuous improvement of instruction. The analysis stage within ADDIE focuses on understanding the goal of the team training and how it will improve the team's capabilities, capacity, productivity and performance of one or more tasks [16]. Training increases the knowledge and skills needed to reach a required level of competence. Once the analysis stage is completed, the design process can begin and subsequently, the instructional system can be developed and deployed. The evaluation stage of the ADDIE process provides a structured method to improve the instruction.

The real-time part of the ADDIE process is the *implementation stage* [15]. In an adaptive instructional context, the implementation stage includes real-time management and execution of training. Training management refers to selecting and configuring training simulations and scenarios that meet learners' needs. Training management motivates reusability in assessment design, so that assessment is not locked to a specific scenario and does not increase the cost of authoring scenario changes. During training execution, the team is exposed to an experience or scenario intended to exercise the required knowledge and skills according to a set of defined training objectives. Team performance may be assessed at various points in the training scenario though observation and then the instructor (human or computer) uses that assessment to intervene (e.g., provide feedback or change the difficulty of the task). Assessments may also be used to determine competency and recommend future training experiences.

Assessment refers to observing and measuring performance, then comparing it to a standard for learners given the simulated conditions [15]. Many instructional systems today assess performance in order to infer learners' progress toward training objectives. However, in contrast to expert human instructors, most computer training systems only adapt the instruction based on triggers in the observed performance rather than based on the resulting inferences [17, 18]. Also, little consideration is given to the estimation of other individual differences (e.g., emotions) and their impact on desired training outcomes. Adaptive training systems offer an opportunity to use assessments instead of simple triggers in selecting interventions like immediate feedback messages, AAR, tailored simulation events, or training progression versus remediation.

Recapping, analysis is a pre-instructional process, evaluation is a post-instructional process and assessment is a real-time instructional process. Good assessment can inform training evaluation by quantifying training effectiveness in relation to the original analysis and design, targeting specific training objectives and learner audiences. Now that we understand these differences, our next step is to evaluate current manual team training concepts and then analyze how current team training concepts might be improved through automation.

### 4.2 Operational Process for Manual Team Assessment

As noted above, the real-time team training process involves immersion of the team in a relevant experience, assessment of progress toward defined training objectives, and selection of appropriate interventions to provide feedback and maintain engagement. Assessment in today's military training systems is largely a manual process. For example, live training exercises typically depend on human observers who assess when or if a required action is completed and whether that action was timely. Checklists for mission scenarios are a common assessment tool, but completing the checklist is not always an accurate measure of performance or knowledge/skill acquisition, and requires a good deal of attention from the observer.

It is even more difficult for a human observer to assess training during a scenario in a simulated environment, as there are many different computers/views to observe. In order to move toward personalized assessment and feedback, ITS frameworks such as GIFT can be leveraged to incorporate real-time automated assessment into the simulations. For virtual simulations and serious games (e.g., VBS3), predetermined sequences of events are used to infer whether the individual or team successfully completed the training mission, but AARs are usually manually built for each domain by comparing the expected and actual events in the simulation. In other words, manual authoring processes provide data to support prescriptive assessments. This prescriptive process is limiting in that it is not always apparent to users other than the author (e.g., subject matter experts) how the objectives of the training were met by scenario conditions or trainee performance.

Compared to manual processes, automation of authoring processes may offer additional flexibility by making the relationship between learning objectives, scenario conditions and trainee behaviors more apparent than any prescriptive approach. Automation may also provide increased transparency to authors and learners by highlighting learner behaviors that were not explicitly identified as measures of assessment, but nonetheless influenced the team's successful performance.

### 4.3 Operational Process for Automated Team Assessment

The goal of automating team assessment is to reduce the human resources required to conduct training exercises, but also to offer additional flexibility and evidentiary power for inferring team states. If the data is available to support automated team assessment, then the automated approach can be a significant improvement over any manual assessment process. Automated processes using AI also offer the advantage of inferring team states without a comprehensive set of data, generalizing to work in situations that have not been predetermined at design time. However, acquiring behavioral and physiological data to support team state inference is an important phase of the ADDIE analysis process.

Next, we discuss how the automated assessment process might work in an operational context. As noted, the essential real-time elements of team training include an immersive experience, rigorous and accurate assessment, and selection of interventions to optimize learning outcomes. In one-to-one tutoring processes, a human or computer-based tutor would test the learner's knowledge of the domain and adapt the instruction to the capability of the learner with the goal of fulfilling a set of learning objectives.

In a team tutoring context, the adaptive tutor does the same, but the operational process for automated team assessment is multi-dimensional. The adaptive team tutor must be able to:

- Understand the goal of the training and its associated objectives
- Consider the competency, performance, learning and emotional states of individual members of the team to explain observations and inform training interventions
- Understand the state of the training and recognize trainees' behaviors as inputs to measurement and assessment
- Infer taskwork states (progress toward training objectives) periodically throughout the training process and respond with appropriate interventions
- Infer the competency of the team from the competency of the individual members
- Infer teamwork states (e.g., cohesion, leadership) periodically throughout the training process and respond with appropriate interventions
- Evaluate the accuracy of team and individual learner state classification and the efficacy of its intervention decisions in order to reinforce AIS learning with each experience

To maintain an accurate operational picture of the team and its members, the adaptive team tutor must be able to source data to support the AI methods employed in the automated assessment process. In the next section, we discuss how our project addresses or plans to address these data, AI and adaptive team tutoring requirements.

# 5    Research and Design Contributions to Automated Assessment

This section discusses the team assessment process and approaches to address three primary research and development challenges in automated team assessment:

- Capturing how each individual on a team contributes to team assessments
- Developing a scalable data structure to describe team performance that can be generalized across a variety of team tasks and domains (e.g., cognitive, psychomotor)
- Assigning team roles and responsibilities dynamically during scenario execution
- Together these contributions make automation more capable, scalable, and reusable for team assessments.

## 5.1    The Role of AI in Automated Assessment

First, we discuss approaches to automated assessment of teams. Automation that does not require AI might include defining metrics and bounds that quantify good or poor performance. These can make assessment more objective and reduce workload. However, they typically focus on performance outcomes, with the link to underlying reasons for the outcomes either missing or implicit (rather than transparently modeled and shown to users). They are also likely to be tied to the specifics of a scenario. If the definitions of good performance depend on context or on interactions between several factors, then simple assessments can be costly to create and difficult to update for reuse in new or changing scenarios.

An alternative is to use AI methods to collect data and context from available sources and infer progress toward assigned objectives. AI is better able to handle states that were not implicitly defined, and AI is better able to infer states even with incomplete datasets. We include in the set of AI approaches both authored and machine-learned models of good behavior that can assess complex interactions or context that arise in team training settings.

Several capable approaches have been demonstrated in GIFT. One example demonstrated automated team assessment by applying the same structures used for an individual learner to a team, thus considering the team to be a single and separate entity for training purposes [19, 20]. Another example went in the opposite direction, creating numerous team entities to evaluate the interactions between all possible combinations of individuals [21, 22]. GIFT offers multiple ways to define and assess teamwork, and the contributions described here structure the assessments in a way intended to make them expressive without high authoring effort, and reusable across training domains.

We have previously described an initial implementation of the present work with a focus on operationalizing TDT in a specific team training scenario [3]. The initial implementation occurred within VBS3 and GIFT, and in it, a team of four infantry carried out a mission with injected events that could compromise team functions. We used TDT to assess team functional resilience and provide adaptive, prioritized support for AAR of the four contributing dimensions. We next present updated information about how AI is making team assessment more reusable for additional scenarios and larger teams.

## 5.2   Capturing Individual Contributions to Team Performance

One challenge in automated assessment is identifying individual contributions to team performance. Examples include identifying when individuals coordinate actions, divide work, fail to provide an expected function, and support each other by taking on a team-mate's functions. Compared to assessing team performance as if the team were a mono-lithic entity, tracking individual contributions requires more work to define all the details to observe during training. Flexible, reusable, scalable definitions of performance and the behavior markers of team competency (Fig. 2) can help reduce this workload. The definitions should be reusable on several levels – enabling changes in the specific scenario events and context, the simulation software, and the instructional domain. While ultimate generality is available in GIFT by making changes in the underlying code, generality of the tools available to non-technical users is also possible. Approaches to let instructors and other observers see how individuals contribute to team performance include identifying the high-level goals of team assessment, organizing and expressing them in ways instructors and other observers use, and reconfiguring parameters automatically without requiring user effort.

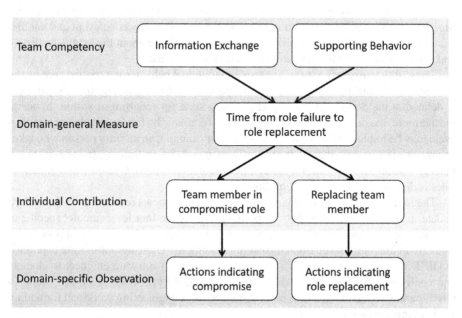

**Fig. 2.** Structure for reusable definitions of team competencies, measures, and observations.

Figure 2 shows four levels of abstraction (rows) that define team assessments in a way that aligns with instructor usage and that AI can reuse across scenarios. At the highest level of abstraction, team competencies from the TDT dimensions categorize all the available assessments and express expert knowledge of what factors the measures load on. Measures, in the second row, are domain-general in the sense that the same measure can be reused in many training domains, from infantry tactical training to workplace decision-making or government crisis response. In order to advance the goal of reusability, the measures are expressed in terms of individual contributions to the team. The structure of the team model (next section) allows domain-general descriptions of the individual contributions that contribute to the measure. For example, to help assess team functional resilience competencies, we would like to measure the time between one team member being compromised and another team member taking corrective action. Then, the required domain-specific knowledge can be filled in with model elements at the bottom row of the figure. For each training domain, we need to define the observations that indicate a compromised function and the observations that indicate corrective action took place.

The generality and reusability of the structure in Fig. 2 is enhanced by defining roles and responsibilities. Roles and responsibilities are concepts that can be reused at all levels of abstraction, tying into domain-specific definitions that capture the specific functionality a team needs in each training domain. They are modeled in our current implementation as follows.

Team members can each have multiple roles. Roles are flexible enough to describe facts about an individual's job specialization, rank in a hierarchy, current knowledge, or actions performed. For example, during training a person who reports an event might be assigned the role of reporter. This example provides an opportunity to assess team functional resilience. If one team member was expected to report an event and another team member actually did, it is likely that we have evidence about the team's resilience and about the two individual contributions to that resilience.

The ability to express expectations about individual behavior is supplied here by the concept of a responsibility. For example, the person who has knowledge of a critical event is defined at the domain-general level as responsible for reporting it within the team. Furthermore, the domain-specific details that determine who has knowledge of a critical event may be implemented using roles again. For example, an infantry person who takes enemy fire is in a role that is dynamically assigned during training (taking fire), and that role carries the responsibility to communicate information. Dynamic assignment of roles is described in the last part of this section.

The four levels of abstraction in defining team assessments reduce the work required to determine individual contributions because three of the four levels are not specific to the instructional domain and can be reused. It is also possible to create opportunities for reuse in the fourth level, domain-specific definitions. These definitions are expressed in GIFT as a combination of Java code, which requires a software engineer to change, and configuration parameters, which can be changed by instructors or end users. In GIFT, parameterization is a best practice that reduces engineering workload for adding or changing scenarios.

In addition, the present work links some parameters at the domain-specific level to be filled with roles and responsibilities. As a result, values for those parameters can be set automatically by events during training and do not need to be configured by humans. The workload on instructors and end users is reduced, and the automated assessments are hypothesized to be reusable in more training scenarios.

In conclusion, training that only assesses team outcomes will miss diagnostic characteristics of how the overall performance was achieved. The same overall mission success is different if one person carried the team or if the team effectively divided duties. Defining the importance of individual contributions to team performance and competency in a generalizable way with a reusable structure creates advantages when authoring assessments. The advantage of concrete feedback that includes objective examples during the AAR (post training) enables the traceability of individual behaviors that are markers of team states and objective team competencies.

### 5.3 Implementing a Scalable Model for Team Assessment

A second challenge is structuring a scalable model for assessing larger teams. The team assessment data structure should enable describing how any team members interact in pairs or larger groups. However, creating explicit data for every possible combination would create an exponential explosion in data size and sustainment effort. Team roles and responsibilities create a more scalable data structure to calculate and record team assessments. Model structures we introduce to GIFT efficiently define expert behavior and simulation events, enabling assessment at scale (Fig. 3).

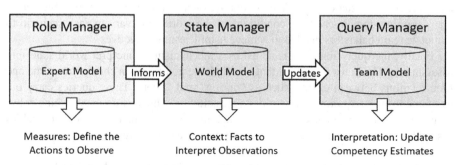

**Fig. 3.** Roles and responsibilities inform how observations update team assessments.

The coloring of Fig. 3 suggests how implementation aligns with the four levels in Fig. 2. Referring to Fig. 1, these components are implemented within the domain module of GIFT and operate on inputs from the training via the gateway module. Adding them makes team assessment possible to code and configure efficiently.

First, the role manager defines what team roles exist and, for roles that change during training, how they can be recognized. The expert model links roles to responsibilities in the sense described above. As a result, the expert model informs the selection of what facts about the simulated world have value to monitor. During training execution, the role manager reads from the world model to update current role assignments.

Second, the world state manager facilitates storing and sharing information about the training simulation. The world state manager defines what facts about the world are needed to make assessments. When those facts are updated in messages from the simulator, their current values are maintained in a shared world model. The world model has also been called a working memory because it defines a subset of facts that are salient and relates those facts to each other with semantic relationships. For example, if an enemy fires at an infantry team, the simulation will send a message with the spatial coordinates of the shot. The world model can transform the location into a relationship that has semantic meaning, such as the shot was close to a certain team member.

In addition to storing facts with semantic meaning, the world model is also the facility for adding context needed for assessment. When the enemy fires at a person and that person communicates the information, context helps assess the correctness of the behavior. For example, if this is the first shot or the first report of enemy fire, the assessment of team information sharing is likely to be more positive than if there has already been a prolonged firefight. So, another benefit of the shared world model is as a store for facts about past events and for connecting events, rather than operating directly on inputs from the simulator. The logic to record past events could be stored without a world model, such as within the code for specific assessments, but the world model enables encapsulating knowledge about the world separately from interpretation, such as assessment. As a result of the encapsulation, there is no duplication of code needed to layer new assessments on the world model and no updates across the codebase needed to change a definition such as the distance where a shot counts as "close."

Each world model contains information specific to the training domain under instruction. The design decision to impose a world model aids in organizing observable facts and structure as a shared state. This infers that world models may be reusable across many training domains and the conditions of the world may vary in each scenario to stimulate team behaviors needed to achieve team learning objectives.

Finally, the query manager is added as a mechanism to interpret world state into assessments. The kinds of queries that are implemented focus on change over time and time relations between events, such as "during" and "after." These queries carry out assessment by interpreting the world state, including who was assigned which roles, at any given time. The current focus on tracking time and changes over time enables assembling a timeline during AAR which points learners to recorded examples from their training.

The query manager can update the team model at different levels based on the defined measures. For example, a binary measure that records the time between a functional loss and a corrective action would have two individuals who are updated as well as the overall team. To specifically avoid the explosion of all possible relationships between individuals as teams grow larger, the team model is sparse and only records roles and relationships between roles that have measures defined.

The key benefit of the models and components to manage them is the scalability for use with larger teams. The data structures also do not limit the complexity of scenarios and performance that may be observed, which typically need to be complex for effective team training. The design is also intended to increase code encapsulation and ease of encoding measures that are reusable because they work without recoding in more contexts. Finally, reusability across scenarios can be increased if these models are expressive enough to capture doctrine in a code library and automate assessments with reduced authoring needed. So, if future testing in new scenarios and instructional domains succeeds, the design of the scalable models will also increase reusability.

## 5.4  Assigning Team Roles and Responsibilities Dynamically

A third challenge is dynamic role assignment, allowing the roles and responsibilities in the team definitions and team model to change during the execution of training. Context-specific changes allow assessment to work flexibly when different learners can take on different functions within the team. Functional changes are important indicators of team competencies at a high level of abstraction which can therefore be used across many simulations. As examples, a team leader can assign team members to tasks with an optimal or suboptimal balance of responsibilities. Alternatively, as personnel recognize functions that might be missing in the team, their responses or divided attention can suggest characteristics of a team process like trust. Next, changing information within the simulation can help assess complex team cognitive competencies like information sharing and shared situational awareness. Finally, automated assessments also need dynamic roles for optimal reusability across scenarios. The assessments should avoid assumptions about which team member will have information or will take on tasks, in order to work in many possible paths through a simulation.

The baseline for team role assignment is configuring the assignments at the start of training, when the instructor who wanted the training fills in all details (examples of details could be: this person is the highest ranking, this person has medic skills, this person is the one carrying the special equipment). Clearly there are limits to what instructors can assign in advance. For example, in the infantry a squad might have one person with medic skills, but all the team members have first aid skills and the choice of who needs to help an injured person before the medic can get there might depend on who is closest. Similarly, it is not natural to assign roles like which person will go through a door first and who will go second. In current practice, instructors do assign these roles when they configure training, but the training would be more flexible and require less instructor workload if that assignment could be automated.

The process of making role assignment dynamic and automating the assignment leverages the expert role model and the world state model, both described above. The expert model separates roles from responsibilities, but it also maps in the other direction so that responsibilities met can tell what roles a trainee is undertaking. As a result, the corrective actions that involve taking on a teammate's function to keep the team going can be detected using the expert model. The other part of the equation is the world model. One of its key functions is to interpret raw data from the simulation environment, like trainee locations in the world, into semantically meaningful labels. The world state is therefore the place to look for information like who is closest to the injured person and who entered a door second.

Again, properly interpreting the meaningful facts that are added to the world state is specific to the training domain, but their definitions can allow for greater or lesser generality and reuse with proper implementation. For example, a rule to find the second person passing through a door might be hard-coded to one location, or it could define a configurable door location that works for any scenario in the same simulator with a door to pass through. The configurable door location furthermore could be set by the instructor at the start of training, or it could use automation to search the simulation world for all doors and update world state whenever anyone passes through any door. Configuring the door location is required in the current implementation state, but the increased automation that removes this need might be desirable in the future.

Finally, should a truly reusable rule exist that records the second person to pass through any door in a simulation, the need for context in the world state becomes clear. Some doors might be benign areas back at base, where the order trainees enter can be recorded but does not make a difference to training. On the other hand, some doors exist in hostile territory and the infantry passing through must follow doctrinal procedures that define what they do once they are inside. The addition of context to interpret observed actions is one of the key contributions of the world model to automating team assessment.

A final consideration is the scalability of dynamic role assignment when the number of roles, team members, and facts about the simulated world increase. Constantly checking all possible assignments would probably overwhelm any computer. GIFT provides an event-based mechanism to make updates only about facts that changed from moment to moment during training. In addition, updating and rechecking the meaningful labels can be carried out efficiently as well. Rather than long lists of conditional (if-then) logic, a more efficient method for maintaining many such facts is the rete [23]. A rete algorithm implements efficient pattern matching to find the subset of facts that matter to a team assignment. Upcoming work is expected to implement rete to carry out dynamic team assignment in situations that call for real-time responsiveness, as opposed to after-action feedback that can be processed quickly once the full training run is complete.

In conclusion, we described at a functional level the software changes that are enhancing automated team assessment in the GIFT adaptive training framework. The changes build on our initial introduction of assessing team functional resilience. The enhancements described here tend to increase the role of AI in supporting assessment. As a result, the assessments become more general and reusable in more training settings. The assessments also require less workload to define when authoring the training and when configuring it for execution with a particular team. With ongoing implementation work, it may be possible to create a library of team assessments that encode many doctrinal team behaviors and correctly assess them in a range of scenarios and settings.

# 6   Recommended Next Steps

We introduced the concept of adaptive team training using GIFT, but the principles discussed in this paper may be generalized to the design of other adaptive instructional software architectures. To enhance the efficacy and usefulness of adaptive instruction as a tool for team training, we recommend the following team competency research topics as logical next steps:

- Research and develop standard methods to define team-based training scenarios
- Research and develop standard methods to define and operationalize team competency in cognitive and psychomotor domains

- Automate the evaluation process for determining the effectiveness of team tutoring interventions to enhance AIS decision-making with each new experience
- Implement self-improving assessments and interventions that respond to effectiveness evaluations and suggest ways to improve specific training
- Provide instructors and training authors with actionable information about team training effectiveness
- Increase high-level control over training in order to facilitate making training as effective as possible when configuring scenarios and during real-time execution.

The implications of this research are focused on GIFT but may contribute broadly to the design of automating instructional systems. An AIS goal is for collaborative learning support for education settings and team-based systems for training settings to be easily deployed and used for training because of how prevalent teams are in the workplace. The design of automation, capturing individual contributions to team performance, and implementing AI approaches to increase generality and reusability are methods that can be used for teams in GIFT and other technology systems to assess and act on team performance.

**Acknowledgments.** The research reported in this paper was performed under a US Army Contracting Command - Aberdeen Proving Ground (ACC-APG) contract (W912CG-19-C-0009). The views and conclusions contained in this paper are those of the authors and should not be interpreted as presenting the official policies or position, either expressed or implied, of ACC-APG, DEVCOM-SC, STTC or the U.S. Government unless so designated by other authorized documents. Citation of manufacturer's or trade names does not constitute an official endorsement or approval of the use thereof. The U.S. Government is authorized to reproduce and distribute reprints for Government purposes notwithstanding any copyright notation hereon.

# References

1. Sottilare, R.A., Brawner, K.W., Sinatra, A.M., Johnston, J.H.: An updated concept for a Generalized Intelligent Framework for Tutoring (GIFT). Retrieved from GIFTtutoring.org on 1–9 May 2017
2. Sottilare, R., Brawner, K.: Component interaction within the Generalized Intelligent Framework for Tutoring (GIFT) as a model for adaptive instructional system standards. In: The Adaptive Instructional System (AIS) Standards Workshop of the 14th International Conference of the Intelligent Tutoring Systems (ITS) Conference, Montreal, Quebec, Canada, June 2018
3. Folsom-Kovarik, J.T., Sinatra, A.M.: Automating assessment and feedback for teamwork to operationalize team functional resilience. In: Proceedings of the 8th Annual Generalized Intelligent Framework for Tutoring (GIFT) Users Symposium (GIFTSym8) 28 May 2020, p. 126. US Army Combat Capabilities Development Command–Soldier Center (2020)
4. Goldberg, B., Hoffman, M., Graesser, A.C.: Adding a human to the adaptive instructional system loop: integrating GIFT and battlespace visualization. In: Design Recommendations for Intelligent Tutoring Systems Volume 8 – Data Visualization, 191 (2020)
5. Dillenbourg, P.: What do you mean by collaborative learning?
6. Ososky, S.J., Sottilare, R.A.: A Heuristic Evaluation of the Generalized Intelligent Framework for Tutoring (GIFT) Authoring Tools. US Army Research Laboratory Aberdeen Proving Ground United States, 1 March 2016

7. Sottilare, R., DeFalco, J.: Fundamentals of adaptive instructional systems tutorial. In: Interservice/Industry Simulation, Training & Education Conference (IITSEC), December 2020
8. Sottilare, R.A., Burke, C.S., Salas, E., Sinatra, A.M., Johnston, J.H., Gilbert, S.B.: Designing adaptive instruction for teams: a meta-analysis. Int. J. Artif. Intell. Educ. **28**(2), 225–264 (2018)
9. Smith-Jentsch, K.A., Cannon-Bowers, J.A., Tannenbaum, S.I., Salas, E.: Guided team self-correction: Impacts on team mental models, processes, and effectiveness. Small Group Res. **39**(3), 303–327 (2008)
10. Smith-Jentsch, K.A., Zeisig, R.L., Acton, B., McPherson, J.A.: Team dimensional training: a strategy for guided team self-correction. In: Cannon-Bowers, J.A., Salas, E. (eds.), Making Decisions Under Stress: Implications for Individual and Team Training (1998)
11. Salas, E., et al.: Does team training improve team performance? A meta-analysis. Hum. Fact. **50**(6), 903–933 (2008)
12. Meneghel, I., Salanova, M., Martínez, I.M.: Feeling good makes us stronger: How team resilience mediates the effect of positive emotions on team performance. J. Happiness Stud. **17**(1), 239–255 (2016)
13. Fowlkes, J.E., Lane, N.E., Salas, E., Franz, T., Oser, R.: Improving the measurement of team performance: the TARGETS methodology. Milit. Psychol. **6**(1), 47–61 (1994)
14. Fowlkes, J.E., Shawn Burke, C.: Targeted acceptable responses to generated events or tasks (TARGETs). Handbook of Human Factors and Ergonomics Methods, 29 (2005)
15. Allen, W.C.: Overview and evolution of the ADDIE training system. Adv. Dev. Hum. Resour. **8**(4), 430–441 (2006)
16. Peterson, C.: Bringing ADDIE to life: Instructional design at its best. J. Educ. Multimedia Hypermedia **12**(3), 227–241 (2003)
17. Wray, R.E., Folsom-Kovarik, J.T., Woods, A., Jones, R.M.: Motivating narrative representation for training cross-cultural interaction. Procedia Manuf. **3**, 4121–4128 (2015)
18. Graffeo, C., Benoit, T.S., Wray, R.E., Folsom-Kovarik, J.T.: Creating a scenario design workflow for dynamically tailored training in socio-cultural perception. Procedia Manuf. **3**, 1486–1493 (2015)
19. McCormack, R.K., Kilcullen, T., Sinatra, A.M., Brown, T., Beaubien, J.M.: Scenarios for training teamwork skills in virtual environments with GIFT. In: Proceedings of the Sixth Annual GIFT Users Symposium, vol. 6, p. 189. US Army Research Laboratory, May 2018
20. McCormack, R., Kilcullen, T., Sinatra, A. M., Case, A., Howard, D.: Teamwork training architecture, scenarios, and measures in GIFT. In: Proceedings of the 7th Annual GIFT Users Symposium, p. 131. US Army Combat Capabilities Development Command–Soldier Center, May 2019
21. Gilbert, S.B., et al.: Creating a team tutor using GIFT. Int. J. Artif. Intell. Educ. **28**(2), 286–313 (2018)
22. Ostrander, A., et al.: Evaluation of an intelligent team tutoring system for a collaborative two-person problem: Surveillance. Comput. Hum. Behav. **104**, 105873 (2020)
23. Laird, J.E.: The Soar Cognitive Architecture. MIT Press, 13Apr 2012

# Towards the Design and Development of an Adaptive Gamified Task Management Web Application to Increase Student Engagement in Online Learning

Miguel Alfredo C. Madrid$^{(\boxtimes)}$ and David Matthew A. de Jesus

Ateneo de Manila University, Quezon City, Philippines
{miguel.madrid,matthew.dejesus}@obf.ateneo.edu

**Abstract.** With the COVID-19 pandemic postponing face-to-face classes and closing down the doors of educational institutions worldwide, online learning is one of the alternatives which these institutions have been adopting. With the advent of these online learning systems, students face many barriers which include lack of time and motivation. To help address these barriers in online learning, this paper presents the design and development of a gamified task management web application which aims to increase student engagement and motivation. In addition, this paper also aims to determine how these implemented gamified features can further be developed for adaptive learning. The application was developed incorporating design elements from two gamification frameworks which aim to improve users' motivation and engagement while catering to as wide an audience as possible. In addition, data which can be gathered from the application may prove helpful towards the design and development of further adaptive gamified features. Future work on the application includes testing its effectiveness with student audiences and implementation of further adaptive features.

**Keywords:** Interaction design for adaptive instructional systems · Web application · Gamification · Student engagement · Student motivation · Online learning

## 1 Introduction

### 1.1 Context

The closure of educational institutions and the postponement of their physical, face-to-face classes have recently become some of the measures that many countries have taken in an effort to suppress the spread of COVID-19. According to a regularly updated report by the United Nations Educational, Scientific and Cultural Organization (UNESCO), there were currently 107 country-wide school closures as of July 21, 2020, affecting 1,066,817,855 learners worldwide [1]. Due to this, many have started to adopt alternatives to face-to-face classes, one of which is online learning.

© Springer Nature Switzerland AG 2021
R. A. Sottilare and J. Schwarz (Eds.): HCII 2021, LNCS 12792, pp. 215–223, 2021.
https://doi.org/10.1007/978-3-030-77857-6_14

With the advent of the online learning systems that the country has adopted, students face many barriers. According to an analysis by Muilenberg and Berge of 1,056 valid surveys from students, the lack of motivation, lack of time, and lack of family and friends' support are among the most severe barriers that students face in an online learning environment [2]. Motivation in particular is of utmost importance to students as, according to Ryan and Deci, only those who are intrinsically motivated exhibit heightened levels of productivity and innovation [3]. Furthermore, a study by Doherty found that when asked, students who failed or dropped out of online courses answered the lack of time or procrastination as the main causes [4].

In recent years, gamification has been increasingly considered by many as a way to help students overcome these learning barriers via increasing student engagement and motivation [5–7].

### 1.2 Objective

To help address the barriers of motivation and procrastination in the context of online learning, this paper presents the design and development of a gamified task management web application which aims to increase student engagement and motivation. In addition, this study also aims to determine how these implemented gamified features can further be developed for adaptive learning.

### 1.3 Scope and Limitations

As the main focus of the study is online learning, the web application is meant for browsers and will be primarily accessed by personal computers. Support for usage on mobile devices is considered, but is not prioritized. The researchers used the latest version of the Django web framework as the platform to create their web application. In addition, the researchers will connect the web application to Moodle learning management system (LMS) to help obtain data regarding task completion and student scores from their online courses. The target audience of this study are college-level students aged eighteen and above undergoing online learning using an online LMS.

## 2 Related Literature

Currently, the use and effects of gamified applications in educational environments is a growing field, but from studies such as those of Seixas et al. [6], which focused on the effectivity of badging platforms on student engagement, and Snow et al. [10], which focused on the effect of game currency on student performance inside and outside of a gamified system, they found that certain game features can have both positive and negative effects on students' motivation and engagement. Given this, caution and careful consideration should be taken when applying game mechanics in educational settings.

In regards to the creation of a gamified system, some previous works include the frameworks of Marczewski [8] and Chou [9]. Marczewski's Hexad framework revolves around four basic user types: Socialisers, Free Spirits, Achievers, and Philanthropists, with each of these user types being intrinsically motivated by relatedness, autonomy, mastery and purpose respectively [8]. For Yu-kai Chou's Octalysis framework, it revolves around understanding and designing around which type of game mechanics appeal to certain "Core Drives", which drive us towards performing certain actions in either a positive or negative way [9]. In these frameworks, importance was placed in creating balanced systems which primarily cater to intrinsically motivated users while adding reward systems for extrinsically motivated users [8], and in understanding how certain game features can be used to attend to the motivational needs of these users [9].

As for previously published gamified applications, among the most popular of these would be Habitica [11] and Forest [12], which were found to primarily fulfill the motivational needs of its users, but relied on each user to be accountable for their in-game activities and focused on having a more free-form system for a wider audience.

Given these details, the researchers believe that it is possible to further continue the study on the effects of certain game features on student engagement and motivation by creating their own gamified web application similar to Habitica and Forest [11–13], adding connections to online learning courses to add accountability and to have a better focus on an educational context. The developed web application primarily applied the Accomplishment, Meaning, and Empowerment Core Drives of Chou [9] in its features to improve motivation and engagement within its users, and also focused on accommodating the four main user types of Marczewski [8] in order to create a balanced system for a wider audience. The developed web application also allows the researchers to further continue determining the effects of certain game mechanics on the engagement and motivation of students as they use the application.

## 3 Design and Development

In designing the application, the researchers chose to focus on catering to the four basic user types of Marczewski and appealing to the Accomplishment, Meaning and Empowerment Core Drives in order to enhance users' intrinsic motivation and engagement. The application, named Guildhouses of Taskosmos, is a gamified task management application connected to an online learning management system (LMS), taking the form of a base-management RPG. In Guildhouses of Taskosmos, users take the role of a "Guildmaster", whose main purpose is to build up their Guildhouse and increase their Reputation in the Kingdom of Taskosmos.

This narrative was created to appeal to the Meaning Core Drive where users are motivated by a belief that they were chosen to do something [9]. As for the connection to an online LMS, this feature was implemented to add an additional layer of verification to the users' completed tasks, which was one of the limitations found in previous task management applications [11, 13].

Progression in the game application is done through different types of Quests: Adventures, which are inspired by the user-set tasks from Habitica [11] and Forest [13], and Guild Quests, which are tied to tasks students must perform in their LMS. Completion of Quests awards users with Guildcoins, which are used for customization of their Guildhouse, and Fame Points, which increase the Fame Level of the user.

The Quest system was conceptualized to help cater to Achievers [9] and the Accomplishment Core Drive [9], as they allow tasks to be seen as challenges to be overcome.

**Table 1.** Relationship of game design choices to framework concepts

| Design choice | Framework concept/s | Rationale |
|---|---|---|
| Guildmaster Narrative | Epic Meaning and Calling Core Drive [9] | Narrative helps users believe that their tasks are greater than they actually are, or that they were specially chosen to perform their tasks [9] |
| Quests System | Achiever User Type [8] Accomplishment Core Drive [9] | Allow mundane tasks to be seen as challenges for the users to overcome |
| Fame Points and GuildCoin Rewards System | Player User Type [8] Accomplishment and Ownership Core Drives [9] | Acts as extrinsic reward system for the Player user type and the Accomplishment core drive, and as what fulfills a player's feeling of ownership for the Ownership Core Drive |
| Customization System | Free Spirit User Type [8] | Caters to the need of self-expression and autonomy of a Free Spirit |
| Milestone System | Achiever User Type [8] Accomplishment and Empowerment Core Drives [9] | Allow users to see their overall accomplishments and personal progress, and act as goals to be achieved |
| Friend System and Kudos | Socialiser and Philanthropist User Types [8] Epic Meaning and Calling Core Drive [9] Social Influence Core Drive [9] | Allows user interactivity and enrichment with each other for Socialisers and Philanthropists Fulfills a feeling of helping others in the community for the Meaning and Social Influence Core Drives |

The point reward system was considered to address the rewards for the Player user type [8] and for the Accomplishment and Ownership Core Drives [9]. For the customization, this feature was considered to address the self-expression of the Free Spirit user type [8].

Other features implemented include Milestones, which are achievements used to help track personal progress, and a Friend System, which allows users to view each others' profiles and give each other one Kudos daily for motivation. The Milestone system is used to again motivate Achievers and the Accomplishment and Empowerment Core Drive. The Friend System and Kudos are here to cater to Socialisers, Philanthropists, the Meaning Core Drive, and the Social Influence Core Drive giving these users the opportunity to interact and motivate others.

A table summarizing the connections between design choices and framework concepts can be found below (Table 1):

# 4   Discussion

## 4.1   Discussion on the Current Application

A ready-for-testing prototype of the designed web application built on the Django web framework and with a connection to Moodle LMS has already been created. The application and the images it uses are currently deployed using cloud-based platforms and hosting services. The current web application also has all of the design choices described in the previous section implemented into the current web application.

In the current iteration of the web application, users are able to create accounts, connect their accounts with the Moodle LMS, go on the different types of Quests, collect Fame Points and GuildCoins through completion of Quests, customize their Guildhouses with the collected currencies, obtain Milestones based on certain criteria, become friends with other users, and give Kudos to friended users.

With the current application, we expect users to use the application alongside the Moodle LMS, connecting Quests to their Moodle assignments and other academic work to help them manage and gain a better overview of their tasks. We also hope that the usage of the application will positively impact student engagement and motivation through the accommodation of the different user types and Core Drives through the different mechanics implemented in the system, such as the currencies, customization, and Kudos mechanics.

Images of the current web application and some of its features can be found in the figures below. Figure 1 shows the current user homepage of Guildhouses of Taskosmos, which shows the logo and also shows an overview of the current assignments of a particular user, as well as its submission status within the Moodle LMS.

**Fig. 1.** Guildhouses of Taskosmos User Homepage

Figure 2 shows the Guildhouse page, which shows the overview of the user's current Guildhouse and also allows the user to perform their Daily Check-in. We hope that interactions with the Guildhouse will help in student motivation as it was created to appeal to a user's sense of ownership and want for customization, and we hope that the Daily Check-in will help with user retention on the application, which will hopefully in turn help in keeping users up-to-date with their assignments.

**Fig. 2.** Guildhouses of Taskosmos Guildhouse Page

Figure 3 shows the basic Quest interface, which lists down the user's current assignments, their deadlines, and allows them to assign them as either Guild Quests or Epic Quests. Going on a Quest will also give the user an email notification about their Quest, which reminds them about the particular assignment and reiterates the assignment deadline. We hope that this system will aid in online learning as it gives constant reminders to users about their assignments and gives users in-application rewards upon completing their assignments.

In addition to the implemented features, the current web application also has the integrated admin interface of the Django web framework for easy administration and gathering of user information and statistics. The admin interface can also be used for simple addition of new customizations for users to purchase and unique milestone badges for particular users.

### 4.2 Discussion on Adaptability

Regarding adaptability, we find that it is relevant for this application as we believe that it may only serve to further better its goals in increasing student motivation and engagement. Given this, we list down in this section certain aspects of our application that may aid in creating a more adaptive learning environment.

First, user data obtained from the implemented features, such as the completion and punctuality rate of Quests may help in the design and development of an adaptive feature

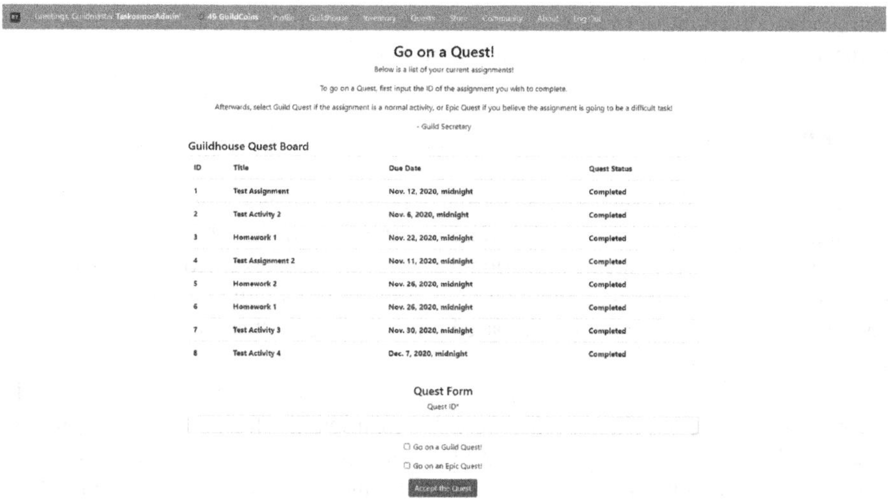

**Fig. 3.** Guildhouses of Taskosmos Quest Page

which could give user-specific feedback to help with motivation and punctuality, as well as further their learning. A system such as this could be implemented with the current email notification system to give weekly reports to a user about their current progress and give them advice on how to improve.

Second, the data gathered from the amount of Guildcoins one user has spent in relation to their current progress within the system may also help in recognizing patterns which may also aid in the development of further adaptive gamified systems such as the one previously mentioned.

Furthermore, the user data obtained from the web application may also aid in making online learning help educators in adjusting their lesson content either for an individual or their classes. More LMS-integrated features may also help in tracking individual progress for each learner by their teachers.

In the creation of an adaptive version of the application moving forward, we feel that it would also be best to first focus on creating a system which adjusts itself according to what it detects as particular Core Drives that best motivates the user [9] or a player type that the user would fall under [8]. For example, a user that accrues or spends a greater amount of Guildcoins than average would be categorized as a Consumer and motivated by the Ownership Core Drive [8, 9]. The amount of Guildcoins they receive could then be automatically adjusted so as to keep the user engaged.

User-specific adjustments could then be further refined using Chou's higher levels of Octalysis, which controls the design focus to appeal to differing Core Drives depending on how far along the user is in the use of the application in addition to their detected player type [8, 9]. This would allow for better user retention for all players at varying Fame Levels.

Current implementations of features could also be modified for user retention and adjusted for adaptivity. For example, the shop which currently has all items available would be modified into a weekly shop rotation which could be fine-tuned depending on the users' tendencies in buying customization options.

## 5 Conclusion

The researchers conclude that they were able to properly create a prototype of a gamified web application meant to aid in increasing student engagement and motivation in online learning while following the gamification frameworks of Marczewski [8] and Chou [9]. The researchers also conclude that there are possible ways in which adaptive systems can be formulated and implemented based on the user data that can be obtained from the current version of the application.

For future work, the researchers plan on testing the effectiveness of the web application in increasing student engagement and motivation via student self-report surveys regarding the matter, which have been used in prior studies as methods to assess student engagement [14], comparing results from before and after the students have used the application. In addition, the researchers also consider conceptualizing and implementing further adaptive features, such as those previously discussed.

## References

1. UNESCO. https://en.unesco.org/covid19/educationresponse. Accessed 21 July 2020
2. Muilenburg, L.Y., Berge, Z.L.: A factor analytic study of barriers perceived by students to online learning. Dist. Educ. **26**(1), 29–48 (2005). https://doi.org/10.1080/01587910500081269
3. Ryan, R.M., Deci, E.L.: Self-determination theory and the facilitation of intrinsic motivation, social development, and well-being. Am. Psychol. **55**(1), 68–78 (2000). https://doi.org/10.1037//0003-066x.55.1.68
4. Doherty, W.: An analysis of multiple factors affecting retention in Web-based community college courses. Internet Higher Educ. **9**(4), 245–255 (2006). https://doi.org/10.1016/j.iheduc.2006.08.004
5. Alsawaier, R.S.: The effect of gamification on motivation and engagement. Int. J. Inf. Learn. Technol. **35**(1), 56–79 (2018). https://doi.org/10.1108/IJILT-02-2017-0009
6. Seixas, L., Gomes, A., Filho, A.: Effectiveness of gamification in the engagement of students. Comput. Hum. Behav. **58**, 48–63 (2016). https://doi.org/10.1016/j.chb.2015.11.021
7. Legaki, NZ., Xib, N., Hamarib, J., Karpouzisa, K., Assimakopoulos, V.: The effect of challenge-based gamification on learning: An experiment in the context of statistics education. In: International Journal of Human-Computer Studies 144, 102496 (2020). DOI: https://doi.org/10.1016/j.ijhcs.2020.102496
8. Gamified UK. https://www.gamified.uk/user-types/. Accessed 21 July 2020
9. Chou, Y., https://yukaichou.com/gamification-examples/octalysis-complete-gamification-framework/. Accessed 21 July 2020
10. Snow, E.L., Allen, L.K., Jackson, G.T., McNamara, D.S.: Spendency: students' propensity to use system currency. Int. J. Artif. Intell. Educ. **25**(3), 407–427 (2015). https://doi.org/10.1007/s40593-015-0044-1
11. Habitica. https://habitica.com/static/home. Accessed 3 Aug 2020
12. Seixrtech Co., Ltd.. Forest. https://www.forestapp.cc/. Accessed 3 Aug 2020

13. Seekrtech Co., Ltd.: Forest - Stay focused (Version 4.20.0). Mobile application. https://apps.
apple.com/app/apple-store/id866450515?mt=8. Accessed 3 Aug 2020
14. Fredericks, J., McColskey, W.: The measurement of student engagement: a comparative analysis of various methods and student self-report instruments. In: Sandra Christenson, S., Reschly,
A., Wylie, C. (eds.) Handbook of Research on Student Engagement. Springer, Boston (2012).
https://doi.org/10.1007/978-1-4614-2018-7_37

# Intelligence Augmentation for Educators, Training Professionals, and Learners

Nkaepe Olaniyi[1]([✉]) [iD] and Jessie Chuang[2]

[1] Kaplan Open Learning, City Exchange, 11 Albion Street, Leeds LS1 5ES, UK
nkaepe.olaniyi@kaplan.com
[2] Classroom Aid Inc., 11100 Chateau Hill, Austin, TX 78750, USA
jessie@classroomaid.org

**Abstract.** "Learning" is a means to an end; the end is to perform. Tools aid human performance. Before electronic computers became commercially available, the term "computer" meant "one who computes": a person performing mathematical calculations. Humans no longer need to do parts of a task that computers or machines can do well. In many industries, intelligent machines with advanced hardware or software have been exploited to augment human performance. In comparison, education and training industries have yet to realize the potential of intelligence augmentation. In this paper, we review case studies of Intelligence Augmentation in industry and in educational institutions, considering common barriers to adoption in the latter. We also explore the possibilities of collaboration between humans and intelligent machines based on Industry 4.0 tools and techniques. Based on industry examples, we propose a model for building collaboration between humans and intelligent machines for improved performance in the development and delivery of teaching and learning.

**Keywords:** Industry 4.0 · Teaching and learning · 4th industrial revolution · Artificial intelligence · Education · Learning engineering · Augmented intelligence · Collaboration · Human-machine collaboration · Augmented Reality

## 1 Introduction

The use of computer and machines to carry out tasks has been increasing in recent years, eventually leading to an age where there is a "blurring of boundaries between the physical, digital and biological" [1], known as the 4th Industrial Revolution or Industry 4.0 (illustrated in Fig. 1). This blurring is attributed to the advances in technologies such as artificial intelligence (AI), quantum computing, robotics, Blockchain, cloud computing, edge computing, 5G/4G, positioning technology, Internet of Things (IoT), and advanced human-machine interface such as Augmented Reality. Combining AI techniques and data analytics with other digital technologies create new digital capabilities including intelligent machines, digitized products and services, as well as new digital business models [2].

The impact of the 4th Industrial Revolution on society is set to be profound, with the development of self-driving cars, greater quality and speed in production processes and

© Springer Nature Switzerland AG 2021
R. A. Sottilare and J. Schwarz (Eds.): HCII 2021, LNCS 12792, pp. 224–242, 2021.
https://doi.org/10.1007/978-3-030-77857-6_15

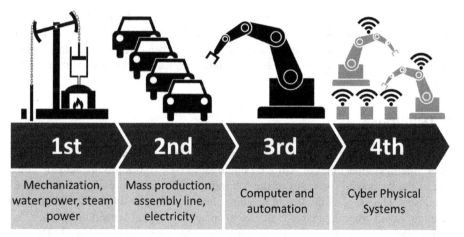

**Fig. 1.** From the First to the Fourth Industrial Revolution (Industry 4.0) – Credit: Christoph Roser at AllAboutLean.com, CC BY-SA 4.0, via Wikimedia Commons

increasing interconnectedness [3]. The COVID-19 pandemic has also meant that there is a growing need to bolster the development of these new technologies, such as cloud computing and IoT, making them more efficient and accessible by all [4–6].

One sector that has been slow in utilizing technologies from this new era is the educational sector. The reasons for this vary from a fear of new technologies to high costs. However, changes are being made and, in many areas, stirred on by the COVID-19 pandemic, particularly in maintaining communication within the University structure. Catering to the variety of learning styles that exist in any class, developing digital citizenship, improving school management efficiency, and enhancing the learning experience as just a few more reasons for the paradigm change [7]. With its prolific growth in industry, the educational sector can be held as duty-bound to delve more into Industry 4.0 tools and techniques in order to help ensure feasible ethical, regulatory and social impacts of this technology, as well as preparing industry-ready graduates [8]. In fact, William Uricchio (professor of comparative media studies at MIT), states that there is a "need to develop AI-literate public, which means a focused attention in the educational sector and in the public-facing media" [9]. So, the use of these disruptive technologies in education is a double-edged sword for these institutions – for delivery and preparation.

The application of advanced hardware and/or software to augment human performance varies widely across education sectors and countries, with equally varied outcomes. Hence, the need to explore success stories, particularly in industry, which will help to create a viable implementation model for any educational institution. This model should be one that is easily adaptable as the aim is to improve teaching and learning with a focus on efficient collaboration between humans and intelligent machines/tools, the key point being **collaboration**. The authors see collaboration as the key shift in paradigm, where new technologies become reliable assistants to educators and trainers in their delivery [10].

This paper will review case studies in industry in Sect. 3. Given the extensive nature of Industry 4.0 tools and techniques, the focus of this section will be on AI-based tools and technologies as these have been acknowledged as having significant impact on human capacities by 2030 [9]. We will then review the use of 4th Industrial Revolution tools in Education via various case studies (Sect. 4). Section 5 then discusses our proposal for intelligence augmentation, applicable to teaching and learning environment. Then the conclusion will summarize the paper.

## 2  Definitions

Before moving on, there is a need to review some key definition of terms used in this paper. Intelligent machines or Artificial Intelligence (AI) algorithms are actually at the core of the successful use cases of the 4th Industrial Revolution tools and techniques in industry. The usage of intelligent machines here is a broader scope of combining AI techniques with other digital technologies to create new digital capabilities [11].

For so-called AI, there are two major approaches as depicted in Fig. 2. The first approach is called symbolic approach where we actually teach AI how to think, the definitions, ontologies and rules required, and then it can do logical reasoning. One application is in expert systems. The other approach called non-symbolic approach and uses various methods and algorithms to find patterns in huge data sets. This kind of approach just became possible because of the advancements made in increasing computing power.

## A Primer on AI

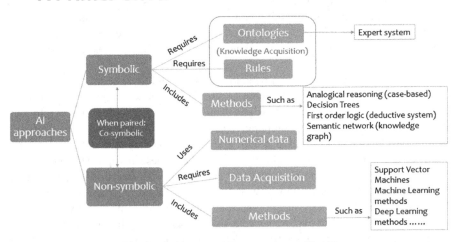

**Fig. 2.** A primer on AI – concept map [2, 12]

In the non-symbolic approach, there's a subset of AI called Machine Learning (ML), referring to a machine's ability to learn using data and without explicit programming. A subset in ML is called Deep Learning (DL), which refers to machine learning based on very large datasets. DL is very useful to process massive unstructured data without being provided the important features (variables).

AI is ideal for processing and analyzing large amounts of data collected from a connected workforce with digital tools, it can help capture heterogeneous data, digest them, find outliers, cleanse data and find correlations and patterns that can be used to identify opportunities for improvement. As our focus is on the collaboration between humans and intelligent machines, Augmented Reality (AR) is a tool regularly used in creating this collaborative environment. AR can be seen as an interface to combine the strengths of humans and machines for augmented intelligence. AR works by overlaying images, schematics, multimedia, 3D objects, animation, location data, and other forms of digital content on real-world objects. Hence, most AR content is interactive.

## 3   AI-Based Tools in Industry

### 3.1   AI in Manufacturing

The use of intelligent machines has taken many forms in industry. Smart manufacturing collects real-time data across the factory to help manufacturers identify and prevent trouble before it happens by pinpointing the root cause of issues before they disrupt production and predicting when faults will occur or when equipment is likely to fail. Actionable insights help manufacturers optimize their production and increase manufacturing productivity by reducing downtime or events that harm yield or increase costs.

IoT-enabled manufacturing units are now able to monitor and regulate themselves. They can detect anomalies in process parameters such as temperature, power output, speed and positioning during machining operations, etc., and adjust themselves for energy management, inventory control, equipment maintenance, and worker safety among others. Using a combination of IoT sensors to inspect manufactured goods and identify any defects automatically, the systems can either make adjustments to the process parameters or notify the concerned personnel to take remedial action. This enables factory personnel to immediately fix any issues and get the system functioning back at top efficiency.

Digital Twin is a digital representation (model) of a physical asset or the whole factory. It allows engineers to do simulations to find better plans in real-time and keeps learning from real data for iterations. For example, Tesla has a Digital Twin for every car manufactured from the factory. Then each day, thousands of miles of data is being fed back to the factory to continuously optimize the algorithms. Using digital twins, enterprises can gain production visibility and planning that improves operational agility, increases throughput, and optimizes process efficiency throughout the supply chain.

With predictive modeling and project designing and planning, General Motors workers can visualize the next steps in a building or assembly process with the overlay of digital content, seeing the final product before physically completing it. Volvo has implemented a digital thread from design through manufacturing processes. Volvo is now connecting front-line worker processes to the thread, to create quality assurance tasks. The benefits include improved operational effectiveness, and cost savings, and getting closer to 0 Part Per Million (PPM) quality goal. Updating and validating engine configuration and QA (Quality Assurance) checklist process reduced from more than a day to less than an hour. Digitization of the QA process is anticipated to save thousands of euros per workstation per year [11].

## 3.2  AI in Healthcare

Elekta, the global medical technology provider for treatment of cancer and brain disorders, unveiled a Connected Field Service program streamlined with digital twins of its customers' deployed equipment to improve customer experience and increase service revenue. The result is increased equipment uptime, 20% of service issues are resolved without dispatching a technician, and improved customer satisfaction with uninterrupted treatments for more than 14,000 patients in the program's first year. This improves business agility by optimizing service delivery network and processes [11].

For AI to process personal health data, the stakes of data privacy and security are very high. Without a trustworthy approach, it is impossible for any new technology to be accepted. Federated learning (also known as collaborative learning) is a machine learning technique that involves the use of multiple decentralized devices rather than computing ML models on large centralized machines. The use of decentralize devices or servers in federated learning means that multiple actors can work on the build of a common, robust machine learning model without sharing data. Hence, critical issues such as data privacy, data security, data access rights and access to heterogeneous data are clearly addressed. It is currently utilized in various industries including defense, telecommunications, Internet of Things (IoT), and healthcare [13].

## 3.3  Augmented Reality (AR) in Industry

Using AR combined with AI has the potential to provide better interactive training and performance support to their employees directly in their field of work instead of a theoretical setting. The AI system aims to provide each worker with exactly what they need, when they need it, and how they need it to perform each job at their peak. It closes the skills gap by providing personalized guidance where instructions are matched to the proficiency of each worker as well as remote mentors. Successful implementations can make the outcomes of some very complex procedures very repeatable for operators at all skill levels. The AR aspect provides an interface between humans and machines. This, for example, allows the AI/AR system to capture successful problem-solving processes, thereby accumulating tacit knowledge. In such a factory setting, using AR glasses would mean that when a problem occurs, the AI/R system can recommend (and also show) previous case solutions to junior/new workers to help them resolve the issue. This helps prevent the loss of precious domain knowledge as workers age or leave.

Jet engine makers estimate they lose millions of dollars each year because nuts that seal fluid lines and hoses, called b-nuts, are not screwed on just right. If the b-nuts are deemed too loose or too tight during testing, the engine must be fixed before it can power a plane with paying passengers. Until recently, there were very few effective ways to tell if the nut had hit that "sweet spot". Workers with torque wrenches had to rely on their skill and judgment to nail the delicate balance.

GE Aviation uses an AR tool with smart glasses or mobile devices to assist mechanics when they need to use a torque wrench. Next, when the Wi-Fi-enabled torque wrench starts to apply torque, it shares the information with the AR server. It then tells the mechanic whether they are properly tightening and sealing crucial jet engine b-nuts. It will also verify the correct value in real time before the mechanic moves on to the next step [14].

Boeing uses head-up displays in cockpits so that pilots could obtain critical information without looking down. It applied the technology to its manufacturing operations to free workers from flipping through instruction manuals. BAE Systems produced a visual training tool that takes workers, step by step, through the process of assembling green energy bus batteries.

GE Healthcare warehouse workers are using AR to complete pick list orders up to 46% faster. Delivering vision picking directly in the worker's line of sight, the AR solution gets real-time information on item location by connecting to warehouse systems and provides workers with clear, easy-to-follow instructions for where to locate items throughout the building [15].

Newport News Shipbuilding designs and builds U.S. Navy aircraft carriers. The company uses AR near the end of its manufacturing process to inspect a ship, marking for removal steel construction structures that are not part of the finished carrier. Historically, engineers had to constantly compare the actual ship with complex 2-D blueprints. Now with AR, they can see the final design superimposed on the ship, which reduces inspection time by 96% - from 36 hours to just 90 min. Overall, time savings of 25% or more are typical for manufacturing tasks using AR [16].

### 3.4 Further Augmentation to Process Complex Problems in Industry

More technologies can augment related capabilities to raise productivity, reduce risk and even achieve missions that are impossible for humans, such as flying to remote locations while being remotely controlled by workers. For example, unmanned aerial vehicles (drones) are getting popular at construction sites for mapping and surveying as drones shorten the data-collection process significantly. Sites that may have taken days or weeks to survey by hand can be surveyed in a matter of hours using this aerial technology.

Drones can be equipped with a digital camera or a thermographic camera, or a combination of both. The former can identify visual defects and damages, while the thermographic camera (with infrared or UV light) is a non-contact and non-destructive inspection method to examine for weaknesses and potential structural defects (e.g., rust) in objects. It has been used in inspecting construction sites, bridges, buildings, farms, solar energy arrays and wind turbines. This is just one example of how tools can augment human's capabilities to collect data. Overlaying a defect scan on top of the 3D model of constructions, workers can easily analyze the causes of defects. If the data are fed into Machine Learning algorithms, this can help find patterns in massive data. Combined with Geographic Information System, positioning information can be layered with other data.

In logistics, inventory management has long had hidden costs built into it. It has always been the case that asset-picking and tracking of inventory inevitably requires manpower and heavily relies on the human eye for discernment. However, the human element often comes with the cost of human error. Leveraging a low power asset tracker and beacon can automatically track inventory and eliminate this kind of human error.

AR glasses and barcode rings with Bluetooth enable workers to receive information about the package at hand instantly. Furthermore, radar technology with mmWaves can monitor restricted areas with efficiency and accuracy.

Hyper-connectivity based on WiFi, 5G, Enhanced Mobile Broadband, Massive Machine Type Communication, Low Power Wide Area networks, etc. and platforms connecting users, data and insights in real time is another key to augmenting human performance. Connected data, insight and remote mentoring can be readily available on-demand. The advancement of computing power and storage capability with low costs, make it possible to process and store the massive data collected and shorten the time needed to take action. However, the torrent of information produced by billions of smart, connected products (SCPs) can become impossible for human cognitive capability to handle.

So, the other possibility of augmentation is to help humans process complex data. One example is IBM Immersive Data, an augmented reality visualization tool that allows data scientists and business executives to quickly explore and understand data using iOS mobile devices [17]. Existing studies have confirmed that task performance effectiveness rises by more than 50% with a 3D stereoscopic view of data that enhances perceptions of spatial dimensions. Gesture interaction aids fluidity of manipulation of the images to be able to probe from multiple directions [18]. Sometimes AI algorithms are black boxes - decision-makers used to explore, simulate and predict by looking at the presentation of critical parameters of performance on a single virtual interface to arrive at conclusions with confidence. 3D or multidimensional visualizations are cognitive agents for human brains and support team communications, both are very valuable.

Startups such as Nanome, Interactive Scientific and C4X Discovery created VR platforms in life sciences to accelerate drug discovery [19]. Using the collaborative VR platform, scientists can "physically" interact with molecules, allowing users to reach out and touch a molecule, and even manipulate force fields in the virtual environment. The Interactive Scientific team concluded that the VR environment was about 12 times faster than conventional interfaces such as a desktop or using tinker toys. The VR platform built by C4X Discovery is an AI-powered platform that analyzes human genetic datasets and visualizes data in 4D [19]. Other use cases for 3D interactive graphics are construction, network visuals, supply chains, IoT analytics, cybersecurity, medical/surgical training, and mine planning with geospatial data.

AI implementation, like all new technology, has a significant barrier, a major one being the lack of AI talents. Can AI help build AI? Yes. Google proved that deep learning neural nets can help design neural nets. This is called AutoML and is based on neural architecture search [20]. Based on AutoML, there are now quite a few Automated Machine Learning products that help people use machine learning and automate a lot of steps in the production process, including data collection, preparation, feature engineering, model selection, training, model performance monitoring after the deployment, and the overall optimization according to business goals. Due to these, data scientists save a lot of time while non-technical people or business analysts can start using ML/DL to solve their problems directly. Furthermore, an array of Augmented Analytics tools let business operators get insights from data by asking questions using natural languages (Natural Language Processing, NLP) and making use of AI or automation capabilities with no-code or low-code user-interface (UI). AI can therefore lessen the skill gap issues, democratizing AI, and enable human-machine collaboration, if well-designed [21].

For successful AI implementations to augment human capabilities, the combination of symbolic and non-symbolic elements is usually necessary. Good design is crucial and should incorporate domain expertise and an effective problem-solving model in building the tool or platform that supports workers. Data and analytics (possibly with Machine Learning) collected from the use of the tool or platform can enable continuous itera-tions for validation and optimization. A strategic implementation process and learning on-demand to support adoption are also needed. However, first we need to build digital representations that machines understand and models that represent the matter well (i.e., can predict correctly). For example, to build an AI-based product to support personal-ized learning on-demand or context-aware performance support, good models of skills, domain knowledge and work context are demanded.

Imagine there is an app that can integrate everything people need to perform bet-ter at work, including learning, job aids, business data (automatically collected by AI/automation tools), insights from data, lessons from previous cases, best practice pro-cesses set up by experts or managers, and real-time mentoring. AI would keep capturing tacit knowledge or tribal knowledge under the hood. This kind of AI applications are built for sales enablement, as well as in other domains, such as to augment leadership, HR management, and improve workplace collaboration efficiency. IBM collects employee's digital footprints from 26 data sources and continuously supports the employee's perfor-mance and learning through smart assistance, intelligent workflows, and a digital learning ecosystem [22]. Different to traditional business intelligence, this kind of solution offers learning on-demand and operational intelligence to augment worker's performance in real time.

Intelligent machines can do huge numbers of trials with rich variables for new designs in a short space of time, including in content design, product design and IC design works. They can also read huge amounts of information and provide brief highlights for humans. For example, the current explosion in information availability makes it impossible for researchers to review all documents relevant to their research. Semantic knowledge graph services can trawl through the Internet, digest all elements on all web pages, 24/7 nonstop. Researchers across the globe use this kind of engine to comb through the incredible amount of publications on COVID-19 [23].

# 4   Industry 4.0 Tools in Education

From the development of the modern pencil in 1795 to the development of online degree programmes by many educational and training institutions across the globe, the sector of education and training is no stranger to modern innovations. However, it is widely acknowledged that this sector has not been as quick to pick up recent developments from the 4th Industrial Revolution as other sectors. Bring Your Own Device (BYOD) is only now gaining ground in many institutions across the globe [24]. So, what are the reasons behind this slow uptake? And is there a future for these tools in this sector?

One way to answer these questions is to review various case studies that have taken place in recent years. These will highlight the barriers to adoption, as well as how they have been overcome when adopting these tools. It will also set the scene on the status of human collaboration with these modern tools in this sector, which is necessary for the model development in Sect. 5. It should be noted that these barriers to adoption vary from institution to institution and from country to country. So, some of the more commonly reported barriers are discussed here.

### 4.1 Industry 4.0 Vision for Teaching and Learning

The management team of any educational institution needs to have a clear vision for the for Industry 4.0 becoming Education 4.0 [25–27]. The vision needs to be clearly expressed to all staff so that disruptive technologies like AI and AR do not take educators by surprise or are regarded as unnecessary, particularly where fulfilling the vision may also involve a change in pedagogy. This means staff buy-in might be necessary. The vision could be as "simple" as utilizing these tools and techniques to simplify admin tasks such as class allocation, timetabling, preparing plans and grading [28]. Providing personalized learning, smart content, global learning, as well as closing the attainment gap [29, 30], can be seen as long-term goals for some institutions, depending on the resources available to them.

The example goals stated above have two (2) key data management tools to help fulfil them: Learner Analytics (LA) and Educational Data Mining (EDM) [31]. LA refers to the "measurement, collection, analysis and reporting of data about the progress of learners and the contexts in which the learning is taking place" [32]. This tool is now more widely used in Higher Education institutions. Kaplan Open Learning provides 100% online degree programmes. Working with Vitalsource (the digital textbook provider), they used learning analytics to examine the relationship between a student's final grade and their engagement with their module e-textbook [33]. The results show a statistically significant positive relationship between the two items, regardless of discipline or level of study. With this insight, educators can now highlight to learners the readily available tools that can promote positive learning behavior and result in positive outcomes for the learners.

In another case study, the University of Maryland, Baltimore County analyzed students' VLE activity and determined that those with low grades utilized the VLE 40% less that those with C grades or higher [34]. This information was then used to develop a tool for students to compare their VLE activity with other students on their course. The analytics were also used to identify effective teaching strategies, such as the use of pre-requisite tests and courses in some disciplines.

While LA is focused on data analytics, EDM utilizes other tools as well, such as machine learning and visualization to identify learners in need and provide educators with information on how to approach these needs. This would bring about significant change in pedagogical design and delivery [31] and is discussed further in Sect. 4.3.

### 4.2 Cost

This is the most reported barrier to adoption among teaching and learning institutions [26, 27, 35]. Many such institution depend on government funding and new technologies can be seen as an unnecessary luxury. Even if technology is seen to aid the teaching and learning process or make small work of tedious admin tasks, the costs of such technologies will hold many back from adoption.

There are a number of cases where this issue has been resolved using familiar tools. Google for Education offers various packages with competitive costs for Chromebooks, as well as providing free G Suite for Education resources [36]. This has meant schools in less well-off districts in the United States, for example, have been able to provide this technology to students in every class which in turn aided students learning [37]. For one school in Wales, using Google's cloud-based email system meant it saved £30,000 in licensing and maintaining the existing email server system [38]. A foundation in the Netherlands also found the use of Google's network infrastructure meant that they needed less manpower for network maintenance and ensuring an easy to manage infrastructure in all schools under the foundation's management [39].

Some institutions are using freely available software and tools to enable greater collaboration between learners based on their interaction with Industry 4.0 tools. For example, the University of Edinburgh has embedded Wikipedia, and other Wikimedia, into their curriculum just for this purpose [40]. The outcome has been an improvement in students' 21st century skills, such as teamwork, digital research and communication skills, a key requirement for the adoption of AI in any classroom [31]. Educators also reported greater student interest in subject matter and greater success in achieving the required learning outcomes of that subject.

The question then is, how is this affecting educational institutions in developing countries? For many countries insufficient infrastructure (such as a lack of network infrastructure or a lack of internet access) is a serious issue.

The other question to be answered is when will an educational institution use adaptive instructional or AI systems when the initial layout can be quite substantial [28]? It is essential that the investment must lead to a valuable return (such as reduced attrition and positive student outcomes) for this to make economic sense to any educational institution. This will be discussed further in Sect. 5 when reviewing the proposed collaboration model.

### 4.3 Dealing with Change

Resistance to change is found mostly in educators. This is usually based on a lack of training and/or familiarity with/understanding of the new technology, as well as a lack of institution support [26, 27, 35]. So, educators, need to be aware of the role of Industry 4.0 technologies, such as AI in this new era – "lifelong learning companions" [28]. The aim in using AI in the teaching and learning process is not to remove educators from their role (which is actually impossible given the limitations of AI, such as facilitating personal development) but to assist educators in their key aim - to provide learners with a valuable learning experience.

The Flipped Classroom is an example of how Industry 4.0 technologies is being used to facilitate learning and bringing about a change in educational institutions. Flipped learning (or the flipped classroom) refers to the pedagogical model of reversing the elements of lecture/lesson and homework [39, 40]. Various studies have shown its use to be a key factor in learner progression [41, 42], such as one provided by one of the authors [43]. Here, tools such as interactive videos with H5P and self-assessed online tests were used for the at-home sessions while problem-solving seminar sessions were held in class. The result was an increase in grades and greater self-efficacy among the students. In another case study from the University of Northampton (UK), the flipped classroom forms part of the Active Blended Learning approach based on various digital technologies [44]. The result here was greater engagement from students and a gold rating (the highest possible) that year, by the Teaching Excellence Framework for the UK [45].

In all examples of flipped or blended learning, the aim can be seen as collaboration with technology to ensure better outcomes for the learner. The educator is never "out of the picture" but instead their presence and expertise continue to provide much needed reassurance and guidance for learners.

In terms of training and support, some institutions prefer to provide in-house delivery, depending on available funding. There are also various software development companies which offer the required training and support to help institutions make the leap into Industry 4.0 technologies. This helps to ensure a healthy customer base and that the tools get the needed feedback input for future developments. Querium has produced an AI virtual tutor – StepWise – and the development was based on teacher contributions and feedback. The tool provides students with hints and instant feedback on homework set by the teacher and the teacher gets a detailed report on various aspects of the homework to help them decide on targeted intervention where necessary [46]. Teachers are reported as saying the tool is indeed useful for their teaching delivery, being able to provide what is necessary for each student (personalized learning) and saves them time [46]. The scope of the tool has reach into various STEM disciplines.

Century Tech is another company that utilizes AI/Machine Learning, neuroscience and learning science in a tool called Century [47]. The tool provides personalized learning for students and provides teachers with resources that help to further develop the student's learning. The aim here is to ensure learners are more confident and helps them develop lifelong learning. The company provides training and support to institutions who take up the tool.

One AR company seeking to ensure classrooms are more interactive is Blippar (AR). Their AR tool is used in museums and discovery-based learning, interactive reading in textbooks and the Gamification of learning [48]. One teacher in Wales has used the app to make his high school Geography case studies more interactive [49]. With all the information being readily available to students, this has also meant he no longer needed to provide reams of handouts. The students were pleased with the tool, mentioning that the interactivity and personalization made it an enjoyable tool to use. The students also commented on preferring to have all their work in AR format.

Finally, Cognii is another company that has developed a virtual learning assistant to help learners and educators. The tool uses Natural Language Processing (the ability of computers to analyze natural language data), AI and Machine Learning to provide one-to-one tutoring. The use of NLP means that it can also provide feedback to open response questions, almost conversing with the learner. For educators, time is saved as the tool provides automated assessment marking. They are also provided with an administrative dashboard to view aspects of the curriculum where learners are struggling and need further support or learning materials. The company aims to provide its tool in areas with a shortage of educators. A survey of students from two institutions where Cognii is used showed that over 95% of students were highly satisfied with the product [50] are reported as finding the AI very helpful, particularly in terms of the feedback it provides.

### 4.4 Speed of Change

There is no denying that Industry 4.0 does involve rapid progression. This can create another barrier as educators feel unable to cope with the pace of change [27]. However, this is one of the reasons why educational institutions should not be left behind in their integration of these tools and technologies, ensuring graduates are industry-ready.

The viable solution to this issue is continued and effective collaboration with industry [27]. This collaboration would also mean there would be an understanding of business issues and industry requirements from graduates. This collaboration would also mean that educational institutions would also be able to see first-hand where the development of AI and AR is heading and determine how this would impact learning. This would include strategies to develop the required competencies in graduates. This can be seen in various forms Advisory Boards in various institutions where employer representatives can provide valuable input to course design and development. The question remains, can more be done? We explore this further in Sect. 5 as part of our proposal.

### 4.5 Ethics and Data Protection

This is a veritable concern for educators due to the responsibility we have to our learners [51]. As much as the tools already described in previous sections provide positive results to help educators in their design and delivery, where is the line drawn? What level of tolerance can be given when it comes to learner data, in providing effective teaching and learning? Currently, institutions follow various guidelines for data protections, such as GDPR and codes of ethics from Professional, Statutory and Regulatory Bodies, but these are not necessarily global in reach. So, there is a need to find alternatives which can be applied in a varied range of scenarios and locations, as complete coverage might be impossible. The case studies from industry (Sect. 3) have highlighted some resolutions to this issue and our proposal (Sect. 5) will cover more on this topic.

## 5   Collaboration Model

Machines can carry out trial and error steps, provide a workflow of best practices, as well as provide logical reasoning on data and knowledge, among other tasks. Although AI and intelligent machines are used in so many use cases, they have their strengths and weaknesses and are far from being the perfect assistant we desire. For example, if training data quality is bad, its prediction will be bad. When there are outliers that the AI has never encountered, that could create misleading results. The best model is to combine the strength of humans and intelligent machines to augment human intelligence, performance and productivity. Users need to learn the basics of how AI works so that they can train the AI to work better for their own context and needs.

Enterprises are aiming to create value for their clients and the society, and the speed of iteration toward maximizing the value creation is crucial for competitiveness and survival. Learning is integrated in the flow of work to augment worker's intelligence and performance. The adoption of augmented intelligence solutions is faster in industry than in educational institutions.

In fact, many educational institutions seem more comfortable with the data/learning analytics aspect of Industry 4.0. Some of these have been highlighted in Sect. 3. So, this can be seen as a first step towards the adoption of AI-based tools in teaching and learning. So, what is the next step? How do educational institutions move forward with Education 4.0 when concerns remain regarding data protection and ethics, and access in remote areas of the world?

The IEEE ICICLE (the Institute of Electrical and Electronics Engineers Industry Connections Industry Consortium on Learning Engineering) defines "Learning Engineering (LE)" as "a process and practice that applies the learning sciences using human-centered engineering design methodologies and data-informed decision making to support learners and their development." [52]. The ideal LE process is proposed by Aaron Kessler and IEEE ICICLE Design SIG (Fig. 3).

## Learning Engineering Process

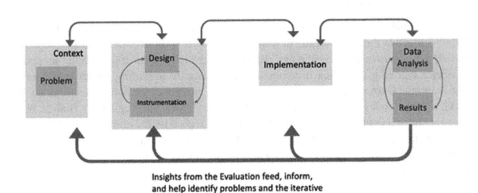

**Fig. 3.** The learning engineering process [52]

The Engineering methodology is crucial to scale up successful learning models efficiently, including personalized learning at scale. Iteration loops with data, analytics and ML/DL are essential, and cross-discipline domain knowledge and competencies are needed, as illustrated in Fig. 4. It should be noted that this collaboration between various teams could be a significant barrier for stakeholders (educators, learners, training professionals, learning program providers), as well as time-to-value.

Based on the AI enablement definitions in Sect. 2, using pre-built tools, algorithmic approaches and ML could augment learning designers, educators, learners and training

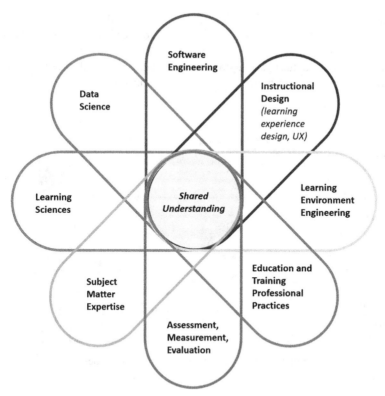

**Fig. 4.** Core knowledge expertise required for the learning engineering process – Credit: Jim Goodell, CC BY 4.0

professionals to ensure a more effective delivery of teaching and learning with Learning Engineering. This culminates into the model proposed by authors - **Augmented Learning Engineering** (see Fig. 5). This will facilitate the human-machine collaborative process, also providing automated feedback loops for stakeholders to enable real time intelligence augmentation.

Learning from industry experience, there is a need to think strategically about how to leverage the strength of intelligent machines to support humans (computing power, unlimited storage, executing repetitive tasks and rules fast, finding patterns from massive data for optimization, etc.). Hence, we can outline a model that can act as a reference for intelligence augmentation in the education or training industry. There are several key elements in the model:

- Digital tools to support productive workflows and team collaboration which can also capture data.
- Domain knowledge, engineering principles, good digital models for problem-solving (e.g. skill modeling) and learning on-demand are integrated in the tools.
- Intentional design to enable huma-human and human-machine collaborations with good human-machine interaction interface.

- Required data and value metrics are identified and defined.
- Plans for building iteration loops with data toward goals and improving the system itself are in place.
- Automated data capturing, integration, processing and analytics for automated iterations by machines or human-in-the-loop optimization.

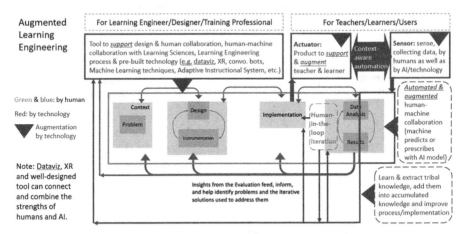

**Fig. 5.** Augmented learning engineering model

### 5.1 Suggestions for Education

Various aspects of the model (such as the data insights loop) have been highlighted in Sect. 4 as being actively utilized in various institutions. Being process based, the emphasis will then be on utilizing available resources.

As part of the process of establishing the overall vision for augmented learning, senior management would also need to clearly illustrate the role educators would play in the model. This would help to determine the tools and training (for staff and students) required. Therefore, the cost of tools used would have to align to the given vision of the institution and the available funding. This may result in taking up the services of a 3rd party vendor and/or developing tailor-made solutions in-house. The latter may require the employment of more staff to handle the development and deployment of the new infrastructure. As the case studies highlighted, there are several companies who are keen to work with educational institutions on projects of this nature.

The pace of change can be reviewed by establishing closer collaborations with industry to ensure delivery in these institutions can continue evolving. Each institution would have to decide at what point in the learning engineering and/or automation process an industry expert(s) can provide key input. Hence, making the academia-industry collaboration more structured and practical in its application.

In terms of ethics, whether utilizing in-house development or 3rd party tools, an educational institution is still responsible for the data protection of its staff and learners.

This model would provide a platform for ensuring that the data stays in-house. Depending on the vision of the institution, the data collected would only be that necessary for the final deployment. There would have to be clear communication with all stake-holders involved to ensure informed consent is received prior to any development. This in turn could result in better collaboration between educators and learners, which is seen as essential to augment learning and develop learning communities, particularly in online learning [53].

This proposed development model to be used within educational institutions could therefore overcome the barriers discussed in Sect. 4 and move educational institutions towards a more collaborative future with AI-based technologies. It should be noted that this is one possibility to enable educators, learners and training professionals to adopt the LE process as a new paradigm. Hence, the proposal intends to initiate a starting point of exploration, a viable first step in the move to achieve Education 4.0, rather the final answer to the questions posed in Sect. 4.

## 6 Conclusion

There is a need to understand that the technologies and tools of the 4th industrial revolution are being developed to augment human work rather than replacing humans entirely. For example, taking up the role normally considered drudgery due to their repetitive nature and lack of creativity [10] and in enhancing communication between stakeholders [16]. These tools are currently being used as an augmentation strategy in various industries.

Being ubiquitous, attention is now turned to the field of teaching and learning. In is anticipated that by 2030, there will be a greater dependence on AI - "Lack of education in AI and inclusiveness of individual in their own decision-making will make most people worse off in 2030." [9]. Hence, the need to ensure more than a basic familiarity with these Industry 4.0 tools and technologies.

This paper has highlighted current barriers to adoption in the teaching and learning sector, as well as case studies of ongoing development in this area. The authors have also reviewed various case studies from industry which highlight the progress made in recent years when it comes to the collaboration between humans and intelligent machines. The collaboration model proposed in this paper is derived from good practice seen across various industries. It highlights further steps educational institutions can take in further utilizing Industry 4.0 tools and techniques, as well as limitations to process implementation. The purpose here is to help ensure that the educational sector also benefits from this collaboration between humans and Industry 4.0 technology and tools, which is widely acknowledged as a way forward for this sector.

## References

1. McGinnis, D.: What is the Fourth Industrial Revolution? (2020). https://www.salesforce.com/blog/what-is-the-fourth-industrial-revolution-4ir/. Accessed 05 Feb 2021
2. Chuang, J.: AI + Human: A Total Reimagination of Learning and Work (2020). https://www.linkedin.com/pulse/ai-human-total-reimagination-learning-work-jessie-chuang/ Accessed 05 Feb 2021

3. Schwab, K.: The Fourth Industrial Revolution: what it means, how to respond (2016). https://www.weforum.org/agenda/2016/01/the-fourth-industrial-revolution-what-it-means-and-how-to-respond/. Accessed 18 Feb 2021
4. Millward, D., Olaniyi, N., Peoples, C.: The new normal: cybersecurity and associated drivers for a post-Covid-19 cloud. In: Daimi, K., Peoples, C. (eds.) Advances in Cyber Security Management (in print). Springer, Cham (2021)
5. Vodafone: 2020 IoT Spotlight (2020). https://www.vodafone.com/business/news-and-insights/white-paper/iot-spotlight-2020#the-impact-of-covid19. Accessed 05 Feb 2021
6. Nasajpour, M., Pouriyeh, S., Parizi, R.M., Dorodchi, M., Valero, M., Arabnia, H.R.: Internet of things for current COVID-19 and future pandemics: an exploratory study. J. Healthc. Inf. Res. 4(4), 325–364 (2020). https://doi.org/10.1007/s41666-020-00080-6
7. Educational Technologies Infographics: Teaching with Digital Technologies Infographic (2015). https://elearninginfographics.com/teaching-digital-technologies-infographic/. Accessed 05 Feb 2021
8. Shahroom, A.A., Hussin, N.: Industrial revolution 4.0 and education. Int. J. Acad. Res. Bus. Soc. Sci. 8(9), 314–319 (2018)
9. Anderson, J., Rainie, L.: Artificial intelligence and the future of humans (2018). https://www.pewresearch.org/internet/2018/12/10/artificial-intelligence-and-the-future-of-humans/. Accessed 12 Feb 2021
10. Davenport, T., Ronanki, R.: Artificial intelligence for the real world. In: Harvard Business Review's 10 Must Reads, pp. 67–84 (2018). https://hbr.org/2018/01/artificial-intelligence-for-the-real-world. Accessed 24 Feb 2021
11. Immerman, D., Lang, J.: Top use cases for digital twin technology to drive digital transformation (2019). https://www.ptc.com/-/media/Files/PDFs/IoT/J12599_DigiTwin_Use_Cases_ebk_v8_lowres.pdf Accessed 19 Feb 2021
12. Trent, S., Lathrop, S.: A Primer on Artificial Intelligence for military leaders. Small Wars Journal (2018). https://smallwarsjournal.com/jrnl/art/primer-artificial-intelligence-military-leaders. Accessed 24 Feb 2021
13. Rieke, N., Hancox, J., Li, W. et al.: The future of digital health with federated learning. NPJ Digit. Med. 3, 119 (2020). https://doi.org/10.1038/s41746-020-00323-1
14. Kloberdanz, K.: Smart specs: OK glass, fix this jet engine (2017). https://www.ge.com/news/reports/smart-specs-ok-glass-fix-jet-engine. Accessed 19 Feb 2021
15. Upskill: GE Uses Skylight to Improve Vision Picking (2017). https://upskill.io/landing/ge-healthcare-case-study/. Accessed 19 Feb 2021
16. Porter, M., Heppelmann, J.: Why every organization needs an augmented reality strategy. In: Harvard Business Review's 10 Must Reads, pp. 85–108 (2017). https://hbr.org/2017/11/why-every-organization-needs-an-augmented-reality-strategy. Accessed 24 Feb 2021
17. Ruiz, A.: IBM Immersive Data: Augmented Reality for data visualization (2019). https://medium.com/design-ibm/ibm-immersive-data-augmented-reality-for-data-visualization-898587b2a57c. Accessed 19 Feb 2021
18. Bach, B., Sicat, R., Beyer, J., Cordeil, M., Pfister, H.: The hologram in my hand: how effective is interactive exploration of 3D visualizations in immersive tangible augmented reality? IEEE Trans. Vis. Comput. Graph. 24, 457–467 (2018)
19. Nanalyze: Virtual reality for drug discovery is for real (2019). https://www.nanalyze.com/2019/07/virtual-reality-drug-discovery/. Accessed 19 Feb 2021
20. Hu, J.: Understanding AutoML and neural architecture search (2018). https://medium.com/aifrontiers/understand-automl-and-neural-architecture-search-4260a0942116. Accessed 24 Feb 2021
21. Gonfalonieri, A.: No-code/low-code AI: new business models and future of data scientists (2020). https://towardsdatascience.com/no-code-low-code-ai-new-business-models-and-future-of-data-scientists-a536beb8d9e3. Accessed 24 Feb 2021

22. Wise Ocean: The Big Blue's Way of Learning Engineering – IBM (2020). https://wiseocean. tech/the-big-blues-way-of-learning-engineering/. Accessed 24 Feb 2021
23. Semantic Scholar CORD-19 webpage. https://www.semanticscholar.org/cord19. Accessed 19 Feb 2021
24. Sundgren, M.: Blurring time and place in higher education with bring your own device applications: a literature review. Educ. Inf. Technol. **22**(6), 3081–3119 (2017). https://doi. org/10.1007/s10639-017-9576-3
25. Jisc Blog – Member stories: moving towards Education 4.0. https://www.jisc.ac.uk/blog/mem ber-stories-towards-higher-education-40-15-jan-2019. Accessed 18 Feb 2021
26. Al-Senaidi, S., Lin, L., Poirot, J.: Barriers to adopting technology for teaching and learning in Oman. Comput. Educ. **53**(3), 575–590 (2009)
27. Mokhtar, M., Noordin, N.: An exploratory study of industry 4.0 in Malaysia: a case study of higher education institution in Malaysia. Indonesian J. Electr. Eng. Comput. Sci. **16**(2), 978–987 (2019)
28. Pixelplex Blog: Artificial Intelligence in Education: Use Cases and Applications (2020) https://pixelplex.io/blog/top-use-cases-of-ai-in-education/. Accessed 05 Feb 2021
29. Crawford, C., Gregg, P., Macmillan, L., Vignoles, A., Wyness, G.: Higher education, career opportunities, and intergenerational inequality. Oxford Rev. Econ. Policy **32**(4), 553–575 (2016). https://doi.org/10.1093/oxrep/grw030
30. Hung, M., Smith, W., Voss, M., Franklin, J., Gu, Y., Bounsanga, J.: Exploring student achieve-ment gaps in school districts across the united states. Educ. Urban Soc. **52**(2), 175–193 (2020). https://doi.org/10.1177/0013124519833442
31. Woolf, B.P., Lane, H.C., Chaudhri, V.K., Kolodner, J.L.: AI grand challenges for education. AI Mag. **34**(4), 66–84 (2013)
32. Jisc: Learning Analytics in higher education (2016). https://www.jisc.ac.uk/reports/learning-analytics-in-higher-education. Accessed 18 Feb 2021
33. Vitalsource Webinar Recordings: Engagement and learning outcomes in an online learning environment. https://learn.vitalsource.com/LG68-Kaplan-Webinar-Recording.html. Accessed 18 Feb 2021
34. Jisc - Case Study B: Analysing the use of VLE at the University of Maryland, Bal-timore County. https://analytics.jiscinvolve.org/wp/files/2016/04/CASE-STUDY-B-Univer sity-of-Maryland-Baltimore-County.pdf. Accessed 18 Feb 2021
35. CASBO: Top Five Barriers to Education Technology (2017). https://www.casbo.org/content/ top-five-barriers-education-technology. Accessed 17 Feb 2021
36. Google for Education. https://edu.google.com/. Accessed 17 Feb 2021
37. Impact Portraits: Charlotte-Mecklenburg Schools. https://drive.google.com/file/d/0B_ OTXR_u3RbUElRa19QTWZnMlU/view. Accessed 17 Feb 2021
38. Google for Education Case Studies – Gowerton School. https://edu.google.com/why-google/ case-studies/gowerton-school/. Accessed 17 Feb 2021
39. Google for Education Case Studies – SOPOGO. https://services.google.com/fh/files/misc/ sopogo_case_study_en.pdf. Accessed 17 Feb 2021
40. Jisc Case Study: Wikimedia in the curriculum. https://repository.jisc.ac.uk/7129/11/edinbu rgh-uni-wikimedia-in-the-curriculum-case-study.pdf. Accessed 17 Feb 2021
41. Khoo, E., Peter, M., Scott, J., Round, H.: Flipped classroom learning in a first-year undergrad-uate engineering course. In: Bastiens, T. et al. (eds.) Proceedings of EdMedia: World Confer-ence on Educational Media and Technology, pp. 1275–1280. Association for the Advancement of Computing in Education (AACE), Amsterdam (2018)
42. Bergmann, J.: Sams, A: Flip Your Classroom: Reach Every Student in Every Class Every Day. International Society for Technology in Education, Eugene (2012)

43. Olaniyi, N.E.E.: Threshold concepts: designing a format for the flipped classroom as an active learning technique for crossing the threshold. Res. Pract. Technol. Enhanc. Learn. **15**(1), 1–15 (2020). https://doi.org/10.1186/s41039-020-0122-3
44. Jisc: Active blended learning. https://repository.jisc.ac.uk/7129/10/uni-of-northampton-active-blended-learning-case-study.pdf. Accessed 17 Feb 2021
45. University of Northampton: Gold – Teaching Excellence Framework 2017. https://www.northampton.ac.uk/about-us/gold-teaching-excellence-framework-2017/. Accessed 17 Feb 2021
46. Querium: Making STEM Learning smarter with A.I.-based virtual tutor engine. http://querium.com/stepwise-virtual-tutor/. last accessed 17 Feb 2021
47. Century – Our Story. https://www.youtube.com/watch?v=HOO0DT62UqQ&feature=emb_logo. Accessed 17 Feb 2021
48. Blippar Blog: Bringing the Augmented Reality Education to your home for free. https://www.blippar.com/blog/2020/04/07/bringing-the-augmented-reality-education-to-your-home-for-free. Accessed 17 Feb 2021
49. Blippar Blog: Teacher Rhys Corcoran on using Blippar for GCSE Geography. https://www.blippar.com/blog/2016/11/11/blippar-educators-rhys-corcoran-using-blippar-gcse-geography. Accessed 17 Feb 2021
50. Cognii Virtual Learning Assistant. https://application.reimagine-education.com/the-winners-individual/2015/392/f16ba8c8f771cafe824c648e61dfd6a3/Cognii%2C+Inc. Accessed 17 Feb 2021
51. Digiteum Blog - How IoT Is Used in Education: IoT Applications in Education (2020). https://www.digiteum.com/iot-applications-education/. Accessed 18 Feb 2021
52. IEEE ICICLE: Learning Engineering Process. https://sagroups.ieee.org/icicle/learning-engineering-process/. Accessed 19 Feb 2021
53. Healey, M., Flint, A., Harrington, K.: Engagement through partnership: students as partners in learning and teaching in higher education (2014). https://www.advance-he.ac.uk/knowledge-hub/engagement-through-partnership-students-partners-learning-and-teaching-higher. Accessed 24 Feb 2021

# A Generic CbITS Authoring Tool Using xAPI

Jinsheng Pan[1], Lijia Wang[2(✉)], Keith Shubeck[2], and Xiangen Hu[2,3(✉)]

[1] The Ohio State University, Columbus, USA
[2] The University of Memphis, Memphis, USA
{lwang3,xhu}@memphis.edu
[3] Central China Normal University, Wuhan, China

**Abstract.** Intelligent Tutoring Systems (ITSs) are considered among the most effective and efficient learning systems. The difficulty of authoring content limits the use of ITSs and creates a bottleneck for most ITS researchers and related industries. AutoTutor, a conversation-based ITS, faces the same problem. This paper will introduce the new improvement of AutoTutor Lite using xAPI and its potential as a generic CbITS authoring tool.

**Keywords:** ITS · AutoTutor · Authoring · xAPI

## 1 Introduction

Intelligent Tutoring Systems (ITSs) has been a hot topic for more than 30 years. Many researchers' work have demonstrated that ITSs are among the most effective and efficient learning systems compared to other learning systems (Fletcher 2005; Vanlehn 2006). As a type of adaptive instructional systems (AIS), conversation-based intelligent tutoring systems (CbITS) have seen much progress using cloud computing and widespread mobile devices like smartphones and laptops (Wang et al. 2020). Due to the COVID-19 pandemic, online education has, at the very least, been strongly encouraged, and in many cases has been required. This has caused demand for AISs to increase in order to satisfy remote education purposes and goals.

## 2 AutoTutor

AutoTutor is a conversation-based intelligent tutoring system. AutoTutor is an effective AIS that has been used for research in the learning sciences for over 20 years (Nye et al. 2014). AutoTutor has shown average learning gains of $0.8\sigma$ during its nearly two decades researches (Nye et al. 2014). It has been applied to a wide range of domains such as computer literacy (Graesser et al. 1999; Person 2003), physics (Graesser et al. 2003; Rus et al. 2014), mathematics (Nye et al. 2018, 2015), electronics (Graesser et al. 2018; Morgan et al. 2018), adult literacy (Cai et al. 2015; Graesser et al. 2016), critical thinking (Graesser et al. 2010; Wallace et al. 2009), biology (Olney et al. 2010), and medical (Wolfe et al. 2016). However, the difficulty of content authoring is a persistent issue for most researchers and industries (Cai et al. 2019; Sottilare et al, 2015; Wang

© Springer Nature Switzerland AG 2021
R. A. Sottilare and J. Schwarz (Eds.): HCII 2021, LNCS 12792, pp. 243–253, 2021.
https://doi.org/10.1007/978-3-030-77857-6_16

et al. 2020), especially when there is a high demand for remote education and ITSs during the pandemic. Researchers may need to consider how to move a step forward by lowering the barrier and difficulties of authoring (Wang et al. 2020). This paper will introduce the new improvement of AutoTutor Lite to demonstrate the power of xAPI and the potential ability as a generic content authoring tool editor. We also want to provide some thoughts on the application of xAPI in an effort to inspire the people who work on the development of ITS authoring tools.

### 2.1  AutoTutor Lite

AutoTutor Lite is the web version of the AutoTutor family (Cai et al. 2015). AutoTutor Lite does not require downloading of any files for its web users to use it online. Additionally, it has nearly no system requirements. It only requires a browser and internet access, so there is almost no barrier for people to use an ITS like AutoTutor. The light weight also saves CPU and internet resources, which improves the system performance and stability. AutoTutor Lite uses an XML file as input to execute an AutoTutor learning object. The XML format is good at data presentation and supports validation, which can prevent syntax errors and incorrect data structures. Most recently, a new version of AutoTutor was released based on Html5 integrated with xAPI statements, which also includes new features to AutoTutor Lite.

### 2.2  xAPI

Another important part of the design is the integration of xAPI to the authoring tool. xAPI is a standard to deliver data statements. The format of the xAPI follows the "actor verb object" (https://adlnet.github.io/, Serrano-Laguna et al. 2017, Nye. et al. 2014) structure, which can well-describe the activities within the system or system-user interactions. As a widely accepted standard, it is very easy for ITSs to share xAPI data with other ITSs using the same data pipeline. In addition to the general usage of xAPI on recording user activities in ITSs, it can also be used to record the actions during the content authoring process. The xAPI records the behavior of the ITS system as well as the content author's interactions with the AutoTutor Lite editor. Thus, besides the regular system behavior, the content details are also recorded in detail as part of the object in xAPI statements sent by the editor. A learning record store (LRS) can hold and manage all the xAPI statements generated during the activities between users and ITSs or authoring tools. LRS also provides data visualization tools to demonstrate the data trends among the xAPI data. Therefore, there is no need to save additional files on another server for AutoTutor Lite. One can easily extract one's own script from xAPI data. This can avoid saving duplicate scripts and reduce storage space waste. Also, this feature can be used to build a version control system (VCS) which we will discuss in the later section.

## 3  Framework

As an ITS, AutoTutor Lite consists of two parts. One is the learning objects player. The other is the content authoring editor. AutoTutor Lite uses an HTML5 based editor rather

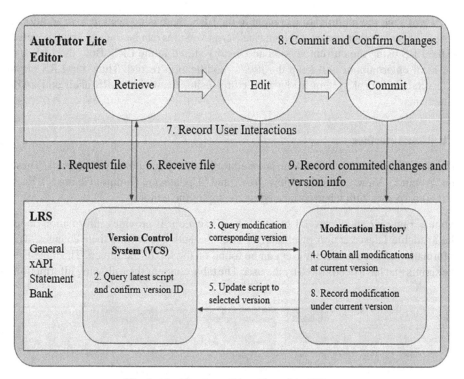

**Fig. 1.** Architecture of AutoTutor Lite Editor

than the outdated flash player. Compared with previous versions, the new version works as a generic tree structure editor with the capability to hold multimedia for different experimental purposes. Figure 1 shows the architecture and workflow of the AutoTutor Lite editor. The new AutoTutor Lite editor integrates the xAPI and associates the system with the LRS. xAPI statements will record the system and users' activities as well as function as the VCS and script storage. As Fig. 1 shown, the editor will retrieve XML files under one's account from LRS. Each file in the LRS is assigned with a unique id (GUID). This allows the AutoTutor editor to retrieve the target file accurately by searching the GUID. After the XML file is successfully loaded, the AutoTutor editor will display the whole script by the selected major component (element) in a tree structure. This simplifies the UI design to adapt the generic XML file modification. The tree structure can also reveal the parent-children relationships among each element in the AutoTutor script structure. It may enhance one's understanding of the system and improve the authoring strategy in general. The AutoTutor Lite editor builds the tree structure with jsTree, an open source jquery plugin which provides interactive trees using json files. The XML format will be converted into a json format to use the jsTree plugin after schema validation. Json is a direct source format that is widely accepted and supported by many open source plugins. Additionally, many other input formats (such as .word, .txt, .xml) can be transformed into json with a low cost. After modifications, users are able to commit what they have done and save the changes into LRS. Considering that xAPI will send the modification content to the LRS, there is no need to save additional script files on another server. All historical script versions can be tracked and recovered in the LRS using the current version and history stored in the LRS. Both the LRS and the local environment will keep the user's modification record. Thus, the LRS plays as a version control system in our new editor using features of LRS itself and xAPI statements.

## 3.1   User Interface

The User Interface (UI) of the AutoTutor editor is mainly composed of four parts. These are "About", "View Outline", "View Tree", and "Update and Commit Changes". Each part corresponds with a button located on the top of the editor.

**About.** Figure 2 shows the UI of the "About" section. It provides information about the available latest version of all scripts after the author commits their changes. The information about the current user can be found on the top of the screen. The table lists the scripts that have been edited by the user. The table contains the following information:

**Fig. 2.** Commit record in local

- Action: the available action button(s) to the script.
- Last Author: the user who most recently edited the script.
- #: number of total changes committed to the script.
- Last Time Edited: the last date and time the user made the modifications;
- Title: the title of the script.

**View Tree.** With the "VIEW TREE" button, users are able to overview the structure of the input file in either a tree view (left of Fig. 3) or an XML view (right of Fig. 3). Under "VIEW TREE", the editor provides users with two additional layers of functional buttons. The first layers, or the second row of buttons in Fig. 3, are the major components of an AutoTutor script. The AutoTutor Lite editor splits the script into parallel components. This can prevent users' frustration brought by the unwieldy tree structure displayed due to the complex content from all the sections. Therefore, users can focus on their target section (such as information delivery, abbreviated as ID to author the educational content. Others, like the environment setting, media and other multimedia information are located in the "RUNNING ENVIRONMENT". With these parameters, one can trigger a desired running model with media information under the customized intelligent agent features. The second layer contains the "SEARCH" function to allow users to search and highlight a specific element quickly. The "SHOW XML/TREE" button can transform the display model between a regular tree structure and an input format. Users can edit in either format.It is easier to refine a few elements of a script in the tree view while it is quicker to replace and update large portions of the script with the XML view.

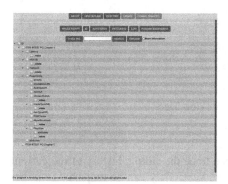

**Fig. 3.** Tree View Left: the tree view of the script under editing, Right: the XML view of the script under editing.

The editorial part allows users to directly edit the file with the operations of edit, copy/paste, insert, and delete under the tree view (see Fig. 4).

- Edit: users could modify the content of an item. However, not every item is allowed to be edited. Only items whose parent is "cdata" or "value" are allowed to be edited by right clicking on.
- Copy/Paste: users can copy an existing item and its children then paste the copy in the current tree at the same level. However, like the edit function,, not every not every item is allowed to be copied.
- Insert: users are capable of inserting a new selected item into the tree.
- Delete: users can delete the selected item including its children from the current tree.

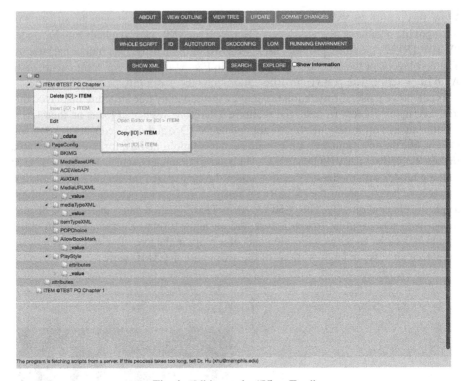

**Fig. 4.** Editing under "View Tree"

**View Outline**

With the "VIEW OUTLINE" button, users can trace the editing history of the current input file. The different versions of a script are kept. They can be reopened in either player or editor. The detailed information such as title, author, co-owner, commit, and description are kept and displayed to help users better locate the targeted version. Thus, "View Outline" is a key part of the VCS (Fig. 5).

**Update and Commit Changes**

The "UPDATE" "COMMIT CHANGES" buttons allow users to submit their modifications to the LRS. After users finish their editing, they can click the "UPDATE" button first to temporarily change the whole script and then confirm the changes are satisfactory. Users can then click the "COMMIT CHANGE" button which opens the "Commit Changes" window where they can commit changes, which updates the modified version to the LRS. Figure 6 shows the wrapped basic information that users can edit before updating the LRS. The wrapped information includes title, co-owners, collaborators, viewer, and descriptions. Additionally, if users check "save as new SKO", AutoTutor will save a new copy of the current script under their own account with a new GUID (Fig. 8).

**Version Control System.** To help users track and retrieve previous versions, AutoTutor Lite has a VCS that uses xAPI. The old VCS would create an extra copy of an AutoTutor

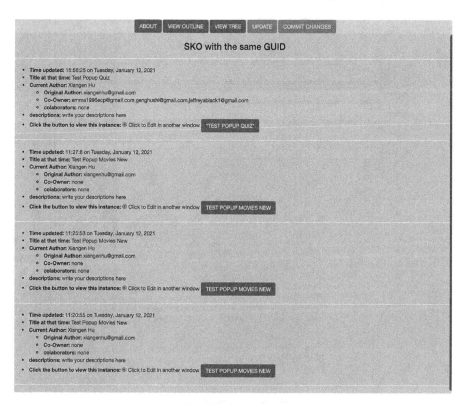

**Fig. 5.** View outline

script and then save it in the backup server. If someone needed to restore a previous version, it simply obtained the corresponding saved file from the backup server. while this cancan solve the issue, it is not a sustainable plan for long term use due to the limits on memory. with the current VCS. AutoTutor first receives the latest version of the file and the history from LRS, then starts to recover the previous version. As Fig. 6 exhibits, both the latest script and history objects are stored in LRS in JSON format. This is in part due to the ease at which the JSON'format can build Js. Tree. Additionally, it is generally easy to use and occupies less space for long objects. In the "history" object, each modification contains a unique id and is placed in descending order. It also keeps the ID, operation, original content, and any new content belonging to a modified element. To restore the most recent script , AutoTutor will first create an empty script called the

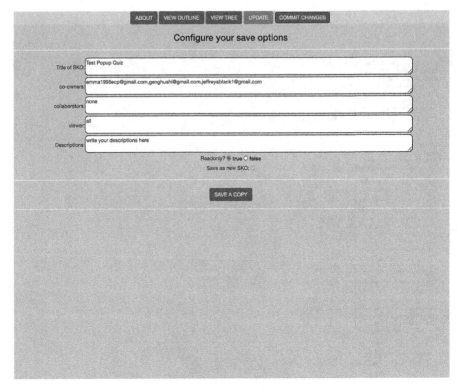

**Fig. 6.** Commit change

recovery script. Then the history of the modified elements (Fig. 7.) will be extracted and compared with the latest script version. AutoTutor will keep the elements not found in its history, because they are not modified. The overlapping elements will be updated based on the type of operations from the following actions:

- Edit: if the element's operation is "edit", AutoTutor will copy the element from latest-version script to recovery script and then in recovery script, change the original content of element to new content recorded in history.
- Insert/paste: if an element's operation is "insert/paste", then AutoTutor and the recovery script will ignore it since the item doesn't exist in the previous version.
- Delete: if an element's operation is 'delete', then AutoTutor will make up a new object with json format and content in the item. Then AutoTutor will add the object to the recovery script, which is also in json format.

```
▼ "JSON_script" : [ 🔁
  ▼ 0 : { 🔁
      "id" : "j1_1"
      "text" : "ID"
      "icon" : true
    ▼ "li_attr" : { 🔁
        "id" : "j1_1"
      }
    ▼ "a_attr" : {
        "href" : "#"
        "id" : "j1_1_anchor"
      }
    ▼ "state" : {
        "loaded" : true
        "opened" : true
        "selected" : false
        "disabled" : false
      }
    ▸ "data" : {}
      "parent" : "#"
      "type" : "default"
  }
  ▼ 1 : {
      "id" : "j1_2"
      "text" : "ITEM @null"
      "icon" : true
    ▼ "li_attr" : {
        "id" : "j1_2"
      }
    ▼ "a_attr" : {
        "href" : "#"
        "id" : "j1_2_anchor"
      }
    ▼ "state" : {
        "loaded" : true
        "opened" : false
        "selected" : false
        "disabled" : false
      }
    ▸ "data" : {}
      "parent" : "j1_1"
      "type" : "default"
  }
  ▼ 2 : {
      "id" : "j1_3"
      "text" : "TITLE"
```

**Fig. 7.** Latest version history

| | | | | |
|---|---|---|---|---|
| ▸ ☑ | John Doe | saved | AT PAL3:FL_KC_Q4 | 2 weeks ago *(Tue Jan 19 2021)* |
| ▸ ☑ | John Doe | saved | AT PAL3:FL_KC_Q4 | 2 weeks ago *(Tue Jan 19 2021)* |
| ▸ ☑ | John Doe | saved | AT PAL3:FL_KC_Q4 | 4 weeks ago *(Sat Jan 09 2021)* |
| ▸ ☑ | John Doe | saved | AT PAL3:FL_KC_Q4 | 1 month ago *(Mon Dec 21 2020)* |
| ▸ ☑ | John Doe | saved | AT PAL3:FL_KC_Q4 | 2 months ago *(Sat Dec 19 2020)* |
| ▸ ☑ | John Doe | saved | AT PAL3:FL_KC_Q4 | 2 months ago *(Sat Dec 19 2020)* |
| ▸ ☑ | John Doe | saved | AT PAL3:FL_KC_Q4 | 2 months ago *(Thu Dec 17 2020)* |
| ▸ ☑ | John Doe | saved | AT PAL3:FL_KC_Q4 | 2 months ago *(Thu Dec 17 2020)* |
| ▸ ☑ | John Doe | saved | AT PAL3:FL_KC_Q4 | 2 months ago *(Wed Dec 16 2020)* |
| ▸ ☑ | John Doe | saved | AT PAL3:FL_KC_Q4 | 2 months ago *(Wed Dec 16 2020)* |
| ▸ ☑ | John Doe | saved | AT PAL3:FL_KC_Q4 | 2 months ago *(Wed Dec 16 2020)* |
| ▸ ☑ | John Doe | saved | AT PAL3:FL_KC_Q4 | 2 months ago *(Wed Dec 16 2020)* |
| ▸ ☑ | John Doe | saved | AT PAL3:FL_KC_Q4 | 2 months ago *(Wed Dec 16 2020)* |
| ▸ ☑ | John Doe | saved | AT PAL3:FL_KC_Q4 | 2 months ago *(Wed Dec 16 2020)* |
| ▸ ☑ | John Doe | saved | AT PAL3:FL_KC_Q4 | 2 months ago *(Wed Dec 16 2020)* |

**Fig. 8.** Save/commit history

## 4    Conclusion

AutoTutor Lite has successfully integrated xAPI within the system. By taking advantage of the xAPI statements, a new VCS was built to remove unnecessary copies and save space by removing redundant information. The whole editor is built using the JSTree plugin, which functions as a generic tree editor and is indifferent to the file's content. We believe this aids users with their understanding of the AutoTutor system and reduces the burden resultingfrom the addition of a long script. However, the new editor could not really solve the difficulties of the content authoring. For example, it is still challenging for new users to develop a truly qualified and effective AutoTutor script (i.e., expectation-misconception tailored). Moving forward, some new modules will be integrated to the new system like emotion detection, which further expands the research application of AutoTutor.

## References

Cai, Z., Hu, X., Graesser, A.C.: Authoring conversational intelligent tutoring systems. In: Adaptive Instructional Systems, pp. 593–603 (2019)

Fletcher, J.D.: The advanced distributed learning (ADL) vision and getting from here to there. INSTITUTE FOR DEFENSE ANALYSES ALEXANDRIA VA (2005). http://www.dtic.mil/docs/citations/ADA452053

Wang, L., Shubeck, K., Shi, G., Zhang, L., Hu, X.: CbITS Authoring Tool in GIFT. In Proceedings of the 8th Annual Generalized Intelligent Framework for Tutoring (GIFT) Users Symposium (GIFTSym8) (p. 69). US Army Combat Capabilities Development Command–Soldier Center (2020)

Wang, L., Shubeck, K., Hu, X.: Google service-based CbITS authoring tool to support collaboration. In: Stephanidis, C., Harris, D., Li, W.-C., Schmorrow, D.D., Fidopiastis, C.M., Zaphiris, P., Ioannou, A., Fang, X., Sottilare, R.A., Schwarz, J. (eds.) HCII 2020. LNCS, vol. 12425, pp. 605–616. Springer, Cham (2020). https://doi.org/10.1007/978-3-030-60128-7_44

Murray, T.: Authoring intelligent tutoring systems: an analysis of the state of the art (1999). https://telearn.archives-ouvertes.fr/hal-00197339/

Nye, B.D., Graesser, A.C., Hu, X.: AutoTutor and family: a review of 17 years of natural language tutoring. Int. J. Artif. Intell. Educ. 24(4), 427–469 (2014)

Sottilare, R., Graesser, A., Hu, X., Brawner, K.: Design Recommendations for Intelligent Tutoring Systems: Authoring Tools and Expert Modeling Techniques. US Army Research Laboratory (2015)

Vanlehn, K.: The behavior of tutoring systems. Int. J. Artif. Intell. Educ. 16(3), 227–265 (2006)

Wolfe, C.R., et al.: Understanding genetic breast cancer risk: processing loci of the BRCA Gist intelligent tutoring system. Learn. Ind. Diff. 49, 178–189 (2016)

Moundridou, M., Virvou, M.: Analysis and design of a web-based authoring tool generating intelligent tutoring systems. Comput. Educ. 40(2), 157–181 (2003)

ADL Initiative, "xAPI Specification," (2016). https://github.com/adlnet/xAPISpec/blob/master/xAPI.md

Serrano-Laguna, Á., Martínez-Ortiz, I., Haag, J., Regan, D., Johnson, A., Fernández-Manjón, B.: Applying standards to systematize learning analytics in serious games. Comput. Stand. Int. 50(February), 116–123 (2017)

Nye, B., Hu, X., Graesser, A., Cai, Z.: Autotutor in the cloud: a service-oriented paradigm for an interoperable natural-language ITS. J. Adv. Distrib. Learn. Technol. 2(6), 49–63 (2014)

Cai, Z., Graesser, A.C., Hu, X.: ASAT: AutoTutor script authoring tool. In: Sottilare, R., Graesser, A.C., Hu, X., Brawner, K. (eds.) Design Recommendations for Intelligent Tutoring Systems: Authoring Tools, pp. 199–210. Army Research Laboratory (2015)

# Intelligence Augmentation for Collaborative Learning

Jeremy Roschelle[(✉)] [iD]

Digital Promise, San Mateo, CA 94403, USA
jroschelle@digitalpromise.org

**Abstract.** Today's classrooms can be remarkably different from those of yesteryear. In place of individual students responding to the teacher from neat rows of desks, today's innovative schools have students working in groups on projects, with a teacher circulating among groups. AI applications in learning have been slow to catch up; most available technologies are described as personalizing or adapting instruction to needs of individual learners. Meanwhile, an established science of Computer Supported Collaborative Learning has come to prominence, with clear implications for how collaborative learning can be supported. In this contribution, I consider how intelligence augmentation could evolve to support collaborative learning. A focus on AI role in automating, adding to awareness, assisting and augmenting is suggested, extending the field's prior tendency to focus on assessing, assigning and adapting.

**Keywords:** Intelligence augmentation · Collaborative learning · Learning sciences

## 1 Introduction

Artificial Intelligence (AI) has been applied to education for 50 years. A classic early AI & education paper proposed extending computer-aided instruction systems with question-answering capabilities based on a representation of knowledge [1]. In the subsequent decades, intelligent tutoring systems (ITS) emerged as a dominant paradigm [2], in which AI was used to infer differences between the knowledge state of a student and the knowledge state of an expert, and to adjust instruction to address these differences [3]. This paradigm contemplated one student interacting with one computer. A continuation of the ITS paradigm was reflected in the most common metaphor used AI-inspired educational technology in the past decade: personalized learning [4]. By personalized, innovators most often mean an automated decision-making process that changes each student's students individual experience on their own device to better suit their learning needs. Learning engineers can continue to develop this "personalized learning" approach as they develop intelligence augmentation for learning—yet to address current educational goals it may be necessary to go beyond this metaphor toward a collaborative, social learning mindset.

© Springer Nature Switzerland AG 2021
R. A. Sottilare and J. Schwarz (Eds.): HCII 2021, LNCS 12792, pp. 254–264, 2021.
https://doi.org/10.1007/978-3-030-77857-6_17

## 1.1   Changes in Educational Goals

Over the last 50 years, the goals of education have changed. Because machines can increasingly automate routine work, it has become more important to help humans to master skills for situations that are non-routine, team-oriented, complex and all of the above. Across all sectors, including higher education, the military, and K-12 education, 21st century skills have become important and infused our understanding of subject matter [5].

For a detailed example, consider the topic of K-12 mathematics. In the United States, the National Assessment of Educational Progress (NAEP) has been used since the 1970s to measure the trend in American student's understanding of mathematics at grades 4, 8, and 12. Over the course of 50 years, NAEP has diverged into two subtests. So that we can compare scores from 1970 to those today, NAEP maintains a subtest specifically to measure the long term trend. This test focuses on knowledge of basic facts, paper and pencil computations, basic measurement formulas, and applying mathematics to everyday life situations (e.g. using money). In the 1970s, a typical mathematics classroom focused on individual students who were learning to use standard procedures to do mathematics quickly and accurately.

The main portion of NAEP today uses a framework has multiple additional dimensions (following changes in the mathematics curriculum standards that have been adopted by states in the US, based on similar international standards). *Conceptual understanding* of mathematics is understood to be a goal that is equally important to procedural problem solving [6]. Students are expected to show understanding by using tools beyond paper-and-pencil, including not only calculators but interactive geometric figures and graphs. Mathematical reasoning is important, and students are expected to make sound arguments, to identify counter-examples to false conjectures, and to use logic. Likewise, there is concern with investigating whether students can make and use mathematical models of real world situations—a much more sophisticated demand than using math in simple real-world situations with money.

Correspondingly, today's best mathematics classrooms look different than they did 50 years ago. Students are expected to work in groups to solve more challenging problems (for example, building a statistical mathematical model to make a recommendation to a soccer coach as to which players should be among the five to take end-of-game penalty kicks). They are expected to discuss and argue over concepts. They will likely make drawings, use mathematical tools (perhaps a spreadsheet or a simulation), and present their work in a broader classroom discussion. Some work is still individual (as procedural fluency in mathematics does require practicing skills), but work also occurs in groups and moves into modes where the teacher leads a discussion with student participation. A teacher, for example, may lead a discussion that compares and contrasts the mathematical strategies that different groups employed for modeling penalty-kick data, and how the different models might help or not help the soccer coach make a decision.

## 1.2   Intelligence Augmentation Must Evolve to Fit Educational Goals

Not surprisingly, early ITS systems likewise on supporting students to do standard procedures quickly and accurately. For example, *model-tracing*, an important approach, followed a student's steps in comparison to what an expert would do, and intervened as soon as the student deviated from an expert approach [3]. AI for learning today has evolved to include many other techniques to helping individual students, often under the banner of "personalization." However, many of these techniques reference a vision of educational goals that better fits 1970s goals than the goals for today. For example, giving each student their own "playlist" of mathematical problems based on the speed and accuracy of their work in the prior playlist makes sense for the goal of learning to do mathematical procedures quickly and accurately. Having students work alone on their own personal problem set does NOT make sense when the goal is to learn to work with team-mates to build a mathematical model that solves a complex challenge. Working alone at your own pace does not make sense when the goal is to learn how to make a mathematical argument or how to explain mathematical concepts to another person.

### 1.3   Intelligence Augmentation and CSCL Fits Today's Goals

As previously discussed, ITS systems beginning in the 1970s addressed 1970s educational goals. They also used 1970s information processing psychology as their theoretical framework. To address today's goals, we need a different theoretical framework. Computer-Supported Collaborative Learning (CSCL) is a body of theory, recently summarized in an international handbook [7], that is appropriate to today's educational goals and can provide a basis for conceptualizing what Intelligent Augmentation [8] for learning can look like today. CSCL fits for three reasons.

First, it contemplates students working together on more complex intellectual challenges (which may be in any academic subject, not just mathematics). It portrays students as being involved together in knowledge building [9], which can apply to the situation of building a mathematical model together, or figuring out a scientific theory, or finding a coherent framework that explains the progression in a series of historical events.

Second, it imagines a classroom where students are engaged in explaining, discussing and arguing with each other. CSCL reflects a "social turn" in learning theory [10], which sees learning not just as something that individuals do on their own, but also a human act that is profoundly social and linguistic. This image reflects what high quality instruction is expected to look like today: teachers are expected to get their students actively and socially engaged.

Third, it envisions a progression of classroom experiences that interweave individual, small group, and full-classroom modalities. The work of making a coherent progression among these modalities is termed "classroom orchestration" [11] – an imperfect analogy where the teacher leads the classroom of students just as a conductor leads an orchestra of musicians.

All three of these characteristics are hard for teachers to achieve. It is difficult to organize and support "productive struggle" among students as they try to solve complex problems. It is difficult to facilitate useful discussions among students and to shape that towards an approximation of "mathematical reasoning" or "scientific argumentation." And it is difficult to orchestrate classrooms so that the different experiences—individual, small group, and full group—connect in meaningful and useful ways.

## 1.4  The Pandemic Highlighted Gaps

When teaching suddenly shifts online, as during the recent pandemic, achieving high quality collaborative learning becomes even more difficult. Although many schools and teachers have shifted to video-conference-based classrooms, interaction patterns have tended to emphasize one teacher talking to multiple students. Even though tools to support online collaboration are available and well-used in the workplace, it is difficult to find examples of schools and teachers who have shifted to been able to maintain classrooms that fulfil today's educational goals, for example, where students work together on more complex challenges, that feature participatory discourse among students, that leverage small group work, and smoothly shift among individual, small group and community-level activities.

## 1.5  A New Vision for Intelligence Augmentation Can Build on CSCL

The difficulties that teachers and students experience in achieving today's educational goals or in participating in what today's instruction is expected to look like—along with the body of research on theory and design for CSCL—provide a way to specify a vision for Intelligence Automation that can meet today's needs. The remainder of the paper elaborates how this could occur.

# 2  Framing Computer Support for Collaborative Learning

## 2.1  About CSCL

CSCL [7] is a subfield of the learning sciences that has a history dating back to the late 1980s. Broadly, the field launches from a recognition that (a) collaborative learning both increases how much students learn (b) learning to collaborate and collaborating to learn are both important (b) yet, most students require support to learn how to collaborate and to engage in effective collaborative learning. An early definition describes collaborative learning as "coordinated, synchronous activity that is the result of a continued attempt to construct and maintain a shared conception of a problem" [12]. To coordinate student activity, the field has developed a robust theory of "scripts" [13] which are supports that organize for student roles, responsibilities and shape the dynamics of collaborative learning. CSCL has led to understanding of how computer-based visualizations and representations can support constructing and maintaining a shared understanding through tools like shared concept maps [14]. More recently, CSCL has documented the supports that students need as they learn to self-regulate their own behavior and their group's work in collaborative learning [15].

Overall, a strong empirical track record documenting the effectiveness of collaboration learning when the work is adequately structure and students are supported. In 2015, the well-known OECD international assessment, PISA, gave students tests of both their ability to collaborate and their skills in academic subjects. The results show a strong correlation between collaboration and learning in science, mathematics, and other subjects [16]. Empirical research has been summarized by meta-analysis (combining the weighted the results of many independent studies), and has found impressive impact of

CSCL on science learning [17]. Today's teachers are also broadly supportive of collaborative learning; for example, when asked how they cognitively engage their students, the top strategies of teachers worldwide focused on giving open-ended challenges to students in small groups [18].

### 2.2   How CSCL Frames Opportunities for Intelligence Augmentation

Kirschner and Erkens [19] provide a useful 3 × 3 framework for describing the role of tools in collaborative learning. They first discuss three aspects of learning, *cognitive, social,* and *motivational.* Tools that support the cognitive aspect would help students with reasoning and with building their knowledge. Tools for the social aspect help students work together. Tools for the motivational aspect help to maintain student interest and engagement during collaborative learning.

A second dimension reflects the grouping of students, which may be at the *community* (or classroom) level, the *small group/team* level, or the *individual* level. A classic research-based community tool in CSCL is called "Knowledge Forum" and is a shared discussion board that has specific supports for a classroom not only to map its collective knowledge about a focal question but also to build on each other's thoughts, to work through disagreements, and to pose collective questions for further investigation.

A third dimension discusses types of pedagogical supports. *Discourse-oriented* tools may facilitate better learning in student discussions, for example, by providing prompts, organizing students into roles, and the like. *Representational* tools help students to visualize and operate on the shared state of knowledge within their group. *Process tools* can facilitate collaborations working through team work phases, such as going from a brainstorm to more focused project work.

## 3   Scenarios for Intelligence Augmentation for Collaborative Learning

Building on the above discussion, we now envision directions for intelligence augmentation that would specifically respond to collaborative learning goals and situations. Although thinking through each of the nine cells in the aforementioned 3 × 3 matrix would be productive, it would also exceed the scope available here. Instead we use the matrix to develop a few contrasting opportunities.

### 3.1   Actionable Awareness of Discussion Patterns

This scenario is community-level, discourse-oriented, and social.

Advances in natural language and vision processing are making it possible to automatically detect patterns in group discussions. For example, the commercially available tool called "TeachFx" provides teachers with colorful visualizations of the pattern of talk in their classrooms, based on a recording the teacher makes using an app on their smartphone. An early feature summarized how much time the teacher or students spends talking during class periods; teachers were often surprised with just how little time was devoted to student talk. Of course, an enabling condition for collaborative learning is

# You had 27 Student Talk highlights

- **What do you think about the quality of Student Talk in this class?** Were your students participating in the way you hoped? Using academic language? Engaging with one another's ideas?
- **What do you think about the equity of Student Talk in this class?** Did you hear a diverse array of voices? Whose are missing?

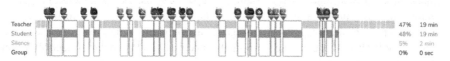

| | | | |
|---|---|---|---|
| Teacher | | 47% | 19 min |
| Student | | 48% | 19 min |
| Silence | | 5% | 2 min |
| Group | | 0% | 0 sec |

**Fig. 1.** Assisting a teacher by finding student talk highlights.

giving students time to talk, and TeachFx has documented that teachers can improve on this metric by paying attention to simple reports (Fig. 1).

Intelligence augmentation can go beyond documenting overall talk-time. For example, TeachFx already automatically suggests classroom highlights. A highlight is a span of classroom talk that featured high-levels of student engagement and interaction. A teacher can quickly listen to the recording of that span of activity or review a rough transcript of what was said. This automation can greatly reduce the time it would take a teacher to review a recording of the classroom and can enable the teacher to make plans to build on successful discussions in future lesson plans.

In related research, investigators have already demonstrated the ability to detect other kinds of interactional patterns among students, for example, relating to eye-gaze, body posture, and particular features of speaking patterns [20]. One can imagine additional forms of assistance that build on this data. For example, classroom teachers seek for inclusive and equitable classroom participation; intelligence automation could help with monitoring who is participating and who has been silent, suggesting opportunities to draw students into the fray. An assistant might also help a teacher recognize which kinds of questions or activities most often lead to effective social engagement, and might suggest opportunities to use those moves in an upcoming lesson.

## 3.2 Maintaining Student Effort Across a Sequence of Activities

This scenario is process-oriented, motivational and spans different team sizes.

In a well-established routine for peer learning, students first respond to a few challenging questions individually (for example, in a lecture that uses "clickers" to capture student responses). Then each student meets with a peer who gave a different response than their own, with the instruction to work towards agreement. This routine uses cognitive dissonance to motivate student discussion of their varied points of view.

One can imagine extrapolating from this scenario to additional forms of augmentation for classroom orchestration, in particular, for enabling the shift from one grouping size of work (individual, group, community) to another while maintaining continuity and motivation. For example, in shifting from group work to a broader discussion, an intelligent assistant might suggest an order of presentation for groups based on the work they did. Hearing about several groups that did roughly the same thing would be less interesting and evocative than discussing contrasting approaches. A full group might brainstorm conjectures that they would like to explore and an intelligent assistant might help with assigning students to conjecture teams while maintaining desired characteristics of the groups (for example, that each group should have a team lead who is good at getting the group engaged).

Motivation may also go astray in a small group for any number of reasons of personal dynamics and yet, unless a teacher is in a group, it can be quite difficult for them to know which groups are struggling. Intelligence augmentation, therefore, can add to the teacher's awareness—for example, alerting the teacher to groups that may need attention and possible reasons to check.

### 3.3 Developing Skill in a Collaborative Learning Role

This scenario is individual, cognitive, and representational.

Although this may seem paradoxical, supports at the individual level may also be useful for supporting collaborative learning. In one implemented example, students are charged to give feedback to a peer about an essay. A technological support system for the feedback-giver results in better feedback and better learning [21]. One kind of cognitive support can be a tool for analyzing and representing the argument that an essay-writer is making. An appropriate tool could help students to diagram the argument and to better see addressable flaws; this kind of tool could potentially benefit from an AI assistant. Tools to support individuals as they participate in collaborations may also address neurodiversity. Some students may benefit from supports for executive function as they collaborate, for example, helping them attend to important details, strengthening short term memory, or scaffolding a multistep process. An automated system of supports could build on well-known Universal Design for Learning principles, such as providing information relevant to the collaboration in alternative representational modalities (e.g. automatic captioning or transcription of a video stream that students are watching together). Online agents can also help a child with autism to develop social skills [22].

Peer agents can also help in preparing students for a later social learning event. For example, an agent could coach a student on how to effectively communicate their question or idea in a forthcoming group or classroom discussion. A student who may be uncomfortable verbalizing their idea could be supported by a role play – or by a tool that helps them to build a graphic or other form of communication to share their idea. Another aspect of the challenge, especially for younger learners, is maintaining an awareness of alternative ideas that others in the team may have. A representational tool could help an individual team member remember that other students have ideas which are different from their own. Overall, learning to collaborate and collaborating to learn are intertwined competencies that develop over years. Tools for individuals can support the growth of these competencies.

# 4  Discussion: Commonalities that Deserve Attention

Looking reflectively across the scenarios suggests commonalities.

## 4.1  Automate, Add Awareness, Assist and Augment

Although there has been some interaction between the field of CSCL and Artificial Intelligence, this intersection is still emerging.

In the personalized learning era, three very common verbs for the role of an intelligent agent were assessing, assigning, and adapting. Agents might assess or track what students are learning and where they need support. On this basis, they might assign new playlists of work to students (or assign specific modules to the student for their further study). Further, the agents might adapt to students' needs by providing each student with the hints, supports, or guidance they most need.

As we shift from an individualized focus to a collaborative learning focus, these verbs are not likely to suffice. Based on reviewing the scenarios, we suggest three additional verbs:

1. *Automate.* Because collaborative learning is complex, teachers and students may need help that automates more routine aspects of the work, so that they can focus their cognitive effort on building shared knowledge. For example, a computer could can efficiently score last night's individual homework, allowing a teacher and students to quickly determine which problems were difficult for students and thus deserving of further group discussion.
2. *Add awareness.* As collaborative learning situations have lots going on for participants, including both relationships and tasks, intelligence augmentation can help by adding support for awareness of key features that might otherwise go unnoticed (for example, who has not been speaking).
3. *Assist.* In a collaborative learning situation, intelligence augmentation is likely to take the form of a helpful assistant who is present during a group work. Perhaps in a lull in conversation, the assistant might suggest an activity or topic to get students' back on track. Or it might draw students to a discrepancy worthy of their shared attention.
4. *Augment.* The phrase "augmentation" in collaborative learning and teamwork has a long history dating back to Englebart's seminal work [11]. As a verb, augmentation recognizes that high-quality teamwork is not easy for students to accomplish, and thus agents might help a group accomplish more than they otherwise would. For example, augmentation could note key concepts as students discuss them verbally and suggest the concepts as nodes which need to be organized on a concept map. Or it might clean up a partial concept map to make it easier for students to work with it together.

## 4.2  Context-Sensitive, Longitudinal and Hybrid

Looking across the scenarios, one can also observe three general challenges for the field of Intelligence Augmentation which a focus on a collaborative learning could address.

1. *Context-sensitive.* As the 3 × 3 matrix should make clear, collaborative learning activities occur in a rich context. Collaborations have a past, present, and future. They should reference not only the team's trajectory, but also how it connects to individual- and community-level learning activities. Learning has motivational, social, and cognitive aspects. In general, designing intelligence augmentation to be appropriately aware of context is an important challenge for AI.

2. *Longitudinal.* Supporting collaborative learning is not just about figuring out what a team of students need know right now. It is also about supporting long-term development of the ability to be a good collaborator and a good collaborative learner. For example, students should be learning how to self-regulate their emotions, cognition and participation in challenging collaborative learning situations. How intelligence augmentation could facilitate longer term development of individual and groups is an open question.

3. *Hybrid.* Collaborative learning also shifts our focus from the one-student-one-computer scenario of early ITS systems to teamwork in agency includes multiple students and multiple intelligent agents. One can readily imagine an agent serving as a "participation coach" (in reference to the first scenario) alongside an agent that may support a teacher in orchestrating a motivating sequence of activities alongside an agent that helps an individual student with their role in the collaboration Working towards a hybrid future of work with multiple forms of agency, both human and computational, is another long-term vector of growth for the field.

### 4.3  Responsible, Human-Centered AI

To realize a positive future of learning based on these ideas will require much attention to issues of ethics, equity, safety, privacy and related concerns. To stay within page limits, this paper deferred the thorough discussion these issues deserve.

## 5  Conclusion

Collaborative learning is a match to today's educational goals. These goals go beyond fast and accurate reproduction of basic and routine procedures. Driven by what is needed by future societies, educational goals more often feature teamwork, tackling complex problems, and developing the ability to work together effectively.

Further, a body of prior designs and theories can inform how innovators explore intelligence augmentation for collaborative learning. In particular, the field of CSCL has summarized its knowledge in a recent handbook of research-based knowledge. A 3 × 3 framework that illuminates the range of possible objectives for learning engineering. Designs may aim to address cognitive, social, or motivational aspects; they may target individual, group, or community level processes; they may offer discourse, representational, or process supports. Reflecting on potential scenarios for intelligence augmentation suggests that the field must also push for capabilities that are context-sensitive, support long-term development and that support hybrid teams of multiple human and computational agents.

As we consider both the shortfalls in learning during the pandemic and how learning may look as we move into the future, innovators and engineers who develop learning technology could create powerful new intelligence augmentations by tackling the needs of teachers and students in support of collaborative learning.

**Acknowledgements.** This material is based upon work supported by the National Science Foundation under grant #2021159 (CIRCLS). Any opinions, findings, and conclusions or recommendations expressed in this material are those of the author(s) and do not necessarily reflect the views of the National Science Foundation.

# References

1. Carbonell, J.R.: AI in CAI: An artificial-intelligence approach to computer-assisted instruction. IEEE Trans. Man-Mach. Syst. **11**(4), 190–202 (1970). https://doi.org/10.1109/TMMS.1970.299942
2. Sleeman, D., Brown, J.S.: Intelligent Tutoring Systems. Academic Press, London (1982)
3. Corbett, A., Anderson, J.R.: Knowledge tracing: Modeling the acquisition of procedural knowledge. User Model. User-Adap. Inter. **4**, 253–278 (1995). https://doi.org/10.1007/BF01099821
4. Pane, J.F., Steiner, E.D., Baird, M.D., Hamilton, L.S.: Continued progress: Promising evidence on personalized learning. Santa Monica, CA, RAND Corporation (2015). https://doi.org/10.7249/RR1365
5. Trilling, B., Fadel, C.: 21st Century Skills, Enhanced Edition: Learning for Life in Our Times. Josey-Bass, San Francisco (2009)
6. National Research Council and Mathematics Learning Study Committee: Adding it up: Helping children learn mathematics. Washington, DC: National Academies Press (2001)
7. Cress, U., Oshima, J., Rosé, C., Wise, A.: International Handbook of Computer-Supported Collaborative Learning. Springer, Berlin. ISBN 978-3-030-65291-3 (in press)
8. Engelbart, D.: Augmenting Human Intellect: A Conceptual Framework; Summary Report, Contract AF 49–1024; SRI International: Palo Alto (1962). https://doi.org/10.21236/AD0289565
9. Scardamalia, M., Bereiter, C.: Computer support for knowledge-building communities. J. Learn. Sci. **3**(3), 265–283 (1994). https://doi.org/10.1207/s15327809jls0303_3
10. Lerman, S.: The social turn in mathematics education research. In Boaler, J. (ed.) Multiple Perspectives on Mathematics Teaching and Learning, pp. 19–44 (2000)
11. Roschelle, J., Dimitriadis, Y., Hoppe, U.: Classroom orchestration: synthesis. Comput. Educ. **69**, 523–526 (2013). https://doi.org/10.1016/j.compedu.2013.04.010
12. Roschelle, J., Teasley, S.D.: The construction of shared knowledge in collaborative problem solving. In: Computer Supported Collaborative Learning, pp. 69–97. Springer, Berlin (1995). https://doi.org/10.1007/978-3-642-85098-1_5
13. Fischer, F., Kollar, I., Stegmann, K., Wecker, C.: Toward a script theory of guidance in computer-supported collaborative learning. Educ. Psychol. **48**(1), 56–66 (2013). https://doi.org/10.1080/00461520.2012.748005
14. Ainsworth, S., Chounta, I.A.: The roles of representation in computer supported collaborative learning. In: Cress, U., Oshima, J., Rosé, C., Wise, A. (eds.) International handbook of computer-supported collaborative learning. Springer, Berlin. ISBN 978-3-030-65291-3 (in press)

15. Järvelä, S., et al.: Enhancing socially shared regulation in collaborative learning groups: designing for CSCL regulation tools. Educ. Technol. Res. Dev. **63**(1), 125–142 (2015). https://doi.org/10.1007/s11423-014-9358-1 https://doi.org/10.1016/j.edurev.2019.100284

16. OECD. PISA 2015 results (volume V): Collaborative problem solving. Paris, OECD. https://doi.org/10.1787/9789264285521-en (2017). https://doi.org/10.1787/1d0bc92a-en

17. Jeong, H., Hmelo-Silver, C. E., Jo, K: Ten years of computer-supported collaborative learning: a meta-analysis of CSCL in STEM education during 2005–2014. Educ. Res. Rev. **28** (2019). https://doi.org/10.1016/j.edurev.2019.100284

18. OECD: TALIS 2018 Results (Volume I): Teachers and school leaders as lifelong learners, TALIS, Paris, OECD Publishing.https://doi.org/10.1787/1d0bc92a-en

19. Kirschner, P.A., Erkens, G.: Toward a framework for CSCL research. Educ. Psychol. **48**(1), 1–8 (2013). https://doi.org/10.1080/00461520.2012.750227

20. Ramakrishnan, A., Ottmar, E., LoCasale-Crouch, J., Whitehill, J.: Toward automated classroom observation: Predicting positive and negative climate. In: 14th IEEE International Conference on Automatic Face & Gesture Recognition, pp. 1–8. IEEE (2019). https://doi.org/10.1109/FG.2019.8756529

21. Latifi, S., Noroozi, O., Talaee, E.: Peer feedback or peer feedforward? Enhancing students' argumentative peer learning processes and outcomes. Br. J. Educ. Technol. e13054 (2021). https://doi.org/10.1111/bjet.13054

22. Tartaro, A, Cassell, J.: Playing with virtual peers: bootstrapping contingent discourse in children with autism. In: Proceedings of International Conference of the Learning Sciences (ICLS), Utrecht, Netherlands, 24–28 June (2008)

# Designing Ethical Agency for Adaptive Instructional Systems: The FATE of Learning and Assessment

Jordan Richard Schoenherr$^{(\boxtimes)}$

Department of Psychology, Institute for Data Science, Carleton University, Ottawa, Canada
jordan.schoenherr@carleton.ca

**Abstract.** Adaptive Instructional Systems (AIS) have the potential to provide students with a flexible, dynamic learning environment in a manner that might not be possible with the limited resources of human instructors. In addition to technical knowledge learning engineering also requires considering the values and ethics associated with the creation, development, and implementation of instruction and assessment techniques such as fairness, accountability, transparency, and ethics (FATE). Following a review of the ethical dimensions of psychometrics, I will consider specific ethical dimensions associated with AIS (e.g., cybersecurity and privacy issues, invidious selection processes) and techniques that can be adopted to address these concerns (e.g., differential item function, $l$-diversity). By selectively introducing quantitative methods that align with principles of ethical design, I argue that AIS can be afforded a minimal ethical agency.

**Keywords:** Adaptive instructional systems · Ethical AI · FATE · Responsible AI

*"Shallow understanding from people of good will is more frustrating than absolute misunderstanding from people of ill will." – Rev. Dr. Martin Luther King, Jr.*

## 1 Introduction

Autonomous systems[1] are perhaps the most impressive artifact humans have created. The proliferation of these systems stems from their promise in performing tasks accurately and rapidly (intelligence) and to do so with little or no human intervention (autonomy). As we become more reliant on autonomous systems, we must consider the implications of shifting responsibility – in whole or in part - from human to nonhuman agents in terms of how these systems can be used, misused, disused, or abused [1–4]. For instance, in UX design, dark patterns (design decisions that de-emphasized user's values and interests in favour of other stakeholders) that represent conflicts between user and client interests have become an increasing concern [5]. These observations have led to a greater emphasis

---

[1] To avoid terminological issues and overlap between the acronym for adaptive instructional systems and autonomous/intelligence systems, I will simply refer to the latter as autonomous systems in that all of these systems have some level of autonomy, i.e., a subset of operations are carried on without user control or supervision.

© Springer Nature Switzerland AG 2021
R. A. Sottilare and J. Schwarz (Eds.): HCII 2021, LNCS 12792, pp. 265–283, 2021.
https://doi.org/10.1007/978-3-030-77857-6_18

on responsible innovation, including considerations of values and ethics during design and implementation [6–8].

Nowhere are these considerations more relevant than in learning technologies. Education is a value-laden domain wherein instructors must actively select what to provide to learners. In that educators provide a social scaffolding for learners, they are in a critical position to shape their knowledge, strategies, attitudes, and behaviours. Learning technologies such as adaptive instructional systems (AIS) and related approaches (e.g., Intelligent Tutoring Systems)[2] substitute a nonhuman agent (e.g., instructor, tutor) for a human agent [9]. In that learner-educator dyads are typically defined by asymmetric power relationships, these relational structures will likely persist, albeit in a modified form, when learners engage with an AIS. Moreover, given the consequential nature of instruction and assessment, [10, 11] poor design can lead to significant ethical (e.g., fairness) and social challenges (e.g., discrimination). Thus, the ethical status of AIS must be considered.

The recognition that education is value-laden [12, 13] and the identification of essential features of moral education [14–16] are important first steps, however, the development of learning technologies like AIS requries a set of concrete practices that can be *embedded within* these systems. In the present review, I consider the implementation of ethical design through operationalization of ethical principles [17] using available approaches. In contrast to some domains, learning technologies are uniquely positioned to develop principled approaches to ethically aligned design. Specifically, research in assessment methodologies has identified frameworks that incorporate statistical techniques that operationalize ethical and social values [10, 11] in a manner required to develop ethical AIS [18]. However, in that learning technologies are only one component of larger socio-technological systems, broader issues such as security and privacy should also be addressed with existing approaches to anonymization (e.g., $k$-anonymization and $l$-diversity) and cybersecurity.

## 2  Ethical Agency in Human and Nonhuman Agents

Efforts to develop standards for ethical autonomous systems are arguably older that the systems themselves, e.g., Asimov's (1942) fictional "Laws of Robotics". Contemporary accounts range from lists of rules and guidelines to proposals for plausible ethical agents [19, 20]. Fundamentally, ethics is concerned with the intentions and behaviour of agents. Thus, prior to considering how an AIS might have anything like ethical agency, I consider human ethical agency, or *ethical sensemaking*.

Ethical sensemaking can be understood in terms of developmental stages, affective and cognitive processes, and knowledge of the social context [21]. For instance, Kohlberg [22] identified three broad stages of moral competency development, defined by a progression from a focus on the receipt of reward and the avoidance of punishment, to interpersonal and social accord, to the use of consequentialist or non-consequentialist principles. Crucially, not all learners progress to the final stages of moral development,

---

[2] For the purpose of brevity, I will refer to both of these systems as adaptive instruction systems as the technical distinction is not relevant to the present discussion.

with many continuing to use group-based norms for ethical reasoning. Despite considerable empirical support for the general features of Kohlberg's theory, evidence from cross-cultural studies has challenged his original formulation [23, 24]. This led Kohlberg to accept that numerous ethical principles could be used in the final stages of moral development [25–27]. This suggestion is also compatible with the observation that humans maintain a number of relational models [28]. Crucially, numerous values inform our ethical judgments, [29] often leading to cross-cultural differences [30]. These norms and conventions must be accounted for when implementing AIS. For instance, studies have demonstrated that academic misconduct is affected by peer influences, such that individual cheating behaviour is positively associated with that of their peers. [31, 32] Learning engineers must therefore understand how learners perceive their relationship with these systems.

Even when individuals have knowledge of the appropriate norms and conventions that apply to a specific context and have adequate moral reasoning abilities, the limitations of cognitive processes can undermine moral judgments and behaviour. For instance, a number of studies have demonstrated that the division of attention can reduce prosocial behaviour [33] whereas directing an individual's attention to standards prior to a task reduces cheating behaviour [34]. Although conscious processing does not necessarily guarantee ethical behaviour (i.e., rationalization), [29] ethical agency requires some kind of active monitoring and regulation of behaviour relative to internal standards. Thus, learning engineers must also be aware of factors that can divide a learner's attention or prime norms that are incompatible with the current context [78].

## 2.1 Metacognition and Machine Morality

Rather than understanding ethical competencies in terms of humans, a general model of ethical agency in computer systems was provided by Moor [20, 35]. He considers four levels of ethical agency. *Ethical impact agents* are autonomous systems that have ethical consequences regardless of the intentions of the designers. *Implicit ethical agents* are systems that have ethical considerations embedded within them. The actions of these systems follow from ethical principles but they are not themselves aware of the ethical principles. *Explicit ethical agents* can identify the ethical affordances of a situation and respond appropriately. The actions of these systems come from a recognition of ethical patterns. Finally, *full ethical agents* have additional features that make them true agents: free will, intentionality, and consciousness. Crucially, Moor suggests that the realization of full agency need not be required to have an ethical system. Instead, he recommends that an explicit ethical agency is a more realistic goal [20]. Thus, a crucial feature of ethical agency is the ability to identify and match patterns within a data set, [36] which requires computable ethical principles that are operationalizable [17, 35, 37].

In Moor's framework, AIS currently reflect ethical impact agents. If AIS are to have a more advanced form of ethical agency, they require at least some dedicated means for ethical pattern classification. Rather than assuming that full ethical agency requires intentionality, consciousness, and free will, ethical sensemaking would seem to be *minimally* based on self-monitoring [19, 36, 38]. Namely, moral agency neither requires mental states, moral responsibility, nor free will [39]. In this way, an ethical AIS must perform primary tasks (i.e., instruction, assessment, feedback) [9] while also identifying patterns in its operations or output that match operationalized patterns which align with ethical principles. If an AIS is not used as a fully autonomous training and assessment system, humans might function as the monitoring and regulation system. If an AIS is granted a high level of autonomy during training and assessment, these systems require a minimal ethical agency to operate.

If minimal ethical agency only requires the incorporation of ethical principles and processes, three possible configurations for these systems appear to be principled following from models of metacognition: [40] systems can have integrated rules for learning, assessment, and ethics (Integration Model), independent, non-interactive systems for learning and assessment and ethics (Consecutive Model), or independent, interactive systems for learning and assessment and ethics (Interactive Model; See Fig. 1).

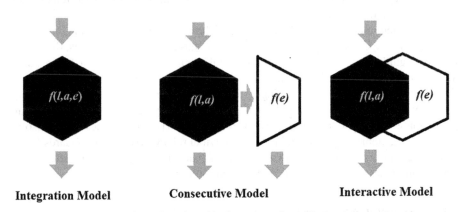

**Integration Model**     **Consecutive Model**     **Interactive Model**

**Fig. 1.** Three general configurations for ethical systems where $f(l,a)$ represents algorithms associated with learning and assessment of the learners performance, and $f(e)$ represent the algorithms associated with assessment of learning. Modified from Schoenherr [41].

*An Integration Model* assumes that we need to clearly demarcate general values associated with learning engineering and ethical values. In this way, deontic principles are not separated from learning and assessment algorithms. Here, an AIS would alter training and assessment in terms of these operationalized values, with all elements defining a single, integrated approach. This can be likened to Moor's notion of an implicit ethical agent as the rules that have ethical implications are not explicitly represented within the system as distinctly ethical. However, values have been considered and incorporated during the design process, i.e., value-sensitive design [6, 78]. Examples would include pre-defined outcomes based on population norms, e.g., performance for learners should be normally distributed defined by a specific mean and standard deviation, where these values are defined in the basis of prior performance. This scenario is likely what defines many current strategies in learning engineering.

*A Consecutive Model* assumes that the operations of an AIS should function independently of any evaluation of social and ethical issues. This approach requires that an ethical monitoring system identifies ethical or social issues based a set of pre-specified patterns. However, the monitoring system would not adjustment performance. Problematic operations or outputs would be identified in order to draw the user's or educator's attention to potential issues. In this way, a consecutive model monitors but does not regulate learning and assessment methods, i.e., an ethical auditor. Examples would include assessing all learners and providing the outcomes of this assessment to an instructor, e.g., an item analysis (described below). Alternatively, in an analogous manner to the original design purpose of intelligence tests, learners that fall below a threshold could also be identified and offered additional assistance, e.g., additional time, or instructional aids. At present, most AIS should be capable of performing these functions.

Finally, *An Interactive Model* assumes that the operations of an AIS might be altered by an ethical regulator. Here, an ethical monitoring system would identify patterns within the data during training and assessment and adjust the parameters of the primary learning and assessment algorithms. Unlike the Integrated Model, criteria related to social and ethical values are clearly demarcated, thereby facilitating modifications to the codes for ethical and non-ethical algorithms. Unlike the Consecutive Model, human intervention is not required. In this way, an interactive model monitors and regulates learning and assessment methods. To ensure transparency, the adjustment procedures used by this model can also be made available to instructors. For instance, if questions of a certain type are associated with biased responses for one group of learners from a specific social category (e.g., Differential Item Function; see Sect. 4.1), these questions and responses might be removed from testing or scores adjusted. Complex variants of this model could function like a generative adversarial network (GAN) or competition models of category learning [79]. In these cases, AIS could learn, and attempt to optimize, patterns associated with ethical norms, e.g., distributive justice principles like equality of outcome. As I will describe below, the adoption of an Interactive Model also requires a consideration of the trade-offs that will be introduced to learning and assessment as a result of adjustments, e.g., accuracy versus fairness. [42].

# 3   Modeling Metaethical Traditions

Metaethical theories define the objects, processes, outcomes, and the communication of moral judgments [43]. Three metaethical theories are considered here: non-consequentialism, consequentialism, and virtue theory. In addition to informing ethical sensemaking process, ethical AIS design should consider how each of these approaches can be implemented within autonomous systems.

*Rules and Duties: Non-consequentialism.* Concepts such as duties, rights, and justice are located at the center of non-consequentialism. Rather than the (positive or negative) outcomes of an action being the proper object of ethics, non-consequentialist accounts of ethics assume that the assessment of an action's ethicality is based on the use of appropriate rules and the intentions of the agent. Philosophers such as Locke and Aquinas argued that objective moral principles are discoverable through rationality. For Kant this principle is referred to as the *categorical imperative* (CI). The CI assumes that all individuals must be treated as autonomous, rational moral agents. Individuals must not be treated as a means to an end, but rather we must respect them as an end in themselves. The CI requires that people act as if they live in the 'the Kingdom of Ends,' i.e., that rational agents must adhere to universal laws regardless of their own motivations or desires to the contrary [44, 45]. In contrast to Kant's account, others have proposed a number of duties including fidelity, reparation, gratitude, non-injury, harm prevention, beneficence, self-improvement, and justice [46]. Contemporary theories often frame these principles as universal rights. For instance, Rawls' theory of justice assumes that all individuals within a society must be regarded as equal, with the rights of individuals conceived of from a position of neutrality. Challenges for non-consequentialist theories are apparent when multiple principles or duties conflict. If values cannot be prioritized (e.g., supervening principles), a means to resolve value conflicts is required in terms of differentially weighting principles.

In the context of AIS, non-consequentialism can be implemented in a straightforward manner. Bringsjord et al. [47] describe these systems as those that can "only perform actions that can be proved ethically permissible in a human-selected deontic logic." (p. 1). Learning engineers must first identify the underlying values and principles that define the social and ethical issues and operationalize these principles within a system. Support for this approach in AIS is evidenced in the increasing interest in incorporating principles that consider the distribution of the benefits of autonomous systems and their relative accessibility [48]. For instance, some approaches to learning engineering might require infrastructure (e.g., telecommunications, power) that rural populations do not have access to, as well as design features that limit the accessibility of these systems for particular persons, e.g., those who have a physical or mental disability. This issue was brought to light in the context of the COVID-19 pandemic [49]. How engagement can occur will depend on interactions between the content, learners, the social and physical environment, and learning technologies being deployed.

*Pleasure and Pain: Consequentialism.* In sharp contrast to non-consequentialism, consequentialism is concerned with the outcomes of actions or rules rather than the intentions behind the action. For instance, Jeremy Bentham assumed that each action is associated with good and bad outcomes. In order to determine the best course of action, one simply needs to sum up the possible outcomes over all of the individuals impacted be an action. Bentham referred to this approach as a 'hedonic calculus' because he assumed that our pleasure and pain responses were sufficient guides to moral actions. In contrast, John Stuart Mill advocated for a qualitative form of consequentialism (utilitarianism) that assumed that there were higher- and lower-order pleasures, such that only higher-order pleasures (e.g., utility) were used as guides to ethical behaviour.

Much like non-consequentialism, a consequentialist approach to AIS has a significant appeal given that it is rooted in an empirical approach that considers outcomes. Considering welfare from a general Bayesian approach, Harsanyi [50, 51] argued that truly impartiality members of a society would favour social contracts that maximize the outcomes for the group.[3] In addition to the static principles of non-consequentialism, learning engineers adopting a consequentialism framework would consider the extent to which specific learning and assessment strategies improve learner outcomes and efficiently use resources as well as the extent to which they provide evidence to support the construct validity of the approach. Such an approach would consider which groups of learners experience proportionally greater gains in performance with the introduction of AIS, or specific algorithms.

---

[3] Namely, his approach to welfare economics assumes that the goal should be to maximize expected utility.

*Virtues and Vices: Virtue Theory.* Virtue ethics assumes that there are essential individual characteristics that define the good, i.e., virtues. Ethical behaviour requires a constant striving to realize these characteristics in order to become a virtuous agent. In Aristotle's formulation, ethical behaviour requires both rationality, practical wisdom, and passion. In terms of this account, virtuous behaviour requires competencies that allow us to identify what features of a situation are ethically relevant, which principles are applicable, what the outcomes of actions will be, and how context affects both [21]. Beyond Aristotle, Maimonides, and Aquinas, virtue theory has been advanced in contemporary and cross-cultural framework. For instance, Confucianism emphasizes the development of moral competency in knowing when and how to act as well as our obligations to others based on prototypical relationships (e.g., father-son).

Virtue ethics has also been adapted to technology, with some arguing for specific 'technomoral virtues' including honesty, justice, courage, empathy, care, civility [52]. Virtue theory likely represents the most difficult approach to implement within AIS given its exclusive focus on ethical agency. Although autonomous systems can use static principles and modify them through experience, the inclusion of an affective component to ethical judgment represents an important hurdle.[4] However, monitoring for patterns in data that reflect social and ethical dimensions does appear to be feasible. For instance, the need for a monitoring capability in terms of an "ethical governor," [19, 53] formal verification procedures, or ranking processes [54]. One solution to designing an AIS informed by virtue ethics would be to operationalize both the principles (e.g., learning and assessment strategies) and outcomes (e.g., performance and social effects) of these systems. Although nonhuman agents might lack the ethical sensemaking ability of human agents, it might be possible to develop a *minimal* moral agency [20].

A useful guide to address these concerns is provided by He [55]. Writing in the New Confucian tradition, He's work is directed toward addressing what he considers to be the practical deficiencies of contemporary Chinese society. Specifically, He expresses concerns over growing corruption within organizations and losses of interpersonal cohesion in society more generally. Despite his focus on China, these concerns apply to all countries. To address these issues, He goes on to suggest that social ethics should adopt criteria for ethical judgments based on the 'moral minimum.' In contrast to Aristotelian virtue ethics that suggests that individuals should attempt to self-actualize by continuously striving for betterment, He's account instead assumes that we should identify the *minimal* standards that permit an individual to function as a member of society.

## 4    Explainable Ethical Standards for Assessment

Beyond general principles, ethical agency requires identifying specific features of a domain and technical affordances of autonomous systems [18]. If we assume that autonomous systems like AIS require ethical agency, we must find some means to evaluate and operationalize ethical standards. In this way, ethically aligned design reflects a

---

[4] Current work in autonomous systems that demonstrate 'empathy' are promising. However, at present these systems are generally focused on cognitive empathy rather than affective empathy. It remains an open question though whether affect cannot simply be modelled by differentially weighting variables or outcomes.

form of explainable AI (XAI) [56, 57] wherein designers must specify *how* specific processes reflect human values and operations [6–8]. Although not advanced as an XAI approach, Yu and Cysnerios [17] develop a compatible method. For instance, they assume that specific values like privacy and security can be operationalized into nontechnical (soft) goals which can further be decomposed into specific functional goals within the design. As Fig. 2 illustrates, the concept of 'privacy' can be operationalized in terms of a number of operational goals including minimizing the amount of personal data collected, restricting access, and adopting data retention techniques based on *l*-diversity. This reflects a mapping from high-level ethical affordances to low-level technical affordances. However, this also requires that developers understand *how* each concept is understood within a given cultural context as well as how specific users understand this concept. Thus, by understanding ethical design as a form of XAI, it recognizes the need to bridge the competencies of the developer and the user [58] reflecting a participatory design process [78].

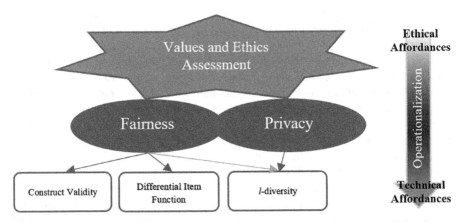

**Fig. 2.** Ethically aligned design operationalization framework. Examples are provided to demonstrate the operationalization of ethical affordances within an autonomous system.

In order to illustrate the kinds of technical affordances that reflect ethical design outcomes, we can consider values identified in guidelines. A number of ethical principles have been considered, e.g., IEEE [59] eight principles: human rights, well-being, data agency, effectiveness, transparency, accountability, awareness of misuse, and competence. To simplify this discussion, I consider affordances in terms of FATE: Fairness, Accountability, Transparency, and Ethics. In the remainder of this paper, I use the FATE framework to consider how minimal ethical agency can be implemented within learning engineering, including AIS.

### 4.1   Fairness

Fairness is typically defined in terms of two dimensions: the application of principles to all individuals (e.g., equality of opportunity) or in terms of distributive justice (e.g., equality of outcomes). Accuracy in learner assessment is a key feature of AIS [9]. Moreover, as Schoenherr [60, 78] has argued, Messick's [10] framework provides a comprehensive means to understand the ethics of psychometrics and its implications for novel learning technologies, e.g., integrated learning records. This is especially true in terms of the FATE value of fairness. Messick's approach has the added benefit of bypassing definitional issues of what constitutes ethical and non-ethical (e.g., social) values in that he considers all assessment a value-laden process. Messick [11] summarized his approach to construct validity by noting that it:

"requires validation not only of score meaning but also of *value implications and action outcomes*, especially appraisals of the *relevance and utility of the test scores* for particular applied purposes and of the *social consequences of using the scores for applied decision making*," (p. 13).

Crucially, Messick recognized that his "distinctions may seem fuzzy because they are not only interlinked but overlapping." [11, p. 22] Consequently, the facets of construct validity reflect pragmatic analytic categories. They nevertheless provide a useful means to structure discussions about the values that inform psychometrics.

**Construct Validity and Relevance/Utility: A Moral Minimum?** Messick provides crucial insight when he notes that various traditional notions of 'validity' (e.g., concurrent, convergent, discriminant, predictive) represent facets of construct validity. Moreover, construct validity represents the amount of evidence that supports the truth claims made within a given context rather than being an all-or-none property of a learning an assessment instrument, i.e., an argument-based approach to validity [61]. In contrast to construct validity, the relevance and utility of a test is determined by factors including the costs and benefits, e.g., administering, processing, interpreting [62]. In this way, the objectives and values of the individual or institution necessarily inform test construction and interpretation. For instance, private organizations might want to develop relatively simple learning technologies to support annual credentialing for ethics training. In this case, while a more extensive psychometrically validated instrument might ultimately be more accurate at discriminating performance, it might not be necessary for the intended purpose within an organization.

He's [55] concept of the moral minimum provides a useful means to understand Messick's argument about construct validity and relevance/utility. Namely, learning engineers' ability to understand how their systems will be used (i.e., value implications and social consequences, see below) are limited by their role within an organization and the availability of information. However, they can nevertheless ensure that their learning and assessment instruments adequately represent the constructs or competencies that they purport to, and that these learning and assessment instruments and the constructs they measure are relevant for their intended purpose. They represent a minimal standard in that they do not consider the wider consequences of assessment, only those for which a learning engineer has *intended* applications. This by no means implies learning engineers should not consider the larger impact of their systems once implemented, rather that this is the most elementary ethical standard that they must meet. This moral minimum is also addressed by the both the IEEE (e.g., 4. Effectiveness; 7. Awareness of Misuse; 8. Competence) and ACM principles (e.g., 2. Professional Responsibilities).

**Value Implications.** Messick's [10] notion of value implications requires a consideration of the consequences of score interpretation. Value implications can be understood in
terms of the *meaning* of the construct label, the explanatory framework used to interpret
the meaning of a learner's performance, and "the ideologies"[5] in which the explanatory
framework is embedded. For instance, a learning engineer might design a training system within an organization to develop a specific competency within a user (construct
validity). During the design process, they must consider whether the instrument supports
an organization's mandate (relevance/utility) but must also consider how an employee's
performance will be understood by management in terms of judging their merit and
value to the organization (value implications).

Learning engineers can assess value implications by examining the extent to which
the information from AIS influence the decision-making processes of an organization.
For instance, an employee's failure to perform adequately on a test might *simply require*
that they make another attempt, fail to receive a promotion or raise, or result in their termi-
nation. Moreover, there are additional value implications if the resulting records contain
personal information that, if breached, could have far reaching impacts on employees
within and outside of the organization. This approach is also addressed by the IEEE (e.g.,
3. Data agency) and ACM principles (e.g., 1.6 Respect privacy; 1.7 honor confidentiality;
2.9 Design and implement systems that are robustly and usably secure).

**Social Consequences.** Messick's notion of social consequences requires a consideration of all three previous facets of construct validity while situating them within the
larger social context. For instance, an employee or student that fails a test can lose their
job or fail to satisfy entry requirements. Thus, tests can adversely impact the position of
an employee or student. For Messick, social consequences were intimately connected to
construct validity such that if individuals from a specific social category (e.g., 'females,'
'gay men') are adversely affected by the use of their test scores, this either reflects a
source of bias within the test or reflects a feature of the construct being investigated.
Any beneficial or detrimental effects that result from the interpretation of test scores
are thus a crucial feature that needs to be considered by learning engineers. Indeed,
learning engineers and service providers share in the accountability for these systems
(see Sect. 4.2). Social consequences are also addressed by the IEEE (e.g., 1. Human
Rights and 2. Well-being) and ACM principles (e.g., 1.1 Contribute to society and to
human well-being, acknowledging that all people are stakeholders in computing; 1.2
Avoid harm).

Many aspects of social consequences might be difficult to embedded within learning
engineering. Discussions concerning social justice tend to focus on discriminatory practices that disadvantage one or more groups, or social category. However, social categories
can vary between groups and can change over time. One means to operationalize this
in the context of learning technologies is to examine Differential Item Function (DIF)
[63–65]. Based on Item Response Theory, [66, 67] DIF assumes that specific test items
might demonstrate differential performance for learners from different social categories,
e.g., socioeconomic status. Moreover, if left unaddressed, social categories might reflect
latent variables that might be predictors of performance. If the social consequences

---

[5] Messick's use of ideologies might reflect a comparable concept to Foucault's episteme.

for specific groups are deemed relevant, learning engineers can use statistical methods like DIF to examine whether AIS unintentionally favour members of specific groups. However, such adjustments are typically associated with trade-offs, [42] requiring that learning engineers have considered how changes in learning and assessment algorithms will impact accuracy and other associated outputs, e.g., feedback.

## 4.2 Accountability

Like fairness, accountability requires considering the obligations of learning engineers, the organizations that sell these technologies, and the institutions that use these technologies have to learners, educators, and organizations that use these technologies. Moreover, by choosing to employ AIS, individuals and organization do not simply shift moral responsibility to these systems. Accountability also requires considering how the innovations of learning engineers are situated within the social and legal structures of a society. This requires not only an understanding of the potential benefits and harms of the particular operations of an AIS (see Sect. 4.3), but also what regulations are available. For instance, in addition to ensuring that competencies are developed and assessed in an accurate manner (see Sect. 4.1) [80], the standards for the acquisition, retention, use, and reuse of records must also be considered. At a high-level, this requires considering standards at a prefecture/province/state, national, or international level such as the General Data Protection Regulation (GDPR) in Europe or the California Consumer Privacy Act (CCPA). A number of specific standards and recommended practices have also emerged addressing how learner record should be managed. Comprehensive Learner Records (CLR) or Integrated Learner Records (ILR) reflect institutional approaches to standardizing records [50]. In addition to technical affordances such as verifiability, interoperability, and portability, these records also require considering issues related to cybersecurity standards and privacy. Specifically, poor network security can increase the vulnerability to data breaches [68, 69] or destruction of information, e.g., ransomware [70, 71].

Learning engineers must ensure that learner data is secure relative to the extent that a system is connected to a network and information is accessible. Much like the requirements of confidentiality within experimental data, the identity of the learner and their performance can be retained in separate locations to ensure that the two are difficult to associate. Even when critical information (identifiers such as names, addresses, and phone numbers) is removed, unique combinations of other information (quasi-identifiers) can be used to infer the identity of a user. For instance, although many students might take an Introduction to Psychology course, few might take that course in conjunction with Geology, Western Philosophy, Hinduism, and Economics. Conjointly knowing all of these courses might allow a malicious attacker to identify an individual within a compromised data set. When these considerations are prevalent, privacy preserving algorithms can be used in the event that aggregated information is required. For instance, approaches such as $k$-anonymization [72] and $l$-diversity [73] describe means that can decrease the likelihood of de-anonymizing field structured data.[6] This value is also addressed by the IEEE (e.g., 3. Data agency; 6 Accountability) and ACM principles (e.g., 1.6 Respect privacy; 1.7 Honor confidentiality; 2.9 Design and implement systems that are robustly and usably secure).

### 4.3 Transparency

Within recent decades, there has been a growing recognition that advances in autonomous systems (specifically, machine leaning and deep neural networks) have created challenges for understanding and assessing their operations. Understanding the technical affordances of AIS are especially important for determining the extent to which they are accurately assessing a learner's performance (see Sect. 4.1) and assessing them against existing standards (see Sect. 4.2). Two prominent ethical issues have been identified as key impediments to autonomous systems: black box algorithms and black data [74, 75]. The opacity of algorithms and data sets tend to be understood in terms of two different dimensions. First, the proprietary nature of the of autonomous system or data set(s) used during training or within the automated decision process. Second, the relative impenetrability of the algorithm or data structure even when they are accessible. For instance, 'big data' sets likely exceed the capacity of any individual to identify quasi-identifiers or understand any relationships between variables. Similarly, the complexity of the algorithm can be such that the information and computer science professions that develop them do not necessarily fully understand their operations. These concerns have led to the need for explainable AI (XAI) [57].

Explainability has proven to be a difficult construct to operationalize in both the computer and cognitive sciences [56, 57, 76]. For instance, whereas interpretability reflects the extent to which an input-output relationship can be described, explainability relies on existing knowledge and analogical reasoning to supplement this process. As Schoenherr [58, 76] has argued, the extent to which a system can, or should be, explainable will be based on the context of the explanation, e.g., the message, audience, and reason for the explanation. Explanations that might work within one community of practice might not be informative in another [76]. Thus, learning engineers must ensure that the learning and assessment algorithms that define AIS are explainable to the learners and educators that use them. Similarly, educators must ensure that they understand the learning and assessment methods that define an AIS. In both cases, this might require training in scientific communication and relevant computer science methods for learning engineers and educators, respectively. This value is also addressed by the IEEE (e.g., 5. Transparency) and ACM principles (e.g., 1.6 Respect privacy).

### 4.4 Ethics

Finally, the metaethical frameworks described above (see Sect. 3) highlight a number of general social and ethical issues that can be addressed by AIS. Consequently, deeper ethical consideration such as 'human rights' and 'well-being' outlined in design frameworks

---

[6] Due to the potential for attacks resulting from homogeneity of a dataset or associations between multiple variables for $k$-anonymization, $l$-diversity promises to be a more effective means to preserve anonymity for low-diversity datasets wherein there is little diversity.

(e.g., IEEE, ACM; see also, [6–8]) would require operationalizing specific rules. As I've noted above (see Sect. 4.1), a number of these issues are computationally tractable. In addition to existing tools (e.g., DIF), there is also the possibility that dedicated ethical monitoring algorithms (e.g., Consecutive or Integrated Models; Sect. 2.1) might find novel ethical issues or discriminatory patterns within the data sets. For instance, these systems could be developed to provide users with structural equation models that represent the relationships between variables, to help educators better understand latent variables that affect learner performance. Similarly, using available data, AIS could model what changes in instructional design might increase learner performance given specific variables. For instance, a series of integrated AIS across multiple sections of the same course could be used to assess the effect of instructional style, question format, and environmental factors such as time of day.

The promise of dedicated ethical models introduces the possibility of greatly enhancing the ethicality of AIS. However, we must approach the design and development of these systems with caution. The multidimensional patterns that they identify or the algorithms that are used for identification, might be beyond the understanding of designers, educators, and administrators. This lack of opacity might make it difficult to identify the underlying ethical issues (see Sect. 4.3). In addition to a general need for transparency of AIS, this also highlights the continued role for human agents in learning engineering. Thus, even if full ethical agency is realizable in autonomous systems, [20] humans should retain responsibility in learning engineering. However, this requires that we ensure that educators have foundational skills in psychometrics and autonomous system design. Learning engineers must review and select appropriate value-based design frameworks that incorporates available laws and guidelines while accommodating ethical sensemaking through participatory design [78].

# 5   Conclusion

In contrast to claims that 'academic approaches' are not appropriate for developing an ethics of autonomous systems, [18] a review of the psychometrics tool currently available in learning technology suggest that ethical design of AIS can greatly benefit from theoretical approaches that have identified and operationalized social and ethical issues within learning engineering and instructional design. This paper has presented a framework that considers operationalization of values and ethics within AIS.

**Ethical Sensemaking and Agency in AIS.** Prior to designing ethical agents, we must first consider the *kind* of ethical agency that these systems should have. Using Moor's [20] framework, *AIS are ethically impactful agents* in that their operations have value implications and social consequences. The adoption of ethical design principles can ensure that AIS are implicit ethical agents in that they do not have a dedicated monitoring and regulatory systems but have incorporated ethical considerations into their operations. Metaethical frameworks can provide insight into how to assess the affordances of these systems in a design process that is sensitive to the values and ethics of users, designers, and organizations [6, 7, 78]. For instance, non-consequentialist approaches might prioritize user privacy and consent. In this case, an AIS would need to have these features embedded within the design. A consequentialist approach would instead emphasize the need to assess learner outcomes using specific criteria. Finally, a virtue ethics approach would instead emphasize ethical agency – whether on the part of stakeholders or the AIS itself. In terms of a learner-centered approach, this would ensure that learners are empowered to participate, and make decisions, about the learning process, with AIS facilitating those processes [7, 78]. Designers and educators must ensure that they take peer influence, division of attention, and conflicting social norms into consider. However, incorporating these features into a design does not make an AIS an ethical agent.

Ethical sensemaking also allows us to understand what features define ethical agency more generally. In terms of Moor's account, explicit ethical agents must, at a minimum, have the ability to recognize ethical patterns whereas full ethical agents require consciousness, intentionality, and free will. As I've argued above, it is not clear that these features are necessary to understand human ethical agency. Rather, I've suggested that we consider ethical agency in autonomous systems in terms of whether systems have ethical monitoring and regulation abilities. If these systems do not, they reflect Integration Models that are comparable to Moor's notion of implicit ethical agents. In order to have a greater level of ethical agency, ethical AIS must incorporate *computable* ethical principles [17, 35, 37, 77] and that ethical systems require a form of ethical pattern recognition, [20] what Moor would refer to as explicit ethical agents. Beyond an ability to audit information for ethical relevance, ethical agency also requires the ability to regulate – to respond in real-time to potential ethical concerns.

The ethical AIS framework proposed here suggest that ethical agency of autonomous systems should consider a system's ability to monitor and regulate its own operations. Consecutive Models make a distinction between algorithms associated with learning and assessment as algorithms associated with ethics. Here, an ethical module will assess each solution provided by an algorithm in terms of a set of ethical criteria. Human operators are then provided with all of the information about student performance and can then evaluate the respective outcomes of learning. More advanced versions of Consecutive Models could also suggest how to correct these patterns, by consider the trade-offs between the multiple criteria provided to the system, e.g., balancing accuracy with equitable outcomes for groups of learners [42]. If AIS can not only monitor but also regulate their operations of learning and assessment algorithms, they would then reflect Interactive Models. In that an essential feature of AIS is their adaptivity, this approach reflects a logical extensive of AIS. An AIS would be able to proactively respond to ethical patterns while altering how information is presented to a learner or how to asses a learner. Ideally, all AIS should have this capacity in that education is value-laden, however, there will be practical limits based on the data available to develop standards for specific learners or groups of learners.

**Ethical Standards for Assessment.** Any model of ethical AIS ultimately requires identifying and operationalizing a set of human values. Whether these reflect distinct values [52] remains an open question. A simple framework for considering values in the design of autonomous systems like AIS is FATE: fairness, accountability, transparency, and ethics. FATE is not the only framework available (e.g., IEEE, ACM). However, FATE presents a high-level set of values and ethics issues related to autonomous systems. Existing quantitative learning and assessment and methods can be aligned with FATE in order to incorporate elements of ethical agency into AIS. *Fairness* in assessment can be informed by Messick's validity framework. In terms of assessment, the moral minimum requires that learning engineers ensure that their learning and assessment strategies have sufficient evidence supporting their construct validity. More specific ethical standards would require considering how AIS are used within an organization, the value implications of assessment, and how these translate into social consequences for those being evaluated. This requires an understanding how social-technological systems function. In contrast, *accountability* requires considerations of how learner records are managed and used. Concerns such as interoperability, accessibility, and security require an understanding of the infrastructure that AIS will be used within. Criteria related to *transparency* are concerned with the intelligibility of these systems to various stakeholders. Namely, it is not only sufficient that a system is designed with principles such as construct validity and satisfies organizational requirements, rather the data and operations used by these systems must be open to evaluation to the respective stakeholders, corresponding to the notion of XAI [56, 76]. Simply because learners' performance is interpretable (e.g., pass or fail, A+ or D−, 67% or 81%) does not provide an explanation of how that value was determined. Transparency is also important in terms of avoiding dark patterns. In the context of design, dark patterns reflect behaviours such as behavioural nudging that result in users engaging in behaviour that benefits an organization rather than the user. In learning engineering, dark patterns might reflect satisficing heuristics such that learners develop strategies that allow them to pass tests without understanding the materials, e.g., selecting a familiar response rather than understanding the meaning of the terms and why a response is correct. If AIS reinforce these superficial studying strategies, learners will be more likely to apply these strategies in other equally consequential parts of their lives.

Finally, *ethics* requires broader concerns that pertain to abstract principles, the values and conventions of a society, and the nature of ethical agency. In many respects, this aspect of FATE is captured by value implications and social consequences of Messick's framework [10]. Designers and educators must consider how learners understand a situation and ensure that learners are provided with the opportunity to critically reflect on the ethical aspects of the educational experience provided by AIS. Concurrently, developers must also engage in ethical sensemaking to ensure that they have identified the ethical affordances on an AIS. Namely, they must consider how ethical affordances ('soft' or 'nonfunctional' goals) can be implemented within the design and where vulnerabilities are present within a system [78]. This point underscores the importance of considering the kind of ethics training provided to developers and learners. Broad metaethical traditions provide insight into what principles should be applied (non-consequentialism), what, and how, outcomes should be assessed (consequentialism), and what core competencies should be promoted in learners and built into autonomous systems (virtue theory).

**Ethical AIS: Humans-in-the-Loop.** By highlighting the importance of virtue theory and the ethical sensemaking abilities that it embodies, this framework promotes the continued role for humans in ethical AIS. Designers and educators should not delegate more responsibility to these systems even if they have the ability to monitor and regulate their own operations based on ethical pattern recognition. Following a similar approach to value sensitive design [6] or reflective design, [7] ethical sensemaking is ultimately participatory: learners, designers, and educators must consider the ethical affordances of these system [21, 78]. In some cases, learners might not be capable of understanding either the technical or ethical affordances of AIS, due to a lack of domain specific knowledge or moral reasoning ability, [25] respectively. Thus, while instructional designers and learning engineers should ensure that their systems are transparent, the process of knowledge translation associated with XAI has limits [58, 76]. Crucially, this framework attempts to highlight how social and ethical issues can be operationalized with existing educational technologies. For instance, fairness can be operationalized in terms of the construct validity of the approach adopted for learning and assessment [9, 10]. Similarly, statistical techniques such as DIF illustrate the ability to assess discrepancies between subgroups within a sample population. However, identifying these subgroups in terms of social categories requires humans that are knowledgeable of categories that have *psychological realism*, i.e., meaningful labels. Moreover, adjusting algorithms to compensate requires that humans consider the trade-offs in adopting one approach over another: by correcting for biases that affect a specific category, the overall accuracy of an algorithm might decrease. In the end, designer and instructors will be required to determine which values are most important in the educational context whether they are embedded within the design or are patterns of performance that result from AIS use.

# References

1. Lee, J.D., See, K.A.: Trust in automation: designing for appropriate reliance. Hum. Factors **46**, 50–80 (2004)
2. Parasuraman, R., Riley, V.: Humans and automation: Use, misuse, disuse, abuse. Hum. Factors **39**, 230–253 (1997)
3. Parasuraman, R., Mouloua, M., Hilburn, B.: Adaptive aiding and adaptive task allocation enhance human-machine interaction. In: Automation Technology and Human Performance: Current Research and Trend, pp. 119–123 (1999)
4. Moor, J.H.: What is computer ethics? Metaphilosophy **16**, 266–275 (1985)
5. Gray, C.M., Kou, Y., Battles, B., Hoggatt, J.T.A.L.: The dark (patterns) side of UX design. In: Proceedings of the 2018 CHI Conference on Human Factors in Computing Systems, pp. 1–14 (2018)
6. Friedman, B., Kahn, P.H., Borning, A.: Value sensitive design and information systems. In: The Handbook of Information and Computer Ethics, pp. 69–101
7. Sengers, P., Boehner, K., David, S., Kaye, J.J.: Reflective design. In: Proceedings of the 4th Decennial Conference on Critical Computing: between Sense and Sensibility, pp. 49–58 (2005)
8. Cummings, M.L.: Integrating ethics in design through the value-sensitive design approach. Sci. Eng. Ethics **12**, 701–715 (2006)
9. Sottilare, R.A.: A comprehensive review of design goals and emerging solutions for adaptive instructional systems. Technol. Instr. Cogn. Learn. **11**, 5–38 (2018)
10. Messick, S.: Validity of psychological assessment: validation of inferences from persons' responses and performances as scientific inquiry into score meaning. Am. Psychol. **50**, 741–749 (1995)
11. Messick, S.: Validity. In: Linn, R. L. (ed.) Educational Measurement, 3rd edn., pp. 13–103. American Council on Education/Macmillan Publishing Company, New York
12. Feather, N.T.: Values in Education and Society. Free Press, New York (1975)
13. Halstead, J.M., Taylor, M.J.: Values in Education and Education in Values. Psychology Press, Hove (1996)

14. Dill, J.S.: Durkheim and Dewey and the challenge of contemporary moral education. J. Moral Educ. **36**, 221–237 (2007)
15. Kohlberg, L.: Moral education in the schools: a developmental view. School Rev. **74**, 1–30 (1966)
16. Maosen, L., Taylor, M.J., Shaogang, Y.: Moral education in Chinese societies: changes and challenges. J. Moral Educ. **33**, 405–428 (2004)
17. Yu, E., Cysneiros, L.: Designing for privacy and other competing requirements. In: 2nd Symposium on Requirements Engineering for Information Security (SREIS 2002), Raleigh, 2002, pp. 15–16 (2002)
18. Blackman, R.: A practical guide to building ethical AI. Harvard Bus. Rev. 15 October 2020. https://hbr.org/2020/10/a-practical-guide-to-building-ethical-ai
19. Arkin, R.C., Ulam, P., Duncan, B.: An ethical governor for constraining lethal action in an autonomous system. Technical report GIT-GVU-09-02 (2009)
20. Moor, J.: Four kinds of ethical robots. Philos. Now **72**, 12–4 (2009)
21. Schoenherr, J.R.: Ethics Sensemaking and Autonomous and Intelligent Systems: Ethical Features of A/IS Affordances. In: Frontiers of AI Ethics (DeFalco, J. & Hampton, A.). Routledge Publishing, forthcoming
22. Kohlberg, L.: Moral stages and moralization. In: Lickona, T. (ed.), Moral Development and Behavior: Theory, Research and Social Issues, pp. 31–53. Rinehart and Winston, New York (1976)
23. Snarey, J.R.: The cross-cultural universality of social-moral development: a critical review of Kohlbergian research. Psychol. Bull. **97**, 202–232 (1985)
24. Al-Shehab, A.J.: A cross-sectional examination of levels of moral reasoning in a sample of Kuwait University faculty members. Soc. Behav. Pers. **30**, 813–820 (2002)
25. Kohlberg, L.: A current statement on some theoretical issues. In: Modgil, S., Modgil, C. (eds.) Lawrence Kohlberg Consensus and Controversy, pp. 485–546. Falmer Press, Philadelphia (1986). https://doi.org/10.1007/978-94-6300-079-6_11
26. Gibbs, J.C., Basinger, K.S., Grime, R.L., Snarey, J.R.: Moral judgment development across cultures: revisiting Kohlberg's universality claims. Dev. Rev. **27**, 443–500 (2007)
27. Thoma, S.J., Rest, J.R.: The relationship between moral decision making and patterns of consolidation and transition in moral judgment development. Dev. Psychol. **35**, 323–334 (1999)
28. Fiske, A.P.: The four elementary forms of sociality: framework for a unified theory of social relations. Psychol. Rev. **99**, 689–723 (1992)
29. Haidt, J.: "The moral emotions," in. In: Davidson, R.J., Scherer, K.R., Goldsmith, H.H. (eds.) Handbook of Affective Sciences, pp. 852–870. Oxford University Press, Oxford (2003)
30. Baek, H.: A comparative study of moral development of Korean and British children. J. Moral Educ. **31**, 373–391 (2002)
31. Hughes, J.M., McCabe, D.L.: Understanding academic misconduct. Can. J. High. Educ. **36**, 49–63 (2006)
32. Kisamore, J.L., Stone, T.H., Jawahar, I.M.: Academic integrity: the relationship between individual and situational factors on misconduct contemplations. Academic integrity: the relationship between individual and situational factors on misconduct contemplations. J. Bus. Ethics **75**, 381–394 (2007)
33. Darley, J.M., Batson, C.D.: From Jerusalem to Jericho: a study of situational and dispositional variables in helping behavior. J. Pers. Soc. Psychol. **27**, 100–108 (1973)
34. Mazar, N., Amir, O., Ariely, D.: The dishonesty of honest people: a theory of self-concept maintenance. J. Mark. Res. **45**, 633–644 (2008)
35. Moor, J.H.: Is ethics computable? Metaphilosophy **26**, 1–21 (1995)
36. Wallach, W., Allen, C.: Moral Machines: Teaching Robots Right from Wrong. Oxford University Press, Oxford (2008)

37. Pereira, L.M., Saptawijaya, A.: Programming Machine Ethics. Springer, Cham (2016). https://doi.org/10.1007/978-3-319-29354-7

38. Vanderelst, D., Winfield, A.: An architecture for ethical robots inspired by the simulation theory of cognition. Cogn. Syst. Res. **48**, 56–66 (2018)

39. Floridi, L., Sanders, J.W.: On the morality of artificial agents. Mind. Mach. **14**, 349–379 (2004)

40. Schoenherr, J.R.: Metacognitive assessments of performance: the psychometric properties of confidence scales and confidence models. In: Proceedings of Fechner Day, Antalya, p. 71 (2019)

41. Schoenherr, J.R.: Trust in the Age of Entanglement. Routledge Publishing, London (2022)

42. Kearns, M., Roth, A.: The Ethical Algorithm: The Science of Socially Aware Algorithm Design. Oxford University Press, Oxford (2019)

43. Miller, A.: Contemporary Metaethics: an Introduction. Wiley, Hoboken (2014)

44. Hill, T.E.: The kingdom of ends. In: Proceedings of the Third International Kant Congress: Held at the University of Rochester, March 30–April 4, 1970. Springer, Dordrecht (1972). https://doi.org/10.1007/978-94-010-3099-1_26

45. O'Neill, O.: Acting on Principle. Columbia University Press, New York (1975)

46. Ross, D.: The Right and the Good. Oxford University Press, Oxford (1930)

47. Bringsjord, S., Arkoudas, K., Bello, P.: Toward a general logicist methodology for engineering ethically correct robots. IEEE Intell. Syst. **21**, 38–44 (2006)

48. Roscoe, R.D., Chiou, E.K., Wooldridge, A.R.: Advancing Diversity, Inclusion, and Social Justice Through Human Systems Engineering. CRC Press, Boca Raton (2019)

49. Korman, H.T.N., O'Keefe, B., Repka, M.: Missing in the Margins: Estimating the Scale of the COVID-19 Attendance Crisis. Bellwether Education Partners, 21 October 2020. https://bellwethereducation.org/publication/missing-margins-estimating-scale-covid-19-att endance-crisis#How%20did%20you%20estimate%201-3%20million%20missing%20stud ents? Accessed 17 Dec 2020

50. Harsanyi, J.C.: Morality and the theory of rational behavior. Soc. Res. **44**, 623–656 (1977)

51. Hill, J.C.: Bayesian decision theory and utilitarian ethics. Am. Econ. Rev. **68**, 223–228 (1978)

52. Vallor, S.: Technology and the Virtues: A Philosophical Guide to a Future Worth Wanting. Oxford University Press, Oxford (2016)

53. Winfield, A.F., Jirotka, M.: Ethical governance is essential to building trust in robotics and artificial intelligence systems. Philos. Trans. R. Soc. A Math. Phys. Eng. Sci. **376** (2018). https://doi.org/10.1098/rsta.2018.0085

54. Dennis, L., Fisher, M., Slavkovik, M., Webster, M.: Formal verification of ethical choices in autonomous systems. Robot. Auton. Syst. **1**, 1–4 (2016)

55. He, H.: Social Ethics in a Changing China: Moral Decay Or Ethical Awakening? Brookings Institution Press, Washington (2015)

56. Došilović, F., Brčić, M., Hlupić, N.: Explainable artificial intelligence: a survey. In: 2018 41st International Convention on Information and Communication Technology, Electronics and Microelectronics (MIPRO) (2018)

57. Gunning, D.: DARPA XAI BAA, DARPA (2016). https://www.darpa.mil/attachments/DARPA-BAA-16-53.pdf. Accessed 20 Feb 2020

58. Thomson, R., Schoenherr, J.R.: Knowledge-to-information translation training (KITT): an adaptive approach to explainable artificial intelligence. In: International Conference on Human-Computer Interaction, pp. 187–204. Springer (2020). https://doi.org/10.1007/978-3-030-50788-6_14

59. IEEE Global Initiative on Ethics of Autonomous and Intelligent Systems, Ethically Aligned Design: A Vision for Prioritizing Human Well-being with Autonomous and Intelligent Systems. IEEE (2019)

60. Schoenherr, J.R.: Ethics of psychometrics: value implications of validity and integrated learner records in AIS. In: Learning Technology - Where we are Today (2021)
61. Kane, T.: An argument-based approach to validity. Psychol. Bull. **112**, 527–535 (1992)
62. Taylor, H.C., Russell, J.T.: The relationship of validity coefficients to the practical effectiveness of tests in selection: discussion and tables. J. Appl. Psychol. **23**, 565–578 (1939)
63. Cohen, A.S., Bolt, D.M.: A mixture model analysis of differential item functioning. J. Educ. Meas. **42**, 133–148 (2005)
64. Holland, P.W., Thayer, D.T.: Differential item functioning and the Mantel-Haenszel procedure. ETS Research Report Series, pp. i-24 (1986)
65. Osterlind, S.J., Everson, H.T.: Differential Item Functioning, vol. 161. Sage Publications, London (2009)
66. Nunnally, J.C., Bernstein, I.H.: Psychometric Theory. McGraw-Hill, New York (1994)
67. Rasch, G.: Studies in mathematical psychology: I. Probabilistic models for some intelligence and attainment tests. Nielsen & Lydiche (1960)
68. News, B.: University of York students targeted in data hack. BBC News, 1 July 2019. https://www.bbc.com/news/uk-england-york-north-yorkshire-49182179. Accessed 1 Aug 2020
69. Association, P.: Lancaster University Students Data Stolen in Cyber Attack. The Guardian, 23 July 2019. https://www.theguardian.com/technology/2019/jul/23/lancaster-university-students-data-stolen-cyber-attack. Accessed 1 Aug 2020
70. Doran, L.: Ransomware Attacks Force School Districts to Shore Up—or Pay Up. Education Week, 10 January 2017. https://www.edweek.org/ew/articles/2017/01/11/ransomware-attacks-force-school-districts-to.html. Accessed 3 July 2020
71. Erazo, F.: University of Utah Pays Ransomware Gang to Prevent Student Data Leak, Cointelegraph, 22 August 2020. https://cointelegraph.com/news/university-of-utah-pays-ransomware-gang-to-prevent-student-data-leak. Accessed 4 Sept 2020
72. Sweeney, L., Samarati, P.: Protecting privacy when disclosing information: k-anonymity and its enforcement through generalization and suppression. Technical report SRI-CSL-98-04. SRI Computer Science Laboratory, Pal Alto (1998)
73. Machanavajjhala, A., Kifer, D., Gehrke, J., Venkitasubramaniam, M.: l-diversity: Privacy beyond k-anonymity. ACM Trans. Knowl. Discov. Data (TKDD) **1**, 3-es (2007)
74. Schoenherr, J.R., Thomson, R.: Insider threat detection: a solution in search of a problem. In: 2020 International Conference on Cyber Security and Protection of Digital Services (Cyber Security), pp. 1–7. IEEE (2020)
75. Pasquale, F.: The Black Box Society, Harvard University Press (2015)
76. Schoenherr, J.R.: Black boxes of the mind: from psychophysics to explainable artificial intelligence. Proc. Fechner Day **2020**, 46–51 (2020)
77. Anderson, M., Anderson, S., Armen, C.: Towards machine ethics: implementing two action-based ethical theories, pp. 1–7. In: Proceedings of the AAAI 2005 Fall Symposium on Machine Ethics (2005)
78. Schoenherr, J.R.: Learning engineering is ethical. In: Goodell, J. (ed.) Learning Engineering Toolkit, pp. 193–221 (2022)
79. Ashby, F.G., Valentin, V.V.: Multiple systems of perceptual category learning: theory and cognitive tests. In: Handbook of Categorization in Cognitive Science, pp. 157–188. Elsevier (2017)
80. Schoenherr, J.R.: Adapting the zone of proximal development to the wicked environments of professional practice. In: International Conference on Human-Computer Interaction, pp. 394–410. Springer, Cham (2020)

# The Role of Participatory Codesign in a Learning Engineering Framework to Support Classroom Implementation of an Adaptive Instructional System

Kelly J. Sheehan, Meagan K. Rothschild[✉], and Sarah J. Buchan

Age of Learning, Inc., Glendale, CA 91203, USA
Meagan.rothschild@aofl.com

**Abstract.** This paper examines the role of participatory codesign in the creation of parent, teacher, and administrator dashboards for a game-based adaptive instructional system designed to teach math to young children. Taking a learning engineering approach, our team of researchers, curriculum specialists, and UX designers engaged in an iterative design process with six primary school teachers and 4 school administrators with the goal of understanding the appropriateness and effectiveness of the dashboards for different role types. Using ongoing interviews and a participatory codesign workshop, we engaged with teachers and administrators over several months and worked with them to understand how the dashboards could serve and be used by role types at varying levels (parent, teacher, principal, administrator, superintendent). We found that the effectiveness and appropriateness of the dashboard stemmed from its ability to communicate information across systems, like allowing teachers to communicate with parents on how to help their child, allowing principals to check-in on teachers on student progress, and allowing superintendents to review school-wide learning goals with principals. In sum, the participatory codesign process was highly successful, leading to a rich understanding of how the dashboards can be better designed to connect information across systems to better serve different role types.

**Keywords:** Participatory codesign · Educational technology · Learning engineering · Adaptive instructional systems

## 1 Introduction

Regardless of the technological innovation, the process for developing high-quality learning environments is, at the end of the day, about real people with their own experiences, needs and goals. And while digital media may offer a promising platform to support young learners with personalized, adaptive instructional systems at scale, contextual diversity ranges across individual learner variability, school learning environments, and home environments. Human-centered design practices are a key to an effective learning engineering framework that aims to respond to variance in human need and experience.

© Springer Nature Switzerland AG 2021
R. A. Sottilare and J. Schwarz (Eds.): HCII 2021, LNCS 12792, pp. 284–297, 2021.
https://doi.org/10.1007/978-3-030-77857-6_19

In our learning engineering framework (Fig. 1), we include participatory codesign with key stakeholders to maximize user engagement, learning outcomes, product scalability/stability, and implementation fidelity across stakeholder groups (Age of Learning 2020; Penuel et al. 2011). This paper will document the process of participatory codesign activities used to develop parent and educator dashboards for use with My Math Academy, a game-based adaptive instructional system designed to help young learners build mastery of early number sense and operations.

"Learning engineering," originally introduced by Herbert Simon (1967), was recently formalized as "a process and practice that applies the learning sciences using human-centered engineering design methodologies and data-informed decision making to support learners and their development" (ICICLE 2019). To create My Math Academy, we apply learning sciences research to inform pedagogy and initial design, as well as in applications of user-centered research methodologies, evidence-centered design, and learning analytics to drive learning outcomes. The goal of this process is to derive insights to inform pedagogy and foster playful engagement of children in real learning contexts.

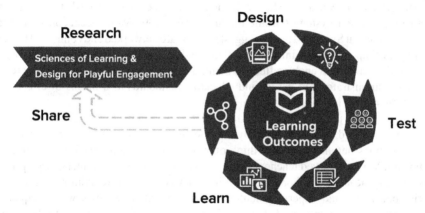

**Fig. 1.** Learning Engineering Framework for the Development of My Math Academy (Age of Learning 2020)

My Math Academy is both a home consumer and school-based learning tool. Parents and their children between 3 and 8 years old supported the design process through game iterations, participating in user testing from concept exploration to design validation over the course of multiple years of product development (Druin 2002). Efficacy research also provided product validation through documented learning gains (Bang and Li 2020; Thai et al. 2018, 2019) and provided new insights to be folded into the next product iterations, such as the development of parent and educator dashboards and resources available for the educators that support the math development of young learners using My Math Academy.

Along with validating the design of My Math Academy as a teaching tool for young learners to gain number sense and skills in numeric operations, it was also important for us to validate the design of My Math Academy for optimal in-classroom implementation. Studies of technology-supported curricula have long shown that teacher adoption depends on how well education practitioners perceive learning tools "fit" within their goals for students, teaching strategies, and expectations for student learning (Shell et al. 2020; King et al. 2016; Blumenfeld et al. 2000). Therefore, while our previous research validated the efficacy of My Math Academy and its appropriateness for use in the hands of young learners, the current research sought to investigate the appropriateness and effectiveness of dashboards for communicating relevant information about student performance.

### 1.1 Approaching Learning Engineering from an Ecological Systems Perspective

Our approach to this research was based on Bronfenbrenner's theory on Ecological Systems. Specifically, we took a multi-dimensional view, aiming to deeply understand the roles of teachers, administrators, parents, and students in using the My Math Academy dashboards. According the Bronfenbrenner's Ecological Systems Theory, a student is not only influenced by proximal factors in their microsystem but also by distal factors and interactions between systems (Bronfenbrenner 1986, 1999). More recent conceptualizations of Ecological Systems Theory suggest systems are networked and connected to each other by participants' social interactions (Neal and Neal 2013). We realize this theory in our work by seeking to enable effective communications across systems (e.g., parents, teachers, administrators) in parent and educator dashboards as a means of effectively supporting student learning (Betts et al. 2020).

To account for the various factors that affect how an individual might use the product, we investigated each role group by interviewing them about their own experiences and perceptions but also how they think other role groups might perceive and use the dashboard; We interviewed teachers about the parent dashboard, we interviewed principals about the teacher dashboard, and we interviewed a state-level administrator about a principal-facing and superintendent-facing dashboard. Interviews were frequently active, where participants used their rich contextual knowledge of day-to-day experiences in their role group to map the ways data fuels decision-making, working through affordances of specific feature sets (Norman 2002). In this sense, we used participatory codesign as a vehicle for understanding participants' microsystems and macrosystems, and how they interact.

### 1.2 Using Participatory Codesign to Create *My Math Academy* Dashboards

We used participatory codesign to understand how different role groups understand and potentially use the My Math Academy dashboards. Participatory codesign is an approach to design that helps bridge the work of those actually making products with the expectations of the users that will engage with the final product. The goal of participatory design was described by Suchman (1993) to be "a more human, creative, and effective relationship between those involved in technology's design and its use, and in that way between technology and the human activities that provide technological systems with their reason for being" (p. viii). In the case of My Math Academy, our team included the product owner, UX designer, curriculum specialist, and design researcher. The team worked closely with six elementary school teachers, three elementary school principals, and a state-level administrator across multiple sessions during which they provided feedback as to the differing information needs across grade-level, school, district, and state leadership.

Our approach to codesign during these sessions followed Roschelle et al. (2006)'s approach, which described "a highly-facilitated, team-based process in which teachers, researchers, and developers work together in defined roles to design an educational innovation, realize the design in one or more prototypes, and evaluate each prototype's significance for addressing a concrete educational need. (p. 606)". In the current research, we follow the three basic stages of participator design proposed by Spinuzzi (2005): exploration, discovery, and prototyping. Our initial exploration took place during a study where teachers were testing the efficacy of My Math Academy in their classrooms, which we used as an opportunity to explore the contexts of use and implementation. We then worked with teachers who had participated in the efficacy study to engage them further in the codesign process. In stage two, our team worked with teachers and administrators in several iterative one-on-one sessions to evaluate the appropriateness of dashboards for their own needs as well as their perceptions of the dashboard meeting the needs for other role types. While we were able to test various prototypes in this research, stage three is ongoing as we continue to develop dashboards for the various role types identified in this research.

# 2 Method

The goal of this research was to understand potential effectiveness, appropriateness, and perceived utility of the My Math Academy Dashboards for different role groups (i.e., parents, teachers, administrators). To understand the needs and experiences of our users, participants engaged in research sessions with team members during which they defined shared objectives, mapped role groups and information needs, and responded to multiple prototypes. Insights from these sessions were iterated on and contributed to the design of the My Math Academy dashboards.

## 2.1 Participants

Our sample included six elementary school teachers and four school administrators (three elementary school principals and one state-level administrator). Teacher participants were all classroom teachers and had previously participated in a My Math Academy efficacy study and expressed continued interest in participating in research. Administrator participants had personal connections with members of the research and design team and agreed to participate. All teacher participants were located in Los Angeles, CA or Orange, CA while the administrator participants were located in the Los Angeles, CA (n = 2), Moorpark, CA (n = 1), and Baltimore, MD (n = 1).

## 2.2 Materials

Materials include prototypes of the My Math Academy Parent Dashboard and Teacher Dashboard (Fig. 2). The prototypes were created on Marvel and accessed through an online browser. They were fully interactive and mimicked the dashboard experiences other than a few subpages that were missing some text. Both the parents and teacher dashboards were structured similarly, with participants first landing on a home screen that showed overall progress and activity in terms of minutes of use. For the Parent Dashboard, parents could scroll down on the home screen to see what learning concepts their child had completed or were in progress. For each concept, parents could click into a How to Help section, which provided suggestions for offline activities that could reinforce learning outside the application.

For the Teacher Dashboard, the home screen shows student activity as well as weekly usage. Teachers could click on each icon to identify students who are struggling, stuck, inactive, or in progress. They could also click the icons at the bottom of the page to navigate to Progress, Groups, Timer, and Overview sections.

### 2.3  Procedure

We used both remote, one-on-one semi-structured interviews as well as an in-person participatory codesign workshop to evaluate the potential appropriateness, effectiveness, and perceived utility of the My Math Academy dashboards.

**Interviews.** Interviews were structured around five general questions that addressed perceptions and potential use of the dashboard. The UX designer, curriculum designer, and design researcher were present at each interview session and took turns asking questions and probing for meaning when needed. Prior to each session, teachers and administrators were instructed to spend one hour independently interacting with the prototype on their personal device. They were sent the interview questions and prototype links beforehand to guide their exploration and help them prepare for the interview (See Table 1 for example interview questions for teachers). Sending the participants questions beforehand helped them focus their responses during the interview sessions, which freed up time for the team to probe for pain points and different use cases, and to brainstorm additional areas for improvement.

Teachers participated in two, one-hour-long sessions during which they provided feedback on dashboard prototypes via video conferencing and sharing screens. In the first session, teachers provided feedback on a prototype of the parent dashboard and discussed how it could be adapted to be appropriate and effective for teachers. In the second sessions, teachers provided feedback on a prototype of the teacher dashboard and discussed how it could be adapted to be appropriate and effective for administrators.

Administrators also participated in two, one-hour long sessions during which they provided feedback on dashboard prototypes. The structure of these sessions was similar to the teacher sessions. However, in the first session, administrators provided feedback on the teacher dashboard and discussed how it could be adapted for administrators, and in the second session, they viewed a prototype of the administrator dashboard and provided feedback relevant to their own use case and whether they thought it would be effective and appropriate for other administrators.

**Participatory Codesign Workshop.** One administrator participated in a 1.5 h-long, in-person participatory codesign workshop. We decided to conduct an in-person codesign

**(a)**

**(b)**

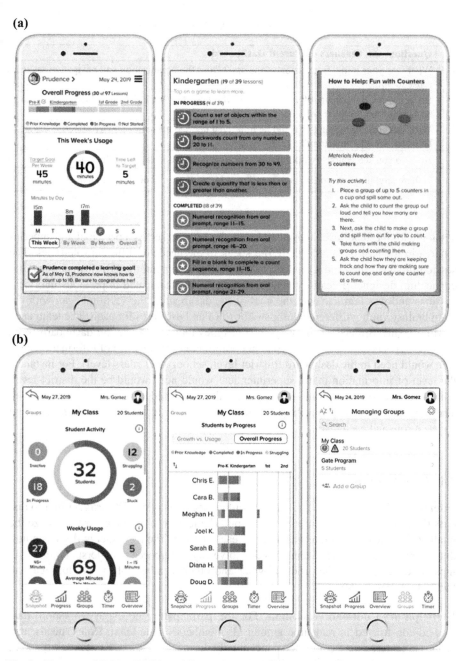

**Fig. 2.** Pictures of Parent Dashboard Prototype (overall progress, lessons, and How to Help sections) and Teacher Dashboard Prototype (snapshot, progress, and groups sections) which participants reviewed in multiple interview sessions.

**Table 1.** Examples of interview questions

| Questions for Teachers on Parent Dashboard |
|---|
| What was your initial impression of the app? Does the organization and navigation make sense to you? |
| Do you think the parents of your students who used My Math Academy will find this to be a useful tool? Why or why not? |
| What features are missing or could be improved upon to make this a more effective bridge between you and the parent? |
| How do you see yourself working this into your flow as a classroom educator? |
| Is there anything else you want to mention, add, or suggest about the prototype? |

session with the state-level administrator as she had worked as a principal and superintendent in the past and could therefore speak to the needs of different role types. The session included the product owner, two design researchers, the UX designer, and the curriculum designer. Because the administrator had participated in previous interview sessions and was familiar with the goal of the dashboards, the session began with the team brainstorming different administrator roles and use cases for each. The team used a white board to map out the varying role types that would use the dashboard (e.g., principal, coach, superintendent, content coordinator) and the level of information each role would need in the dashboard (district level, school level, class level). For instance, the level of information that a superintendent would need would be the district-level, while the level of information that a principal would need would be the school-level. The team then moved into ideating how the features of the dashboard would be different for each role and each level.

### 2.4  Data Analysis

**Interviews.** The design researcher, curriculum specialist, and UX designer met to discuss their notes after each interview session. The team worked together to analyze the qualitative data and generate themes after each session. The team met to discuss notes, draw connections between themes, and resolve any differences in understanding. Findings were shared with the product owner and other members of the product team to facilitate design iterations.

**Participatory Codesign Workshop.** For the participatory codesign workshop, data was co-constructed in real time among all members of the team. Roles, needs, and proposed features were connected conceptually during the session. Key takeaways were agreed upon and any disagreements were discussed during the session.

# 3 Results

## 3.1 Interviews

**Parent Dashboard.** For the parent-facing dashboard, teachers expressed the importance of having the dashboard provide useful and actionable information to the parent about their child's performance. After reviewing the dashboard prototype, one teacher talked about the importance of the dashboard providing parents with specific (rather than general) feedback on their child's performance.

"I love these (referencing the Highlights section, which outlines the student's accomplishments)! It's good for you to know the positive comments and to just help parents with the positive reinforcement. But it ties something specific to what the child did, because you should be specific about the feedback and not just say 'good job,' but say why it was good."

More so, teachers appreciated that the prototype included a How to Help section, which suggests to parents offline activities they can do with their child that can reinforce learning. Another teacher said, "I thought it was pretty neat for the parents to be able to get involved. Because sometimes a lot of the parents always ask 'What can I do? My child is struggling, how can help?' And it was just right there, they didn't have to go anywhere else. You guys are giving them all the tools that they need."

For the parent dashboard, teachers perceived its utility as being a resource for parents, providing parents with information about their child and suggesting ways they can support and grow math learning at home.

**Teacher Dashboard.** For the teacher-facing dashboard, teachers highlighted two important user needs for the dashboard: 1) having connection points between teacher-facing dashboards and parent-facing dashboards, and 2) allowing teachers to easily identify students who need more help.

First, teachers wanted to send e-mails and texts through the dashboard so they could easily communicate with parents, allowing parents to quickly see where their child is struggling and succeeding. They then wanted to use the app to suggest materials for parents and students to do at home. One teacher said, "I recommend a message center where I could communicate with parents and indicate which skill their child needs to practice or provide materials for their child to practice that skill at home. I feel that this would encourage parents to provide one on one instruction at home." Because our teacher participants viewed both the parents and teacher dashboard prototypes, they saw opportunities to connect the parent-facing and teacher-facing dashboards. Teachers not only want to communicate information to parents through the My Math Academy dashboard, but they also want to use it as a place to connect parents with additional resources, activities, and tools.

Second, teachers saw the dashboard's potential effectiveness in providing quick information on which students need more help or intervention. Teachers discussed using the dashboard – specifically the information on the Snapshot page - to cluster their students into small groups based on performance, and then working with the group of children that needed the most help. One teacher said, "[Using the dashboard] freed me up to work with a small group of struggling kids." In this sense, the teacher dashboard helped teachers personalize their teaching; they could easily identify the children who needed help and then provide them with one-on-one instruction while the other children continued to progress their learning in the game.

Compared to teachers, administrators saw the teacher dashboard's utility as being a platform to demonstrate how the product is yielding benefits. In this sense, administrators thought the key use of the My Math Academy dashboard would be to serve as a starting point for teachers and administrators to discuss how their students were doing in math. One principal said, "I could have [had the teacher] pull it up in a meeting I had the other day and said, 'Hey, let's take a look at how we're doing right now.' That's what would help me. If I had access to the objectives we were struggling with, that's what I would want to focus on with my grade level. [I would say to them] 'What are you guys going to do to bring this up?'".

While teachers primarily see the teacher dashboard as being a connection point to parents and a tool to identify which students need intervention, principals saw themselves using the teacher dashboard to check in on progress and ensure learning objectives are being met.

**Administrator Dashboard.** For the administrator-facing dashboard, administrators expressed needing the dashboard to slice, filter, and export data on different levels (e.g., by grade, class, student) as well as by various student characteristics (e.g., English-language learners, Title 1, Gifted and Talented Program students, Special Education students). One principal said, "I am looking for sub-population information like EL status... I am looking to be able to see all kids at one grade level in one shot. I couldn't seem to make that happen." Another administrator, talking about wanting to see data for a subset of kids, expressed the desire for the dashboard to do this with little input from him. "If I am responsible for creating these groups because it's not tied into my student data, then it's not happening." Administrators linked their need to easily access and export specific dashboard data to their roles as administrators and having to communicate learning progress to a variety of people, including parents, teachers, Parent Teacher Association (PTA) members, and the Superintendent of the school district. While the dashboard did not at the time have the ability to slice and export data in this way, it was clear that this was an important feature that aligned with administrator's roles as liaisons between their school and other members of the community.

### 3.2 Participatory Codesign Workshop

The codesign workshop highlighted the need for administrator dashboards to highlight progress but resulted in different information structuring and designs for superintendents or content creators versus principals or coaches.

Across role types and use cases, the codesign participant (a state-level administrator) expressed the need for the dashboard to communicate progress or Return on Investment (ROI). Regardless of role type, administrators have to be able to show how their students' learning has changed from the start of using the educational product to the present state to justify cost and effort needed to implement. A vital aspect of communicating progress and ROI is making the data interface easy for busy administrators to use and also simple for different stakeholders to understand (e.g., families, community members, politicians, senior leadership). Our participatory design participant expressed, "Don't make me maintain my data – help me use it!".

However, it became clear that how administrators will use the dashboard depends on their role group. For superintendents and content creators, they likely will not need to access data frequently, and therefore might need push reminders to prompt them to check on progress. But for principals and coaches, it is important that they can pull data when they need it, likely on a weekly basis when they are making classroom rounds, meeting with other administrators, or running workshops.

More so, it became apparent that principals and coaches not only need to see the performance, but also get suggestions on next steps to take. Our participant labeled this concept of responding as *bright spots* (achievements) and *hot spots* (points of struggle), with bright spots being displayed on the dashboard as percent of class or school succeeding on certain concepts and hot spots being displayed as percent of class or school struggling on certain concepts. For principals, we mapped out how the dashboard could go further and make suggestions for how to help: For bright spots, we brainstormed opportunities to discuss achievements at schoolwide events and recognition opportunities. For hot spots, we talked about opportunities for coaching sessions and staff activities focused on addressing the sticking point. The important takeaway for the administrator dashboard when used by principals was to present opportunities to celebrate successes while providing actionable suggestions for responding to students struggling.

## 4  Discussion

By conducting iterative, participatory codesign with teachers and administrators, we were able to more deeply understand the needs, expectations, and use cases for our parent, teacher, and administrator dashboard users. Our analyses revealed important findings for each role type. We found that teachers saw the parent-facing dashboard as being an important resource for parents because it can provide specific information on children's progress and targeted areas where parents can supplement learning at home. There were three key findings related to the teacher-facing dashboard. First, we found that the teachers saw the teacher-facing dashboard as being important for identifying students who need the most help so they can personalize learning. Second, teachers wanted to utilize the dashboard to connect with parents to share additional information and resources. Third, principals identified another use case for the teacher dashboard, seeing themselves using it when meeting with teachers to check in on learning progress and goals. For the administrator-facing dashboard, we found the dashboard needs to be flexible and allow them to look at data across levels, but that the type of information shared and how it is accessed depends on role group. Administrators also want the dashboard to go one step further by recommending how to address problem areas and successes, which can help them communicate how they are taking action to their many stakeholders.

In total, our team learned that the critical benefit of the My Math Academy dashboards was allowing teachers and administrators to personalize their approach to learning, whether that be how they communicate progress and learning goals across levels or how they approach learning with their students (see Fig. 3). Our multi-system approach provided us insights into how potential dashboard use spans ecological systems, and how different role types saw themselves using the dashboard in different ways when interacting with each other (Betts et al. 2020; Bronfenbrenner 1986, 1999; Neal and Neal 2013).

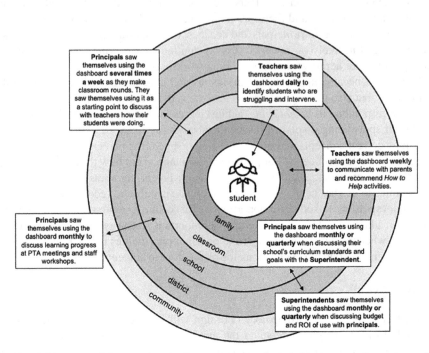

**Fig. 3.** Multi-systems Diagram showing how teachers and administrators saw themselves using the dashboard to connect information across levels and with varying frequencies.

### 4.1  Implications for Educators

Participatory codesign harnessed teacher and administrator expertise to ensure My Math Academy dashboards "fit" within goals for students, teaching strategies and expectations for student learning (Blumenfeld et al. 2000). It was only through working with teachers and administrators that we came to understand how vital it was that they could use the dashboard to identify struggling students and know exactly what students are struggling on. My Math Academy populates this information in the dashboard using student in-game learning data. We learned that the accessibility and utility of such data in a dashboard can enable teachers to further personalize learning by, for example, creating flexible focus groups to provide support. Without a dashboard that populates such information, purposeful grouping can consume a lot of teachers' time. The dashboard can, therefore, empower teachers with more availability to focus on helping struggling students and providing further individualized learning opportunities. Indeed, research on another math learning system, IXL, found that teachers felt that using the technology increased student independence and allowed teachers to personalize learning and provide more corrective feedback to students (Schuetz et al. 2018). It was only by interviewing teachers and asking them how they would use the dashboard that we realized the immense power of having access to a dashboard with individual student learning information that also provided teachers with data-driven recommendations.

In addition to connecting teachers to actionable data, the dashboard also provides offline content and resources per learning objective that teachers can readily access and choose to use, thus providing another means of reducing time spent sourcing supportive content. The offline content feature (i.e., the How to Help section) of the dashboard can also serve to connect teachers with parents, which we found was an important feature that teachers desired. Oftentimes, limited resources and anxieties around math render parents unsure on how to best help their children (e.g., Betts 2021). Teachers can use the dashboard content to enhance teacher-parent communication and foster positive parent engagement in their child's learning (McCarthy et al. 2020).

On a greater scale, it is our hope that working with teachers and administrators will increase support for the dashboard since the design is authentic to the lived experiences and needs of all teachers. It is possible that there is some resistance to using adaptive tools like My Math Academy because of concerns and anxieties around ease of use (Sánchez-Prieto et al. 2019). Long term, participatory codesign with teachers could potentially reduce such concerns and increase digital tool adoption—knowing the dashboard was designed in-collaboration with teachers for teachers may increase levels of trust regarding ease of implementation, authenticity, and effectiveness.

### 4.2 Making Insights Accessible, Meaningful, and Actionable for Dashboard Implementation

Engaging in iterative, participatory design with teachers and administrators was critical for bringing the team in line with practitioner expectations. The educators brought to light design affordances and implications that will impact the ways designers create the my math academy dashboards not just for classroom use, but for connecting information and communication between home, school, and beyond. While the creation and testing of the dashboards with different role groups is still ongoing, the dashboard design iterations that have emerged through Age of Learning's learning engineering framework has made student data accessible, meaningful, and actionable for teachers tasked with creating math-rich environments for early learners, which is the foundation for designing educational products for children that then make sense to the adults in their ecology of learning experiences, whether at home or at school (M. Rothschild, personal communication, April 21, 2017). Ultimately we are working to build toward a personalized learning ecosystem, which learning engineering enables through an iterative design process.

While we hope this research can lend insight into how to use participatory codesign to understand how educators use adaptive instructional systems, our study had several limitations. Of note, our sample was one of convenience and does not fully represent teachers' experiences across the U.S. It is also possible that because we gave teachers prototypes before the interview sessions, their ideation was constricted to what they saw compared to if we had not provided any dashboard prototypes before the interviews. It will be important for future research to expand on this research and explore additional questions, like how teachers are actually using dashboards in their classroom. For example, it is possible our teachers envision themselves using the dashboard in a way that ends up not fitting their needs in the moment, especially given recent shift in remote learning and hybrid classrooms (Darling-Hammond et al. 2020). It will be important for our team and future researchers to investigate the utility of dashboards in connecting educators to parents and connecting teachers to offline content. We plan to continue to work with educators to determine what is working well and what requires improvements, thus enabling an authentic iterative participatory codesign cycle to continue.

### 4.3 Conclusions

Deeply understanding the lived experiences of educators is essential to creating products that not only meet their needs, but foster a trust in the product's appropriateness, effectiveness, and usefulness. Using participatory codesign iteratively not only provided us with deep expertise into the experiences of teachers and administrators, but it allowed us to see the unique ways in which educators saw themselves using the product to interface with each other, parents, and other members of their community. However, educators' experiences are constantly evolving and can change drastically. It is important for researchers who are designing adaptive instructional systems for educators to continuously connect with their users to ensure their products are authentically reflecting their experiences. By detailing here how we integrate participatory codesign in a learning engineering framework, we hope to inspire other researchers and designers take a similar approach when working with educators who are using their learning products, with the ultimate goal of deriving more authentic insights that inform pedagogy and foster meaningful student learning in real learning contexts.

## References

Age of Learning, Inc. (2020). My Math Academy: A research-driven design approach to personalized learning for young children. https://www.ageoflearning.com/research/MM%20Development%20Process.pdf

Bang, H.J., Li, L.: My Math Academy significantly accelerates early elementary children's math skills and fosters greater engagement in math: a replication of a randomized control trial. Research brief (2020). https://learningpolicyinstitute.org/sites/default/files/product-files/Restart_Reinvent_Schools_COVID_Priority2_Distance_Learning.pdf

Betts, A.: The RESET framework: examining critical factors in parent-child math participation. Paper presented at the IAFOR International Conference on Education, Honolulu, Hawaii (2021)

Betts, A., Thai, K.-P., Gunderia, S., Hidalgo, P., Rothschild, M., Hughes, D.: An ambient and pervasive personalized learning ecosystem: "smart learning" in the age of the internet of things. In: Sottilare, R.A., Schwarz, J. (eds.) HCII 2020. LNCS, vol. 12214, pp. 15–33. Springer, Cham (2020). https://doi.org/10.1007/978-3-030-50788-6_2

Blumenfeld, P., Fishman, B.J., Krajcik, J., Marx, R.W., Soloway, E.: Creating usable innovations in systemic reform: scaling up technology-embedded project-based science in urban schools. Educ. Psychol. 35(3), 149–164 (2000)

Bronfenbrenner, U.: Ecology of the family as a context for human development. Dev. Psychol. 22(6), 723–742 (1986)

Bronfenbrenner, U.: Environments in developmental perspective: Theoretical and operational models. In: Friedman, S.L., Wachs, T.D. (eds.) Measuring Environment Across the Life Span: Emerging Methods and Concepts. American Psychological Association, Washington, D.C. (1999)

Darling-Hammond, L., Edgerton, A.K., Truong, N., Cookson, P.W.: Restarting and reinventing school: learning in the time of COVID and beyond. Learning Policy Institute, Palo Alto, CA, USA (2020). https://learningpolicyinstitute.org/sites/default/files/product-files/Restart_R einvent_Schools_COVID_Priority2_Distance_Learning.pdf

Druin, A.: The role of children in the design of new technology. Behav. Inf. Technol. **21**(1), 1–25 (2002)

IEEE Industry Connection Industry Consortium on Learning Engineering (ICICLE), December 2019. https://www.ieeeicicle.org

King, M., Rothberg, S., Dawson, R., Batmaz, F.: Bridging the edtech evidence gap: A realist evaluation framework refined for complex technology initiatives. J. Syst. Inf. Technol. **18**(1), 18–40 (2016)

McCarthy, K.S., Crossley, S.A., Meyers, K., Boser, U., (Under Review). Toward More Effective and Equitable Education: A Call for Innovations in Educational Technology. Submitted to Education Research Journal

Neal, J.W., Neal, Z.P.: Nested or networked? Future directions for ecological systems theory. Soc. Dev. **22**(4), 722–737 (2013). https://doi.org/10.1111/sode.12018

Norman, D.: The Design of Everyday Things. Basic Books, New York (2002)

Penuel, W.R., Fishman, B.J., Cheng, B.H., Sabelli, N.: Organizing research and development at the intersection of learning, implementation, and design. Educ. Res. **40**(7), 331–337 (2011)

Roschelle, J., Penuel, W.R., Shechtman, N.: Co-design of innovations with teachers: Definition and dynamics. In: Proceedings of the International Conference of the Learning Sciences, pp. 606–612. International Society of the Learning Sciences, New Brunswick (2006)

Sánchez-Prieto, J.C., Cruz-Benito, J., Therón, R., García-Peñalvo, F.J.: "How to measure teachers' acceptance of AI-driven assessment in elearning: a TAM-based proposal. In: Conde-González, M.Á., Rodríguez-Sedano, F.J., Fernández-Llamas, C., García-Peñalvo, F.J. (eds.) TEEM 2019 Proceedings of the Seventh International Conference on Technological Ecosystems for Enhancing Multiculturality (Leon, Spain, October 16th-18th, 2019), ICPS: ACM International Conference Proceedings Series, New York, NY, USA pp. 181–186. ACM, (2019). https://doi.org/10.1145/3362789.3362918.

Schuetz, R.L., Biancarosa, G., Goode, J.: Is technology the answer? Investigating students' engagement in math. J. Res. Technol. Educ. **50**(4), 318–332 (2018). https://doi.org/10.1080/15391523.2018.1490937

Shell, A., Tare, M., Blemahdoo, E.: Incorporating research and educator voice in edtech design. In: Gresalfi, M., Horn, I.S. (eds.) The Interdisciplinarity of the Learning Sciences, 14th International Conference of the Learning Sciences (ICLS) 2020, vol. 3, pp. 1549–1552. International Society of the Learning Sciences, Nashville (2020)

Simon, H.A.: Job of a college president. Educ. Rec. **48**(1), 68–78 (1967)

Spinuzzi, C.: The methodology of participatory design. Tech. Commun. **52**(2), 163–174 (2005)

Suchman, L.: Forward. In: Schuler, D., Namioka, A. (eds.) Participatory Design: Principles and Practices, pp. vii–ix. Lawrence Erlbaum Associates Inc., Hillsdale (1993). https://doi.org/10.1057/9781137360823_9

Thai, K.P., Li, L., Schachner, A.: My Math Academy significantly accelerates early mathematics learning. Research brief, October 2018. https://www.ageoflearning.com/case_studies/Master ing-Math-Research-Brief-11.pdf

Thai, K.P., Bang, H.J., Li, L.: Accelerating early math learning with research-based personalized learning games: A cluster randomized controlled trial. Submitted to Journal of Research on Educational Effectiveness (Under Review)

# Scaling Adaptive Instructional System (AIS) Architectures in Low-Adaptive Training Ecosystems

Robert A. Sottilare[1]([✉]) [iD] and Keith W. Brawner[2]

[1] Soar Technology, Inc., Orlando, FL, USA
bob.sottilare@soartech.com
[2] US Army CCDC-STTC, Orlando, FL, USA

**Abstract.** This paper reviews horizontal and vertical scaling methodologies for adaptive instructional system (AIS) software architectures. The term *AIS* refers to any instructional approach that accommodates individual differences to facilitate and optimize the acquisition of knowledge and/or skills. The authors propose a variety of scaling methods to enhance the interaction between AISs and low-adaptive training ecosystems with the goal of increasing adaptivity and thereby increasing learning and performance. Typically, low-adaptive training systems only accommodate differences in the learner's in-situ performance during training and do not consider the impact of other factors (e.g., emotions, prior knowledge, goal-orientation, or motivation) that influence learning. AIS architectures such as the Generalize Intelligent Framework for Tutoring (GIFT) can accommodate individual differences and interact with low-adaptive training ecosystems to model a common operational picture of the training relative. These capabilities enable AISs to track progress toward learning objectives and to intervene and adapt the training ecosystem to needs and capabilities of each learner. Finding new methods to interface AISs with a greater number of low-adaptive training ecosystems will result in more efficient and effective instruction.

**Keywords:** Adaptive instruction · Horizontal scaling · Vertical scaling

## 1   Introduction

Today, much of the infrastructure for corporate, military and K-12 training is minimally adaptive. Minimal adaptivity refers to training systems which intervene with learners of equivalent performance identically, present all users with the same initial content, provide prescriptive interventions based only on assessed performance, and use the same interventions for common errors for all users. While this minimal adaptivity approach is more efficient and less expensive to author instruction, this approach fails to account for individual differences in experience, workload (stress), emotions, and domain competency. Further, it relies upon a human element for higher level adaption, be it the self-regulation ability of the learner or the regulation of the learner by a teacher, instructor, or trainer. Whether a human or computer-based instruction, the instructor must have

© Springer Nature Switzerland AG 2021
R. A. Sottilare and J. Schwarz (Eds.): HCII 2021, LNCS 12792, pp. 298–310, 2021.
https://doi.org/10.1007/978-3-030-77857-6_20

knowledge of the learner to be responsive and tailor the experience of each learner with the goal of optimizing their learning.

## 2 Adapting to the Learner in Training Ecosystems

Learning experience includes on-the-job experiences, training, education, reading and informal learning (unassessed experiences). Incongruence between experience and workload (e.g., low experience with high workload) often results in stress that hinders learning. The zone of proximal development (ZPD) is the range of abilities that an individual can perform with assistance but cannot yet perform independently [1]. They are *proximal* because the individual is approaching a level of mastery, but still requires additional training to be able to perform these tasks without assistance. Workload is the amount of work assigned to or expected from an individual, team or machine within a specific period [2]. Low adaptive systems are often unable to assess the level of workload, which renders them unable to mitigate its negative effect on learning outcomes. Without the input data on learner experiences and workloads, systems must rely on broad guesswork or heuristics to regulate each learner's instructional experience.

There has been a long history of research seeking to understand the connection between learning and emotions [3]. Emotions influence learning efficiency and effectiveness. The fundamental emotions associated with learning are boredom, confusion, frustration, anger, fear, and joy [4] and these emotions are usually associated with reward, punishment, or stress [5]. The most effective AISs are those that can adapt to each learner's prior knowledge needs, preferences, and goals. The ability to mitigate negative emotions begins with detection and recognition/classification of emotions. Behavioral and physiological data support learner state detection and is accomplished using either external hardware-based sensors, internal software-based sensors, or a combination of the two [6]. The sensor data is collected and analyzed to classify the learner's emotional state and then an intervention is selected to mitigate the risk associated with emotions that are negatively impacting learning and encourage positive emotions.

Finally, domain competency or prior knowledge accounts for the skills and abilities of an individual (or a team) with respect to the required knowledge, skills, experience, attitudes, values, behaviors, or defined standards required to complete the assigned task. While there is significant evidence to support the positive influence of adaptive instruction on learning outcomes in terms of effectiveness, efficiency, engagement, and flow [7–11], there are currently few systems able to tailor/adapt instruction based on the learner's domain competency, behavior (e.g., emotional), physiological states (e.g. arousal), interests, preferences, situational awareness, self-regulation or spatial ability.

While it doesn't make economic sense to start over and scrap most of the existing and very scalable instructional solutions in the marketplace, it does make sense to increase their adaptivity and learning effectiveness. We should be evaluating options to scale adaptive solutions and enhance the performance of existing minimally adaptive or low training systems [12–14]. Overcoming this major hurdle will help us realize the global acceptance of adaptive instruction as a practical tool of choice. This paper examines methods to enhance the scalability of adaptive strategies in low-adaptive training ecosystems.

Scalability is the property of a system to handle growing amounts of work by adding resources to the system [15]. In an economic context, a scalable business model implies that a company can increase sales given increased resources. In a system engineering context, scalability implies that you can either multiple the existing capability or increase the functional capability of the existing systems through innovation. To meet this design goal, scalability methods for low-adaptive training ecosystems should focus on improving authoring, content curation, instructional delivery methods, real-time instructional management or even evaluation processes. The next section identifies a variety of scaling methods and approaches.

## 3 Scaling Dimensions

Since the goal is to expand the adaptivity of low adaptive training ecosystems, we must also consider the accessibility of these systems and how we might scale AISs to interoperate with both standalone and distributed training systems. For standalone low adaptive training ecosystems (e.g., a classified military training system or system behind a K-12 update policy), we should consider how to enhance interoperability with the system to drive adaptivity in the design. One way would be to natively design and embed adaptive instructional loops in the existing training system and its processes. Another way would be to have an interface which is external to the system that uses training system variables to assess the progress of the learner or team toward a set of learning objectives.

For distributed training ecosystems, such an interface must already exist, and it may support interoperation between a AIS architecture and the lower-adaptivity distributed low adaptive training ecosystem. If not, enhancement to the existing ecosystem for bidirectional AIS communication can be undertaken. Which of these approaches provide the best opportunity to scale the training ecosystem? When we discuss scaling, the terms *horizontal* and *vertical* scaling are often methods that we consider in designing or redesigning these systems.

*Horizontal scaling* (also known as scaling out) means that you can scale by expanding or duplicating your current pool of resources [16], whereas vertical scaling means that you scaled by adding more capability to the existing system. In horizontal scaling approaches, each parallel subsystem is highly independent and do not share assets, interfaces, or operating systems. This makes it unlikely that any single failure significantly affects the performance of the overall system. Figure 1 shows a horizontal approach where 10 independent subsystems run in parallel and a failure in any subsystem results in only a 10% reduction in performance while a failure in the vertical system results in a 100% reduction in performance until the problem is fixed.

*Vertical scaling* (also known as *scaling up*) refers to adding resources (e.g., computing power, servers, memory) to your system as the demand grows [17]. However, there are some challenges and risks associated with vertical approaches. Unlike horizontal approaches that can almost scale infinitely, vertical strategies have limited effect due to design tradeoffs. Also, vertical scaling strategies usually have a much higher risk of downtime and experience longer down times than horizontal scaling methods. There is also greater frequency of system outages and hardware failures. The design of vertical approaches limits the ability to upgrade the system in the future or move to other

**Horizontal Scaling Approach**                    **Vertical Scaling Approach**

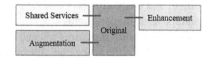

| | | | | |
|---|---|---|---|---|
| Original | Duplicate | Duplicate | ... | Duplicate |

1        2        3              10

*Identical, but independent subsystems*          *Different and interdependent subsystems*

**Fig. 1.** Horizontal vs. Vertical scaling approaches

solutions/hardware in the marketplace due to compatibility issues. Finally, the cost of implementing a vertical approach is usually much higher than horizontal approaches.

Horizontal scaling methods increase system output by duplicating the existing system to provide parallel capabilities. Using an example of electromechanical systems, horizontal scaling of an electrical generation at a dam can be increased by increasing the number of water turbines that generate power. The technology and the methods are the same. There are just more subsystems working in parallel. In contrast, a vertical scaling approach might use methods to increase the performance of each water turbine (e.g., reduce friction) so individually they can process more water, turn faster and produce more electricity.

Another example of a horizontally scaled system is a web-server farm which can be expanded by adding servers as demand increases. Each of the servers in the farm host copies of the same software and work in parallel. Tasks can be moved from servers that have high workload to those with lower workload. Vertical scaling approaches might use more streamlined processes or higher performing components to scale. While we have focused mainly on horizontal and vertical scaling methods, it is worth noting that there are several dimensions beyond horizontal and vertical scaling [18]:

- *Administrative scaling*: increasing the number of organizations or users who have access a system
- *Functional scaling*: enhancing the system by adding new functionality without disrupting existing activities
- *Geographic scaling*: expansion from a local area to a larger region
- *Load scaling*: accommodating changing (heavier or lighter) loads
- *Generation scaling*: adopting new generations of components
- *Heterogeneous scaling*: adopting components from different vendors

For AISs, we might think about scaling their ability to author more adaptive courses, curate more content, serve more learners or influence the adaptivity of more low-adaptive systems by using the same processes we have now, but enabling them to run in parallel or innovating those processes. Mostly, we see opportunities to increase the efficiency of these AIS processes and increase their output through automation. Consider the efficacy of methods to support our goal to scale AISs both horizontally and vertically in low-adaptive training ecosystems:

- *artificial intelligence (AI) techniques* to automate authoring, instructional management and evaluation processes – vertically enhances the performance of existing low adaptive training systems
- *interoperability standards* to enable the stimulation of existing low-adaptive training systems by AISs – horizontally increases the number and type of systems that AISs can interact and exchange data with
- edge, fog, and cloud architectures for *distributed processing* of learner states and traits to enable real-time assessment and intervention with learners – horizontally distribute the workload associated with classification and assessment calculations
- leverage *interoperability standards* like Distributed Interactive Simulation (IEEE 1278) or High-Level Architecture (IEEE 1516) to facilitate entity data interoperability between AISs and low adaptive training systems
- *standardized conceptual models* to facilitate the use of alternative adaptive recommender engines, instructional strategies, and policies via evolving AIS family of standards (IEEE 2247)
- *standardized external interfaces* to support interoperability between AISs and with Learning Management Systems - the use of IMS Global Learning Technology Interoperability (LTI) standard to facilitate interaction between AISs and LMSs like edX, Blackboard and Canvas

The following sections elaborate on the methods listed above with the goal of identifying opportunities to extend AIS technologies (tools and methods) to interoperate with existing low-adaptive training ecosystems.

## 4   Scaling Methods

The goal in this section is to examine methods to scale AISs both horizontally by increasing interoperability with existing training ecosystems and vertically by increasing the capacity of AIS technologies through innovation. In this way, we anticipate the design of standards and processes which will improve the accessibility, usability, effectiveness, and efficiency of future AISs.

### 4.1   Scaling to Increase Accessibility to Low-Adaptive Systems

Sottilare, Hoehn & Tanaka [19] examined the theory, design, application methods and recommended standards needed to exploit AISs as drivers for tailoring military training in existing (low-adaptive) training simulation ecosystems. Two approaches were explored: 1) external stimulation and 2) embedded solutions. Both solutions depend upon the interoperation of a number of subcomponents such as the stimulating or embedded subsystem, the instructional subsystem, and the simulation.

The external stimulation approach depends upon the interoperation of a few different components with methods and standards to enable the exchange of data between the simulation environment and the AIS to support learner assessment and adaptive interventions by the AIS. The first of these components is used to stimulate the training simulation (e.g., an aircraft/tank cockpit, a VR helmet performance aid for repairing

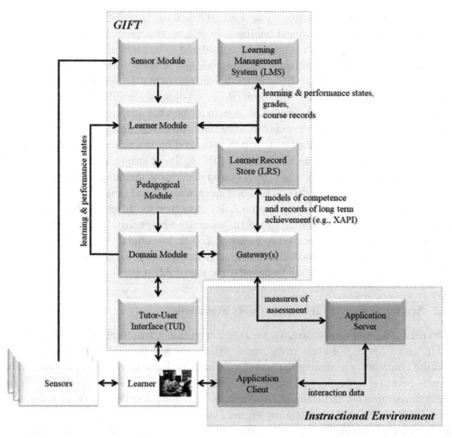

**Fig. 2.** Using an AIS to stimulate a low-adaptive instructional environment

systems or an operational sonar/radar system). This stimulator can be used to adapt the complexity of any training scenario.

The second of these components is a simulation model used to generate and present information to the learner or team (e.g., a model of the simulated behaviors on a tactical display, a model of an item to be analyzed and repaired, or a radar/sonar picture to display. The third of these components is the AIS and the instructional model by which it changes the simulation in a manner which is instructionally useful and responsive to each individual learner's needs. Each of these components/subsystems must have a method to communicate forward and backward with the other components in the ecosystem. The AIS must act on the simulation which feeds the live processing system which communicates changes back to the simulation and the actions back to the AIS. The interfaces between these systems need to have a standard method in which to communicate to be responsive to changes in other parts of the training ecosystem and take effective actions to help each learner achieve their goals. Figure 2 illustrates the interaction between an external AIS architecture, the Generalized Intelligent Framework for Tutoring (GIFT) [20, 21], and a low-adaptive instructional environment (e.g., training simulation). This is accomplished via a standardized gateway that consumes measures of assessment from the instructional environment and intelligently selects appropriate interventions.

The embedded approach is generally considered to be more effective and efficient, but may be more difficult to add to existing designs or support distributed simulation ecosystems where the training simulations that are part of that ecosystem change depending on the goal of the training. This limits the ecosystems scalability. Designing the AIS to be a native element of the simulation system enables the adaptive interventions to be designed to operate within the simulation system's processes and its limitations.

Alternatively, the stimulation approach is limited by the availability of assessment data within the simulation and the ability of the AIS to consume and use that data. In other words, you could only assess states using data that is measured in the system. All that said, the stimulation approach is much more adaptive and scalable.

Before well leave this scaling approach, let's touch on the difference between stimulating a single training simulation versus stimulating a whole ecosystem. Distributed simulations, multiple geographically separated, heterogenous simulations that exchange data using a common set of protocol data units, and share a common simulated environment. This is discussed in more detail in the next section of this paper.

### 4.2  Scaling Using AIS Interoperability Standards

The IEEE 1278 series of standards for Distributed Interactive Simulation and the IEEE 1516 series for High Level Architecture (HLA) are widely used in the training simulation community to enable the transfer of information about simulated entities and events between disparate, geographically-separated simulations to support shared synthetic environments and training experiences. Assuming a collective (team) scenario-based training ecosystem, extending the use of these standards to other simulation-based learning environments in corporate, adult, and K-12 training would enable a standardize method of sharing entity state data. State data includes descriptors of learner states (e.g., position, location, physical state) and events occurring during a scenario. It is likely this would require extensions of the current standards to support a broader variety of event types.

IEEE under Project 2247, AIS standards, is currently defining the functionality of AIS models and the types of data and format required to support interoperability between AIS components and external systems. Common AIS components include the Individual Learner Model (ILM), Adaptive (or pedagogical) Model (AM), Domain Model (DM), and Interface Model. Standards for interface models will facilitate data definition and exchange with low-adaptive ecosystems, allowing the later improvement from a low-adaptivity system as described above into a full AIS. Standardized models may also be used to facilitate the use of alternative adaptive recommender engines, instructional strategies, and policies in much that same way that IEEE 802-compliant wireless devices (e.g., laptops, tablets) enable the exchange of data on home or organizational networks.

### 4.3  Scaling to Reduce Workload via AIS Process Automation

The introduction mentions that most of the current training systems tend to focus on a single domain of instruction, lack the ability to repurposed to instruct other domains, and lack sufficient adaptivity to tailor instructional experiences to the goals, needs (learning gaps) and preferences of any individual learner or team. Most of these training systems simply don't model learners or teams at a sufficient level of detail to support tailoring. The effort to create a textbook or any instructional content is significant, but if each student were to receive their own customized version of a textbook that would naturally require almost as many textbooks as students – quite a significant increase in the total time and workload to curate (search and find content) or author (create content), manage/store and maintain content.

"Working material" available to accomplish the task of AIS development may be sourced in two ways – 1) curation of existing content which must be searched, retrieved and evaluated for relevance and then stored for later use or 2) the creation of new content. Most of the instructional content in existing training ecosystems can remained relatively unchanged for many years – reading, writing, arithmetic, chemistry, physics, history, drawing, and other "stable" domains so curation may be the most efficient method of amassing appropriate content for adaptive instruction. Automating this process would help scale the use and reuse of content and reduce the workload associated with the curation process. Making it easier to produce adaptive instruction along with the effectiveness and efficiency of adaptive instructional methods will increase its appeal and its use as an instructional tool of choice.

There already exist large bodies of content in learning content management systems [22, 23] related to the above-listed instructional domains. How to search, index, sort, aggregate, import, or otherwise make such content available to an AIS and subsequently the student is an open question involving who controls the instructional process – the computer-based tutor, a human instructor, the learner or is it a mixed initiative system where all can influence content selection? Mixed initiative systems with this level of flexibility usually involve greater development costs because of the expertise required to make effective selection decisions. The ability to automate curation process can help reduce workload and cost.

The second method to supply working material to the AIS is content creation – but the authors consider such tools to be out of scope for the subject of AIS – the number and variety of content creation tools already numbers in the thousands with many such systems outputting content that is useable by other systems and in a variety of interactive multimedia instructional (IMI) levels [24]. Again, developing systems with greater flexibility usually comes at a cost, but again that cost can mitigated by automation to provide more efficient instruction and lower overall ownership costs.

Another consideration in the scaling of adaptive instruction for training is the extent which content which can be synthesized, remixed, recombined, or otherwise generated from the original content. AIS content creation tools should be designed to support the adaptive features of the AIS rather than just selecting a media type (e.g., audio, video, graphics) that is available and redundant of media presented to the learner. In other words, we should design AISs to adapt media for the purpose of keeping individual learners and teams engaged in the learning process.

Finally, the authoring of AIS capabilities is currently a major factor limited the development and the widespread use of AIS technologies. AI can be used to automate AIS processes and reduce the time/cost and knowledge required for authoring, instructional management and evaluation. Specifically, intelligent agents can be used to observe and guide AIS authors or even directly manage content curation and creation/modification processes. AI can also be used to enhance the effectiveness and efficiency of adaptive instruction by optimizing adaptive decisions governed by AIS strategies and policies as discussed further in the next section of this paper.

### 4.4   Dynamic AIS Architectures for Real-Time Assessment and Intervention

Another way to scale AIS architectures is to make them more flexible in how they support system goals. As training environments move from fixed facilities to mobile devices and from virtual to live training, there are challenges in identifying and acquiring the data needed to assess learning in AISs. For example, a virtual simulation at a fixed site essentially has all the reference (ground truth) data needed for assessment. Live environments require sensors to acquire learner behavioral data and datastreams may be subject to loss in quality or availability. Augmented and mixed reality environments fall somewhere in between virtual and live systems. Data architectures are usually evaluated to determine where data is available and where it should be processed to support system goals. For AISs, the goals are to optimize learning and intervene with the learner and the environment in real-time. Where the data is captured and processed matters for the purposes of making it available to systems which can make meaningful instructional decisions (e.g., AISs).

AIS system recommendations and interventions in a distributed training ecosystem may require multiple datastreams to support a variety of responses at different levels (labeled here as edge, fog, cloud) in the training ecosystem. The goal in a distributed computing environment is to determine how close that computational processes and data storage need to be to maintain adequate response times or save network bandwidth [25]. In edge computing, processing happens on the device where the data is generated, and this reduces latency that might be incurred when processing and data used in that processing are on different devices or nodes in a network. In fog computing, processing happens across multiple nodes in the network. Cloud computing provides on-demand availability of resources (data storage and computing power) and usually involves moving data from where it is generated to a central location where processing happens. In training ecosystems, cloud-based solutions may result in latency that is unable to support real-time interaction with the learner. Let's review how this all works in distributed training.

At the edge level – responsiveness to engagement or boredom as measured by learner gaze [26] or emotions or mood measured by physiological sensors [27, 28] is needed to moderate the live experience. This generates large amounts of data, but advancements in edge (local) processing have allowed the large amount of sensor-based information to be communicated succinctly for responsive action. At the fog level, data may be moved to a central and perhaps secure local node on the training network. This is particularly desirable when protection of learner data is a priority in the training ecosystem.

At the cloud level, it is usual to have adaptive instruction select the next homework problem, access and structure content, and perform the typical roles of the AIS. Such cloud processing systems warehouse large amounts of data for analysis, and while they are much less responsive (slower than edge processing), it is a designer decision about what should and should not be processed in the cloud. If the timescale by which a response is needed is typically much longer than the expected latency it is usually processed in the cloud.

One process that may often be executed offline is the training of models which are used in the other systems, and the bulk-data processing required to make fine-grained sense of trace data across multiple training experiences, and update the various systems used across the rest of the architecture – actions which are enormously sensitive to latency. The varying levels of data-processing discussed here are not new, but currently industry standard in webhosted audio/visual systems.

### 4.5  Scaling Between Systems Using LTI Standards

Another way to scale AISs is to enable data sharing through established information standards. The IMS Global Learning Tools Interoperability (LTI) standard was established to support the exchange of learner assessment data with learning management systems (LMSs) such as edX, Blackboard and Canvas. In 2018, Aleven et al. [29] conducted research that shared assessment data from the edX LMS and two AIS architectures: GIFT and the Cognitive Tutor Authoring Tools. This extended AIS solutions to previously low-adaptive LMSs.

### 4.6  Scaling Between Systems Sharing Intelligent Agents

Finally, in examining methods to scale AISs, we discuss the role of intelligent agents in the evaluation of effectiveness of adaptation strategies and policies. Intelligent agents are autonomous entities which acts to achieve a defined set of goals in an environment. In the case of adaptive instruction, an intelligent agent observes conditions in the environment and then acts to either change the conditions to be more favorable to achieving its goals. Conditions include conditions of the learner at any point in the instruction and includes conditions under which learning is taking place (e.g., level of problem or scenario difficulty).

Each interaction is weighted to determine its value in achieving the agent's goals and in this way the agent learns and improves its decision-making processes. Over time, self-improving agents within AISs can enhance the accuracy of their classifications or predictions and optimize learning outcomes. This supports tailoring and learner goal achievement. Enhanced and validated (trusted) agent capabilities in AISs will improve their acceptance and improve their value in the learning technology marketplace.

### 4.7  Scaling Horizontally Through Content Understanding

Content can be scaled both vertically and horizontally. Horizontal scaling, discussed previously, hinges upon being able to import and evaluate (curate) pre-existing content. For most domains there is a significant amount of pre-existing content available in various forms of writing, videos, images, and other media. Systems can proliferate through the automated ingestion and re-packaging of the content while linking content from one domain to another. As an example, middle school biology textbook content can be linked to its elementary and high school versions. Automated processing and linking can allow a single system to link a wide variety of content, which scales a single system into many related domains to support the learning of students of varying capabilities.

### 4.8 Scaling Vertically Through Content Understanding

While horizontal scaling allows for the system to cover additional domain content, vertical scaling within a domain of instruction involves the processing of content to create the additional artifacts regarding the original content set. This improved AIS performance can take the form of feedback (e.g., mid-lesson reporting) [30], question asking [31], generated scenarios [32], or remixed content [33]. If technology capabilities can be adjusted appropriately, the combination of horizontal and vertical scaling can create a positive feedback loop – where vertical scaling can create a potentially infinite amount of content on a single subject and horizontal scaling technologies can link it appropriately to related content.

## 5   Next Steps

Having review several viable scaling approaches, a recommended set of next steps to enhance the scalability of low-adaptive training ecosystems is discussed in this section. First, it would be appropriate to examine the impact of these scaling approaches (and others) on AIS design, performance (e.g., responsiveness) and maintenance. Empirical experiments are needed to fully understand how scaling influences performance and will help develop a set of recommended practices and perhaps standards for AIS design. Second, the authors recommend also examining the impact of scaling approaches on system cost, usability, and credibility in the marketplace. A third step is to continue the development of standards through IEEE and other standards bodies to ease the burden of bringing effective solutions to the AIS marketplace. This will increase the ubiquity of AISs as an instructional tool of choice and provide exposure to a broader user base. Finally, AIS researchers and developers must be committed to support the needs and experiences of end users (learners) and instructors/teachers/trainers. Scaling approaches should enhance trust in AIS solutions and support user goals.

## References

1. Doolittle, P.E.: Vygotsky's zone of proximal development as a theoretical foundation for cooperative learning. J. Excell. College Teach. **8**(1), 83–103 (1997)
2. Merriam-Webster Dictionary. Definition of Workload
3. Graesser, A.C., McDaniel, B., Chipman, P., Witherspoon, A., D'Mello, S., Gholson, B.: Detection of emotions during learning with AutoTutor. In: Proceedings of the 28th Annual Meetings of the Cognitive Science Society 2006, pp. 285–290 (2006)
4. Pekrun, R.: Emotions and learning. Educ. Pract. Ser. **24**, 2–31 (2014)
5. Barrett, L.F.: How emotions are made: The secret life of the brain. Houghton Mifflin Harcourt, 7 March 2017

6. Aleven, V., McLaughlin, E.A., Glenn, R.A., Koedinger, K.R.: Instruction based on adaptive learning technologies. In: Mayer, R.E., Alexander, P. (eds.) Handbook of research on learning and instruction, 2nd edn., pp. 522–560. Routledge, New York (2017)
7. Baker, R.S.: Modeling and understanding students' off-task behavior in intelligent tutoring systems. In: Proceedings of the SIGCHI Conference on Human Factors in Computing Systems, pp. 1059–1068 (2007)
8. Csikszentmihalyi, M., Abuhamdeh, S., Nakamura, J.: Flow (1990)
9. VanLehn, K.: The relative effectiveness of human tutoring, intelligent tutoring systems, and other tutoring systems. Educ. Psychol. **46**(4), 197–221 (2011)
10. Vygotsky, L.S.: The collected works of L. S. Vygotsky: Vol. 2. The fundamentals of defectology (abnormal psychology and learning disabilities) (J. E. Knox & C. IB. Stevens, Trans.). Plenum, New York (1993)
11. Sottilare, R.A.: Applying adaptive instruction to enhance learning in non-adaptive virtual training environments. In: Bagnara, S., Tartaglia, R., Albolino, S., Alexander, T., Fujita, Y. (eds.) IEA 2018. AISC, vol. 822, pp. 155–162. Springer, Cham (2019). https://doi.org/10.1007/978-3-319-96077-7_16
12. Sottilare, R., Hoehn, R., Tanaka, A.: Adapting existing simulation architectures to enhance tailored instruction. In: Proceedings of the Interservice/Industry Training Simulation & Education Conference, Orlando, Florida, December 2019 (2019)
13. Roessingh, J.J., Poppinga, G., van Oijen, J., Toubman, A.: Application of artificial intelligence to adaptive instruction - combining the concepts. In: Sottilare, R.A., Schwarz, J. (eds.) HCII 2019. LNCS, vol. 11597, pp. 542–556. Springer, Cham (2019). https://doi.org/10.1007/978-3-030-22341-0_43
14. Bondi, A.B.: Characteristics of scalability and their impact on performance. In: Proceedings of the Second International Workshop on Software and Performance – WOSP 2000, p. 195 (2000). https://doi.org/10.1145/350391.350432. ISBN 158113195X
15. Idziorek, J.: Discrete event simulation model for analysis of horizontal scaling in the cloud computing model. In: Proceedings of the 2010 Winter Simulation Conference 2010 December 5, pp. 3004–3014. IEEE (2010)
16. Mondesire, S.C., Stevens, J., Maxwell, D.B.: Vertical scalability benchmarking in three-dimensional virtual world simulation. In: Proceedings of the Conference on Summer Computer Simulation, 26 July 2015, pp. 1–7 (2015)
17. El-Rewini, H., Abd-El-Barr, M.: Advanced Computer Architecture and Parallel Processing. Wiley, Hoboken (2005)
18. Sottilare, R., Hoehn, R., Tanaka, A.: Adapting existing simulation architectures to enhance tailored instruction. In: Proceedings of the 2019 Interservice/Industry Training Simulation & Education Conference (IITSEC), Orlando, Florida (2019)
19. Brawner, K.: Individualised modelling of affective data for intelligent tutoring systems: lessons learned. Int. J. Simul. Process Model. **14**(3), 197–212 (2019)
20. Sottilare, R.A., Brawner, K.W., Goldberg, B.S., Holden, H.K.: The generalized intelligent framework for tutoring (GIFT). US Army Research Laboratory–Human Research & Engineering Directorate (ARL-HRED), Orlando, FL, 31 July 2012
21. Sottilare, R.A., Brawner, K.W., Sinatra, A.M., Johnston, J.H.: An updated concept for a Generalized Intelligent Framework for Tutoring (GIFT). GIFTtutoring.org. 1–9 May 2017
22. Ostrow, K.S., Selent, D., Wang, Y., Van Inwegen, E.G., Heffernan, N.T., Williams, J.J.: The assessment of learning infrastructure (ALI) the theory, practice, and scalability of automated assessment. In: Proceedings of the Sixth International Conference on Learning Analytics & Knowledge, 25 April 2016, pp. 279–288 (2016)
23. Lust, G., Collazo, N.A., Elen, J., Clarebout, G.: Content management systems: enriched learning opportunities for all? Comput. Hum. Behav. **28**(3), 795–808 (2012)

24. Schwier, R., Misanchuk, E.R.: Interactive multimedia instruction. Educ. Technol. (1993)
25. Shi, W., Cao, J., Zhang, Q., Li, Y., Xu, L.: Edge computing: vision and challenges. IEEE Internet Things journal. **3**(5), 637–646 (2016)
26. D'Mello, S., Olney, A., Williams, C., Hays, P.: Gaze tutor: A gaze-reactive intelligent tutoring system. Int. J. Hum Comput Stud. **70**(5), 377–398 (2012 )
27. Sottilare, R.A., Proctor, M.: Passively classifying student mood and performance within intelligent tutors. J. Educ. Technol. Soc. **15**(2), 101–114 (2012)
28. DeFalco, J.A., et al.: Detecting and addressing frustration in a serious game for military training. Int. J. Artif. Intell. Educ. **28**(2), 152–193 (2018 )
29. Aleven, V., Sewall, J., Andres, J.M., Sottilare, R., Long, R., Baker, R.: Towards adapting to learners at scale: integrating MOOC and intelligent tutoring frameworks. In Proceedings of the Fifth Annual ACM Conference on Learning at Scale, pp. 1–4, June 2018
30. Brawner, K., Sottilare, R.: Proposing module-level interoperability for adaptive instructional systems. In: Artificial Intelligence in Education, p. 11, June 2018
31. Efron, M., Winget, M.: Questions are content: a taxonomy of questions in a microblogging environment. Proc. Am. Soc. Inf. Sci. Technol. **47**(1), 1 (2010 )
32. Folsom-Kovarik, J.T., Rowe, J., Brawner, K., Lester, J.: Toward automated scenario generation with gift. Design Recommendations for Intelligent Tutoring Systems, p. 109
33. Magalong, S.J., Palomar, B.C.: Effects of flipped classroom approach using gooru learning management system on students' physics achievement. In: Proceedings of the 10th International Conference on E-Education, E-Business, E-Management and E-Learning, 10 January 2019, pp. 75–78 (2010)

# HyWorM: An Experiment in Dynamic Improvement of Analytic Processes

Ethan B. Trewhitt[1]([⊠]) [ID], Elizabeth T. Whitaker[1] [ID], Elizabeth Veinott[2] [ID], Rick Thomas[3] [ID], Michael Riley[1], Ashley F. Mcdermott[4] [ID], Leonard Eusebi[4] [ID], Michael Dougherty[5], David Illingworth[5] [ID], and Sean Guarino[4]

[1] Georgia Tech Research Institute, Atlanta, GA 30332, USA
ethan.trewhitt@gtri.gatech.edu
[2] Michigan Technological University, Houghton, MI 49931, USA
[3] Georgia Institute of Technology, Atlanta, GA 30332, USA
[4] Charles River Analytics, Cambridge, MA 02138, USA
[5] University of Maryland, College Park, MD 20742, USA

**Abstract.** HyWorM is an approach and implementation for guiding analytic sensemaking processes using the HyGene model of human hypothesis generation. It is an evolution of the RAMPAGE Workflow Monitor (WorM) that monitors and guides analysts in the production of counterfactual forecasts, dynamically adapting work prompts and the revelation of new evidence to broaden and narrow analyst attention, then controlling the schedule of specific forecast problems. WorM also monitors and controls the timing of workflow steps to ensure that attention is distributed effectively across counterfactual problems and other analysis tasks. The inclusion of HyGene theory in WorM to yield the HyWorM process shows potential to broaden analysts' attention to a variety of evidence by using results from the HyGene simulation. Based on previous studies with HyGene, we hypothesize that this will improve the quality of counterfactual forecasts.

**Keywords:** Counterfactual forecasting · Sensemaking analysis · Workflow monitoring · Hypothesis generation · Probability judgment · Working memory

## 1 Introduction

### 1.1 RAMPAGE, GLOW, and WorM

At the core of this project is the Reasoning About Multiple Paths and Alternatives to Generate Effective Forecasts (RAMPAGE) process, a flexible process framework to support hypothesis generation. The RAMPAGE process was developed as part of the Forecasting Counterfactuals in Uncontrolled Settings (FOCUS) program run by IARPA, in which the goal was to develop and empirically evaluate systematic approaches to counterfactual forecasting processes. Analysts were presented with challenge problems that involved counterfactual forecasting scenarios using simulated worlds, such as the game Civilization V or a simulation of a flu epidemic. The teams were provided data of variable reliability and accuracy and a series of questions to forecast. Each team was to

© Springer Nature Switzerland AG 2021
R. A. Sottilare and J. Schwarz (Eds.): HCII 2021, LNCS 12792, pp. 311–320, 2021.
https://doi.org/10.1007/978-3-030-77857-6_21

use a predefined counterfactual forecasting process, which could be modified between challenges.

GLOW is the frontend user interface that provides evidence, problem details, and other information, and prompts the users (analysts) to provide their counterfactual forecasts. The Workflow Monitor (WorM), which is the main focus of this paper, is the backend workflow monitoring component of the GLOW-WorM RAMPAGE platform.

## 1.2  Hygene + WorM = HyWorM

WorM guides analysts through the RAMPAGE process, which provides a set of analysis methods to be performed sequentially by an analyst to produce counterfactual forecasts. The theory and design of these methods is guided by the psychologists on the RAMPAGE team. The methods are designed to be ordered and configured dynamically by WorM, whose design and implementation is guided by HyGene to form a composite approach known as HyWorM. HyGene is a model of the mechanisms by which humans generate hypotheses using long-term memory, as well as a model of human forecasting based on those hypotheses [1] and related research [2]. In the HyWorM integration, the HyGene is a simulation and plays the role of the human analyst. Based on the hypothesis generation of the simulated analysts in HyGene, WorM responds with dynamic analytic process method selections. The simulation is used to explore multiple analytic process method choices and compare the results. The envisioned long-term goal is to design an approach to perform real-time HyGene simulations and to dynamically select the most effective analytic method based on the results of the HyGene simulations.

WorM guides the analyst by selecting and configuring the appropriate methods that maximize the effectiveness of their counterfactual process. This tool models the general process and uses that model to encourage dynamic iteration through the methods of the process based on an assessment of the state of the analysis. Initially, this tool tracked the methods used and guided the analyst (via the RAMPAGE interface called GLOW) to select the next method with the greatest potential to further the analysis within the context of previously executed methods to avoid overlap. By monitoring the progress of the forecasting process in later versions, WorM has been refined to customize specific analysis steps, as well as to direct the analyst to repeat methods or skip to later steps in the process. Our hypothesis is that this approach encourages the analyst to explore more of the hypothesis space and results in a greater diversity of hypotheses generated and evaluated than with a more static or problem-independent workflow.

## 2  Key WorM Features

The RAMPAGE process, and WorM as a component of that process, was developed in five (5) cycles. Each cycle consisted of a development, then user testing, followed by evaluation. Through this iterative process, WorM has been tested and improved to include a number of innovative dynamic methods.

WorM operates based on a specification of the overall workflow for analysts, including the definition of static steps, steps with multiple analysis methods, optional steps based on time, optional steps based on analysts' work products (for correction or support), and pseudorandom assignment of evidence and forecasts to ensure diverse prompts across analysts for evaluation of the statistical significance across users.

### 2.1 Pseudorandom Assignment of Evidence and Counterfactual Forecast Problem Presentation

To evaluate whether the order of evidence presentation and/or counterfactual forecast problems might affect overall performance, WorM builds a set of pseudorandom orders for these items. The order schedules are allocated evenly across users so that roughly the same number of samples exist to test the quality of each order schedule. This ordering takes place both for revealing subsets of evidence to users, and in asking users to give forecasts for the official counterfactual problems.

### 2.2 Dynamic Timing Control

WorM is tasked with scheduling workflow steps based on an overall time limit, proportionally allocating time to each step based on the time used on previous steps, the time remaining in the analysis process, and the proportional value and level-of-effort of upcoming steps. While the user is ultimately in control of the time taken during the process, WorM estimates the ideal time for each step and GLOW shows the user their progress during each step. The system warns users who are running behind or have exceeded the allocated time for a given step.

### 2.3 Writing and Reading Memoranda as a Method of Cross-Pollination

The RAMPAGE process introduced the idea of analysts creating written memos to serve two key purposes: to solidify their own thinking and justify the reasoning they used to produce their forecasts, and to persuade other analysts to come to the same conclusions. RAMPAGE provided writing prompts to each analyst as an imitation/role-play of a character within the simulation, then shared the written memos with other analysts to read. Each analyst produced forecasts before and after this process so that the quality of forecasts could be compared before and after the memo writing and reading steps.

WorM dynamically assigns memo-writing prompts and assigns the written memos to specific other analysts for their review. This ensures that the memo information was using only memos that were meaningful and provides an opportunity for the users to complete any missing pieces. The checks were as follows:

- Collaboration stages are rebuilt using known memo data. Only memos that have been populated will be shown to other users for reading.
- Memo contents are checked for length, with warning messages created that are shown to the user (by GLOW) before they may continue.

## 2.4  Dynamic Method Selection Based on the Analyst's Work Products

WorM uses a collection of dynamic methods, assigned to specific points in the workflow, to react to the analyst's work up to that point. In some cases, this means reacting to potential mistakes that can be discovered in the analyst's prior work and scheduling a specific method to remediate the potential issue. This check happens multiple times throughout the workflow, so it is designed to maximize the remediation value by avoiding duplication of methods when possible. WorM integrates with GLOW to implement the dynamic processes, as shown in the figure below. The integration interaction is as follows, and the full decision tree is shown in Fig. 1:

1. At the end of each step, GLOW gives WorM an opportunity to update the next step
2. WorM determines whether the next step is dynamic
3. For dynamic steps, WorM evaluates the user's workbook products
4. Based on the evaluation, WorM creates the full set of instructions for the next step
5. GLOW presents the next step to the user

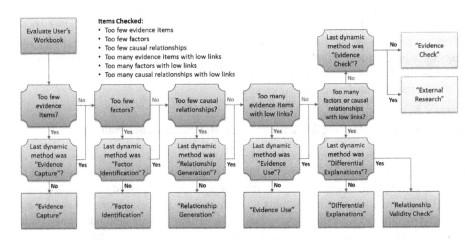

**Fig. 1.** Dynamic method selection

## 2.5  Customized Instructions Based on Previous Analyst Work

WorM can select dynamic methods using two approaches. One approach is optional remediation instructions. After certain steps, user work is checked against a set of rules aimed at recognizing shortcomings. Each rule that is triggered will add another text section to the dynamic instructions. If no rules are triggered, a set of review instructions are included, as shown in the figure below (Fig. 2).

The other approach provides suggestions using user content. At certain steps, instructions are supplemented with a set of starting point suggestions pulled from the user's own work. For example, we ask users to select malleable factors, and to start them off,

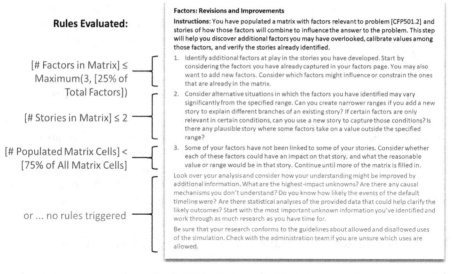

**Rules Evaluated:**

[# Factors in Matrix] ≤ Maximum(3, [25% of Total Factors])

[# Stories in Matrix] ≤ 2

[# Populated Matrix Cells] < [75% of All Matrix Cells]

or ... no rules triggered

**Factors: Revisions and Improvements**

**Instructions:** You have populated a matrix with factors relevant to problem [CFP501.2] and stories of how those factors will combine to influence the answer to the problem. This step will help you discover additional factors you may have overlooked, calibrate values among those factors, and verify the stories already identified.

1. Identify additional factors at play in the stories you have developed. Start by considering the factors you have already captured in your factors page. You may also want to add new factors. Consider which factors might influence or constrain the ones that are already in the matrix.

2. Consider alternative situations in which the factors you have identified may vary significantly from the specified range. Can you create narrower ranges if you add a new story to explain different branches of an existing story? If certain factors are only relevant in certain conditions, can you use a new story to capture those conditions? Is there any plausible story where some factors take on a value outside the specified range?

3. Some of your factors have not been linked to some of your stories. Consider whether each of these factors could have an impact on that story, and what the reasonable value or range would be in that story. Continue until more of the matrix is filled in.

Look over your analysis and consider how your understanding might be improved by additional information. What are the highest-impact unknowns? Are there any causal mechanisms you don't understand? Do you know how likely the events of the default timeline were? Are there statistical analyses of the provided data that could help clarify the likely outcomes? Start with the most important unknown information you've identified and work through as much research as you have time for.

Be sure that your research conforms to the guidelines about allowed and disallowed uses of the simulation. Check with the administration team if you are unsure which uses are allowed.

**Fig. 2.** Remediation instructions

WorM evaluates their factors and provides the top 3 that may satisfy the step objectives, as shown below (Fig. 3).

In this example step, the user's existing factors are evaluated.

- Candidate factor requirements:
  - *Is not* included in their current matrix
  - *Is* included in another story in which other factors in this matrix also have values.
- Candidates are ranked by diversity, which is defined as the total number of distinct cell values for stories in which this factor appears.
- The user's titles for their top *n* = 3 factors (highest diversity) are written into the instructions.

**Analysis: Missing Factors**

**Instructions:** You have developed a matrix of stories and factors for problem [CFP502.1]. This step will help you focus only on those factors that potentially affect the outcome of each story, but which are not captured in your matrix. Consider the factors you have identified but not linked to any stories in the matrix. Are any of those factors affected by the counterfactual? Does the change in their value affect the outcome of any of your stories? If so, link the factors to a story and fill in their ranges in the matrix.

Based on your matrix so far, these factors may be useful to consider:

1. Relationship between Greece and Venice
2. Additional unit capabilities
3. Arabian - Shoshone relationship

After identifying new malleable factors, does it suggest a new forecast story? If so, make a note, you will add the story in a future step.

**Expected Output:** Check and add new malleable factors to a forecast matrix if relevant.

**Fig. 3.** Customized instructions using user-generated content

Similar to the earlier process, the integration with GLOW works as follows:

1. At the end of each step, GLOW gives WorM an opportunity to update the next step

2. WorM evaluates the user's workbook products with multiple specific rules
3. Based on the evaluation, WorM customizes the instructions to include or exclude specific remediation steps, or support steps if no remediation is needed
4. GLOW presents the next step to the user

### 2.6 Explicit Warnings Based on the Detection of Errors in User Content

As users interact with the GLOW frontend, WorM has a number of rule checks for explicitly-defined mistakes the user may make. These may be as simple as insufficient length of text responses, or as complex as redundancy of one response by the analyst when compared to their previous work whenever diversity is required. GLOW provides analyst work regularly to WorM as an event, then WorM analyzes the work for errors and provides text warnings for presentation by the user by GLOW, if needed.

## 3   HyGene Theory as a Basis for Analyst Workflow Guidance

During the RAMPAGE Project, the HyGene simulation was used offline to run experiments and to provide input into the design of analytic methods and processes. An innovative approach that we are beginning to implement is real-time simulation of analysts in HyGene to provide data and guidance to WorM to dynamically choose the best method for the analyst to perform next. WorM will:

- Use AI reasoning based on HyGene models
- Reason about the steps that the user has taken and model the user's activity
- Attempt to determine, e.g., whether users are evaluating all available evidence, avoiding cognitive biases, creating diverse hypotheses.
- Use this model to suggest appropriate narrowing or broadening steps

This will be the first software integration between HyGene and WorM The concept of operations for WorM + HyGene consists of the following steps:

1. The digital analyst is given a process step (or a few process steps) to begin analysis of the Civ 5 question.
2. The digital analyst produces notes, memos, hypotheses, causal influences, or forecasts.
3. WorM analysis of the diversity takes place.
4. WorM sets up parameters in HyGene with the state and estimates of diversity.
5. HyGene produces forecasts based on several alternative next steps in the process.
6. WorM manages the selection of the next process step or method.
7. WorM sends it to the analyst for continuation of the process.

For this experiment a digital analyst surrogate will produce the analytic products in collaboration with a human in what is commonly called a "pay no attention to the man behind the curtain" (PNAMBC) demonstration. GLOW is intended to be used as the frontend visualizer, though it will not be integrated as part of this demonstration (Fig. 4).

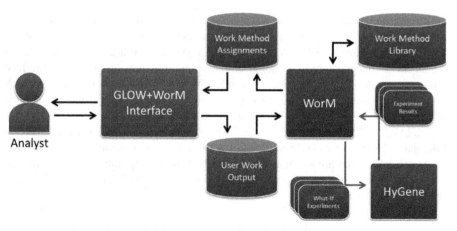

**Fig. 4.** GLOW + WorM + HyGene combined architecture and components

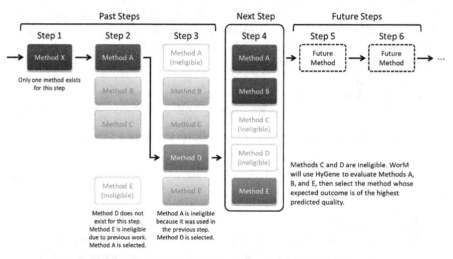

**Fig. 5.** Steps in the WorM + HyGene dynamic method selection process

The figure below shows the steps in the WorM method selection as described in the concept of operations (Fig. 5).

One objective of the inclusion of HyGene in the FOCUS project has been to explore the effectiveness of including the brain-based mental analysis models of memory (from HyGene) with the workflow customization enabled by WorM within the RAMPAGE process. With a robust model of human sensemaking provided by HyGene, WorM would be able to more accurately predict the best sensemaking approach at many times throughout the RAMPAGE process, and thus provide users with the best reasoning method at each step, customized to their individual needs at each moment.

As an initial evaluation of the concept, we conducted an experiment in which HyGene was used to model semantic and episodic memory of the Civ 5 diplomatic cable dataset, plus a simplified model of WorM to guide the selection of a cable to present to the virtual user at multiple steps, in order to maximize user attention to concepts within the cables. This is driven by one hypothesis that underlies HyGene: that a user who considers a broader set of concepts within the solution space of a problem is more likely to produce accurate forecasts within that space. Thus, if WorM can use HyGene to determine which data, when presented to the user, is likely to most broaden the user's thinking at each step, that user is more likely to produce accurate forecasts.

The FOCUS T&E team created and delivered a customized FOCUS configuration of the game *Sid Meier's Civilization V*, a.k.a. "Civ 5". This version of Civ 5 contains diplomatic cables that are simulated letters written from a diplomat in one country to the corresponding diplomat in another country within the virtual Civ 5 world. One such cable appears as in Fig. 6:

Foreign Secretary's Office,
Our hearts are always hearty after hearing from you. The Koreans' military force has arrived at an average status, according to our intelligence officers. Insofar as we can decipher, the Koreans estimates we are a neutral party. A neutral manner with the Koreans is what we maintain. We perceive the Koreans to be an average target for attack.
Yours in service,
Charge d'affaires in Korea

**Fig. 6.** Example diplomatic cable from FOCUS Civilization 5 problem set

Another cable is shown in Fig. 7:

Correspondent,
Not a day goes by where we do not think highly of your zeal for your work. We estimate the Assyrians to be pursuing unknown dominance now. Our spies are not at all certain in this report. Whatever the Assyrians' advertised position may be, the Greeks regard the Assyrians as a neutral civilization. Please send word on the Assyrians' military ambitions, as the foreign office is thoroughly alarmed about the Assyrians' doings. We believe that the Assyrians have become a moderate danger to our strategies. We published that transactions between us and the Assyrians are currently friendly.
All the best,
The Honorable Foreign Secretary

**Fig. 7.** Second example diplomatic cable from FOCUS Civilization 5 problem set

In the WorM + HyGene experiment, we consider each cable to comprise one episode in memory, and the words in the cable form the semantic space of the mental model.

We use natural language processing (NLP) to tokenize and lemmatize the words in each cable, excluding stop words (like 'the', 'with', 'and', etc.) and punctuation. Tokenization separates words from each other, while lemmatization converts each word to its lemma, which is the canonical form of each word (e.g. "tracing" becomes "trace", and "was" becomes "be"). This reduces the complexity of the dataset and equates terms that are conceptually identical without losing information that is meaningful to this experiment.

In the Cycle 5 problem set, the Civ 5 diplomatic cables are stored in a CSV file containing 3445 cables, and thus the constructed HyGene model contains 3445 episodes. After NLP, the model contains 526 entries in semantic memory. To simulate slightly imperfect memory, the HyGene model is configured with $L_{prob} = 0.9$ and $L_{gauss\_var\_factor} = 20$, with a vector length of 10000 entries for episodic memory and semantic memory.

## 3.1 Primary WorM Mechanism

The experiment uses a simulated workflow of 20 steps, with 30 candidate cables chosen at random to be considered for each step. For the first step, the HyGene model is queried to determine the extent to which each candidate episode would activate all terms in semantic memory, if selected. WorM then selects the candidate in which the absolute value of all semantic memory activation values was greatest. This represents the episode with the broadest coverage of concepts, as defined by memory activation.

For each subsequent step, WorM performs the same prediction with a new set of 30 randomly selected cables, again asking HyGene to predict the semantic activation that would occur if each were selected. However, distinct from the first step, this time WorM selects the episode whose activation most increases the span of memory activated so far, across all entries in semantic memory. This means it is effectively optimizing to increase the area under the curve, where the curve is the defined span between min and max activation for all terms in semantic memory. In doing so, WorM is attempting to create the broadest possible activation in semantic memory using the episodes made available to it throughout the 20 steps of the workflow.

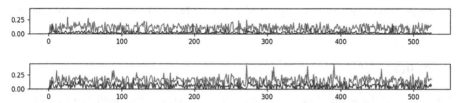

**Fig. 8.** Activation range (strongest) for each semantic term number after 1 (blue, lower) and 20 (red, higher) workflow steps. Top plot shows the baseline condition, using random episode selection for each workflow step, whereas the lower plot shows the results after intelligent episode selection for each workflow step. Note that both the positive and negative activation levels are higher for the intelligent selection condition (Color figure online).

The plot in Fig. 8 shows the activation range after 20 workflow steps for two conditions. The top plot shows the baseline condition, using random episode selection for each workflow step, whereas the lower plot shows the results after intelligent episode selection for each workflow step. In these plots, the X axis is the semantic term number (0 to 525) and the Y axis is the span from lowest to highest activation value. Note that activation can take any value, negative or positive. An activation value of "zero" effectively means no activation, whereas highly negative or positive activation is desired in this experiment. The "span" value for each semantic term is the difference between the highest positive and lowest negative values seen so far, clipping each at zero. The blue series (lower) represents the activation spans following the first step, and the red series (higher) represents the final activation spans after the final step. In the baseline configuration, the same process is performed but with one cable selected at random for each step, with no consideration for its effect prior to selection.

The baseline plot shows that the overall activations are lower, indicating narrower thinking, which (as hypothesized) would lead to lower quality forecasts from this user, whereas the intelligent selection process yields equal or greater activation ranges across all of the semantic terms.

This experiment shows that HyGene can be used as an underlying model to improve performance in the RAMPAGE process executed by WorM. By guiding the user's thought processes toward evidence that broadens their thinking (as defined by equal or greater span of activation ranges across all semantic terms), we hypothesize that the user will, in turn, create more accurate forecasts.

## 4   Conclusion

This paper describes an initial integration and exploration into the use of a hypothesis generation simulation, HyGene, to simulate the behavior of a human analyst during the process of receiving evidence and generating hypotheses using analysis methods being managed by WorM. This first experiment provided results that show that using HyGene to guide WorM's presentation of episodic evidence to analysts suggest that those analysts would have broader attention in memory that would lead to improved hypotheses and counterfactual forecasts. Next steps include further experimentation that would investigate whether HyWorM is able to broaden attention to evidence, and would translate to a measurable real-world improvement in forecast accuracy.

## References

1. Thomas, R.P., Dougherty, M.R., Sprenger, A.M., Harbison, J.I.: Diagnostic hypothesis generation and human judgment. Psychol. Rev. **115**, 155–185 (2008). https://doi.org/10.1037/0033-295X.115.1.155
2. Jamieson, R.K., Avery, J.E., Johns, B.T., Jones, M.N.: An instance theory of semantic memory. Comput. Brain Behav. **3**, 126–127 (2020). https://doi.org/10.1007/s42113-019-00046-x

# Investigating Adaptive Activity Effectiveness Across Domains: Insights into Design Best Practices

Rachel Van Campenhout$^{(\boxtimes)}$, Bill Jerome, Jeffrey S. Dittel, and Benny G. Johnson

VitalSource Technologies, Pittsburgh, PA, USA
Rachel.Vancampenhout@vitalsource.com

**Abstract.** Courseware as an adaptive instructional system is a complex environment to develop. The student will encounter lessons of content with integrated formative practice, adaptive activities, and assessments in their learning path. The alignment of all course features, including the scaffolding structure of the adaptive activities, may vary between courses and the teams who created them. In a previous analysis of adaptive activities [1], these activities had net positive effects on student learning estimates and summative assessment scores. In this paper, we will analyze three additional non-STEM courses that had less effective adaptive activities using the same methods as the original study, and further investigate course features that could be influencing their effectiveness, such as alignment, difficulty, and amount of practice. The results of this analysis can provide guidance on how to best create content for adaptive courseware and provide an example of the critical role data analysis has in the evaluation and iterative improvement of student learning environments.

**Keywords:** Adaptive activities · Adaptive courseware · Formative practice · Learning by doing · Learning outcomes

## 1 Introduction

The Acrobatiq by VitalSource platform delivers data-driven courseware that provides a comprehensive learning environment for students, from text content and media to formative practice and summative assessments. In particular, the courseware utilizes real-time student data to deliver adaptive practice activities throughout a student's learning path. The adaptive activities are personalized for each course learning objective and provide students scaffolded questions adapted to fit their needs. Previous analysis of a Probability and Statistics course investigated how the adaptive activities impacted student learning by analyzing their impact on two metrics: learning estimates and summative assessment scores [1]. It was found that the adaptive activities helped increase students' learning estimates. It was also found that the adaptive activities helped students increase their summative assessment scores. Students who were able to increase their learning estimates via the adaptive activities also scored higher on summative assessments than their peers who did not increase their learning estimates.

© Springer Nature Switzerland AG 2021
R. A. Sottilare and J. Schwarz (Eds.): HCII 2021, LNCS 12792, pp. 321–333, 2021.
https://doi.org/10.1007/978-3-030-77857-6_22

This study aims to build upon this research in two ways. First, we will replicate the analysis done for the previous study's research questions on several other non-STEM courses (Project Management, Finance, and Macroeconomics) that had less effective adaptive activities. For each of these courses, we will answer the following research questions: "How do the adaptive activities affect learning estimates for students?" and, "How do the adaptive activities affect student scores on summative assessments?".

Second, by analyzing a variety of courses with variation in results, we can investigate a second line of inquiry on the features of the courseware that could influence the degree of effectiveness for these adaptive activities. The research question we will seek to answer is: "What features of courseware design influence the effectiveness of the adaptive activities for increasing student learning estimates and outcomes?" As this second area of investigation concerns course features, the original Probability and Statistics course from previous research will be used to compare results with the additional courses analyzed for the first research questions. To answer this research question, we will investigate course features such as question alignment, difficulty, and the amount of adaptive practice for each course. The question difficulty for each course can be analyzed for the formative questions, adaptive questions, and summative questions separately to examine any potential relationship to the effectiveness of the adaptive activities. For example, if the summative question difficulties are substantially different from the formative or adaptive practice, then it is possible the adaptive practice may not have a measurable effect on summative scores.

By analyzing these course features in relation to the effectiveness of the adaptive activities, we can identify a set of guidelines for authoring and developing course features. While tools such as the adaptive practice can be used to help students learn and improve outcomes, implementation of these tools can vary and impact their effectiveness. By evaluating both the effectiveness of adaptive activities and course features which could impact their effectiveness, we can suggest implementation guidance for adaptive activities across subject domains. Understanding course design through data is needed to continue data-driven iterative improvements that benefit the learner. Courseware should be able to maximize learning benefits for students no matter the domain. It is critical for features—especially adaptivity—to be effective regardless of content area.

## 2   Methods

**The Courseware.** The courseware analyzed were all developed on the Acrobatiq platform using the same learning methodology and design. Each course includes units of content, broken down into modules, broken down further into individual lesson pages. Each lesson page is organized around a learning objective, and all content and formative practice aligns—and is tagged to—that learning objective. The formative practice provides students with opportunities to practice what they have learned as they work through the content, receiving immediate targeted feedback. Formative practice is a foundational learning method shown to increase learning for different age groups and different subjects [2] and feedback increases the benefits of formative practice [3]. The formative practice integrated with the content is a type of learning by doing, which has been shown to have about six times the effect size than reading alone [4]. This learning by doing approach has also been shown to be causal for learning [5–7].

The formative practice questions are not graded, but student responses contribute to their learning estimate—a predictive measure generated for each student on each learning objective. This learning estimate is based on a machine learning model which uses item response theory (IRT) [8, 9] to predict how well the student might perform on a learning objective in a summative assessment. This IRT approach takes into account the psychometric properties of questions when constructing the ability estimate: the difficulty and discrimination of questions is modeled by a two-parameter logistic model. A Bayesian approach [10] estimates the posterior distributions of the IRT question parameters from data in addition to the student ability posterior distribution from the formative and adaptive questions students answered. The learning estimate value between 0 and 1 is derived from the ability posterior, with higher values indicating a higher probability of obtaining a passing score on that learning objective's summative assessment. The model will assign a category of low, medium, or high as long as there is enough data for the model to have sufficient confidence in its prediction.

The learning estimate drives the personalization in the adaptive activities. Placed after a series of lesson pages in the module, the adaptive activity uses the student's learning estimate for each learning objective to determine the set of questions the student will receive. Students with high learning estimates will only see the most difficult questions which should mirror those on an assessment. Students with low or medium learning estimates receive those same question in addition to easier questions that will help to scaffold knowledge gaps leading to the hardest questions. The low and medium level questions can provide steps or sub-steps toward the hard questions, reducing cognitive load for those students much like a worked example [12]. The purpose of the scaffolding is to meet students at their ability level and build from there, much like Vygotsky's zone of proximal development [11]. The adaptive activities are formative in nature. They do not produce a score for the gradebook, but are graded on completion only, regardless of accuracy. Like the formative practice, students receive immediate, targeted feedback and can continue answering the questions until they get them correct. Responses on the adaptive activity contribute to the final learning estimate calculations as well.

**The Population.** Each of the three courses selected were run at the same traditional four-year institution in 2019. The courseware was used as the primary learning resource in introductory courses led by faculty. No experimental manipulations were used for this population; students engaged in the courseware as a natural part of their credit-bearing course. The platform did not collect demographic information for students.

**The Data.** The courseware data necessary for this analysis are the formative question attempts, accuracy, learning estimate states, adaptive activity attempts and accuracy, and summative assessment attempts and accuracy. The unit of analysis for this study were the student-learning objective pairs, I.E., a single student's work on a single learning objective. As in the original study, the data set for each course was reduced to only include learning objectives with formative, adaptive, and summative question attempts. The final data for each course is listed in Table 1.

**Table 1.** The data for each course analyzed.

| Course | Students | Learning objectives | Total Data records |
|---|---|---|---|
| Project management | 72 | 47 | 2798 |
| Macroeconomics | 84 | 58 | 2797 |
| Finance | 76 | 50 | 3053 |

# 3  Results

## 3.1  RQ 1: How Do the Adaptive Activities Affect Learning Estimates for Students?

**Overall Learning Estimate Change.** The first analysis was to evaluate the overall learning estimate changes from before to after the adaptive activity for all student-learning objective pairs. This same analysis was done on all three courses. For project management, there were 1,589 instances in which a learning estimate was available immediately before and after the adaptive practice, and the mean learning estimate change was −0.024, which was overall negative. for finance, there were 1,623 instances of learning estimate changes, with a mean change of −0.024 as Well. For macroeconomics, there were a total of 1,695 instances of learning estimates with a mean of − 0.007. As in the original study, for each course a shapiro-wilk test showed the learning estimate differences were not normally distributed. A one-sample wilcoxon signed rank test showed the median learning estimate change was statistically different from 0 (P < < < 0.001) for all courses (Table 2).

**Table 2.** The learning estimate increases and decreases for each course.

| | Project management | | Finance | | Macroeconomics | |
|---|---|---|---|---|---|---|
| Statistic | Learning estimate increase | Learning estimate decrease | Learning estimate increase | Learning estimate decrease | Learning estimate increase | Learning estimate decrease |
| Count | 619 | 970 | 709 | 914 | 778 | 917 |
| Mean | 0.045433 | −0.068897 | 0.046014 | −0.077883 | 0.026653 | −0.036113 |
| Std | 0.045714 | 0.052469 | 0.060242 | 0.075473 | 0.037764 | 0.036812 |

We can compare these learning estimate changes to those found in the Probability and Statistics course [1]. In that course, 62% of all learning estimate changes were positive with a mean increase of 0.132, while the learning estimate decreases had a mean of − 0.064. The learning estimate increases were twice as large compared to the decreases. For these three business courses, there are more decreases in learning estimates than increases, and the mean decrease is 1 to 3% points larger than the mean increase. This tells us that further investigation is needed to understand why the results are contradictory to the original analysis. Misalignment of course features such as question difficulty or the design of the adaptive activities themselves could be affecting these overall learning estimate changes.

**Learning Estimate Change by Category.** The second analysis was to evaluate the learning estimate changes according to each category of learning estimate before and after the adaptive activity. A student's learning estimate categories immediately prior to starting the adaptive activity determines the level of scaffolding they receive for each learning objective. The questions in the adaptive activity are formative as well, so contribute to the learning estimate and therefore students can change learning estimate categories after completing the adaptive activity

*Project Management.* In Project Management, the majority of all student estimates remained in their category. The largest change in category was the medium learning estimate category—after completing the adaptive activity, approximately 20% of medium learning estimates shifted to high and 20% shifted to low. The high and the low category both only had a small portion of estimates change to the next available category. This does not tell an overwhelmingly clear story. It seems that learning estimate category changes after the adaptive activities nearly balance out (Table 3).

**Table 3.** The number of instances of learning estimate changes after completing adaptive questions, grouped by learning estimate category.

| Learning estimate category | High (after adaptive) | Medium (after adaptive) | Low (after adaptive) |
|---|---|---|---|
| High (before adaptive) | 471 | 77 | 2 |
| Medium (before adaptive) | 112 | 284 | 104 |
| Low (before adaptive) | 1 | 41 | 453 |

*Finance.* The learning estimate category groups for Finance show a similar pattern when compared to Project Management. The majority of all student learning estimates remained in the same category. The medium category had the most change, with approximately 40% changing category at a nearly equal split between high and low. Nearly 17% of high learning estimate instances changed from high to a lower category, while only 7% of low learning estimate instances changed from low to a higher category (Table 4).

*Macroeconomics.* There was less movement between categories in this course, compared to the others. For both the high and low categories, no students had learning estimate instances move 2 categories (high to low or low to high). Very few students even moved one category. The medium category had the largest move, but more to low than to high (Table 5).

**Table 4.** The number of instances of learning estimate changes after completing adaptive questions, grouped by learning estimate category.

| Learning estimate category | High (after adaptive) | Medium (after adaptive) | Low (after adaptive) |
|---|---|---|---|
| High (before adaptive) | 541 | 99 | 10 |
| Medium (before adaptive) | 95 | 296 | 101 |
| Low (before adaptive) | 1 | 26 | 341 |

**Table 5.** The number of instances of learning estimate changes after completing adaptive questions, grouped by learning estimate category.

| Learning estimate category | High (after adaptive) | Medium (after adaptive) | Low (after adaptive) |
|---|---|---|---|
| High (before adaptive) | 861 | 33 | 0 |
| Medium (before adaptive) | 50 | 214 | 69 |
| Low (before adaptive) | 0 | 30 | 420 |

## 3.2   RQ 2: How Do the Adaptive Activities Affect Mean Summative Assessment Scores for Students?

The learning estimate is a predictive measure generated for each student on each learning objective, but the more traditional method of evaluating student learning is through a summative assessment. Students completed a quiz shortly after the adaptive activity. We compared the mean summative assessment scores for each learning estimate category.

**Project Management.** The first—and most surprising—result was the overall range of mean summative scores. All categories averaged over 0.9 (90%) from low to high, with a range of 0.044 (4.4%). Students performed very well on the summative assessments, though the reason for this is yet unknown. When looking at the upward movement within a category, we find that students who increased their learning estimate after the adaptive practice (students who changed from medium before to high after; low before to medium/high after) scored higher than their peers who did not increase their learning estimate. There are a few anomalies in the trend, but those are mostly where there are small amounts of data (i.e. the high before adaptive to low after adaptive category has a higher mean summative score than any other high category, but that score is also created from only 2 instances) (Table 6).

**Table 6.** Mean summative scores by learning estimate category before and after the adaptive activity questions.

| Learning estimate category | High (after adaptive) | Medium (after adaptive) | Low (after adaptive) |
|---|---|---|---|
| High (before adaptive) | 0.932 | 0.921 | 0.958 |
| Medium (before adaptive) | 0.937 | 0.902 | 0.908 |
| Low (before adaptive) | 1.00 | 0.922 | 0.914 |

**Finance.** The mean summative assessment scores for each learning estimate category before/after the adaptive activity show the same trends as the Project Management. Students who had a high category after the adaptive activities had higher summative assessment scores than those who had medium or low learning estimates after the adaptive activities. Students with medium learning estimates after the adaptive activities had higher scores than those with low learning estimates. These trends are also consistent within the high, medium, and low category before the adaptive activity: within each of those categories, mean summative scores increased as the learning estimate categories increased after the adaptive activities. The range of mean scores is more consistent with expectations, ranging from 0.733 (73.3%) to 0.863 (86.3%) (the mean score of 1.00 was generated from one data point so was not used as the mean high score) (Table 7).

**Table 7.** Mean summative scores by learning estimate category before and after the adaptive activity questions.

| Learning estimate category | High (after adaptive) | Medium (after adaptive) | Low (after adaptive) |
|---|---|---|---|
| High (before adaptive) | 0.863 | 0.817 | 0.733 |
| Medium (before adaptive) | 0.844 | 0.814 | 0.706 |
| Low (before adaptive) | 1.00 | 0.767 | 0.748 |

**Macroeconomics.** The mean summative assessment scores for Macroeconomics do not follow the trends of Project Management and Finance. Instead of higher learning estimate categories corresponding to higher summative assessment scores, these scores appear to be a more random pattern. The spread of these scores is also very close: all categories fall between 0.844 and 0.882, less than 4% difference (Table 8).

**Table 8.** Mean summative scores by learning estimate category before and after the adaptive activity questions.

| Learning estimate category | High (after adaptive) | Medium (after adaptive) | Low (after adaptive) |
|---|---|---|---|
| High (before adaptive) | 0.882 | 0.863 | NA |
| Medium (before adaptive) | 0.857 | 0.872 | 0.874 |
| Low (before adaptive) | NA | 0.882 | 0.844 |

Overall, the analysis of all three courses for the first two research questions shows general inconsistencies with the original study. All three courses showed the adaptive activities had a net negative impact on the learning estimates. Two of the three courses (Project Management and Finance) confirmed the trend that students who increased their learning estimate after the adaptive practice increased their summative assessments compared to their peers who did not. Two of the three courses (Project Management and Macroeconomics) showed unusual results in the summative assessment scores as well, with all ranges of students performing high and with a very narrow spread of scores. Course features for each course will be investigated to help contextualize these findings.

### 3.3   RQ 3: What Features of Courseware Influence the Effectiveness of the Adaptive Activities?

**Alignment.** To gain a bigger-picture understanding of what could be influencing some of these unexpected findings, we will look at the difficulty alignment of question types: formative, adaptive, and summative. Question alignment ensures that the students receive learning benefits from formative practice questions and adaptive questions, while also being fairly evaluated in the summative assessment. A misalignment between question difficulty in different question types could be affecting the benefit of the adaptive activities. For instance, if the adaptive activities were more difficult than the formative practice questions, then on average students would not do as well on them and learning estimates would decrease. If summative assessment questions were much more difficult, then the formative and adaptive questions would not have sufficiently prepared students and they would not do as well on the summative questions (Fig. 1).

For all four courses, the relationship between the formative practice and adaptive practice mean accuracy was close despite differences in direction. In Probability and Statistics, students in all categories did slightly better in the adaptive activities than the formative practice. In the other three business courses, students had slightly lower mean accuracy scores on adaptive activity questions than from the formative questions. This could suggest that the formatives were easier than the adaptive activities (or the adaptive activities were more difficult than the formatives).

The mean accuracy/scores on formatives, adaptive activities, and summative assessments are unaligned for some courses. For instance, Project Management had formative

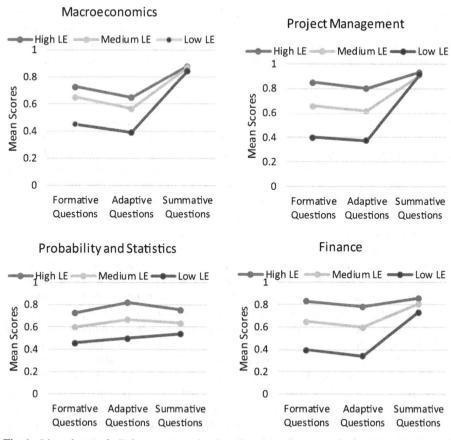

**Fig. 1.** Line charts of all four courses showing the mean scores on formative, adaptive, and summative questions by learning estimate category.

and adaptive mean scores which were relatively parallel for students at all learning estimate levels, but then the summative mean scores for all learning estimate categories were extremely high. Students at the low level had a mean accuracy in the 40% range for formatives and adaptive activities, yet scored in the 90% range for the summative assessments. It is unlikely that this increase in accuracy was caused by the formative practice. It is also unlikely that the summative assessments (which were written by the same subject matter experts who wrote the formative practice) were so easy that all students scored within a few percentage points of each other. This leads us to hypothesize that some external variable is the cause for this misalignment, such as the assessments being treated as practice tests taken collaboratively in class. Different implementation practices of the courseware between courses could easily affect the data seen here, but would not be captured via the platform itself so only inferences can be made.

The alignment of practice across the course is a good indicator of how effective the course design is, as well as when external factors may be influencing outcomes. Probability and Statistics is visibly the most challenging course with about a 20-point mean accuracy/score spread between low and high learning estimate groups, with changes under 8 points between formative questions and summative questions across all groups. However, the business courses show a dramatic misalignment between the formative and adaptive questions and the summative questions, for reasons not yet known.

**Amount of Adaptive Practice.** We also compared the average amount of adaptive practice available for each learning objective across all courses. The Probability and Statistics course had an average of 14.05 adaptive practice questions per learning objective. Project Management averaged 6.69, Finance averaged 5.17, and Macroeconomics averaged 4.85. Probability and Statistics had approximately double the available adaptive practice and also had a positive net change in learning estimate scores with a mean increase three times higher than any other course. This suggests that the amount of available practice is related to the possible increase of learning estimates. While the amount of practice may not be sufficient to guarantee increased learning estimates, it is a necessary component.

The next feature we investigated was the amount of scaffolded practice in the adaptive activities, i.e. how many questions were tagged for delivery at the low, medium, and high level. The goal of the scaffolding questions is to provide a series of questions on a learning objective that start easy and increase in difficulty to help students who were struggling on that learning objective make more incremental steps in difficulty. There were guidelines for the development of the activities, but the number and level of scaffolded questions was up to the discretion of the subject matter experts writing the activities. It was reasonable to expect some learning objectives would need more or fewer scaffolded questions depending on how complex the learning objective was. However, the breakdown of adaptive questions by level showed surprising results compared to our expectations. Each course had learning objectives with no scaffolding questions at all (all questions for the learning objective were set to high) effectively meaning they were non-adaptive for that learning objective. The breakdown of adaptive questions per course by quartile revealed that several courses had far fewer low and medium level questions than others. To illustrate the differences between courses, we will look at the amount of adaptive practice available for learning objectives at the 75th percentile (Table 9).

**Table 9.** Adaptive practice available at the 75th percentile for each scaffold level.

| Course | Low questions | Medium questions | High questions |
|---|---|---|---|
| Project management | 1 | 1 | 7 |
| Macroeconomics | 1 | 1 | 4 |
| Finance | 1 | 1 | 3.75 |
| Probability and statistics | 5 | 5 | 9 |

Given that all courses had learning objectives without scaffolded questions, none of them meet the expectations for the design of the activities. However, there are meaningful differences in the amount of scaffolded practices for learning objectives in each course.

At the 75th percentile, the three business courses each only have a single question per objective at the low and medium level. The ratio of scaffolding questions to high questions favors the high questions in all three courses. At the 75th percentile, the Probability and Statistics course had the highest number of low and medium-level questions (5 and 5, respectively) which puts the number of scaffolding questions higher than the number of high-level questions. Struggling students received more scaffolded support in Probability and Statistics and had more positive learning estimate changes and more instances of increased summative assessment scores.

**Learning Estimate Changes by Learning Objective.** Given that the mean adaptive scores for all three business courses trended down and there were learning objectives without scaffolding, we approached the data from a different perspective. What were the adaptive characteristics of learning objectives that increased and decreased learning estimates the most? To illustrate this, we will start with examples from Finance, which had a mean learning estimate change of $-0.024$. The learning objective that had the largest decrease in learning estimates had a mean learning estimate change of $-0.245$, about ten times larger than the mean decrease. When we look at the adaptive questions for this objective, we find that there was 1 low question, 1 medium question, and 27 high questions. The ratio of scaffolded questions is extreme. The learning objective that had the next largest decrease had a mean change of $-0.114$ (four times the mean) had 2 low, 0 medium, and 6 high. This ratio also favored difficult questions. When we look at the learning objectives that increased learning estimates, we find a different trend. The two learning objectives that increased learning estimates the most each had a total of 9 adaptive questions: 2 low, 4 medium, 3 high and 2 low, 3 medium, 4 high respectively. More than half of the questions were at the low and medium level for these learning objectives. Seeing similar trends in all courses, this indicates that the ratio of scaffolded questions matters for how helpful the adaptive set is for students on a given learning objective. This analysis also shows how specific learning objectives that are outliers can shift the aggregated means for all learning objectives.

**Alignment of Adaptive Scaffolding.** Considering the alignment of formative question accuracy to adaptive question accuracy from previous analysis combined with the lack of scaffolded questions on some learning objectives in all courses, we analyzed the difficulty level of the adaptive questions according to the difficulty level at which they were tagged. We compared how different learning estimate categories performed on different levels of scaffolded questions. For Probability and Statistics as well as Finance, the questions tagged to low, medium, and high did perform according to the expected trend (high-level questions were more difficult to answer and low-level questions were easier to answer, across all groups). However, we found that for Macroeconomics and Project Management that each level of question was almost equally as difficult for students (meaning a student in the low learning estimate category did not find the easy questions any easier than the hard questions). Scaffolded questions not being written at the intended level of difficulty likely contributed to the overall lack of effectiveness of those adaptive activities.

# 4 Conclusion

There are many factors that can influence the success of adaptive instructional systems. In the comparison of courseware in this paper, we saw varying results for the effectiveness of the adaptive activities. The features that seemed to have the largest impact on the effectiveness of the adaptive activities were the design of the adaptive activities themselves—the number of adaptive questions as well as item analysis of the questions at each level. Adaptive activities with more questions per learning objective and high ratios of scaffolded questions to hard questions were most successful in increasing learning estimates. This isn't to say that other course features such as alignment of formative, adaptive, and summative questions are not important. It is likely that alignment will always impact the effectiveness of adaptivity and assessment more generally, but the effects of alignment were obscured by the findings of the adaptive activity design itself. There are also complicating external factors—such as how the courseware features are used in the classroom environment or individual student engagement behaviors—which cannot be accounted for in this paper.

Courseware is a complex learning environment to design. The initial design of adaptivity within courseware was research-based yet imperfect, and iterative improvement is vital to the development process of courseware in general, and adaptivity specifically [13]. The analysis in this study identified that the effect of adaptive activities will vary depending on their design and content. By identifying the variables which could influence the success of adaptivity for students and their learning, best practices can be identified for future development and current courseware can be improved for the betterment of the students. The analysis of these courses suggests that the adaptive activities:

- Should have more than eight questions per learning objective, generally
- Should have a minimum ratio of 50% scaffolding questions to high questions for every learning objective
- Should ensure low and medium questions are written to their respective level

This paper also shows how critical the use of data is for the improvement of student learning. Consider the earlier design note that the number and level of scaffolding questions was up to the discretion of the subject matter expert. It's likely that the subject matter expert evaluated some learning objectives and considered them simpler, therefore not in need of as much scaffolding. Yet the data showed that some students struggled on all learning objectives and that less scaffolding was less helpful. This can be a symptom of "expert blindness;" it can be challenging for experts to imagine the first-time learning experience of students, especially those who are struggling. The data remind us to never make assumptions on whether or not students may need additional support. Data can also help to adjust the difficulty level of the adaptive questions over time, as subject matter experts may intend on writing to a specific difficulty level and yet it may be more or less difficult for students in practice when completed in the end environment. This analysis has provided valuable insights and guidance for how to scaffold practice for students to optimize the benefits of adaptive practice. These insights can benefit many courses and many more students in future iterations of design.

**Acknowledgements.** The authors sincerely thank Leandro Ucha for his assistance in preparing the data for the analysis of the adaptive activities.

# References

1. Van Campenhout, R., Jerome, B., Johnson, B.G.: The impact of adaptive activities in Acrobatiq courseware - investigating the efficacy of formative adaptive activities on learning estimates and summative assessment scores. In: Sottilare, R.A., Schwarz, J. (eds.) HCII 2020. LNCS, vol. 12214, pp. 543–554. Springer, Cham (2020). https://doi.org/10.1007/978-3-030-50788-6_40
2. Black, P., William, D.: Inside the black box: raising standards through classroom assessment. Phi Delta Kappan **92**(1), 81–90 (2010). https://doi.org/10.1177/003172171009200119
3. Dunlosky, J., Rawson, k., Marsh, E., Nathan, M., Willingham, D.: Improving students' learning with effective learning techniques: promising directions from cognitive and educational psychology. Psychol. Sci. Public Interest **14**(1), 4–58 (2013). https://doi.org/10.1177/152910 0612453266
4. Koedinger, K., Kim, J., Jia, J., McLaughlin, E., Bier, N.: Learning is not a spectator sport: doing is better than watching for learning from a MOOC. Learning at Scale, Vancouver, Canada, pp. 111–120 (2015). https://doi.org/10.1145/2724660.2724681
5. Koedinger, K., McLaughlin, E., Jia, J., Bier, N.: Is the doer effect a causal relationship? how can we tell and why it's important. Learning Analytics and Knowledge. Edinburgh, United Kingdom (2016). https://doi.org/10.1145/2883851.2883957
6. Koedinger, K.R., Scheines, R., Schaldenbrand, P.: Is the doer effect robust across multiple data sets? In: Proceedings of the 11th International Conference on Educational Data Mining, EDM 2018, pp. 369–375 (2018)
7. Olsen, J., Johnson, B.G.: Deeper collaborations: a finding that may have gone unnoticed. Paper presented at the IMS Global Learning Impact Leadership Institute, San Diego, CA (2019)
8. Baker, F. The basics of item response theory. ERIC Clearinghouse on Assessment and Evaluation. College Park, MD (2001). http://echo.edres.org:8080/irt/baker/
9. Embretson, S., Reise, S.: Item Response Theory for Psychologists. Erl-baum, Mahwah (2000)
10. Fox, J.: Bayesian Item Response Modeling: Theory and Applications. Springer, New York (2010). https://doi.org/10.1007/978-1-4419-0742-4
11. Sanders, D., Welk, D.: Strategies to scaffold student learning: applying Vygotsky's zone of proximal development. Nurse Educ. **30**(5), 203–204 (2005)
12. Sweller, J.: The worked example effect and human cognition. Learn. Instr. **16**(2), 165–169 (2006). https://doi.org/10.1016/j.learninstruc.2006.02.005
13. Goodell, J., Thai, K.-P.: A learning engineering model for learner-centered adaptive systems. In: Stephanidis, C., Harris, D., Li, W.-C., Schmorrow, D.D., Fidopiastis, C.M., Zaphiris, P., Ioannou, A., Fang, X., Sottilare, R.A., Schwarz, J. (eds.) HCII 2020. LNCS, vol. 12425, pp. 557–573. Springer, Cham (2020). https://doi.org/10.1007/978-3-030-60128-7_41

# Croatian POS Tagger as a Prerequisite for Knowledge Extraction in Intelligent Tutoring Systems

Daniel Vasić[1,4(✉)] ⓘ, Branko Žitko[2,4] ⓘ, Ani Grubišić[2,4] ⓘ,
Slavomir Stankov[2,4] ⓘ, Angelina Gašpar[3,4] ⓘ, Ines Šarić-Grgić[3,4] ⓘ,
Suzana Tomaš[3,4] ⓘ, Ivan Peraić[2] ⓘ, and Matea Markić-Vučić[2,4] ⓘ

[1] Faculty of Science and Education, University of Mostar, 88000 Mostar,
Bosnia and Herzegovina
daniel.vasic@fpmoz.sum.ba
[2] Faculty of Science, University of Split, 21000 Split, Croatia
{branko.zitko,ani.grubisic,insaric}@pmfst.hr,
ivan.peraic@skole.hr
[3] Catholic Faculty of Theology, University of Split, 21000 Split, Croatia
[4] Faculty of Humanities and Social Sciences, University of Split, 21000 Split, Croatia
suzana@ffst.hr

**Abstract.** In this article we present an knowledge extraction approach that can be used in systems that implement teaching in a fully automated manner. These systems are called Intelligent Tutoring Systems (ITS) and are conceived around the idea of one-to-one teaching. Many such systems use natural language processing to improve the communication interface between student and the system. These techniques can be also used on the content creator side to semi-automate or fully automate the task of teaching content creation. In such systems the knowledge representation plays a crucial role to successfully implement teaching and encourage learning. The output of the knowledge extraction phase is a knowledge in the form of a hyper graph that can be used for adaption to the students current knowledge level. We present a deep neural network architecture for precise POS tagging of words written in languages that are morphologically rich. Using sparse representations for words in this task increases the vector space and makes learning more complex. This problem can be solved to some extent by using traditional vector representations but there is also the problem with representing words that are ambiguous. Proposed architecture uses a Bidirectional Encoder Representations from Transformers (BERT) model that is pre-trained on Croatian language to achieve state-of-the-art accuracy for POS tagging.

**Keywords:** Natural language processing · Knowledge extraction · Part of Speech tagging · Intelligent Tutoring Systems

The paper is part of the work supported by the Office of Naval Research Grant No. N00014-20-1-2066.

© Springer Nature Switzerland AG 2021
R. A. Sottilare and J. Schwarz (Eds.): HCII 2021, LNCS 12792, pp. 334–345, 2021.
https://doi.org/10.1007/978-3-030-77857-6_23

# 1   Introduction

Natural language processing involves a series of tasks that could be applied within a variety of systems that make everyday life easier. E-learning systems are also a class of such systems. A component that determines part of speech tags from text in natural language provides such systems with a number of new functionalities. POS tagging is usually the first step in natural language pipeline and the first step of text structuring in knowledge based systems. Such systems use tasks such as automatic generation of questions, generation of sentences, text similarity checks and a number of other applications. All of these tasks start their processing steps usually by using some kind of POS tagger first to process the texts into structures that can be used in further stages.

## 1.1   Research Motivation and Background

Recent improvements in machine learning methods, the availability of various data sets, and the increase in computer processing capabilities have contributed to various methods that can be used to process the text in a semantically rich way. Also with improvements in precision of methods for syntactic text processing, methods for knowledge extraction that use these models are also being enhanced. There are methods for knowledge representation that use only syntactic information from dependency parse tree and POS tags [29, 30].

One of these approaches that uses this information to build ordered recursive hypergraph called semantic hypergraph is presented in [4]. In the article authors propose a novel rule based model for knowledge extraction using only information syntactic information. This knowledge representation model can be used in many knowledge based systems. E-learning is one area that could benefit by using knowledge extraction methods. In such systems many tasks like knowledge assessment and question answering could be supported by knowledge extraction based methods.

Within e-learning systems, there is a subclass of systems based on the assumption that one-on-one paradigm learning yields the best results. Such systems are ITS's, and they are used to try to achieve one-on-one teaching effects. One of the most well-known examples of the application of natural language processing techniques in ITS's is AutoTutor [1]. AutoTutor uses a variety of natural language processing algorithms to enable natural language teaching. Various tests of the application of AutoTutor in teaching show very good results [2].

In this article we propose an model for syntactic text processing on our native language, Croatian. Croatian language is morphologically rich language that belongs to Balto-Slavic family of languages. The most famous intelligent tutor which combines natural language processing techniques in the Croatian literary language is ColabTutor [3]. This system, over a defined area of knowledge, applies various natural language processing techniques to enable the student to communicate with the system in natural language. To achieve this type of communication in the stages of teaching and testing knowledge, ColabTutor uses various lexical resources and a series of manually defined rules.

## 1.2  POS Tagging for Under-Resourced Morphologically Rich Languages

Automatically determining the type of words from a text written in the Croatian language is not an easy task. To automatically determine the type of word, it is necessary to define the concept of morphosyntactic description and morphosyntactic designations that represent the basis for such word processing. In the Croatian language there are ten word classes that are divided into open and closed words. Open and closed words characterize those words that change their form depending on the position. Although they change their form, their meaning remains the same. All changeable word types consist of a stem and a suffix. The base is the part of the word that does not change depending on the morphological changes, except in cases where some phonetic change occurs at the end of the base. To develop an model for knowledge extraction the first main challenge is to develop method for POS tagging.

Most method for POS achieve an accuracy of more than 95%. According to these figures, it can be concluded that POS tagging is almost impossible to further optimize, and that with this precision POS tagging can be done almost entirely by a machine. But at the level of the whole sentence, and these are the sentences that the system has completely hit exactly, it is obvious that further improvements are possible. Occurrence-level precision will certainly be above the 90% limit because points are earned on non-variable occurrences. Accuracy needs to be observed at the level of the number of sentences that the system has completely hit, because every small mistake spoils the results in the further processing. The latest methods report an accuracy of 55% to 60%, these numbers can be reduced by changing the domain of the text on which the system is trained, changing the writing style, etc.

POS tagging itself is not in a solution to any natural language processing problem, but in most cases it is a prerequisite for other tasks such as naming Entity Recognition, Sentiment Analysis, Question Answering and a number of other applications. In this article we present our preliminary research on using advancements in deep neural networks for POS tagging in Croatian language.

## 2  Related Research

A person learns the task of determination of word class by listening and connecting, and then by replicating like any other skill. POS tagging is mainly based on methods that learn based on a large amount of text. Approximating word type labels or POS tags without a large amount of highlighted text is an impossible task. It is very important that there are corpora available. The existence of labeling procedure of a word class is also important. A set of POS tags is a list of all word type tags, i.e. labels used to determine the type of word, and sometimes other grammatical categories (case, tense, etc.) of each occurrence (token) in the text. The existence of a standard for POS tagging and the existence of manually annotated texts are the basic preconditions for building a system for POS tagging of text in any language.

MULTEXT-East [5] is a standard for annotating the word class, which is also used for texts in the Croatian language, and defines over 1000 word classes. Morphosyntactic specifications determine the grammar and vocabulary of morphosyntactic features and descriptions. They determine what a set of morphosyntactic descriptions (MSDs) is suitable for each language and which features they correspond to. For example, the Ncnp description also applies to the English language and is mapped to the structure of the feature Class: noun, Type: general, Gender: neuter, Number: plural.

The hr500k corpus [6] is one of the lexical resources in the Croatian language that contains 506,457 occurrences, and is marked according to the MULTEXT-East specification, with a total of over 1000 types of POS tags. Precisely this speaks in favor of how much more complex the development of a method for POS tagging in the Croatian language is than building a method in English. Although, POS tagging is a seemingly trivial task of matching a word type with its tag. This is often not the case in practice because the type of word is often context dependent, and often the same word (a word that is spelled the same but has a different meaning) has a different tag in different sentences. The first methods for automatic word type recognition used mathematical models based on statistics to approximate the word type based on the probability distribution of the tags for a particular word.

Fortunately, in most languages, most words are unambiguously defined, so the accuracy of these models in the beginning reached the accuracy of 93% to 95%. This fact is not surprising because if we were to assign a personal noun label to all unknown words we would have an accuracy of 90% [7].

In 1987, authors at Brown University proposed a model [8] for POS tagging that is based on dynamic programming similar to the Viterbi algorithm. The approach itself achieved good results, and at the same time it was twice as fast as the approaches of that time. This word processing method was based on a table of pairs and triplets used to estimate certain phenomena that are non-existent or very rare.

A number of machine learning methods can be applied to this task, and are typically based on a set of manually defined features. Those skilled in the POS task include information in the POS tagging that makes it easier for the system to identify the POS tag. Commonly used classification methods are the Support Vector Machine method [9], the Perceptron neural network [10]. The latest methods are based on deep learning methods are currently achieving the best results. The main problem is that they largely depend on the amount of text available for training. A major shift in natural language processing for different languages, even those languages that are poor in terms of training resources. This has been made possible by using transfer learning and deep neural networks.

For the Croatian language, a number of methods for POS tagging in English can be applied. In paper [11], the authors use the hidden Markov model (HMM) to predict word type designations. Newer approaches include the use of conditional random fields (CRF) [12] and deep neural networks models [13] that approach to state-of-the-art results.

Deep learning based methods mostly use recurrent neural networks. The basic recurrent neural network consists of neurons that use the output from the previous neuron as input to the next layer. This way of training the neural network allows coding words that previously appeared in the sequence. Today the increasingly popular models are created by adaptation of attention based mechanisms. Some of the most popular models of this type are BERT (Bidirectional Encoder Representations from Transformers) [14] and ELMo (Deep Contextualized Word Representations) [15]. Models for ELMo [16] and BERT vector [17] representation for Croatian language has been also published recently allowing the development of transformer based models for POS tagging but also other NLP tasks.

## 3    The Proposed Architecture

The model for POS tagging presented in this paper is a type of statistical model based on neural network. The system tries to determine the word class based on the words learned during the training process. A prerequisite for the development of a statistical model is the existence of training data. In this case, these are the words and the corresponding tags for each word. The statistical model is developed by training and is presented in the form of weight values. The weight values are updated based on the model predictions, and the difference between the model prediction and the values from training data set is called the error gradient resulting from the loss function. The goal of training a statistical model is to minimize the loss function by the gradient descent method or the less computer-demanding stochastic gradient descent.

A single-layer neural network can approximate any function, but that layer must be impractically large and may have difficulty generalizing the model. Deep neural networks are developed by increasing the layers and the number of parameters. These models have been proven to be excellent approximators and in theory a sufficiently large neural model can solve any problem [18].

A simple neural network doesn't use recurrent connections to encode long range dependencies and as such it is not adapted to many natural language processing tasks. The basic characteristic of data in natural language processing is the interdependence and the connection of distant words in the text. Mechanisms in the form of LSTM (Long-Short Term Memory) and GRU (Gated Recurrent Unit) [20] cells are used to solve the problem of the disappearing and exploding gradient. To achieve better accuracy and to encode features from two directions bidirectional connections within the layers of the neural network are mostly used.

### 3.1    Convolutional Neural Network Based Feature Extraction

The word embedding for our POS tagging approach consists of dividing a word into four different parts, namely: a normalized word form, a word prefix, a word suffix, and information about whether a word contains a capital letter, special character, or digit. This kind of word partitioning provides a representation of words that is suitable for morphologically rich languages. Also, instead of simply assigning a vector to a corresponding word, Hash embedding [21] is used. This trick provides a unique vector representation for each word, and also effectively solves the problem of words that are not in the dictionary. The length of the prefix and suffix used during the training phase is 3. All of the obtained vectors are merged into one vector and further converted into a single representation using a MLP layer. This layer uses the MaxOut [22] operation which converts this array of multidimensional representations into a 128 dimensional vector. The next step is to embed these contextually independent vectors into the context-dependent matrix that represents the sentence. A common step is to encode word strings using LSTM and GRU cells, but some implementations also use convolutional neural networks. Most natural language processing tasks use a two-way LSTM (BiLSTM) architecture to encode a sentence first from left to right and then from right to left in order to produce vector sequence representation. The result of these passages is one vector in whose parts the context of the whole sentence is embedded. This makes it possible to solve the problem of unambiguity because each occurrence in the sentence gets a unique representation depending on the context in which they are located.

When building features, a sliding window is used to get the context taking a two adjacent occurrences on both sides of the word that is being tagged. The advantage of using this approach is less sensitivity to long-term relations in the text, which allows more precise processing of short texts and incomplete sentences. Residual connections are used to connect convolutional layers, which enable learning of more complex structures without losing information during learning. After passing the vector through the convolutional layers, specially defined functions are used to extract the features. These features take into the account the obtained vectors of the surrounding words and words from other sentences. A simple single-layer perceptron is used to predict the probability distribution over a series of tags. Figure 1 shows the complete system architecture.

### 3.2   Training of the Convolutional Neural Network

The proposed architecture is implemented within the spaCy tool[23], which, unlike classical approaches, uses a transition based method for tagging. This strategy uses sequential steps to add a single tag or change the state until it reaches the most likely tag.

As the training corpus is quite small, for obtaining good results, the weight values were initialized with vector representations of Clarin.Sl-embed.hr ?. The system was trained on a training set in 30 iterations with different sample sizes in the range from 4 to 32. Dropout layers were used in the neural network that discard some neurons during training to prevent overfitting of the training data set. The rejection rate in the dropout layers used during training is adjustable and ranges from 0.20 to 0.60. An SGD [26] optimizer with a learning rate of 0.001. The width of the convolutional layer is 4. The number of parts within the MaxOut layers is 4, the number of rows in the table of vector space for sentences

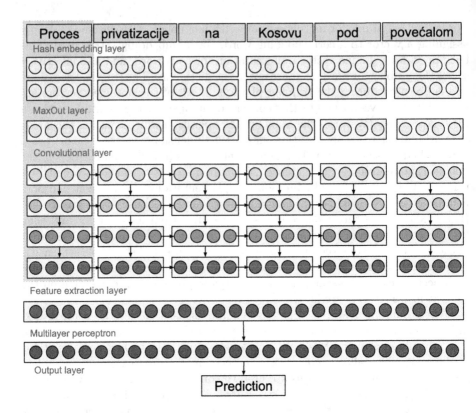

**Fig. 1.** Convolutional neural network architecture feature extraction for POS tagging of texts written in Croatian language.

is 2000. Figure 2 shows the validation loss on the left and the F1 measure on the right during 30 epochs of training.

### 3.3   Attention Based Feature Extraction

The improvement of results can be achieved by using a model based on attention or the so-called transformer model. For feature extraction, pre-trained vectors are used extracted from large data set by using transformer model. These vectors are fine-tuned on a smaller set of manually annotated data. Such models are ideal for resource-poor languages because they allow network training in an unsupervised way to obtain text representation. In other words, the system first learns the meaning of each word based on text that is not manually annotated, and then could be fine tuned to specific task on smaller data set.

The proposed convolutional neural network architecture used special vectors that were pre-trained on shallow neural networks based on context. The problem with these representations is that they do not involve long-term dependencies within the text but only a narrow context, and do not look at the sentence as a whole.

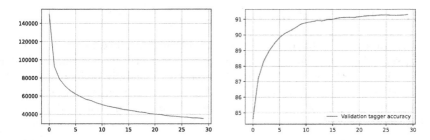

**Fig. 2.** Validation loss and accuracy of the proposed CNN model architecture.

This problem is solved by using an attention-based transformer model where vector representation is generated based on the whole sentence by paying attention to individual parts of the whole sentence so that the word vector contains parts of other words in the sentence.

It is important to emphasize that BERT and similar models do not use a one-dimensional attention structure applied over latent RNN states, but use several layers of attention. The BERT model uses a total of 384 different attention mechanisms, and in addition uses other layers, such as residual connections, fully connected layers, and vector normalization layers. But we can say with certainty that attention is the most important part. Output vectors are further used to classify text using MLP as described previously.

### 3.4  Training of the Attention Based Neural Network

The BERT model was trained in a slightly different way than the previous model. It primarily uses the Adam [27] optimizer instead of the SGD algorithm with an adjustable learning rate and $L2$ regularization. The $beta1$ parameter is set to 0.9, $beta2$ to 0.999 and the training uses 10 warm up steps. The reason for this approach for training is that the pre-training data will certainly be very different from the training data. If the system would immediately adjust the weight values with a fixed learning rate, it is very likely that it will overfit the learning data and give worse results. The neural network training process based on the neural network architecture using BERT weight values is shown in Fig. 3.

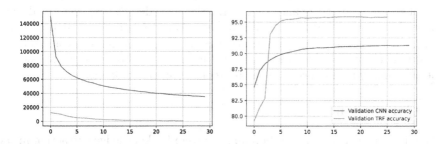

**Fig. 3.** Validation loss and accuracy of the proposed CNN model and attention based model.

# 4   Results and Future Work

In this section we present comparison of the obtained results evaluated on hr500k testing set. The table shows the results of the currently most accurate models for Croatian POS tagging. The Reldi tagger uses manually defined features in combination with Conditional Random Fields. It is the only approach that is not based on neural network. Another neural network approach called Parser-V3 is also included for comparison. Parser-V3 [25] uses the BiLSTM architecture to extract features and, in order to improve the model and reduce resilience to words outside the dictionary, this model uses character embeddings (Table 1).

**Table 1.** Comparison of the result for proposed models and state of the art models for POS tagging of texts written in Croatian language.

|  | Precision | Recall | F1 score |
|---|---|---|---|
| CNN model* | 91.92% | 91.92% | 91.92% |
| **BERT model*** | **95.23%** | **95.23%** | **95.23%** |
| Classla model [13] | 94.60% | 94.60% | 94.60% |
| Reldi tagger [12] | 91.91% | 91.91% | 91.91% |
| Parser-v3 [25] | 94.29% | 94.29% | 94.29% |

The accuracy of the BERT-based model is better than accuracy of the convolutional neural network model. The reason for the better results compared to the proposed models is that BERT produces better representations of words from which the neural network learns to generalize data, especially for the task of POS tagging.

For the successful implementation of the knowledge extraction component, the accuracy of the model for POS tagging is of great importance. Therefore, the aim of the research conducted as part of this paper was to make a component for POS tagging that will achieve just as good results as the currently state of the art methods. We plan to integrate this component for syntax based knowledge extraction. The knowledge extraction method developed in by using POS tagger proposed in this article can be evaluated on SemCRO [28] data set. By using this data set, the quality of the proposed model on out-of-domain data can be obtained and also the quality of generated knowledge can be quantified. The knowledge extracted can be used in many artificial intelligence based systems. The goal is to develop natural language based ITS system that can communicate with user in natural way. Allowing the student to focus on subject matter and not on communication errors that are frequent in such systems.

# 5   Conclusion

There is a great motivation in building a system for knowledge extraction in the Croatian language so that it can be applied in ITS's. From the linguistic part of view Croatian language is highly inflected so other equally complex languages could also benefit from these models. On the other side such component would enable the creation of an image of the student's knowledge based on the entered answers to the tutor's questions. Based on the extracted knowledge the system could, automatically generate questions from text written in natural language. There are numerous other applications that could benefit from such approach. It is very important to develop a method for knowledge extraction that is precise so that it can be applied in a system that independently perform a complex teaching process. Semantic hypergraphs are knowledge representation technique that uses syntactic information to represent knowledge and allow unstructured text processing in semantically rich way. The process of converting text into a semantic hypergraph begins with segmentation of words and with POS tagging. After that subsequently the first step for the creation of semantic hypergraph is text parsing. Although complete model for knowledge extraction is beyond the scope of this article, we present preliminary research on POS tagging. This is a first and very important step in the global goal of creating semantically rich knowledge representations. These representations can then be used in numerous intelligent systems. We also present state of the art model for POS tagging based on deep neural network architecture. This model can be used in many artificial intelligent based systems that process natural language texts.

# References

1. Graesser, A.C., VanLehn, K., Rose, C.P., Jordan, P.W., Harter, D.: Intelligent tutoring systems with conversational dialogue. AI Mag. **22**(4), 39 (2001). https://doi.org/10.1609/aimag.v22i4.1591
2. Graesser, A.C., Chipman, P., Haynes, B.C., Olney, A.: AutoTutor: an intelligent tutoring system with mixed-initiative dialogue. IEEE Trans. Educ. **48**(4), 612–618 (2005). https://doi.org/10.1109/TE.2005.856149
3. Žitko, B.: Model inteligentnog tutorskog sustava zasnovan na obradi kontroliranog jezika nad ontologijom, Fakultet elektrotehnike i računarstva, Zagreb (2010)
4. Menezes, T., Roth, C.: Semantic hypergraphs, CoRR, vol. abs/1908.10784 (2019). http://arxiv.org/abs/1908.10784
5. Erjavec, T.: "MULTEXT-East: morphosyntactic resources for Central and Eastern European languages. Lang. Resour. Eval. **46**, 131–142 (2012). https://doi.org/10.1007/s10579-011-9174-8. LNCS, vol. 9999, pp. 1–13
6. Ljubešić, N., Agić, Ž., Klubička, F., Batanović, V., Erjavec, T.: Training corpus hr500k 1.0. In: Slovenian Language Resource Repository CLARIN.SI (2018). http://hdl.handle.net/11356/1183
7. Charniak, E.: Statistical techniques for natural language parsing. AI Mag. **18**(4) (1997). https://doi.org/10.1609/aimag.v18i4.1320
8. DeRose, S.J.: Grammatical category disambiguation by statistical optimization. In: Computational Linguistics, vol. 14, pp. 31–39 (1988). https://www.aclweb.org/anthology/J88-1003
9. Giménez, J., Màrquez, L.: SVMTool: a general POS tagger generator based on Support Vector Machines. In: Proceedings of the 4th International Conference on Language Resources and Evaluation (2004)

10. Spoustoví, D., Hajič, J., Raab, J., Spousta, M.: Semi-supervised training for the averaged perceptron POS tagger. In: Proceedings of the 12th Conference of the European Chapter of the Association for Computational Linguistics (EACL 2009), pp. 763–771 (2009)
11. Agić, Ž., Ljubešić, N., Merkler, D.: Lemmatization and morphosyntactic tagging of Croatian and Serbian. In: Proceedings of the 4th Biennial International Workshop on Balto-Slavic Natural Language Processing (BSNLP 2013), Sofia, Bulgaria, pp. 48–57. Association for Computational Linguistics (2013)
12. Ljubešić, N., Klubička, F., Agić, Ž., Jazbec, I.: New inflectional lexicons and training corpora for improved morphosyntactic annotation of Croatian and Serbian. In: Proceedings of the Tenth International Conference on Language Resources and Evaluation (LREC 2016), pp. 4264–4270. European Language Resources Association (ELRA). https://www.aclweb.org/anthology/L16-1676
13. Ljubešić, N.: The CLASSLA-StanfordNLP model for lemmatisation of standard Croatian 1.1, Slovenian language resource repository CLARIN.SI (2020). http://hdl.handle.net/11356/1287
14. Jacob, D., Ming-Wei, C., Kenton, L., Toutanova, K.: BERT: pre-training of deep bidirectional transformers for language understanding. In: Proceedings of the 2019 Conference of the North American Chapter of the Association for Computational Linguistics: Human Language Technologies, Volume 1 (Long and Short Papers), vol. 1, pp. 4171–4186 (2019). https://doi.org/10.18653/v1/N19-1423, https://www.aclweb.org/anthology/N19-1423
15. Peters, M., et al.: Deep contextualized word representations. In: Proceedings of the 2018 Conference of the North American Chapter of the Association for Computational Linguistics: Human Language Technologies, Volume 1 (Long Papers), vol. 1, pp. 2227–2237. https://doi.org/10.18653/v1/N18-1202, https://www.aclweb.org/anthology/N18-1202
16. Ulčar, M., Robnik-Šikonja, M.: High Quality ELMo embeddings for seven less-resourced languages. In: Proceedings of the 12th Language Resources and Evaluation Conference (2020). https://www.aclweb.org/anthology/2020.lrec-1.582
17. Ulčar, M., Robnik-Šikonja, M.: FinEst BERT and CroSloEngual BERT. In: Sojka, P., Kopeček, I., Pala, K., Horák, A. (eds.) TSD 2020. LNCS (LNAI), vol. 12284, pp. 104–111. Springer, Cham (2020). https://doi.org/10.1007/978-3-030-58323-1_11
18. Zarita, Z., Ong, P.: Function approximation using artificial neural networks, pp. 140–145. World Scientific and Engineering Academy and Society (WSEAS) (2007). https://doi.org/10.5555/1376368.1376392
19. Hochreiter, S., Schmidhuber, J.: Long short-term memory. Neural Comput. **9** (1998). https://doi.org/10.1162/neco.1997.9.8.1735
20. Cho, K., et al.: Learning phrase representations using RNN encoder-decoder for statistical machine translation. In: Proceedings of the 2014 Conference on Empirical Methods in Natural Language Processing (EMNLP), pp. 1724–1734 (2014). https://doi.org/10.3115/v1/D14-1179
21. Svenstrup, D., Hansen, J., Winther, O.: Hash embeddings for efficient word representations. In: Proceedings of the 31st International Conference on Neural Information Processing Systems, pp. 4935–4943 (2017). https://doi.org/10.5555/3295222.3295246
22. Goodfellow, I., Warde-Farley, D., Mehdi M., Courville, A., Bengio, Y.: Maxout networks. In: Proceedings of the 30th International Conference on International Conference on Machine Learning - Volume 28, vol. 28, pp. 1319–1327 (2013)
23. spaCy - Industrial-strength Natural Language Processing in Python. https://nightly.spacy.io/. Accessed 14 Jan 2021

24. Ljubešić, N.: Word embeddings CLARIN.SI-embed.hr 1.0, Slovenian language resource repository CLARIN.SI (2018). http://hdl.handle.net/11356/1205
25. Dozat, T., Manning, C.: Simpler but more accurate semantic dependency parsing. In: Proceedings of the 56th Annual Meeting of the Association for Computational Linguistics (Volume 2: Short Papers), pp. 484–490 (2018). https://doi.org/10.18653/v1/P18-2077
26. Ruder, S.: An overview of gradient descent optimization algorithms, CoRR, vol. abs/1609.04747 (2016)
27. Kingma, D., Ba, J.: Adam: a method for stochastic optimization. In: Proceedings 3rd International Conference on Learning Representations, ICLR 2015 (2015). http://arxiv.org/abs/1412.6980
28. Vasić, D., Žitko, B., Gašpar, A., Ljubešić, N., Štrkalj Despot, K., Merkler, D.: Semantic hypergraph corpus SemCRO 1.0, Slovenian language resource repository CLARIN.SI (2020). http://hdl.handle.net/11356/1377
29. Baisa, V., Kovář, V.: Information extraction for Czech based on syntactic analysis. In: Vetulani, Z., Mariani, J. (eds.) LTC 2011. LNCS (LNAI), vol. 8387, pp. 155–165. Springer, Cham (2014). https://doi.org/10.1007/978-3-319-08958-4_13
30. Straková, J., Pecina, P.: Czech information retrieval with syntax-based language models. In: Proceedings of the Seventh International Conference on Language Resources and Evaluation (LREC 2010) (2010)

# Evaluation of AIS

# Evaluating the Question: The Instructor's Side of Adaptive Learning

James Bennett[✉], Leila Casteel, and Kitty Kautzer

Herzing University, Menomonee Falls, WI, USA
jambennett@herzing.edu

**Abstract.** Many people in the education sector are aware of the benefits students derive from adaptive learning systems. Unfortunately, what is not well known is that an adaptive learning system can also augment the instructor's understanding of what learning has occurred. Valid and relevant questions used by the adaptive learning system can provide an instructor with real-time insight into the level of knowledge attained by each individual student. Similarly, the same sort of knowledge can also indicate learning deficits that might affect an entire class and allow for an instructor to accurately respond to the student's learning needs in an informed way.

The key to this is an understanding and confidence on the part of the instructor for each assessment delivered by the adaptive learning system.

In this paper, we will demonstrate how to use information gained through the implementation of an adaptive learning system to augment knowledge. In it, we will propose a methodology for evaluating adaptive learning questions given as assessments.

The intent is to produce a tool for determining the validity, reliability, and standardization of the questions asked by the system in a way that gives the instructor specific knowledge about student learning. This tool will approach a question's evaluation, both before the question is asked and then after, using basic psychometric principles. While this paper will focus on the use of such a tool by the instructor, it should be understood it would serve very well to evaluate questions by instructional designers and curriculum developers.

**Keywords:** Adaptive learning · Psychometrics · Intelligence augmentation · Artificial intelligence

## 1 Introduction

Adaptive Learning is finally making serious inroads into organized learning. While this is a boon for the learner, instructors can be left feeling at a loss and marginalized by not being directly involved in all a student's learning activities.

Often, the instructor treats what happens inside the adaptive learning system as separate from their own interaction with learner. This should be avoided since an adaptive learning system can provide information on the learner's attainment of knowledge beyond what may demonstrated in the classroom. An adaptive learning system will

© Springer Nature Switzerland AG 2021
R. A. Sottilare and J. Schwarz (Eds.): HCII 2021, LNCS 12792, pp. 349–360, 2021.
https://doi.org/10.1007/978-3-030-77857-6_24

not only serve the learner, but can also provide superior augmented information to the instructor in a way that makes it one of the most valuable resource available.

This paper will not only demonstrate that but will make recommendations for a tool to assess the questions and input from adaptive learning assessments - a tool that will be both useful for the instructor and invaluable to an instructional designer that needs to validate the accuracy of the adaptive learning taking place.

## 2  What Information is Provided by the Augmented Knowledge

While this paper will focus on the development of a tool to augment the knowledge of instructors and instructional designers, it is important to understand what knowledge this tool can provide. At our university we use the methods described in this paper to evaluate assessments delivered in an adaptive learning platform. The results can serve as guiding data for the following actions:

- Informs instructor where there are knowledge deficits and if intervention is needed for each learner.
- Informs instructor where there are knowledge deficits and if intervention is needed across an entire cohort.
- Informs instructor where grade and learner scoring adjustments are required due to error or lack of fairness.
- Informs the instructor/instructional designer when assessments are not accurate.
- Provides analysis and guidance toward areas where the assessment may need correction.

In essence, the evaluation tool serves a dual purpose in helping educators recognize and fill learning gaps as well as make improved adjustments to an adaptive learning system.

## 3  Methodology

The recommendations put forth in this paper come from three years of inductive analysis. Herzing University first introduced adaptive learning in 2017 and began by employing it in the General Education courses offered at the university. In 2018 Herzing University launched a Nursing program built on the Realizeit adaptive learning platform. This was a milestone for education since there were very few instances at that time of adaptive learning being used across an entire degree program of study.

To Herzing University's advantage, Nursing education traditionally focuses on the accuracy of exam questions using psychometric principles. This provided a ready and detailed data set that allowed for the analysis of thousands of questions answered by hundreds of learners. Since these question items were delivered through the adaptive learning platform, we were able to follow question evaluation protocols that provided insight into each question. We found that analysis could be used to directly augment the knowledge of the instructor regarding areas where an individual learner or an entire class might need remediation. Just as important, the data provided augmented information to instructional designers concerning the validity, reliability, and standardization of the questions used. This made for greater accuracy and directed improvements to each question.

The details and specific methods for each type of analysis will be covered in the respective sections later in this paper.

## 4 Defining Intelligence Augmentation for This Paper

While most people have heard of Artificial Intelligence (A.I.), the related term of Intelligence Augmentation (I.A.) is not nearly as well known or is often misunderstood as a topic limited to the field of cybernetics.

The popular definition between A.I. and I.A. comes from Peter Skagestad's The Mind's Machines: the Turing Machine, the Memex, and the Personal Computer [1]. Simply put, the difference is that A.I. is purposed with replacing the human mind and I.A. can be said to "increase the reliability of human thought by extending and assisting it." [2].

At first read, these definitions may give the impression that A.I. and I.A. are in conflict, but in cases such as the one presented here, the artificial intelligence system (the adaptive learning engine) will also serve as an intelligence augmentation for both instructors and instructional designers.

## 5 Background on Adaptive Learning: The Context of Why This is Important

The primary component in any system that delivers true adaptive learning is an accurate alignment between the learner's input and what is being measured. A simple example of this would be content that presents what is to be learned, followed by one or more questions that assess whether or not the student learns the required knowledge. In most adaptive learning systems, if the assessment determines that the student has not attained the knowledge required, it would then redirect the student back to the appropriate content for additional instruction.

For this process to work, the adaptive learning system must have a programmed association between the assessment and the knowledge be measured. It is of the utmost importance that the association be relevant and valid. Unfortunately, traditional learning assessments are notoriously inaccurate in this area and often not as specific as needed. An example of this would be a multiple-choice quiz question like the one below.

The intent is to assess whether the learner can explain a specific concept, such as how to bake a cake. But, in this example the quiz question misses the mark:

Which of the following ingredients are found in nearly all cakes? Select all that apply.

A.  Eggs
B.  Flour
C.  Milk

D.  Vanilla extract

While this may assess a learner's knowledge about cake ingredients, a correct answer in this question is not evidence that the learner knows how to bake a cake, let alone that they can explain how to do it.

The instructor may have an intuitive sense that a learner who answers such a question correctly has attained the appropriate knowledge, but not because of any direct evidence provided by the question results. This would be more likely due to the instructor's awareness of other activities learners may have performed. For example, each person in a class may have also written cake recipes for another assignment, so in the mind of the instructor the above question is related since all students completed both activities. But in an adaptive learning system, the A.I. would have to be told to how to account for both assignments in its assessment of student performance.

# 6  Why Choose These Particular Evaluation Methods?

In the science of psychological assessment there are four principles used to judge the quality of a given assessment [3]. These principles are irreplaceable as standards when it comes to using adaptive learning questions to augment instructor evaluation of student knowledge. A brief description of each is given below. It is worth noting that each of these principles is usually divided into subcategories (e.g. Standardization falls into two categories: norm referencing and criteria referencing) but for the purposes of the tool recommended here, it is not necessary to define those nuances.

**Validity.** For use as an augmentation tool, this is the most critical principle and should always be the first criteria. It focuses on whether an assessment captures and measures what is intended to be assessed. While this may seem obvious, it is also something that is too often taken for granted. Test item writers do not always understand the details of this principle and can make assumptions that a test item assesses some specific knowledge, when it measures something completely different. A simplified example of this can be seen in the cake baking question given earlier.

**Reliability.** This concept focuses on the dependability of the assessment. Does it perform consistently and do the scores demonstrate the assessment is measuring more accurately than mere chance? Do the conditions and the context of the assessment influence the measurement? An example of a test item that would be unreliable in this way would be a question that gave away its own answer in its wording or inadvertently gave the solution to another question in the same exam.

**Standardization.** From a simplified perspective, standardization as a principle of analysis looks to ensure that if all things are equal, that performance on any given question or assessment will be uniform from one student to another. In other words, if an above average learner answers a specific question correctly, most of the other above average learners should also answer the same question correctly.

**Freedom from Bias.** Bias is present in assessments when scores differ based on group membership. While this is generally thought of in terms of anti-discrimination and regarding protected groups such as those based on gender, ethnicity, disability, etc. bias can it be found toward any group. In an organized education setting the group could also include a cohort or class.

# 7 Methods for Evaluating the Assessments

In this next section, we will explain the various methods for evaluating the assessments. As a part of the explanation we will identify which of the four psychometric fundamentals is being addressed and what either the instructor or instructional designer would gain from this knowledge.

## 7.1 Validity

The most important evaluation of any learning assessment is its validity. If an assessment is *valid*, it is measuring what it is supposed to measure.

The simplest way to determine an assessment's validity is to make certain it aligns with a specific course outcome, learning objective, or required competency and then evaluate whether the assessment measures a learner's performance in that area. A first step in this can be to compare the cognitive domain of what is being measured to what is being assessed. This can be done using Bloom's Taxonomy.

Table 1 provides a list of common verbs and their corresponding cognitive domain as categorized in Bloom's Taxonomy.

In Table 1, cognitive domains are represented in one of six rows. To the right of each domain are several verbs that can be used to describe an action of a learner as a part of an assessment. For example, if an assessment requires that a learner describe and explain a concept, it would be measuring *understanding*. If understanding is what the assessment was intended to measure, then the assessment is likely valid. Note that the lists of verbs here are not exhaustive. There are many verbs that fall within these domains.

Unfortunately, there can be a misalignment when questions and answers are programmed into an adaptive learning system. Assessments may be about a specific topic, or may be tied to key content, but are not direct measures of a learner's performance toward an outcome or objective. Returning to the example of the cake baking question given earlier, the question is only really testing if a learner can remember ingredients. It does not measure if the learner has attained any outcomes or objectives that are in the higher domains. For example, remembering ingredients does not indicate a learner knows why each of the ingredients are required (understand) or what ingredients might be added or substituted (analyze, evaluate, create).

Which of the following ingredients are found in nearly all cakes? Select all that apply.

A. Eggs
B. Flour

**Table 1.** Original work: Bloom, B.S. (1956). Taxonomy of educational objectives: The classification of educational goals. New York, NY: Longmans, Green. or Bloom's revised taxonomy: Anderson, L.W. & Krathwohl, D.R. (2001). A taxonomy for teaching, learning, and assessing: A revision of Bloom's taxonomy of educational objectives. New York, NY: Longman.

| Cognitive Domain | Verb used in outcome or objective |
|---|---|
| Create | Produce new or original work<br>Design, construct, develop, formulate, author |
| Evaluate | Justify a stand or decision<br>Appraise, argue, defend, judge, select, support, value, critique |
| Analyze | Draw connections among ideas<br>Differentiate, compare, examine, experiment, test |
| Apply | Use information or skill<br>Execute, implement, operate, use |
| Understand | Explain ideas or concepts<br>Explain, translate, describe, classify |
| Remember | Recall facts or basic concepts<br>list, name, define, identify |

C.  Milk
D.  Vanilla extract

From the instructor and instructional designer's perspective, what makes the question valid is if it is measuring knowledge or an ability within the proper domain. Why this is valuable information for the instructor and why it is an important first step in evaluating any assessment is because some assessments in an adaptive learning system do not need to be valid at this level or they may not be actually measuring what first appears due to the system's programming. An example would be a quiz question or other assessment that is simply there to measure the learner's retention of content - not the attainment or mastery of a particular learning objective.

If the question does align with a skill or objective or exactly what it measures can be identifies, the student's score may be considered valid and the data from the item serves as augmented information. For the instructor, it lets them know if they need to intervene on the student's behalf or remediate. For the instructional designer, if the assessment is determined to be invalid its use as a measurement of learning may need to be reconsidered.

Again, assessment evaluators should be aware that in some cases there may not be an exact alignment. This is because what the assessment measures is the attainment of knowledge or skills that support an objective as prerequisite knowledge. An example of this would be a question asked by the adaptive learning system that required learners to order a sequence of steps in a specific procedure. While such a question would not actually measure the learner's ability to perform the procedure, it could provide insight into the learner's abilities in a sub-objective that directly supports a main learning objective.

Because of this the evaluation tool recommended by this paper will include a designation for that consideration.

It should be noted that of all the analysis techniques employed by this tool, an of evaluation of validity is the only one that can be completed before or after learners have used the assessment.

## 7.2  Reliability

After it has been determined that an assessment is valid, the next step is to analyze its reliability. This review is begun by examining the Difficulty Index of a question or other assessment.

The Difficulty Index (sometimes referred to as P value) is obtained by using a simple formula of dividing the number of correct answers by the number of all the learners that answered the item [4].

$$P = \frac{\# \text{correct item } answers}{\# \text{ all item } answers}$$

While the formula is presented here for clarity, it should be noted that many adaptive learning systems can provide this data in some form or another.

This formula produces a number from 0.00 to 1.00. A lower number is indicative of a more difficult item. For example, if 100 learners answered the item and 56 of them answered correctly, the Difficulty Index would be .56. The value of the Difficulty Index can then be used as an indicator for the need to look at an item more closely.

Contrary to a common misconception, the Difficulty Index value does not determine the reliability of the question on its own. An overly low or high Difficulty Index can be caused by any number of factors. The point here is to use the designated value as a trigger for further analysis.

Another commonly held misbelief about the Difficulty Index is which exact value should initiate an evaluation of the assessment.

Due to the confusion around what a Difficulty Index statistically means regarding learner performance, there are a number of well-intentioned Web sites that offer advice on which numeric value indicates a need for review of question items. Too often, a value of 0.50 is given as the review threshold but is unfounded in both the psychometric literature and basic statistics. This is illustrated by determining the Difficulty Index of a hypothetical multiple-choice question with one correct answer and three distractors. If each individual learner answering the question selected a completely random answer, the Difficulty Index would be close to 0.25. A threshold of 0.5 is far above what would be expected by even random answer selection. As a tool, the use of a 0.5 Difficulty index would be extremely inefficient.

During our two years of question reviews for reliability, we found that the standard recommendation of a 0.30 Difficulty Index served best to determine if any particular item needed to be reviewed. This is the typical threshold for item results that are interpreted in a norm-referenced way [5].

It should be noted that even using a Difficulty Index of 0.30 is just an indicator to examine an item further. Different question types can result in very different Difficulty

Index values and evaluators should be aware of this. For example, we found that it was rare that a "choose all the apply" question type ever attained a number as high as 0.30. Anyone using this method to check for reliability should feel free to narrow down the Difficulty Index threshold based on the question type, but again, we found that 0.30 served well as an all-purpose number.

After the Difficulty Index threshold is reached the question is then brought for review before one or more subject matter experts. The reviewers are looking to make certain that the assessment is written in a way that does not mislead learners and that the answer key is correct with no unintended problem distractors. It is this review that determines if any given assessment is reliable enough to be accepted as augmented data for the instructor - something that an instructor can act upon in the classroom.

For an instructional designer, the more important knowledge gained by performing a reliability check is the identification of problems or errors for correction in the assessment.

It is worth mentioning at this point that we have found just determining these two attributes of an assessment (validity and reliability) can be enough information to provide actionable direction for both the instructor and the instructional designer.

### 7.3  Standardization

When it comes to evaluating the standardization of an assessment item, what we have found to work best is the use of a Discrimination Index. The Discrimination Index can provide insight into norm-referencing for a specific question item.

The basic explanation of a Discrimination Index is that it compares learner responses to other learner scores on other assessment items (such as all the questions on an entire exam). If an item is "positively discriminating" it means that the item was more often answered correctly by learners with high scores than low scores [5].

Much like the Difficulty Index, the Discrimination Index is a calculation that is often produced by exam software or the adaptive learning system. Unfortunately, there is a great deal of variation in different systems and sometimes professionals disagree on which formula to use. In our assessment analysis, we use the Discrimination Index as a simple warning sign that an item may not truly measure what it was intended to measure and therefore learner answers cannot be used to augment instructor information about learner knowledge.

What follows is the formula we use.

$$D = (P_u - P_l)/\text{the number of students in each group}$$

In the above equation $P_u$ is the fraction of students in the upper scoring group (upper 27%) that answered correctly, and $P_l$ is the fraction of students in the lower scoring group (lower 27%) that answered correctly. Often, exam software will further extrapolate this data to produce what is referred to as *Point Biserial Correlation*. The point biserial value is between $-1.0$ to $1.0$. There are other methods and formulas that can be used to produce some form of Difficulty Index. For example, some software produces a score that divides learner scores in the middle (e.g. upper 50% scoring group/lower 50% scoring group). We considered this formula too inefficient to use in spotting the need for assessment review because learners approaching mean performance on a larger collection of questions could answer any given item correctly or incorrectly, without much discrimination showing in the numbers.

What we found was the need for a clear indicator and not nuanced detail because we were using the Discrimination Index to look for issues in standardization. How this was done was by looking at the values of both the high and low scoring groups, using the Discrimination Index. This number was already produced by the adaptive learning system we were using and it served well as an indicator of spotting possible anomalies in standardization. This creates a sort of norm-referenced look at each item.

For example, if an item seems to have a score that is contrary to expectations (such as more underperforming learners answering the question correctly than higher-performing learners) then it should be reviewed. Another example would be an item that consistently showed no clear discrimination in either $P_u$ or $P_l$. The closer the two numbers are to representing only 50% of either group, the more likely the question does not discriminate in a standard way across learners.

In a review of literature on question item analysis, it is possible to find any number of publications that point to a wide variety of specific Discrimination Index values to serve as triggers for analysis. The point being made here is that unexpected anomalies rather than a given number should be used to determine the need for item review.

# 8   The Tool

While there are many other methods and formulas for analyzing learner answers, we chose these for their efficiency and their ability to indicate potential disparities quickly. We have compiled these methods to produce a single tool for both the instructor and the instructional designer.

By using this tool, an instructor can gain direct and detailed insight into learner attainment of knowledge, rather than leaving the adaptive system to completely judge learner performance and remediation. The instructional designer can also use this tool to fine tune the adaptive learning assessment, thus ensuring efficacy.

In practice we use these approaches in meetings where all instructor and designer stakeholders are present to participate in the review. This ensures that not only is everyone evaluating the same assessments, but that the subject matter experts are on hand to put the augmented information to immediate use.

While the version of the tool shown below is used in a more manual process, the same could be automated in either a script or a spreadsheet macro with the data pulled from the assessment results. If automation were to be used, this manual tool could serve as an outline for such a script. It would be important to note that the script or macro would only indicate those assessment items that met the suggested review threshold. Once the threshold was met, further analysis would still require review by experts.

| Validity | Yes | No |
|---|---|---|
| Does the item truly assess the knowledge or skill assigned to it? (e.g. Bloom's verb, practical performance, etc.) | Item appears valid | Further review required |
| Does the item assess prerequisite or necessary supporting knowledge/skill? | Item may be valid as part of the body of knowledge for subject domain | Item does not appear valid |

Instructor/Instructional Designer: If the item appears valid, the instructor may use this information as augmented knowledge concerning learner performance, and adjust learner activity accordingly (e.g. review material, etc.). If the item's validity is suspect, it should be corrected as a learning object so that it is valid

| Reliability | Yes | No |
|---|---|---|
| Is the P value less than .30 or over .80? Note that .30 is simply a trigger. Different assessment types may trend to other P values | Further review required | Item appears reliable, but further review can be performed |
| Are there any distractors or other elements of the item that appear to generate an unusual number of incorrect answers? E.g., larger number of learners selecting the same incorrect distractor, miskeyed element, etc. | Item may not be reliable. Further review required. SME review should seek to determine why this is occurring | Further review required |
| Is there something unclear or misleading in the question stem that could account for the low P value? | Item is not reliable and may not be valid (misleading stems can misalign an item with what is intended to be measured) | Item may not be reliable. Further review required. SME review should seek to determine why this is occurring |
| Is there something in the question stem that could account for an unusually high P value (e.g., question gives away the answer)? | Item is not reliable and may not be valid (misleading stems can misalign an item with what is intended to be measured) | Item may not be reliable. Further review required. SME review should seek to determine why this is occurring |
| Are learners presented with content required to learn this concept? | Further review required. The assessment may simply be beyond appropriate expectations for learners at this level | Ensure content is presented to learner and review assessment again with new data |

Instructor/Instructional Designer: If the item appears reliable, the instructor may use this information as augmented knowledge concerning learner performance, and adjust learner activity accordingly (e.g. review material, etc.). If the item's reliability is suspect, it should be corrected as a learning object. This may include adjusting learner scores if they are influenced by an unreliable assessment

| Standardization | Yes | No |
|---|---|---|
| Are there anomalies indicated in the Discrimination Index? E.g., point biserial score below 0.0, | Further review required | Assessment item may be standardized |
| Are there any distractors or other elements of the item that appear to generate an unusual number of incorrect answers? E.g., larger number of learners selecting the same incorrect distractor | Item may not be standardized or reliable. Further review required. SME review should seek to determine why this is occurring | Further review required. SME review should seek to determine why this is occurring |
| Are there any other anomalies (such as stem or distractor bias) that might explain the lack of standardization? | Further review required. SME review should seek to determine why this is occurring | Assessment item may be standardized |

Instructor/Instructional Designer: If there appears to be standardization with the item, the instructor may use this information as augmented knowledge concerning learner performance, and adjust learner activity accordingly (e.g. review material, etc.). If the item's standardization is suspect, it should be corrected as a learning object

# 9  Conclusion

Earlier and less formal versions of this tool have been used with success in providing augmented knowledge to both faculty and instructional designers. Instructors have the ability to react with confidence in regard to the effectiveness of instruction and learning activities within the adaptive learning system, and those working in an instructional design capacity have been able to use this information to refine assessment items to make them more accurate. We believe that a more structured version of the tool, such as this, will further enhance this augmentation.

Nursing education has proven to be an ideal testing ground for this tool and its components since learners are required to pass a licensure exam with clearly outlined domains of knowledge. With similar attention to any learning objectives, this tool could be used for assessments in any subject or course.

In fact, with some modification a tool such as this could be used to evaluate human input and computer judgment in other situations including consumer targeting or even threat assessment.

# 10  Recommendation for a Review by an Artificial Intelligence

Though it is outside the scope of this paper, this tool could be further refined by developing an A.I. system that performed the assessment evaluations. This could be done by incorporating as many of the steps of the analysis process as possible.

For example, to review a test item for validity, the A.I. would compare any learning objectives the item was written to measure with the assessment itself and then provide a probability score of the item's validity. Teaching an A.I. system to evaluate something like this would be a matter of seeding in the Bloom's levels and possibly a substantial list of the action verbs from the taxonomy to correlate against assessments. Using standard A.I. teaching methods should be sufficient.

In the end a tool like this would present a series of probability scores (e.g., 98% valid, 87% reliable, etc.) which would enhance the augmentation provided to an instructor or instructional designer. Just as with the more manual tool presented in this paper, there would still need to be expert review of any assessment that did not meet predetermined threshold score, but the process would be simplified by predetermining which assessments or items needed review.

# References

1. Skagestad, P.: The mind's machines: the turing machine, the memex, and the personal computer. Semiotica **111**(3/4), 217–243 (1996)
2. Advances in Artificial Intelligence, Software and Systems Engineering: Joint Proceedings of the AHFE 2018 International Conference on Human Factors in Artificial Intelligence and Social Computing, Software and Systems Engineering, The Human Side of Service Engineering and Human Factors in Energy, 21–25 July 2018, Loews Sapphire Falls Resort at Universal Studios, Orlando, Florida, USA "Redefining the Role of Artificial Intelligence AI in Wiser Service Systems", p. 163

3. Discussion Piece: The Psychometric Principles of Assessment, Professor John Rust Psycho-metrics Centre, Research Matters; Issue 3, January 2007
4. Lord, F.M.: The relationship of the reliability of multiple-choice test to the distribution of item difficulties. Psychometrika **18**, 181–194 (1952)
5. Oermann, M.H., Gaberson, K.B.: Evaluation and Testing in Nursing Education, 6th edn. Springer, Heidelberg (2019).ISBN 978-0-8261-3574

# Why Not Go All-In with Artificial Intelligence?

Kristen DiCerbo[(⊠)]

Khan Academy, Mountain View, CA 94041, USA
Kristen@khanacademy.org

**Abstract.** Despite decades of research and significant current investment, AI-based applications in education have not gotten traction at scale in a way that transforms learning. The most common learning and assessment applications are intelligent tutoring systems that adjust content based on a student profile and automated essay scoring systems that apply "learned" models of scoring to score written assignments. Among the challenges facing these applications in achieving classroom implementation are: trust, existing systems of teacher and student roles and responsibilities, and fairness. This paper discusses these issues and then examines a case study of the use and subsequent removal of artificial intelligence in Khan Academy offerings.

**Keywords:** Artificial intelligence · Trust · Activity theory · Fairness

## 1 Introduction

AI-based technologies have led to change in many industries and there has been a relatively constant drum beat over at least the past decade predicting their move into education. Although advocates have pushed a wide variety of potential applications, there remain few examples of AI-based applications present in classrooms at scale. While venture capital money pours into potential new solutions, it is worth looking at reasons to be cautious about artificial intelligence in education.

Murphy [16] identifies two categories of AI in use in education applications: rule-based expert systems and machine learning. Rule-based expert systems are those that mimic the decision making of experts by first assembling a knowledge base that captures and encodes expert knowledge and then creating an inference engine which applies programmed decision rules to incoming data streams. Machine learning systems build a model based on large amounts of data (rather than modeling expert thinking). The most common use of rule-based expert systems is in intelligent tutors which attempt to adjust the content presented to each student based on a profile of their knowledge and skills. The most common use of machine learning systems in education is in automated essay scoring, which attempts to build a model that uses features of student-written essays to replicate the scoring of a human rater.

There have been decades of research into both intelligent tutoring systems and automated essay scoring. Despite this, there are a number of issues that remain, particularly related to the implementation of these technologies in classrooms. This paper will explore

© Springer Nature Switzerland AG 2021
R. A. Sottilare and J. Schwarz (Eds.): HCII 2021, LNCS 12792, pp. 361–369, 2021.
https://doi.org/10.1007/978-3-030-77857-6_25

three of these: lack of trust in the systems, lack of consideration of the existing classroom relationships, norms, roles, and responsibilities, and issues of fairness. This paper will outline these three issues and see how they apply to a case study of artificial intelligence at Khan Academy.

## 2  Reasons for Caution

### 2.1  Trust

A major issue in the use of artificial intelligence across domains is user trust of the system. Trust as related to AI has been defined as a state in which a person willingly depends on the AI agent, after having taken its characteristics into account [13]. Using survey methodology, researchers have confirmed that people can feel trust toward machines [5, 10, 11]. However, trust is a complicated construct and there are many factors that contribute to levels of trust and change in trust over time. McKnight and Chervany [15] propose a model of trust that suggests three large buckets of these factors: an individual's disposition to trust, the level of trust in institutions, and interpersonal (or in this case person-machine) trust. They posit that the latter tends to fluctuate more than the other two. AI systems will need to satisfy many criteria in order to earn the trust of users, including: fairness, reliability, privacy, and usability. Systems may attempt to provide assurances about these factors explicitly by, for example, publishing information about the system's prediction performance or informing users about how the underlying models work. In the absence of these explicit assurances, or in addition to them, users will use other perceived properties and behaviors in order to inform both their beliefs and their trust-related behavior [13].

One way to examine trust in AI is to look at the extent to which the person accepts and follows the recommendations of an AI system. For example, college students used an AI tool designed for the military to judge the presence or absence of a camouflaged soldier in a view [6]. After observing the automated aid make errors, participants distrusted even reliable aids, unless an explanation was provided regarding why the aid might make mistakes. Knowing this explanation increased trust in the decision aid and increased reliance on the tool. This desire for users to understand models underlying systems has led to work in explainable artificial intelligence. However, some AI methods, such as deep neural networks, don't provide simple explanations for how the developed models work. In addition, trying to quantify the uncertainty in models is often a difficult task and communicating about that uncertainty in ways that are understandable to the general public is even more daunting. In general, the research on the effects of assurances and explanations in combination with observed functioning of a system on trust beliefs and behaviors is in a nascent phase [13].

One area specific to education where AI and trust have come into focus is the use of automated essay scoring. In 2013, the National Council for Teachers of English released a position statement strongly against the use of automated essay scoring with end of year tests. They say in part, "Computers are unable to recognize and judge those elements that we most associate with good writing (logic, clarity, accuracy, ideas relevant to a specific topic, innovative style, effective appeals to audience, different forms of organization, types of persuasion, quality of evidence, humor or irony, and effective uses of repetition, to name just a few). Using computers to "read" and evaluate students' writing (1) denies students the chance to have anything but limited features recognized in their writing; and (2) compels teachers to ignore what is most important in writing instruction in order to teach what is least important" [17]. Whether their judgements of the capabilities of automated scoring are correct or not, it is clear that this organization of teachers does not trust that AI-enabled scoring is capable of accurately performing the task that humans do.

## 2.2  System Change

Learning, especially in the context of educational efforts, is a social process that unfolds as a complex system. Learning occurs in the interaction between educators, students, and others in a community. These communities develop tools, like digital learning environments, and create rules and norms for using them in ways that make sense for their system. We can represent these systems in a way suggested by Activity Theory [7] (see Fig. 1).

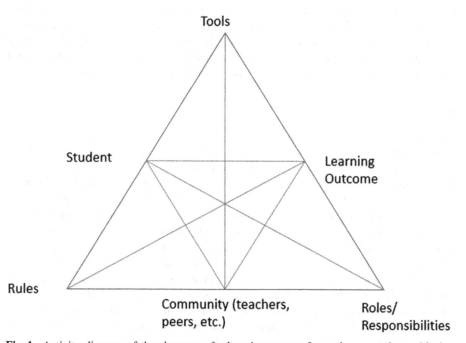

**Fig. 1.** Activity diagram of the elements of a learning system focused on a student achieving learning outcomes.

In discussions of AI-based learning systems, conversation frequently incorporates only a portion of the system, often the top part of the triangle above involving students, digital tools, and learning outcomes. This leaves out the interactions of students and teachers with each other and with technology. The norms and rules of interactions between students and teachers and the roles and responsibilities of both are long-standing and entrenched in the system. If they are going to be changed there will need to be convincing reasons to make that change. AI-designers who believe they can drop technology into the classroom and transform education are likely to join the long list of technology evangelists who thought the same but have failed to disrupt the system [18]. Education as a system is slow to change, in part because its work is so important that experiments that might not work have the potential to have lasting negative impact on students' lives.

A big instructional question that arises in learning is who gets to select the next activity. AI-driven tools are often developed to create individual student profiles, identify content that meets particular criteria related to difficulty levels, and serve that up to students. However, teachers often see it as their role to drive the pace and sequence of learning. They have a course specific scope and sequence designed to get students through the standards expected of students at a particular grade level. On top of that, students have their own interests and understandings of what they know. Teachers and parents want students to be owners of their own learning, to have agency, and to be lifelong learners. We know that students who are self-regulated learners tend to have better learning outcomes [8]. Looking at the situation from the activity theory perspective highlights the challenges an AI-drive recommendation engine may face when placed into a classroom system. This same analysis of the actors, rules, and roles and responsibilities can be done for many instructional activities and should be examined by those designing AI-based tools for the classroom to determine how it will fit in the existing system and the extent to which change in the system is needed for the tool to succeed.

## 2.3   Fairness

Education is replete with evidence of unequal outcomes for learners from historically under-resourced communities. If we are to use AI-based solutions in education, it must be clear that these solutions are not replicating and reinforcing the systematic biases that lead to these unequal outcomes. Unfortunately, examples abound outside the education sphere of how AI does just that. In the classic example of Amazon's attempt to build a resume-screening tool, the training data reflected that men had historically been chosen as the successful candidate far more often than women, so women were seldom represented as successful candidates in the data set. Although developers did not include gender as a variable to be used in selection, they used resumes and hiring decisions from the past to train the resume screening model. As a result, the model ended up identifying proxies for gender, like attending a women's college, and replicating past decisions, resulting the screening out more women than men [4]. In the realm of education, several studies have documented differing performance of automated scoring models for test-takers with different native language or disabilities [1, 20].

Recall that automated essay scoring relies on the AI system learning how to score written work through the use of human-graded text corpora. Researchers looking at patterns of AI language learning found that corpora of text from the internet often used to train semantic language systems contained language reflecting historic biases around race and gender [2]. Training with these texts is likely to reproduce the same biases we have now. For this reason, some have recommended preventative auditing of training data to help ensure fairness [9].

In evaluating automated essay scoring, researchers use humans as the "gold standard" of comparison and report the relationship between human scoring and machine scoring as part of the evidence of the validity of the automated scoring. When differences are found, such as students with a foreign language background scoring higher with automated scoring techniques, scoring methods were developed to minimize the impact of these differences [1]. However, humans are not without bias, particularly in regard to their own linguistic backgrounds and evaluation of language skill [3].

Rather than a comparison to a human standard, some researchers have suggested using evidence of disparate impact, or evidence of different outcomes, to investigate bias [9]. In order to do this, a basic confusion matrix can be constructed with the categories to be examined (e.g., male and female) against a particular outcome (e.g., grade level skill recommended or not). From this, measures of accuracy, sensitivity, and specificity can be examined. This method aligns to legal definitions of bias where the standard is to demonstrate that there are unequal outcomes for unequal groups. In the assessment realm, psychometric guidelines require that if automated scoring models are to be used for making high-stakes decisions for college admissions or employment, their developers must perform validation procedures to ensure demographic factors are not producing significant differences in scores across subgroups of test-takers [21].

A variety of methods have been suggested to improve the fairness of AI models, including modifying training data, changing algorithms to optimize for fairness as well as selection criteria, and changing output decisions after the fact [19]. Efforts are made to evaluate fairness in high stakes testing environments. However, little attention is paid in the research literature to these issues in the learning and assessment-for-learning spaces.

## 3 Case Study: Khan Academy

Khan Academy is a nonprofit organization that provides free online instruction and practice for an array of K-14 disciplines and test preparation for the SAT, LSAT, and other tests. As of the end of 2020 the site had 109 million registered learners who logged billions of learning minutes on the site. The site encourages a mastery learning approach in which learners practice skills until they demonstrate a high level of proficiency, allowing learners to establish a solid foundation of skills and fill in gaps they may have from previous learning experiences. In a recent study of 5,348 students, after controlling for prior knowledge and demographic characteristics, using Khan Academy for 30 min or more per week resulted in a 22 point score on the Smarter Balanced Assessment math score, an effect size of .22 [12].

Khan Academy began with Sal Khan tutoring a cousin in mathematics. As more cousins became interested, he began making videos of himself explaining concepts and soon afterward wrote a basic software application to allow them to practice solving problems. He posted the videos on YouTube and they soon became popular, and Khan decided to quit his investment banking job and establish Khan Academy as a nonprofit aimed at providing "a free world class education for anyone, anywhere." Khan also wrote a book, *The One World Schoolhouse* that lays out a vision of personalized, mastery-based learning [14].

Given this orientation, the team looked for ways to use technology and data to better personalize learning, including identifying learning gaps and recommending content.

Work began on a system to identify student proficiency based on their performance on questions in the system. This information was fed into a statistical model that predicted their probability of answering another question on that skill correctly. Based on those probability estimates, students would be placed at a particular level of a skill (not started, practiced, level one, level two, or mastered). Students would monitor their progress toward mastery on a set of related skills in a "mission" (see Fig. 2). Missions also had a recommendations system so that when students mastered some skills, the system recommended which next skills in the mission they should tackle based on their performance on other skills.

**Fig. 2.**   Screenshot of Khan Academy's tracking of skill mastery in missions.

Another key component of early Khan Academy was the knowledge map (see Fig. 3). This was a visual depiction of all the skills taught on Khan Academy and how they relate to each other. Viewers could zoom out to see all the skills or zoom in and focus on a particular area. Skills would change color as students mastered them. The visualization promoted student agency as students could see the relationships among skills and choose for themselves which skills they wanted to tackle next by clicking on one of the circles to be taken to videos and exercises about that skill.

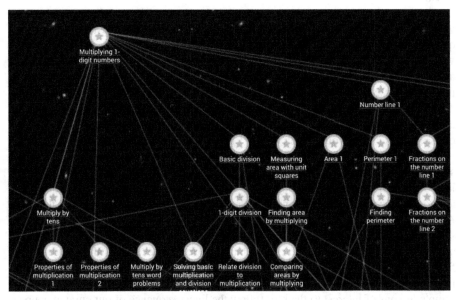

**Fig. 3.** Screenshot of Khan Academy's (now deprecated) knowledge map.

The interesting fact for the purposes of this paper is that neither missions nor the knowledge map exist on the current version of Khan Academy, due in large part to the difficulty in fitting these into the implementation models of classrooms (but in part also due to difficulties scaling as the amount of content on the site exploded). The issues related to scaling included the difficulty of keeping the knowledge map up to date as new content was added. There were difficulties in keeping up with the added complexity of adding new nodes and edges but there were also conceptual difficulties as new domains were added that do not have the networked skill structure that math does. Similarly, the recommendation engine required constant tuning as new skills were added into the system.

However, there were also issues related to implementation described above in the section on cautions. Initially, most of the learners at Khan Academy were individuals seeking out additional assistance or interested in acquiring new skills on their own. These learners were generally relatively self-directed and motivated. However, over time, in order to reach the students who needed help the most, and who were likely less self-directed and motivated, Khan Academy began pursuing a strategy of classroom use. This meant entry into a new system, the classroom described above in the abstract.

There were teachers trying to manage individual recommendations and pathways for all the learners in their classes while they had set pacing guides and sequences of activity. It was not feasible to put students in front of a computer and expect them to be able to work independently all the time and get to proficiency on grade level skills. Teachers wanted to have at least some control over what students were working on and had deeply embedded schemas around giving assignments to students. Assignments also made sense to students in classes who wanted to know when they were finished for the day or the week.

On top of this, there were issues of trust of the system. First, students could not tell what it would take to get them to mastery of a skill other than "just keep answering questions correct until the system tells you it is mastered." While this worked for motivated independent learners, it was untenable for students trying to complete a homework assignment. Second, the recommendation system would give recommendations for the next skill to tackle that teachers, and often experts, did not agree with. There was no easy way to determine, much less explain, the reasons why the underlying model made a given recommendation. It should not be a surprise that after a few cases of this in a classroom, a teacher would begin to lose trust in the recommendation system.

Given the growing "debt" of falling behind on the mapping and recommendation system with new content, the difficulty fitting into the classroom system, and the growing lack of trust in the recommendations, the decision was made to simplify. Today, there are no AI-based recommendations being made outside of test preparation on the Khan Academy platform. There is a mastery system with clear rules about how many questions students need to get right on which kinds of activities to move up levels. Teachers make assignments for students, which can be based on recommendations the system makes from static pre-requisite maps, but can also be based on the teacher's curriculum or judgement. Learners still also have the agency of being able to click through courses and sample lessons of interest to them or follow the linear sequence of our curated courses.

Even with these changes, there is room to improve to fit into classrooms. The notion of practice to mastery is not common in schools. It can conflict with grading systems that require a percentage score to input into an average. Requiring students to achieve mastery can still conflict with a teacher's need to keep a certain pace to cover all the topics in a year. However, Khan Academy fits better with the understood roles and responsibilities of the classroom, continues to provide students with choice and agency, and does not have issues of trust in the system.

## References

1. Bridgeman, B., Trapani, C., Attali, Y.: Considering fairness and validity in evaluating automated scoring. In: Annual Meeting of the National Council on Measurement in Education (2009)
2. Caliskan, A., Bryson, J., Narayanan, A.: Semantics derived automatically from language corpora contain human-like biases. Science 356(6334), 183–186 (2017)
3. Carey, M.D., Mannell, R.H., Dunn, P.K.: Does a rater's familiarity with a candidate's pronunciation affect the rating in oral proficiency interviews? Lang. Test. 28(2), 201–219 (2011)

4. Dastin, J.: Amazon scraps secret AI recruiting tool that showed bias against women. https://www.reuters.com/article/us-amazon-com-jobs-automation-insight/amazon-scraps-secret-ai-recruiting-tool-that-showed-bias-against-women-idUSKCN1MK08G. Accessed 12 Feb 2021

5. Desai, M., et al.: Effects of changing reliability on trust of robot systems. In: 7th ACM/IEEE International Conference on Human-Robot Interaction, pp. 73–80 (2012)

6. Dzindolet, M.T., Peterson, S.A., Pomranky, R.A., Pierce, L.G., Beck, H.P.: The role of trust in automation reliance. Int. J. Hum. Comput. Stud. 58(6), 697–718 (2003)

7. Engeström, Y.: Expansive learning at work: toward an activity theoretical reconceptualization. J. Educ. Work. 14, 133–156 (2001)

8. Ergan, B., Kanadli, S.: The effect of self-regulated learning strategies on academic achievement: a meta-analysis study. Eurasian J. Educ. Res. 69, 55–74 (2017)

9. Feldman, M., Friedler, S.A., Moeller, J., Scheidegger, C., Venkatasubramanian, S.: Certifying and removing disparate impact. In: KDD 2015: Proceedings of the 21st ACM SIGKDD International Conference on Knowledge Discovery and Data Mining, pp. 259–268 (2015)

10. Freedy, A., DeVisser, E., Weltmant, G., Coeyman, N: Measurement of trust in human-robot collaboration. In: International Symposium on Collaborative Technologies and Systems, pp. 106–114 (2007)

11. Groom, V., Nass, C.: Can robots be teammates?: benchmarks in human-robot teams. Interact. Stud. 8(3), 483–500 (2007)

12. Hill, K., Weatherholtz, K., Chattergoon, R.: Use of Khan Academy and mathematics achievement: a correlational study with Long Beach Unified School District. In: Glick, D., Cohen, A., Chang C. (eds.) Early Warning Systems and Targeted Interventions for Student Success in Online Courses, pp. 37–63. IGI Global, Hershey (2020)

13. Israelsen, B.: "I can assure you… that it's going to be all right"—a definition, case for, and survey of algorithmic assurances in human-autonomy trust relationships. arXiv preprint arXiv:1708.00495 (2017)

14. Khan, S.: The One World Schoolhouse. Twelve, New York (2012)

15. McKnight, D.H., Chervany, N.: While trust is cool and collected, distrust is fiery and frenzied: A model of distrust concepts. In: Amcis 2001 Proceedings, p. 171 (2001)

16. Murphy, R.F.: Artificial intelligence applications to support K-12 teachers and teaching: a review of promising applications, opportunities, and challenges. RAND, Santa Monica (2019)

17. National Council of Teachers of English: NCTE position statement on machine scoring. https://ncte.org/statement/machine_scoring/. Accessed 12 Feb 2021

18. Reich, J.: Failure to Disrupt. Harvard University Press, Cambridge (2020)

19. Romai, A., Ruggieri, S.: A multidisciplinary survey on discrimination analysis. Knowl. Eng. Rev. 29, 582–638 (2013)

20. Wang, Z., von Davier, A.: Monitoring of scoring using the e-rater automated scoring system and human raters on a writing test. ETS Research Report Series. ETS, Princeton (2014)

21. Williamson, D.M., Xi, X., Breyer, F.J.: A framework for evaluation and use of automated scoring. Educ. Meas. Issues Pract. 31(1), 2–13 (2012)

# Core to the Learning Day: The Adaptive Instructional System as an Integrated Component of Brick-and-Mortar, Blended, and Online Learning

Lynelle Morgenthaler$^{(\boxtimes)}$(iD) and Michelle D. Barrett(iD)

Edmentum, Bloomington, MN 55437, USA
lynelle.morgenthaler@edmentum.com
https://www.edmentum.com

**Abstract.** Advanced technologies for individualized learning present intuitively appealing opportunities to provide students with exactly what they need, when they need it. However, observed challenges with implementations of adaptive instructional systems in K–12 education to date point to a need to better articulate the theory of change for the incorporation of individualized pathways and teacher-led grade-level learning, removing incongruities. This paper first examines separate exemplar theories of change underlying each of the adaptive instructional system and blended learning models. It then discusses associated pedagogical and setting considerations, identifying several areas of incongruity to be addressed when bringing these models together. An exemplar theory of change for integrating the adaptive instructional system as a component core to the learning day is proposed. Finally, the paper reflects on research required to test the proposed model and changes in interactions, pedagogy, and curriculum that may be required.

**Keywords:** Adaptive instructional system · Intelligent tutoring system · Blended learning · Curriculum · Pedagogy · Individualized learning

## 1 Introduction

Over the last 50 or so years, the education system in the United States has evolved with the aspiration to ensure that all students are able to achieve, evident in policy language such as "No Child Left Behind" and "Every Student Succeeds" and in accountability procedures intended to guarantee all students have access to high standards of education. Simultaneously, computer technologies have advanced to allow for a higher degree of personalization of services than ever before. Combined, it isn't surprising to witness the relatively recent emergence of adaptive instructional systems, individualized and/or personalized learning paths, and instructional models which blend human teachers with technology.

© Springer Nature Switzerland AG 2021
R. A. Sottilare and J. Schwarz (Eds.): HCII 2021, LNCS 12792, pp. 370–381, 2021.
https://doi.org/10.1007/978-3-030-77857-6_26

Although these efforts were well underway prior to 2020, in 2020 the COVID pandemic served as a forcing function for the rapid adoption of technology in schools as they sought to enable remote and socially-distanced learning. It also highlighted ongoing structural inequities that caused the pandemic to have differential impact on students based on socio-economic, racial/ethnic, metro classification, disability, and other opportunity gaps. Post-COVID, teachers will be presented with tremendous challenge as they work to remediate widespread and uneven gaps due to interrupted learning opportunities. Individualized and personalized learning tools are seen as an important component of equitably meeting the remediation challenges presented by the pandemic, with advocates calling for policy changes that remove perceived blockers to pre-pandemic adoption, such as strict seat time requirements [1].

In a Delphi study designed to identify areas in tension in the advancement of technology-enhanced learning [2], calling upon a large sample of experts from learning sciences, psychology, computer sciences, and educational technology fields, an area of tension emerged opposing individualized to standardized learning paths. This indicates that there are arising possibilities and opportunities for improving learning through introducing technologies to individualize learning paths as well as possible downsides or pitfalls for the same. In order to address the tension, both positions need to be understood and acknowledged. The authors of this study further found that the latter positions often reflected aspects highly relevant to the implementation in actual educational practices. Resolving this tension requires changes across multiple layers of the educational ecosystem, including student interactions, tactical pedagogical practices, and curriculum and teaching strategies. Some changes require shifts in educational policies, such as seat time requirements, to resolve the tension [1]. Indeed, a recent case study revealed that navigating institutional pressures to improve state grade-level standardized test scores while implementing tasks and technologies designed to personalize student learning presented great challenge to teachers [3], indicating policy shifts in accountability measures may need to occur to relieve the tension.

As the authors of the Delphi study point out, when the tension is considered in light of observed time-frames for change in educational systems [4], it should be expected that even once an approach to remedy the tension is identified, the resolution of this tension will take time given the hierarchy of changes required. Typically, changes in curriculum and teaching strategies take the longest time, often spanning several years and multiple generations of teachers, followed by changes in tactical pedagogical practices, which can take weeks to months for teachers to embed in their practice, followed by changes in technology-mediated student interactions, which can take hours for teachers to master. However, the pandemic may not afford us the luxury of waiting to support students who experienced unfinished learning, and it is therefore of high urgency to address the tension as educators return to teach a post-COVID population of students with a wide and unprecedented opportunity gap in learning.

Two areas of research relevant to understanding and addressing the tension include adaptive instructional systems and blended learning. This paper first examines separate exemplar theories of change underlying each of the adaptive instructional system and blended learning models. It then discusses associated pedagogical and setting considerations, identifying several areas of incongruity to be addressed when bringing these models together. An exemplar theory of change for integrating the adaptive instructional system as a component core to the learning day is proposed. Finally, the paper reflects on research required to test the proposed model and changes in interactions, pedagogy, and curriculum that may be required.

## 2    Instructional Theory

### 2.1    Adaptive Instructional System Theory of Change

Adaptive instructional systems (AIS), are defined as

> ... artificially-intelligent, computer-based systems that guide learning experiences by tailoring instruction and recommendations based on the goals, needs, and preferences of each individual learner or team in the context of domain learning objectives [5].

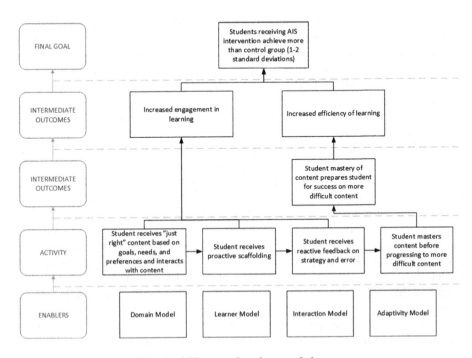

**Fig. 1.** AIS exemplar theory of change

Prevailing theories of change for adaptive instructional systems tend to be situated in notions of the effectiveness of mastery learning and of tutoring that arose from studies conducted by Bloom and his graduate students Anania and Burke [6–10]. In this research, students who received one-to-one tutoring were found to be two standard deviations above a control group receiving regular classroom instruction, and students who were instructed with mastery learning methods were found to be about one standard deviation over the control group. Although the challenge issued by Bloom was to search for methods of group instruction as effective as one-to-one tutoring, some attention turned to the creation of intelligent tutoring systems (ITS) that could tutor individual students in a way that mimics the effectiveness of expert human tutors.

In a meta-analysis of later studies examining the relative effectiveness of human tutoring and intelligent tutoring systems (ITS), ITS were found to function nearly as effectively as human tutoring when they use a step-based approach in which proactive scaffolding and reactive feedback are provided at grain sizes that reflect the steps a learner must take to solve a problem [11]. Unfortunately, however, the effect sizes of human tutoring and mastery learning were lower on average than found in Bloom's studies, for a number of reasons. Studies have also found evidence that adaptive instructional systems yield positive effects on student learning outcomes when adapting to student knowledge, strategies, and errors [12]. These studies focus on adaptive instructional systems as supplemental tutors, and many use advanced technologies to emulate the behavior of expert tutors. Figure 1 illustrates an exemplar theory of change for such a system.

## 2.2   Blended Learning Theory of Change

Blended learning does not have a consistent definition across the literature. Most definitions include some allowance for technology and teachers working together to advance student learning. An iNACOL (International Association for K–12 Online Learning) report in 2015 describes blended learning as an instructional delivery model, not a technology plan [13]. Work by the Clayton Christensen Institute came to the following definition:

"... a formal education program in which a student learns at least in part through online learning with some element of student control over time, place, path, and/or pace and at least in part at a supervised brick-and-mortar location away from home. The modalities along each student's learning path within a course or subject are connected to provide an integrated learning experience." [14]

A key aspect of this definition is the connection between the modalities of online and in-person instruction to provide an integrated learning experience. It should be noted that constraints on location (i.e., "away from home") may no longer be as relevant as they once were, given the advent of wide-spread synchronous teacher-led online instruction that accompanied school shutdown during the COVID pandemic. We might reframe blended learning as a combination of synchronous, teacher-led instruction and independent online learning.

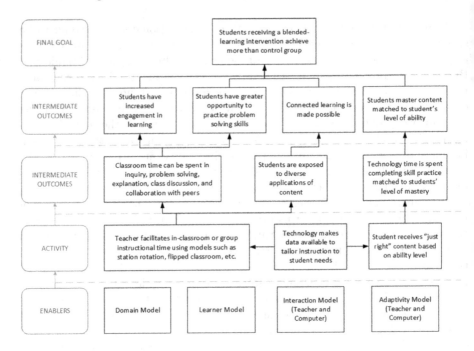

**Fig. 2.** Blended learning exemplar theory of change

One study [15] outlines a theory of action of one such blended system that includes classroom time envisioned to provide students with experiences in inquiry, problem-solving, explanation, class discussion, and collaboration with peers while technology provides practice matched to student's level of mastery accompanied by immediate feedback. Together, the eco-system is theorized to increase student achievement by increasing engagement, exposure to diverse applications of the content, and greater opportunity to practice problem-solving skills. Connected learning experiences [16] then become possible. In addition, the availability of data from such an ecosystem to enable learning analytics has been proposed as a key factor of success in the proposed system [17]. Figure 2 illustrates an exemplar theory of change based on these hypotheses. An implementation of a system purported to be built for this ecosystem found significant positive effects in year two [15].

## 3   Bringing Blended Learning and Adaptive Instructional Systems Together

### 3.1   Pedagogical Considerations

Implementation of technology in the classroom requires a number of conditions for success, including knowledge and skills, resources, time, rewards, participation, commitment, leadership, and dissatisfaction with the status quo [18].

The integration of an adaptive instructional system into a blended learning implementation further requires coherence in these systems' theories of change, such that the components of the combined theory are not in conflict with one another. As will be illustrated below, it appears that implementations to date place the teacher at the heart of the tension between the individualized and standardized learning paths described earlier in this article.

Empirical research is now beginning to emerge from blended instructional models in which adaptive instructional systems are components of an overall learning eco-system [19–24]. However, few studies to date examine the details of implementation in order to test the theory of change that informs the actions, intermediate outcomes, and long-term goals of the overall ecosystem. In addition, most of these studies document a lack of fidelity to the recommended implementations of the adaptive instructional systems, which may indicate that even if the adaptive instructional system itself had a strong theory of change, it was unlikely to have materialized in an instructional reality.

For example, a recent study designed to capture details of implementation [24] found that blended AIS implementations can be fraught with challenge. Low fidelity appears to occur especially when time constraints drive teachers to use the adaptive instructional system at a lower-than-recommended dosage in order to accommodate their ability to adequately instruct grade-level standards. A recent case study found that time was a serious constraint to teachers' use of an adaptive instructional system as a component of instruction [3].

Perhaps time constraints experienced by teachers in implementing digital solutions could have been predicted, as they had precursors in time variables outlined in Carroll's model of school learning [25] and in the mastery-versus-coverage dilemma described by Slavin [26]. Frameworks such as Multi-Tier System of Supports (MTSS) [27] and Response to Intervention (RTI) [28] propose approaches to allocating additional instructional time for students requiring remediation. Typically, these systems "borrow" instructional time from other less academic portions of the school day. Recommendations for students returning from COVID interruptions to learning have focused on a "double dose" of extra time [29] and on additional small-group interventions (defined by size of group or instructional intensity) for the majority of students [30].

In addition to these identified time constraints, the majority of teachers in the aforementioned studies kept teacher-led and computer-led instruction as distinct entities and did not use student data from one modality to inform the other, finding it difficult to incorporate data from an adaptive instructional system into their daily synchronous instructional practices. In addition, many teachers expressed a desire to override the adaptive algorithm so that the content assigned would better align with content being taught in the course. One teacher hypothesized, "Students would [experience] better growth if they worked on topics that supported standards covered in class and homework. They would get more out of both [instructional modalities]." [24] The concept of connected interventions as opposed to disconnected interventions is a topic much discussed in intervention literature.

Given these findings, this paper proposes that the challenges in implementations seen to date are not simple issues of better professional development or teacher willingness to change, and that treating them as such is a great disservice to the field. Rather, they stem from multiple areas of incongruity:

1) Educators are expected to provide students opportunities to learn grade-level standards in their core instruction and often follow a number of practices in creating standards-aligned instructional units that provide an integrated curriculum [31] rather than a hierarchical list of discrete standards to be taught one by one in a way often favored by adaptive instructional systems. As a tangible example, English language arts units are often based in themes, allowing learners to make connections across text and centering standards from disparate domains in a single piece of complex literature. When this type of dissonance between systems and everyday practice occurs, teachers opt to not use data from one modality of discrete skills to inform their synchronous instruction of integrated curriculum.

2) Most examples of successful blended learning point to logistics—when and where students are learning—rather than how coherence is achieved among social learning opportunities, integrating grade-level and intervention instruction, and the individual recommendations made by an adaptive instructional systems [13]. Case studies pointing to success to date typically engage students that greatly value the flexibility in time and place over perceived benefits of social classroom learning experiences [14].

3) Past blended-learning research has tended to focus on the role of the student, technology, and content rather than the role of the teacher [32]. Yet, the theories of change expressed to date in a blended-learning ecosystem consider the teacher at least an equal partner to the technology. It stands to reason then, that the teacher-mitigated learning experience of grade-level synchronous instruction and the computer-led AIS instruction should be considered equally as well.

4) Opportunity to learn rigorous grade-level standards is an issue of equity, and one of the driving factors in educational policies calling for accountability in legislation such as "No Child Left Behind." Teachers are faced with a complicated calculus when it comes to balancing the mastery of pre-cursor lower-level skills and access to on-grade learning opportunities in an instructional day of real time constraints.

An astute reader will note that these incongruities first appear in the lowest levels of the theory of change presented in Fig. 2.

## 3.2  Impact of Setting

In addition to the pedagogical considerations outlined above, teachers face increasing complexities associated with physical settings. Blended learning can occur in brick-and-mortar settings with students participating in face-to-face teacher interactions and in-person supported computer-time; in hybrid settings with students in brick-and-mortar classrooms some of the time and in remote locations for computer-time; and in settings with students online 100% of the time for both synchronous learning with teacher/peers and asynchronous, independent computer-time. In these examples, both the nature of support in the teacher-led instruction varies and the support during the computer-led instruction varies.

There are very likely interactions of each of these blended-learning scenarios that points to elements of success for an AIS component. For example, one might expect that an AIS that is easy to use in both brick-and-mortar and home settings might allow for more seamless integration by teachers and students than one that requires considerable technical support by a teacher and is, therefore, unlikely to be successful in the home. Future research testing for proposed theories of change should take care to incorporate setting data into analysis in order to better understand these interaction.

## 3.3    Toward a Congruent Theory of Change

This paper asserts that in order to be successfully actualized and tested, theories of change need to evolve to address the incongruities educators experience when blending teacher instruction with AIS.

Each AIS has an adaptive model that is designed to optimize learning against a domain objective at the individual level. Hence, these algorithms tend to focus relentlessly on mastery along an individualized learning path. This is evident in reviewing the exemplar theory of change for an AIS: There is not an explicit activity that involves the teacher. While many developers of these systems would claim they are not trying to replace a teacher, they haven't explicitly built the role of the teacher into the system. The challenges teachers face in implementing these systems point to an algorithmic problem: The solutions are optimizing for only one facet of student outcomes.

In the blended-learning exemplar theory of change, while the teacher is certainly present, the relationships between and among enablers and activities tend to fall apart when the technology has adaptive algorithms optimized to the individual student. Teachers find it difficult to use data presented by the AIS; the AIS doesn't interact with other learning components; the level of mastery of specific content nodes required within the AIS may be out of alignment with instructional goals; and ultimately, there isn't enough time in the day to do it all.

It is too easy (and flawed) to point to this problem as one of "progressive" personalized learning versus "conservative" standardized learning. Looking deeper into the underlying theories of change of AIS and blended learning, the truth may be that the tension between individualized and standardized learning paths is a false dichotomy; that learning paths should neither be individual, nor standardized, but rather optimized across individual and social learning, across equitably filling gaps and equitable on-grade instruction, and across time, to yield the best learner growth and achievement the system as a whole can produce.

A congruent theory of change for the use of adaptive instructional systems blended with teacher-led instruction can establish a new teacher-full AIS as core to the learning day by clarifying, extending, and incorporating a robust role for the teacher. It also must account for resolution of the tension across these twin goals of the educational system, i.e., on-level instruction and intervention to remediate unfinished learning. Therefore, the proposed theory of change allows for explicit application of hierarchical optimization decisions by district and school administrators, teachers, and learners. Figure 3 illustrates the changes in enablers, activity, and intermediate outcomes required for this revised model.

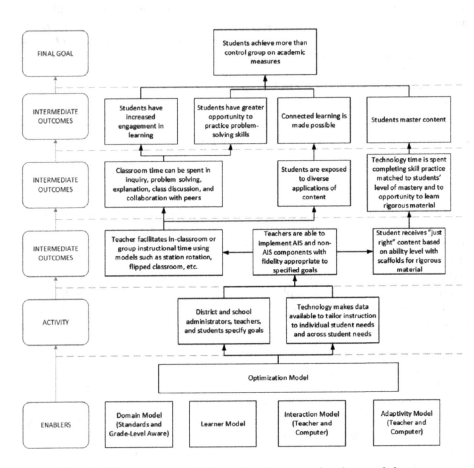

**Fig. 3.** AIS as component of core learning exemplar theory of change

First, note that an optimization model has been added to the enablers. Second, note that the activity layer includes explicit indication of goals by district and school administrators, teachers, and students. Third, note that the reconciliation of goals by the system is expected to result in an intermediate outcome in which teachers are better able implement both the AIS and non-AIS components of instruction with fidelity appropriate to the specified goals. Finally, note that the optimization model, teacher and student input, and data from the system is expected to result in an outcome in which technology of the AIS allows for both mastery of precursors and for scaffolded exposure and access to on-grade, rigorous content.

A robust research agenda is required to test the causal linkages in this proposed theory of change. While the authors are aware of some attempts at optimization across students in a school to date [33–35], these models have tended to focus on optimizing student assignment to specific learning nodes for the following school day due to constraints in school resources (e.g., classrooms, computer labs, teachers), leaving teachers and students with little agency.

In a traditional AIS, information from the system is designed to inform teacher-led instruction. In contrast, the theory of change proposed here is intended to provide teachers with more agency as they work in tandem with technology to optimize learning for their students. In this model, an AIS will continue to inform teacher-led instruction, but in a more dynamic, time-sensitive model, and, more importantly, information from teacher-led instruction would also be taken as input by the AIS to inform its behavior in the form of scaffolds offered to the learner. One important potential is the ability of the interventions in an AIS to more directly support the content presented in teacher-led grade-level instruction, even if the computer-led instruction offers below-level support for the learner. In this type of AIS, a computer would use both information about the student as a learner and information about offline instruction to provide the right supports at the right time in a way that meshes seamlessly with the teacher's goals.

# 4    Conclusion

Consistent with the evolution of application of artificial intelligence to complex problems, in which system designs that purposefully include human-in-the-loop are emerging, the proposed theory of change represents an evolution of AIS from one-to-one intelligent tutors to components of a complex educational ecosystem in which human and computer learning work in tandem. Emerging practices in learning engineering, which apply the learning sciences, human-centered engineering design methodologies, and data-informed decision-making to support learners and their development hold great promise in iterating on increasingly effective solutions. An important and developing area of focus is providing the teacher, who has a personal relationship with the student and knows the student as a whole learner, agency in serving the best interests of students, aligning system supports with their teacher-led grade-level instruction, and bringing AIS out of the isolated computer lab and into the core of the learning day.

**Acknowledgements.** The authors are grateful to Cheryl Dodge for her thoughtful review and comments during the preparation of this paper.

# References

1. Jenkins, S.: Policy solutions that foster competency-based learning (2020). https:// eric.ed.gov/?q=personalized+learning+and+core&pg=2&id=ED607346
2. Plesch, C., Kaendler, C., Rummel, N., Wiedmann, M., Spada, H.: Identifying areas of tension in the field of technology-enhanced learning: results of an international delphi study. Comput. Educ., 92–105 (2013). https://doi.org/10.1016/j.compedu. 2013.01.018
3. Daruwala, I., Bretas, S., Ready, D.D.: When logics collide: implementing technology-enabled personalization in the age of accountability. Educ. Res. (2020). https://doi.org/10.3102/0013189X20960674
4. Riley, D.: Educational technology and practice: Types and timescales of change. Educ. Technol. Soci. 10, 85–93 (2007). https://citeseerx.ist.psu.edu/viewdoc/ download?doi=10.1.1.99.983&rep=rep1&type=pdf
5. Sottilare, R.: A comprehensive review of design goals and emerging solutions for adaptive instructional systems. Technol. Instr. Cogn. Learn. 11, 5–38 (2018)
6. Bloom, B.S.: Learning for mastery. instruction and curriculum. regional education laboratory for the carolinas and virginia, topical papers and reprints, number 1. Eval. Comment 1(2), n2 (1968)
7. Bloom, B.S.: The 2 sigma problem: the search for methods of group instruction as effective as one-to-one tutoring. Educ. Res. 13, 4–16 (1984)
8. Anania, J.: The effects of quality of instruction on the cognitive and affective learning of students. Ph.D. thesis, University of Chicago (1982)
9. Anania, J.: The influence of instructional conditions on student learning and achievement. Eval. Educ. Int. Rev. Ser. 7, 1–92 (1984)
10. Burke, A.: Students' potential for learning contrasted under tutorial and group approaches to instruction. Ph.D. thesis, University of Chicago (1982)
11. VanLehn, K.: The relative effectiveness of human tutoring, intelligent tutoring systems, and other tutoring systems. Educ. Psychol. 46, 197–221 (2011). https:// doi.org/10.1080/00461520.2011.611369
12. Aleven, V., McLaughlin, E.A., Glenn, R.A., Koedinger, K.R.: Instruction based on adaptive learning technologies. In: Handbook of Research on Learning and Instruction, 2nd edn., pp. 552–560. Routledge, New York (2017)
13. Powell, A., et al.: Blending learning: the evolution of online and face-to-face education from 2008–2015. promising practices in blended and online learning series (2015). https://eric.ed.gov/?q=personalized+learning+and+core&pg=3& id=ED560788
14. Christensen, C.M., Horn, M.B., Staker, H.: Is k-12 blended learning disruptive? An introduction of the theory of hybrids (2013). http://www.christenseninstitute. org/wp-content/uploads/2013/05/Is-K-12-Blended-Learning-Disruptive.pdf
15. Pane, J.F., Griffin, B.A., McCaffrey, D.F., Karam, R.: Effectiveness of cognitive tutor algebra i at scale. Educ. Eval. Policy Anal. 36, 127–144 (2014). https://doi. org/10.3102/0162373713507480
16. Ito, M., et al.: Connected learning: an agenda for research and design (2013)
17. Snodgrass Rangel, V., Bell, E.R., Monroy, C., Whitaker, J.R.: Toward a new approach to the evaluation of a digital curriculum using learning analytics. J. Res. Technol. Educ. 47, 89–104 (2015)
18. Ely, D.: Conditions that facilitate the implementation of educational technology innovations. J. Res. Comput. Educ. 23, 298–305 (1990). https://doi.org/10.1080/ 08886504.1990.10781963

19. Amro, F., Borup, J.: Exploring blended teacher roles and obstacles to success when using personalized learning software. J. Online Learn. Res. **5**, 229–250 (2019)
20. Brasiel, S., Jeong, S., Ames, C., Lawanto, K., Yuan, M., Martin, T.: Effects of educational technology on mathematics achievement for k-12 students in Utah. J. Online Learn. Res. **2**, 205–226 (2016)
21. Brodersen, R.M., Melluzzo, D.: Summary of research on online and blended learning programs that offer differentiated learning options (2017). https://eric.ed.gov/?id=ED572935
22. Karam, R., Pane, J.F., Griffin, B.A., Robyn, A., Phillips, A., Daugherty, L.: Examining the implementation of technology-based blended algebra I curriculum at scale. Educ. Technol. Res. Dev. **65**(2), 399–425 (2016). https://doi.org/10.1007/s11423-016-9498-6
23. Fazal, M., Panzano, B., Luk, K.: Evaluating the impact of blended learning: a mixed-methods study with difference-in-difference analysis. TechTrends **64**(1), 70–78 (2019). https://doi.org/10.1007/s11528-019-00429-8
24. Phillips, A., Pane, J.F., Reumann-Moore, R., Shenbanjo, O.: Implementing an adaptive intelligent tutoring system as an instructional supplement. Educ. Tech. Res. Dev. **68**(3), 1409–1437 (2020). https://doi.org/10.1007/s11423-020-09745-w
25. Carroll, J.: A model for school learning. Teach. Coll. Rec. **64**, 723–733 (1963)
26. Slavin, R.: Mastery learning reconsidered. Rev. Educ. Res. **57**, 175–213 (1987). https://doi.org/10.3102/00346543057002175
27. Batsche, G.: Multi-tiered system of supports for inclusive schools. In: Handbook of Effective Inclusive Schools: Research and Practice, pp. 183–196. Routledge Publishers, New York (2014)
28. Fuchs, D., Fuchs, L.S.: Introduction to response to intervention: what, why, and how valid is it? Read. Res. Q. **41**, 93–99 (2006)
29. Morgenthaler, L.: Start smart: Reopening school after covid learning loss (2020). https://www.edmentum.com/resources/white-papers/start-smart-reopening-school-after-covid-learning-loss
30. Schneider, M., Garg, K.: Operation reverse the loss, redux (2020). https://ies.ed.gov/director/remarks/12-9-2020.asp
31. Wiggins, G., McTighe, J.: Module I: Unpacking standards. In: The Understanding by Design Guide to Advanced Concepts in Creating and Reviewing Units, pp. 5–20. ASCD, Virginia (2012)
32. Wang, Y., Han, X., Yang, J.: Revisiting the blended learning literature: using a complex adaptive systems framework. Educ. Technol. Soc. **18**, 380–393 (2015)
33. Kemple, J.J., Segeritz, M.D., Cole, R.: Assessing early impacts of school-of-one: evidence from the three school-wide pilots. https://eric.ed.gov/?q=%22school+of+one%22&id=ED528799
34. van der Linden, W., Barrett, M., Lie, J., Diao, Q.: A system to optimize learning and educational resource availability. Paper presented at Annual Meeting of the National Council on Measurement in Education, Vancouver, Canada, April 2012
35. Margolis, J.: Three-year map growth at schools using teach to one: math (2019). https://www.newclassrooms.org/wp-content/uploads/2019/02/Three-Year-MAP-Growth-at-TtO-Schools-1.pdf

# Learner Characteristics in a Chinese Mathematical Intelligent Tutoring System

Kai-Chih Pai[1]([✉]), Bor-Chen Kuo[2], Shu-Chuan Shih[2], Huey-Min Wu[2], Hsiao-Yun Huang[3], Chih-Wei Yang[2], and Chia-Hua Lin[2]

[1] Tunghai University, Taichung, Taiwan
kcpai@thu.edu.tw
[2] National Taichung University of Education, Taichung, Taiwan
[3] Fu Jen Catholic University, New Taipei City, Taiwan

**Abstract.** The present study aims to explore the effectiveness and learner characteristics of Chinese Mathematical intelligent tutoring system in multiple mathematics subjects. Data were collected from primary school, secondary school, and college. The students' interactions were recorded in database as log files. The data were coded to fit the format of Datashop, which is a data repository and web application for researchers analyzing learning sequence of data. A learning curve visualizes changes in student learning state over interactions on different mathematics subjects. The results of learning characteristics of students were discussed. Furthermore, the study compared students' learning patterns in three different score groups (high, medium, and low). The results found that students with lower pre-test score received more prompting in their interaction comparing students with higher pre-test score. More learning patterns were discussed.

**Keywords:** ITS · Learning analytics · Learner characteristics · Learning curve

## 1 Introduction

Artificial intelligence (AI) has been implemented in the educational environment through intelligent tutoring systems (ITSs). ITSs aim to provide adaptive instruction and feedback to learners without teachers. In the past, ITSs have been developed in various fields, such as computer literacy, reading literacy, mathematics, and so on. Moreover, the development of ITSs in mathematics has been widely implemented in different learning stages and programs, such as Cognitive Tutor (grades 9 to 12), Mathia (grades 6 to 8), and ALEKS (K to grade 12) [1, 2]. When students need assistance with a math problem, ITSs can provide step-by-step problem-solving instructions or simply offer hints [3].

Conversational intelligent tutoring systems have been developed to help students learn domain knowledge by inputting phrases, words, or choosing a correct answer. One examples of such a system is AutoTutor [2]. Previous studies have implemented conversational ITSs in multiple domains, including physics, computer literacy, and mathematics [4].

© Springer Nature Switzerland AG 2021
R. A. Sottilare and J. Schwarz (Eds.): HCII 2021, LNCS 12792, pp. 382–393, 2021.
https://doi.org/10.1007/978-3-030-77857-6_27

ITS applications have shown significant learning improvement when compared with conventional instruction [5]. In recent years, the study of the effectiveness of ITSs has apparently moved from instruction experiments to explore students' learning characteristics. For example, research has analyzed the learner interaction data from different perspectives (learner, teacher, and material designer), here by exploring the different user interfaces of the system [6]. According to an analysis of the learner process based on interaction data, they could provide important information to determine the learner's learning status during the learning steps. On the other hand, some studies have explored the difference between the instructional vision and learners' learning performance by analyzing the interaction data through PSLC DataShop [7]. These studies have explored the relationship between a learning sequence and learning performance.

The present study aims to explore the effectiveness and learner characteristics of a Chinese mathematical intelligent tutoring system used in multiple mathematics subjects at different learning stages.

# 2 Method

## 2.1 Chinese Conversational Mathematical Intelligent Tutoring System

The Chinese Conversational Mathematical Intelligent Tutoring System was developed based on the concept framework of ITSs and AutoTutor [8]. The system consists of four main modules: domain model, tutoring model, student model, and interface model. Figure 1 demonstrates the procedure of the system. The four modules are described below.

**Domain Model.** The domain model is designed based on knowledge structures. The knowledge structures are constructed by domain experts. Figure 2 demonstrates an example of the sequence of the concepts in one topic: the application of linear equations with one unknown. Each topic contains several main concepts with main practice problems. For each problem, there was an ideal answer, some expected answers, misconceptions, and instructional contents.

**Tutoring Model.** The system develops the tutoring model based on the human tutor and expectation and misconception-tailored dialogue (EMT) dialogue in AutoTutor [2, 9]. Each expectation contains a series of instructional information to assist students in constructing their mathematics concepts. Four types of tutoring feedbacks are provided for each expectation: pump, hint, prompt, and assertion and construct a cycle of tutoring loop. Students interact with one or two conversational agents to learn mathematics by typing equations, texts, drag-and-drop objects, and choosing correct answers [8]. The system immediately gives instructional feedbacks based on the students' responses and assesses whether they are correct, incorrect, or if there are any misconceptions. For one agent design, the computer agent as a tutor to assist students to solve the math problems. For two agents design, a teacher and a peer student will interact with students. Students collaborate with peer student to solve the problem. The peer student sometimes gives wrong answer that need students to correct. The teacher agent is designed to provide

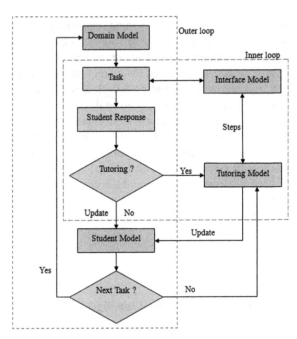

**Fig. 1.** The procedure of Chinese Conversational Mathematical Intelligent Tutoring System [8].

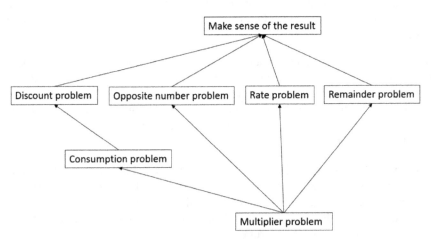

**Fig. 2.** The knowledge structure for the application of linear equations with one unknown.

instructional explanation and correct information for assisting students to enhance learning. In general, the system provides a series of dialogue moves and instructional prompts for students to articulate the expectations and identify the misconceptions.

**Fig. 3.** The interface of math ITS (input math equation)

**Student Model.** In the Chinese conversational mathematical intelligent tutoring system, some different algorithms were implemented to evaluate students' answers and update their learning styles. A block-based matching analysis for matching mathematical equations was used [10]. On the other hand, a latent semantic analysis and regular expression were used for evaluating students' natural language [2].

**Interface Model.** The interface of the Chinese Conversational Mathematical Intelligent Tutoring System consists of four major interface components, including one or two conversational agents, dialogue window , content or questions display, and response typing [8]. For one computer agent, the agent was designed as a tutor to help students understand the math concepts and solve the problem. In contrast, for two agents, a teacher and peer student will interact with learners on each topic. The peer student agent may provide incorrect answers as a way to have learners try to correct the answer. The teacher tutor will give the correct answer when the learner makes incorrect answers over several attempts. In the content or questions display, the questions are shown as pictures for the learner to review, and the system also provides the instruction video or content for the learner to observe. In the response typing, the students can input their answers, include math formula, phrases, words, drag-and-drop objects, or choose one or two answers, which is displayed in the lower area. Figures 3, 4, and 5 demonstrate the interface of our math ITS, including the type of math equations, input phrases, and drag-and-drop objects (Fig. 6).

**Fig. 4.** The interface of math ITS (input phrases, words)

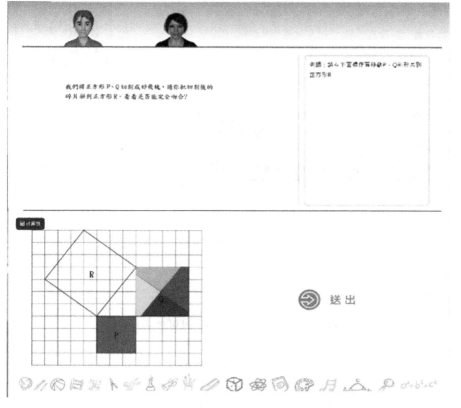

**Fig. 5.** The interface of math ITS (drag and drop)

## 2.2 Experiment Topics

The present study developed several learning topics in primary school, secondary school, and college. Some major math knowledge components (KCs) (see Fig. 7) can be found in each topic, which also contains the main problems, and instructional feedback was designed for each KC. Each problem consists of four instructional scripts: ideal answer, expected answers, misconceptions, and instruction content (Table 1).

## 2.3 Data Analysis

Looking at the effect size, the present study detected significant differences between the pretest and posttest. The effect size helps researchers understand the magnitude of the differences found in learning performance. Moreover, the study further analyzed stu-

**Fig. 6.** The instructional material of math ITS

**Table 1.** Experiment topics.

| Topic | Domain school |
|---|---|
| Fraction multiplication and division | Primary school |
| Application of linear equations with one unknown | Secondary school |
| Pythagoras theorem | Secondary school |
| Calculus limit | College level |

dents' learning patterns through a learning curve tool, which was developed by Carnegie Mellon University. The learning curve visualizes the changes in student learning status in the interactions on different mathematics topics. According to the results of the learning curve, we could better understand the learning patterns in each topic; here, the shape of the learning curves may reveal opportunities for improving the domain model, the instructional activities, and their sequence [11]. On the other hand, the present study further explored the relationship between the different learning performance groups and interaction frequencies to examine the internal validation of the Chinese conversational math ITS.

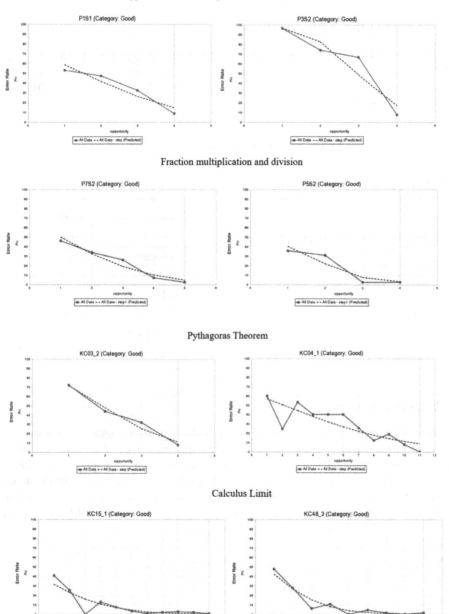

**Fig. 7.** Learning curves in the "good" category

# 3 Results

## 3.1 Learning Effectiveness

Table 2 presents the learning effect size on the different learning topics. The results of the ANCOVA indicated a significant difference between the means of the two instruction groups. Compared with conventional instruction, the students learned using the math ITS showed better performance.

**Table 2.** The effect size of different math subjects

| Subject | Condition | Effect size |
|---|---|---|
| Fraction multiplication and division | Math ITS | 0.794 |
| | Classroom | 0.599 |
| Application of linear equations with one unknown | Math ITS | 1.074 |
| | Classroom | 0.823 |
| Pythagoras theorem | Math ITS | 0.514 |
| | Classroom | 0.369 |
| Calculus limit | Math ITS | 1.169 |
| | Classroom | 0.875 |

## 3.2 Learning Curve

In total, three types of learning curves were found in our study. Figure 7 shows that the learning curve reveals improvement in student performance (i.e., error rate decreases) as the opportunity count (i.e., practice with a given knowledge component) increases. This indicates that the tutoring interaction is helpful for students learning mathematics concepts. However, Fig. 8 shows that the learning curve among some KCs is not declining and still showing a high error rate from the start; this pattern indicates that KCs are needed

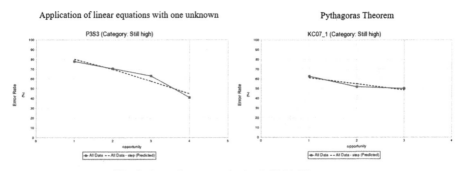

**Fig. 8.** Learning curves in the "still high" category

to have more instructional interactions with students. Figure 9 shows that the KC curve is not declining, but it is already at a low error rate from the start. This pattern indicates that the KC is already known and mastered; therefore, little to no learning is expected. For these KCs, it may be valuable to reduce the number of opportunities in the student model or take them in the tutoring model.

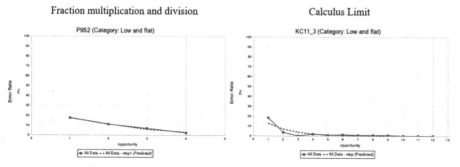

**Fig. 9.** Learning curves in the "low and flat" category

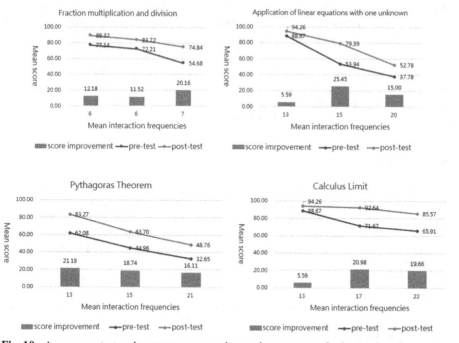

**Fig. 10.** Average pretest and posttest scores and score improvement for interactions by number of turns.

### 3.3 Students' Learning Patterns

We looked at the overall interaction behaviors to see how the students performed; this was done by comparing how many interaction turns were involved. The number of interaction frequencies is suggestive of student understanding of the targeted concepts and the practice of scientific explanation. Figure 10 shows that students who received higher scores in the pretest just needed fewer instructional interactions. Students with lower scores in the pretest needed more interactions. Students with lower scores on the pretest improved more after learning by math ITS in most math subjects.

## 4   Conclusions

The present study explored the effectiveness of a Chinese mathematical intelligent tutoring system at different learning stages. The results show that students performed better when using the Chinese Conversational Mathematical Intelligent Tutoring System. Moreover, the results of the learning curve could help us understand which topic is a good fit for mathematics learning. Indeed, some math topic materials should be revised to help students learn efficiently.

Overall, the results indicate that the Chinese Conversational Mathematical Intelligent Tutoring System with personalized feedback is helpful for learning mathematics at different learning stages. These findings are in line with previous studies [3, 4, 8], although previous studies have only focused on learning performance by comparing the pretest and posttest. The current study examined the internal validity of the Chinese Conversational Mathematical Intelligent Tutoring System by analyzing the relationship between the interaction frequencies and different score groups. These findings are additional evidence that the math ITS could improve scores for most of the students. It could also be extremely useful information for teachers to know which students required additional prompting and which topic needed to be revised.

### References

1. VanLehn, K., Graesser, A.C., Jackson, G.T., Jordan, P., Olney, A., Rose, C.P.: When are tutorial dialogues more effective than reading? Cogn. Sci. **31**, 3–62 (2007)
2. Graesser, A.C., D'Mello, S.K., Hu, X., Cai, Z., Olney, A., Morgan, B.: AutoTutor. In: McCarthy, P.M., Boonthum, C. (eds.) Applied Natural Language Processing and Content Analysis: Identification, Investigation and Resolution, pp. 169–187. IGI Global, Hershey (2012)
3. Burch, K.J., Kuo, Y.: Traditional vs. online homework in college algebra. Math. Comput. Educ. **44**, 53–63 (2010)
4. Nye, B.D., Graesser, A.C., Hu, X.: AutoTutor and family: a review of 17 years of natural language tutoring. Int. J. Artif. Intell. Educ. **24**(4), 427–469 (2014). https://doi.org/10.1007/s40593-014-0029-5
5. VanLehn, K.: The relative effectiveness of human tutoring, intelligent tutoring systems, and other tutoring systems. Educ. Psychol. **46**(4), 197–221 (2011)
6. Rudzewitz, B., Ziai, R., Nuxoll, F., Kuthy, K., Meurers, W.D.: Enhancing a web-based language tutoring system with learning analytics. In: EDM (2019)

7.  Harpstead, E., Aleven, V., MacLellan, C.J., Koedinger, K.R.: Using data to explore the differences between instructional vision and student performance. In: the 32nd SIGCHI Conference on Human Factors in Computing Systems (2014)
8.  Pai, K.C., Kuo, B.C., Liao, C.H., Liu, Y.M.: An application of Chinese dialogue-based intelligent tutoring system in remedial instruction for mathematics learning. Educ. Psychol. (2020)
9.  Graesser, A.C.: Conversations with AutoTutor help students learn. Int. J. Artif. Intell. Educ. 26(1), 124–132 (2016). https://doi.org/10.1007/s40593-015-0086-4
10. Yang, C.W., Kuo, B.C., Liao, C.H.: A HO-IRT based diagnostic assessment system with constructed response items. Turk. Online J. Educ. Technol. TOJET 10, 46–51 (2011)
11. Koedinger, K., Booth, J.L., Klahr, D.: Instructional complexity and the science to constrain it. Science 342(6161), 935–937 (2013)

# Evaluation Methods for an AI-Supported Learning Management System: Quantifying and Qualifying Added Values for Teaching and Learning

Lisa Rerhaye[1]([⊠]), Daniela Altun[1], Christopher Krauss[2], and Christoph Müller[2]

[1] Fraunhofer FKIE, Zanderstraße 5, 53225 Bonn, Germany
lisa.rerhaye@fkie.fraunhofer.de
[2] Fraunhofer FOKUS, Kaiserin-Augusta-Allee 31, 10589 Berlin, Germany

**Abstract.** Artificial intelligence offers great opportunities for the future, including for teaching and learning. Applications such as personalized recommendations and learning paths based on learning analytics [i.e. 1], the integration of serious games in intelligent tutoring systems [2], intelligent agents in the form of chatbots [3], and other emerging applications promise great benefits for individualized digital learning. However, what value do these applications really add and how can these benefits be measured?

With this article, we would like to give a brief overview of AI-supported functionalities for learning management system as well as their possible benefits for future learning environments. Furthermore, we outline methods for a comprehensive evaluation that meets the users' needs and concretizes the actual benefit of an AI-supported LMS.

**Keywords:** Artificial intelligence · Learning management systems · Evaluation

## 1 Trend Toward Intelligent Learning Environments

The design and development of digital learning environments has gained tremendous momentum. Current constraints due to the Corona pandemic are fueling the development of multifunctional, intelligent learning platforms that will give a new face to the future of learning. Shengquan Yu describes the following trends that challenge creators of learning environments: Future education (1) should consider the individualization and diversity of students, (2) can promote all-round development of learners, (3) is lifelong and comprehensive learning in real life, and (4) will be increasingly social. Personalization, adaptability, and selectivity are the keywords associated with future education. "Students in the future will not have to follow a fixed curriculum, sit in a fixed class, and learn in a fixed rhythm" [4]. Instead, future education will be more flexible. New technology will support future schools by accurately judging the learner's cognition, capability, and emotion to present strategies and methods most fit for a learner, and artificial intelligence will co-work with teachers to highlight their respective advantages [4].

© Springer Nature Switzerland AG 2021
R. A. Sottilare and J. Schwarz (Eds.): HCII 2021, LNCS 12792, pp. 394–411, 2021.
https://doi.org/10.1007/978-3-030-77857-6_28

Although some modern school formats already exist, they are far from being widespread. Furthermore, the increasing demand for lifelong learning in the future means that more learning will take place at work or during leisure time. The challenges for the school of the future are thus transferable to all areas of life in which learning takes place.

Many learning technologies are flooding the market before their clear benefit is determined. This is where this article comes in. In the following, we would like to present popular examples of AI functionalities for digital learning environments and possibilities for its evaluation.

### 1.1 Terms and Definitions in the Context of Learning Environments

The digitization of learning is particularly evident in the proliferation of digital learning environments such as Learning Management Systems (LMSs). LMSs are the central entry points to the educational content for learners and teachers. Schulmeister [5] summarized what is meant by LMSs: In contrast to mere collections of teaching scripts or hypertext collections on web servers, LMSs are software systems that have the following functions:

- a user administration (login with encryption);
- course management (courses, content management, file management)
- a role and rights assignment with differentiated rights;
- communication methods (chat or forums) and tools for learning and note taking (e.g. whiteboard, notebook, calendar, etc.);
- the presentation of course content, learning objects and media in a network-compatible browser;
- the ability to create learning content yourself without programming knowledge (not a mandatory component of an LMS, but quite a few of these systems include tools for so-called authoring) and
- storage of learning level data.

Current developments of learning platforms include intelligent functionalities. "An Intelligent Learning Management System (ILMS) is a personalized adaptive (reactive) and pro-active LMS which displays contents to the current user, based on his or her exhibited knowledge, skills and chosen learning style" [6]. ILMS should support features and tools like automation, mapping, scaffolding, mobility, reporting and knowledge generating to be able to provide the best learning-path and learning-content to the learner. Despite all these functionalities, it is important to provide its users the ability to keep under control his/her own learning and be able to turn off the AI functionalities to allow full access to all materials. Usability and time consumption should not be affected negatively [6].

Mavrikis and Holmes [7] use the term Intelligent Learning Environments (ILE) "(…) as a broad category of digital educational interactive applications equipped with features that enable the provision of personalized, adaptive support to students (either by means of task selection or adaptation, or dynamic assistance while students are undertaking a task)". Among other components (such as the actual learning environment or user interface), an intelligent system usually involves three 'models': The learner model, the pedagogy model and the domain model. The learner model represents information about the students, i.e. preferences, achievements, challenges, and emotional states (both for all the students who have used the system so far and for the individual student). The pedagogy model represents strategies for teaching and learning, i.e. collaborative learning, feedback and approaches to assessment. The domain model represents knowledge about the subject that the system is aiming to help the student learn, i.e. mathematical procedures or the laws of physics. "The system's algorithms draw on these three models to adapt the learning content to the individual student" [7]. Mavrikis and Holmes conclude that systems like these are far from displacing teachers or tutors, but instead they are able to augment the human aspects of teaching.

Another term used in the context of digital learning platforms is Learning Experience Platform (LXP). Learners receive a kind of personal learning cockpit on an LXP, in which they can control and monitor their learning content themselves. A personal profile, planned career paths, and individual challenges and tasks provide structure to the system. Human Resources Development should also be involved here. An LXP also promotes collaboration and social learning within the company [description adapted from 8].

Kuo and Hu [9] stress, that all three terms intelligent, learning, and environment are heavily loaded, and their meanings are changing as a function of theoretical (cognitive psychology, computer sciences and AI) breakthroughs and technological (learning technology) advances. Intelligent is no longer just people but increasingly systems, learning is no longer just the learner but also the system, and the learning environment is shifting more and more from face-to-face to online courses or a mix of both [9]. Smart or Intelligent Learning Environments, intelligent learning platforms, learning experience platforms, etc. have in common that they all strive for a digital learning environment that makes learning, teaching, creating and administering learning content as efficient, effective and fun as possible.

### 1.2 AI-Supported Functionalities in LMS and Their Possible Benefits

**AI-supported Chatbots/Virtual Tutors.** In the context of LMS's, an AI-supported chatbot is a digital chat solution, sometimes referred to as a "virtual tutor" [10] or "virtual coach", that can respond to user questions in regards to learning courses, present current knowledge levels and/or present simple contents and definitions (e.g., from a glossary) [11].

*Functionality.* The AI backend is responsible for understanding the text input by the user. Natural Language Understanding (NLU/NLP) and Intent Classification with supervised deep learning are commonly used in the scenario. Examples of this include usual greetings or introductionary messages like "Hello", "What should I learn today". These systems generate answers/responses to the users input with common dialogue management and Natural Language Generation (NLG) and Supervised Deep Learning or Reinforcement Learning. Common generated answers can be, for instance "I have similar topics you might be interested in: […]", "Based on your profile and test history, you should learn […] today" or simple definitions, e.g. "A vector is a geometric object".

*Benefits.* Chatbots or virtual tutors are integrable into external messenger applications, such as Slack or Telegram, and they have a motivating effect. Furthermore, recommender systems, that are based on predicted future behavior of concerned learners and strengthen students that have a more difficult time in academia, can provide helpful learning suggestions via those Chatbots. Moreover, statistics from chatbots can increase training data for recommender systems.

**Personal Learning Recommendations/Adaptive Learning/Content Curation.** Recommender Systems help to personalize learning environments through individual content suggestions that fit the learner's needs and help to identify suitable items for learning and teaching tasks from a wide range of available learning resources [12]. Individual suggestions for learning content are usually based on the learner's interaction with the LMS as well as his/her past performance (e.g. through evaluated tests). Recommended items are [13]: Learning Objects within a course, entire courses or learning modules, suggested groups or single classmates for collaborative learning, or external material. Recommender Systems in the context of LMS can also support custom content curation to boost content relevance and content accessibility for individual learner types [14].

Recommendations can be determined by the following principles [13]:

- Content-based Filtering (CbF) based on items, the metadata of those items and the attributes of the user profile.
- Collaborative Filtering (CF) is usually based on consumption histories of similar users. However, in educational contexts it is essential to first identify successful learning patterns in the users' histories and then transfer those patterns to other learners.
- Knowledge-based Filtering (KbF), based on the extracted understanding of the user's needs. This can be based on the learner's preferences – as known from the entertainment domain. However, in learning environments it is more effective to first analyze the learning need of a user for a learning object and recommend items based on this relevance score. "For instance, learners tell the system that they are beginners in specific topic areas, and the system starts filtering appropriate items based on this information."
- Hybrid Filtering (HF), based on a combination of the previous approaches.

*Benefits.* Learner-tailored guidance that helps learners reach a course goal can help to make the content selection more efficient and effective; it allows learners to reach course objectives, like passing an exam. It utilizes collaborate filtering approach to consider successful and 'weak' learners, 'personal' aspect comes into play when learner types and successes of each are differentiated. Furthermore, it changes LMS from "static" to dynamic platform, which adapts to its users individual needs and preferred learning styles [15].

**(Personalized) Learning Paths.** Learning paths represent the sequence and set of the available learning objects that are essential to study in order to reach the course goal or a personal learning goal. Personalized learning paths can be automatically determined individually for each learner based on factors like existing skills and prior interaction with the LMS, like test results, to best fit his needs and to ensure an optimal learning experience.

Determination of a best possible learning path can be based on [1]:

- Content-based analysis,
- Tutor-objectives and didactic sequences,
- Fulfillment of preconditions or exclusion criteria,
- Knowledge or activity-based approaches,
- as well as hybrid combinations.

*Benefits.* Optimal adjustment of the roadmap of training materials, especially in a limited timeframe [16]; individual learning paths, especially those constructed with input from the learner, can boost learning experience [17]. Learning paths, coupled with personal learning recommendations, can also help identify "at-risk students" and offer hints/learning objects, to minimize the risk of course failure [18].

**Learning Analytics.** Learning Analytics enables teachers to observe the overall or detailed progress and performance of students and figure out weaknesses in learning and understanding [19]. It supports the Smart Learning Recommender infrastructure in building a foundation for collecting learning data and integrates educational recommender systems [20].

*Benefits.* Supports several computer-assisted educational tasks [1], such as the course review for accuracy, by collecting and processing students' learning activities, and automatically providing hints for the instructional staff. For instance, knowing which learning objects or courses have a high failure rate can indicate necessary changes to the learning material [21]. It supports the assessment of learners' ability in grasping learning objectives by analyzing learning activity logs and providing automatic feedback for both learners and instructors. Efficiency in course registration: along with payment processors, learning analytics allow interested users to register for courses independently without supervision of educational specialists.

### 1.3   Miscellaneous AI-Based Trends in LMS/LXP

**Educational Data Mining (EDM).** Large-scale data that is derived from educational settings, such as interactive learning environments, computer-supported collaborative learning or administrative data from schools and universities [22].

**Administrative Task Automation.** Description: Administrative Task Automation represents a self-regulated system for educational organizations and administrative staff. Tasks that can be automated include grading (homework, essays, and exams), payments, classification and processing of paperwork, etc. [16].

*Benefits.* Time saved in grading individual student assignments, especially when multiple tests are involved. As a result, educators can spend more one-on-one time with those who require personal assistance in learning [17]. Grading Assessments: Reduction in human-made errors when it comes to grading.

**Smart Testing.** Based on users individual learning types, an AI supported testing module can customize single test questions or entire test modalities to suit the learning style of different learners [23]. "Weaker" learners, sometimes classified as "at-risk students" can get additional quizzes or custom-tailored tests before an evaluated exam, to boost their performance for the final test [17].

# 2  Evaluation of AI-Supported Functionalities in Learning Contexts

Evaluation is the "systematic investigation of the worth or merit of an object" [24]. In more detail, it is "the identification, clarification, and application of defensible criteria to determine an evaluation object's value, quality, utility, effectiveness, or significance in relation to those criteria" [25, see also 26].

Evaluations can aim to achieve four interrelated goals: (1) the acquisition of knowledge, (2) the exercise of control, (3) the creation of transparency in order to enable dialogue, and/or (4) the documentation of success (legitimation) [27]. In addition, evaluations should also ensure comparability.

The requirements for evaluations can be summarized in four guiding principles. Evaluations should:

- be useful, i.e. oriented towards the information needs of the users (usefulness)
- be realistic, well thought-out, diplomatic and cost-conscious (feasibility)
- be legally and ethically correct and pay attention to the welfare of those involved in the evaluation and affected by the results (propriety); and
- produce and convey professionally appropriate information about the quality and/or usability of an evaluated program (accuracy) [27, 28].

A distinction is made between formative evaluations (during an intervention) and summative evaluations (following an intervention) [e.g. in 29]. The so-called design-based research approach according to Wang and Hannafin [30] describes formative evaluation methods during the (further) development of a technology-enhanced learning environment. They define design-based research as "a systematic but flexible methodology aimed to improve educational practices through iterative analysis, design, development, and implementation, based on collaboration among researchers and practitioners in real-world settings, and leading to contextually-sensitive design principles and theories" [30].

According to Stockmann [27], there exist two evaluation paradigms: (1) evaluation as an empirical-scientific procedure that follows the critical-rational research logic and considers all known empirical research methods applicable. (2) The existence of an objectively ascertainable reality by empirical-scientific methods is denied. Instead, "reality" is assumed to be socially constructed from different perspectives of stakeholders that may conflict with each other. In this case, the goal of an evaluation is to change these relations in favor of the disadvantaged.

In principle, according to the first paradigm, all known research methods can be used, be it the collection of qualitative or quantitative data. Qualitative survey methods are suitable for the analysis of process-related data (program control, process, etc.), while quantitative survey and evaluation methods are to be used for the examination of the achievement of objectives, impact and causal considerations [27].

In our use case, we want to evaluate AI functionalities in digital learning environments. However, what do we actually evaluate? Most AI applications in learning environments aim at optimizing learning by making it more efficient and more effective. In context of learning recommender systems for instance, 'efficiency' describes the way to achieve a personal goal. In terms of learning in a closed-corpus setting like a course, a higher efficiency means optimizing the process, saving effort and time to reach the course goal. 'Effectiveness', in turn, directly concerns the result achieved. A higher effectiveness means to reach, e.g., a better mark in the exam or longer lasting knowledge [31].

There are also numerous approaches and attempts to measure the intelligence of a system. Fardinpour, Pedram, Burkle [6], in example, created a fuzzy model to measure the intelligence of LMS that is supposed to help clients to evaluate and choose the best LMS. In terms of evaluating an AI system, Hernández-Orallo [32] distinguishes between traditional task-oriented and ability-oriented evaluation approaches. In the first approach, AI is evaluated according to its task performance. The author names three categories of task-oriented approaches: Human discrimination, problem benchmarks and peer confrontation. In the first approach, the assessment is made by and/or against humans through observation, scrutiny and/or interview. According to the author, this kind of evaluation is not very usual in AI, except for the Turing test and its variants. Problem benchmarking means the assessment is performed against a collection or repository of problems (M), which is very frequent in AI. The peer confrontation approach describes the assessment of AI performance through a series of matches, where AI systems "play" against each other. The result is relative to the other participants. The relative values allow for a numerical comparison and performance metrics can be derived. The latter is the common approach in several domains such as games and multi-agent systems, but other AI domains could also take advantage of it, especially if systems are evaluated according to the best one in terms of resources or accuracy in a competitive way, or when the evaluation is set up as a challenge [32].

Using an ability-oriented approach, an AI-supported system is characterized by its (cognitive) abilities, rather than by the tasks it is designed to solve. The author argues that specialized AI systems require task-oriented evaluation, while general-purpose AI systems require an ability-oriented evaluation [32].

The user interface, user satisfaction and the user experience are also of enormous importance for a system with AI support to ensure user acceptance of the system. In addition, it is essential that the goals for the use of AI are being recorded together with the users. Users of such a system can be learners, teachers, and authors of learning content, but also supervisors who enter an assessment of competence into the system afterwards, as well as training managers who are responsible for the training organization. Possibilities for the use of AI on digital learning platforms can be individualized learning paths, clear learning analyses prepared for learners and teachers, as well as finding engines and authoring systems that support the search and creation of content. The goals pursued with the use of AI should always address the corresponding user needs or interests. These can be, for example, the reduction of learning time, the reduction of the time required for the creation of learning content, the increase of user motivation, the improvement of performance, an improved self-organization, or the generation of own solution paths in the sense of competence orientation.

For this purpose, standardized tests, quantitative and qualitative data collection, as well as the recording of the user state can be considered. The different possibilities of evaluation are presented in the following.

## 2.1 Qualitative Evaluation Methods

Qualitative evaluation is the application of qualitative research methods to questions of practice and program evaluation [33].

"Qualitative research is multimethod in focus, involving an interpretative, naturalistic approach to its subject matter. This means that qualitative researchers study things in their natural settings, attempting to make sense of, or interpret, phenomena in terms of the meanings people bring to them. Qualitative research involves the studied use and collection of a variety of empirical materials – case study, personal experience, introspective, life story, interview, observational, historical, interactional, and visual texts – that describe routine and problematic moments and meanings in individuals' lives" (Denzin & Lincoln, 2005, p. 2; cited in Aspers & Corte (2019). Anastas [33] defines qualitative research as "having key characteristics primarily related to the way in which the research is conducted and only partly by the form in which the data are collected, that is, in textual rather than numerical form. These characteristics are as follows:

1. flexibility of method and procedure during the conduct of the study, often in response to findings as they emerge;
2. the collection of relatively unstructured data to describe the phenomena of interest in the words or actions of those who embody or live them, often but not always implying an inductive process of assigning meaning to the data;
3. a scope of study that includes the observational context of the study, usually the one in which the phenomena of interest naturally occur, as well as the procedural decisions made during the conduct of the study, hence also describing and analyzing them; and
4. a scope of study that includes the subjective experiences of the researcher and the research participant as data while also describing and analyzing them".

Aspers and Corte [34] are defining qualitative research as "an iterative process in which improved understanding to the scientific community is achieved by making new significant distinctions resulting from getting closer to the phenomenon studied". They stress that a qualitative dimension is present in quantitative work as well.

Michael Quinn Patton, author of "Qualitative Research & Evaluation Methods: Integrating Theory and Practice" in fourth edition [35], has created a helpful, open-access checklist for qualitative evaluations [36]. He summarizes that "qualitative methods are often used in evaluations because they tell the program's story by capturing and communicating the participants' stories [...] Qualitative findings in evaluation can illuminate the people behind the numbers and put faces on the statistics to deepen understanding" [36].

In the following, we present examples of how qualitative research methods can be applied in the context of learning environments. Şahin, Yurdugül [37] used self-developed open ended questionnaire and a semi-structured interview to get insights into needs and expectations of users of learning management systems. They performed a content analysis to analyze the qualitative data. It showed that learners want more entertaining and self-monitoring environments, especially with elements of gamification. In addition, learning environments have reporting and predictive capability on student achievement. They conclude that learners' needs and expectations match with third-generation Learning Management Systems, which can be developed through educational data mining and learning analytics.

Regarding the development and implementation of new functionalities for learning environments, it is important to evaluate the perceived value of the tool by the users. Ali, Hatala, Gašević, Jovanović [38], in example, evaluated a learning analytics tool called LOCO-Analyst. They evaluated the tool in two steps: The evaluation of the first version of the tool led to the enhancement of the tool's data visualization, user interface, and supported feedback types, while the purpose of the second evaluation was to see how the improvements affected the users' perceived value of the tool. Therefore, they combined open-ended questionnaires with numerical Likert scales.

## 2.2 Quantitative Evaluation Based on Data Generated by the LMS Itself Using the Example of Recommender Systems

Quantitative evaluations of LMS focus on the analysis of numerical data of predefined outcomes. Therefore, researchers should be able to access the essential data of representative LMS. However, if the developers, e.g., of an educational recommender system, do not have access to courses, participants or learning management systems to gather the needed data, they must reuse existing datasets. Researchers have noted that besides a standardized dataset definition, there is also a lack of standardized definitions relating to evaluation procedures [39]. They suggest approaches but also comment that they must be further researched. In the following, we demonstrate the quantitative evaluation of AI-supported LMSs using the example of recommender systems.

**The Evaluation Framework.** The most important aim of an evaluation "is to measure a certain property or effect of the Recommender System" [40]. Said and Bellogin evaluated common evaluation frameworks and protocols. They conclude that the "performance of an algorithm implemented in one [evaluation framework] cannot be compared to the performance of the same algorithm in another". Their results differ by up to 10% depending on the evaluation framework. Moreover, they noticed that there "are no de facto rules or standards on how to evaluate a recommendation algorithm" [41]. Weibelzahl introduced a framework for a four-tiered evaluation procedure [42] consisting of "evaluation of input data", "evaluation of the inference mechanism", "evaluation of the adaption decision" and "evaluation of the total interaction". Manouselis [26] abstracted this to a multi-layered evaluation approach for recommender systems in technology enhanced learning which can also be reduced to only two layers: the accuracy of the model and the effectiveness of the changes made at the interface. The first layer corresponds to quantitative evaluations, relating to measurements of the algorithm's outputs, the second to qualitative assessments regarding user perceptions.

According to Said, Bellogín [41], the most important evaluation dimensions are (1) the dataset, (2) the data splitting, (3) the evaluation strategies and (4) the metrics. The work of Krauss [13] builds on these four dimensions and follows additionally the approach of Campos et al. who suggest that the following questions should be answered during each experiment:

- "MQ1: What base set is used to perform the training-test splitting?
- MQ2: What [scoring] order is used to assign [relevance scores] to the training and test sets?
- MQ3: How [much data] comprise the training and test sets?
- MQ4: What cross-validation method is used to increase the generalization of the evaluation results?
- MQ5: Which items are considered as target items (in a Top-N recommendation task)?
- MQ6: Which items are considered relevant for each user (in a Top-N recommendation task)?" [43]

The required evaluations can be either performed online - directly in a real course - or offline - with the use of existing data in a simulation. The latter can utilize either simulated data or past real-world data in a simulated environment.

**Data Splitting.** When performing an offline evaluation with historical data, the whole dataset must be split: To guarantee an objective prediction of data, the training dataset must be separated from the test dataset [44]. It is common sense that the split process happens randomly. With one restriction: at least some consumption data of the same user, who will receive recommendations, should exist in the training dataset and test dataset. If there were no data of the user in the training set, a collaborative filtering algorithm would fail because of the cold start problem. More importantly, if there are no activity data available in the test set, this user cannot be evaluated since a prediction cannot be compared with real data. Thus, either the prediction of a relevance score or the evaluation of this prediction would be impossible.

However, a total random split contradicts the specialized paradigm educational recommender systems where time plays a key role [31]. Therefore, Campos et al. suggest different specialized validation approaches for Time-Aware Recommender Systems, where two definitions seem to be appropriate for the evaluation of learning environments [43]. The "increasing-time window" approach splits the whole dataset into training set and test set according to a variable time threshold. Another approach is called the "fixed time-window" approach that works in a similar manner to the "increasing time-window" approach, but using a fixed time interval for both the training dataset and the test dataset. Researchers start considering those alternative data splitting approaches for educational recommender system evaluations because the selection of the time-window size and splitting approach could better represent real world circumstances. However, researchers should keep in mind that time-window evaluations are not comparable to standard cross-validation evaluations [13].

**Key Metrics.** A critical question regarding evaluation is: how to measure "appropriate" or "good" recommendations. Campos et al. pointed out that there is no definition of what constitutes a "good" recommendation, but "a commonly used approach is to establish the quality (goodness) of recommendations by computing different measures that assess various desired characteristics of anu RS output" [43]. Manouselis et al. recommends four high-level measures to define success criteria of Recommender Systems in TEL [26]:

- Effectiveness describes the percentage of consumed Learning Objects during a learning phase.
- Efficiency indicates the time needed by the user to reach the learning goal.
- Satisfaction is a subjective measure that must be assessed by qualitative methods.
- Drop-out rates represent the percentage of users who stop participating in the learning setting and thus do not reach the course goals.

According to Erdt et al. [40], popular performance measures in offline experiments are Mean Absolute Error, Root Mean Square Error, precision, recall and f-score. Moreover, Manouselis et al. [26] incorporated some further measures from Social Network Analysis, such as Variety, Centrality, Closeness and Cohesion, as they seem also to be valid for learning networks. Finally, a timeliness measure can indicate how long it takes between the presentation of an educational recommendation and the time at which the user should actually access this item [31].

### 2.3  Usability and User Experience Evaluation

It is a well-known fact that the usability of a product is relevant for its success and an LMS is no exception. The usability and user experience (UX) have a tremendous effect on the user acceptance and the intention to use an LMS [45]. Accordingly, many recent LMS evaluations include research methods borrowed from the field of usability/UX or even see UX as the primary concern to improve LMS [46, 47].

Usability can be defined as the "extent to which a system, product or service can be used by specified users to achieve specified goals with effectiveness, efficiency and satisfaction in a specified context of use" [48]. UX additionally includes "all the users' emotions, beliefs, preferences, perceptions, physical and psychological responses, behaviors and accomplishments that occur before, during and after use" [48]. The concepts of usability and UX are closely intertwined and so are the associated research methods. The goal of a classic usability test is to ensure that the systems fulfills the targeted users' needs. UX methods focus additionally on the users' emotions and behavior as the likeliness to recommend the used product. While these tests are usually used to improve a product, they can also be used to evaluate the benefit of AI components of an LMS.

There are two approaches to study usability and UX, qualitative and quantitative, each with its own advantages and disadvantages [49]. Qualitative methods, e.g. (semi-structured) interviews, observations, behavioral analyses, or expert evaluations can provide detailed insights, yet are often time consuming. Quantitative measures can be collected through polls, questionnaires or surveys. These methods are efficient to apply and analyze, but they do not always provide tangible insights. Therefore, a mix of quantitative and qualitative methods is recommended.

The most common quantitative methods to analyze usability and UX are questionnaires. Especially standardized questionnaires are a useful tool for A/B tests, where two different versions of a system are compared with each other. There are plenty of usability questionnaires to choose from, e.g. the System Usability Scale (SUS), Software usability Measurement Inventory (SUMI), Questionnaire for User Interaction Satisfaction (QUIS), AttrakDiff or the Usability Metric for User Experience (UMUX). The User Experience Questionnaire (UEQ) has established itself and includes usability as well as UX aspects [50]. Instead of one general score, the UEQ provides scores on the six dimensions Attractiveness, Efficiency, Dependability, Perspicuity, Stimulation, and Novelty and therefore provides a relatively specific picture of what aspects of the LMS have changed due to the artificial intelligence functionalities. These types of questionnaire can also be used to evaluate parts of the LMS, as for example chatbots. In order to do so, half of the participants should interact with a regular chatbot, the other half with an AI chatbot before answering the questionnaire.

Post-task questionnaires, like the After Scenario Questionnaire (ASQ), Subjective Mental Effort Questionnaire (SMEQ), Usability Magnitude Estimation (UME) or the Single Ease Question (SEQ) are to be used directly after completing a task and measure the subjective perception of the difficulty of that recent task. The NASA task load index (NASA TLX) uses six subscales (Mental Demand, Physical Demand, Temporal Demand, Performance, Effort, Frustration) to measure the subjective mental workload [51]. These questionnaires are very short, with most of them containing only one single question (SMEQ, UME, SEQ) with the goal to disrupt the users as little as possible. Therefore, these questionnaires can be used after each task and enable a comparison between those tasks. This makes post-task questionnaires a good tool to evaluate AI-supported LMSs, where the difficulty of the content should adapt to the users knowledge and skills. If the difficulty of the content adjusts to the user perfectly, post task questionnaires should show less signs of insufficient challenge or excessive demand.

Additionally, performance data can be collected, i.e. students' marks. If the performance data improves or stays at the same level while students need less time learning with the LMS, it might indicate that the AI successfully eliminated irrelevant learning content. Users spending less time searching for learning content might indicate a successful recommender system. However, it is important to note that these measures can be ambiguous and falsely interpreted. If the usability/ UX of the LMS declines, users might spend less time on the LMS as well. Therefore, this method should always be combined with other tools, as questionnaires or interviews, to ask directly about the reason of the changed behavior.

While usability tests offer many ways for an evaluation of an AI-supported LMS, there are some disadvantages. First, the usability tests always measure the current state and not the idea behind a functionality. AI components need input to work effectively, meaning that these tests can only discover a benefit if the AI components are evolved. AI components can also complicate the User Interface by adding new functionalities. Therefore, the usability can decline while the AI functionalities still have a benefit for the learners. Accordingly, mixing methods to gain a broader understanding of the users' perception is strongly advised.

### 2.4 Using the Assessment of the Learner's Mental State for Evaluation

Adaptive Instructional Systems (AIS) aim to support the learner by dynamically providing feedback tailored to the individual learner's needs. To select the appropriate type and level of content or support, an adaptive learning system should gather on-task information of the user state, i.e. the learner's current mental state. The Real-Time Assessment of Multidimensional User State (RASMUS) is an example for a rule-based diagnostic framework providing information on task performance and up to six user states affecting performance, namely mental stress, emotional state, motivation, fatigue, attention, and situational awareness [52, 53].

The assessment of user states is not only a method to support the development of AIS; it is also promising in the context of evaluating AI-supported systems. Information on mental state changes can provide insight into whether a learning content is over- or under-challenging, or whether it is time for a break from learning. Under-challenge manifests itself in boredom and mental "shutting down", which can result, for example, in decreased receptivity, decreased motivation, or decreased effectiveness of training. Over-challenge shows itself, for example, through surrender or frustration, which can also lower motivation or the effectiveness of the training.

The disadvantage of an evaluation based on user state detection is the necessity of using specific hardware that makes it possible to measure user states, for example eye-tracking, EEG [54] or a pressure-sensitive mouse [55]. The latter seems to be a promising approach to keep the effort regarding the required hardware as small as possible. Nevertheless, user state assessment is an evaluation method that enables an objective, user-centered, real-time diagnosis of the effect of the learning system on the learner. The results of the user state analysis could also be used to evaluate AI functionalities in LMS following learning periods. Were the tasks set at an adequate level, i.e., neither over- nor under-challenging? What was the course of the learner's emotional and motivational state over the learning period and how does this relate to the AI-support?

## 3 Summary and Best Practice

The result of this paper is an overview of possible evaluation methods for specific AI functionalities integrated in Learning Management Systems. As part of every system evaluation, usability and UX should be considered as the basis of an adaptive, user-centered (learning) system. If the requirements of usability and UX are not met, it can also have a negative impact on the evaluation of the AI functionalities. User state assessment seems to be a promising approach for objective evaluation, but more research is needed in this area. We recommend the combination of qualitative and quantitative, as well as objective and subjective evaluation methods. Involving the actual users of the LMS in the development of appropriate AI functionalities is important to determine the need and the actual benefit.

Artificial intelligence offers a lot of potential to make learning more effective and efficient, to support teachers in teaching and media creators in optimizing teaching materials [56]. However, several prerequisites must be met for the successful use of AI. These are briefly discussed here based on the authors' practical experience.

On the one hand, it is important that the target group and its exact needs can be named. AI projects often fail because although rough requirements are formulated, they are not tailored to a demonstrable benefit for the target group. To this end, it is first necessary to analyze who the actual users of the system are and how the processes to be improved have been carried out to date. Ideally, this is accompanied by qualitative and quantitative studies of the current state. These will also serve later as a starting point and proof of improvement. The specified requirements should result in a demonstrable research question, which can optionally be divided into smaller hypotheses. For a clearly comprehensible methodological procedure, the evaluation criteria must then be designed, which will later serve to compare the old and new systems.

After that, the appropriate foundations for the use of AI must be created. If Artificial Intelligence is to improve learning in closed courses, just to give an example, it should first be possible for the teaching itself to take place digitally. This requires not only appealing digital learning media, for example consisting of machine interpretable texts, interactive exercises, animations and videos, but also the use of a learning management system designed for these media. With AI, it would be difficult to improve learning if much of the learning material is not machine readable (e.g., based on PDFs that are merely scans of handwritten scripts).

Furthermore, it is important that the right data is available to the AI components. To increase reusability, there are interoperable standards and specifications for the respective data types. For the description of skills and competencies, for example, the ESCO [57] format of the European Union is suitable. Learning content can be described by LOM [58] and digital exercises by QTI [59] (both from IMS Global). One of the most important aspects, however, is the recording of learning behavior, via so-called learning records, for which, CALIPER [60] (IMS Global) or xAPI [61] (ADL) can be used. These standards can be used to formally describe a large data set, while at the same time taking data protection into account by the ability of pseudonymizing or anonymizing user data. Some projects, such as the Common Learning Middleware [62], enable interoperable infrastructures and thus support the incorporation of AI features without technical barriers.

The actual work of designing and implementing the AI components follows - always with the research question in mind. At regular intervals, the improvement achieved so far should be iteratively evaluated and the results fed back to optimize the AI algorithms. Finally, the overall result can be evaluated and the answer to the research question can be discussed.

# References

1. Krauss, C., Salzmann, A., Merceron, A.: Branched learning paths for the recommendation of personalized sequences of course items. In: Schiffner, D. (ed.) Proceedings of DeLFI Workshops 2018 co-located with 16th e-Learning Conference of the German Computer Society (DeLFI 2018) (2018)

2. Beyyoudh, M., Idrissi, M.K., Bennani, S.: A new approach of integrating serious games in intelligent tutoring systems. In: Serrhini, M., Silva, C., Aljahdali, S. (eds.) EMENA-ISTL 2019. LAIS, vol. 7, pp. 85–91. Springer, Cham (2020). https://doi.org/10.1007/978-3-030-36778-7_10

3. Nenkov, N., Dimitrov, G., Dyachenko, Y., et al.: Artificial intelligence technologies for personnel learning management systems. In: 2016 IEEE 8th International Conference on Intelligent Systems (IS), pp. 189–195. IEEE (2016)

4. Yu, S., Niemi, H., Mason, J. (eds.): Shaping Future Schools with Digital Technology. PRRE, Springer, Singapore (2019). https://doi.org/10.1007/978-981-13-9439-3

5. Schulmeister, R.: Lernplattformen für das virtuelle Lernen: Evaluation und Didaktik (2003)

6. Fardinpour, A., Pedram, M.M., Burkle, M.: Intelligent learning management systems. Int. J. Distance Educ. Technol. **12**, 19–31 (2014). https://doi.org/10.4018/ijdet.2014100102

7. Mavrikis, M., Holmes, W.: Intelligent learning environments: design, usage and analytics for future schools. In: Yu, S., Niemi, H., Mason, J. (eds.) Shaping Future Schools with Digital Technology. PRRE, pp. 57–73. Springer, Singapore (2019). https://doi.org/10.1007/978-981-13-9439-3_4

8. Köhnen, B.: Learning Experience Plattformen (2019). https://www.haufe-akademie.de/digitales-lernen/magazin/learning-experience-plattformen?chorid=04330006&em_src=kw&em_cmp=google%2Fdl%2Fhlx%2F82119%2F04330006&wnr=04330006&gclid=EAIaIQobChMI0umYtLbk7gIVSuDtCh3KfgsTEAAYASABEgLVS_D_BwE. Accessed 12 Feb 2021

9. Kuo, B.-C., Hu, X.: Intelligent learning environments. Educ. Psychol. **39**, 1195–1198 (2019). https://doi.org/10.1080/01443410.2019.1669334

10. HR Technologist: Emerging Trends for AI in Learning Management Systems (2019). https://www.hrtechnologist.com/articles/learning-development/emerging-trends-for-ai-in-the-learning-management-system/. Accessed 12 Feb 2019

11. Softengi AI-powered LMS (Learning Management System). https://softengi.com/blog/ai-blog/ai-powered-lms-learning-management-system/. Accessed 12 Feb 2021

12. Verbert, K., Drachsler, H., Manouselis, N., et al.: Dataset-driven research for improving recommender systems for learning. In: Long, P., Siemens, G., Conole, G., et al. (eds.) Proceedings of the 1st International Conference on Learning Analytics and Knowledge - LAK 2011, pp. 44–53. ACM Press, New York (2011)

13. Krauss, C.: Time-dependent recommender systems for the prediction of appropriate learning objects. Technische Universität Berlin (2018)

14. BigData MadeSimple: Is artificial intelligence (AI) the next step of smart learning? (2019). https://bigdata-madesimple.com/is-artificial-intelligence-ai-the-next-step-of-smart-learning/. Accessed 12 Feb 2021

15. zeomag: How will AI and Machine Learning revolutionize e-learning? (2018). https://www.zeolearn.com/magazine/how-will-ai-and-machine-learning-revolutionize-e-learning. Accessed 12 Feb 2021

16. docebo: Enterprise E-Learning Trends 2020 A New Era of Learning (2019). https://uhlberg-advisory.de/wp-content/uploads/2019/11/Docebo-Enterprise-E-Learning-Trends-2020.pdf. Accessed 12 Feb 2021

17. GYRUS: What are the must-haves in an AI-based LMS (2020). https://www.gyrus.com/What-are-the-must-haves-in-an-AI-based-LMS. Accessed 12 Feb 2021

18. Kondo, N., Okubo, M., Hatanaka, T.: Early detection of at-risk students using machine learning based on LMS log data. In: 2017 6th IIAI International Congress Juli 2017, pp. 198–201 (2017)

19. eLearning Industry: eLearning Trends To Watch Out For In 2021 (2020). https://elearningindustry.com/elearning-technology-and-content-trends-2021. Accessed 12 Feb 2021

20. forma LMS: E-learning Trends 2021 (2021). https://www.formalms.org/articles/22-elearning-trends-technology/229-e-learning-trends-2021.html. Accessed 12 Feb 2021

21. eThink: Artificial Intelligence in the Workplace: The Future of the L&D Landscape (2020). https://ethinkeducation.com/blog/artificial-intelligence-workplace-future-ld-landscape/. Accessed 12 Feb 2021
22. ideal: AI For Recruiting: A Definitive Guide For HR Professionals (2017). https://ideal.com/ai-recruiter-skillset/. Accessed 12 Feb 2021
23. tituslearning: 5 ways artificial intelligence can be used in eLearning (2020). https://www.tit uslearning.com/artificial-intelligence-elearning. Accessed 12 Feb 2021
24. Sanders, J.R.: The Program Evaluation Standards: How to Assess Evaluations of Educational Programs, 2 edn. SAGE, Thousand Oaks (1998). 6 [printing]
25. Fitzpatrick, J.L., Sanders, J.R., Worthen, B.R.: Program Evaluation: Alternative Approaches and Practical Guidelines, 4th edn. Pearson Education, Upper Saddle River, Montreal (2011)
26. Manouselis, N., Drachsler, H., Vuorikari, R., Hummel, H., Koper, R.: Recommender systems in technology enhanced learning. In: Ricci, F., Rokach, L., Shapira, B., Kantor, P.B. (eds.) Recommender Systems Handbook, pp. 387–415. Springer, Boston, MA (2011). https://doi.org/10.1007/978-0-387-85820-3_12
27. Stockmann, R.: Was ist eine gute Evaluation? Einführung zu Funktionen und Methoden von Evaluationsverfahren: (CEval-Arbeitspapier, 9). Universität des Saarlandes, Fak. 05 Empirische, Saarbrücken (2004)
28. Böttcher, W., Caspari, A., Hense, J., et al.: Standards für Evaluation, Erste Revision 2016, Mainz (2017)
29. Brahm, T., Jenert, T.: Technologieeinsatz von der Bedarfsanalyse bis zur Evaluation. In: Ebner, M., Schön, S. (eds.) Lehrbuch für Lernen und Lehren mit Technologien: [L3T], [Stand:] Mai 2011, pp. 127–134. Books on Demand, Norderstedt (2011)
30. Wang, F., Hannafin, M.J.: Design-based research and technology-enhanced learning environments. ETR&D 53, 5–23 (2005). https://doi.org/10.1007/BF02504682
31. Krauss, C., Merceron, A., Arbanowski, S.: The timeliness deviation: a novel approach to evaluate educational recommender systems for closed-courses. In: Proceedings of the 9th International Conference on Learning Analytics & Knowledge (LAK19), pp. 195–204. ACM, New York (2019). https://doi.org/10.1145/3303772.3303774
32. Hernández-Orallo, J.: Evaluation in artificial intelligence: from task-oriented to ability-oriented measurement. Artif. Intell. Rev. 48(3), 397–447 (2016). https://doi.org/10.1007/s10 462-016-9505-7
33. Anastas, J.W.: Quality in qualitative evaluation: issues and possible answers. Res. Soc. Work Pract. 14, 57–65 (2004). https://doi.org/10.1177/1049731503257870
34. Aspers, P., Corte, U.: What is qualitative in qualitative research. Qual. Sociol. 42(2), 139–160 (2019). https://doi.org/10.1007/s11133-019-9413-7
35. Patton, M.Q.: Qualitative Research & Evaluation Methods: Integrating Theory and Practice, 4th edn. SAGE, Los Angeles (2015)
36. Patton, M.Q.: Qualitative Evaluation Checklist (2003)
37. Şahin, M., Yurdugül, H.: Learners' needs in online learning environments and third generation learning management systems (LMS 3.0). Tech. Know. Learn. (2020). https://doi.org/10.1007/s10758-020-09479-x
38. Ali, L., Hatala, M., Gašević, D., et al.: A qualitative evaluation of evolution of a learning analytics tool. Comput. Educ. 58, 470–489 (2012). https://doi.org/10.1016/j.compedu.2011.08.030
39. Drachsler, H., Bogers, T., Vuorikari, R., et al.: Issues and considerations regarding sharable data sets for recommender systems in technology enhanced learning. Procedia Comput. Sci. 1, 2849–2858 (2010). https://doi.org/10.1016/j.procs.2010.08.010
40. Erdt, M., Fernandez, A., Rensing, C.: Evaluating recommender systems for technology enhanced learning: a quantitative survey. IEEE Trans. Learn. Technol. 8, 326–344 (2015). https://doi.org/10.1109/TLT.2015.2438867

41. Said, A., Bellogín, A.: Comparative recommender system evaluation. In: Kobsa, A., Zhou, M., Ester, M., et al. (eds.) Proceedings of the 8th ACM Conference on Recommender systems - RecSys 2014, pp. 129–136. ACM Press, New York (2014)
42. Weibelzahl, S.: Evaluation of adaptive systems. In: Bauer, M., Gmytrasiewicz, P.J., Vassileva, J. (eds.) UM 2001. LNCS (LNAI), vol. 2109, pp. 292–294. Springer, Heidelberg (2001). https://doi.org/10.1007/3-540-44566-8_49
43. Campos, P.G., Díez, F., Cantador, I.: Time-aware recommender systems: a comprehensive survey and analysis of existing evaluation protocols. User Model. User-Adap. Inter. 24(1–2), 67–119 (2013). https://doi.org/10.1007/s11257-012-9136-x
44. Herlocker, J.L., Konstan, J.A., Terveen, L.G., et al.: Evaluating collaborative filtering recommender systems. ACM Trans. Inf. Syst. 22, 5–53 (2004). https://doi.org/10.1145/963770.963772
45. Eraslan Yalcin, M., Kutlu, B.: Examination of students' acceptance of and intention to use learning management systems using extended TAM. Br. J. Educ. Technol. 50, 2414–2432 (2019). https://doi.org/10.1111/bjet.12798
46. Sahid, D.S.S., Santosa, P.I., Ferdiana, R., et al.: Evaluation and measurement of Learning Management System based on user experience. In: Seminar, I.A.E. (ed.) Proceedings of the 2016 6th International Annual Engineering Seminar, Eastparc Hotel, Yogyakarta, Indonesia, 1–3 August 2016. IEEE, Piscataway, NJ (2016)
47. Takashi Nakamura, W., Harada Teixeira de Oliveira, E., Conte, T.: Usability and user experience evaluation of learning management systems - a systematic mapping study. In: Proceedings of the 19th International Conference on Enterprise Information Systems. SCITEPRESS - Science and Technology Publications, pp. 97–108 (2017)
48. ISO: ISO 9241-11:2018 (2021). https://www.iso.org/standard/63500.html. Accessed 11 Feb 2021
49. Santoso, H.B., Schrepp, M., Utomo, A.Y., et al.: Measuring user experience of the student-centered e-learning environment. J. Educ. Online 13, 58–79 (2016)
50. Laugwitz, B., Held, T., Schrepp, M.: Construction and evaluation of a user experience questionnaire. In: Holzinger, A. (ed.) USAB 2008. LNCS, vol. 5298, pp. 63–76. Springer, Heidelberg (2008). https://doi.org/10.1007/978-3-540-89350-9_6
51. Hart, S.G., Staveland, L.E.: Development of NASA-TLX (Task Load Index): results of empirical and theoretical research. In: Hancock, P.A., Meshkati, N. (eds.) Human Mental Workload, vol. 52. North-Holland; Sole distributors for the U.S.A. and Canada, pp. 139–183. Elsevier Science Pub. Co, Amsterdam, New York (1988)
52. Bruder, A., Schwarz, J.: Evaluation of diagnostic rules for real-time assessment of mental workload within a dynamic adaptation framework. In: Sottilare, R.A., Schwarz, J. (eds.) HCII 2019. LNCS, vol. 11597, pp. 391–404. Springer, Cham (2019). https://doi.org/10.1007/978-3-030-22341-0_31
53. Schwarz, J., Fuchs, S.: Multidimensional real-time assessment of user state and performance to trigger dynamic system adaptation. In: Schmorrow, D.D., Fidopiastis, C.M. (eds.) AC 2017. LNCS (LNAI), vol. 10284, pp. 383–398. Springer, Cham (2017). https://doi.org/10.1007/978-3-319-58628-1_30
54. Schwarz, J.C.: Multifaktorielle Echtzeitdiagnose des Nutzerzustands in adaptiver Mensch-Maschine-Interaktion: Dissertation zur Erlangung des akademischen Grades Doktor der Philosophie (Dr. phil.) (2019)
55. Witte, T., Haase, H., Schwarz, J.: Measuring cognitive load for adaptive instructional systems by using a pressure sensitive computer mouse. In: Sottilare, R., Schwarz, J. (eds.) Adaptive Instructional Systems (2021)

56. Krauss, C., Merceron, A., An, T.-S., Zwicklbauer, M., Steglich, S., Arbanowski, S.: Teaching advanced web technologies with a mobile learning companion application. In: Proceedings of The 16th ACM World Conference on Mobile and Contextual Learning (mLearn 2017), Larnaca, Cyprus, 30 October–1 November 2017. ACM (2017). https://doi.org/10.1145/313 6907.3136937
57. European Union ESCO format. https://ec.europa.eu/esco/portal/home. Accessed 12 Feb 2021
58. MS Global LOM. http://www.imsglobal.org/metadata/index.html. Accessed 12 Feb 2021
59. IMS Global QTI. http://www.imsglobal.org/question/index.html. Accessed 12 Feb 2021
60. IMS Global CALIPER. http://www.imsglobal.org/activity/caliper. Accessed 12 Feb 2021
61. ADL xAPI. https://xapi.com/. Accessed 12 Feb 2021
62. Krauss, C., Hauswirth, M.: Interoperable education infrastructures: a middleware that brings together adaptive, social and virtual learning technologies. In: The European Research Consortium for Informatics and Mathematics (ed) ERCIM NEWS: Special Theme: Educational Technology, pp. 9–10 (2020). ISSN 0926-4981. https://ercim-news.ercim.eu/images/stories/ EN120/EN120-web.pdf. Accessed 12 Feb 2021

# Impediments to AIS Adoption in the Philippines

Ma. Mercedes T. Rodrigo(✉)

Ateneo de Manila University, Quezon City, Philippines
mrodrigo@ateneo.edu

**Abstract.** This paper is a critical examination of four factors that affect widespread adoption of computer-based interventions in general and adaptive instructional systems (AISs) in particular within the Philippine context: Despite government and private sector efforts, hardware diffusion in schools has not reached critical mass. The poorest sectors of society have very limited Internet access. The curriculum tends to focus on computer literacy skills and is generally unable to use information and communication technologies to support specific subjects. Finally, teachers lack the preparation and, as a consequence, the confidence to use technology in innovative ways. The study-from-home necessitated by the COVID-19 pandemic would have been an ideal opportunity to maximize the impact of computer-based interventions such as AISs as these technologies have been shown to compensate for weak teacher-led instruction. However, AISs demand the very same resources that the Philippines educational system does not have, making such deployments impossible. This paper ends with a challenge to design AISs to operate under these difficult circumstances in order to maximize the benefits that they bring to education.

**Keywords:** AIS adoption · Impediments · Philippines

## 1 Educational Outcomes in the Philippines

The Philippines is an archipelago in South East Asia. Composed of over 7000 islands, the country has a population of 106 million people, 55 million of whom are less than 25 years old (UNESCO 2020).

Despite a literacy rate of 99.1% (UNESCO 2020), Filipinos' educational achievement is poor, as measured by several recent international achievement tests. The South East Asia – Primary Learning Metrics (SEA-PLM) Programme, for example, is a UNICEF and South East Asian Ministers of Education (SEAMEO) partnership that aims "to improve the region's capacity to measure learning outcomes, use data, and allow peer exchange on policies and practices" (UNICEF and SEAMEO 2020). Its flagship effort is the SEA-PLM Assessment. Formally launched in 2014, the study attempted to measure the outcomes of Grade 5 students in six participating countries: Cambodia, Lao PDR, Malaysia, Myanmar, Philippines, and Vietnam. Its report dated 2019 (UNICEF and SEAMEO 2020) provided a profile of students in the areas of reading, writing, and mathematics. Only 10% of Philippine students were performing at or above the minimum reading standard prescribed by the United Nations Sustainable Development Goals

© Springer Nature Switzerland AG 2021
R. A. Sottilare and J. Schwarz (Eds.): HCII 2021, LNCS 12792, pp. 412–421, 2021.
https://doi.org/10.1007/978-3-030-77857-6_29

(SDGs). The large majority, 72%, of Philippine students were at the lowest levels of writing literacy, meaning they could only express simple ideas with limited vocabulary. In mathematics, only 17% of students performed at expected levels.

Similar findings emerged in the 2018 Programme for International Student Assessment (PISA; Philippines Department of Education 2019 December). Filipino students scored an average of 340 points in reading literacy while other countries in the Organization for Economic Cooperation and Development (OECD) averaged 487 points. In math literacy, Filipino students averaged 353 points, as compared to an OECD average of 489 points. Finally, Filipinos scored 357 points in scientific literacy, compared to an OECD average of 489 points.

The Trends in Mathematics and Science Survey (IEA 2020) provided further corroboration. The Philippines scored the lowest among 58 countries surveyed for Grade 4 math and science achievement. Filipino students' average score for mathematics was 297 as compared to an overall average of 400. Filipinos' average for science was 249, as compared an overall average of 400 as well. When tested in 2003, Filipinos scored 364 and 332 for math and science respectively. This means that the current cohort of Filipino students performed worse than prior generations from the same country.

Computer-based learning technologies from drill-and-practice modules to adaptive information systems (AISs) have the potential to provide students with individualized, motivating instruction. Indeed, both the public and private sectors have invested heavily in the infusion of technology in schools with the hope that these tools will lead to better educational outcomes. However, is the Philippine educational system capable of adopting these tools? What are the factors that are hindering the widespread use of computer-based teaching and learning tools?

This paper is a critical examination of the factors that affect widespread adoption of computer-based interventions in general and AISs in particular with the Philippine context. Of the various factors that drive and guide the success of any technology intervention, this paper will focus on four (4) main areas: hardware, Internet access, curriculum, and manpower. The paper will discuss how the Philippine educational system coped under the COVID-19 pandemic. The paper will end an assessment of the Philippines' readiness for AISs.

## 2  Hardware

The widespread infusion of ICTs in the Philippine educational system began in 1996 with the Department of Education (DepEd; formerly known as the Department of Education, Culture, and Sports (DECS)) Modernization Program. Among the goals of the program was the introduction of ICTs to transform the teaching and learning process (Philippines Department of Education 2018). To these ends, the government initially invested PhP375 million (Rodrigo 2003), of which 80% was to be allocated to secondary schools, 15% to primary schools, and 5% to administrative offices (Philippines Department of Education, Culture, and Sports 1997). Public primary schools received an e-classroom package consisting of six terminals, an interactive whiteboard, and a projector while secondary schools received anywhere from 11 to 150 terminals, depending on the school's population (Vergel de Dios 2016). Over the years, the government was firm in its commitment to increase computer penetration in schools. In 2009, for example, one of the computerization program's goals was to supply 75% of public secondary schools with multimedia-capable computer laboratories and to train 75% of teachers (Rodrigo 2003).

Initiatives from public and private institutions supplemented these efforts (Vergel de Dios 2016). The Department of Trade and Industry provided 60,000 computers to 4,900 public schools. The Commission on ICT, which evolved into the Department of ICT, provided computer laboratory packages and elearning modules to schools. In 1999, Citibank, NA-Philippines gave US$100,000 to establish computer laboratories in secondary schools (Rodrigo 2003). Coca-Cola, Intel, and Microsoft provided hardware, Internet connectivity, and teacher training (Vergel de Dios 2016). By 2012, 51% of primary schools and 88% of secondary schools had computers (Vergel de Dios 2016) and by 2018, the budget of what came to be called the DepEd Computerization Program (DCP) grew to Php8 billion (Montemayor 2018).

Unfortunately, school and student needs far outstripped the available resources and ICT infrastructure never reached critical mass. In 1996, a school with 3000 students would only receive a computer laboratory with 50 terminals (Vergel de Dios 2016) for a ratio of 60 students per computer. Circa 2012, the ratio of students to computers was still high. Only 1% of primary schools and 35% of secondary schools had less than 20 students sharing one computer. This meant that most students could only use computers for one hour per week. A more recent case study by Castillo (2017) reported that a typical computer laboratory in Davao Oriental, a province in the south of the country, had 6–8 working computers for a class of 30 to 40 students. Teachers would typically have one student working on each computer while 3–5 others watched. Sometimes, teachers had to divide the class into two—half would work on the machines while the other half would work with pen and paper.

Issues with logistics were partly to blame. A report by the Philippine Commission on Audit (2017) found that from 2015 to 2017, the Department of Education had a 99% physical target deficiency, i.e. over 77,000 schools were still awaiting delivery of ICT packages. Deficiencies in deliveries were attributed to poor sales service coupled with unmet readiness requirements within the schools themselves. When ICTs were delivered, they were often not used because they were defective, incomplete, or uninstalled. In some cases, school principals made use of ICTs for purposes other than teaching and there was reported rampant theft of equipment (San Antonio 2019).

Furthermore, most initiatives could not be sustained. A study by Espinosa and Caro (2011) tracked the status of ICT in education initiatives over 10 years. They found that the most infrastructure projects tended to be pilots or one-time-big-time donations without continuing support. One mistake that both schools and donors make in estimating the cost of ICT integration is to focus on the initial costs of equipment and retrofitting of facilities (Tinio 2003). In truth, these only constitute 40% to 60% of total cost of ownership. Maintenance and support costs constitute between 30% to 50% of the cost and these are the costs that are not usually included in technology deployments.

## 3   Internet Access

Internet connectivity has been and continues to be a challenge for the Philippine educational system. In 2016, it was estimated that only 14% of public elementary schools

(5,503 out of 38,683) and 55% of secondary schools (4,360 out of 7,915) had Internet access (Marasigan 2016). When Internet access is donated, subscriptions are usually time-bound. One such program for example donated a one-year subscription (Vergel de Dios 2016). When it expired, no public funds were appropriated to pay for continued connectivity.

In recent years, the proliferation of smart mobile phones has made personal Internet access possible across all socio-economic classes. In the Philippines, as with the rest of the Global South (Nye 2015), the mobile phone is the primary computing platform. As of 2019, there were 155 mobile phone subscriptions for every 100 people in the Philippines (World Bank 2021). It is reasonable to hypothesize, then, that the mobile phone might help bridge the digital divide by enabling people across all socio-economic classes to access the Internet. As of 2017, approximately 60% of individuals in the Philippines were on the Internet (World Bank 2021) and Filipinos were the highest users of social media in the world (Pablo 2018).

However, the country's Internet infrastructure does not compare well to its counterparts in other countries. The Philippines' 4G network was ranked the 4th slowest among 88 countries in 2018 (Mirandilla-Santos et al. 2018). The country generally ranks behind its South East Asian neighbors in terms of Internet cost and accessibility (Pablo 2018). Consumers using fixed broadband services pay about 7.1% of gross national income per capita: the affordability threshold recommended by the International Telecommunications Union is 5% (Mirandilla-Santos et al. 2018).

There is also research that implies that mobile phones and mobile data access seems to reinforce existing digital inequalities (Uy-Tioco 2019). People from the lower socio-economic classes constitute the majority of the population. Their educational attainment is typically secondary or elementary school only. They tend to be unskilled laborers who live in semi-permanent homes in slum areas. The introduction of pre-paid mobile phones in 1998 opened the mobile phone device and service market to those with no credit history. Hence 96% of mobile phones are pre-paid.

To cater to this segment, major telecommunications providers offer low-cost ways to add credit or load to their phones, e.g. PhP20.00 for 15 MB of data, valid for one day (Uy-Tioco 2019). This produces what Uy-Tioco (2019) calls a "metered mindset" where people "sip and dip" rather than browse and surf, carefully conserving airtime and only turning on their data when they need to do so. Telecommunications companies do provide zero-rated services such as certain news sites, Facebook, and Facebook Messenger, but this creates an imbalance in the kinds of content that the digital poor are able to access.

Another means by which the lower classes access the Internet is through Internet cafes that follow a the "Pisonet" format. Internet access in these shops is coin-operated, much like washing machines in other countries: Customers drop 1 peso coins in the machine's coin slot for four minutes of Internet time. It is up to the customers to collect the 1 peso coins for their usage.

The current COVID-19 pandemic has made Internet access all the more essential for student to be able to continue with their studies. Out of 22 million primary and secondary students, 6.2 million have insufficient funds to buy Internet time, 6.9 million have unstable Internet connections, and 6.8 million have no Internet-capable gadgets (Luistro 2021).

# 4  Curriculum

Curriculum is defined as "what, why, how, and how well students should learn in a systematic and intentional way" (IBE-UNESCO 2021b). It takes the form of a planned course of study as well as all the learning experiences that a school is supposed to provide its students. Whenever thinking about curriculum, it is necessary to distinguish among what is intended, implemented, and attained. The intended curriculum refers to a formal document that specifies what educational policy makers expect that students will be taught (IBE-UNESCO 2021d). The implemented curriculum refers to the actual teaching and learning activities that take place in the classroom (IBE-UNESCO 2021c). The attained curriculum refers to outcomes, i.e. the knowledge, skills, and attitudes that learners acquire as a result of the learning activities (IBE-UNESCO 2021a). In an ideal world, the intended, implemented, and attained curricula should be equivalent but, in truth, substantial gaps exist.

Part of the intention of the DepEd Modernization program was for students to learn basic computer skills such as word processing, spreadsheet operations, and the use of the Internet (Philippines Department of Education, Culture, and Sports 1997). ICTs were then supposed to be integrated in subject areas such as English, science, math, and history. The hope was that students would apply these new computer skills to other subject areas, leveraging on whatever advantages these new technologies provided (Bonifacio 2013).

Unfortunately, the intention to use of ICTs within as tools to teach subjects themselves neither implemented nor attained. From the early days of the DCP to the present, ICTs were and are taught as subjects to be learned in themselves rather than as platforms for learning other subjects. The priority of school curriculum then and now is on computer literacy, productivity tools, programming, and multimedia skills (Department of Education 2020; Rodrigo 2003).

# 5  Manpower

The failure to implement the intended curriculum can be attributed in part of the infrastructure and Internet connectivity problems already discussed. An additional cause is the lack of teacher preparation. Recent versions of the teacher pre-service curriculum includes subjects that teach about educational technology and the use of technology for teaching and learning (Cortes et al. 2019). These subjects cover the theories and principles behind the use and development of educational technology interventions. They also include lessons on ethics, social responsibility, and intellectual property. However, more recent technologies such as robotics, augmented reality, virtual labs, and so on are not included, so teachers lack exposure to these alternative platforms.

Teacher in-service training is even more limited. The DepEd structure is divided into a central office, 17 regions and 80 divisions. Training is provided from the central office and at the division level. The teacher training modules are usually limited to productivity tools, e.g. word processing, spreadsheet, presentation tools. Teachers are taught the functions of these tools but they are not taught how to integrate these tools in their lessons (Torii et al. 2019). A study of 383 teachers in the Central Visayas Region in the middle of the country found that teachers have only basic knowledge of ICT tools and how to operate them but teachers do not have the skills to use them in innovative ways (Marcial and Rama 2015). Teachers often also lack the support that they need in order to improve their skills. The ICT coordinator of the division office is supposed to monitor the use of ICTs in school management and in lessons. Leyte, one of the provinces in the Central Visayas Region, has one ICT coordinator to oversee 1258 schools (Torii et al. 2019). This makes the task of monitoring impossible. The ICT coordinators never completely understand the conditions or needs of each school and its teaching staff.

Teachers are short on resources. They have little to no access to subject-specific software (Alcantara et al. 2020). They have no time to prepare their ICT-based lessons during work hours and have to use their own personal time to do so (Torii et al. 2019). When they are in school, they have to compete with other teachers for the use of resources such as projectors or the computer laboratory.

Finally, and perhaps as a result, teachers lack confidence either in the technology or in themselves. Some refuse to use ICTs because they do not see any advantage in doing so, because they have forgotten how to use the applications, or they worry about making mistakes in operation (Torii et al. 2019).

# 6 Philippine Education Under COVID-19

How does an educational system that is already in crisis manage under COVID-19? When schools closed in March 2020, a petition that gathered 360,000 signatories demanded that DepEd cancel the academic school year (Ruins 2020). Their argument was that not all students have access to the technologies they need for online education. They wanted an academic freeze until the digital divide was bridged and until the pandemic curve was flattened. To worsen the situation further, Typhoon Goni made landfall in the Philippines in October 2020. It was the year's strongest cyclone. Typhoon Vamco followed in November 2020, causing severe flooding, power disruptions, and loss of life (Lalu 2020). Student groups again clamored for an academic freeze until flooding cleared and utilities were restored.

However, an academic freeze was not an option. DepEd asserted that an academic freeze would have severe effects on students' economic lives (Hernando-Malipot 2020). Indeed, research from the OECD suggests that income increases from 7.5% to 11.1% for each additional year of schooling (Hanushek and Woessmann 2020). Losing a year of schooling, on the other hand, leads to fewer learning outcomes, diminishes current skills, and weakens the foundation upon which future learning can be built.

DepEd, in cooperation with the local government units and the private sector, pressed on, advocating flexibility in the way schooling is delivered. They prepared self-learning modules which were provided to learners in either digital form or hard copy (Mocon-Ciriaco 2020). Local governments provided learners with free laptops, tablets, and wireless Internet. DepEd also established the DepEd Commons, a collection of digital learning resources and DepEd TV, a YouTube channel with high-quality, curriculum-based content presented by DepEd teachers. To support these efforts, the major telecommunication companies offered zero-rated access to the DepEd Commons. As of October 2020, nearly 25 million learners were enrolled for the school year, representing about

90% of the students population (Mateo 2020). Although this exceeded initial projections, it still indicates that around 3 million learners dropped out of the school system.

By December 2020, teacher advocacy groups noted that student participation was dwindling (ABS-CBN News 2020b). The group claimed that less than half of their students attend online classes. The DepEd offered reassurance saying that students can still use other modalities to access educational content (ABS-CBN News 2020a). If students were having connectivity issues, they could use printed modules, educational television, and radio.

## 7 Discussion and Conclusion

The COVID-19 pandemic would have offered AISs the opportunity to shine. With students forced to study from home, adaptive instruction promises guided, personalized practice opportunities and tutoring, on a variety of platforms (Lee 2008). The Philippine context, with its under-resourced schools and underprepared manpower, offers another perfect circumstance in which these technologies can test their effectiveness.

Note that these technologies offer no guarantees. Results from meta-analyses range from null to slightly positive (Reich 2020). At the same time, these analyses suggest that computer-based instruction may compensate for weak instructional quality as the variance among classrooms using computer-based interventions tended to be smaller than the variance among classrooms not using these interventions at all. Since all computer-based interventions are blended, human educators teach some classes while students use computer-based instruction during others. If a class has a weak teacher, having students devote some class hours to well-constructed educational software can lead to better learning gains. In contrast, traditional classes are completely teacher-led. Hence, students under a weak teacher have limited alternatives. In a country like the Philippines, having students use AISs or similar computer-based materials might be able to strengthen instruction and narrow some of the gaps, both internal and external.

The Philippine educational technology ecosystem, however, does not seem ripe to take advantage of educational technologies such as AISs. The same resources needed to deploy AISs—hardware, the connectivity, the curriculum support, and the skilled manpower—are precisely the resources that the Philippine education system sorely lacks. Access to these technologies and resources is determined by socio-economic standing. Thus, those in the margins who stand to gain the most from these technologies and interventions are also the ones least poised to access them.

This is a challenge, therefore, to those of us working in the field of AISs. We have to find ways to make our technologies usable under even difficult circumstances, as instruments to bring out greater equity rather than a means of reinforcing existing socio-economic structures. If we can design AISs to operate under these circumstances, we open educational opportunities to those who need them most and increase the life outcomes of whose who are otherwise marginalized. It is in this space that we stand to make the most meaningful impact.

**Acknowledgement.** Many thanks to Walfrido David Diy for helpful comments and suggestions.

# References

ABS-CBN News. Alleged dwindling number of students in online learning should not be alarming: DepEd (2020a). https://news.abs-cbn.com/news/12/29/20/alleged-dwindling-number-of-students-in-online-learning-should-not-be-alarming-deped

ABS-CBN News. Number of students participating in distance learning declining: teachers' group (2020b). https://news.abs-cbn.com/news/12/28/20/number-of-students-participating-in-distance-learning-declining-teachers-group

Alcantara, E.C., Veriña, R.U., Niem, M.M.: Teaching and learning with technology: ramification of ICT integration in mathematics education. Southeast Asia Math. Educ. J. **10**(1), 27–40 (2020)

Bonifacio, A.L.: Developing information communication technology (ICT) curriculum standards for K-12 schools in the Philippines. In: The Sixth Conference of MIT's Learning International Networks Consortium (LINC), MIT, Cambridge, Massachusetts, USA (2013)

Castillo, L.S.V.: Call of duty: a case study of ICT integration in Philippine public schools in San Isidro Davao oriental post K-12 implementation. JPAIR Multi. Res. **30**, 1–16 (2017)

Cortes, S.T., Pineda, H.A., Jugar, R.R.: Alignment of the revised secondary teacher education curriculum and the hiring qualifications for SHS teachers in the Philippines: a theoretical gap analysis. J. Educ. Naresuan Univ. **24**(1), 1–19 (2019)

Espinosa, K.J.P., Caro, J.D.: Analysis of ICT integration initiatives in basic education and lessons learned: the case of the Philippines. In: 2011 First ACIS/JNU International Conference on Computers, Networks, Systems and Industrial Engineering, pp. 342–347. IEEE, May 2011

Hanushek, E.A., Woessmann, L.: The Economic Impacts of Learning Losses (2020). https://www.oecd.org/education/The-economic-impacts-of-coronavirus-covid-19-learning-losses.pdf

Hernando-Malipot, M.: DepEd fears 'massive impact' of academic freeze on students. Manila Bulletin, 18 November 2020. https://mb.com.ph/2020/11/18/deped-fears-massive-impact-of-academic-freeze-on-students/

IBE-UNESCO. Attained curriculum (2021a). http://www.ibe.unesco.org/en/glossary-curriculum-terminology/a/attained-curriculum

IBE-UNESCO. Curriculum (2021b). http://www.ibe.unesco.org/en/glossary-curriculum-terminology/c/curriculum-plural-curricula

IBE-UNESCO. Implemented curriculum (2021c). http://www.ibe.unesco.org/en/glossary-curriculum-terminology/i/implemented-curriculum

IBE-UNESCO. Intended curriculum (2021d). http://www.ibe.unesco.org/en/glossary-curriculum-terminology/i/intended-curriculum

IEA. TIMSS 2019 International Results in Mathematics and Science. IEA TIMSS & PIRLS International Study Center (2020). https://timssandpirls.bc.edu/timss2019/international-results/wp-content/themes/timssandpirls/download-center/TIMSS-2019-International-Results-in-Mathematics-and-Science.pdf

Lalu, G.P. Student group wants academic freeze until floods clear, internet fixed, 16 November 2020. https://newsinfo.inquirer.net/1361470/student-group-wants-academic-freeze-until-floods-clear-internet-is-fixed

Lee, J., Park, O.: Adaptive instructional systems. Handb. Res. Educ. Commun. Technol. 469–484 (2008)

Luistro, A.A.: Learning from the Learning Crisis. SoulPH20/20 Webinar Series 9 January 2021. https://www.youtube.com/watch?v=rqxedRQRFyE

Marasigan, L.: Globe: No Internet access in 80% of public schools. Business Mirror. https://businessmirror.com.ph/2016/03/12/globe-no-internet-access-in-80-of-public-schools/. Accessed 12 Mar 2020

Marcial, D.E., Rama, P.A.: ICT competency level of teacher education professionals in the central Visayas region, Philippines. Asia Pac. J. Multidiscipl. Res. **3**(5), 28–38 (2015)

Mateo, J.: As Classes Open, 'Learning Crisis' Highlighted With Millions Of Students Left Behind. One News, 5 October 2020. https://www.onenews.ph/as-classes-open-learning-crisis-highli ghted-with-millions-of-students-left-behind

Mirandilla-Santos, M.G., Brewer, J., Faustino, J.: From Analog to Digital: Philippine Policy and Emerging Internet Technologies (2018). https://asiafoundation.org/wp-content/uploads/2018/ 10/From-Analog-to-Digital_Philippine-Policy-and-Emerging-Internet-Technologies.pdf

Mocon-Ciriaco, C.: The impossible is possible: Covid shut down schools, but learning goes on. Business Mirror, 8 October 2020. https://businessmirror.com.ph/2020/10/08/the-impossible-is-possible-covid-shut-down-schools-but-learning-goes-on/

Montemayor, M.T.: DepEd steps up public awareness on computerization program. Philippine News Agency (2018). https://www.pna.gov.ph/articles/1031175

Nye, B.D.: Intelligent tutoring systems by and for the developing world: a review of trends and approaches for educational technology in a global context. Int. J. Artif. Intell. Educ. 5(2), 177–203. Springer (2015). https://link.springer.com/article/10.1007/s40593-014-0028-6

Pablo, M.: Internet Inaccessibility Plagues "Social Media Capital of the World". The Asia Foundation (2018). https://asiafoundation.org/2018/10/24/internet-inaccessibility-plagues-soc ial-media-capital-of-the-world/

Philippine Commission on Audit. DepEd_ES2017 (2017). https://www.coa.gov.ph/phocadown loadpap/userupload/annual_audit_report/NGAs/2017/National-Government-Sector/Depart ment-of-Education/DepEd_ES2017.pdf

Philippines Department of Education. DepEd Computerization Program Orientation Handbook. Department of Education Tagbilaran (2018). http://www.depedtagbilaran.org/wp-content/upl oads/2019/03/DCP-Handbook-Batches-3536–40-to-44.pdf

Philippines Department of Education. PISA 2018 National Report of the Philip-pines (2019). https://www.deped.gov.ph/wp-content/uploads/2019/12/PISA-2018-Philippine-National-Report.pdf

Philippines Department of Education. Aide Memoire: Accelerating the DepEd Computerization Program in the Light of the COVID-19 Pandemic, 27 May 2020. https://commons.deped.gov. ph/download_oua_document?id=2e58a405-a51f-4f05-8440-f115bddc723c

Philippines Department of Education, Culture, and Sports. JANUARY 17, 1997 – DO 4, S. 1997 – ACTION PLAN FOR DECS MODERNIZATION PROGRAM. Department of Educa-tion (1997). https://www.deped.gov.ph/1997/01/17/do-4-s-1997-action-plan-for-decs-modern ization-program/

Reich, J.: Failure to Disrupt: Why Technology Alone Can't Transform Education. Harvard University Press, Cambridge, MA (2020)

Rodrigo, M.M.T.: Tradition or transformation? an evaluation of ICTs in Metro Manila schools. Inf. Technol. Dev. 10(2), 95–122 (2003)

Ruins. Cancel the Academic Year 2020–2021 (2020). https://www.change.org/p/deped-suspend-the-academic-year-2020-2021

San Antonio, D.M.: Issues and Concerns on School Governance and School Improvement in DepEd CALABARZON. In Ocampo, D., Lucasan, K.L.M. (Eds.), Key Issues in Governance, Finance, School Improvement, and Information and Communication Technology (ICT) in Basic Education. University of the Philippines, Center for Integrative Development Studies (2019). https://www.researchgate.net/profile/Dina_Joana_Ocampo/publication/333309653_ Key_Issues_in_Governance_Finance_School_Improvement_and_ICT_in_Basic_Education/ links/5ce61180a6fdccc9ddc70363/Key-Issues-in-Governance-Finance-School-Improvement-and-ICT-in-Basic-Education.pdf#page=9

Tinio, V.L.: ICT in Education (2003). https://e-learning.tsu.ge/pluginfile.php/183/mod_resource/ content/0/ict_docs/ICT_in_education.pdf

Torii, A., Kamidate-Yamaguchi, M., Kubota, K.: The actual condition of teachers and the teacher training about ICT Utilization in Leyte, the Philippines. In: 2019 International Symposium on Educational Technology (ISET), pp. 87–91. IEEE (2019)

UNESCO. Philippines: Education and Literacy (2020). http://uis.unesco.org/en/country/ph

UNICEF & SEAMEO. SEA-PLM 2019 Main Regional Report, Children's learning in 6 Southeast Asian countries. Bangkok, Thailand: United Nations Children's Fund (UNICEF) & Southeast Asian Ministers of Education. Organization (SEAMEO) – SEA-PLM Secretariat (2020)

Uy-Tioco, C.S.: 'Good enough' access: digital inclusion, social stratification, and the reinforcement of class in the Philippines. Commun. Res. Pract. **5**(2), 156–171 (2019)

Vergel de Dios, B.: Building and sustaining national ICT/education agencies: Lessons from the Philippines. World Bank (2016). http://documents.vsemirnyjbank.org/curated/ru/344311488 908487127/pdf/113217-NWP-PUBLIC-ADD-SERIES-Agencies-Philippines-SABER-ICT no15.pdf

World Bank. (2021). World Development Indicators. https://data.worldbank.org/indicator/IT.CEL. SETS.P2?locations=PH

# Setting Goals in Adaptive Training: Can Learners Improve with a Moving Target?

Bradford L. Schroeder[1]([✉]), Nicholas W. Fraulini[2], Wendi L. Van Buskirk[1],
Cheryl I. Johnson[1], and Matthew D. Marraffino[1]

[1] Naval Air Warfare Center Training Systems Division, Orlando, FL, USA
{bradford.schroeder,wendi.vanbuskirk,cheryl.i.johnson,
matthew.marraffino}@navy.mil
[2] StraCon Services Group, LLC, Fort Worth, TX, USA
nicholas.fraulini.ctr@navy.mil

**Abstract.** The present work explores the effectiveness of goal setting in the context of adaptive training. Previous research has demonstrated that adaptive training approaches that tailor feedback and difficulty based on task performance lead to better learning outcomes than non-adaptive approaches. Likewise, decades of research on goal setting as an instructional technique has shown that setting achievement goals for trainees to improve also increases learning outcomes. In particular, challenging, specific goals have been found to be more effective than generic "try your best" goals. Bridging these techniques together presents an interesting opportunity to examine the effects of goal setting on performance in a training system that adapts both feedback and difficulty. For example, when a scenario's difficulty is adapted up, a specific goal may no longer be attainable, which begs the question – do challenging goals improve performance compared to generic goals in a training system that adapts difficulty? In this experiment, 45 college students were trained to perform a complex radar detection task under two goal setting conditions, specific ("try to improve by 25%") or general ("try your best"). We evaluated performance using a pre- to post-test design across several task measures. Overall, results were mixed, showing advantages for the specific goal condition on some accuracy measures but disadvantages on some timeliness measures compared to the general goal group. Implications for goal setting theory and practical applications for adaptive training are discussed.

**Keywords:** Adaptive training · Goal setting · Feedback

## 1 Introduction

### 1.1 Implementing Instructional Strategies in Adaptive Training

Adaptive training, which is training tailored to the strengths and weaknesses of individual trainees, has been demonstrated as an effective technique for learner-centered instruction in certain contexts [1, 2]. Adaptive training approaches use learner characteristics and/or

This is a U.S. government work and not under copyright protection in the U.S.; foreign copyright protection may apply 2021
R. A. Sottilare and J. Schwarz (Eds.): HCII 2021, LNCS 12792, pp. 422–435, 2021.
https://doi.org/10.1007/978-3-030-77857-6_30

performance during training to individualize the delivery of specific instructional interventions. For example, several different adaptive training systems have utilized the strategies of tailoring scenario difficulty and feedback based on trainee performance during training, leading to improved performance when compared to non-adaptive approaches [3–6].

Though previous research supports the effectiveness of adaptive difficulty and tailored feedback, there is a lack of research examining how goal setting might interact with adaptive features. Broadly, goal setting refers to setting a goal for trainees to achieve on their next assessment. Previous research suggests that specific, challenging goals have greater impacts on task performance compared to general "try your best" goals [7]. This effect has been replicated for decades but has not been examined in adaptive training systems at the time of this writing. Nevertheless, some studies have examined a variation on the specific vs. general goal effect that has particular relevance in adaptive training applications.

One important finding is that assigned goals are more effective than self-set or general goals in a variety of domains [8–11]. Locke and Bryan [10] observed that self-set goals tended to be less challenging than assigned goals and yielded comparatively modest improvements in performance. One reason for this is that self-set goals are naturally subject to influence by an individual's perceived self-efficacy [12]. In turn, this may mislead individuals to self-set a goal that is mismatched with their true ability. An externally assigned goal based on objective measures of performance should not be vulnerable to this effect. Because adaptive training systems observe and assesses performance objectively, they are well suited for assigning goals to trainees. Thus, implementing an assigned goal feature may be an effective way to capture the benefits of goal setting in an adaptive training system.

The purpose of the present study is to examine whether adding a goal setting intervention to an adaptive training system yields performance benefits. This paper investigates whether goal setting provides an added learning benefit in an adaptive training system.

## 1.2 Adaptive Training and Goal Setting

The testbed for this experiment was an adaptive trainer for a complex radar detection and prioritization task that had participants learn to identify and triage incoming target signals based on a complex set of rules. Despite this task's complexity, previous research suggests that goal setting can still facilitate performance improvements as task complexity increases [13]. Therefore, goal setting could be a viable instructional strategy for improving performance.

The adaptive training system that we used in this study provides performance feedback to the trainee at the end of every training scenario. An important theme in the goal setting literature is the interplay between performance feedback and goal setting. Locke [14] argued that feedback alone is not enough to improve performance, unless one uses that feedback to set a goal. In conjunction with performance feedback, the explicit addition of a goal can help trainees make use of feedback to improve their performance [15]. Per Kluger and DeNisi's Feedback Intervention Theory (FIT) [16], when a learner receives feedback comparing their performance against a standard of performance, they cope with any discrepancy in a variety of ways. Learners can change the standard, abandon the standard, reject the feedback, or change their behavior. Kluger and DeNisi [16] argued that the optimal way to resolve this discrepancy is to change one's behavior. Specifically, they claimed that goal setting is the most effective way to trigger behavior change, rather than any other discrepancy coping method. Based on the aforementioned literature, it should be beneficial to add a goal setting intervention to the performance feedback we provide trainees.

### 1.3 The Present Study

The present work investigates the effectiveness of goal setting in a training system that adapts difficulty and provides performance feedback. Specifically, do challenging, specific goals improve performance compared to general goals in a training system that adapts difficulty? Because effective goal setting requires challenging specific goals, there is a possibility that goal setting may not be effective when difficulty is adapted to be easier. On the other hand, when difficulty adapts to be harder, a set goal may become unattainable (cf. Locke [17], which supported that unattainable goals still yield improvement). Therefore, there is reason to believe that the addition of goal setting may not yield a straightforward benefit. Despite this, the literature suggests strong consistent improvement effects in goal setting studies [7]. With this in mind, we hypothesized that participants presented with challenging specific goals for future performance would show greater improvements in performance scores (e.g., accuracy, timeliness) from pre-test to post-test than participants presented with general "try your best" goals.

## 2    Method

### 2.1    Participants

Forty-five participants were recruited using a large southeastern university's research participation system. Participants (N = 45, 22 females) were randomly assigned to one of two experimental conditions: the specific goal setting condition (n = 23) or the general goal setting condition (n = 22). The average age of the participants was 20.93 years (SD = 2.35). Participants were paid $15 per hour for 2.5 h of participation.

### 2.2    Testbed

Participants completed a simulated radar detection and prioritization task using an experimental testbed developed specifically for this study. This task was designed based on a military electronic warfare task. The participants' task during experimental scenarios was to monitor the environment for critical radar events and submit both scheduled and unscheduled reports based on those events. Critical radar events were defined as either the appearance or disappearance of radar signals in the environment. When new signals appeared during a scenario, which is referred to as a "gain," participants were required to determine several of their parameters in order to correctly identify the radar. When existing radar signals disappeared from the environment, which is referred to as a "secure," participants selected the signal from a list of present signals to indicate it had disappeared. The experiment consisted of five 12-min scenarios: a pre-test scenario, three training scenarios, and a post-test scenario. All five scenarios included two stages: Stage 1 and Stage 2. Each scenario began with several radars present in the environment that participants were required to identify as quickly as possible. A Stage 1 Report of all radars present at scenario onset was due at two minutes and 30 s (i.e., a scheduled report), at which time the testbed progressed to Stage 2. If participants did not remember to submit their Stage 1 Report, a message appeared telling them they had not submitted their Stage 1 Report and their score would be penalized as a result. During Stage 2, radars appeared and disappeared based on an underlying adaptive algorithm, and participants were required to submit reports of these events (i.e., gain reports and secure reports, respectively) as quickly and accurately as possible (i.e., unscheduled reports). Stage 2 lasted until participants submitted their Final Report, which was due at 12 min (i.e., a scheduled report). The Final Report consisted of the combined information participants had submitted during their Stage 1 and Stage 2 reports. Similar to the end of Stage 1, the scenario would end at 14 min if the participant failed to submit a Final Report.

## 2.3  Procedure

Upon arrival, participants reviewed and signed a form explaining the safety protocols in place during the COVID-19 pandemic, and then reviewed the informed consent form before providing their consent. Next, participants reviewed an instructional PowerPoint® that provided background information on the task and tutorials for using the testbed. Following completion of the PowerPoint®, participants completed the first of two practice scenarios. The first practice scenario was eight minutes in length and provided participants with hands-on experience completing Stage 1 and Stage 2 reports. During the first practice scenario, the experimenter guided participants through the process of analyzing radar parameters, interacting with the testbed interface, and submitting reports. After completing the first practice scenario, participants completed a knowledge quiz to gauge their ability to complete the task and interact with the testbed. If participants answered items in the quiz incorrectly, the experimenter would review these items with the participant before progressing.

After completing the knowledge quiz, participants completed the second practice scenario. The second practice scenario was six minutes in length and progressed similarly to the first practice scenario except that the experimenter did not guide participants' actions. Following the second practice scenario, participants were offered the opportunity to take a short break. Participants then completed the five full 12-min scenarios. The pre-test and post-test scenarios were set to an intermediate difficulty for all participants. However, the difficulty for the three training scenarios was adapted for all participants based on their performance, such that the difficulty increased with high performance and decreased with low performance. Prior to the three training scenarios, participants were shown either specific goals or general goals based on experimental condition. Participants in the specific goals group were encouraged to improve their score by 25%

(which is a combined score of accuracy and timeliness), whereas participants in the general goals group were encouraged to try their best to improve performance on the next scenario. The specific goal of improving overall performance by 25% was chosen based on Locke and Latham's [7] suggestion for specific, challenging goals, as well as participants' performance during pilot testing. The maximum overall score for scenarios was 100%, and the specific goal changed to reflect the maximum improvement participants could achieve on their next scenario (i.e. if a participant scored 90% on the previous scenario, their goal statement would encourage them to improve 10% to an overall score of 100%). At the end of all scenarios, participants were provided end-of-scenario feedback detailing their performance on the previous scenario (see Fig. 1). After completing the five scenarios, participants provided ratings on the feedback and goal setting messages on a Likert scale (e.g., "The goal setting feedback I received helped me to improve my performance on the next scenario"), as well as demographic information. Participants then read a debriefing form detailing the study's purpose, and were provided a receipt confirming their participation.

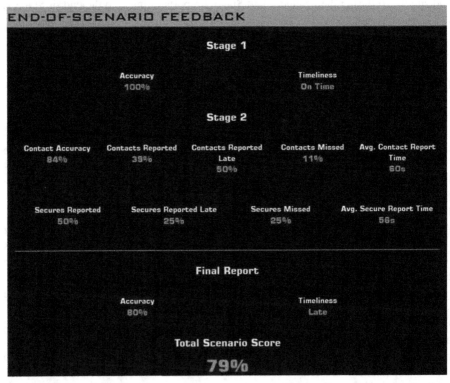

**Fig. 1.** End of scenario feedback example. Each stage consists of performance metrics for timeliness and accuracy. The Total Scenario Score is the average score across Stage 1, Stage 2, and Final Report.

# 3  Results

To test our hypothesis that trainees receiving specific goal setting interventions would show greater performance improvements, we compared our two groups on several performance measures. Because our hypothesis was directional, we performed one-sided t-tests on difference scores which were calculated by subtracting pre-test performance

**Table 1.** Descriptive statistics and *t*-test results

|  | Group | Mean | SD | *t* (43) | *d* |
|---|---|---|---|---|---|
| Stage 1 |  |  |  |  |  |
| Report accuracy | General | 23.39% | 25.15% | 0.57 | 0.16 |
|  | Specific | 27.18% | 19.07% |  |  |
| Report timeliness[a] | General | 8.48 s | 41.26 | −0.98 | 0.29 |
|  | Specific | −4.27 s | 45.64 |  |  |
| Stage 2 |  |  |  |  |  |
| Gain reports accuracy | General | 15.07% | 13.98% | 1.69* | 0.50 |
|  | Specific | 24.03% | 21.03% |  |  |
| Gains reported on time | General | 23.67% | 36.59% | −0.55 | 0.16 |
|  | Specific | 18.69% | 22.32% |  |  |
| Gains reported late[a] | General | −12.56% | 44.61% | 1.64† | 0.49 |
|  | Specific | 7.58% | 37.31% |  |  |
| Gains missed[a] | General | −11.11% | 22.47% | −1.84* | 0.54 |
|  | Specific | −26.26% | 32.08% |  |  |
| Gain report timeliness[a] | General | −62.57 s | 81.61 | 0.66 | 0.20 |
|  | Specific | −47.50 s | 71.59 |  |  |
| Secure reports accuracy | General | 5.80% | 37.13% | 0.68 | 0.12 |
|  | Specific | 10.61% | 40.35% |  |  |
| Secures reported on time | General | 34.78% | 35.50% | −1.68† | 0.50 |
|  | Specific | 18.18% | 30.39% |  |  |
| Secures reported late[a] | General | −8.99% | 33.79% | 1.73† | 0.51 |
|  | Specific | −7.58% | 48.17% |  |  |
| Secures missed[a] | General | −5.80% | 37.13% | −0.42 | 0.12 |
|  | Specific | −10.61% | 40.35% |  |  |
| Secure report timeliness[a] | General | −33.61 s | 52.98 | 0.46 | 0.13 |
|  | Specific | −18.05 s | 153.82 |  |  |
| Final report |  |  |  |  |  |
| Report accuracy | General | 19.61% | 20.95% | 1.63* | 0.48 |
|  | Specific | 32.05% | 29.62% |  |  |
| Report timeliness[a] | General | −34.43 s | 48.30 | 0.77 | 0.23 |
|  | Specific | −23.55 s | 45.90 |  |  |

*Note.* Measures were calculated by taking posttest scores and subtracting them by pretest scores.
[a]A lower difference score reflects better improvement
**p* < .05; †effect with *p* < .05 in opposite of hypothesized direction; *d* = Cohen's *d* effect size

from post-test performance. Since the radar detection task was comprised of multiple reports, and those reports were assessed on their accuracy and timeliness, we examined accuracy and timeliness separately for each. These analyses are summarized in Table 1.

### 3.1 Stage 1

There were no significant differences between goal setting groups in Stage 1 accuracy and timeliness. However, both differences were in the hypothesized direction (see Table 1).

### 3.2 Stage 2: Gain Reports

There was a significant improvement in accuracy for gain reports, such that those receiving specific goals improved nearly 10% points greater than those who received general goals (see Fig. 2). This group also significantly reduced the percentage of gain reports that they missed (see Fig. 3), showing a decrease of 15% points greater than those who received general goals.

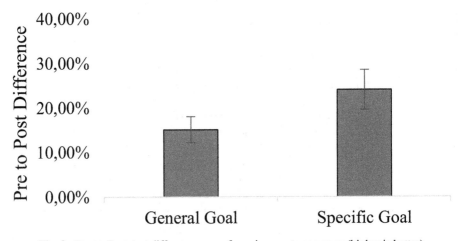

**Fig. 2.** Pre-to-Post-test difference score for gain reports accuracy (higher is better)

However, these benefits for the specific goal setting group were accompanied by an increase in late gain reports, such that the specific goal group increased their late gain reports by 8% points, while the general goal group decreased their late gain reports by 13% points (see Fig. 4). This effect was opposite of the hypothesized direction. There was no significant difference for gain report timeliness.

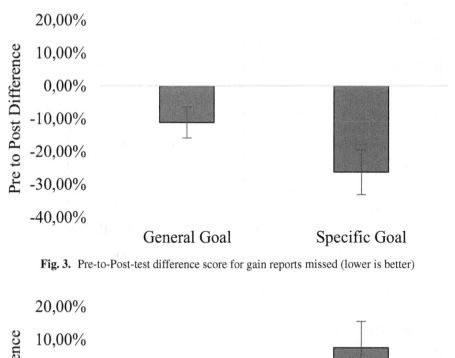

**Fig. 3.** Pre-to-Post-test difference score for gain reports missed (lower is better)

**Fig. 4.** Pre-to-Post-test difference score for gain reports late (lower is better)

### 3.3   Stage 2: Secure Reports

There were opposing effects for secure performance between both goal setting groups, such that the general goal group showed greater increases in secures reported on time and greater decreases in secures reported late (see Fig. 5 and Fig. 6). These effects were opposite of the hypothesized direction. There were no significant differences for secure reports accuracy, secure report timeliness, or secure reports missed.

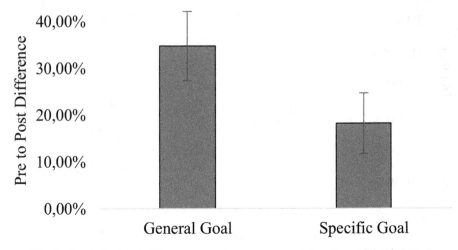

**Fig. 5.** Pre-to-Post-test difference score for secures reported on time (higher is better)

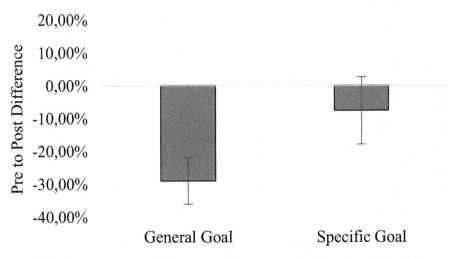

**Fig. 6.** Pre-to-Post-test difference score for secures reported late (lower is better)

### 3.4    Final Report

The specific goal group had a significantly greater improvement in accuracy compared to the general goal group, with a greater improvement of 12% points (see Fig. 7). The difference in final report timeliness was not statistically significant. However, both groups improved from pre-test to post-test.

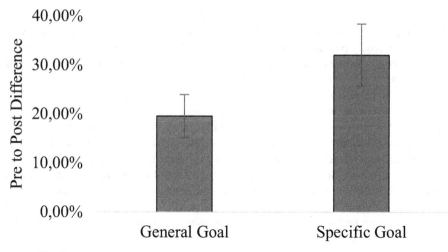

Fig. 7. Pre-to-Post-test difference score for final report accuracy (higher is better)

### 3.5 Exploratory Analysis: Were Goals Met?

Within the specific goal group, we were curious whether participants met the goals they were assigned. Additionally, because of the nature of adaptive difficulty, any goal could magnify in either its ease or difficulty depending on the direction of the difficulty adaptation. With 22 participants in the specific goal group, there were 66 goals assigned during their three training scenarios. Only 11 of these goals were met. We also examined whether any goals that had been met were preceded by an increase or decrease in difficulty. We observed that 6 goals were met after a decrease in difficulty, 5 goals were met after no change in difficulty, and 0 goals were met after an increase in difficulty.

Additionally, we queried participants' perceptions of the goal setting messages they received during the experiment. We identified a significant difference in perceptions of the goal setting messages. For the statement "The goals I received were reasonable," those in the specific goal group (M = 3.95, SD = 1.29) showed significantly lower agreement than those in the general goal group (M = 5.00, SD = 1.09; $t(43) = 2.94$, p = .005).

Taken together, these results suggest that our goal of a 25% improvement in overall score may have been too challenging for participants, particularly when preceded by an increase in difficulty. However, further analyses will examine these effects in detail as more data are collected, particularly to assess the impact of adaptation on the benefits of goal setting.

## 4  Discussion

### 4.1  A Comment on the Use of Directional Tests

The goal of this experiment was to examine the effects of goal setting feedback in an adaptive training system. More specifically, we attempted to assess the relative effectiveness of specific and general goal setting statements. We hypothesized that participants presented with challenging specific goals for future performance would show greater improvements in performance scores than participants presented with general goals. Our hypothesis was only partially supported; we observed effects consistent with our hypothesis on three performance measures; however, we observed three other performance measures that were counter to our hypothesis.

In general, the literature suggested a consistent positive effect on performance when adding a goal setting intervention to a training program. With this in mind, we followed Kimmel's [18] recommendations for the use of directional, one-tailed tests to test our hypothesis that specific goals would lead to greater performance improvements after training than general goals. However, Field's [19] recommendation is that one-tailed tests that return a result in the opposite direction should be ignored and treated as a failure to reject the null hypothesis. Therefore, the results we presented in the direction opposing our hypothesis should be interpreted with caution (specifically, where the general condition had better improvements in gains reported late, secures reported on time, and secures reported late).

### 4.2 Evaluating the Impact of Goal Setting

When contemplating why we did not find performance improvements for Stage 1 and secures, we considered the nature of the task as well as the end of scenario feedback. In Stage 1, participants had to identify as many radars as possible in a short amount of time. It may have been overwhelming for participants to process all the contacts at once, leaving the feedback or goal setting interventions less effective for this stage.

In contrast, during Stage 2, radars appeared in the environment somewhat sequentially over a longer period; therefore, participants had more time to classify individual contacts. Additionally, the Final Report includes all of the information submitted for both the Stage 1 and Stage 2 reports. Therefore, Final Report accuracy included the gain data from Stage 2 and any data that participants corrected or updated from the initial Stage 1 report. Further, as can be seen in Fig. 1, the end of scenario feedback provided only an overall score for accuracy and timeliness for Stage 1 and the Final Report, but Stage 2's feedback contained more detailed data on the gain and secure reports. It is possible that participants were better able to make use of this information in conjunction with the specific goals to improve their performance.

The different accuracy results on gains versus secures may have occurred due to frequency. In our scenarios, gains were 3 times more frequent than secures. Therefore, participants had more opportunities to report gains versus secures. The high rate of occurrence may have enabled participants to try out different strategies and learn from trial and error. However, it was encouraging to see that secure accuracy was in the hypothesized direction. That said, there may be a simpler perceptual explanation for secures. It may be more difficult to detect and attend to the absence of a radar signal, rather than the appearance of a new one.

Regarding timeliness, we did not identify significant improvements in report timing across all aspects of the task (i.e., no reports were being submitted significantly faster in post-test). Our speculation is that our feedback, which provided more detail pertaining to accuracy (see Fig. 1) may have motivated participants to improve their accuracy, sacrificing reporting speed. Despite this, it is important to note that participants were instructed that timeliness and accuracy were equally important, and performance would be penalized for late reports. Though goal setting has shown a strong reliable effect in a wide range of domains in previous research, we found conflicting evidence in our experiment. One reason we may not have found effects on all performance measures may relate to the unfamiliarity of the task our participants had to perform (despite it being complex). In Neubert's [20] meta-analysis, he argued for research investigating the effect of goal setting feedback for complex tasks that involved large amounts of learning on behalf of the student. In most of the goal setting and complexity studies included in his meta-analysis, the tasks performed were somewhat familiar to the participants. This was not the case in our experiment; the task was entirely unfamiliar to participants.

### 4.3   Feedback and Goal Setting

Several of our results are consistent with Kluger & DeNisi's [16] seminal work on feedback interventions. First, Kluger and DeNisi found evidence that feedback (in particular, outcome feedback) can hurt performance on unfamiliar tasks. They suggested that this is especially true with tasks performed for a short duration – consistent with Neubert's [20] argument above.

Second, Kluger and DeNisi found that outcome feedback can impede learning complex tasks. Indeed, completing Stage 1, identifying secures, and submitting reports in a timely manner are the most complex sub-tasks of our radar detection task. Though Kluger and DeNisi found that goal setting augmented performance when combined with outcome feedback, it may not have been enough to help participants on our most complex subtasks - especially when combined with the difficulty adaptation.

Third, Kluger and DeNisi argued that feedback has to help students abandon incorrect strategies. From a cognitive perspective, the combination of the end of scenario outcome feedback and goal setting feedback may not have been sufficient to help participants improve on Stage 1, secure, and timeliness performance. In particular, if they are performing poorly, feedback informing them what strategies are detrimental and/or which ones are beneficial for improving performance (also known as Process feedback [16]) may have been more effective. In fact, several authors have found a benefit for process feedback for training complex military tasks [21, 22].

Despite not supporting our hypothesis on all performance measures, the combination of outcome feedback and specific goal setting appears to be beneficial and helped students improve performance on some parts of the task. As this was the first study to investigate the use of goal setting in adaptive training systems, these results are promising.

### 4.4   Limitations and Future Research

There were a few limitations of our study. First, despite providing participants with outcome feedback on timeliness and informing them in the instructional PowerPoint® that the total score was a combination of accuracy and timeliness, we should have provided two specific goals in the feedback - one for accuracy and one for timeliness. Second, as can be seen in Table 1, there was a large amount of variance in the performance data. This large variability in the scores may have decreased the probability of finding significant results. This may be a result of the complexity or unfamiliarity of our experimental task. Results with adaptive training and simpler tasks may be clearer cut. Lastly, we did not include an adaptive training alone nor a no-feedback control group in order to assess the incremental value of goal setting above that of the other feedback interventions.

Therefore, future research should take a value-added approach to assessing incremental value of goal setting in adaptive training systems in order to tease apart its unique value. Further, our exploratory results showed that none of the specific goals were met when there was an increase in the difficulty level of the task. Thus, future research should investigate whether it would be advantageous to change the specific goal (i.e., to be "easier" in this case) when the task is adapted to be more difficult. Research is also needed to determine if the same pattern of results would occur if we had used Fleet personnel. Fleet personnel would be more familiar with the task and would allay the concern of task unfamiliarity posed by Neubert [20]. Lastly, future research should investigate the use of goal setting feedback in combination with process feedback, especially for complex tasks where the task is novel for trainees.

As Cohen [23] stated, though feedback is one of the most potent instructional tools, it continues to be the least understood. Continued research is necessary to investigate the myriad combinations of feedback parameters and provide practitioners with guidance on effective feedback strategies.

**Acknowledgments.** We gratefully acknowledge Dr. Kip Krebs and the Office of Naval Research who sponsored this work (Funding Doc# N0001420WX00540). We also wish to thank Robert Veira, Jason Hochreiter, Marc Prince, and Jacob May for their significant contributions during testbed development, and Matthew Pierce and Jacob Entinger for their assistance with data collection. Presentation of this material does not constitute or imply its endorsement, recommendation, or favoring by the U.S. Navy or Department of Defense (DoD). The opinions of the authors expressed herein do not necessarily state or reflect those of the U.S. Navy or DoD. NAWCTSD Public Release 21-ORL007 Distribution Statement A – Approved for public release; distribution is unlimited.

# References

1. Kelley, C.R.: What is adaptive training? Hum. Factors **11**(6), 547–556 (1969)
2. Wickens, C.D., Hutchins, S., Carolan, T., Cumming, J.: Effectiveness of part-task training and increasing difficulty training strategies: a meta-analysis approach. Hum. Factors **55**(2), 461–470 (2013)
3. Landsberg, C.R., Mercado, A.D., Van Buskirk, W.L., Lineberry, M., Steinhauser, N.: Evaluation of an adaptive training system for submarine periscope operations. Proc. Hum. Factors Ergon. Soc. **56**(1), 2422–2426 (2012)
4. Marraffino, M.D., Johnson, C.I., Whitmer, D.E., Steinhauser, N.B., Clement, A.: Advise when ready for game plan: adaptive training for JTACs. In: Proceedings of the Interservice/Industry Training, Simulation and Education Conference (2019)
5. Marraffino, M.D., Schroeder, B.L., Fraulini, N.W., Van Buskirk, W.L., Johnson, C.I.: Adapting training in real time: an empirical test of adaptive training frequency algorithms. Military Psychology (in press)

6. Van Buskirk, W.L., Fraulini, N.W., Schroeder, B.L., Johnson, C.I., Marraffino, M.D.: Application of theory to the development of an adaptive training system for a submarine electronic warfare task. In: Sottilare, R.A., Schwarz, J. (eds.) HCII 2019. LNCS, vol. 11597, pp. 352–362. Springer, Cham (2019). https://doi.org/10.1007/978-3-030-22341-0_28
7. Locke, E.A., Latham, G.P.: A Theory of Goal Setting & Task Performance. Prentice-Hall, Inc., Hoboken (1990)
8. Boyce, B.A., Wayda, V.K.: The effects of assigned and self-set goals on task performance. J. Sport Exerc. Psychol. 16(3), 258–269 (1994). https://doi.org/10.1123/jsep.16.3.258
9. Elston, T.L., Ginis, K.A.M.: The effects of self-set versus assigned goals on exercisers' self-efficacy for an unfamiliar task. J. Sport Exerc. Psychol. 26(3), 500–504 (2004). https://doi.org/10.1123/jsep.26.3.500
10. Locke, E.A., Bryan, J.F.: The effects of goal setting, rule-learning, and knowledge of score on performance. Am. J. Psychol. 79(3), 451–457 (1966)
11. Locke, E.A., Latham, G.P.: New directions in goal setting theory. Curr. Dir. Psychol. Sci. 15(5), 265–268 (2006)
12. Bouffard-Bouchard, T.: Influence of self-efficacy on performance in a cognitive task. J. Soc. Psycho. 130(3), 353–363 (1990)
13. Wood, R.E., Mento, A.J., Locke, E.A.: Task complexity as a moderator of goal effects: a meta-analysis. J. Appl. Psychol. 72(3), 416–425 (1987)
14. Locke, E.A.: Toward a theory of task motivation and incentives. Organ. Behav. Hum. Perform. 3(2), 157–189 (1968)
15. Latham, G.P., Baldes, J.J.: The practical significance of Locke's theory of goal setting. J. Appl. Psychol. 60(1), 122–124 (1975)
16. Kluger, A.N., DeNisi, A.: The effects of feedback interventions on performance: a historical review, a meta-analysis, and a preliminary feedback intervention theory. Psychol. Bull. 119(2), 254–284 (1996)
17. Locke, E.A.: Motivation by goal setting. In: Handbook of Organizational Behavior, pp. 43–56 (2000)
18. Kimmel, H.D.: Three criteria for the use of one-tailed tests. Psychol. Bull. 54(4), 351–353 (1957)
19. Field, A.: Discovering Statistics Using IBM SPSS Statistics, 5th edn. SAGE Publications, London (2018)
20. Neubert, M.J.: The value of feedback and goal setting over goal setting alone and potential moderators of this effect: a meta-analysis. Hum. Perform. 11(4), 321–335 (1998)
21. Astwood, R.S., Van Buskirk, W.L., Cornejo, J., Dalton, J.: The impact of different feedback types on decision-making in simulation based training environments. In: Proceedings of the 52nd Annual Meeting of the Human Factors and Ergonomics Society, vol 52, pp. 2062–2066. Santa Monica, CA: Human Factors and Ergonomics Society (2008)
22. Buff, W.L., Campbell, G.E.: What to do or what not to do?: Identifying the content of effective feedback. In: Proceedings of the 46th Annual Meeting of the Human Factors and Ergonomics Society, vol. 46, pp. 2074–2078. Santa Monica, CA: Human Factors and Ergonomics Society (2002)
23. Cohen, V.B.: A reexamination of feedback in computer-based instruction: Implications for instructional design. Educ. Technol. 25(1), 33–37 (1985)

# Teachers' Perspectives on the Adoption of an Adaptive Learning System Based on Multimodal Affect Recognition for Students with Learning Disabilities and Autism

Penny J. Standen[1] ⓘ, David J. Brown[2] ⓘ, Gosia M. Kwiatkowska[3] ⓘ,
Matthew K. Belmonte[2] ⓘ, Maria J. Galvez Trigo[1] ⓘ, Helen Boulton[2] ⓘ,
Andrew Burton[2] ⓘ, Madeline J. Hallewell[1] ⓘ, Nicholas Shopland[2(✉)] ⓘ,
Maria A. Blanco Gonzalez[4] ⓘ, Elena Milli[5] ⓘ, Stefano Cobello[5] ⓘ,
Annaleda Mazzucato[6,7] ⓘ, and Marco Traversi[8] ⓘ

[1] University of Nottingham, University Park, Nottingham, UK
[2] Nottingham Trent University, Nottingham, UK
{david.brown,nicholas.shopland}@ntu.ac.uk
[3] University of East London, London, UK
[4] Consejería de Educación. Junta de Castilla y León. Avenida del Real Valladolid s/n,
Valladolid, Spain
[5] Polo Europeo della Conoscenza - IC BoscoChiesanuova, Boscochiesanuova, Italy
[6] Fondazione Mondo Digitale, Rome, Italy
[7] University of Naples Federico II, Naples, Italy
[8] La Cometa Del Sud, Salerno, Italy

**Abstract.** Adoption of e-learning for those with special needs lags that for mainstream learners. Not much is known about barriers and facilitators that drive this disparity. The present study used focus groups and interviews to collect the views of 21 teachers taking part in preliminary evaluations of an adaptive learning system based on multimodal affect recognition for students with learning disabilities and autism. The system uses multimodal detection of affective state and scoring of performance to drive its adaptive selection of learning material. Five themes captured the teachers' views of the system's potential impact, especially regarding learning and engagement but also on factors that might influence adoption. These were: the potential of the system to transform their teaching practice; the ability of the system to impact on learning outcomes; the potential impact on teacher-student/peer to peer relationships; usability issues; and organisational challenges. Despite being highly motivated as volunteer testers, teachers highlighted barriers to adoption, which will need addressing. This finding underscores the importance of involving teachers and students in the design and development process.

**Keywords:** Adaptive learning systems · Mulitmodal affect recognition · Barriers to adoption

---

The original version of this chapter was revised: Authors affiliation has been corrected. The correction to this chapter is available at https://doi.org/10.1007/978-3-030-77857-6_45

© Springer Nature Switzerland AG 2021, corrected publication 2021
R. A. Sottilare and J. Schwarz (Eds.): HCII 2021, LNCS 12792, pp. 436–452, 2021.
https://doi.org/10.1007/978-3-030-77857-6_31

# 1  Introduction

2020's COVID-19 restrictions led to a surge in uptake of language apps, virtual tutoring, video conferencing tools and online learning software, as educational establishments struggled to meet the needs of their students remotely [1]. Pre-pandemic, the adoption of computer-based learning for those with special educational needs lagged that for mainstream users [2]. This is in spite of obvious advantages.

E-learning is seen as an antidote to the challenges experienced by these learners in accessing the educational opportunities and support they need but are often denied. Types of intervention vary, from the device-based such as games or other software on laptops or mobile devices, to web based virtual learning environments. Depending on configuration they confer the advantages of a variety of multimedia content, and flexible scheduling both in time and location [3], all of which would seem to allow individualised instruction to meet the specific needs of the most cognitively challenged learners. Learners can progress through content at their own pace, spending as long as is needed on concepts that have not been fully grasped but skipping over those that have [4].

These interventions are generally well received by both special needs teachers and their students, being seen as fun and with the potential to improve student motivation [5]. However, in education widely, in spite of teacher training programmes, an increase in ICT resources, and the requirements of national curricula, there has been disappointingly slow uptake of ICT in schools by the majority of teachers [6].

Goodyear et al. [7] define online teaching and learning in general as "teaching and learning that takes place over a computer network of some kind" which includes "both synchronous and asynchronous forms of interaction as well as interaction through text, video, audio, and in shared virtual worlds". Such methods recently have been augmented with affect recognition to optimise the presentation of learning material. Recent reviews [8, 9] have highlighted an explosion of work on the use of artificial intelligence tools for education (AIEd) that detect affective states relevant to learning. These affect-detecting interventions operate via various sensors and machine learning models, and promote learning in corresponding ways: they can apply real-time data on student engagement to trigger an on-screen agent (e.g. [10]), or a human teacher to implement "just-in time" personalised interventions [11], or to drive the machine-assisted selection and presentation of learning material so that it adapts to the learner's current needs [12].

The majority of studies on AIEd have been carried out with university students. The meta-analysis by Wu, Huang & Hwang [13] did report on type of participant yet did not identify any with special needs. Given the potential of affect sensitive adaptive learning systems to provide personalised support, school-aged students with learning disabilities and autism were identified as a stakeholder group of the MaTHiSiS project [14] which aimed to use affective state and performance to drive the presentation of learning material in an adaptive learning system.

For the project, a library of learning material was developed with teachers from the different schools. From this library teachers could create their own learning activities and learning graphs: an online equivalent of a specific lesson in traditional learning environments, where several learning goals are defined and are expected to be acquired. To reach these goals, the learning experience is divided into several Smart Learning

Atoms, which are representations of small pieces of knowledge [14]. These reusable learning objects are self-contained learning components that are stored and accessed independently. In accordance with each atom's prerequisite atoms, they can be assembled and re-assembled into new learning graphs, or sequenced to form individual learning paths. For MaTHiSiS this level of granularity enables a higher degree of personalisation, as changes in affect detection can immediately drive changes in presentation of learning material directed by the learning graph. The long-term intention is that teachers will continue to develop their own library and learning materials to support the continued learning of their students and to cater for the wide variety of learners with whom they work.

Before a learner can start to use MaTHiSiS, their teacher must complete a profile detailing their characteristics such as age, gender, time in school, preferences and abilities. From these profiles, MaTHiSiS determines a starting level of challenge for whatever learning graphs the teacher has identified or constructed for them. As the learner works with MaTHiSiS, the selection and change in the learning content are based on their performance (calculated from correct and incorrect responses) and their affective state, maintaining them in an optimal affective state thereby maximizing their learning. MaTHiSiS requires a computer with Windows 8.1 operating system or above, a connection through the school's Internet or an external wireless portable router. This hardware enables initiation of sessions and upload of live data during sessions. Learning material can be displayed on the computer screen, an Android tablet, or a NAO robot. In addition to the accelerometer in the tablet, sensory data are collected from a Kinect V2 sensor and a high-definition web camera connected to the computer.

Developing such systems takes considerable investment in resources and, however much they may cost to buy and to maintain, evidence for their effectiveness is required before teachers can be expected to adopt them. In the field of health innovation, implementation science explores how interventions for which there is sound evidence get taken up and put into practice, identifying factors that influence uptake from all relevant sectors such as patient, provider and the broader community and policy environment [15]. The MRC framework for complex interventions [16] sees the promotion of effective implementation as the final phase in the development of an intervention, following the collection of evidence for effectiveness. However, there is a strong argument for considering implementation at the earlier stages of the process especially in the design of devices, technology or software. The widely adopted concept of user-sensitive inclusive design was formulated specifically to facilitate the design for heterogeneous user groups such as those with disabilities or the elderly, to ensure that the final product meets their requirements and adoption is more likely. Input from users is sought from the very start of the design process. In the words of Newell et al. [17] "Rather than suggesting that designers rely on standards and guidelines, it is suggested that designers need to develop a real empathy with their user groups" (p. 235). These authors emphasise the importance of getting the design right: "In a field where so many everyday needs go unmet, however, the idea of design that does not provide direct solutions may seem wasteful and self-indulgent" (p. 238). In the case of MaTHiSiS, though many researchers bought into this vision, challenges nevertheless arose from a disconnect between the classroom-based researchers who were scoping user requirements and the laboratory-based engineers who were designing the core systems. At least as far as MaTHiSiS's use cases, to which this core system was to be applied, the design intention was that teachers and students should be involved from an early stage of the design process adopting the USERfit approach [18] to determine the user, task and environmental requirements for the intervention.

Studies from higher or mainstream education have already highlighted a number of factors that may hamper or promote the adoption of computer based or e learning (e.g. [19, 20]) although none specifically on AIEd. Few studies have explored barriers to adoption in special-needs teaching. From a review of the literature, Abed [21] concluded that the ability of computer technology to facilitate personalisation may be its crucial element, as studies with negative findings were those where personalisation was absent and this lack of personalisation would lead to abandonment of the technology. The review focussed on ICT's potential to include students with special needs into mainstream classes; views expressed by the 20 teachers interviewed centred on the challenge of providing extra support for students with special needs who are taught alongside typically developing peers. The findings were not transferable to classes comprising only special needs students.

The review by Liu, Wu and Chen [5] identified 26 publications on technology in special education from 2008 to 2012 and found that although negative outcomes were reported much less than positive ones there were challenges to incorporating such technologies into the curriculum. These challenges had been highlighted in the study by Campigotta, McKewen & Demmens Epp [22] and included integration of such devices into the classroom, the effort required to populate the application with learning material and the limitations of the devices. Teachers may also experience time constraints setting up the technology, limited access to the necessary technology, and difficulties in managing the class.

Given the lack of information about barriers and facilitators to the adoption of e-learning for those with special needs, the present study set out to collect the views of teachers who were taking part in preliminary evaluations of the MaTHiSiS system. The information obtained was intended to feed back into the ongoing design process to enhance the probability that the final product would meet the needs of teachers and learners and thus improve its adoption. Such a user-centred product would also facilitate recruitment to a larger scale evaluation whence definitive information of the effectiveness of the intervention would be sought.

The aim of the present study was to discover what teachers see as the barriers and facilitating factors to the adoption of an affect sensitive adaptive learning system for their students with learning disabilities and autism.

## 2 Methods

### 2.1 Design

Single semi-structured interview conducted either one-to-one or in a focus group.

### 2.2 Participants

Twenty-one (21) participants were recruited from the staff at schools and educational centres at six different sites (Nottingham and London in the UK, Rome, Salerno and

Fumane in Italy and Valladolid in Spain) who had taken part in the development and evaluation of the MaTHiSiS system (for more detail see [14]).

### 2.3  Procedure

Before the study commenced, ethics approval was received from the first author's University Faculty of Medicine and Health Sciences Research Ethics Committee, B16122016.

After meetings between research staff and teachers at each testing site to explain this phase of the project, teachers who expressed an interest in taking part were given information packs and consent forms, and times and locations for the data collection were agreed.

Five focus groups of between two and four participants were held, but at one testing site a series of individual interviews took place as it was not logistically possible to organise a focus group.

If required, a brief description of the MaTHiSiS system was given at the beginning of the session to remind teachers of the different components of the system. A semi-structured interview approach was adopted and the topic guide, with prompt questions, was structured according to the four types of factors found by Minocha [23] to influence the adoption of social software. These are:

- social (e.g., issues related to collaboration and group working)
- educational (factors that have a bearing on learning and teaching)
- organisational (the way in which the institutions involved deal with the introduction and use of the tools)
- technological (factors related to access, implementation and maintenance of the tools and services).

The focus groups and individual interviews lasted between 20 min and an hour and were audio recorded, transcribed at the pilot sites and translated into English language. These transcripts were then sent to the UK partners responsible for carrying out the analysis.

### 2.4  Analysis

Four members of the research team analysed the transcripts using thematic analysis following the stages described by Braun and Clarke [24]. First, all four members of the team independently read the same three transcripts selected because they presented particularly lengthy and detailed answers to the prompt questions. They assigned initial codes to sections of text relevant to the research aims and made suggestions how these might be combined to form an overarching theme. According to Braun & Clarke [24] (p. 82) a theme captures something important about the data in relation to the research question and represents some level of patterned response or meaning within the data set. The team then met to discuss their potential themes and agreed an initial set of themes with clear definitions and names for each theme. Then each team member independently analysed a subset of three or four of the transcripts so that each transcript was analysed by at least two team members. A final discussion agreed an updated set of themes from the first tentative set and a selection of text extracts that vividly conveyed the meaning of each theme.

# 3  Results

The team of four researchers agreed on five themes that captured the teachers' views of the system's potential impact, especially regarding learning and engagement but also on factors that might influence adoption. The following five themes emerged from the analysis:

1. Transformative potential
2. Ability to impact learning outcomes
3. Potential impact on teacher-learner/peer-learning relationships
4. Ease of use/usability issues
5. Organisational challenges

References to original transcripts are made using the convention: (name of interviewing partner, page number), where:

UoN: University of Nottingham (UK)
NTU: Nottingham Trent University (UK)
RIX: Rix Research and Media from the University of East London (UK)
PE: Polo Europeo della Conoscenza (Italy)
JCYL: Consejería de Educación Junta de Castilla y León (Spain)
LCS: La Cometa del Sud (Italy)
FMD: Fondazione Mondo Digitale (Italy)
Participants are referred to in the results collectively as "teachers".

## 3.1  Theme 1: Transformative Potential

Interviewees observed that the nature of the system might exert a long-term effect on their teaching practice in two ways. The first was on the way teachers saw their students, as use of the system revealed students' skills, knowledge and abilities that they had not otherwise understood or realised. The second was on the way they taught: the MaTHiSiS system was based on "non-linearity" (the ability to create learning experiences that are decoupled from the traditional progression of learning goals but that support highly individualised goal-oriented learning experiences), seen as very different to current classroom practice.

**Changes in Teachers' Perceptions of Students.** Teachers had observed that use of the system revealed students' skills, knowledge and abilities that they had not otherwise understood or realised. Students sometimes had not been afforded the opportunity to show their true range of skills and abilities. The system allowed them to demonstrate these.

*"Students (names) for instance demonstrated much more skills, than you would otherwise (realise) without the computer system. And also people/students like L. who seems very social and engaging but sometimes you think or maybe she, you know... but she was able to demonstrate what she can do, showing you much more than you would think."* (RIX, P2).

The instances where this observation had been made arose because the support given by MaTHiSiS had allowed the teachers to relinquish a degree of control:

*"I like it that there are certain activities where students can become independent. So, a lot of students I worked with probably might not have the confidence, or might not have the opportunity to, but I think now there are several of them from the group we had who would be able to sit and do this independently. And I think that's really important for the students but it's also important for the staff. I had to step back a little bit and let them do that. And I realised that they are progressing themselves as well"* (RIX, P4)

This led to the realisation that maybe they should increase their expectations of the students' achievements:

*"I keep going back to the sequencing with the lights, but that was my light bulb moment, that we don't push our students enough. We are not giving them a chance if they can't do it doesn't mean that they never do."* (RIX, P11)

**Changes in Teaching Practice.** Interviewees found the whole notion of an affect sensitive adaptive learning system and the construction of teaching material that it required as something very different from their current practice:

*"well, MaTHiSiS uses a quite different approach to teaching, compared to our system ... what you define "non-linearity"* (the ability of MaTHiSiS to create learning experiences that are decoupled from the traditional progression of learning goals but that support highly individualised goal-oriented learning experiences), *"isn't that? Non-linearity is something completely different, compared to our methodologies"* (FMD, P3)

It would change the way teachers prepared lessons:

*"if I think to a future use of the system...well...I imagine that MaTHiSiS could help me with my job. I would prepare the lessons in terms of learning graphs, include the LMs I want... it would be a different way to prepare and plan the lessons"* (FMD, P4)

as well as allowing teaching staff to better share out their finite time between a large, probably heterogeneous, group of students:

*"[I]f you have the chance that while you [students] are doing an activity that is appropriate to your level and you can be with others."* (JCYL, P4)

or, for critical thinking and reflection:

*"This would actually give staff more time to think critically, more time to develop really good learning materials for the students."* (RIX, P6)

## 3.2 Theme 2: Ability to Impact Learning Outcomes

Prompting interviewees to consider the educational implications of introducing something like MaTHiSiS revealed four sub-themes illustrating the way interviewees saw the potential impact on learning outcomes. These were: maximising engagement/minimising boredom and frustration; improved teacher knowledge of students' progress; empowerment of learners; impact on achievement and behaviour.

**Maximising Engagement/Minimising Boredom and Frustration.** Teachers were aware that this was the aim of the intervention but emphasised the importance to them of maintaining engagement in their students, especially so for those with ASD:

*"... because "to be engaged" does not simply mean "to be there, to pay attention", it means to be prepared and to be willing to learn, it's related to motivation in my opinion and it's very hard to understand this with ASDs students."* (FMD, P1)

The ability of MaTHiSiS to detect and use information about affective state was described by one teacher thus:

*"An increased concentration and opportunity to achieve something is greater. Rather than getting frustrated and giving up the student is more likely to stay engaged and learn for longer – because of the adjustment to the level. So the student will be engaged for longer. And I would hope that because of this the child will be able to learn more."* (RIX, P1)

Additionally, teachers appreciated the feedback they could obtain about their student's affective state:

*"The monitoring of the learner has been shown to PE02's teachers and I think that this can be a support for them since they can check the level of motivation and the level of not... where is absent the boredom in a certain activity, if this will be generalised to the traditional school activity, the school activity can be more effective in terms of learning for the student"* (PE, P2)

**Improved Teacher Knowledge of Students' Progress.** Teachers commented that MaTHiSiS facilitated enhanced tracking of student progress:

*"And also having the data and seeing them really progressing I think it's fantastic for staff."* (RIX, P3)

and this knowledge could be used to personalise their learning pathways:

*"The MaTHiSiS system has lots of potential for teachers to know their students much better and understand their level and provide materials that are suitable for them and stretch them."* (RIX, P4)

The particular monitoring that MaTHiSiS provided was seen as especially useful in special education where student progress was better seen in terms of small steps:

*"Because in mainstream you have your levels, whereas in special needs it's really hard to assess the little jumps but it's really important to assess the little jumps"* (RIX, P3)

**Empowerment of Learners.** Teachers described their students as having begun to construe themselves as actors in their learning experiences and hence having achieved some sense of control over the learning process.

*"The other learner was a very severe PMLD I think that his involvement has been reached when he started to perceive himself as able to perform an act, in his case to touch, to be able to give the correct answer in a physical way."* (PE, P1)

**Impact on Student Achievement and Behaviour.** Teachers reported several benefits for their students. In common with other computer mediated learning, the opportunities for frequent repetition had noticeable benefits for some students:

*"I think repetition…. Repetition [of learning material] is very useful for ASDs students especially with new things to learn. For example, E cannot read as you know, he [pause] memorizes the words as images. With MaTHiSiS I noticed that he started to memorize new words as the [learning material] appeared again!"* (FMD, P2)

And that while this learning took place using a specific system it could generalise:

*"Yes, definitely, like I said, it has the real potential for generalising learning to another situation"* (RIX, P9)

Some teachers noticed an effect on terminating disruptive behaviour and exploited this:

*"….so actually you could send – if they are getting to that point where they're disruptive, "Tell you what, would you like to go and do a bit of MaTHiSiS in the corner… And actually then they're still hitting learning objectives, they're still learning."* (NTU/UoN, P18)

### 3.3 Theme 3: Potential Impact on Social Relationships

Even before the remote learning imposed by pandemic precautions, the role in learning of social contact had been recognised. When considering the impact of a system like MaTHiSiS, interviewees highlighted the importance of relationships between teacher and student, between students but also between the school and family.

**Teacher Student Relationships.** MaTHiSiS was never intended to be used without supervision yet strong views were expressed that such a system could never replace a teacher:

*"If we are talking of a model that foresees the disabled child alone in front of a screen or a robot, I'm completely against this idea."* (PE, P3)

In support of this, participants highlighted the role of emotional closeness to facilitate the learning process and that this was something only a human teacher provided:

*"The emotional closeness is very important more than fundamental, the child is reassured by the presence of the adult. Personally I use the emotional closeness in my profession, in the formal learning situation and in the group activity because it's a condition that eases the learning process. The machine, the computer, in short, technology can support what is the help and therefore what the adult can do to get to the development potential of each student. The machine can support this, but I do not think it can be substituted"* (PE, P5)

Participants also stressed the need for interventions to avoid frustration, although the system was specifically designed to do just this:

*"I needed to be side by side with the pupil in order to favour learning without error, since he gets very frustrated with failures."* (JCYL, P6)

While the system was designed to utilise machine learning to recognise patterns in noisy data using a series of features (for instance eye gaze, body posture, facial expression) across a large sample of users and then making predictions and inferences, teachers were not always confident this could reliably match the sensitivity of a human:

*"If we are talking about decision-making, I believe that an algorithm can never substitute the human eyes and the ability to feel the child's emotion that a teacher develops in the relationship with the pupil. A system can provide hints, and can be useful in a group condition – when the whole class is working and the teacher cannot follow the progression of all. But with the disabilities or the autism we are working in an individual way, sometimes the change of the affective state is so slight and depends on the individual and unique expressions of the child that only a teacher that knows him very well can interpret."* (PE, P3)

It was also felt that the salience of different channels varied between children, especially for those with very limited physical ability:

*"You have to get to know them sometimes as well to understand that yeah, they are, brain, motor skills, it's all there, but sadly they can't use their arms, their legs, they can't get that across with anything other than eyes and head."* (NTU/UoN, P6)

Likewise, informativeness of various channels varied for users with autism, corroborating findings that many individuals with autism in many situations will use gaze aversion as a strategy to manage cognitive load, and actually can think better when they are not looking at the object of their attention [25, 26]:

*"And the one thing interestingly enough about the eye gaze, tracking eye movements, I think it's interesting because – but then sometimes I think children with*

*autism may not actually give you the most accurate data in that sense. Because I've got a child in my class who will just not look at what he's doing, no matter what."* (NTU/UoN, P6)

Because of these differences between autistic and non-autistic learners, and also heterogeneity within the broad rubric of the autism spectrum, the within-subjects evaluation of MaTHiSiS raised a question as to whether affect detection and its precise role in determining the presentation of learning material, may need to take a different form for learners with autism [14]. In spite of reservations, teachers recognised that the technology had the potential to act as a 'social mediator' between themselves and students, especially those on the autistic spectrum:

*"yes, using the system could help a new ASD student to gradually know and meet the teacher, you know? To reduce his/her anxiety with new people"* (FMD, P6)

Teachers acknowledged that the nature of their relationship with the learner would change but primarily in the type of interactions they had and how they targeted their support:

*"I don't have any worries that the robot takes away the role from the teacher, but the way technology is going it's good if technology could help with some of the decision making and we can support learners that need that support and others might be working away with our support"* (RIX, P6)

**Student-student Interactions.** Some collaborative scenarios had been developed for the system whereby two students could work together taking it in turn to make a move or a choice. However not all centres had access to these. Those teachers who did experience them welcomed the introduction of the collaborative scenarios which scaffolded constructive social interaction (see [27]):

*"Collaborative option - it is really nice, there are few things, you know, the students wanted to interact with me, especially the monsters and the mazes and things like that. They were trying get me involved and I would say 'that's your maze, carry on' but if they were actually doing it together, supporting each other or racing against each other to do it, or something, that would be very nice social activity and learning, building confidence and having fun"* (RIX, P9)

Special attention should be given to the selection of collaborating partners:

*T1: "Yes, but with students who have similar characteristics or difficulties or development."*

*T2: "It is good to make them progress in a similar way, but you can also use one or two children from the class and let them be the helpers."*

*T3: "Yes, but you have to select them very well. Otherwise they will not help they will answer instead of him".* (PE, P5)

**Parent's Involvement with their Child's Education.** The positive effect of parental involvement in a learner's progress is well known but difficult to achieve especially in pecial education. Teachers saw the potential of using the analytics engine of MaTHiSiS (e.g. graphs of affect state and learning progression) as a medium for sharing student progress with their parents or caregivers:

*"For me the graphs of each student... have been very useful. I'm thinking of showing them to the parents in order to let them know about their children's work at school. Also collaborating with the class teacher showing her these results will be interesting."* (PE, P2)

## 3.4    Theme 4: Ease of Use

A range of characteristics of the system impinged on the ability of both teachers and students to use it with ease. Teachers recognised that they were participating in a research project and that the system with which they were working was still in development but raised several points which were crucial in promoting the adoption of a system like MaTHiSiS.

**The Need for Training and Support.** Teachers welcomed the training that they had received in using the system at the beginning of the evaluation phase but thought that this on its own was not enough to support adoption. What was needed was ongoing training rather than purely initial training and support:

*"[T]he equipment, and probably the staff taking it on as well, as it would be something else new and sometimes that quite scary and daunting, and even though they had the training it still doesn't get adopted by staff. So I think that would be the main barrier."* (RIX, P5)

**Time Investment.** At the beginning of the evaluation phase, teachers had access to a selection of learning material that would be suitable for their nominated students for the period of the evaluation. For ongoing use, though, they would need to develop more learning material to ensure all lesson plans could be fulfilled by the system. This investment in time was seen by some as daunting but could be offset by a range of other aspects of the system.

For example, once produced, material could be reused:

*"In theory the possibility to reuse the material can quicken the preparation work."* (PE, P2)

And shared between teachers and between schools:

*"But I think that means you could distribute it across the – like encourage other people to take on the software and if they took it on as well, then you would say – right, what about this? What about that?"* And – *"It's like teachers always are little magpies, we take things off each other all the time, we take ideas – Oh, can I just – I found this online the other day, and just bring it over to someone."* (NTU/UoN, P30)

In addition to time saving from the reusability of learning material, teachers' time could also be freed through the support to students the system provided. This assistance would give teachers time to attend to more vulnerable learners and to other critical teacher roles such as developing appropriate learning materials:

> *"I think once the teacher got used to using it, I think it could definitely save them time. I think initially, they might not notice the difference but they have realised what it was able to do then it would give them more time to prepare other things and create other activities in the classroom, definitely."* (RIX, P11)

**Accessibility for Learners.** As far as student use was concerned, there was definitely a feeling that some groups would be able to use the system with minimal support:

> *"I mean, like I say, students with autism, I think they'd need help to start with but then they'd be able to do it straightaway. I mean, students with more severe learning – you'd probably always need a staff member with them, depending on how severe their learning need was."* (NTU/UoN, P24)

Teachers made it clear, however, that for some students, there remain motor (physical) and cognitive barriers to using the system. These obstacles are functions both of the core system and of the learning materials developed for it:

> *"Pupils need to have a minimum cognitive ability (too deep PMLD maybe it is not fine), apart from having good motor skills. Here we are working with children that had limited mobility to interact with the tablet. It's also a barrier that they (pupils) have not yet acquired reading skills, although I could solve it by reading them the words or texts."* (JCYL, P2)

### 3.5   Theme 5: Organisational Challenges

Teachers' views on possible constraints to adoption alluded to the physical environment and the organisation's current practices and to attitudes towards the introduction of such a system.

**School Environments.** Environments have been designed and organised to enable the predominant teaching practice of the time. For many, the organisation of the physical environment would need rethinking.

> *"It's not even the behaviour, it's just some of the – it's just manoeuvring wheelchairs around the classroom as well, you've got that, and some classrooms are bigger than others. Thankfully I've got quite a big classroom now but there are some classrooms where you're manoeuvring wheelchairs and equipment might just not fit in that room."* (NTU/UoN, P19).

However, some teachers face an even bigger challenge in the inadequacy of the school's technology infrastructure:

*"We have worked with quite 'precarious' conditions, I mean, in the school we do not have too nice WiFi conditions, when we change to the other building, with nice and speedy WiFi connection I think it would be easier. It is clue to have a good Internet connection and also nice devices."* (JCYL, P4)

**Fitting into Existing Practices.** One challenge is the need to sustain a system that is set up for one learner while having to cater for the needs of a whole class. Teachers had varying opinions on whether they could run MaTHiSiS on a whole class basis:

*"But you couldn't do it as a whole class setting could you really, because the sensors would have to be on every child and you wouldn't – it would be a huge thing. It would have to be like a lab full of the same sensor. And I don't know whether a school would buy into that because it would be a lot of money I'm assuming (laughs). So it's kind of a case of on a one to one target level I think it could work."* (NTU/UoN, P14).

Introducing new technology was felt to be challenging if some colleagues were resistant to change:

*"Yeah, so I think in terms of a lot of those things would put up a barrier in some teachers' heads to begin with, particularly with the organisation of it. I think it would take a while to get people in the MaTHiSiS way, that it became a thing in the school. It would be like eventually it could be really useful, but the organisation of it would probably – when people are rushing around there's just no time: I can't do it, there's just no time. I don't want to do it in my time."* (NTU/UoN, P16)

This reluctance was even more marked when it came to embracing digital technology in their teaching practice although this was seen to be a characteristic of the older generation or those who had not encountered IT during their training:

*"There are certain teachers... who don't want to do anything IT wise, ICT wise, that might be too advanced for a teacher maybe. They think it's too advanced for themselves but it isn't. And they're just not open to new things. Whereas I think you'll find that maybe the younger generation of teachers, or teachers that might not be younger generation, but they might not have been a teacher, they might have qualified late, they're just maybe open to things like this more."* (NTU/UoN, P16)

**School Budgets.** If schools did not already have access to the components of the system, initial set up costs seemed daunting:

*"Well... no! [laughs] as T1 said, we don't know the cost of the system, so... let me think... I imagine that MaTHiSiS is going to be quite expensive, right? Because it's a new system, because of its complexity etc. Not to mention the costs of the equipment!"* (FMD, P8)

However, although the costs of equipment were often seen as high, they were offset by longer-term gains:

*"If you have to buy the laptop, the tablets, put a high speed WiFi network... this is an economic investment that, although it is profitable in the long run, it is not easy."* (JCYL, P9)

If any colleagues were still reluctant to adopt such a system, one participant felt the crucial argument would be the cost-effectiveness of a system that could reliably interpret student engagement:

*"So something that's measuring their engagement, all that sort of pressure, oh gosh, what if this child doesn't listen and learn because he never does it in lessons, they're going to find out. Whereas actually if you put them on a software where you know they're going to engage, you know that the software is measuring their engagement, I can't see how that wouldn't be a successful argument. In a situation where they're trying to balance cost effectiveness."* (NTU/UoN, P34)

## 4 Discussion

Given the slower rates of adoption of computer-based learning in special education, the intention of the current study was to elicit the views of teachers on factors that would influence implementation. Resolving these factors at an early stage in development was considered important in order to modify the design in ways that would make adoption more likely. In spite of being highly motivated by virtue of having volunteered for a research project, teachers highlighted a range of issues that need addressing in order to promote adoption of this type of technology. There were design issues such as accessibility for learners and accuracy of the algorithm but these had been largely addressed by the time these final interviews took place (although affect detection and its precise role in determining the presentation of learning material, may need to take a different form for learners with autism). This experience underlines the importance of involving end users directly in the design and development process. Of more interest are the factors on which implementation depends but which are usually considered to be outside the designer's remit. These factors operate at an individual (teacher) level (e.g. the potential of the system to transform the way they worked) or at an organisational level [28].

An expensive technology-based intervention must be seen as worth the initial outlay in training, purchase of equipment and development of teaching material. Teachers were acutely aware of the educational advantages enabled by the technology which may be strong enough for initial adoption. However, they frequently referred to the investment in time required not only to prepare material but also to rethink the way the system could be incorporated into their day-to-day practice, a factor also identified by Campigotto et al. [22], Basak [19] and Cox et al. [6]. They cited organisational barriers such as the budgets, reluctance of colleagues and the school environment. Some of these factors have been highlighted in implementation science and by the researchers cited above. For perceived advantages in pedagogic practice and educational outcome to outweigh the perceived disadvantages in retraining time, financial outlay, environmental restructuring and organisational inertia, teachers need to be assured that these would be offset by longer-term savings in both time and financial investment.

However, of equal importance to these barriers to adoption are the factors that promote ongoing use. Teachers need ongoing support. Additionally, they need time to reflect and plan: to rethink their lesson plans, to share material with others and to engage and solve organisational issues. Developers can anticipate these challenges and should make every effort to not only address usability issues (including the ease with which teachers can input and update their teaching material) but also to design approaches for ongoing training and support as well as keeping component costs low.

Teachers are not the only stakeholders who determine the adoption of a new technology or other practice. Students and their families also have a perspective as do local managers and educational policymakers. At this stage of development of the MaTHiSiS system, teachers were the group that had the most experience of it and could also provide their observations on the other perspectives. If such educational technologies are to succeed practically, future research should involve other stakeholders to ensure barriers at all levels are identified.

**Acknowledgements.** This research was funded by the European Research Council Horizon 2020#687772 "Managing Affective-learning THrough Intelligent atoms and Smart InteractionS".

# References

1. World Economic Forum, 29 April 2020. https://www.weforum.org/agenda/2020/04/corona virus-education-global-covid19-online-digital-learning/. Accessed 08 Jan 2021
2. Cinquin, P.-A., Guitton, P., Sauzéon, H.: Online e-learning and cognitive disabilities: a systematic review. Comput. Educ. **130**(March), 152–167 (2019)
3. Rose, R.M., Blomeyer, R.L.: Access and equity in online classes and virtual schools, North American Council for Online Learning (2007). https://www.inacol.org/resource/access-and-equity-in-online-classes-and-virtual-schools. Accessed 08 Jan 2021
4. Bertini, E., Kimani, S.: Mobile devices: opportunities for users with special needs. In: Chittaro, L. (ed.) Mobile HCI 2003. LNCS, vol. 2795, pp. 486–491. Springer, Heidelberg (2003). https://doi.org/10.1007/978-3-540-45233-1_52
5. Liu, G.Z., Wu, N.W., Chen, Y.W.: Identifying emerging trends for implementing learning technology in special education: a state-of-the-art review of selected articles published in 2008–2012. Res. Dev. Disabil. **34**, 3618–3628 (2013)
6. Cox, M., Preston, C., Cox, K.: What Factors Support or Prevent Teachers from Using ICT in their Classrooms? Paper presented at the British Educational Research Association Annual Conference, University of Sussex at Brighton (1999)
7. Goodyear, P., Salmon, G., Spector, J.M., Steeples, C., Tickner, S.: Competences for online teaching: a special report. Educ. Technol. Res. Dev. **49**, 65–72 (2001)
8. Narayanan, S.A., Kaimal, M.R., Bijlani, K., Prasanth, M., Kumar, K.S.: Computer vision based attentiveness detection methods in e-learning. In: Proceedings of the 2014 International Conference on Interdisciplinary Advances in Applied Computing—ICONIAAC 2014. ACM Press, New York, pp 1–5 (2014)
9. Yadegaridehkordi, E., Noor, N.F.B.M., Ayub, N.M.B.A., Affal, H.B., Hussin, N.B.: Affective computing in education: a systematic review and future research. Comput. Educ. **142**, (2019)
10. Thompson, N., McGill, T.J.: Genetics with Jean: the design, development and evaluation of an affective tutoring system. Educ. Technol. Res. Dev. **65**, 279–299 (2017)

11. Aslan, S., et al.: Investigating the impact of a real-time, multimodal student engagement analytics technology in authentic classrooms. In: Presentation at Computer Human Interaction (CHI) 2019 (paper 304), Glasgow, Scotland (2019)

12. Scheiter, K., et al.: Adaptive multimedia: using gaze-contingent instructional guidance to provide personalized processing support. Comput. Educ. **139**, 31–47 (2019)

13. Wu, C.-H., Huang, Y.-M., Hwang, J.-P.: Review of affective computing in education/learning: trends and challenges. Br. J. Educ. Technol. **47**(6), 1304–1323 (2016)

14. Standen, P.J., et al.: An evaluation of an adaptive learning system based on multimodal affect recognition for learners with intellectual disabilities. Br. J. Educ. Technol. **51**(5), 1748–1765 (2020)

15. Bauer, M.S., Damschroder, L., Hagedorn, H., Smith, J., Kilbourne, A.M.: An introduction to implementation science for the non-specialist. BMC Psychol. **3**(1), 32 (2015)

16. Campbell, M., et al.: Framework for design and evaluation of complex interventions to improve health. BMJ **321**, 694–696 (2000)

17. Newell, A.F., Gregor, P., Morgan, M., Pullin, G., Macaulay, C.: User-sensitive inclusive design. Univ. Access Inf. Soc. **10**, 235–243 (2011)

18. Poulson, D.F., Waddell, F.N.: USERfit: user centred design in assistive technology. In: Nicolle, C.A., Abascal. J. (eds.) Inclusive Design Guidelines for HCI, pp 143–150. London: CRC Press (2001)

19. Basak, S.K.: A comparison of barriers and enhance factors on the adoption and use of ICT into teaching and learning for teachers. In: International Conference on Information Society (i-Society 2014), pp. 244–247, London (2014)

20. Rikala, J., Hiltunen, L., Vesisenaho, M.: Teachers' attitudes, competencies, and readiness to adopt mobile learning approaches. In: IEEE Frontiers in Education Conference (FIE) Proceedings, pp. 1 – 8, Madrid (2014)

21. Abed, M.G.: Teachers' perspectives surrounding ICT use amongst SEN students in the mainstream educational setting. World J. Educ. **8**(1), 6–16 (2018)

22. Campigotto, R., McEwen, R., Demmans Epp, C.: Especially social: exploring the use of an iOS application in special needs classrooms. Comput. Educ. **60**(1), 74–86 (2013)

23. Minocha, S.: A study of the effective use of social software to support student learning and engagement. The Open University, Milton Keynes (2009). UK. http://oro.open.ac.uk/16141/3/Effective-use-of-Social-Software-in-Education-CaseStudies.pdf. Accessed 11 Feb 2021

24. Braun, V., Clarke, V.: Using thematic analysis in psychology. Qual. Res. Psychol. **3**(2), 77–101 (2006)

25. Chen, G.M., Yoder, K.J., Ganzel, B.L., Goodwin, M.S., Belmonte, M.K.: Harnessing repetitive behaviours to engage attention and learning in a novel therapy for autism: an exploratory analysis. Front. Educ. Psychol. **3**, 12 (2012)

26. Doherty-Sneddon, G., Riby, D.M., Whittle, L.: Gaze aversion as a cognitive load management strategy in autism spectrum disorder and Williams syndrome. J. Child Psychol. Psychiatry **53**(4), 420–430 (2012)

27. Legoff, D.B., Sherman, M.: Long-term outcome of social skills intervention based on interactive LEGO play. Autism **10**(4), 317–329 (2006)

28. Locke, J., et al.: Individual and organizational factors that affect implementation of evidence-based practices for children with autism in public schools: a cross-sectional observational study. Implementation Sci. **14**, 29 (2019)

# Adaptive Modules on Prerequisite Chemistry Content Positively Impact Chiropractic Students' Proficiency in Biochemistry

Verena Van Fleet[(✉)]

Northwestern Health Sciences University, Bloomington, MN 55116, USA
vvanfleet@nwhealth.edu

**Abstract.** Students entering the doctor of chiropractic program at Northwestern Health Sciences University were offered three adaptive units on chemistry concepts deemed foundational for the two-course biochemistry series offered in the first two terms of the program. The effects of this remedial intervention offered to 3 incoming cohorts were assessed in a retrospective case-control approach by comparing several outcomes with a control group of similar size who started the program before the implementation of the adaptive units. Our calculations suggest that there is a positive effect of these adaptive units, in that the odds ratio for students to end the course with a grade of D or F decreased. The biggest impact on performance among 4 summative exams in the course was observed on the final exam, with an odds ratio of 2.3 to earn an A or B on the final, indicating that students who had access to the adaptive units had a substantially higher chance to earn a good grade. The odds ratio for students to earn an F or D on the final was 0.5, indicating a 50% lower risk for a low or failing score.

**Keywords:** Adaptive learning · Chemistry pre-requisites · Health science education

## 1 Introduction

### 1.1 Chiropractic Education

As is typical for curricula in graduate health sciences professions, chiropractic curricula start out with an emphasis on basic sciences, such as Gross Anatomy, Histology, Physiology, Biochemistr, followed by courses involving patient interaction as well as specific techniques within the scope of practice of chiropractic, culminating in a focus on internships in last terms of the educational path. Chiropractors are trained as primary care providers, who will refer to other healthcare professions, if they recognize that a condition requires interventions that lie outside of their scope of practice. At Northwestern Health Sciences (NWHSU), the program can be completed in 10 trimesters, with 3 fifteen-week trimesters offered each year. In order to properly diagnose patients, chiropractors have to first understand how the human body works from the molecular all

© Springer Nature Switzerland AG 2021
R. A. Sottilare and J. Schwarz (Eds.): HCII 2021, LNCS 12792, pp. 453–465, 2021.
https://doi.org/10.1007/978-3-030-77857-6_32

the way up to the whole organism. A sequence of two biochemistry courses (Biochemistry 1 and Biochemistry 2) is placed in the first two trimesters. Before graduates can get licensed and practice (in the United States), they have to pass four national board examinations, with the first one as is typical for graduate level health care professions, focused on the basic sciences, with 6 distinct parts: Gross Anatomy, Spinal Anatomy, Physiology, Biochemistry, Pathology, and Microbiology.

## 1.2 Variation in Student Readiness

It is common in many graduate professional degree programs that some students enter these programs with varying degrees of proficiency in pre-requisite content for various reasons. Most commonly, students are underprepared because they are several, sometimes many years removed from any science courses they took during their undergraduate education, especially those who spent some time in the workforce and are pursuing a second career. The following two reasons are specifically pertaining to some students pursuing a doctorate in chiropractic: 1. they have misconceptions about the chiropractic profession, never reviewed a chiropractic curriculum and are surprised about the rigor and extent of the basic science curriculum. 2. In the U.S., chiropractic programs are accredited by the Council on Chiropractic Education (CCE), which also sets the minimal requirements for students to be eligible for admission into doctor of chiropractic programs. When the PI started teaching at NWHSU in 2004, the minimal requirements included two terms of general chemistry, as well as organic chemistry; and that provided a solid foundation on which to build the biochemistry courses. In the late 2000, the CCE decided to open up chiropractic programs to a wider population of students and changed the minimal standards for admission to—among other criteria—no longer specifically require general chemistry and organic chemistry, just a minimal number of science credits. NWHSU has continued to require general chemistry and organic chemistry; however, over the course of the last decade has admitted an increasing number of students with waved requirements, most commonly, the chemistry requirements. The CCE historically has allowed chiropractic programs to waive incoming requirements, but schools have to report how they support these students and on their progress.

## 1.3 Performance Trends in Biochemistry at NWHSU

The changed admissions criteria showed disconcerting trends among the lowest performing students. When there rarely used to be an exam score below 55% (there are 3 summative exams and one final exam), scores as low as in the 30% range were all of a sudden popping up. The instructor responded by adding a homework assignment on important foundational chemistry concepts critical especially for the lecture component of Biochemistry 1, based on the first two introductory chapters of the course textbook [1]. The lab component of Biochemistry 1 had always started out with one unit on 'Basic Calculations' and one unit on 'pH and Buffers' (the 2 h per lab was designed to review foundational chemistry concepts, such as calculations and pH/buffer, as well as conduct experiments to further deepen the lecture content). While regularly teaching a few lab sections, the instructor gleaned more insight into students' proficiency levels. Here it also became evident that quite a few students were lacking some very fundamental skills. In general, in lecture and lab, the gap between the highest performers and the lowest performers had widened, but there was no room to add foundational content to the Biochemistry 1 course or a remedial course into the curriculum. It also did not seem fair that students who were well prepared would have to sit through foundational content again. NWHSU offers tutoring services and the instructor also made time to meet with some students on an individual basis, but kept searching for more substantive means of support to help students succeed.

### 1.4 Adaptive Learning

At the 2016 WCET (WICHE Cooperative for Educational Technologies; WICHE = Western Interstate Commission for Higher Education) Annual Conference in Minneapolis, the PI learned about Adaptive Learning for the first time, became intrigued with the potential of a remedial intervention that would provide individualized resources to those students who needed it and would bring all students to a common minimal level of chemistry understanding. The instructor successfully lobbied the administration to explore adaptive learning as an option. After exploring several possible vendors, it was decided to partner with Acrobatiq® (now owned by VitalSource®) and in the fall of 2017 work started on developing adaptive units specifically tailored to prime students for biochemistry.

### 1.5 Effect of Adaptive Units on Students' Performance in Biochemistry

After several terms of incorporating the adaptive units, it was time to investigate whether there is actually a measurable effect. Are students participating? Do they perform better? Are they less likely to earn a low grade or fail? Do the adaptive units, which are a demanding task for some students, impact their decision to choose to 'split' (spread their first trimester over 2 terms)?

## 2 Methods

### 2.1 Description of Adaptive Chemistry Units

Acrobatiq provided leadership and guidance through a project manager and an instructional designer in the process of development of the adaptive units.

*The first task* was to a list of learning outcomes in conjunction with skills that include chemistry terminology, concepts and knowledge fundamental to biochemistry.

*The second task* entailed the writing of 10 multiple choice questions for each learning outcome to be randomly usable in the pre-assessment. (This is different from the creation of a typical quiz that tests usually multiple learning outcomes with maybe two questions coming from different angles; in this case, the questions can bear similarities; e.g. a calculation question can use the same words, just modified numbers; or two questions can have the same stem and correct answer, but different distractors).

*The third task* for the instructor was to create educational content for each learning outcome. The course textbook's [1] first and second chapter were the source of some of the content built, but the majority of content was built using an open educational resource by OpenStax [2]. The most time-consuming part in each of the resource pages was the selection and creation of enough adequate practice questions to give students plenty of opportunity to practice and also for Acrobatiq's analytics to work well.

The learning outcomes were grouped into three units:

1. Basic Lab Calculations: focused on teaching students how to perform calculations they will need primarily for lab exercises, including dimensional analysis, molar concentration and dilution calculations.
2. pH and Buffer: Grasping pH and buffer is needed in some of the lab exercises, as well as some lecture units, and is also critically important in certain contexts in physiology, pathology and clinical pathology.
3. Foundations for Biochemistry: Addresses primarily organic chemistry concepts, such as functional groups and stereochemistry, but also takes a fundamental look at redox reactions, thermodynamics, and chemical equilibrium

*The fourth task* for the instructor was to create a post-assessment quiz for each unit.

### 2.2 Embedding the Adaptive Units into the Course

The incorporation of all components in order to function in the ways described in this paragraph was performed by the Acrobatiq team. On the landing page (Fig. 1), Students see an introductory unit with a welcome message and a description of the principle of adaptive learning, the flow of the process, as well as the purpose of the three adaptive units (Units 2, 3 and 4).

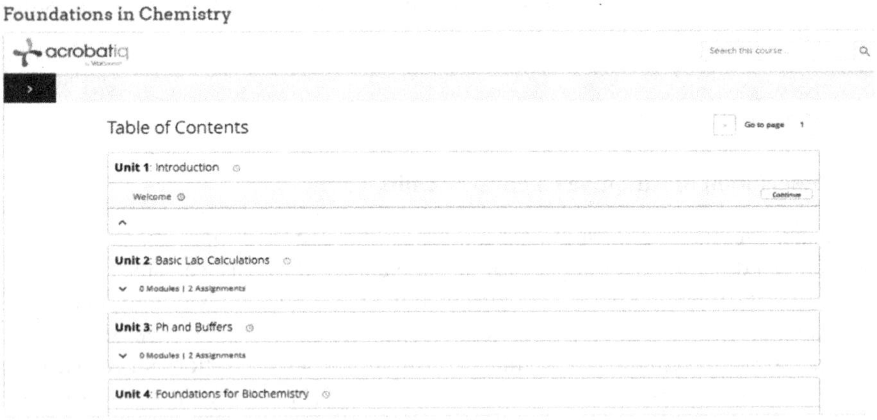

**Fig. 1.** Student view of the landing page in Acrobatiq (link is embedded in LMS, Moodle).

In the expanded module view (Fig. 2), the student can select two options:

**Fig. 2.** Student view of expanded unit (a unit can have more than one module, but this unit happens to have only one).

The 'Module 1' link will take students to the pre-assessment. Students are instructed to not look up answers to any questions, but to go through them pragmatically, and to take their best guess if they are not sure about or do not know the correct answer. Students are assured that the pre-assessment does not count for anything, but has the sole purpose to feed the algorithm that determines, which content pages the student needs to study to eventually succeed in the post-assessment quiz and also build a solid foundation for the course content that follows. Students are also asked to complete the pre-assessment individually to make sure that they will get assigned the appropriate content pages. In order to incentivize students to participate in the adaptive learning units, the 3 unit quizzes are bundled with other low point formative assessments and count towards the final grade. In addition, a small participation credit is also offered. To provide time for students to work through the units, two of the units are taking the place of a former paper lab activity (Basic Calculations) in week 1, and a former wet lab (pH and Buffers) in week 2, while two hours of lecture are allocated for students to work on the third unit (Foundations for Biochemistry) in the first week of each term. Liu *et al.* [3] were also looking to level the playing field for students entering a professional degree program in pharmacy by providing remedial units in biology, chemistry, math, and information literacy. In their approach, students got access to the adaptive units for 6 weeks prior to the start of the first semester of the program, participation was optional, and there was no credit associated with the participation.

The Acrobatiq platform provides the instructor with a lot of insights into study habits, learning, amount of time spent, and much more for each cohort, as well as individual students.

## 2.3  Studying the Effects of the Units

**Participants.** Some data reported stems from cohort aggregate scores (no focus on individual students) from cohorts taught between 2010 and 2019. Due to the COVID-19 pandemic, courses switched to remote teaching and learning during the winter term of 2020. Due to theses altered circumstances, data from cohorts who entered the program during the year 2020 were excluded from this study.

Comparative data were retrospectively analyzed in various ways, including a case-control approach. In the case-control study, the 'intervention' group is comprised of students who entered the program in the fall of 2018 (the first term the units were implemented), winter of 2019, and the fall of 2019 (a total of 258 students. The control group (a total of 267), students who did not experience the adaptive learning 'intervention', were chosen as close as possible to the time of implementation of the adaptive units, but also to include two fall and one winter cohort (fall 2016, winter 2017, fall 2017). The fall cohorts are typically more than twice as large as the winter cohorts, so by also choosing two fall and one winter cohort, the size of the compared groups was very similar. In the case of the Liu *et al.* study [3], the intervention and control groups were generated within one cohort of 128 pharmacy students, by offering their remedial units before the start of the semester on an optional basis, with some students choosing not to participate becoming the control group.

**Data Sources.** Performance and participation data can easily be accessed and exported from the Acrobatiq platform. For each term cohort a spreadsheet is created by the instructor, where scores on formative and summative assessments, including Acrobatiq quiz scores and an adaptive participation credit are collected.

**Calculations.** Measuring small changes, as expected regarding the impact of these three adaptive units (which make up a small fraction of the 5 credit Biochemistry 1 course) and the outcome measure affects a relatively small number of individuals compared to the intervention and control groups studied, the odds ratio (OR) can be calculated as a measure of the impact of the intervention. The odds ratio is the ratio of the odds of an outcome found in one group to the odds of it found in another group. The set-up of the data and the formula are described below:

|  | Students **with** the Outcome (e.g. final grade F) | Students **without** the Outcome (e.g. final grade not F) |
|---|---|---|
| Intervention (adaptive learning) | a | b |
| No Intervention (Control) | c | d |

$$OR = \frac{a}{c} \div \frac{b}{d} = \frac{ad}{bc}$$

# 3  Results

### 3.1  Student Participation and Performance on Adaptive Units

According to the Acrobatiq dashboard, the activity completion and the number of pages viewed regularly lies above 95%. Figure 3 shows an example of analytics from the dashboard giving the instructor information how often students have accessed the course. One can also choose to show data for individual students regarding their learning, time spent, number of times they accessed the course, etc. 65% or more students in each cohort have accessed the course 6 or more times.

**Performance on Adaptive Unit Post Assessments (Quizzes).** The average score on all Unit quizzes (post-assessments) is over 99%, as students are given 3 attempts with feedback on each attempt and the highest attempt scores counting toward the final grade.

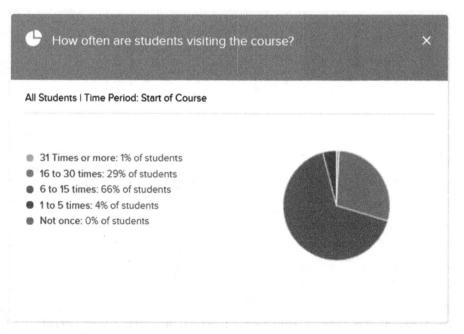

<comment>pie chart with legend</comment>

**Fig. 3.** Shows one example of Acrobatic dashboard information.

## 3.2   Effect on Final Grade

**Final Grade Trend over 10 Years.** Figure 4 shows the final grade trend over 10 years for each cohort, showing the percentage of students grouped by grades A and B, then C, and lastly D and F.

**Odds Ratio for Final Grades in Biochemistry 1.** In order to determine whether there was an effect on final grades in Biochemistry 1, the odds ratio was calculated for all grades, as well as D and F combined (Table 1).

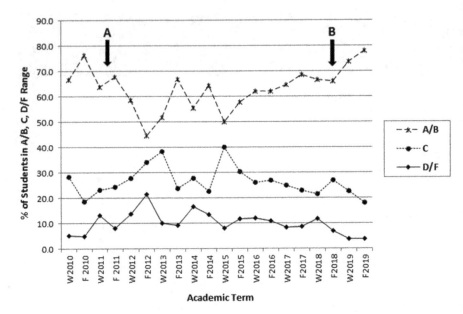

**Fig. 4.** Percentage of students in each term who ended the course with a grade of F or D, C, and B or A between the winter term of 2010 and the fall of 2019. Also indicated are A: the approximate time, when the CCE changed the admissions requirements (the author could not find a record of when exactly the change occurred) and B: when the adaptive units were incorporated into Biochemistry 1.

**Table 1.** Total number of students (n), number of students for each grade, and odds ratio of finishing Biochemistry 1 with a certain grade, given for the Intervention Group, which used the adaptive units and the Control Group, which did not use the adaptive units.

|  | n | A | B | C | D | F | D + F |
|---|---|---|---|---|---|---|---|
| Intervention group (with adaptive units) | 258 | 56 | 131 | 58 | 9 | 4 | 13 |
| Control group (without adaptive units) | 267 | 59 | 115 | 66 | 18 | 7 | 25 |
| Odds ratio | – | 1.0 | 1.4 | 0.9 | 0.5 | 0.6 | 0.5 |

### 3.3 Effect on Exam 1 Performance

**Exam 1 Grade Trend over 10 Years.** Figure 5 shows the grade trend on exam 1 over 10 years for each cohort, showing the percentage of students grouped by grades A and B, then C, and lastly D and F.

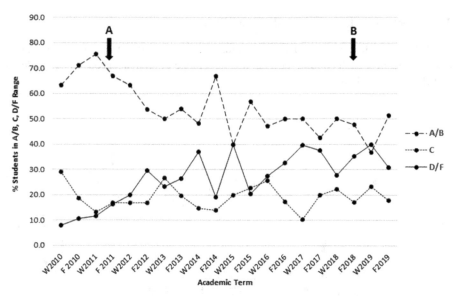

**Fig. 5.** Percentage of students in each term who scored a grade of F or D, C, and B or A on Exam 1 between the winter term of 2010 and the fall of 2019. Also indicated are A: the approximate time, when the CCE changed the admissions requirements (the author could not find a record of when exactly the change occurred) and B: when the adaptive units were incorporated into Biochemistry 1.

**Odds Ratio for Grades on Exam 1.** As for the final grade, the odds ratio was determined for grades on exam 1. This exam always includes several questions similar to the quiz questions at the end of adaptive Unit 4 (specifically functional groups and stereochemistry).

**Table 2.** Total number of students (n), number of students for each grade, and odds ratio of earning a certain grade on Exam 1, given for the Intervention Group, which used the adaptive units and the Control Group, which did not use the adaptive units. The total number of students is higher for both groups than for the final grade, as it includes students who ended up dropping the course after the first exam.

|  | n | A/B | C | D + F |
|---|---|---|---|---|
| Intervention group (with adaptive units) | 272 | 127 | 51 | 94 |
| Control group (without adaptive units) | 283 | 132 | 49 | 102 |
| Odds ratio | – | 1.0 | 1.1 | 0.9 |

### 3.4   Effect on Performance on the Final Exam

Final Exam Grade Trend over 10 Years. Figure 6 shows the grade trend on the final exam over 10 years for each cohort, showing the percentage of students grouped by grades A and B, then C, and lastly D and F.

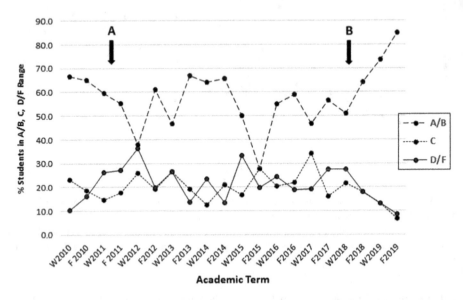

**Fig. 6.** Percentage of students in each term who scored a grade of A or B, C, and D or F on the final exam between the winter term of 2010 and the fall of 2019. Also indicated are A: the approximate time, when the CCE changed the admissions requirements (the author could not find a record of when exactly the change occurred) and B: when the adaptive units were incorporated into Biochemistry 1

**Odds Ratio for Grades on the Final Exam.** As for the final grade, the odds ratio was determined for grades on the final exam. This exam includes questions on the last two units covered in lecture as well as comprehensive questions.

**Table 3.** Total number of students (n), number of students for each grade, and odds ratio of earning a certain grade on the final exam, given for the Intervention Group, which used the adaptive units and the Control Group, which did not use the adaptive units.

|  | n | A/B | C | D + F |
|---|---|---|---|---|
| Intervention group (with adaptive units) | 258 | 192 | 32 | 34 |
| Control group (without adaptive units) | 264 | 147 | 57 | 60 |
| Odds ratio | – | 2.3 | 0.5 | 0.5 |

## 3.5   Are Students Deciding to Take It Slower?

**Odds Ratio for Decision to Split.** Table 2 shows the odds ratio for students to decide to go on a split schedule Table 4.

**Table 4.** Number of students in intervention and control group, number of students who decided to split and odds ratio of a student to decide to go on a split schedule.

|  | Total number of students | Number of students who decided to split |
|---|---|---|
| Intervention group (with adaptive units) | 258 | 20 |
| Control group (without adaptive units) | 267 | 22 |
| Odds ratio | – | 0.9 |

# 4   Discussion

## 4.1   Student Participation and Performance in Adaptive Units

**Participation.** The strategy of counting the Unit quiz scores (post-assessment scores), towards the final grade, as well as offering a small number of points for participation turned out to be motivating and led to 100% of students completing the pre-assessments (minimal requirement for participation points) and the Unit quizzes (post-assessments). It certainly also helped, that there was time allocated for students to work on the units in the first two weeks of the term. In addition, they occurred at the very beginning of the very first trimester students were enrolled in a program pursuing a career, or a second career, which means the work load from other courses was not yet very heavy and the motivation was high. Liu *et al.* [3] offered their remedial adaptive units for incoming students of a pharmacy program for 6 weeks before the start of the semester, made it voluntary and did not offer any credit. They ended up with lower participation rate, with the advantage that the intervention and the control groups were part of the same cohort, which made them very similar in that they ended up going through the exact same instruction in the course and were all taking the same exams, which is not the case in this study. The advantages of our study is that the number of students in the compared groups are substantially higher (>200) and all students in the intervention group got the benefit of the remedial material.

**Performance.** The post-assessment quizzes were treated as formative assessments and students were allowed to try up to three times with the highest score counting, so they could learn from mistakes. Due to the high achievement of averages of >99% on all three unit quizzes, it is not possible to correlate these quiz scores with students' efforts, time and efficiency dedicated to the adaptive units. Therefore, performance on two summative assessments (exam 1 and the final exam), as well as the final grade in the course (Biochemistry 1) were used to determine, whether the intervention had any effects on outcomes.

## 4.2 Effect on Final Grades

**Final Grades over Time.** Observing final grades (As and Bs bundled, Cs, and Ds and Fs bundled), depicted as percentage of students in each cohort, there seems to be an upward trend in As and Bs since the winter of 2015, potentially a steeper upward trend since the implementation of the adaptive units (Fig. 4). Of more interest though is the trend in Ds and Fs, as those are students at risk of eventually not being able to progress in the program. Students with 3 terms of academic difficulty, which includes failing a course and/or a low GPA, are dismissed from the program.

**Odds Ratios for Final Grades.** Since the percentage of students completing Biochemistry 1 with a D or F has been relatively low, it was decided to calculate odds ratio for students ending the course with certain grades (Table 1). The odds ratio of 0.5 for Ds and Fs is an encouraging result that means students have a 50% reduced risk of finishing the course with a D or F (since 2020, the program no longer allows students scoring <70% to pass a course; in other words, as is typical for most graduate programs, there is no more grade of D). On the other hand, with the OR = 1.4 for a grade of B, the odds for a grade of B is about 40% higher. The odds to finish the course with an A or a C are about the same for the control and the intervention group. In the grade trend over time graph the trends seem to go in the same direction even before the adaptive units were implemented, so there may be other reasons for the beneficial odds at play.

A question that arose from the beneficial odds ratios on final grades was, whether there was an impact on a specific summative assessment; thus the same approach was taken to see how grades were trending over time and what odds ratios were obtained in the case of exam 1 and the final exam (there are two more summative exams in this course, data not shown).

## 4.3 Effect on Two Summative Exam

**Exam 1.** In the grade trend of Exam 1 over time graph (Fig. 5), an upward trend for grades D and F and a downward trend for grades A and B since about the winter of 2011 can be observed. However, over the time interval during which the two compared groups started the program (between fall 2016 and fall 2019) the trends seemed fairly flat. This also becomes apparent in the OR values, which are hovering around 1 (Table 2), meaning that the intervention likely had not effect. This result was surprising, as exam 1 occurs only about 3 weeks after students complete the adaptive units and about 15% of the exam questions are very similar to the Unit 4 post-assessment questions. Considering though that this is one of the first big exams in a new program, with a new instructor, the impact of the adaptive units may just not be substantive enough to make a difference compared to these bigger challenges for these incoming students.

Since there is an effect on the final grade, the positive effects seen in case of the final course grade had to occur in one or more of the remaining summative assessments.

**Final Exam.** Figure 6 shows the most impressive trend with respect to increasing percentage of As and Bs and decreasing percentages for Cs, Ds, and Fs. The distinctly lower OR of 0.5 for both Cs, as well as Ds and Fs combined (Table 3), and OR = 2.3 for an A and B, are indicators that the adaptive units support students in building a solid foundation on which they can build their biochemistry knowledge. Of course, there could be other factors playing a role, and give rise to new research questions.

Among others, it will be interesting to investigate correlations with incoming GPA. In addition, is there a correlation between waved admissions criteria and if so, is it correlated to a low GPA or waved chemistry pre-requisite, and/or a combination of both? It will also be interesting to find out whether there is a measurable impact on students' performance on the chemistry portion of the Part I National Board Examination.

### 4.4  Effect on Decision to Split

Subjectively, it seemed that once the adaptive units were implemented, that a higher number of students was deciding to split the first term, an officially offered option for students to spread trimester 1 courses over two terms. Thus the odds ratio for students splitting was determined (Table 4). The hypothesis was that students may realize that they need extra time to catch up and make the decision to take it slower. However, the odds ratio of 0.9 does not suggest that there was a significant difference between the intervention and the control group.

# References

1. Nelson, D.L., Cox, M.M.: Lehninger Principles of Biochemistry. 7$^{th}$ (edn.) W.H. Freeman and Co. (2017)
2. Flowers, P., Robinson, W.R., Langely, R., Theopold, K.: Chemistry. OpenStax (2015)
3. Liu, M., McKelroy, E., Corliss, S.B., Carrigan, J.: Investigating the effects of and adaptive learning intervention on students' learning. Educ. Tech. Res. Dev. **65**, 1605–1625 (2017)

# Using Adaptive Flashcards for Automotive Maintenance Training in the Wild

Daphne E. Whitmer[1]([⊠]), Cheryl I. Johnson[1], Matthew D. Marraffino[1],
and Jeremy Hovorka[2]

[1] Naval Air Warfare Center Training Systems Division, Orlando, FL 32826, USA
{daphne.whitmer,cheryl.i.johnson,matthew.marraffino}@navy.mil
[2] Motor Transport Maintenance Instructional Company, Logistics Operations School, Marine
Corps Combat Service Support Schools, Camp Johnson, Jacksonville, NC 28542, USA
jeremy.hovorka@usmc.mil

**Abstract.** The U.S. military is interested in modernizing its training and educational technology resources to support tailored, learner-centric experiences more consistent with the digital-age. The goal of this research was to explore the benefits of adaptive training in the context of a USMC course. To this end, we describe the development of an adaptive flashcard system to help Marines study during an automotive maintenance course. Specifically, the system incorporated techniques, such as adaptive sequencing and the use of mastery criteria to drop flashcards from study. These techniques have been effective in the context of short-term laboratory studies but not for longer-term course performance. Therefore, we conducted an initial pilot study to compare course performance outcomes between cohorts before and after the addition of the adaptive training system in the course. Overall, there was a 50% reduction in exam learning objective failures in the adaptive training cohort compared to the cohort without adaptive training. Furthermore, we found that greater usage of the system was related to higher course GPA. Taken together, these results demonstrate a promising use-case for an adaptive training solution implemented successfully "in the wild," and future research plans for this system are discussed.

**Keywords:** Adaptive training · Flashcards · Spacing effect · Criterion learning · Classroom intervention

## 1 Introduction

Recently, both the Chief of Naval Operations [1] and the Commandant of the Marine Corps [2] have stressed the requirement to move away from a one-size-fits-all, industrial-age approach to training to a digital-age approach with flexible, learner-centric training available at the point of need. A current challenge faced by United States Navy (USN) and United States Marine Corps (USMC) schoolhouses is the expanding training curricula and rise of student throughput without the accompanying increase in training days and available instructors [3]. Therefore, instructors are encumbered to teach more material in fewer days to larger classrooms, while also identifying and remediating students who need additional support. Likewise, students must bear some responsibility to study on their own during minimal free time to keep up with these new demands. Unfortunately, in many cases instructors and students alike currently lack the digital-age resources they need to overcome these challenges. To this end, the goal of the present research was to develop an adaptive training tool to support students during this shift to self-paced, student-centered learning and evaluate its effectiveness in the context of a USMC course (i.e., "in the wild").

In order to accomplish this goal, we partnered with Automotive Maintenance Technician Basic Course (AMTBC) instructors at the Marine Corps Combat Service Support School. The AMTBC is a fast-paced, 52-day course that covers eight automotive systems across three different vehicle type families, including light, medium, and heavy fleet vehicles. The course is comprised of six sections that advance through the complexities of these automotive systems. Early in the course, students learn the theory of all the automotive systems and spend the rest of the course applying that knowledge by performing hands-on activities necessary to maintain and repair the vehicles, going in-depth for each system. In addition, incoming students' experience with automotive maintenance is highly variable, with some students having no experience at all prior to this course. Given these time constraints and students' variability in prior experience, success in this course often requires students to study actively during their own time to keep up with the pace of the course. Flashcards are a useful tool to help emerging mechanics and technicians become proficient with the basics, given the amount of rote memorization required to advance through the course.

Based on the need for learner-centric training and promising research findings, we took an adaptive training approach when designing a flashcard training testbed. Adaptive training (AT), which is training that is tailored to an individual's needs [4], provides a unique training experience for an individual learner, rather than a one-size-fits-all approach more commonly used in traditional classrooms. This learner-centered technique tailors the training experience to individual students by targeting their strengths and weaknesses in performance. AT has been demonstrated to be beneficial in several domains, including learning a new language [5], physics [6], problem-solving [7], and medical skills [8]. Furthermore, AT approaches have been successful in military domains, such as periscope operations [9], close air support decision-making skills [10], and electronic warfare operations [11]. For example, Marraffino and colleagues [10] described an adaptive scenario-based training system for a complex, military decision-making task that tailored both feedback and scenario difficulty based on trainee performance. During an evaluation of this system with USMC students, they found that the adaptive condition led to the largest pre- to post-test learning gains compared to both a non-adaptive condition (i.e., trainees received the same feedback and scenario difficulty regardless of performance) and a control condition (i.e., slideshow refresher on the task). The authors argued that AT approaches can help train students with different levels of experience so that novice students can "catch up" to their more experienced peers.

Overall, AT approaches seem well-suited to fulfill the goals outlined by the Chief of Naval Operations and Commandant of the Marine Corps, but more research is needed to determine whether the benefits of AT extend to military classroom learning. At present, few studies report on how AT interventions affect learning outcomes in a real-world course, but rather focus on test events specific to the adaptive trainers themselves (i.e., pre to post-test outcomes). Therefore, the current research aims to address this gap and explores the potential benefits of incorporating AT during a USMC course on key course outcomes, such as number of exam failures and course GPA.

In the present paper, we report a pilot study in which an adaptive flashcard system was used as an intervention in a real-world military classroom. First, we review the relevant literature that informed the design decisions of the AT system. Next, we discuss the implementation of the AT system "in the wild" to meet the instructional goals of an automotive maintenance course. In this case, the AT system adaptively sequenced the flashcards and dropped them from study based on how the student performed on each flashcard using specific mastery criteria. Lastly, we present the results of a pilot study examining the effects of the AT system on course learning outcomes and discuss lessons learned and future research directions.

## 1.1   The Benefits of Flashcards for Learning

Flashcards are a popular study strategy, and instructors commonly encourage their students to use flashcards to prepare for exams [12–15]. In fact, flashcards have been demonstrated to be a helpful tool for learning, and students often report that they use flashcards to memorize information, test themselves, and get feedback or assess what they know [13, 15]. Additionally, using flashcards as a tool for self-testing is related to the *testing effect*, a well-studied phenomenon in which long-term retention is enhanced as a result of repeated testing as opposed to repeated studying [16–21]. For example, Roediger and Karpicke [20] demonstrated the powerful advantages to repeated testing on learning as compared to repeated studying in a series of studies using prose passages. They found benefits to repeated studying at immediate retention, but repeated testing led to higher memory performance one week later. That is, after a one-week delay, those who re-studied forgot significantly more information than those who repeatedly tested. A possible explanation for this effect is that repeated testing gives students the opportunity to practice retrieving the learned information (i.e., known as *retrieval practice*) and also enhances the number of retrieval cues, whereas re-reading text while studying makes it easier to process the material each time it is re-read [13]. In other words, flashcards give learners an opportunity to self-test repeatedly, practice retrieval, and increase the strength and number of retrieval cues to enhance long-term memory of the material, whereas re-studying may only improve the speed and fluency at which the material is processed.

## 1.2   Flashcard Sequencing

A classic technique often explored in the flashcard training literature to improve long-term memory involves expanding the spacing interval between individual flashcard presentations. This technique is called the *spacing effect* or *distributed practice* [22–27], in which spacing out one's study over several study sessions in a longer period of time leads to improved long-term retention, as opposed to cramming information in one (or few) study sessions [see 29, 30 for a review]. For example, students using an effective, spaced study strategy would space their flashcard studying by practicing for one hour every week. However, students generally use poor metacognitive strategies when it comes to studying [30] and they prefer to cram rather than space their study [31]. Cramming, or repeating information over and over in a short period of time, only enhances short-term memory prior to assessment with a rapid rate of decay [25]. Students may prefer to cram because the time interval between studying and assessment is short, so they perceive it as efficient, or they have less of a concern about long-term knowledge retention. Both methods result in information acquisition, but the critical difference between spacing and cramming is that spacing one's study leads to long-term retention of the material whereas cramming leads to faster forgetting.

Recently, there has been an increased interest in the literature exploring whether spacing or sequencing flashcards can be performed adaptively, based on the learner's in-training performance during short-term training periods. The rationale behind this adaptive sequencing approach is that it allows learners to focus on concepts that they need more practice with by re-sequencing incorrectly recalled items towards the "top" of the flashcard deck and the less difficult items towards the "bottom" of the deck. By implementing adaptive sequencing, the flashcard deck is being reshuffled constantly based on a learner's last response to a flashcard in an attempt to optimize the spacing intervals for each individual flashcard. Several studies have shown that adaptively sequencing the flashcards, or increasing the time interval between correctly answered flashcards, led to better learning outcomes than randomly sequencing flashcards or having fixed learning intervals [32–34]. For example, Mettler, Massey, and Kellman [34] used a geography task and found that adaptively sequencing trials based on trial accuracy and reaction time led to larger pre- to post-test changes than pre-determined spacing that was not based on the learner's performance. Additionally, Mettler and colleagues [35] showed adaptive sequencing to be more efficient than random sequencing using the same geography task (Experiment 2). Using the student's accuracy and reaction time during training as a method to space the flashcards has been demonstrated as a way to improve the effectiveness and efficiency of training. However, most of this research has been conducted in the laboratory with limited investigations into the efficacy of these techniques in real-world classrooms.

## 1.3 Flashcard Mastery

Another technique examined in the flashcard training literature is dropping flashcards from future study. Students must make the most of limited study time, and one way to achieve this is by using a criterion to assess their knowledge and drop well-known flashcards from the deck to focus on the harder flashcards that have not yet reached this criterion. This type of assessment used to perform dropping is known as *criterion learning* or *mastery learning* [e.g., 15, 36–38]. Past research has demonstrated that increasing the mastery criterion, or number of correct recalls required to drop a flashcard, is associated with improved long-term retention [15, 30, 38–40]. However, research has shown that students typically choose to drop a flashcard after only one correct recall [25, 30], rather than waiting for several successful recall attempts to make a more informed metacognitive judgment. When studying independently, employing this technique requires students to perform metacognitive monitoring (i.e., asking oneself, "How well do I know this flashcard?"), which students struggle to do effectively [30,

39–41]. With these considerations in mind, a flashcard training system can be designed for students so that they do not need to make these decisions of how and when to study.

A more learner-centered, adaptive approach to mastery learning would perform flashcard dropping based on a student's in-training performance and would require several correct recalls for an item to be considered "mastered." Furthermore, past research has shown that using objective mastery criteria as a method to drop flashcards (e.g., 4 out 4 correct responses within 7 s per trial), is more effective than not dropping any flashcards or allowing the learner to decide when to drop a flashcard [30, 35, 39–41]. This adaptive mastery approach removes concepts from the flashcard deck once they have been "mastered" so learners can focus on the concepts they are struggling with rather than restudying flashcards that they already know. This approach to dropping flashcards adaptively may increase engagement with the task and optimize task difficulty to prevent learners from getting bored [42], as concepts that are already well-known are retired. A recent study by Whitmer and colleagues [41] compared three conditions that differed based on how flashcards were dropped during training the visual identification of armored vehicles. Participants were either in a condition that included mastery criteria to drop flashcards, a condition in which flashcards were never dropped, or a condition in which the learners decided when they mastered a flashcard and dropped it from the deck. Those in the condition with mastery criteria had the lowest forgetting rates after a two-day retention interval compared to the other two conditions. Additionally, learner-control over the flashcards led to the poorest learning outcomes [see also 30]. In sum, previous work has shown that using objective mastery criteria to drop flashcards can improve retention and efficiency of training. However, like much of the spacing literature, there have been few studies that have looked at this technique in the setting of classroom learning outcomes.

## 2   Current Research

For the present work, the AT system was examined as an AT intervention "in the wild" to determine whether it was an effective additional training resource for an automotive maintenance course in a military schoolhouse. With a high-volume roster of students with varying backgrounds and needs, an AT system can help support the instructional goals of the course. For instance, one student entering this military occupational specialty (MOS) may have little knowledge of automotive systems, whereas another student may have been a mechanic prior to entering the Service, but both students are expected to achieve similar performance standards by the end of the course. The AT system can provide an individualized training experience to both trainees, such that the novice student may need extra reps and sets to get up-to-speed (e.g., completing the same flashcard deck multiple times), whereas the more experienced student may only need a refresher on certain topics. Additionally, it is essential in this type of course to master the early information (e.g., function of different vehicle parts) because it informs later training (e.g., diagnosing a malfunction). Not only can this adaptive intervention help the less experienced students achieve a similar level of knowledge as their more experienced peers, it can also benefit instructors by freeing up classroom time to train advanced topics.

In this study, we compared learning outcomes in a USMC course from two different class cohorts: one before and one after the AT system was implemented in the course. Prior to the implementation of the AT system, instructors strongly recommended that students make their own flashcards for independent study. Instructors typically reviewed these flashcards only when students were having difficulty during the course, thus the research team did not have access to the students' flashcards for evaluation. Students in the cohort after the AT system was implemented had access to the adaptive flashcard trainer, but they were free to develop their own flashcards as desired. The goal of implementing the AT system was to add another tool for students to use for studying. We expected that providing students with an adaptive flashcard training system to supplement their course instruction and replace the need to create their own flashcards could improve the effectiveness and efficiency of their valuable study time. Likewise, the training system could support students by helping them make good study decisions, which the literature suggests that students do not do well on their own [see 30, 41, 43], such as how to order flashcards, how often to study the flashcards, and which flashcards can be removed from further study. We built the AT system with these instructional needs in mind. Our main research goal was to determine if using the AT system was associated with better course performance. We hypothesized that students who used the AT system would have better course performance than students who did not use the AT system. Additionally, we explored usage trends and hypothesized that increased use of the AT system would be associated with better course performance.

## 2.1 Adaptive Flashcard System

The AT system was developed using lightweight scripting software that could be installed on each student's course-issued laptop. When students first opened the AT system, a student dashboard provided background information about the system and allowed students to select a flashcard deck for training. Once a training session was initiated, the AT system would begin collecting performance data that were later used for analysis. When students completed a training session by mastering out of the deck, meeting the maximum time (i.e., 20 min) or maximum number of trials (i.e., 300 trials) allowed for the session, or quitting the session, they were returned to the dashboard and could select a different (or the same) flashcard deck. The following sections describe the design of the AT system, which was guided by the goals of the course and previously discussed research.

**Flashcard Content.** Using course material provided by instructors, ten flashcard decks were available to students within the AT system. The flashcard decks covered four out of eight automotive systems in the course, including the power train, electrical systems, hydraulic systems, and compressed air systems. These topic areas were identified by instructors as four particularly challenging topics for students in the course. Overall, the ten decks covered more than 160 course learning objectives.

Within each content area, there were three different types of flashcards that asked participants to either: identify the automotive part (identification), identify the function of the part (function), or locate the part on a vehicle (location). Figure 1 presents an example of each flashcard for the Air Governor part in the compressed air system. Both identification and function flashcards used a multiple-choice format in which students were presented with an image of a component and four options. For identification flashcards, the goal of the flashcard was to label the component depicted in the image. For function flashcards, the image contained a label and the goal was to identify the correct function of that component. Feedback was provided after each flashcard. For incorrect flashcards, the correct answer was highlighted in green and the incorrect answer in red (see Fig. 2). For correct flashcards, the correct answer that the student selected was highlighted in green. Location flashcards used either a multiple-choice format or a click-to-locate format. For location flashcards that used multiple-choice format, the AT system displayed a picture of a part and students had to choose from four options that described a spatial location (e.g., "on top of the transmission" or "passenger side, underneath the exhaust muffler"). For click-to-locate flashcards, as shown in Fig. 3, the AT system presented an image depicting an area of a vehicle system, and the student's task was to locate the specified component by clicking on the corresponding area of the image. Feedback was provided by circling the correct location with the text, "correct" in green or "incorrect" in red under the picture (see Fig. 3). For all flashcard decks, a feedback prompt appeared when a flashcard was mastered that read, "You mastered this card. It will be removed from the deck. Good job!"

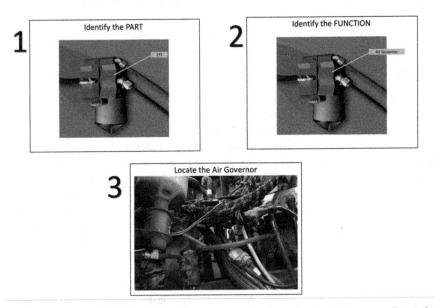

**Fig. 1.** Examples of the three different flashcard question types for the Air Governor. Part 1 shows the identification flashcard, Part 2 the function flashcard, and Part 3 the location flashcard.

**Sequencing and Mastery.** The research literature previously discussed and the instructional goals of the course guided the design decisions for the training system. Specifically, the sequencing was determined based on a student's accuracy and reaction time for individual flashcards. For example, items answered incorrectly were presented sooner than

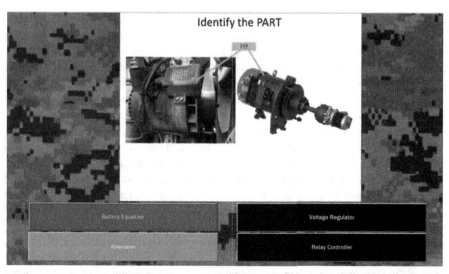

**Fig. 2.** Example multiple-choice flashcard with feedback for an incorrect response to an identification question. The correct answer is highlighted in green and the incorrectly selected response is highlighted in red. (Color figure online)

**Fig. 3.** Example of a click-to-locate flashcard with feedback for an incorrect response. After clicking the wrong area of the image, incorrect feedback is displayed in red and a yellow circle highlights the correct location of the component. (Color figure online)

items answered correctly with fast reaction times. The literature suggests that adaptively sequencing flashcards gives a learner additional opportunities to study difficult items by reshuffling the deck and prioritizing these incorrectly recalled items [e.g., 32–35]. Additionally, the mastery criteria for dropping flashcards was 3 out of 4 correct responses within 20 s per trial. Based on past research [e.g., 35, 41], the system adaptively dropped flashcards using this mastery criteria so that well-known items could be retired and students could focus their study time on items with which they needed more practice. Likewise, we hoped to keep students engaged by matching the difficulty level to their performance so that they would continue to use the AT system to study for their course exams. A more experienced student could "master out" early whereas a novice student may need extra trials to reach the same criterion. The accuracy criterion was less strict than our previous work [41] to minimize frustration and encourage participation. It should be noted that the reaction time was extended to allow students enough time to read the function flashcards, which included 1–2 short sentences per answer choice.

The maximum time allotted per flashcard deck was 20 min or a maximum of 300 trials. A deck would be completed if a student either mastered all of the flashcards, the maximum time had elapsed, or the maximum number of trials had occurred – whichever happened first (although students had the option to end training early if they desired). We wanted to ensure that sufficient time had passed for the adaptive instructional techniques to function, so we determined the maximum time and number of trials based on pilot testing. Students were encouraged to repeat content areas as many times as they wanted to help them study. When they completed a flashcard deck, the AT system returned them to the dashboard where they could select from one of the ten decks again.

## 3   Longitudinal Pilot Study

### 3.1   Comparison of Two Cohorts

The purpose of this pilot study was to explore the potential benefits of training with an adaptive flashcard system on course outcomes in a USMC course. Specifically, we compared a cohort that used the AT system to a previous cohort that did not have access to the AT system. The cohort that used the AT system included 45 students (2 students dropped out of the course) and the cohort that did not have the AT system included 46 students (3 students dropped out of the course). Demographic information was not available for either cohort.

All 45 students had access to the flashcards in the AT system on their course-issued computers, which included these two AT strategies – adaptive sequencing and mastery criteria to drop flashcards. At the beginning of the course, instructors informed students in this cohort what the AT system was, how to access it, and encouraged them to use the system as a study tool. Students in the cohort who did not receive the AT system were encouraged to make their own flashcards and study them as they saw fit.

Throughout the course, students completed graded written exams and practical hands-on exercises, which were used to calculate their overall course GPA. Instructors provided these data related to course performance to the research team for both cohorts. In addition, they provided the data from the AT system, which offered insights on how much students used it during the course.

## 3.2 Written Exam Performance Results

One particular metric that instructors were interested in was the number of learning objective failures on exams during the course. Each exam is composed of a number of learning objectives with a passing criterion specific to each, as determined by course managers and subject matter experts. If students do not meet the passing criterion, they are required to take that portion of the test again. If students fail a particular learning objective three times, they could be dismissed from the course; therefore, this is a key metric for instructors to monitor. For the first analysis, we wanted to explore whether the AT cohort experienced fewer learning objective failures than the cohort without AT.

For this study, we focused on learning objective failures from the second section of the course, which is concentrated on understanding the theory of automotive systems and learning the specific functions of individual vehicle parts. The vast majority of the material covered by the flashcards was contained within this section of the course, therefore these data were the most relevant.

The cohort without AT had 41 learning objective failures, whereas the cohort who used the AT system had 20 learning objective failures. Overall, there was a 50% reduction in course learning objective failures in the cohort who used the AT system compared to the previous cohort who did not use the AT system. This difference was statistically significant, $\chi^2 (1, N = 90) = 7.23, p = .007$. These data suggest that using the AT system helped students on their written exam performance.

## 3.3 AT System Usage and Course Performance Results

Next, we explored the relationship between usage of the AT system and performance in the course for the cohort who had access to the AT system. For these analyses, we examined whether completing more flashcard trials and mastering more flashcards in the AT system were associated with higher course GPA. There was a strong, positive relationship between all three variables (see Table 1). In other words, those who had a higher course GPA also completed more flashcard trials in the AT system and mastered more flashcards. Likewise, those who completed more flashcards also mastered more flashcards during training.

**Table 1.** Correlation table between adaptive system usage and course performance

|  | Number of flashcards completed | Number of flashcards mastered |
|---|---|---|
| Number of flashcards completed | – | |
| Number of flashcards mastered | .92** | – |
| Course GPA | .52** | .48* |

Note: Pearson correlation values are reported. **$p < .001$, *$p = .001$

Usage rate of the AT system was also examined to understand how students utilized the training resource during the course. As shown in Fig. 4, the total number of flashcards completed by each student varied widely, such that some students completed over 1000 flashcards and others completed fewer than 10 flashcards. Table 2 includes descriptive statistics of several usage metrics that were captured during the evaluation. Consistent with the number of flashcards completed, each of the other usage metrics indicated a wide distribution of engagement with the AT system.

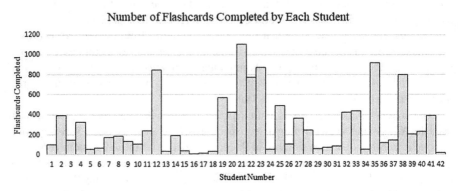

**Fig. 4.** Number of flashcards completed for each student during evaluation.

**Table 2.** Descriptive statistics of usage data

| Metric | M | SD | Min | Max | Description |
|---|---|---|---|---|---|
| Unique decks | 4.69 | 2.62 | 1 | 10 | *The number of unique decks that a student completed at least a single flashcard* |
| Days used | 3.88 | 1.86 | 1 | 8 | *The number of days that a student completed at least a single flashcard* |
| Training sessions | 9.60 | 7.30 | 1 | 30 | *The number of times a student opened the system to complete at least a single flashcard* |
| Total flashcards | 287.20 | 290.10 | 1 | 1106 | *The number of total flashcards completed by students across all training sessions* |
| Avg. flashcards/Training session | 26.53 | 13.13 | – | – | *The average number of flashcards completed by students during each training session* |
| Total flashcards mastered | 22.55 | 35.12 | 0 | 102 | *The number of flashcards mastered across all training sessions* |

### 3.4 Instructor and Student Reactions

At the end of the course, instructors provided their feedback and they shared what they heard from the students. Overall, the instructors and students were very positive about the AT system. Instructors reported that they observed noticeable differences on course exams and during practical application exercises in the cohort who used the AT system compared to previous cohorts. Likewise, the instructors have explained that the AT system has had a positive "ripple effect" in the course, in addition to the positive effects on course performance metrics. This ripple effect from the AT system has provided the instructors with a new method to train foundational topics, saving hours of instructional time that can be repurposed for more hands-on training in critical or difficult to train areas. This improvement in training efficiency has provided opportunities to expand training to other learning objectives. Additionally, students reported that they found the AT system helpful and easy to use. Instructors told the research team, "The students have nothing but great things to say about using the system!" As a result of the positive findings and feedback, instructors have continued to use the AT system in the course after the conclusion of this pilot study.

## 4  Discussion and Future Research

In this initial pilot study, the AT system was used as an intervention in a real-world military classroom to determine if using the AT system was related to improved course learning outcomes in an automotive maintenance course and whether the AT system was an effective classroom training resource. We were motivated to build the AT system to help students study for their exams effectively and efficiently while also providing instructors with a digital-age resource to get their students proficient on the basics. In addition to the instructional goals of the course, the expansive flashcard training literature provided significant guidance for the design of the AT system. Specifically, we concentrated on implementing adaptive strategies that improve long-term retention, which is critical for success in this MOS. Findings related to the testing effect, the spacing effect, and criterion learning influenced the sequencing and dropping techniques implemented within the AT system.

The results of this pilot study showed that the cohort that used the AT system had significantly better course performance in the section of the course regarding the theory of automotive systems and specific functions of individual vehicle parts than the cohort who did not have the AT system. Additionally, greater use of the AT system was positively associated with higher overall course performance. It should be noted, however, that data regarding system usage and course performance were correlational, and therefore it is unclear whether students who had a desire for high course performance were also more likely to use course resources. Next, an examination of the usage trends was conducted to understand how students used this type of training resource, which showed a high degree of variability in how students interacted with the AT system. Some students completed many flashcards across multiple training sessions, and other students completed only a single flashcard. We would expect that students who completed more flashcards in a deck would receive a larger benefit from the adaptive interventions. That is, students who completed fewer flashcards may not be in training long enough to experience the positive effects of the AT. This hypothesis is supported by the positive correlation between the number of flashcards completed and course performance.

Due to the success of the pilot study, additional studies are planned with future AMTBC cohorts to help address some limitations and incorporate lessons learned from this initial evaluation. First, we plan to incorporate a formal pre/post-test design to improve our understanding of the AT system's effects on long-term retention during the 52-day course and collect demographics and other questionnaires related to perceptions of the AT system. The present research is limited because we were unable to draw conclusions regarding characteristics of the students and improvements with specific flashcards. Surveying students about their perceptions of training may help us better understand how and why students use the AT system. For instance, usage data showed a wide range in how many times students engaged with the AT system. In a future evaluation, additional survey data may help identify individual difference characteristics that predict usage rates. This type of student data will help inform future iterations of the AT system and facilitate increased engagement.

The second future research plan will use a formal experimental approach to examine how each adaptive strategy influences course outcomes. Our pilot study is limited because it did not include a comparison group from which to explore the unique effects of the adaptive flashcard strategies. A future study will include a non-adaptive version of the flashcard system to understand how adaptive sequencing and mastery contribute to long-term learning and retention in a real-world course. Third, we plan to examine whether these strategies are similarly effective across different categories of learning materials. The current research is unable to determine whether the adaptive algorithm in the AT system was comparably advantageous for identification, function, and location flashcards, as well as across the different topic areas.

This pilot study represented an application and investigation of AT techniques into a flashcard-based training resource "in the wild." The results showed a promising use-case that these types of learner-centric technologies are effective in military schoolhouses and can meet the digital-age objectives set by the Chief of Naval Operations and Commandant of the Marine Corps. The use of adaptive flashcard training systems can support students by providing them with an opportunity to study basic concepts and practice rote memorization independently and outside of the classroom to prepare for their exams. Likewise, this individualized training approach is tailored to each student's needs so that it can provide novice students with the extra reps and sets necessary to get up-to-speed to their more experienced classmates, who may only need a shorter review.

**Acknowledgments.** We gratefully acknowledge Dr. Peter Squire and the Office of Naval Research who sponsored this work (Funding Doc# N0001420WX00227) and Natalie Steinhauser for her helpful insights throughout the course of the project. We would also like to thank the instructors and students from the Automotive Maintenance Technician Basic Course (AMTBC) for their support of this pilot study and Rebecca Pharmer for her contributions to the development of the adaptive training system. Presentation of this material does not constitute or imply its endorsement, recommendation, or favoring by the U.S. Navy or Department of Defense (DoD). The opinions of the authors expressed herein do not necessarily state or reflect those of the U.S. Navy or DoD.

# References

1. Richardson, J.M.: A Design for Maintaining Military Superiority (2016). https://www.navy.mil/cno/docs/cno_stg.pdf
2. Berger, D.H.: 38th Commandant's Planning Guidance (SSIC No. 05000 General Admin & Management) (2019). https://www.marines.mil/news/Publications/MCPEL/Electronic-Library-Display/Article/1907265/38th-commandants-planning-guidance-cpg/
3. Barto, J., Daly, T., Lafleur, A., Steinhauser, N.: Adaptive blended learning experience (ABLE). In: Proceedings of the Interservice/Industry Training, Simulation & Education Conference (I/ITSEC). National Training Systems Association, Orlando (2020)
4. Landsberg, C.R., Van Buskirk, W.L., Astwood, R.S., Mercado, A.D., Aakre, A.J.: Adaptive training considerations for simulation-based training. Special report No 2010–001, NAWCTSD. Naval Air Warfare Center Training Systems Division, Orlando (2011)
5. Peirce, N., Wade, V.: Personalised learning for casual games: the 'language trap' online language learning game. Lead. Issues Games Based Learn. **159**, 170 (2010)
6. VanLehn, K., et al.: The Andes physics tutoring system: lessons learned. Int. J. Artif. Intell. Educ. **15**(3), 147–204 (2005)
7. Narciss, S., et al.: Exploring feedback and student characteristics relevant for personalizing feedback strategies. Comput. Educ. **71**, 56–76 (2014)
8. Romero, C., Ventura, S., Gibaja, E.L., Hervás, C., Romero, F.: Web-based adaptive training simulator system for cardiac life support. Artif. Intell. Med. **38**(1), 67–78 (2006)
9. Landsberg, C.R., Astwood Jr., R.S., Van Buskirk, W.L., Townsend, L.N., Steinhauser, N.B., Mercado, A.D.: Review of adaptive training system techniques. Mil. Psychol. **24**(2), 96–113 (2012)
10. Marraffino, M.D., Johnson, C.I., Whitmer, D.E., Steinhauser, N.B., Clement, A.: Advise when ready for game plan: adaptive training for JTACs. In: Proceedings of the Interservice/Industry Training, Simulation & Education Conference (I/ITSEC). National Training Systems Association, Orlando (2019)
11. Van Buskirk, W.L., Fraulini, N.W., Schroeder, B.L., Johnson, C.I., Marraffino, M.D.: Application of theory to the development of an adaptive training system for a submarine electronic warfare task. In: Sottilare, R.A., Schwarz, J. (eds.) HCII 2019. LNCS, vol. 11597, pp. 352–362. Springer, Cham (2019)
12. Hartwig, M.K., Dunlosky, J.: Study strategies of college students: are self-testing and scheduling related to achievement? Psychon. Bull. Rev. **19**(1), 126–134 (2012)
13. Karpicke, J.D., Butler, A.C., Roediger, H.L.: Metacognitive strategies in student learning: do students practise retrieval when they study on their own? Memory **17**, 471–479 (2009)
14. Kornell, N., Bjork, R.A.: The promise and perils of self-regulated study. Psychon. Bull. Rev. **14**(2), 219–224 (2007)
15. Wissman, K.T., Rawson, K.A., Pyc, M.A.: How and when do students use flashcards? Memory **20**(6), 568–579 (2012)
16. Carrier, M., Pashler, H.: The influence of retrieval on retention. Mem. Cogn. **20**(6), 633–642 (1992)
17. Johnson, C.I., Mayer, R.E.: A testing effect with multimedia learning. J. Educ. Psychol. **101**(3), 621–629 (2009)
18. Karpicke, J.D., Roediger, H.L.: The critical importance of retrieval for learning. Science **319**(5865), 966–968 (2008)
19. Roediger, H.L., Butler, A.C.: The critical role of retrieval practice in long-term retention. Trends Cogn. Sci. **15**(1), 20–27 (2011)
20. Roediger, H.L., Karpicke, J.D.: Test-enhanced learning: taking memory tests improves long-term retention. Psychol. Sci. **17**(3), 249–255 (2006)

21. Toppino, T.C., Cohen, M.S.: The testing effect and the retention interval: questions and answers. Exper. Psychol. **56**(4), 252–257 (2009)
22. Bahrick, H.P., Bahrick, L.E., Bahrick, A.S., Bahrick, P.E.: Maintenance of foreign language vocabulary and the spacing effect. Psychol. Sci. **4**(5), 316–321 (1993)
23. Ebbinghaus, H.: Memory: A Contribution to Experimental Psychology. Ruger, H.A., Bussenius, C.E., Hiligard, E.R. (trans.) Dover Publications, New York (1964)
24. Glenberg, A.M., Lehmann, T.S.: Spacing repetitions over 1 week. Mem. Cogn. **8**(6), 528–538 (1980)
25. Kornell, N.: Optimising learning using flashcards: spacing is more effective than cramming. Appl. Cogn. Psychol. **23**(9), 1297–1317 (2009)
26. Paivio, A.: Spacing of repetitions in the incidental and intentional free recall of pictures and words. J. Verbal Learn. Verbal Behav. **13**(5), 497–511 (1974)
27. Shaughnessy, J.J., Zimmerman, J., Underwood, B.J.: The spacing effect in the learning of word pairs. Mem. Cogn. **2**(4), 742–748 (1974)
28. Cepeda, N.J., Pashler, H., Vul, E., Wixted, J.T., Rohrer, D.: Distributed practice in verbal recall tasks: a review and quantitative synthesis. Psychol. Bull. **132**(3), 354–380 (2006)
29. Dempster, F.N.: The spacing effect: a case study in the failure to apply the results of psychological research. Am. Psychol. **43**(8), 627–634 (1988)
30. Kornell, N., Bjork, R.A.: Optimising self-regulated study: the benefits—and costs—of dropping flashcards. Memory **16**, 125–136 (2008)
31. Son, L.K.: Spacing one's study: evidence for a metacognitive control strategy. J. Exper. Psychol. Learn. Mem. Cogn. **30**(3), 601–604 (2004)
32. Kornell, N., Bjork, R.A.: Learning concepts and categories: is spacing the "enemy of induction"? Psychol. Sci. **19**(6), 585–592 (2008)
33. Mettler, E., Kellman, P.J.: Adaptive response-time-based category sequencing in perceptual learning. Vis. Res. **99**, 111–123 (2014)
34. Mettler, E., Massey, C.M., Kellman, P.J.: A comparison of adaptive and fixed schedules of practice. J. Exper. Psychol. Gen. **145**(7), 897–917 (2016)
35. Mettler, E., Burke, T., Massey, C.M., Kellman, P.J.: Comparing adaptive and random spacing schedules during learning to mastery criteria. In: Denison, S., Mack, M., Xu, Y., Armstrong, B.C. (eds.) Proceedings of the 42$^{nd}$ Annual Conference of the Cognitive Science Society, pp. 773–779. Cognitive Science Society (2020)
36. Bloom, B.: Learning for mastery. Eval. Comm. **1**(2), 1–12 (1968)
37. Pyc, M.A., Rawson, K.A., Aschenbrenner, A.J.: Metacognitive monitoring during criterion learning: when and why are judgments accurate? Mem. Cogn. **42**(6), 886–897 (2014)
38. Vaughn, K.E., Rawson, K.A.: Diagnosing criterion-level effects on memory: what aspects of memory are enhanced by repeated retrieval? Psychol. Sci. **22**, 1127–1131 (2011)
39. Pyc, M.A., Rawson, K.A.: Testing the retrieval effort hypothesis: does greater difficulty correctly recalling information lead to higher levels of memory? J. Mem. Lang. **60**(4), 437–447 (2009)
40. Pyc, M.A., Rawson, K.A.: Costs and benefits of dropout schedules of test–restudy practice: implications for student learning. Appl. Cogn. Psychol. **25**(1), 87–95 (2011)
41. Whitmer, D.E., Johnson, C.I., Marraffino, M.D., Pharmer, R.L., Blalock, L.D.: A mastery approach to flashcard-based adaptive training. In: Sottilare, R.A., Schwarz, J. (eds.) HCII 2020. LNCS, vol. 12214, pp. 555–568. Springer, Cham (2020)
42. Van Merriënboer, J.J., Sweller, J.: Cognitive load theory and complex learning: recent developments and future directions. Educ. Psychol. Rev. **2**, 147–177 (2005)
43. Scheiter, K., Gerjets, P.: Learner control in hypermedia environments. Educ. Psychol. Rev. **19**(3), 285–307 (2007)

# Revealing Data Feature Differences Between System- and Learner-Initiated Self-regulated Learning Processes Within Hypermedia

Megan Wiedbusch[1]([✉])(ID), Daryn Dever[1](ID), Franz Wortha[2](ID), Elizabeth B. Cloude[1](ID), and Roger Azevedo[3](ID)

[1] Department of Learning Sciences and Educational Research, University of Central Florida, Orlando, FL 32816, USA
{meganwiedbusch,ddever,elizabeth.cloude}@knights.ucf.edu
[2] Department of Psychology, University of Greifswald, Franz-Mehring -Str. 47, 1789 Greifswald, Germany
franz.wortha@uni-greifswald.de
[3] School of Modeling, Simulation, and Training, University of Central Florida, Orlando, FL 32816, USA
roger.azevedo@ucf.edu

**Abstract.** Self-regulated learning (SRL) with advanced learning technologies has shown to significantly augment learners' performance across contexts. Yet studies find learners lack sufficient SRL skills to successfully implement strategies (e.g., judgments of learning, note taking, self-testing, etc.). Current research does not fully explain how and why this failure of effective strategy deployment occurs. We used principle component analysis (PCA) on process data (i.e., log files) from 190 undergraduates learning with MetaTutor, a hypermedia-based intelligent tutoring system, to explore underlying patterns in the frequency of strategy deployment occurring with and without pedagogical agent scaffolding to better understand any underlying structures of system- and learner-initiated cognitive and metacognitive SRL strategy use. Results showed that the system's underlying architecture deploys processes corresponding to both the phases of learning and type of effort allocation according to Winne's (2018) Information Processing Theory of SRL. However, learner-initiated processes for those who received scaffolding only displayed strategy deployment that corresponded to the type of effort allocation required of the processes (i.e., more effortful constructionist processes like note-taking versus short canned responses for judgements of learning). Additionally, results suggest all learners deploy strategies based on the familiarity of processes. Regression models using these principle components outperformed raw frequency models for capturing post-test learning performance across all participants.

This research was supported by funding from the National Science Foundation (DRL#1661202, DUE#1761178, DRL#1916417, IIS#1917728), the Social Sciences and Humanities Research Council of Canada (SSHRC 895-2011-1006). The authors would also like to thank members of the SMART Lab at UCF for their contributions.

© Springer Nature Switzerland AG 2021
R. A. Sottilare and J. Schwarz (Eds.): HCII 2021, LNCS 12792, pp. 481–495, 2021.
https://doi.org/10.1007/978-3-030-77857-6_34

**Keywords:** Self-regulated learning · Metacognition · Intelligent tutoring systems

# 1    Introduction

Self-regulated learning (SRL) assumes learners are active as they monitor and regulate their cognitive and metacognitive processes [1–3]. However, studies find learners demonstrate difficulty effectively employing SRL processes with advanced learning technologies (ALTs) [2,4–6]. To help learners address these difficulties, various ALTs were specifically developed to foster SRL in learners by integrating scaffolding, such as guidance provided by externally regulating pedagogical agents [2,7]. Current research on SRL with these types of ALTs must make assumptions across all learners about the role of scaffolding and its influence on SRL during complex learning. For example, they assume that ALTs will model, prompt, and support learners to engage in specific strategy use throughout complex learning [8], but it is not always known which strategies should be employed, how learners should be prompted, or when scaffolding should occur to optimize learning.

Our study aimed to address these questions by examining how learners deploy strategies and explore the underlying features of both system-initiated and learner-initiated processes. While the system we studied, MetaTutor– a hypermedia intelligent tutoring system (ITS), was designed with specific theoretical considerations of SRL (described below), we sought to provide evidence that the system did in fact prompt learners in a theoretically based way and understand what features of these processes might have influenced their deployment (e.g., familiarity of processes). Furthermore we sought to understand what features of cognitive and metacognitive processes learners self-initiated and how these compared to the system. Finally, we wanted to understand if dimension reduction utilizing any potentially underlying features could better capture learning compared to models using raw frequencies of process deployment which might lend credence to an argument that the underlying features of similarly deployed processes are important for both understanding current ITSs and the future design of ALTs.

## 1.1    Theoretical Foundations

Winne's (2018) Information Processing Theory (IPT)of SRL models the phases and processes that cyclically occur throughout learning and provides potential guiding principles for prompting scaffolding [2,3,6]. According to this theory, learners process information throughout four (not necessarily sequential or exhaustive) phases of learning: (1) task definition (2) goals and planning (3) strategy use, and (4) adaptation. Within phase 1, *task definition*, learners define their current context and goals by developing a perception of task demands and requirements compared to previous experiences of similar tasks or metacognitive judgments about the context. During phase two, *goals and planning*, learners use their *task definition* to set goals and plan how to accomplish those goals. Entering phase 3, *strategy use,* learners then enact those plans, updating the *task definition* and goals as necessary. In this phase learners can use a variety of cognitive and metacogntive strategies that are often constrained based on the tools available to them (e.g., the ability to record and revisit notes is only possible when provided a recording tool). We further expand on relevant strategies afforded in the MetaTutor environment below (see Section **1.2 MetaTutor**). During phase 4, *adaptation,* learners adapt their goals, plans, and SRL strategies if necessary. For example, if the learner felt that their original plan of highlighting all new vocabulary was overwhelming and was not contributing to their general knowledge, the learner might choose to instead develop and draw a concept map to connect the new vocabulary going forward.

Throughout these four phases, learners monitor the conditions, operations, products, evaluations, and standards (COPES) features of their learning in order to effectively deploy SRL strategies. *Conditions* refer to the external (e.g., tools, note-taking applications, limited time) or internal (e.g., prior knowledge) resources and constraints learners encounter throughout learning. *Operations* are the specific cognitive and metacognitive processes and strategies a learner has in their toolkit to help them learn (see Section **1.2 MetaTutor** for more information on specific cognitive and metacognitive operations). *Products* are developed from *operations* as defined by both external and internal *conditions.* This includes new knowledge that emerges from the searching, monitoring, and assembly of new and prior information. *Standards* are the internal and external metrics by which learners evaluate, monitor, and describe the quality of *products* as they pertain to both their goals and *conditions.*

Despite both conceptual [12] and empirical support for this model [13], more research is needed to understand why, how, and when different phases, and strategies within those phases, occur successfully and when they fail. Greene and Azevedo (2009) showed that one key distinction between successful and unsuccessful learners was the frequency of metacognitive monitoring skills [13]. However, the environment learners were in did not regulate or offer regulating features that might have influence or encouraged the use of certain SRL processes. This raises the question if optimal learning according to the IPT framework still holds when external regulation is present and how this might influence learning choices and behaviors regarding which and how to deploy different SRL processes. Many studies have addressed this question [6,7,14], but did not provide evidence to support the assumption that systems augmented learner strategy deployment through external regulation in the way that they were designed. That is, when co-regulating with the learners during learning, did the deployment of strategies (i.e., operations) actually have learners augment their behavior in a way that would have them deploy strategies encouraging underutilized or more effective strategies that might otherwise have been ignored according to the phases and COPES features as specified in IPT? Perhaps learners just completed the prompted strategies to accommodate the environment requirements but did not augment their own behavior outside of these requirements. For example, a learner might complete metacognitive judgements of learning when asked by the system to, but fail to initiate this operation outside of prompting even if it would be effective towards completing their learning goals. There is evidence that learners who fail to effectively self-regulate may do so due to limitations in knowledge and skills about metacognition and metacogntive strategies [9–11] which could be contributed to the familiarity of these concepts. More work is needed to see if avoidance of these types of strategies still occur within environments that provide scaffolding and assistance with less familiar or unfamiliar processes or if the external regulation and encouragement of these operations influences internally regulated strategy deployment.

Other research within environments that do provide external regulation have been used by some researchers to argue that the failure of learners to effectively self-regulate could be attributed to high informational load limiting cognitive resources [15,16], but empirical evidence is still needed to support these claims. Furthermore, even when using systems that were designed using theoretical models of SRL to guide the production rules of strategy deployment, there is still not a clear understanding of how to handle when there are multiple processes that could be effective during a particular point in a session, or how features should be considered for deployment. For example, is it more important to try and guide the student to a more rigid looping through the four phases of learning and only push phase transitions when either a certain amount of time has passed or are there certain conditions or standards that need to be met before a phase transition should occur? What type of operations should be considered and when? Do all COPES features influence strategy deployment, and if so to what extent? These are all questions that still need to be addressed by the current development and evaluation of ALTs that support SRL.

## 1.2    MetaTutor

MetaTutor, a hypermedia-based ITS, detects, models, traces, and fosters learners' SRL while they learn about human body systems [2]. The system's underlying architecture was designed to have pedagogical agents prompt various SRL strategies and then provide the learner feedback on their performance of that strategy. These production rules were both event (i.e., prompted based on specific learner actions) and time-based (i.e., prompted after a pre-specified amount of time) that would trigger various cognitive (i.e., prior knowledge activation [PKA], planning, summarizing, and taking notes) and metacognitive (i.e., JOL, feelings of knowing [FOK], concept evaluations [CE], and monitoring progress towards a goal [MPTG]) strategies (see Table 1). The system was designed with several assumptions about SRL that are grounded in Winne's (2018) theory and empirical evidence, but currently work has not shown whether the system actually prompts learners in a way that aides them to follow the intended learning strategy deployment [2]. For example, learners are prompted to provide two subgoals while they learn in the environment and are initially prompted to set them at the beginning of the learning session (i.e., during Phase 1). But work still needs to be done to show whether or not these goals are revisited during Phase 4, adaptation, and what strategies might encourage updates to a learners subgoals. Additionally, if these changes do exist, is the frequency with which they adapt similar when provided scaffolding versus not?

## 1.3    Current Study

The goal of this study was to address the gaps raised above and extend previous research. Specifically, we wanted to provide evidence of an ITS (i.e., MetaTutor) augmenting learners SRL behaviors and examine features underlying system- and learner-initiated SRL process. Because of the complexity of the IPT model, we chose to use principle component analysis (PCA) to explore data features using the IPT model to ground our interpretations. Furthermore, we explored if these components could be used to better predict learning compared to raw frequency regression models.

We posed the following broad research questions:

- RQ1: *Are there theoretically explainable principle components for the frequency system-initiated metacognitive and cognitive processes?*
- RQ2: *Are there theoretically explainable principle components for the frequency of learner-initiated metacognitive and cognitive processes?*
- RQ3: *Can the principle components for the frequency of both system- and learner-initiated metacognitive and cognitive processes model learning?*

Given that our first two research questions were exploratory, we did not have any specific hypothesis about the underlying features of process deployment. However, after identifying several underlying features, we hypothesized that using these components as dimension reduction in regression modeling, would outperform models that only used the raw frequencies of strategy deployment.

## 2    Methods

### 2.1    Participants and Conditions

190 (Age: M = 20, SD = 3.2; 53% female) undergraduates from three North American universities participated in a two-day laboratory study in which they learned about the human circulatory system with MetaTutor. Participants were randomly assigned to either a prompt and feedback (i.e., experimental; N = 94) or control condition (N = 96). Participants in the experimental condition, were prompted to engage in SRL processes by the system and given immediate feedback on their performance. Several pedagogical agents embedded in MetaTutor prompted specific SRL strategies (e.g., Mary the Monitor prompted monitoring strategies, Pam the Planner prompted planning strategies, etc.). Feedback was provided by the pedagogical agent which varied depending on the strategy. For example, Sam provided feedback on summaries where he either congratulated the participant on submitting a content-rich summary, or requested the participant take more time to include more information on the topic. Participants in the control condition were neither prompted nor provided feedback. However, all participants across conditions could self-initiate the same SRL processes by using an SRL palette (see Fig. 1). All participants were compensated $10/hour, up to $40 for their participation.

**Table 1.** Deployable cognitive and metacognitive processes within MetaTutor definitions adapted from Greene & Azevedo (2009).

| Process type | Process | Operational definition |
|---|---|---|
| Cognitive | Prior Knowledge Activation (PKA) | Searching for relevant prior knowledge for a current task |
| | Planning | The coordination and selection of operators for a learner to make behavioral actions to move from current conditional states to goal and sub-goal states |
| | Summarizing | Providing brief statements about the main points about what a learner just read, inspected, or heard |
| | Taking notes | Copying (and potentially extending) text from the environment |
| Metacognitive | Judgments of Learning (JOL) | The assessment of how well a learner believes they have learned the material |
| | Feeling of Knowing (FOK) | The feeling of being aware something is familiar with some understanding of the topic, but not able to recall on demand |
| | Content Evaluations (CE) | Monitoring the quality of content relative to goals |
| | Monitoring Progress Towards a Goal (MPTG) | Assessing if a goal has been completed or met |

## 2.2 Materials

Participants all interacted with MetaTutor, a hypermedia-based ITS (see Section **1.2 MetaTutor**). Additionally, they completed a demographics questionnaire, several self-report measures[1], and a 30-item pre-test about the human circulatory system. After the learning session, participants completed a 30-item post-test and another set of self-reports.

## 2.3 Experimental Procedure

Our study occurred over two days. On day one after consenting, participants completed the demographics questionnaire, several self-report measures, and the 30-item pre-test. On day two, participants learned about the human circulatory system using MetaTutor for 90 min as we collected facial expression data via a web-camera mounted on the participant's screen. While in the environment, learners were first introduced to their task through a series of introductory videos before they were asked to set a series of sub-goals. Following this, participants

---

[1] For brevity and clarity, these measures are not specified as we did not consider them in this current analysis. Readers are encouraged to contact the corresponding authors for more information about specific items.

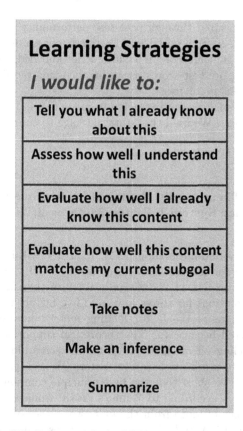

**Fig. 1.** MetaTutor's SRL Palette with the SRL processes users can deploy at any time during learning.

watched another series of videos covering various SRL strategies before they began completing their task to learn as much as they could about the human circulatory system. Once participants finished within the environment, they completed a counterbalanced 30-item post-test and another series of questionnaires. All participants were debriefed, paid, and thanked for their participation and feedback.

## 2.4   Coding and Scoring

The frequency of cognitive and metacognitive SRL processes were used as measurements of process deployment based on the use of the SRL palette (see Fig. 1). Cognitive processes included PKA, planning, summarizing, and taking notes. Metacognitive processes included JOLs, FOKs, CEs, and MPTGs. While inference making was measured and available during the learning session, due to low initiation (both learner and system), this was not considered for our analysis.

Learning was measured through post-test performance (i.e., number of correct responses on the 30-item post-test). Post-test scores ranged from 16.67% to 96.67% correct, with a mean score of 68.40%. Prior knowledge was accounted for in RQ3 by including pre-test scores as an independent variable but was found to be a non-significant predictor.

Data used in our analysis was extracted from log files in Python and analyzed using R (version 3.5.1). We used the 'stats' package to conduct our PCA [17].

## 3   Results

### 3.1   Are There Theoretically Explainable Principle Components for the Frequency System-Initiated Metacognitive and Cognitive Processes?

We used PCA on system-initiated process frequency within the experimental condition (N = 94) for feature extraction. Initial eigen values indicated that the first two factors explained 25.9%, and 19.2% of the variance respectively, or 45.1% overall. Solutions for three, four, and five factors were each examined using oblimin rotations of the factor loading matrix, however the two-factor solution was preferred because (a) The theoretical support of the components (b) The visual leveling off of eigen values on the scree plot after two factors, and (c) Difficulty interpreting subsequent factors. We interpret the examination of the biplot (Fig. 2) to show that the first principle component (PC1) reflects the ordering of phases according to Winne's (2018) framework. Specifically, we see that the components move from the first two phases of task definition and goals and planning (PKA and planning) into processes regarding content and strategy use (JOL, summarizing, taking notes) and finally into the final phases of learning and adaptation of strategy use (feeling of knowing, content evaluations, and monitoring progress towards goals).

We have interpreted the second PC (PC2) to represent the type of effort allocation or the operations and product factors according to Winne's (2018) framework. Summarizing and taking notes requires learners to construct knowledge and verbalize knowledge through free form responses while all the other processes require learners to answer short questionnaires. This suggests that the deployment of strategies was influenced by the type of effort required of the learner to use that strategy.

In sum, these analyses provide evidence that the MetaTutor system is initiating SRL processes according to Winne's (2018) theoretical assumptions. While the type of scaffolding and their respective production rules had been designed into the system, MetaTutor did not have any explicit timing or set number of deployments required of each process. Instead, these processes were event-based production rules determined by the learner's actions. Furthermore, we see that the phase of SRL and type of effort required for a process seem to be significant underlying factors for the frequency of process deployment.

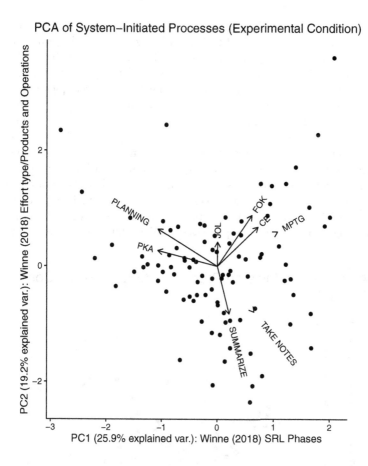

**Fig. 2.** Principle component biplot for system-initiated processes within the experimental condition.

### 3.2 Are There Theoretically Explainable Principle Components for the Frequency of Learner-Initiated Metacognitive and Cognitive Processes?

We used PCA of MetaTutor learner-initiated process frequency within both the experimental condition (N = 94) and control condition (N = 96) for feature extraction. Analysis was done separately on each condition to account for any differences the system might have on learner behavior and to allow for between condition comparisons. Solutions for three, four, and five factors were each examined using oblimin rotations of the factor loading matrix, however the two-factor solution was preferred because of the same reasoning as our first research question in addition to the ability for comparison both across conditions and across system and learner initiated prompts within the experimental condition.

Initial eigen values for the experimental condition indicated that the first two factors explained 19.4%, and 15.2% of the variance respectively, or 34.6% overall. We interpret the examination of the biplot (Fig. 3) to reveal that PC1 reflects the type of effort allocation or the operations and product factors according Winne's (2018) theory (the same as PC2 in our first research question) with the notable exception of prior knowledge activation moving towards more external and constructive effort. While we acknowledge this could be an artifact of the data, it could also be explained as prior knowledge activation required more recall and could be more cognitively effortful than the other questionnaires.

Learner-initiated processes in the experimental condition was interpreted as the familiarity of these processes. Specifically, we see that the components that are most indicative of traditional learning strategies (test tasking [MPTG], planning, summarizing, PKA, and taking notes) are more or less grouped while unfamiliar but highly metacognitive processes (JOLs, FOKs, and CEs) are grouped.

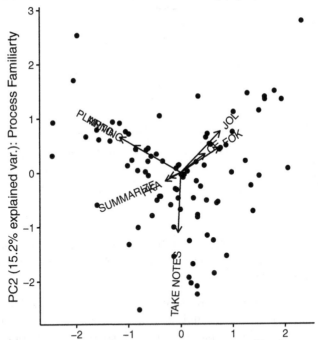

**Fig. 3.** Principle component biplot for learner-initiated processes within the experimental condition.

Initial eigen values for the experimental condition indicated that the first two factors explained 23.9%, and 19.9% of the variance respectively, or 43.8% overall.

We were not able to interpret the PC1 through examination of the biplot (Fig. 4). However, we suspect further analysis into either the quality or time spent on these processes might help explain this dimension. Specifically, as most learners spend a great deal of time taking notes, but less time picking out subgoals (planning) or taking quizzes (MPTG), this dimension might be data-driven, and not theoretically explained, but further analysis is needed to substantiate this claim. PC2 for learner-initiated processes in the control condition was interpreted as the familiarity of these processes (similar to the experimental condition). Specifically, we see that the components that are most indicative of traditional learning strategies (test tasking [MPTG], planning, summarizing, PKA, and taking notes) are grouped while unfamiliar, highly metacognitive processes (JOLs, FOKs, and CEs) are grouped.

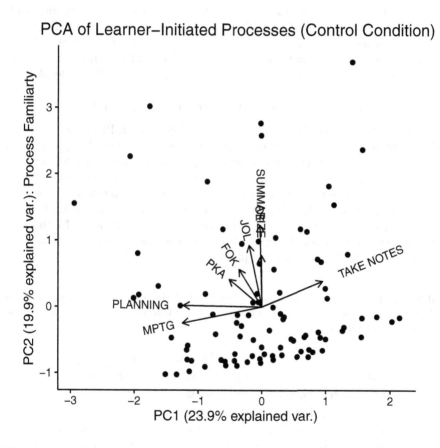

**Fig. 4.** Principle component biplot for learner-initiated processes within the control condition.

In sum, while learners do share a similar PC for the frequency of the self-initiated processes, the system is encouraging different behaviors for participants in the experimental condition. Simply, the system is encouraging a bit more exploration outside of familiar concepts, but levels of effort that are required are still a factor. Can the principle components for the frequency of both system- and learner-initiated metacognitive and cognitive processes model learning?

### 3.3 Can the Principle Components for the Frequency of both System- and Learner-Initiated Metacognitive and Cognitive Processes Model Learning?

A Poisson distribution regression model using the raw frequencies of SRL process deployment (both learner and system initiated) was found to be a non-significant model for learning for all participants ($p > 0.05$). A significant simple linear regression model was found ($F(5, 93) = 17.83$, $p < 0.005$) to predict learning based on the PCs from both system- and learner-initiated processes in the experimental condition, with an $R^2$ of 0.50 (see Table 2 for coefficients and predictor significance). Learning (i.e., performance on the posttest) modeled as

$$Learning = 0.40 - 0.02 * (LearnerInitiatedPC1) \tag{1}$$

in which Learner Initiated PC1 was interpreted as SRL Phases according to IPT. A simple linear regression using the PCs for learner-initiated processes in the control condition was found to be a non-significant model for learning for all participants ($p > 0.05$). These findings suggest that models using the raw frequencies of cognitive and metacognitive process deployment by the system were unable to capture learning but that models using the underlying features of these processes by the system were able to capture learning. Neither the raw frequency models nor the principle component models were able to capture learning using the learner-initiated processes.

**Table 2.** Parameter estimates, standard error, $t$-statistics, and $p$ for a regression model of learning based on the PCs from both system- and learner-initiated processes in the experimental condition.

|  | $\beta$ | Std. Error | $t$ value | $p$ |
|---|---|---|---|---|
| (Intercept) | 0.399 | 0.034 | 11.622 | <0.005* |
| PC1 (System-Initiated) | −0.021 | 0.009 | −2.277 | 0.025* |
| PC2 (System-Initiated) | −0.006 | 0.011 | −0.586 | 0.559 |
| PC1 (User-Initiated) | 0.004 | 0.010 | 0.394 | 0.695 |
| PC2 (User-Initiated) | 0.001 | 0.012 | 0.064 | 0.949 |

# 4    Discussion

This study extends previous SRL research by addressing the lack of empirical evidence around why learners fail to effectively deploy SRL strategies and how/if ALT environments with external scaffolding does influence learner deployment of cognitive and metacognitive strategies. Specifically, we examined which dimensions of SRL contribute to this failure by inspecting the deployment of strategy use by both the system and the learner. Using dimension reduction through PCA, our work suggests that well-researched systems (i.e., MetaTutor) do follow underlying theoretical models in their prompting. In other words, specific processes were prompted by the system according to the phases and the type of effort (i.e., operations and products) of Winne's (2018) IPT of SRL. This has important implications for two reasons. First, while the system had been designed with some elements of this framework (i.e., what type of scaffolding to offer and production rules indicating what events can trigger scaffolding), the environment was not explicitly designed to deploy certain strategies over others or at certain timepoints. That is, the system did not need to hit a certain quota of one strategy type within a time period (e.g., five JOLs throughout the entire session), but rather responded to the learner's decision and interaction with the environment. Our results highlight that the deployment of strategies was highly driven by the learning phase and type of effort learners the system felt was being underutilized and potentially avoided. That is, processes deployed during task definition and goals and planning (i.e., PKA and planning), the first two phases according to Winne's (2018) PIT framework, were deployed similarly. This was also found for the content and strategy use phase processes (JOL, summarizing, taking notes) and the final phase of learning, adaptation of strategy use, with FOKs, content evaluations, and MPTG processes being deployed similarly. Additionally, the system deployed strategies that were similar in their effort type (i.e., free response constructionist processes versus canned responses metacognitive processes).

This is an important finding to help the future development of externally regulating systems. We suggest that process and scaffolding should be designed to support the intended learning phase that they are deployed during. For example, we can imagine a system's underlying production rules prioritizing note taking during the strategy use phase of the learning session more then when the learner first enters the environment or is about to finish their learning session. Or alternatively, when a system must decide between processes to deploy, the architecture should consider both the phase and type of effort required by the learner to complete that process. This would help avoid and unnecessary or intruding process from being prompted that would otherwise interrupt learning. It would also allow for more theoretically justified production rules to exist in systems that support SRL. We suggest that future systems consider such processes together in future design.

Our second set of analysis suggest learners, however, did not share these same dimensions in their own deployment of processes. Instead, their deployment appears to be driven by the familiarity of strategies. That is complex metacognitive processes (e.g., FOKs, JOLs, etc.) that are less common in traditional education were less likely to be deployed. This could be contributed to the lack of standards or products that these processes provide learners. If the learner does not understand or see the benefit of using these strategies, they would be less likely to use them in comparison to familiar strategies taught throughout their educational career (e.g., note taking and quizzes). Previous research has argued that failure to use SRL effectively could be contributed to high informational load limiting cognitive resources [15,16] and these results show some support for such an argument. Processes that require more internal metacognitive effort were deployed less than familiar externally demanding processes. That is, limited cognitive and metacognitive resources were being allocated by familiarity, and not by strategy efficiency.

In conjunction with our previous findings, we argue that future systems should be designed to help facilitate and encourage unfamiliar strategy use. For example, the system could highlight the utility of using a FOK and encourage users to metacognitively monitor by explaining how and when an FOK could be useful or rewarding the user for trying unfamiliar strategies. We also suggest that when the system must determine which of two similar processes (e.g., from the same phase or requiring similar effort types) to prioritize, less familiar strategies to learners as practice for future learning sessions. Interestingly, participants in the experimental condition had slightly different strategy use, sharing a PC with the system (i.e. type of effort or the products and operations as defined in Winne's (2018) model). This finding suggests that learners who received scaffolding were deploying processes in a similiar manner they were being prompted in. We use this as evidence that the system was influencing self-regulated behaviors of learners even when external regulation was not being explicitly used all the time.

Finally, we found that models of learning using agent-induced PCs outperformed models using only raw frequencies for the experimental condition suggesting that dimension reduction, when theoretically explainable, could help build better models for adaptive intelligent scaffolding and analysis. That is, when considering the future development of ALTs using scaffolding and externally regulating pedagogical agents, process deployment should not focus on individual processes but rather the underlying features and mechanisms of the processes. Further research and analysis is needed to examine why learners fail to use SRL processes efficiently, and which theoretical factors system architectures should use for scaffolding learners' SRL.

# References

1. Winne, P.H.: Cognition and metacognition within self-regulated learning. In: Schunk, D.H., Greene, J.A. (Eds.) Educational Psychology Handbook Series. Handbook Of Self-regulation of Learning and Performance, pp. 36–48. Routledge/Taylor & Francis Group (2018)

2. Azevedo, R., Taub, M., Mudrick, N.V.: Understanding and reasoning about real-time cognitive, affective, and metacognitive processes to foster self-regulation with advanced learning technologies. In: Handbook of Self-regulation of Learning and Performance, pp. 254–270. Routledge New York, NY, USA (2018)

3. Greene, J.A., Schunk, H.: Handbook of self-regulation of learning and performance. In: Historical, Contemporary, and Future Perspectives on Self-regulated Learning and Performance, pp. 17–32. Routledge (2018)

4. Kramarski, B.: Teachers as agents in promoting students' SRL and performance: applications for teachers' dual-role training program. In: Schunk, D.H., Greene, J.A. (Eds.) Educational Psychology Handbook Series. Handbook of Self-regulation of Learning and Performance, pp. 223–239. Routledge/Taylor & Francis Group (2018)

5. Paans, C., Molenaar, I., Segers, E., Verhoeven, L.: Temporal variation in children's self-regulated hypermedia learning. Comput. Hum. Behav. **96**, 246–258 (2019)

6. Taub, M., Azevedo, R.: How does prior knowledge influence eye fixations and sequences of cognitive and metacognitive SRL processes during learning with an Intelligent Tutoring System?. Int. J. Artif. Intell. Educ. **29**(1), 1–28 (2019)

7. Biswas, G., Segedy, J.R., Bunchongchit, K.: From design to implementation to practice a learning by teaching system: Betty's Brain. Int. J. Artif. Intell. Educ. **26**(1), 350–364 (2016)

8. Azevedo, R., Moos, D.C., Johnson, A.M., Chauncey, A.D.: Measuring cognitive and metacognitive regulatory processes during hypermedia learning: issues and challenges. Educ. Psychol. **45**(4), 210–223 (2010)

9. Taub, M., Azevedo, R., Bouchet, F., Khosravifar, B.: Can the use of cognitive and metacognitive self-regulated learning strategies be predicted by learners' levels of prior knowledge in hypermedia-learning environments? Comput. Hum. Behav. **39**, 356–367 (2014)

10. Duffy, M., Azevedo, R.: Motivation matters: interactions between achievement goals and agent scaffolding for self-regulated learning within an intelligent tutoring system. Comput. Hum. Behav. **52**, 338–348 (2015)

11. Harley, J.M., Bouchet, F., Hussain, S., Azevedo, R., Calvo, R.: A multi-componential analysis of emotions during complex learning with an intelligent multi-agent system. Comput. Hum. Behav. **48**, 615–625 (2015)

12. Greene, J.A., Azevedo, R.: A theoretical review of Winne and Hadwin's model of self-regulated learning: new perspectives and directions. Rev. Educ. Res. **77**(3), 334–372 (2007)

13. Greene, J.A., Azevedo, R.: A macro-level analysis of SRL processes and their relations to the acquisition of a sophisticated mental model of a complex system. Contemp. Educ. Psychol. **34**(1), 18–29 (2009)

14. Bannert, M., Sonnenberg, C., Mengelkamp, C., Pieger, E.: Short- and long-term effects of students' self-directed metacognitive prompts on navigation behavior and learning performance. Comput. Hum. Behav. **52**, 293–306 (2015)

15. Azevedo, R.: Issues in dealing with sequential and temporal characteristics of self- and socially-regulated learning. Metacognition Learn. **9**(2), 217–228 (2014)

16. Moos, D.C.: Note-taking while learning hypermedia: cognitive and motivational considerations. Comput. Hum. Behav. **25**(5), 1120–1128 (2009)

17. Team, R.C.: A language and environment for statistical computing. R Foundation for Statistical Computing, Vienna, Austria (2019). www.R-project.org/

# Adaptation Strategies and Methods
# in AIS

# Collecting 3A Data to Enhance HCI in AIS

Faruk Ahmed[1], Genghu Shi[1], Keith Shubeck[1], Lijia Wang[1], Jeffrey Black[1],
Emma Pursley[1], Iqbal Hossain[1], and Xiangen Hu[1,2(✉)]

[1] The University of Memphis, Memphis, USA
[2] Central China Normal University, Wuhan, China

**Abstract.** 3A refers to content aware, context aware, and learner aware intelligent tutoring system (ITS) [2]. The idea behind this is that any ITS should be delivering content intelligently by knowing about the state of the user. The state of the user could be emotional or even physical.

Almost all the ITS are more or less intelligent to deliver content. But less intelligent to know whether the learner is accepting the content. In addition, the context consists of two components: context of the content and context of the environment. It is easy for an ITS to be aware of the context of the content (e.g., calculus in case of integrals) but very few ITS take into account the context of the environment. For example, a learner is accessing content in a crowded environment from her cell phone and a learner is accessing content inside a library where it is calm. Contexts of these two learners are different. Moreover, the learner awareness includes emotional states as well as physical states of a learner.

In this research our focus is to collect data by enabling a 3A learning system in AutoTutor [11]. AutoTutor is a conversation-based ITS that uses an expectation-misconception tailored dialogue to promote learning. Several questions involved in designing 3A enabled AutoTutor. How to collect 3A data without violating learners' privacy is the most important one. All other design questions revolve around this.

**Keywords:** Adaptive instructional system · Intelligent tutoring system · Content context and user awareness · Learning environment

## 1 Introduction

3A data contains an aggregated history of learner's emotions. It also contains continuous system event data. For example, mouse movements and clicks, the delay between mouse movements and clicks, and the delay between receiving a question and providing an answer. The 3A data also consists of inertial measurement unit (IMU) sensor data, when present, noise level data in the surrounding area, and audio-visual clues which can be used to identify learner's with disabilities (e.g., hard of hearing).

There are off-the-shelf technologies [3,4] to recognize generic emotion from the facial image. These generic emotions of a user is an excellent source of

© Springer Nature Switzerland AG 2021
R. A. Sottilare and J. Schwarz (Eds.): HCII 2021, LNCS 12792, pp. 499–508, 2021.
https://doi.org/10.1007/978-3-030-77857-6_35

valuable information for learner awareness. Our pilot implementation uses AWS Recognition API. It provides an eight-dimensional vector along with confidence score of user emotion from facial expression. At a certain interval we obtain those vectors and store them into a learning record store (LRS) using xAPI. Other information is also stored in LRS through xAPI.

The Rekognition API returns more information e.g., bounding box, landmarks, and the pose of faces. As we already mentioned each attribute has a value and a confidence score. The engine provides a binary prediction of gender male or female based on the physical appearance. It does not indicate a person's gender identity. Interesting attributes for 3A are age, smile, eyeglasses, sunglasses, eyesopen, mouthopen.

In this paper we are reporting a prototype framework that collects individualized 3A data from question-answer sequences along with the student's facial expressions. This framework is also used to explore 3A in a collective environment, like a classroom. Finally, this framework can be used to provide an avenue to conduct Wizard of Oz-type experiments that blend human tutoring in an ITS (e.g., human tutors take over tutor agent avatars). We believe this framework can be used to provide insights into several research questions. For example, what is the optimal delay between providing an answer to a question as a tutor? How many students can human tutors handle in a collective blended learning environment? Other research questions could focus on the engagement strategies used by tutors when interacting with multiple students in a blended ITS.

The 3A data we collect will also help us understand and improve the quality of tutor answers to student questions, trace student learning, and ultimately provide smooth transitions from questions and answers and vice versa. The emotion data can be used to create a baseline for generic emotion expressions for comparisons to more specific learning related emotions. Our 3A framework was also designed to observe the student's cognitive process of knowing, applying, and reasoning when answering mathematical questions, as defined in the Trends in International Mathematics and Science Study (TIMSS) framework. Through this framework a reliable and timely trend data on the mathematics and science achievement of the students in united states compared to that of students in other countries.

From a theoretical and methodological perspective, we are interested in how 3A-enabled HCI might impact learners psychologically. Given that a 3A-enabled HCI will provide a more realistic imitation of human educators, how might this affect the learners' experience? What are the potential benefits or detriments here? From a technological perspective, we established an efficient method for storing and retrieving historical emotion history by using a LRS. However, to make this work we developed new xAPI statements. With this in mind, we are interested in how to standardize these statements so that they could be used by all 3A-enabled ITSs. If this is accomplished, it would make it possible for a student's emotional and learning history to be used across multiple learning systems.

# 2   Related Literature

Adaptive instruction refers to the educational activities that accommodate to individual students and their unique behaviors so that each student can develop the necessary knowledge and skills [5,12]. Currently, many remarkable ITSs are available for teaching STEM subjects as well as computer technologies [8,13]. ITSs are moving towards adaptive instructions to accommodate exceptional learners [9]. Additionally, there are ongoing efforts and research toward defining AIS standards [16]. 3A has huge potential in AISA [1,2].

A few ITSs, like ALEKS, are Content-Aware and Context-Aware. ALEKS is "Assessment and LEarning in Knowledge Spaces" and "is a Web-based, artificially intelligent assessment and learning system [7]". Using adaptive questioning techniques, ALEKS quickly and accurately determines "exactly what a student knows and doesn't know in a course" and instructs the student on the most suitable topics. A 3A enhancement in ITSs (e.g., in ALEKS) by incorporating learner behavior will produce the next-generation adaptive instruction systems (AIS) which are Learner-Aware. For Learner-Aware, we are able to monitor learning performance both at the mastery levels of the skills and emotional changes (through emotion classification by processing their facial expressions). Moreover, this enhancement will contribute to evaluate the fourteen cognitive procedures defined by Trends in International Mathematics and Science Study (TIMSS) framework [10] along with three important cognitive domains; knowing, reasoning, and applying. Furthermore it would be a proof of concept to identify correlation between TIMSS cognitive process and facial emotion of a learner. This correlation can determine a user's boredom, inattentiveness, as well as weakness in the learning process.

Monitoring emotions distributed over time provides an aggregated cognitive state of the learner. We can track distributed emotions that map to distributed cognitive states. Analyzing those cognitive states would give deeper insight about the learning content. It may contribute to improving the design of the content.

# 3   3A Data Collection

We have implemented 3A technology in AutoTutor for collecting face details during learning. We also experimented with 3A in a collective environment e.g., classroom. Another exciting addition to these is keeping a human behind an avatar through chat environment.

## 3.1   Individualized 3A Data

The goal of this experiment is to collect 3A learning data especially the facial expressions during students' learning. It includes what students are studying which is content, in what context e.g., algebra in math or algebra in physics, and emotional states of learner from the physical appearance.

In the study a within-subject design with block randomization will be used to assess learners' emotional reactions towards various difficulty levels of questions. The study uses Autotutor - a conversation-based ITS that supports a mixture of vicarious learning and interactive tutoring. In this study, both the information delivery mode and the interactive tutoring mode is used. The information delivery mode is used to teach undergraduate students who major in psychology statistics. The lectures are were scripted by several experts in statistics. While students interactive with AutoTutor, it collects students' anonymized facial expressions and it does not store any recorded video. A demographic survey accompanies this experiment to collect information including age, sex, and ethnic background.

The experiment's procedure is as follows. Participants were recruited from a statistics and methods course. They first received an informed consent and after agreeing they received a demographic survey which asked for their age, gender, and ethnicity. When students logged into AutoTutor, they are asked by the system to provide permission to use any available webcam (e.g., built in webcams in a laptop, desktop webcam, or cell phone camera). If the participants granted permission, AutoTutor begins to capture the facial images, which are then sent to AWS Rekognition for scoring emotions at a given interval (e.g., 3 s). The system receives eight emotion-related scores which are then stored in the LRS. The emotion data collection process continues until the participant completes a learning module or closes the ITS. Each participant has a unique user ID and a secured authentication system through Google. To provide additional security, the internet communication happens through "HTTPS", an SSL-enabled web protocol. A flowchart of our method is provided in Fig. 1. There is an IRB submitted for this study at the University of Memphis (PRO-FY2021-279).

## 3.2   Collective 3A Data

We define classroom as a collective environment where multiple students interact with the instructor. The instructor could be virtual. In a classroom, there should be a high resolution camera to capture students' faces.

We performed an analysis of classroom video with AWS Rekognition shown in Fig. 2. In this video almost all the faces with landmarks are identified.

There are more information available which are not drawn on the picture. Those are gender (male/female), age range, smile, emotion, if wearing glasses, if mouth is open, pose of the face e.g., which direction he/she looking at.

It is possible to find out if a student is yawning, or looking away from the instructor, or talking. There are research works to detect and track speaker using 3D triangulation [6,14] along with dataset [15]. In a classroom environment we are able to combine the 3D triangulation, pose, and mouth landmarks (e.g., mouthopen) to find out who is talking. Speech recognition is there to know what he/she is talking about. With these advance technologies establishing the collective 3A environment in a classroom is promising for advance research.

There is one hurdle we found in collective 3A data collection. As in the individualized 3A each user is traceable whenever he/she logs into the system. But

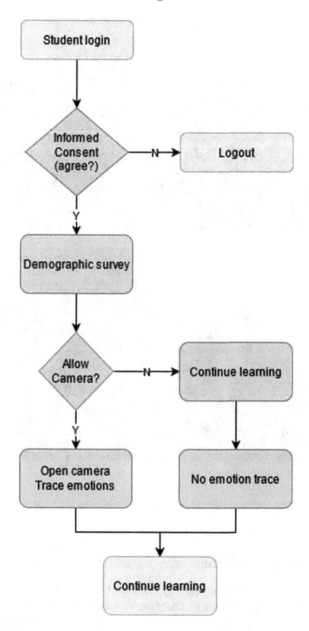

**Fig. 1.** Flowchart of the experimental procedure

for collective 3A data collection tracking individual is difficult because they are not logging in individually rather they are performing collective interaction with ITS. One possible workaround is that to obtain collective statistics of the learners state instead of individualized state. For example, what percent of students are focused, what percent of students are yawning or not focused. What percentage of students are asking questions and so on.

(a)

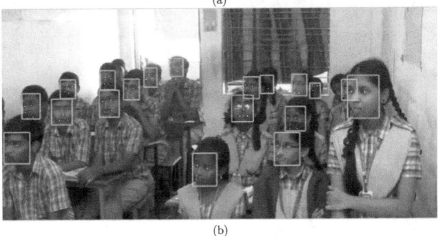

(b)

**Fig. 2.** A classroom image analyzed through AWS Rekognition (image collected from internet).

### 3.3 Blended Human Tutor

We have explored another technology to conduct Wizard of Oz experiments, that is blending human tutor in ITS. The idea is that a student interacts with ITS through chat or speaking. The chat takes place between student and ITS avatar. But, if students want to talk to a human tutor then there will be tutors available to answer questions. For an experiment it is also done that student does not know if there is a human tutor behind the avatar and when he/she sees humanoid answers either he/she gets excited or surprised. We are yet to find the actual behavior of a student when he/she comes to know about blended human tutor. We have two prototypes for this chat by text and video chat.

**Chat by Text.** AutoTutor system successfully integrate chat function with real human during one's interaction with any AutoTutor. We have explored python3 asynchronous http as chat server which is complex to implement and integrate. But the one without server is easiest to integrate and implement. This new chat module is realized using xAPI statements and learning record store (LRS) without setting a chatting server. This design reduces the effort and cost spending on developing and maintaining the chat server. Meanwhile, the chat function runs well with in a small group learning.

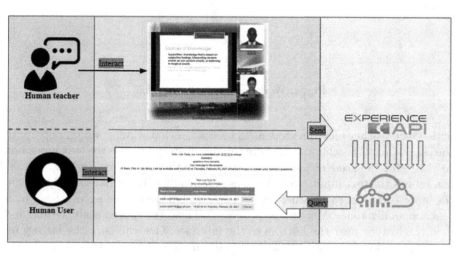

**Fig. 3.** Framework of chat function using xAPI and LRS

As shown in Fig. 3, the chat module query the statement from LRS regularly (once per 3 sec, for example). Through this method, there is not much effort needed to set up a chat function to have a similar function and behavior with in a small group of question and answering session as a normal chat server does. It reduces the barrier of non-engineering or non-programming major to achieve the same goal. Because there is no server to push the message directly to the target user immediately. This innovative chat function is not a real-time chat. The web page does a time trigger to obtain and query corresponding LRS to check whether there is any existed interaction.

**Chat Workflow.** When one interacted with an AutoTutor conversation, he/she would observe multiple agents avatar's head images shown on the interface. Below each avatar, the button with question mark (Fig. 4) would turn on the text input box for user to chat with the human teacher if there is one available. Then a learner is able to chat with the teacher as the regular text chatting room.

On the real human teacher side, he/she would open the special website designed for teacher role (Fig. 5). Teacher could choose a student to interact

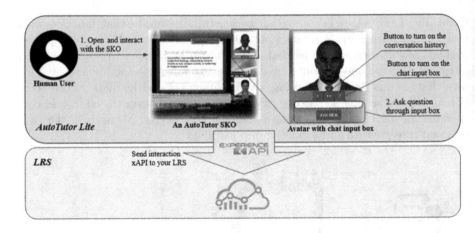

**Fig. 4.** Workflow on the student role

with. Once teacher picked a student to interact, a chat window would pop up. In the chat window, teacher can observe the chat history and use the text input box to chat with the student. As a chat module, both the student and the teacher can submit the text input multiple turns continually without pausing. By design, the input text from the teacher will be spoken from the virtual agent's head with real human like tones. Meanwhile, student will hear the spoken sentence and find it in the history near the bottom of the interface. One call turn the history on by click the double cross button located downside of the avatar (either of them in the figure). It will only determine the parameters of the selected avatar such as the voice, language, tone, speech speed and etc. In the view of the teacher, he/she could chat with multiple students during the same session. To better improve the user-experience of the chat function, we recommend a teach to chat within 2 students at the same time.

**Video Chat.** The video chat functionality is explored by combining WebRTC with TURN server, SIGNALING server along with http server. The video chat is not as simple as serverless chat because it has overhead of having multiple servers for real time audio-visual communication.

In case of video chat, when students start interacting by clicking button, the avatar is replaced by the video feed of the tutor. Tutor and student can see each other and talk to each other.

## 4   Future Direction

After obtaining the experimental data we will analyze those and try to find out the answers of optimum delay between question-answers, sentences for seamless transition from question to answer, capacity of tutor in terms of technology, and cognitive capacity of a tutor. We will also look at the possibility of monitoring

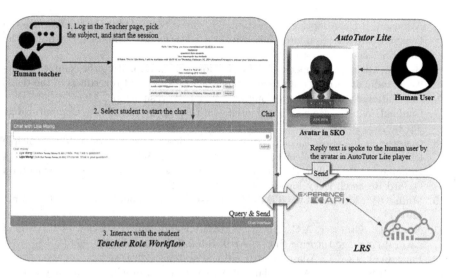

**Fig. 5.** Workflow on the teacher role

quality of answers provided tutors. If there is any repeated question, we will find a way to reuse the answers. In addition we will look at where in the content most questions are generated, are those questions similar, if so how much similar. If dissimilar then we will look for why those are dissimilar. Is it because of different level of learning of students or presentation of content.

## 5    Conclusion

In this research we built the framework to collect 3A data in individual setting and collective setting. In both cases we integrate Wizard of Oz experiment with blended human tutor.

## References

1. Ahmed, F., Shubeck, K., Andrasik, F., Hu, X.: Enable 3A in AIS. In: Stephanidis, C., Harris, D., Li, W.-C., Schmorrow, D.D., Fidopiastis, C.M., Zaphiris, P., Ioannou, A., Fang, X., Sottilare, R.A., Schwarz, J. (eds.) HCII 2020. LNCS, vol. 12425, pp. 507–518. Springer, Cham (2020). https://doi.org/10.1007/978-3-030-60128-7_38
2. Ahmed, F., Shubek, K., Hu, X.: Towards a GIFT enabled 3A learning environment. In: Goldberg, B.S. (ed.) Proceedings of the Eighth Annual GIFT Users Symposium(GIFTSym8), pp. 87–92, May 2020
3. Amazon Web Services: Amazon rekognition developer guide. https://docs.aws.amazon.com/rekognition/latest/dg/rekognition-dg.pdf. Accessed 30 May 2020
4. API, M.A.F.: Facial recognition software— microsoft azure. https://azure.microsoft.com/en-us/services/cognitive-services/face/. Accessed 30 May 2020

5. Atkinson, R.C.: Adaptive Instructional Systems: Some Attempts to Optimize the Learning Process. Stanford University, Institute for Mathematical Studies in the Social Sciences, Stanford (1974)

6. Ban, Y., Girin, L., Alameda-Pineda, X., Horaud, R.: Exploiting the complementarity of audio and visual data in multi-speaker tracking. In: Proceedings of the IEEE International Conference on Computer Vision Workshops, pp. 446–454 (2017)

7. Canfield, W.: Aleks: a web-based intelligent tutoring system. Math. Comput. Educ. **35**(2), 152 (2001)

8. Graesser, A.C., et al.: Electronixtutor: an intelligent tutoring system with multiple learning resources for electronics. Int. STEM Educ. **5**(1), 15 (2018)

9. Hallahan, D.P., Pullen, P.C., Kauffman, J.M., Badar, J.: Exceptional learners. In: Oxford Research Encyclopedia of Education (2020)

10. Mullis, I.V., Martin, M.O.: TIMSS 2019 Assessment Frameworks. ERIC, Germania (2017)

11. Nye, B.D., Graesser, A.C., Hu, X.: AutoTutor and family: a review of 17 years of natural language tutoring. Int. J. Artif. Intell. Educ. **24**(4), 427–469 (2014)

12. Park, O.C., Lee, J.: Adaptive instructional systems (2004)

13. Perez, R.S., Skinner, A., Sottilare, R.A.: –a review of intelligent tutoring systems for science technology engineering and mathematics (stem). Assessment of Intelligent Tutoring Systems Technologies and Opportunities, p. 1 (2018)

14. Qian, X., Brutti, A., Lanz, O., Omologo, M., Cavallaro, A.: Multi-speaker tracking from an audio-visual sensing device. IEEE Trans. Multimedia **21**(10), 2576–2588 (2019)

15. Roth, J., et al.: Ava active speaker: an audio-visual dataset for active speaker detection. In: ICASSP 2020–2020 IEEE International Conference on Acoustics, Speech and Signal Processing (ICASSP), pp. 4492–4496. IEEE (2020)

16. Sottilare, R., Brawner, K.: Component interaction within the generalized intelligent framework for tutoring (gift) as a model for adaptive instructional system standards. In: The Adaptive Instructional System (AIS) Standards Workshop of the 14th International Conference of the Intelligent Tutoring Systems (ITS) Conference, Montreal, Quebec, Canada (2018)

# Enhance Conversation-Based Tutoring System with Blended Human Tutor

Faruk Ahmed[1], Keith Shubeck[1], Liang Zhang[1], Lijia Wang[1], and Xiangen Hu[1,2(✉)]

[1] The University of Memphis, Memphis, USA
[2] Central China Normal University, Wuhan, China

**Abstract.** Conversation-based learning technology is playing important role in adaptive instructional systems (AIS). As a part of the adaptivity of an instructional system it would be ideal to incorporate a human tutor to deal with conversation that is beyond the capability of a chat-bot or virtual tutor. Moreover, it is possible to answer many research questions if experiments are performed with a blended human tutor. In this research we have implemented a prototype that blends a human tutor with a virtual tutor in a typical conversation-based tutoring system (i.e., AutoTutor). We performed R&D with server-based and serverless implementations. Additionally, we have implemented audio-visual blending through WebRTC so that the conversation between students and teachers can take place through spoken language with video. We found that the serverless chat blending with AutoTutor is fast, easy to implement, and reliable. We made the so-called serverless implementation possible by using some very powerful features of a learning record store (LRS).

**Keywords:** Adaptive instructional system · Intelligent tutoring system · Conversation-based tutoring · Serverless chat application · Blend human tutor

## 1 Introduction

Organizations like Apple, Google, Whatsapp, Instagram, Amazon, and Facebook are promoting conversational user interface based applications. Most of the applications are text-based, speech-based or both.

Learning technologies also implemented conversation-based tutoring system e.g., AutoTutor [7]. With conversational learning technology, the students communicate with virtual agents which are backed by artificial intelligence. In their study, Person et al. (2002) had students chat with virtual agents. In the middle of the conversation the real human took over the virtual agents. Afterwards, the scripts where shown to students who were asked if they could differentiate between the sentences provide by the tutor agent and the human tutor. They could not identify which sentence is from a virtual agent, or which sentence is from human the human tutor [8].

Blending human tutoring along with virtual tutor has a enormous possibility of answering many research questions. Specifically, this provides a new way to

© Springer Nature Switzerland AG 2021
R. A. Sottilare and J. Schwarz (Eds.): HCII 2021, LNCS 12792, pp. 509–518, 2021.
https://doi.org/10.1007/978-3-030-77857-6_36

perform Wizard of Oz-type experiments. These experiments are often fruitful and provide interesting insights into human-computer interactions in learning environments.

## 2  Related Literature

There is ongoing research to make intelligent tutoring systems (ITS) aware of 3A [1,2]. The 3A in ITSs means the context, content, and the learner aware-ness. In 3A learning environment the ITS is more aware of these parameters from the video camera by looking at the facial expressions and emotions of the learner. Researchers are continuing their efforts to improve the quality of the awareness. This is one reason why chat applications are getting more and more attention to integrate with ITSs. There are many chat frameworks which are within reach in features e.g., RASA, Microsoft Bot, Google Dialogflow. Cur-rently, chat applications are integrated in many websites. These conversations with a virtual chat-bot typically end with the bot contacting a human agent.

In this work, we are blending human tutor and chat with an ITS for the benefit of learning technologies. Specifically, we are referring to a mechanism that allows a student to carry on a conversation with the tutor agent, but the student can communicate with the human tutor when necessary.

When we think of chat applications we often assume a client-server model, however there are many applications without a so-called server. In the book chapter [4] the authors mentioned a month long case study of a serverless chat application. There is another group of researchers presented multi-user chat that works in a distributed, serverless fashion over named data networking [9]. In [3], Bakouan et al. implemented a system in which a human agent is used when the ITS does not have right information. In their application, the contribution of human tutor is primarily for enriching the computer system.

## 3  Experience API and Learning Record Store

xAPI [5] is developed and adopted by the US Department of Defense and accepted internationally as a technical specification and data standard to describe learning behavior. In short, xAPI statement follows the format "actor verb object" (https://adlnet.github.io/). It is used to records the activities and interactions among systems and their users. xAPI was introduced about 10 years ago has been introduced and become one of the most widely used data standards for learning activities [6]. The backbone of this serverless implementation is the xAPI Learning Record Store (LRS).

LRS is an xAPI echo system where the user receives and stores xAPI state-ments. LRS is defined in the xAPI specification as, "a server (i.e. system capable of receiving and processing web requests) that is responsible for receiving, stor-ing, and providing access to Learning Records." It does not store only learning data, but it can be extended to enable any system to store an xAPI state, store and retrieve xAPI statements, and store various xAPI metadata.

LRSs are not limited to simply storing xAPI data. It has been expanded to provide many other functionalities such as dashboard, control panel, learning analytics, recommendation, etc. In this research we implemented the serverless chat application using LRS.

In a client-server application, model the client requests for data and server serves. The initial idea was to integrate this client server model in a conversation-based tutoring system, so that a student can interact with a virtual agent blended real human agent. It is possible to conduct a wizard of Oz experiment by setting up a human tutor behind a virtual tutor when a student wants to ask, for example, a trigonometry or calculus question to the tutor agent. The student may have no idea whether the answer is provided by the program or from a real human. This will enable a huge pathway to answer important research questions.

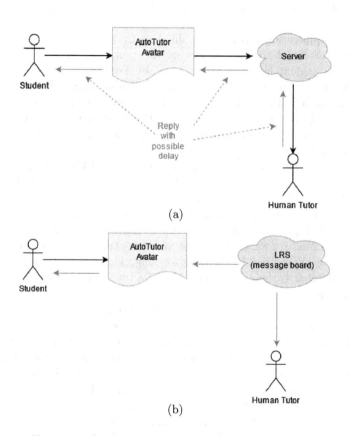

**Fig. 1.** Client server model and the serverless model of chat application

Implementing these ideas in the client-server model of http or https is difficult. This is because http is a stateless protocol. Even if we implement an API to request server, server has to post the request to a human tutor and wait for the answer. As soon as the answer arrives, it should deliver to the client (Fig. 1a).

The delay between the request and response could take longer, and holding a http session that long is not practical. While there are many alternatives, like push notifications, implementing these involves a good deal of overhead.

There is a very simple but powerful model for this architecture. Simply use LRS as a message board. The client will post questions to the message board while other clients (human tutors) will check if there are any messages for them. Any human tutor can answer that question and post it to the message board. The client will then pull that answer. While this is a simple solution, it serves the purpose of blending human tutor with a virtual avatar (Fig. 1b).

With this blended chat in AutoTutor, data could be collected and many research questions can be answered. Those research questions ranging from the technological channel capacity to human tutor tutoring capacity, from smooth transition of questions to answers to logical delay, or even how to engage students.

The chat application repeatedly pulls data from the message board in LRS. Right now it is fixed to 0.5 s. However, the pulling should be dynamic. For example, if a student asked question from an AutoTutor terminal, he will be waiting for the answer. Then it is logical that terminal scans LRS frequently. On the other hand, if a student received an answer and until he asks next question there is no need to scan LRS frequently. In this case, the student is not eagerly waiting for any information. Yes, student might look for "language art" tutor who is not online yet.

Currently, on the tutor side, a tutor can chat with 10 students. This number of 10 students is fixed. This is a technology capacity. It remains to be seen how many students a human tutor can handle within this framework at a given time. Human tutors naturally have a cognitive capacity limitation. One tutor can not answer unlimited questions, in part because questions will have variation. A tutor cannot be in a mode of answering those for a long time. In fact to maintain high quality, a tutor should not be tutoring for long. This poses a potential research of, in general, what is the optimal capacity of a tutor, and is this something that can be measured?

Another research topic could be the smooth transition from question to answer. If a student ask a question that is not acknowledged, the student may turn their attentions to something else. In this case, there can at least be a simple response that lets the student know the question was received (e.g., "let me think"). Furthermore, it remains to be seen what efficient acknowledgments are or how there can be a smooth and engaged transition from asking a question to receiving an answer. In summary, student engagement is very critical question which may get answer from this blended chat environment.

Further research questions can focus on monitoring the quality of the answers. This can be done through AI, but to train AI, the data from this type of environment is necessary. In fact, the AI can gradually learn how to monitor and improve the quality of the questions or answers. More interestingly, from the pattern of students' questions, it is possible to know how a student is learning.

During face to face instruction, an instructor can know how much the student is learning from that student's questions.

What is right amount of delay between question and answer? If a student asks a question and suddenly a full paragraph is returned as the answer, this does not resemble human behavior. Students will know that this is an answer from computer. That is why it is necessary to know what is correct amount of delay between question and answer, which also depends on the type of question being asked.

## 4  Server Based Implementation

We started with server based implementation of blended chat in AutoTutor. In the server-based architecture we thought about an API which will be integrated by AutoTutor. Every time a student ask a question, that question will be transferred to the server. The server posts this question to the available teachers and waits for answers in an asynchronous fashion. Once it receives answer, it push back to the AutoTutor terminal from where the API was called. We used Sanic asynchronous framework for this, which is similar to a modern version of Flask or Django framework with asynchronous mode built in. This means each and every method is by default asynchronous. In the server side, it uses a redis database to keep track of the question and answer with a publisher, subscriber model. When each teacher logs in, they are registered as publisher and there is an internal method which is registered as subscriber. Each teacher connects to the server through a web socket which provides bi-directional communication facility. Ultimately, teachers replies by publishing an answer and subscriber gets a notification. That notification is pushed back to the API call. This architecture is shown in Fig. 2a.

The server-based blended chat is complex in structure. It requires an http server and an in-memory database e.g., redis. Moreover, pushing the answer back to the API caller is unreliable because if the delay of receiving a reply is more than the timeout then the API caller will not get reply. The API was kept in this architecture so that AutoTutor does not have to connect through a web-socket.

## 5  Serverless Implementation

To overcome the drawbacks of server-based chat for AutoTutor the great idea of server less technology was thought. It is fast, reliable, stateful, and easy to integrate. Although http is stateless and xAPI call happens through http, the chat communication is stateful. The main advantage is that it does not require an extra server in the architecture. AutoTutor is already communicating with LRS for storing learning data, so this question-answer is just another channel to that.

In this architecture students login to AutoTutor and can see the teachers who are online. Students can choose a teacher to direct their questions to and

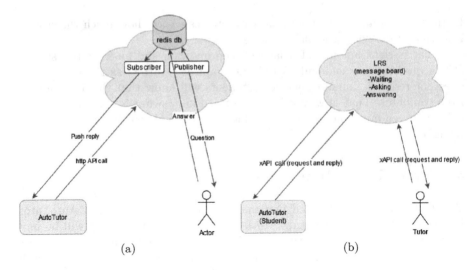

**Fig. 2.** Internal structure of a server-based and serverless chat for the AutoTutor

get replies from. Each student can communicate to each individual teacher a like point-to-point protocol.

On the other hand, teachers can publish their session details, such as availability and subject in the message board. Students get that information and then ask questions. The internal structure of serverless implementation is shown in Fig. 2b.

There are three types of objects in this architecture "Asking", "Waiting", and "Answering". **Asking** and **Waiting** are for the students; **Waiting** and **Answering** is for teacher. The LRS stores each question with URL, and that URL refers back to the content where the question originated. This is method is exciting because it allows the questions to be mapped onto the content. In other words, AutoTutor will know the context of the questions. It is also possible to see which of the questions are generated at which content and what time. The teacher launcher is shown in Fig. 3 and the student launcher is shown in Fig. 4.

A history of the questions connected to content and context can provide more insight about the content as well as students' learning progress. The content can be interpolated with expected questions from the students. If students do not ask questions, then this may indicate students skipped some content, was disengaged, or uninterested.

## 6   WebRTC for Audio Visual Chat

We have made more progress on the blended chat for AutoTutor to integrate audio-visual features. This idea was tested as a prototype so that students can also communicate by talking and seeing the tutor right from the AutoTutor terminal. In previous sections we mentioned that students can interact by typing

Hello, Xiangen Hu, you have **committed** until <u>17:42:55</u> to answer
**Statistics**
questions from students.
Your message to the students:
Hi there, This is Xiangen Hu, I will be available until 17:42:54 on Friday, February 26, 2021 (America/Chicago) to answer your Statistics questions.

Now it is 17:33:17
Time remaining 9.6 minutes

| Student 0 | Student 1 | Student 2 | Student 3 | Student 4 | Student 5 | Student 6 | Student 7 | Student 8 | Student 9 |

Chat with Hu Lab

[Submit]

- *Hu Lab:* (*17:31:11 on Friday, February 26, 2021*) How are you! [ Link ]
- **Xiangen Hu:** (*17:31:11 on Friday, February 26, 2021*) hello [ Link ]
- *Hu Lab:* (*17:31:11 on Friday, February 26, 2021*) Hello! [ Link ]
- *Hu Lab:* (*17:31:11 on Friday, February 26, 2021*) hello [ Link ]
- **Xiangen Hu:** (*17:31:11 on Friday, February 26, 2021*) What are you doing? [ Link ]
- *Hu Lab:* (*17:31:11 on Friday, February 26, 2021*) How are you? [ Link ]
- *Hu Lab:* (*17:31:11 on Friday, February 26, 2021*) Hello [ Link ]
- *Hu Lab:* (*17:31:11 on Friday, February 26, 2021*) Can you answer me? [ Link ]
- **Xiangen Hu:** (*17:31:11 on Friday, February 26, 2021*) Who are you? [ Link ]

**Fig. 3.** Teacher launcher

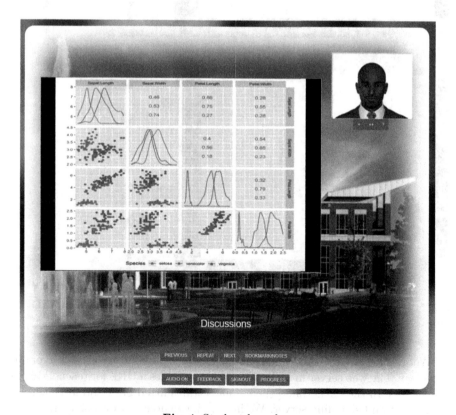

**Fig. 4.** Student launcher

questions. Students interacting with AutoTutor by conversation is already there, but the blending of the tutor into the instructional system is not yet available. That is why we have tested this features and found that this can be integrated as well. This requires a signaling server, turn server, and a web server.

**Fig. 5.** If student wants to talk the avatar will be replaced by audio/video feed of the tutor.

WebRTC uses real time audio and video transmission so extra servers are necessary. The web server in audio visual chat provides a URL for teachers as well as students. In the background the media is transmitted back and forth through turn server and signaling server. We have implemented our own signaling server and used **Coturn** as turn server. The web server is also implemented using python3's **http.server** module. The modern browsers does not allow media transmission (e.g., does not allow to open camera and microphone) unless the communication is secured (e.g., https). This is why in this audio visual chat https was used with **Let's Encrypt's**[1] ssl certificates.

The goal is when a students ask question by talking, the avatar will be replaced by the video of the tutor. Work for integrating WebRTC with AutoTutor is ongoing. AutoTutor with WebRTC audio-visual conversation is shown in Fig. 5.

# 7   Conclusion

In this research we have developed a prototype for blended chat in both a server-based, serverless, and audio visual chat for conversational learning technologies, in this case AutoTutor. This prototype development is an integral part of improving Adaptive Instructional System (AIS). Next, we will be conducting experiments with this tutoring system blended tutors to find answers of the research questions mentioned above.

The contribution of this approach would be 1) Maximize the utility of the LRS. The intended usage of the LRS has been storing of learning activity. We are able to use it as "bulletin board", by keeping track of the behaviors of "posting questions", and "waiting for answers", so that learners and tutors can use it to communicate with each other. This mimics functions that can usually only be achieved by designated servers. Another contribution is 2) that this enhancement is made for an already well developed conversation-based ITS. This implementation will help to answer some of the research questions that were previously incapable of addressing. For example, how much of a "human-touch" is really needed in a conversation-based ITS? Can this enhancement achieve true "mixed-initiative" dialog of ITS? This is something that has been particularly difficult for conversation-based ITSs to fully implement. Finally, 3) our enhancement makes it possible for educators to continue engaging in teaching with the technology. Specifically, this technology places the teachers in a key position to directly interact with their students on an as-needed basis. This blended framework can turn a hands-off individualized learning environment into a highly effective tool driven by the pairing of a teacher and technology.

**Acknowledgment.** This research was sponsored by the National Science Foundation under the award The Learner Data Institute (award #1934745). The opinions, findings, and results are solely the authors' and do not reflect those of the funding agencies.

# References

1. Ahmed, F., Shubeck, K., Andrasik, F., Hu, X.: Enable 3A in AIS. In: Stephanidis, C., et al. (eds.) HCII 2020. LNCS, vol. 12425, pp. 507–518. Springer, Cham (2020). https://doi.org/10.1007/978-3-030-60128-7_38

---

[1] Let's Encrypt is a non profit organization providing ssl certificates free of cost. URL is https://letsencrypt.org/.

2. Ahmed, F., Shubek, K., Hu, X.: Towards a GIFT enabled 3A learning environment. In: Goldberg, B.S. (ed.) Proceedings of the Eighth Annual GIFT Users Symposium(GIFTSym8), pp. 87–92, May 2020

3. Bakouan, M., Kone, T., Kamagate, B.H., Oumtanaga, S., Babri, M.: A chatbot for automatic processing of learner concerns in an online learning platform. Int. J. Adv. Comput. Sci. Appl. **9**(5), 168–176 (2018)

4. Choudhary, B., Pophale, C., Gutte, A., Dani, A., Sonawani, S.S.: Case Study: use of AWS lambda for building a serverless chat application. In: Bhalla, S., Kwan, P., Bedekar, M., Phalnikar, R., Sirsikar, S. (eds.) Proceeding of International Conference on Computational Science and Applications. AIS, pp. 237–244. Springer, Singapore (2020). https://doi.org/10.1007/978-981-15-0790-8_24

5. Kevan, J.M., Ryan, P.R.: Experience API: flexible, decentralized and activity-centric data collection. Technol. Knowl. Learn. **21**(1), 143–149 (2016)

6. Lim, K.C.: Using XAPI and learning analytics in education. In: Elearning Forum Asia, pp. 13–15 (2016)

7. Nye, B.D., Graesser, A.C., Hu, X.: AutoTutor and family: a review of 17 years of natural language tutoring. Int. J. Artif. Intell. Educ. **24**(4), 427–469 (2014)

8. Person, N., Graesser, A.C.: Human or computer? autotutor in a bystander turing test. In: Cerri, S.A., Gouardères, G., Paraguaçu, F. (eds.) ITS 2002. LNCS, vol. 2363, pp. 821–830. Springer, Heidelberg (2002). https://doi.org/10.1007/3-540-47987-2_82

9. Zhu, Z., Bian, C., Afanasyev, A., Jacobson, V., Zhang, L.: Chronos: Serverless multi-user chat over NDN. Technical report NDN-0008 (2012)

# Adapting to the Times: Examining Adaptive Instructional Strategies in Preferred and Non-preferred Class Types

Meredith Carroll(✉) 📵, Maria Chaparro 📵, Summer Rebensky 📵,
Kendall Carmody 📵, Rian Mehta 📵, and Warren Pittorie 📵

Florida Institute of Technology, Melbourne, FL 32901, USA
mcarroll@fit.edu

**Abstract.** Adaptive training can take place across multiple learning contexts, such as in-person or online class types, and in classroom or simulation environments [1]. Given the COVID-19 pandemic, institutes of higher education were forced to adapt and make instruction available both online and in-person; providing the opportunity to examine how adaptive learning strategies faired in different class types. When examining adaptive strategies across class types, of particular interest are individual learner characteristics and preferences, as students who typically would not take online classes found themselves taking classes in this medium [2]. We sought to evaluate the effectiveness of adaptive learning strategies across preferred and non-preferred class types. A significant interaction was found between instructional strategy presence and preferred class type, with students primarily attending classes in their preferred class type self-reporting significantly lower stress and workload levels than those who did not receive the adaptive instructional strategies. For students attending class primarily in their non-preferred learning environment, the opposite was true. Additionally, students in their preferred class types achieved higher exam scores. The methods, results, discussion and implications are discussed in the context of how to effectively conduct adaptive training.

**Keywords:** Preferred class type · Learner engagement · Performance · Feedback · Metacognitive intervention

## 1 Introduction

Adaptive training allows for skill acquisition by adjusting training to an appropriate level needed for a group or individual to improve towards the desired end skill level [3]. Adaptive training can take place across multiple learning contexts, including various: (a) class types (e.g., in-person, synchronous online, and asynchronous online) (b) learning environments (e.g., classroom, simulation, live), and at different scales (e.g., one-on-one, large classes of learners; [1, 4]. Adaptive training can also take place at different levels, for example, micro-adaptive training allows instructors to make real time modifications based on a student's current on-task performance of the training tasks

© Springer Nature Switzerland AG 2021
R. A. Sottilare and J. Schwarz (Eds.): HCII 2021, LNCS 12792, pp. 519–536, 2021.
https://doi.org/10.1007/978-3-030-77857-6_37

(i.e., intelligent tutoring system), whereas macro-adaptive training, modifies training based on assessment prior to instruction [5]. Macro-adaptive training allows instructors to modify using strategies such as alternative goals, content granularity, and/or delivery methods [5]. A wealth of research supports the finding that adaptive training leads to favorable learner improvements, such as, increased engagement and deeper learning by providing appropriate feedback, the optimization of challenge levels, and increased goal clarity [6–9].

There are a range of instructional strategies that can be utilized to adapt training in order to increase learner engagement and learning outcomes [10]. For example, feedback such as providing students with incorrect responses or grades based on their performance, can be adapted at the micro-level to facilitate students understanding which topics or skills they need to revisit, and can be delivered through various methods (e.g., outcome, process-level feedback) and class types (e.g., classroom, online; [11]. Feedback has been shown to result in higher levels of engagement, effective learning, and information retention [12–14]. Advanced organizers, which can provide an overview of the content to be covered in upcoming lessons, is an instructional strategy that can be used to adapt training at the macro-level in order to increase goal clarity [15] and facilitate metacognitive strategies where students reflect on material and engage across learning instances [16, 17]. Increasing the granularity of advanced organizers and content outlines for students struggling to connect topics, can increase the student's understanding of how to organize information, and the components of difficult topics [18, 19]. Goal clarity can result in increased engagement levels and improved performance [20, 21]. An additional instructional strategy which can be utilized to increase engagement and learning strategies are metacognitive interventions such as display prompts and student polls that can be adapted at the micro- or macro- level to encourage students to reflect on learning and revisit materials [22, 23]. Metacognitive strategies have been found to re-engage students, increase learning engagement, and task value [22, 24].

However, when adapting learning experiences, instructors must take into consideration the individual characteristics of the learner. Research has indicated interactions occur between individual difference variables (e.g., state anxiety, metacognitive abilities), and learning contexts [3, 25, 26]. Individual learners have different needs and class type preferences, which can impact the effectiveness of various instructional strategies [27]. These differences are especially important during the COVID-19 pandemic, which introduced many challenges for instructors and learners. Institutions across the world were forced to redirect instruction to online, and many learners found themselves in a class type that was not only novel, but that did not align with their preferred class type. Students forced into online learning are likely to yield negative experiences that can lead to frustration and incomplete learning [28]. This introduces a need to understand how the effectiveness of the above presented instructional strategies is impacted by whether a student is learning within their preferred class type. Studies have found that students who choose to take online classes and perform well in those contexts are more independent, typically exhibit metacognitive skills, and enjoy autonomy compared to those who do not choose online classes [27–33]. Diaz and Cartnall [27] compared students who self-selected into a health education class on-campus compared to those who self-selected into a distance learning class on performance and found that those who chose to enroll and persist in an online class were more independent, intrinsically motivated students, whereas those who chose to enroll on-campus were more dependent, extrinsically motivated students [27]. Additionally, learners who perform well in online contexts are typically good at self-reflective learning and metacognition [28]. This may be due to the fact that students who opt to take online courses are met with more challenges in terms of prioritizing in a non-classroom environment compared to those who self-select into in-person [34]. Additionally, online courses typically report lower retention when compared to face-to-face/in-person courses [35]. Therefore, students who choose online classes may be more independent in their learning, but face issues maintaining pace and progress in online classes. Students who self-select into in-person learning tend to have more of an external locus of control and overall perform better than students who prefer online courses, potentially due to the more structured classroom environment [36]. Those who prefer in-person learning may need social support systems and interactions to succeed in online classes.

Studies examining whether self-selection into class types impacts class performance measures such as grade point average (GPA), final exam scores, and quizzes have yielded mixed results [37–40]. Studies comparing undergraduate students who self-selected to in-person classes (i.e., introductory math and statistics) versus those taking the same course online found that traditional in-person students outperformed online students [3, 38]. Studies comparing students who chose traditional in-person classes versus those who chose online or hybrid found that student performance for undergraduate students in online classes was better in terms of final grades than traditional or synchronous classes [39, 43]. However, the opposite has also been found. A study by Gundlach et al. (37) measured student performance in an undergraduate statistics course and found that students who chose to take the traditional in-person class outperformed the online class type. It is important to note some studies have found no significant difference in performance among online or in-person classes [38, 44, 45].

There is an absence of literature comparing how preferred and non-preferred learning contexts affect learning. Educators have touched on e-learning *preparedness* which explains that students who are not prepared to take online classes and get pushed into online learning are likely to have negative outcomes [28]. Studies typically compare students who self-select into various class types and compare these mediums. However, this may not necessarily indicate whether they prefer this class type as there are likely other factors at play, for example, most people who take online classes do so out of necessity [31]. A report covering online education found that observational studies typically make comparisons between students who opt to take the course online and those who self-selected into the traditional face-to-face/in-person format without controlling for factors such as true preference, common personal characteristics, and school circumstances, which may jointly influence decisions regarding online course enrollment and course outcomes [31, 46]. This begs the question, will adaptive instructional strategies be as effective in preferred and non-preferred class types? Or are common instructional strategies used to adapt the learning content beneficial in only some learning contexts?

To examine this research question, we conducted a study that examined the effectiveness of three instructional strategies implemented in various class types, and used by instructors to adapt learning content, across both preferred and non-preferred class types. Instructional strategies included advanced organizers, engagement queries, and knowledge checks with feedback. An initial pilot study was conducted to examine the feasibility of delivery of the instructional strategies in an online learning context and to evaluate and adjust data collection methods prior to conducting the primary data collection. Thirty-five students participated in the pilot study received three learning interventions (advanced organizers, engagement queries, and knowledge checks) related to their class content during the second half of a college-level aeronautics course. Four primary findings resulted from the pilot study that triggered adjustments to how the primary data collection was to be conducted. First, results indicated that students were not taking the time to read through the survey questions as completion times were extremely fast and far below baseline survey completion times. Therefore, the decision was made to add attention checks, wherein the user was asked not to select an answer to a question. Second, pilot study results revealed that perceived goal clarity and level of feedback were important predictors of learning engagement; as such, knowledge checks were updated to provide immediate feedback on correct answers as well as target the topics with which student's commonly had difficulty. Third results of the pilot study suggested that students appeared to be missing the social component of learning during online classes. Therefore, outlines were updated to include a discussion component to facilitate reflection on the upcoming topics, provide instructors with ways to personalize material based on student experiences, and promote peer to peer discussion. Additionally, in an attempt to increase response rate, all interventions were embedded within the college's learning management system (LMS) and students received survey reminders throughout the study. Finally, to facilitate a deeper understanding of how preferred class type and the unique conditions presented due to the pandemic effected learning, preferred class type and social presence questions were included, along with questions regarding the drawbacks of each class type and whether students faced challenges while trying to participate in class, such as technical difficulties or illness. The following sections present the primary study methods, results and implications for adaptive training.

## 2   Methods

### 2.1   Participants

Seventy-two students from a southeastern U.S. university volunteered to participate in the study, 35 students in treatment and 37 in control. Participants were recruited from four aeronautics courses offered during the Fall 2020 semester. These courses included two sections of Aeronautics 1 taught by one instructor and two sections of Introduction to Human Factors taught by a second instructor. The study was a between subjects design with one section of each course acting as a treatment group and one as a control group. Although initially 72 students signed up for the study, data from only 45 participants (20 control, 25 treatment) were used in the analysis due to missing data. Given the COVID-19 pandemic, students were provided full autonomy in choosing how to attend class, either in-person, online synchronously, or online asynchronously. Twenty- two students chose to attended primarily online (only one of which was asynchronous) and 5 students attended in-person. Eighteen students chose to attend both in-person and online at different points throughout the study, that is they attended in a hybrid manner.

Participation was voluntary and extra credit was offered for participation or completing an alternative task. The study was approved by a university institutional review board.

## 2.2 Interventions

Three interventions were provided to students: advanced organizers, engagement queries, and knowledge checks with feedback. These were delivered via the university's LMS which was available to both online and in-person students. First, the night before each class, the treatment group received advanced organizers through a LMS announcement with a linked discussion board aimed at eliciting metacognitive processes. These outlines were adapted based on the amount of content the instructor covered in each class and whether an instructor indicated a topic needed to be covered again based on student performance. The advanced organizer would introduce the major topics which were scheduled to be covered during the lesson and end with a question related to the content. For instance, if one of the topics to be covered in class was long-term memory, the discussion board would ask the student "Share a time where you recalled a memory with someone who was there and they remember it differently than you? What were some of the differences in how it was recalled?" Second, participants in the treatment group were administered engagement queries via the LMS. These queries were administered to students attending in-person or online synchronously during a pause midway through each class. For participants attending asynchronously online, they were directed to take the engagement query halfway through the recorded lecture. The engagement queries consisted of 10 questions to measure engagement levels and factors that influence engagement, such as challenge, goal clarity, feedback, enjoyment, and meaningfulness. For example, students were asked, "how difficult was this activity?", and provided with choices such as, "the lesson was very challenging, I couldn't keep up" to "the lesson was too easy, I was not challenged" to address challenge level. Third, knowledge checks with feedback were embedded in participants' end of week survey. Knowledge checks were adapted to cover topics from the week's lectures with which students typically struggled. Participants in the treatment group received immediate feedback on which answer was correct. For example, if the student answered incorrectly, the next window would display a prompt stating they had selected the incorrect response, re-display the question, and provide the correct answer. Participants in the control group did not receive advanced organizers or engagement queries, and took the knowledge checks but were not provided any feedback.

Over the course of the 8-week data collection, instructors were provided with a weekly report detailing the results of the engagement queries and knowledge check scores for each topic. Based on the information, instructors could adapt the course, at the macro-level, by providing more examples or readdressing material related to either the chapters students felt were too difficult or knowledge checks many students failed. Instructors could additionally provide examples which required higher-order thinking if the students felt the topics were too easy or use more relevant examples to reengage students who felt the topics were not engaging. We recognize that this resulted in diffusion of some of the treatment to the control group; however, given this was an actual college class, and that the instructors were doing everything they could to improve engagement and learning under the unprecedented circumstances, it was a limitation of the study that was unavoidable.

## 2.3 Measures

Three types of measures were collected: (a) individual difference surveys (b) subjective self-report measures, and (c) performance scores. Surveys were administered at four points within the study via Qualtrics, including (1) at course beginning (pre-surveys) (2) during each lesson (during surveys/engagement queries) (3) at the end of each week (weekly surveys), and (4) at the end of the data collection (post surveys).

Pre-surveys consisted of demographic questions including: age, ethnicity, sex, education, major, occupation, and experience in both school and with mobile devices. The pre-surveys also included the State Trait Anxiety Inventory (STAI) Trait Scale – as a measure of anxiety as a trait, preferred class type questions, and a COVID-19 learning challenge question.

During-surveys were administered mid-way through the lectures or in natural breaks during learning content, and included an engagement query. The engagement query was used to measure cognitive engagement, challenge, goal clarity, feedback, and enjoyment. The engagement query was created for the current study and consisted of 6-items of quantitative nature, derived from Fuller et al. (2018) and 4-items of qualitative nature designed to qualify why the learner was engaged or not.

Weekly-surveys were administered at the end of each week and consisted of: (a) STAI State Scale – as a measure of stress (b) Flow State Scale – as a measure of challenge, goal clarity, and feedback (c) Flow Short Scale (FSS) – as a measure of engagement, and finally the (d) NASA-TLX – as a measure of mental workload. Finally, the social presence questionnaire was used to examine social needs, and questions related to environmental challenges and what environment they attended class in were included.

Post-surveys, were administered at the end of the data collection. The post survey contained all of the scales from the weekly-survey discussed prior, as well as, COVID-19 learning challenge questions. Final test scores were used as a measure of performance.

Instructors were also asked a series of questions related to what they felt was most helpful about the learning interventions, how they used the interventions to adapt their teaching, and whether they felt it was effective in increasing engagement.

## 2.4 Procedure

During the first week of class, a presentation was delivered to each class session to inform students of the study and extra credit available for participation. To provide access to asynchronous, online students, this presentation was recorded and subsequently uploaded to the LMS. To minimize diffusion, participants were asked not to share their extra credit experience with students in other courses. Students were required to enroll in the study by the end of the first week of class to participate. Students who agreed to participate completed the online informed consent form and pre-surveys.

During the first week of class the pre-survey was made available. During each subsequent weeks, weekly surveys were made available for users to complete after the final class of the week or after all materials had been reviewed asynchronously. The post survey was made available at the end of data collection during the final week of the study. The study lasted eight weeks.

Participants in the treatment group received advanced organizers with discussion boards via the LMS the night prior to each class session and were alerted throughout the course, using LMS announcements, to complete engagement queries, weekly surveys, knowledge checks and the post survey. The weekly survey reminders were sent the day after the final lesson for that week, with an additional reminder the Sunday before the following week. The post survey reminder was sent the day after the final lesson for the course. Instructors were provided with instructor reports every Monday morning to allow them to review and update course content and delivery methods. Control classes were prompted throughout the course, using LMS announcements, to complete their weekly surveys with knowledge checks and the post survey. After the study concluded, instructors were interviewed regarding the perceived benefits of the instructor reports and how they used the information to adapt their teaching.

# 3 Results

Although initially 72 students signed up for the study, data from only 45 participants were used in the analysis after removing participants who: (1) failed to participate in over 30% of the surveys (2) failed attention checks throughout the surveys, and (3) failed exams as these students were outliers that precluded an accurate comparison of groups with small sample sizes. This led to the final sample size of 45 participants (20 control, 25 treatment). In order to examine the effectiveness of the instructional strategies with respect to preferred class type, students were then further classified into type of student dependent on how they attended a majority (over 50%) of their classes; i.e., either in-person, online synchronously, or online asynchronously) and their reported preferred class type. Only 27 participants reported their preferred class type, resulting in a sample size of 27 for the primary analysis. Of these 27 students, 22 attended online, with 10 of those students being in their preferred class type. Of the 5 students who attended in-person all were in their preferred environment. Preferred class types and attendance are summarized in Table 1.

**Table 1.** Preferred class type and attendance

| Attended in preferred class type | N | Class type attended > 50% |
|---|---|---|
| Yes | 5 | In-person |
| | 10 | Online synchronously |
| No | 2 | Online synchronously (*Prefer Asynchronously*) |
| | 10 | Online synchronously (*Prefer In-person*) |

*Note.* $N = 27$

## 3.1  Instructor Interview Results

To gain insight into any adaptation that the instructors made to course content and delivery, the instructors were interviewed after the study was complete. The interviews revealed that one instructor adapted their instruction by providing more in-depth examples of the topics for which students had reported the content being "too easy." Additionally, the instructor examined the advanced organizer discussion boards and, based on this, attempted to tailor examples used in instruction to make them more relevant to the students and the current situation due to the COVID-19 pandemic. The instructor felt that these interventions were mildly effective in increasing engagement for the treatment group. The second instructor did not adapt the content based on the feedback as they felt the report validated the topics that, through experience teaching the class, he had come to realize were difficult for students. However, the instructor felt that the report would be most beneficial for those who were novel to teaching a course, as it would allow them to effectively adapt their teaching in ways that normally come about after multiple times teaching the course.

## 3.2  Instructional Strategy and Preferred Class Type Effects on Workload, Stress, Engagement and Performance

A two-way MANOVA with instructional strategy presence and preferred class type was conducted to examine the impact of the adaptive instructional strategies and preferred class type on workload, stress, engagement and performance. The average of the weekly scores over the assessment period from the NASA-TLX, the STAI, and the Flow Short Scale (as the engagement measure) were utilized, along with the final exam score. The MANOVA revealed no main effects of instructional strategy presence $F(4, 19) = 0.392, p > .811$, or attending class in your preferred class type $F(4, 19) = 0.072, p = .990$. However, a significant interaction between instructional strategy presence and attending class in your preferred class type emerged $F(4, 19) = 3.934, p = .017$. Univariate results revealed significant interactions between instructional strategy presence and attending class in your preferred class type for workload $F(1, 22) = 12.298$ $p = .002$ and stress $F(1, 22) = 4.392, p = .048$. Both engagement and exam scores were not found to be statistically significant $F(1, 22) < 0.001, p = .922$ and $F(1, 22) = 2.326, p = .096$, respectively (see Table 2, Figs. 1 and 2).

**Table 2.**  Univariate analyses of interaction between instructional strategy presence and preferred class type on engagement, workload, stress, and exam scores

| Condition*In preferred class type | F | df | p | $\eta^2$ |
|---|---|---|---|---|
| Engagement | .000 | 1,22 | .992 | .000 |
| Workload | 12.3 | 1,22 | .002 | .359 |
| Stress | 4.39 | 1,22 | .048 | .166 |
| Exam | 2.32 | 1,22 | .141 | .096 |

*Note.* $N = 26$. *$p < .05$. **$p < .01$. ***$p < .001$.

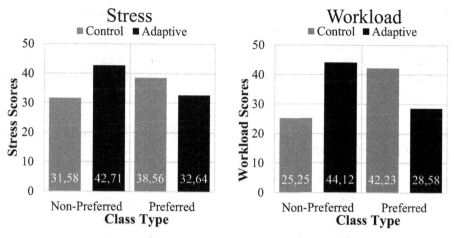

**Fig. 1.** Stress and workload in Non-preferred vs. Preferred class type

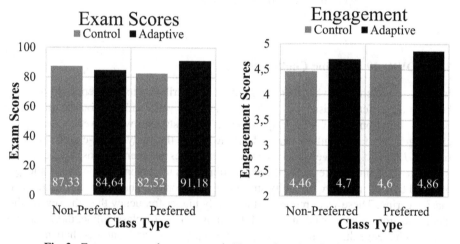

**Fig. 2.** Exam scores and engagement in Non-preferred vs. Preferred class type

### 3.3 Instructional Strategy and Preferred Class Type Effects on Factors that Influence Engagement

A two-way MANOVA with adaptive instructional strategy presence (present/not present), and class type (preferred/non-preferred) was conducted on factors known to influence learner engagement including challenge, goal clarity, and feedback. The average of scores of these flow state scale subcomponents across the weeks of the experiment were utilized. The MANOVA revealed no significant main effects of instructional strategy presence $F(3, 21) = 0.684$, $p = .572$, or preferred class type $F(3, 21) = 0.653$, $p = .590$. However, a significant interaction was found between instructional strategy presence and preferred class type $F(3, 21) = 4.48$, $p = .014$ (see Table 3 and Fig. 3).

The univariate results did not reveal any specific measure significantly accounting for the interaction. However, examining the breakdown of each grouping revealed those in their preferred class types experienced marginal increases with respect to perceived challenge (control = 5.18, treatment = 5.52), goal clarity (control = 5.23, treatment = 6.04), feedback (control = 4.98, treatment = 5.89) when in the presence of the instructional strategies.

**Table 3.** MANOVA results of instructional strategy presence and in preferred class type on challenge, goal clarity, and feedback.

| Between subjects effects | $F$ | $df$ | $p$ |
| --- | --- | --- | --- |
| Condition | .684 | 3, 21 | .572 |
| In preferred class type | .653 | 3, 21 | .590 |
| Condition* in preferred class type | 4.48 | 3, 21 | .014 |

*Note.* $N = 27$.
*$p < .05$. **$p < .01$. ***$p < .001$.

### 3.4  COVID-19 Learning Challenges

In order to understand what factors might have contributed to differences in learning between the different class types, a thematic analysis was conducted on the qualitative data resulting from the COVID-19 questions in which students were asked to identify the challenges they faced with respect to learning during the study. Open-ended responses from all 72 participants were analyzed to extract themes and then responses were categorized into the thematic areas. For those attending class in-person, the top two challenges reported by students were difficulty sustaining attention and challenges associated with mask wearing. These were reported at a slightly higher frequency than the seven other challenge areas summarized in Table 4. For those attending class online, there was one primary challenge that the majority of participants reported and that was challenge associated with distraction and focusing. A second challenge area, technical issues, also had a notably higher frequency than the remaining challenge areas summarized in Table 4.

## 4  Discussion

This study sought to evaluate the effectiveness of adaptive learning strategies, specifically: advanced organizers, knowledge assessments, and engagement queries designed to elicit metacognitive processes, at increasing engagement and learning in preferred and non-preferred class types. Due to the unique challenges presented by the COVID-19 pandemic, many students struggled to complete the study. This was expected as many studies conducted during the pandemic have found student enrollment is down, students have delayed taking classes due to economic issues, and all students are anxious and uncertain of what the pandemic will bring [47, 48].

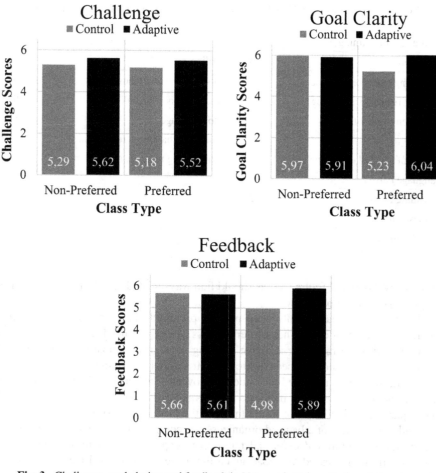

**Fig. 3.** Challenge, goal clarity, and feedback in Non-preferred vs. Preferred class type.

The adaptive learning interventions by themselves did not have an impact on workload, stress, performance, and engagement. This may be due to several reasons. First, the inability to control diffusion between the control and treatment group could have influenced the results. Given that this was an actual college class, the instructor who adapted instruction based on the instructor reports felt compelled to adapt instruction for both the treatment and control groups. This led to diffusion of the treatment. Furthermore, the lack of one of the instructors using the learning and engagement results to adapt instruction prevented the treatment from being fully implemented, potentially diluting the treatment effect. Additionally, the large amount of missing data likely played a role in the lack of significance results. Anecdotal reports from students revealed that they felt the interventions added to the course work, resulting in decreasing response rates as the semester progressed. Potentially, these students faced even more difficulties learning

**Table 4.** Self-reported COVID-19 learning challenges experienced across class types

Challenges of learning

| In-person | N | Online | N |
|---|---|---|---|
| Sustaining attention and Focus | 8 | Distractions and focus issues | 29 |
| COVID-19(masks/breathing) | 4 | Technical issues/challenges | 9 |
| Too much information | 3 | No challenge | 5 |
| Fatigue | 3 | Location challenges (time zones) | 2 |
| Length of time (class/lecture length) | 3 | Completing work (exams/group work) | 3 |
| Language barrier | 2 | | |
| Attending class | 2 | | |
| Homesickness | 1 | | |
| Desk location | 1 | | |

during COVID-19 and future studies should find ways to study students who fall off or become less engaged over time.

However, when participants were in their preferred class type, some interesting patterns emerged. Students in their preferred class type experienced lower levels of stress and workload when receiving adaptive learning strategies, compared to their control counterparts. This could have been due to the instructional strategies directing their focus to areas needed to be reviewed and studied. However, students in their non-preferred class type actually experienced increases in stress and workload compared to their control counterparts. This is likely due to the fact that the instructional strategies did increase task load (e.g., review of advanced organizers and completion of engagement queries); perhaps those in preferred class had more spare capacity and therefore could more easily absorb the increased task load given the decreased workload facilitated by the redirection of attention to relevant learning content. Students are more likely to use learning strategies and less inclined to avoid performance in classes that they feel they belong to and are more motivated in [49]. An alternative explanation is that most students in their non-preferred class type were attending classes online instead of their preferred class type of in-person. These students may have experienced less workload and stress compared to the preferred learners choosing to attend in-person as they did not have the added task load and stress of getting out, getting to and from class, and preparing and wearing personal protective equipment such as masks.

For exam scores, the univariate results, revealed no statistically significant differences based on the presence of instructional strategies or preferred class type. However, the findings had practical significance. For students in their preferred class type, adaptive instructional strategies resulted in an increase of approximately an entire letter grade when compared to the control group participants. For those not in their preferred class type, scores were very similar. This is an interesting finding as many studies only compare those who self-select into either an online or in-person class type without taking their preference into account [31, 46]. Studies have found that higher grades are found in classes where students say they feel a better sense of belonging, motivation, and self-regulation [49]. Studies examining what class type students prefer and why, find that students typically prefer face–to-face, or in-person, instruction [31, 50]. due to the interaction the student is able to obtain with both peers and instructors [51]. Additionally, they feel that online discussion boards are not equivalent to in-person discussions.

There were no significant differences in engagement levels experienced by any of the groups, regardless of instructional strategy presence or preferred class type. Differences in engagement may not have been detected due to the time of measurement. The Flow Short Scale, which was used to capture engagement levels during class attendance, is more appropriate as a measure of deep engagement during the task. However, this measure was captured at the end of the week once all class assignments had been completed. In ideal conditions, the Flow Short Scale would have been captured after each class. However, due to the three modes of attendance, and issues with integrating measures into asynchronous videos, this was not possible. With respect to the factors that influence engagement, including challenge, goal clarity and feedback, although the multivariate analysis revealed a significant interaction between the presence of adaptive learning strategies and preferred class type, none of the measures were significant at the univariate level. It appears that the general pattern across these measures was an increase for the instructional strategy group over the control, but only in the preferred class type. Those in their preferred class type experienced marginal increases in perceived challenge, goal clarity, and feedback.

This study provides some very preliminary evidence regarding the impact of preferred class type on the effectiveness of adaptive instructional strategies. More research is needed on preferred class types to draw any concrete conclusions as there is currently very limited research in this area. The literature tends to compare students who chose online or in-person class types without taking into account why they took the course in that context and that it may not necessarily be their preferred class type (e.g., took online because they needed flexibility to attend work). Throughout the COVID-19 pandemic response, many students are choosing to attend online although it is against their actual preferences [52].

### 4.1 Practical Implications

There are several practical implications of these research findings. First, these results suggest that adaptive instructional strategies might not be equally effective in all class types, especially those that do not align with a learner's preference. Second, this research highlights an interesting side effect that a situation such as a pandemic has on student learning. While instructors across primary, secondary, post-secondary and adult education strive to integrate strategies designed to address the challenges associated with transitioning their content to online platforms, it appears that preference in class type might be a factor, and one outside of the instructors' control, that influences learning effectiveness. Third, this research suggests that special consideration should be given to the added workload associated with instructional strategies and that added workload may become exasperated when a learner is not in their preferred class type.

Instructors should take these findings into consideration when integrating instructional strategies into different class types. For example, instructors could query learners regarding their preferred class type and integrate instructional strategies designed to make up for both class-type shortcomings and lack of learner preference. For instance, instructors could incorporate interactive class polls during synchronous online classes, or provide opportunities for prompts to facilitate in-depth discussions that facilitate personalization. Students could be given a choice regarding how many, when, or which of these activities to participate in, to help manage stress and workload. Additionally, instructors could provide students, who are learning online and are not in their preferred class type, continuous opportunities for self-reflection to allow them to improve their approach to learning in that class type [28]. Finally, it may be beneficial for instructors to encourage students to attend class in the class type in which they feel most comfortable and feel that their learning is most effective.

In the COVID-19 pandemic, many universities offered students the option to attend class in-person, remotely during class time, or asynchronously after class was held. It is possible universities could choose to continue this model moving forward in order to offer learning to a wide variety of students. If this is the case, it may be necessary to ensure that instructors are aware of learner preferences, monitoring learner stress and workload, and adapting teaching methods and strategies to ensure these remain in desirable ranges.

## 4.2   Study Limitations and Future Research

These results should be interpreted with caution given the many limitations associated with this study. First, the large amounts of missing data due to students not completing surveys was the biggest limitation of the study. This resulted in an extremely small sample size when analyses were performed. Future research should incorporate ways to increase student participation and attention during survey completion. For example the use of a chat feature rather than discussion boards. Second, the nature of the study which was conducted "in the wild" resulted in both dilution of the treatment effect as well as diffusion of the treatment effect. That is, the given that this was an actual college class, the instructor who adapted instruction based on the instructor reports felt compelled to adapt instruction for both the treatment and control groups. Furthermore, one of the instructors did not use the engagement results to adapt instruction which prevented the treatment from being fully implemented. Future studies should look at including ways to ensure reports and treatment results are provided in a manner which facilitates all instructors utilizing the material and survey responses in the same manner. Future research should attempt to replicate these findings in a more controlled experimental environment, for a longer period of time, and with different classes. This study was conducted with two college-level aeronautics classes, the results may be different with differing topics and these adaptive interventions should be tested in those contexts. Additionally, a semester long study with adaptive interventions may yield more prominent results. Finally, more research is needed on how non-preferred class types affect students and what adaptive strategies can be implemented to increase and facilitate students in this environment.

# 5   Conclusion

Instructional strategies that allow instructors to adapt learning content based on student needs have many benefits, including increased engagement and learning outcomes [6–9]. However, this research suggests that the effectiveness of these strategies may depend on how closely a class type aligns with a learner's preferences. This study examined the effectiveness of adaptive instructional strategies when students were in their preferred and non-preferred class types. The findings reveal that students preferred class types may have an impact on student learning outcomes, including stress and workload experienced during learning. The results of the study also revealed challenges to increasing engagement and learning outcomes in non-preferred class types. When implemented in a preferred class type, the interventions demonstrated decreased workload and stress, and increased exam performance compared to a control group. However, when compared to a control group, these interventions resulted in increases in workload and stress for participants in their non-preferred class types. These results suggest that introducing instructional strategies that require additional effort of the student, while intended to benefit the student, may lead to negative outcomes if the student is in a stressful and unfamiliar class type. Therefore, educators should consider encouraging students to attend class in the class type in which they feel more comfortable and feel that their learning is most effective.

# References

1. Mueller-Hanson, R.A.: Developing adaptive training in the classroom. US Army Research Institute for the Behavioral and Social Sciences (2009)
2. Lassoued, Z., Alhendawi, M., Bashitialshaaer, R.: An exploratory study of the obstacles for achieving quality in distance learning during the COVID-19 pandemic. Educ. Sci. **10**(9), 232 (2020)
3. Schaefer, P.S., Dyer, J.L.: Bridging the gap between adaptive training research and Army practice. Mil. Psychol. **24**(2), 194–219 (2012)
4. Billings, D.R.: Efficacy of adaptive feedback strategies in simulation-based training. Mil. Psychol. **24**(2), 114–133 (2012)
5. Landsberg, C.R., Astwood Jr., R.S., Van Buskirk, W.L., Townsend, L.N., Steinhauser, N.B., Mercado, A.D.: Review of adaptive training system techniques. Mil. Psychol. **24**(2), 96–113 (2012)
6. Hepplestone, S., Holden, G., Irwin, B., Parkin, H.J., Thorpe, L.: Using technology to encourage student engagement with feedback: a literature review. Research in Learning Technology, vol. 19, no. 2 (2011)
7. Sharek, D., Wiebe, E.: Investigating real-time predictors of engagement: implications for adaptive videogames and online training. Int. J. Gaming Comput.-Mediated Simul. (IJGCMS) **7**(1), 20–37 (2015)
8. Martin, A.J., Lazendic, G.: Computer-adaptive testing: implications for students' achievement, motivation, engagement, and subjective test experience. J. Educ. Psychol. **110**(1), 27 (2018)
9. Sampayo-Vargas, S., Cope, C.J., He, Z., Bryne, G.J.: The effectiveness of adaptive difficulty adjustments on students' motivation and learning in an educational computer game. Comput. Educ. **69**, 452–462 (2013)

10. Carroll, M., Lindsey, S., Chaparro, M.: Integrating engagement inducing interventions into traditional, virtual and embedded learning environments. In: Sottilare, R., Schwarz, J. (eds) Adaptive Instructional Systems (2019)

11. Wollenschlager, M., Hattie, J., Machts, N., Moller, J., Harms, U.: What makes rubrics effective in teacher-feedback? Transparency of learning goals is not enough. Contemp. Educ. Psychol. **44**, 1–11 (2016)

12. Chapman, P., Selvarajah, S., Webster, J.: Engagement in multimedia training systems. In: Proceedings of the 32nd Annual Hawaii International Conference on System Sciences (1999)

13. Issenberg, B.S., McGaghie, W.C., Petrusa, E.R., Gordon, D.L., Scalese, R.J.: Features and uses of high-fidelity medical simulations that lead to effective learning: a BEME systematic review. Med. Teach. **27**(1), 10–28 (2005)

14. Bell, B.S., Kozlowski, S.W.J.: Active learning: effects of core training design elements on self-regulatory processes, learning, and adaptability. J. Appl. Psychol. **93**(2), 296–316 (2008)

15. Bolkan, S., Goodboy, A., Kelsey, D.: Instructor clarity and student motivation. Commun. Educ. **65**(2), 129–148 (2016)

16. Gunstone, F.: The importance of specific science content in the enhancement of metacognition. The Content of Science, pp. 131–146 (2012)

17. Shen, C.Y., Liu, H.C.: Metacognitive skills development: a web-based approach in higher education. Turkish Online J. Educ. Technol.-TOJET **10**(2), 140–150 (2011)

18. Shihusa, H., Keraro, F.N.: Using advance organizers to enhance students' motivation in learning biology. Eurasia J. Math. Sci. Technol. Educ. **5**(4), 413–420 (2009)

19. Lenz, B.K.: Promoting active learning through effective instruction: Using advance organizers. Pointer (1983)

20. Shernof, D.J., Ruzek, E.A., Sannella, A.J., Schorr, R.Y., Sanchez-Wall, L., Bressler, D.M.: Student engagement as a general factor of classroom experience: associations with student practices and educational outcomes in a university gateway course. Front. Psychol. **8**, 994 (2017)

21. Limperos, A., Buckner, M., Kaufmann, R., Frisby, B.: Online teaching and technological affordances: an experimental investigation into the impact of modality and clarity on perceived and actual learning. Comput. Educ. **83**, 1–9 (2015)

22. Schmidt, A.M., Ford, K.J.: Learning within a learner control training environment: the interactive effects of goal orientation and metacognitive instruction on learning outcomes. Pers. Psychol. **56**, 405–429 (2003)

23. Ford, J., Smith, E., Weissbein, D., Gully, S., Salas, E.: Relationship of goal orientation, meetacognitive activity, and practice strategies with learning outcomes and transfer. J. Appl. Psychol. **83**, 218–233 (1998)

24. Kohler, D.B.: The effects of metacognitive language learning strategy training on lower-achieving second language learners. ProQuest Information & Learning (2002)

25. Goska, R.E., Ackerman, P.L.: An aptitude-treatment interaction approach to transfer within training. J. Educ. Psychol. **88**, 249–259 (1996)

26. Mith, L.H., Renzulli, J.S.: Learning style preferences: a practical approach for classroom teachers. Theor. Pract. **23**(1), 44–50 (1984)

27. Diaz, D.P., Cartnal, R.B.: Students' learning styles in two classes: online distance learning and equivalent on-campus. Coll. Teach. **47**(4), 130–135 (1999)

28. Guglielmino, P., Gugliemino, L.: Identifying learners who are ready for e-learning and supporting their success. In: Piskurich, G. (Eds). Preparing Learners for E-learning (2004)

29. Corbeil, J.R.: Online Technologies, Self-Efficacy, Self Directed Learning Readiness, and Locus of Control of Learners in a Graduate-Level Web-Based Distance Education Program. University of Houston, Houston (2003)

30. Guglielmino, P.J., Guglielmino, L.M.: Are Your Learners Ready for E-Learning. The AMA Handbook of E-Learning. American Management Association, New York (2003)

31. Xu, D., Xu, Y.: The Promises and Limits of Online Higher Education: Understanding How Distance Education Affects Access, Cost, and Quality. American Enterprise Institute (2019)
32. Hannafin, M.J., Land, S.M.: The foundations and assumptions of technology-enhanced student-centered learning environments. Instr. Sci. **25**, 167–202 (1997)
33. Yen, H.J., Liu, S.: Learner autonomy as a predictor of course success and final grades in community college online courses. J. Educ. Comput. Res. **41**(3), 347–367 (2009)
34. Howland, J.L., Moore, J.L.: Student perceptions as distance learners in internet-based courses. Distance Educ. **23**(2), 183–195 (2002)
35. Dietz-Uhler, B., Fisher, A., Han, A.: Designing online courses to promote student retention. J. Educ. Technol. Syst. **36**(1), 105–112 (2007)
36. Kahn, P., Everington, L., Kelm, K., Reid, I., Watkins, F.: Understanding student engagement in online learning environments: the role of reflexivity. Educ. Tech. Res. Dev. **65**(1), 203–218 (2017)
37. Gundlach, E., Richards, K.A.R., Nelson, D., Levesque-Bristol, C.: A comparison of student attitudes, statistical reasoning, performance, and perceptions for web-augmented traditional, fully online, and flipped sections of a statistical literacy class. J. Stat. Educ. **23**, 1–33 (2015)
38. Hoffman, J., Elmi, A.: Comparing student performance in a graduate-level introductory bio-statistics course using an online versus a traditional in-person learning environment. Journal of Statistics Education (2020)
39. McFarlin, B.: Hybrid lecture-online format increases student grades in an undergraduate exercise physiology course at a large urban university. Adv. Physiol. Educ. **32**, 86–91 (2008)
40. Tanyel, F., Griffin, J.: A Ten-Year Comparison of Outcomes and Persistence Rates in Online versus Face-to-Face Courses (2014). https://www.westga.edu/~bquest/2014/online courses2014.pdf
41. Paden, R.R.: A Comparison of Student Achievement and Retention in an Introductory Math Course Delivered in Online, Face-to-Face, and Blended Modalities. Ph.D. diss., Capella University, ProQuest Dissertations Publishing, UMI, no. 3237076 (2006)
42. Sue, V.: Comparing online and traditional courses. Acad. Exch. Q. **9**, 30–34 (2005)
43. Faulconer, E.K., Griffith, J., Wood, B., Acharyya, S., Roberts, D.: A comparison of online, video synchronous, and traditional learning modes for an introductory undergraduate physics course. J. Sci. Educ. Technol. **27**, 404–411 (2018)
44. Paul, J., Jefferson, F.: Performance in an Online vs Face-to-face Environmental Science Course from 2009 to 2016. Department of Biology (2016)
45. Caywood, K., Duckett, J.: Online vs on-campus learning in teacher education and special education. J. Teacher Educ. Div. Counc. Except. Child. **26**, 98–105 (2003)
46. Lee, Y., Stringer, D., Du, J.: What determines student's preference of online to F2F class? Bus. Educ. Innov. J. **9**(2), 97–102 (2017)
47. Gallagher, T.H., Schleyer, A.M.: "We signed up for this!" - student and trainee responses to the Covid-19 pandemic. N. Engl. J. Med. **382**(25), e96 (2020)
48. Sundarasen, S., et al.: Psychological impact of COVID-19 and lockdown among university students in Malaysia: implications and policy recommendations. Int. J. Environ.-Ment. Res. Publ. Health **17**(17), 6206 (2020)
49. Farrington, C., Porter, S., Klugman, J.: Do classroom environments matter for noncognitive aspects of student performance and students' course grades? University of Chicago Consortium on School Research Working Paper (2019)
50. Delaney, J., Johnson, A.N., Johnson, T.D., Treslan, D.L.: Students' perceptions of effective teaching in higher education. St. John's, NL: Distance Education and Learning Technologies (2010)

51. Tichavsky, L.P., Hunt, A.N., Driscoll, A., Jicha, K.: It's just nice having a real teacher: student perceptions of online versus face-to-face instruction. Int. J. Sch. Teach. Learn. **9**(2), n2 (2015)
52. Imsa-ard, P.: Thai university students' perceptions towards the abrupt transition to 'forced' online learning in the COVID-19 situation. J. Educ. Khon Kaen Univ. **43**(3), 30–44 (2020)

# Alignment of Competency-Based Learning and Assessment to Adaptive Instructional Systems

Laurie Dunagan[1]([⊠]) and Douglas A. Larson[2]([⊠])

[1] The Boeing Company, St. Louis, USA
laurie.l.dunagan@boeing.com
[2] Purdue University, West Lafayette, USA
douglas.larson@purdueglobal.edu

**Abstract.** The attraction of competency-based learning as a progressive model for newer learning systems has increased significantly over the past several years. It is built around the principle that learner outcomes, defined as what the learner is able to do and master after their learning experiences, are the ultimate measure for evaluation. This improves on earlier learning frameworks which focused on content authoring to develop curricula and instructor delivery techniques that relied heavily on standard grading systems, emphasizing testing only in terms of how much content was consumed and could be recalled by the learner. Thus, the focus was on instructor efficacy instead of on learner needs. A competency-based learning approach encourages tailoring the learning experiences to the learner and using evidence of learning to improve and adapt the learning components, which aligns well with adaptive instructional system approaches. The purpose of this paper is to further expand on competency-based learning, system and student evaluation, the assessment process, and how competency-based learning approaches may be applied to enhance and tailor adaptive instructional systems to achieve higher levels of learning based on individual outcomes. Additionally, it will be shown that there is a close connection between competency-based learning, learning analytics, and adaptive learning systems.

**Keywords:** Adaptive learning systems · Competency-based learning · Learning outcomes · Learning experiences · Evaluation and assessment · Learning analytics · Computerized learning systems · Digital environments

## 1 Introduction

In the past several years, the training community has tried to understand why students after graduating from school and from a variety of training programs are often not sufficiently competent as they progress though the program or when they get to their first job. Confronting this dilemma, many instructional programs have had to try and improve their teaching methods and develop new learning models that offer better ways to assess learning. One of the learning models at the forefront today is competency-based

© Springer Nature Switzerland AG 2021
R. A. Sottilare and J. Schwarz (Eds.): HCII 2021, LNCS 12792, pp. 537–549, 2021.
https://doi.org/10.1007/978-3-030-77857-6_38

learning. Traditionally, a one-size fits all model has been applied to most teaching and learning models. However, since not all learners are the same for a variety of reasons, this approach has proved less than optimal. On the other hand, a competency-based approach encourages tailoring the learning experiences to the learner and using evidence of learning to improve and adapt the learning components, which happens to align well with adaptive instructional system approaches. In order to understand why this learning model has gained so much popularity, it is important to explore several key concepts of the competency learning model.

## 2  Competency-Based Learning Concepts

### 2.1  Principle Design Focus of Traditional Learning Versus Competency-Based Learning

The traditional learning or teaching model places its design theory around the learning content, including authoring, materials, delivery and overall instructor efficacy, which supports teaching to the content. Assessment in this model is largely based on standard grading systems that gauge knowledge acquirement in terms of how much content was consumed and could be recalled by the learner. These assessments are mostly summative in nature incorporating multiple choice, true/false, matching and computational mathematics on an exam at the end of a learning block. With this learning model, the student is often passive and the teaching and learning aspects are time boxed. Course development in the traditional learning model is really focused on the instructor and creating learning objectives, which are defined by Martha Kruy at Central Connecticut State University [11], as discrete units of knowledge, skills and tasks that tend to have statements of intent in terms of the course rather than looking at any demonstrated behavior by the student.

In contrast, the competency-based learning model focuses on active student engagement and the desired outcomes to be achieved by the student. This model suggests a more self-paced learning implementation, where the learning is self-directed and customized until mastery of the outcomes is obtained. The learner is viewed as an individual on his or her own learning path where the time for learning will be adapted as needed, as opposed to being just part of the group on the same learning path with predetermined learning allotments. Figure 1 depicts the main components of a Competency-based Framework Learning System.

The key element of the competency-based learning model is the learning outcomes that describe behaviors which incorporate a wide range of knowledge and skills, which can often be observed and include skillsets that are transferable to a wide range of settings. The learning outcomes can be developed over time through a variety of learning experiences, and can be demonstrations of performance [11]. The measures of mastery attained by the student is in terms of SMART outcomes, and where possible, to look at on the job performance to validate mastery. SMART outcomes provide the basis for measurement because they are Specific, Measurable, Attainable/Appropriate, Relevant/Realistic and Timely. The development of SMART outcomes is best accomplished by applying a cognitive learning taxonomy, such as Bloom's taxonomy [2]. This is a classification system that distinguishes different levels of human cognition or reasoning skills that students use for active learning, and can be applied to levels of learning for

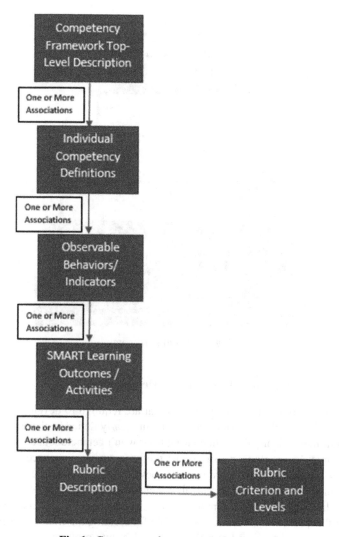

**Fig. 1.** Competency framework learning model

assessment. Figure 2 shows the levels in Bloom's Taxonomy and the progression of a learner from the bottom to the top. This model supports competency-based learning because it explains how the learner starts with the fundamental knowledge piece at the remember state, recalling facts and concepts, and ends at mastery with application of the knowledge that can be observed in terms of analyzing, evaluating and creating original works. Other graphic representations of Bloom's taxonomy can be viewed on the website of Vanderbilt University [15] and Iowa State University [9].

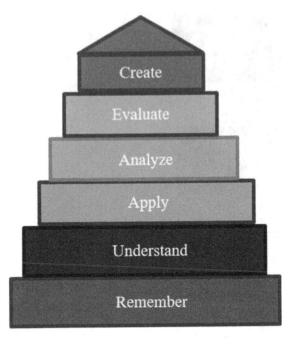

**Fig. 2.** Bloom's taxonomy

## 2.2 Instructional Design and Courseware Development

There are various roles and responsibilities that are required to develop a good learning program along with the courseware. Without clearly defined roles a program may become dysfunctional, and the right contributions won't get included, or important considerations may be overlooked to improve the program. In aerospace education, the competency learning outcomes are typically developed by teams of expert practitioners and regulators. However, it is critical to include an instructional designer to ensure that the quality of the learning outcomes is met. Instructional designers are invaluable partners in this process as they are responsible for creating the training curriculum for students to achieve the desired outcomes. These learning professionals ensure that all the learning elements are constructed to align for the benefit of the students. It is also important to have their input in the design of computerized learning systems so the learning outcomes of the student are not forgotten as the learning becomes automated. This process is most efficient when instructional designers work directly with the expert practitioners, regulators and the developers of the training devices [10].

There are many instructional design frameworks, such as ADDIE, ASSURE, Backward Design, and others. The importance of establishing an instructional design framework is to create a repeatable process for curriculum and program development and ensure that key elements of learning design are addressed. The framework should allow iteration and evaluation to be conducted to effectively revise the learning program. For example, ADDIE, which is a process for instructional design stands for Analysis, Design, Development, Implementation, and Evaluation. It is often applied to technology-based training [8]. ASSURE has similar concepts, and calls out the requirement for established learning outcomes and learner participation. Backward Design emphasizes learning outcomes be developed first, then the rest of the curriculum development. All of these instructional designs fit well within the competency-based learning model. At the onset of curriculum development is the ideal time and opportunity for decisions to be made about including adaptive instruction, as well determining what learning data is required to accomplish these goals.

### 2.3 Assessments in Competency-Based Learning

Understanding and assessing the amount of learning that a student has accomplished is one of the main goals of competency-based learning. Assessments provide evidence of learning that can ideally be used real time to adjust the learning activities for the individual learner. The principle assessment tool that is used is the rubric, which was depicted in Fig. 1. Rubrics provide the basis of assessment and feedback for both the learner and the teacher who has responsibility to adjust the teaching and instructional methods and activities for the learner to achieve desired outcomes. At the outset of a new course design, measurable learning outcomes should be established, assessment criteria developed, and then learning activities to meet those outcomes can be created. Once those are completed, appropriate assessments and rubrics can be constructed to match and assess the learning activities and experiences. The learning outcomes are based on learning levels, and the competencies are built around levels of competence, for example from novice to expert, so the rubrics address these differentiated levels for scoring and measurement purposes.

Another important element in assessment is to incorporate many types of assessments around many learning activities. There are summative and formative assessments that can be used. In competency-based learning, formative assessments are essential as they provide in-process evaluations, are often observation based, and are key to adapting the learning while it is taking place. Summative assessments are conducted at the end of learning and are usually in the form of a final test or project, and do have value, but aren't as valuable for guiding and adapting the learning that is in progress. Summative assessments are more like learning milestones that are achieved and aggregate all the learning objectives and outcomes into a single measure. In this case, a final grade will not provide clarity on what elements of a course or learning block were most or least successful in achieving the instructor's goals or learning outcomes, thus, would not be helpful in adapting the learning. On the other hand, formative assessments which are conducted continually throughout the learning process provide a more responsive, dynamic, and adaptive element to the competency-based framework.

When considering assessment, it is important to distinguish what is meant by assessment versus grading. They are related, but two distinct terms. The definition of assessment according to the University of Massachusetts Amherst [14] is the following: "Assessment is the systematic collection and analysis of information to improve student learning." Whereas, grading is used to score and evaluate an individual's performance on a specific item, which may be rolled up into a final grade. In order for assessment to take place, the grades need to be connected to assessment criteria and learning outcomes to evaluate learning, not task performance. Therefore, the goal of assessment is to identify and improve learning elements based on the established learning goals and outcomes in a holistic manner. It will require the collection of many data and feedback parameters and an analysis of those to produce results about what may need to be changed to improve student learning. This becomes a data-driven change process that can highlight both strengths and weaknesses in a variety of areas, such as in the curriculum, teaching methods, learning activities, or options and pathways in a computerized learning system. In fact, experimentation is welcome within the competency-based framework in order to see what works from one individual to another to achieve the learning outcomes; however, the results must be reviewed continually to guide the direction of both the teaching and learning.

## 2.4  Role of Learning Analytics in Competency-Based Learning

Since competency-based learning depends on data and information to drive change and adaptation, learning analytics plays a lead role. There are two very good definitions of learning analytics. The first one comes from the Society for Learning Analytics Research (SOLAR) organization, and states that "Learning Analytics is the measurement, collection, analysis and reporting of data about learners and their contexts, for purposes of understanding and optimising learning and the environments... [13]". The second definition stated by Professor Erik Duval during a presentation about learning analytics has a strong learner focus and says "Learning Analytics is about collecting traces that learners leave behind and use those traces to improve learning [4]". The second definition also lends itself well to the concept of recording all of the actions within computerized learning systems and using those traces to improve and direct the learning while either engaged in the learning system or to be analyzed afterward to recommend future enhancements.

The collection of learning data will not only include assessments, but also data about the student, the learning environment, computerized logged data, and any feedback that can be provided by the student, instructor or learning system. The more that is known about the learner, learning activities, and the learning environment, the better analysis can be performed. All of the data must be collected, cleaned, stored and made available for analysis. If any of this can be put into an automated process that is ideal. The data will be reviewed, aggregated and analyzed to provide results for decision making. If after analysis, a learning outcome appears to not have been met, then action can be taken to address it. Perhaps, a formative assessment will be revised or a new one added, or a new learning activity may be needed to fill a gap. In the case of a computerized learning system, modifications could be needed in its construction or the direction it takes a student within the program. The rubric may need to be adjusted to better measure the learning outcome. The more clearly all of the elements are tied together, the easier the results can be traced to specific areas that require change or can be improved within the learning environment. Dashboards or a display of the results of the analysis are good ways to make these visible to both the instructors and the learners so that they can take initiative to improve learning outcomes as they progress through the learning process. Learning analytics can and should be performed as soon as adequate data is available at any time during the learning process in order to provide direction for adapting the learning.

At the end of each learning cycle, a re-assessment of learning outcomes with the learning data should occur, and a retrospective should be conducted to see what items may need adjustment. Surveys are another way to collect qualitative measures from the students and instructors on how they feel the learning went, and to highlight any areas that may need to be looked at for improvement. If the surveys can also be tied to the learning outcomes that would provide more evidence to indicate if learning was sufficient. The ultimate measure to validate learning and competency would be to assess the student's performance on the job. If weaknesses are noted, then those could roll back into the course design for further improvement for the next course iteration. Figure 3 is a representation of a course assessment cycle that shows what should be looked at before, during and after a course instance.

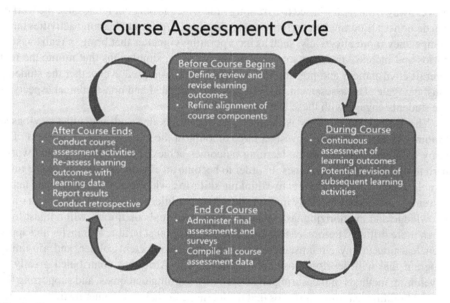

**Fig. 3.** Course assessment cycle, based on the course assessment cycle of Northeastern University [12]

## 3    Competency-Based Learning in the Industry

### 3.1    Application of Competency-Based Learning

The international aviation industry has been leading efforts to apply competency-based learning concepts to pilot training, as well as cabin crew and maintenance training. EASA (European Aviation Safety Agency) and ICAO (International Civil Aviation Organization) have both developed and published their competency frameworks that have been used with many pilot training programs around the globe. The impetus that led to this development came after an analysis was conducted by the UK Civil Aviation Authority (CAA) of several fatal aircraft accidents. It was determined that, "… in more than

50% of these accidents the actions of the flight crew were the primary causal factor (UK CAA, 2013). This analysis shows that flight crew handling skills were a factor in 14% of the accidents whereas flight crew non-technical skills were a factor in more than twice as many (32%) [7]". With this information, the international aviation organizations decided that traditional training, which was a traditional task-based system, should be improved, and the recommendation was to incorporate well-defined competencies into the pilot training that cover both technical and soft competencies. They looked at the healthcare industry as an example of using competency-based training to improve performance. There are a few aspects that are similar, such as both professions are highly task-based, they both require problem solving in various scenarios (normal and non-normal or emergency), and soft skills such as communication and teamwork are very important. Safety is also considered a critical element. With this approach, training moves away from hours-based to a training time which is only complete once the learner can demonstrate competent performance. Additionally, different learning activities build competency more effectively, such as incorporating vignettes that bring in realistic scenarios and increase problem solving abilities, or using simulations that mimic the real aircraft environment and present both normal and non-normal events that the students must navigate. The assessments look at both the technical and non-technical aspects as the students engage with these learning activities.

The United States Army is another sector that has invested in competency-based training. In fact, the Army invests a large amount in the education of its soldiers. The army looks very closely at the learning outcomes achieved by its students, and works hard to optimize those outcomes. In order to become an effective soldier, he or she must be able to apply critical and creative thinking skills to a wide array of problems and under extreme conditions, especially in war time. Thus, a soldier that only learns through route knowledge and memorizing tasks that are done in normal conditions, will not last long when more difficult, unforeseen situations arise. They must be able to transfer and apply their learning to any circumstance. This calls for a competent soldier, and a training program that will develop those competencies. The Army has contributed greatly to developing methods of measuring and improving learning outcomes, and supporting the idea of building learning portfolios that the learner can share with other institutions after graduation from the Army [3].

### 3.2 Emirates Training Use Case

To support the efforts of training organizations to develop new airline pilots more reliably with industry-acceptable levels of competence, Boeing has worked with multiple aviation industry partners to design an ecosystem for learning. The goal of these partnerships is to employ best practices in instructional design and systems development so that educators have reliable data to focus on improving summative and formative outcomes for learners.

Learning professionals from Boeing collaborated with stakeholders from Emirates Airline to document regulatory, industry, and airline requirements to determine competence in students throughout the course of training. This included academic and practical demonstrations of knowledge, skill, and ability to gauge progress and mastery over time. Subsequently, a new application to collect, store, review, and analyze data was developed where expected student outcomes informed the design of the curriculum and learning system. Together, these elements were developed symbiotically as a learning ecosystem. All records about student learning and learning operations are digital and available to the training organization for analysis.

During initial use of the new curriculum and system, the administration of the training organization quickly started to identify patterns in student engagement and performance. Previously, different data points about individual students were held by separate departments, and stakeholders had to request reports on performance. With the new system, any approved stakeholder can view a current snapshot of a student's performance immediately. Early interventions improved student outcomes with reduced impact to administrative resources and instructor staff. The training organization identified that student class attendance issues were an early marker that a student was struggling before it appeared with lower class quiz and test scores. As a result, interventions with students were introduced sooner and performance of the affected students improved with added support.

To make learning more adaptive and personal, enhancements will be introduced, such as individual learning plans. Further performance improvements are expected to be implemented as more students progress through the training program and the administration and instructor staff can analyze the data and recommend changes based on the results.

# 4 Computerized Adaptive Learning Systems

## 4.1 Design Elements

One of the larger goals of an adaptive computerized system is to be able to alter its behavior based on the learner's needs and respond to the user's actions as the learner progresses through the system to reach the desired learning outcomes. In order to tailor to the learner, characteristics about the learner are valuable inputs, such as demographics, learning style, preferences, current skills, and even emotions could be important. A fundamental element is the interaction between the user and the system. There is a need for both static, long term information to represent general information about the student, and dynamic variables that the system can act upon on a short term basis that are changeable, specific and interactive. One of the most common areas for adaptation is the learning content itself and task-based activities. The degree of difficulty can be considered based on the learner's knowledge level and the pace adjusted as the student either excels or struggles. Adaptive links can recommend next steps, or provide other text or multimedia, such as images or videos, depending on what the student does. Additionally, the system may adapt the assistance given to the student by displaying, hiding or deleting learning links based on adaptation rules, or provide help, hints and feedback as needed or requested by the student [6].

In order to work with measurable competencies in a digital environment there must be a way to effectively capture the data points and the learning experiences of the student. The method that has gained traction in this area is Experience API (xAPI), which is an open-source data and interface standard. It is an e-learning software specification that allows interoperability of learning technology products to communicate and work together. It enables recording and transfer of the learning experience data. This specification can track anything the learner does in any learning system that utilizes xAPI [1].

Once the data and learning experience is captured, it must be stored. The learning record store (LRS) is the place that can house the xAPI statements. These statements are easily parsed to understand what actions the student took in the learning experience and in what context. Ideally, this would occur real time in the computer learning system and then adapt to the learner's needs based on the student's actions and performance. However, this data could also be analyzed later to look at ways to improve the system based on how well the learning outcomes were met or not.

### 4.2 Example Computerized Instructional Adaptive System

An example adaptive system that uses a competency framework in its model is called MALO (Model of Adaptation of Learning Objects). Essentially this system tries to adapt the content, the format of presentation displayed, as well as the learning path, taking into account the learner's knowledge background and previous skills in order to adapt the learning objects to the individual. This system starts with the student's previous competencies and sets the desired competence as the source to establish the adaptation process to be executed [4].

At Boeing, there is work ongoing to further develop instructional tutoring and adaptive systems, as well as advanced techniques for authoring those adaptive systems. There are various studies that support the idea that a student can achieve significant learning gains when using an adaptive system. These systems can assist the instructor in performing accurate assessments, particularly on task-based procedures, which is a large component in aviation training. Boeing is also looking at ways to incorporate competency assessment into the adaptive learning systems, and ease the load of instructors by assessing components that can be translated to a digital environment. This may permit the instructors to focus on soft competencies, such as communication, team work, and leadership elements, which are inherently more difficult to capture and assess in a digital environment. In creating the adaptive systems, models are developed of the expert, student and instructional components to make sure the system considers and integrates all of those aspects in the learning model. Boeing has developed an Instructional Tutoring System (ITS) that integrates these concepts. See Fig. 4 that depicts the Boeing ITS architecture. Additionally, many virtual reality (VR) elements have been incorporated into the adaptive systems to make them more realistic, for example in pilot training and flying a plane, there is a VR flight deck, VR captain and a VR Instructor to assist in teaching the lessons. Figure 5 shows an example of one such VR training environment

### 4.3 Challenges to Applying Competency-Based Frameworks to Computerized Learning Systems

The challenges to applying competency-based frameworks to computerized learning systems are two-fold. First, the effort to build successful competency-based education with SMART student outcomes is significant and takes time. Second, combining computerized learning systems with SMART student outcomes requires an advanced collaboration

## Expert Model

- Allows system to solve problems
- Approach
  - ✓ Model solution paths
  - ✓ Encode rationales for and implications of actions

## Student Model

- Estimates student's understanding
- Approach
  - ✓ Maintain dynamic profile of proficiency scores against learning objectives

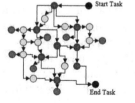

Start Task

End Task

## Instructional Model

- Allows system to implement interventions
- Approach
  - ✓ Manage sequence/selection of training activities
  - ✓ Manage hints and feedback on actions
  - ✓ Summarize performance

**Fig. 4.** The Boeing ITS architecture.

**Fig. 5.** The Boeing integrated VR training environment

between professionals in instructional design and computer learning system developers. In order to overcome this challenge, a strong organizational commitment is required to design, develop, and deliver highly effective training programs that put the student first and measure outcomes.

For the first item, the entire instructional design process (e.g. ADDIE) must be followed for repeatable, effective outcomes to be applied to the training program. Once a program is deployed, a program of continuous improvement is required for long-term success. This is especially critical for complex training programs focused on developing professional competence, like the training of airline pilots. Competency-based frameworks offer greater effectiveness through improved student outcomes, but this adds complexity to the curriculum development process. Additionally, lesson authoring into the adaptive system is often cumbersome and time consuming, and subject matter experts are still required to make sure the content is negotiated correctly by the automated learning system.

It would be simplistic to describe development of a learning ecosystem as sufficient by just applying competency-based frameworks to computerized learning systems. This implies that computerized learning systems are fully developed and immutable. Student outcomes must be the focus of developing the training curriculum and in configuring a learning system. From the start of a new learning initiative, the instructional designers and other learning stakeholders need to coordinate with the developers of the computerized learning system to ensure it contains the right learning focus. The system will need to be able to collect significant data and make it available for analysis to demonstrate that the student has mastered the desired outcomes. Analysis will also be used to direct future program modification.

The expected gains available through methodological and technological capability improvements require that computer learning scientists are welcomed into the team of stakeholders designing, developing, and evaluating learning programs. The close cooperation of specialized professionals across a range of interrelated disciplines is necessary for creating a successful learning ecosystem.

## 5  Summary

Incorporating adaptive elements into the learning process provides students a more personalized experience and lends to a more complete and successful progression through the different levels of learning until mastery is reached. As noted in a paper published by EduCause [5], "… adaptive learning respects their prior knowledge, responds to their learning needs, and reduces gaps in their understanding." Additionally, in an adaptive learning model, the instructor's role moves away from a content provider to a learning facilitator. With the idea that competency-based training is focused on the learner outcomes, and must collect evidence of this learning to adapt and meet the outcomes, it is truly an adaptive learning system. In order to act on the evidence, it must be analyzed which ties in learning analytics. Thus, there is clearly a close connection between competency-based learning, learning analytics, and adaptive learning models. Whether the learning system takes place in a computerized system or not really depends on the learning outcomes and the capacity to capture the data, learning experiences, and assess those in a digital environment. One aspect that must also be considered when implementing these systems, which rely on heavy data collection around the student, is not only handling the data requirements of acquiring and storing it, but also with obtaining the necessary permissions, as privacy and ethics of using people's data is increasingly regulated.

## References

1. Advanced Distributed Learning (ADL). Experience API (xAPI) Standard (2020). https://adl net.gov/projects/xapi/

2. Anderson, et al.: A Taxonomy for Learning, Teaching, and Assessing: A Revision of Bloom's Taxonomy of Educational Objectives. Addison, Wesley, Longman (2001)
3. Delvaux, S.: Measuring Learning Outcomes From Military Service. Inside Higher Ed, June 2017. https://www.insidehighered.com/views/2017/06/16/what-colleges-can-learn-military-about-competency-based-learning-outcomes-essay
4. Duval, E.: Learning Analytics – Tracking Learning, 2 May 2012. https://www.youtube.com/watch?v=OI5FhTcrIsE
5. EduCause. 7 Things You Should Know About Adaptive Learning (2017). https://library.edu cause.edu/resources/2017/1/7-things-you-should-know-about-adaptive-learning
6. Ennouamani, S., Mahani, Z.: An overview of adaptive e-learning systems. In: The 8th IEEE International Conference on Intelligent Computing and Information Systems (ICICIS 2017), December 2017
7. European Aviation Safety Agency (EASA). Terms of Reference for a Rulemaking Task – Evidence-based and Competency-based Training. RMT.0599, no. 1, May 2016. https://www.easa.europa.eu/sites/default/files/dfu/ToR%20%26%20Concept%20Paper%20RMT.0599%20Issue%201.pdf
8. International Society for Educational Technology (ISET) (2021). https://www.isfet.org/pages/addie-model
9. Iowa State University, Center for Excellence in Learning and Teaching. Revised Bloom's Taxonomy (2020). https://www.celt.iastate.edu/teaching/effective-teaching-practices/revised-blooms-taxonomy/
10. Kearns, S.K., Mavin, T., Hodge, S.: Competency Based Education in Aviation: Exploring Alternative Training Pathways. Ashgate Publishing (2016)
11. Kruy, M.: Education Research Guide – Definitions: What is the Difference between Learning Outcomes and Learning Objectives? Central Connecticut State University, Elihu Burritt Library, December 2020. https://libguides.ccsu.edu/c.php?g=736249&p=5262504
12. Northeastern University, Center of Advancing Teaching and Learning through Research (2020). https://learning.northeastern.edu/course-assessment/
13. Society for Learning Analytics Research (SOLAR). What Is Learning Analytics? (2011). https://www.solaresearch.org/about/what-is-learning-analytics/
14. University of Massachusetts Amherst, Office of Academic Planning and Assessment. Course-based Review and Assessment, Methods for Understanding Student Learning (2001). https://www.umass.edu/oapa/sites/default/files/pdf/handbooks/course_based_assess ment_handbook.pdf
15. Vanderbilt University, Center for Teaching. Bloom's Taxonomy (2020). https://cft.vanderbilt.edu/guides-sub-pages/blooms-taxonomy/

# Developing an Adaptive Framework to Support Intelligence Analysis

Ashley F. McDermott[1]([⊠]) (ID), Elizabeth Veinott[2] (ID), Leonard Eusebi[1] (ID),
Elizabeth T. Whitaker[3] (ID), Ethan B. Trewhitt[3] (ID), Shane Mueller[2] (ID),
David Illingworth[4] (ID), Rick Thomas[3] (ID), Michael Dougherty[4] (ID), and Sean Guarino[1] (ID)

[1] Charles River Analytics, Cambridge, MA 02138, USA
amcdermott@cra.com
[2] Michigan Technological University, Houghton, MI 49931, USA
[3] Georgia Tech Research Institute, Atlanta, GA 30332, USA
[4] University of Maryland, University Park, MD 20782, USA

**Abstract.** An essential component to intelligence analysis is inferring an explanation for uncertain, contradictory, and incomplete data. In order to arrive at the best explanation, effective analysts in any discipline conduct an iterative, convergent broadening and narrowing hypothesis assessment using their own tradecraft. Based on this observation, we developed an adaptive framework to support intelligence analysis while being tradecraft agnostic. The Reasoning About Multiple Paths and Alternatives to Generate Effective Forecasts (RAMPAGE) process framework provides a structure to organize and order analysis methods to maximize the number and quality of hypotheses generated, helping to improve final forecasts. The framework consists of five stages of analysis: (1) Information Gathering and Evaluation; (2) Multi-Path Generation; and (3) Problem Visualization; (4) Multi-Path Reasoning; and (5) Forecast Generation. As part of IARPA's FOCUS program, we demonstrated the flexibility of this framework by developing five versions of the process to answer five different sets of counter-factual forecasting challenges. While the FOCUS program concentrated on counter-factual forecasting, this framework was designed to support hypothesis generation and assessment, which is a critical component of analysis across the intelligence domain.

**Keywords:** Intelligence analysis · Adaptive · Analysis framework

## 1 Introduction

At its core, any intelligence analysis process is an inferential process to determine the best explanation for uncertain, contradictory, and incomplete data [1]. Although intelligence tradecraft can vary greatly among people and among disciplines, at a high level, it is an iterative, convergent broadening/narrowing hypothesis assessment process with four cognitive functions (see Fig. 1): framing and contextualization, down-collect, conflict and corroboration, and hypothesis exploration [2, 3].

In this paper, we present our Reasoning About Multiple Paths and Alternatives to Generate Effective Forecasts (RAMPAGE) process, a flexible process framework to

© Springer Nature Switzerland AG 2021
R. A. Sottilare and J. Schwarz (Eds.): HCII 2021, LNCS 12792, pp. 550–558, 2021.
https://doi.org/10.1007/978-3-030-77857-6_39

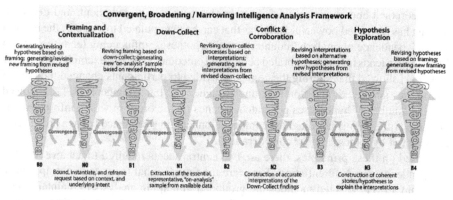

**Fig. 1.** Iterative, convergent broadening/narrowing analysis process [3]

support hypothesis generation. The RAMPAGE process was developed as part of the Forecasting Counterfactuals in Uncontrolled Settings (FOCUS) program run by IARPA. The goal of FOCUS was to develop and empirically evaluate systematic approaches to counterfactual forecasting processes. Over the course of Phase 1 of the program, participating teams were presented with five challenges. Each challenge presented forecasting scenarios and questions from simulated worlds, such as the game Civilization V or a simulation of a flu epidemic. The teams were provided data of variable reliability and accuracy and a series of questions to forecast. Each team was to use a predefined counter-factual forecasting process, which could be modified between challenges.

Over the course of the five challenges we developed five iterations and showed that our RAMPAGE process framework is flexible enough to support adaptive adjustments around the exact analysis methods while ensuring that analysts achieve multi-path reasoning (MPR) in their analysis. Based on analyst feedback and their performance across five challenges in counter-factual forecasting, we developed five separate versions of our process using this framework.

## 2   Hypothesis Generation

The primary foundation of the analytical methods applied in our RAMPAGE process is research surrounding the cognitive processes of hypothesis generation. In RAMPAGE, we consider counterfactual forecasting as an instance of the more general process of hypothesis generation. Hypothesis generation involves the creation, generation, and retrieval of hypothesized states of the world, based on available data. Hypotheses and data can represent anything of theoretical or practical interest. The Canonical example in the literature involves the generation of disease hypotheses [4], but the generation processes are central to many other domains, including intelligence analysis [3, 5]. There is considerable evidence that human hypothesis generation is severely affected by human biases and cognitive limitations [6–9]. Failures in hypothesis generation, including counterfactual reasoning, result from an analytical process that neglects key regions of the hypothesis space.

Theoretical and empirical work in cognitive psychology, judgment, and decision-making has identified powerful variables that can be manipulated to enhance the breadth and independence of analysts' counterfactual hypotheses, influencing them to perform MPR, which leads to better calibrated beliefs and outcomes [10]. For example, Dougherty et al. [11] showed that altering the context provided to participants changed the type of hypotheses generated, and Sprenger and Dougherty [8] and Lange et al. [12] showed that the number of hypotheses generated depends on the order in which information is presented (presenting less diagnostic information later in a sequence led to a broadening of the set of hypotheses under consideration).

Based on these principles, there are two central facets required to achieve MPR—independence and differentiation. These are the foundational features of our approach, and many of our selected methods are grounded in helping analysts to maintain these features. Exploring a wide range of possible outcomes and explanations is important, as is exploring *independent* parts of the hypothesis space [13] and avoiding common biases (framing bias, confirmation bias) that lead to early dismissal of potentially valid alternative explanations [14, 15]. Methods such as *information paucity* and *presentation order* function by driving analysts in the group to independently explore different parts of the hypothesis space. Furthermore, it is not enough to generate many hypotheses; *differential hypotheses* must be generated that enable analysts to determine which forecasts best account for contrasting outcomes and evidence. Methods such as *immersive perspective taking, differential hypothesis checking*, and *pre-mortem analysis* are designed to explore contrasting outcomes and evidence. The RAMPAGE process also includes methods for *narrowing* the hypothesis space into specific forecasts, lessons, and outcomes. Narrowing is a natural process that analysts perform to prioritize and constrain their focus on the hypotheses that they deem most important. If left to their own devices, analysts often perform narrowing with bias, pruning important alternative hypothesis and considerations, and ultimately leading to single-path reasoning [9, 16, 17]. RAMPAGE narrowing methods provide strategies to help the analyst focus without losing an effective set of differential hypotheses (i.e., hypotheses that enable comparative testing of possible forecasts and lessons).

The RAMPAGE framework is designed to support independent analysis and differentiation through selecting iterative broadening and narrowing methods. When using the RAMPAGE process, it is expected that each analyst works independently with minimal, strategic idea sharing. The next section provides a detailed explanation about this framework.

# 3   RAMPAGE Process Framework

This process proceeds through five stages of analysis: (1) Information Gathering and Evaluation; (2) Multi-Path Generation; and (3) Problem Visualization; (4) Multi-Path Reasoning; and (5) Forecast Generation. The process is intended to be run independently for each question being forecast. Table 1 describes the five process iterations we developed under this framework.

In the *Information Gathering and Evaluation* stage of analysis, available data is collected and distributed among analysts in order to minimize anchoring bias – when

**Table 1.** Description of each iteration of the RAMPAGE process

| Stage | Version 1 | Version 2 | Version 3 | Version 4 | Version 5 |
|---|---|---|---|---|---|
| Information gathering and evaluation | Limited information | Limited information | Information order randomized | Information order randomized | Identify initial factors |
| | Evidence checking | Evidence checking | Evidence checking | Identify factors | Team factor check |
| Multi-path generation | Hypothesis generation & validation differential hypotheses | Hypothesis generation & validation differential hypotheses | Hypothesis generation & validation | Identify causal relationships | Hypothesis story generation |
| Visual problem representation | Cognitive mind map | Hypothesis tree | Malleable grouping | Malleable grouping | Matrix of stories |
| Multi-path reasoning | New perspectives (2×) | New perspectives (2×) | New perspectives (2×) | New perspectives (2×) | Identify malleable factors in stories |
| | Hypothesis sharing | Hypothesis sharing | Hypothesis sharing | Keyword sharing | Premortem the explanation |
| Forecast generation | No specific guidance | No specific guidance | Format changes | Strategy guidance & format changes | Strategy guidance & format changes |

multiple analysts are working on a problem, this ensures they all start from different parts of the hypothesis space. This can be achieved multiple ways. In the earlier FOCUS challenges, we decomposed the provided data into conceptually oriented bins for disjoint distribution to the analytical team. Each analyst was provided a subset of available data to broaden their outlook and asked to generate a set of hypotheses relevant to the target forecast based on that data.

In later challenges, we modified the Information Gathering and Evaluation stage so that analysts received all data up front, but were each given different questions to answer first, so each analyst would approach the data from a different initial perspective. This instantiation of the process worked well given that there were several questions to be forecast that all relied on the same dataset but were separate forecasts. If this was not the case for an analyst, then a method akin to the first process we tried would be more appropriate.

Next, the analysts proceed to the *Multi-Path Generation* stage, where analysts generate initial sets of hypotheses. When done in conjunction with the data being distributed into different conceptual bins, the analyst would receive a set of data, review and check the quality of the evidence, and generate hypotheses based on the available data. After completing hypothesis generation for a given subset of the data, the analyst received a new set of data, and performed a fresh round of evidence checking and hypothesis generation with the expanded data. Finally, after performing this for all data bins, the analysts were asked to narrow their focus by characterizing the evidence impact of each hypothesis.

During this stage, analysts work separately to maintain independence and build and evaluate hypotheses working on the subsets of data or specific question provided to them. This stage involves both an initial generation method to maximize the number of independent hypotheses under consideration and an initial narrowing method to focus on the most likely or most informative hypotheses.

Throughout the process, a key stage is *Problem Visualization*. This stage was implemented in a diverse range of approaches, ranging from using an external tool to create a "mind map", structuring the visual collection of hypotheses in a hierarchical scheme or linked directly to supporting evidence or related claims, or having a comparative matrix of the best hypotheses under consideration. Sometimes this was built into how information was captured rather than being a separate stage and other times it was a discrete step in the process. The key to this stage is to assist the analyst in visualizing the hypothesis space, helping them to identify gaps in their knowledge or possibilities they had not considered.

Next, the analysts proceed to the *Multi-Path Reasoning* stage where they are asked to broaden their outlook by considering a range of different perspectives on the analysis. These perspectives could include different roles within the scenario, such as a health official versus a head of state, or roles external to the scenario, such as how would a game developer imagine this scenario into a game, or to shift the focus on the hypotheses to trying to identify malleable factors or creating additional hypotheses after assuming your current analysis is catastrophically wrong. Once these new perspectives have been used to broaden the hypotheses under consideration, the analysts once again narrow the space, making sure to include any newly generated hypotheses they found surprising or interesting.

The final stage is *Forecast Generation,* where analysts reviewed the hypotheses under consideration and translated those into forecasts. The questions presented during the FOCUS challenges asked for a probability distribution across bins of potential answers. We used multiple elicitation methods, ranging from simply having the analysts assign probabilities to each bin, to having them put numbers of marbles in jars corresponding to each bin. This stage included the least empirical support and was the stage analysts found most difficult. The question of how to translate a set of hypotheses into a probability forecast is currently under-researched and is a critical area where forecasting could be improved. When questions are not asked in this format, this translation into a forecast may not be as challenging.

# 4  Framework Adaptivity

## 4.1  Adaptive Timing

Due to the nature of the FOCUS challenges, time was consistently a limiting constraint on the work our analysts were able to do. However, the RAMPAGE framework does not have specific time requirements, so it could be adjusted as needed. We used a software instantiation of the RAMPAGE process for challenges 2–5, which gave us greater control over the time allotted to different steps of the process. This instantiation also demonstrated to us that having an adaptive time allotment was critical. Different analysts would need more or less time on various methods, and the process had to be able to adapt to their needs while ensuring the entire process was completed in the available time. The fifth challenge also included more problems than previous challenges, so that time needed to be adjusted to cover more questions for analysis. While this proved to be a significant stumbling block due to the already limited time, the process itself could easily adjust and by dynamically changing the recommended time throughout the challenge, we were able to support our analysts in completing all challenge questions.

The RAMPAGE framework does not have any explicit timing requirements itself. However, in this fast-paced world timing is often an important factor in analysis. Our experience implementing time-pressured processes within this framework demonstrate that it can be used under time constraints.

## 4.2  Adaptive Methods

The initial concept behind the RAMPAGE framework and driving purpose of the FOCUS program was to support changing methods, remove any methods that appeared not to be working and add new methods to test. In the five iterations, we used this feature of the framework across all stages of our processes.

Under the Information Gathering and Evaluation stage, we began with methods to restrict the amount of information the analysts had available at a time, gradually releasing additional information. The analyst team did not respond well to this and essentially did not begin hypothesis generation in earnest until they had all available information. This caused us to change the approach to randomize the order of information between analysts while allowing all of them to access all information before moving on to hypothesis generation. Under the Multi-Path Generation stage, we changed the methods to add more structure to hypothesis generation, breaking hypotheses into factors and causal relationships and eventually creating stories around factors to explain how those factors could change. The Visual Problem Representation went through the largest changes, requiring different supporting software as well as methods, moving from creating a mind map in external software to creating a matrix of the factor stories that the analyst was considering so that they could be compared side-by-side. Under the Multi-Path Reasoning stage we made several adjustments around which perspectives we used, starting with different decision making roles and changing to perspectives focused directly on the content of the hypotheses, looking for malleable factors and conducting a premortem on the leading hypothesis [18, 19]. Under the Forecast Generation stage, we changed the guidance provided and the interface for recording forecasts. For the challenge problems, forecasts were reported as percent likelihood of each option and the analysts struggled to report forecasts in that form. We provided alternate ways of arriving at the likelihoods, but the overall idea of providing likelihoods of all possible answers remained a struggle for the analysts and would be an interesting avenue of future study.

We were also able to make the methods adaptive to each analyst across the Multi-Path Generation and Multi-Path Reasoning stages of the process. The software we used to support our processes during the FOCUS challenges was able to choose the next method adaptively based on whether the analyst needed to further broaden or narrow their analysis. Due to the timing constraints, in our iterations of the process, a blank method was built into the process, which was filled in adaptively for each analyst. The framework would also support overall expansion or contraction of the process in the absence of timing constraints.

The RAMPAGE framework was developed with method adaptivity as a core concept. Individual processes are expected to differ based on the tradecraft of each intelligence analysis organization and discipline.

### 4.3 Adaptive Complexity

The foundation of the RAMPAGE framework is alternating between broadening and narrowing methods. Processes built with the RAMPAGE framework can vary from simple to complex within this foundation. Depending on the analyst's needs, the process could be as simple as one cycle through this broadening and narrowing, resulting in a data integration stage (i.e. exploring what data are available), a single method to broaden the hypotheses being examined, and a single narrowing method to arrive at a conclusion. Over the course of the FOCUS program, our processes ranged from 5 to 9 distinct methods.

As long as methods can be fit into the role of either broadening or narrowing the hypothesis space, the type of method or tradecraft used during iterations of this cycle can be put in any order. One big change we made in the final challenge was to move the point for collaboration from the end to the beginning of our process. While collaboration is usually intended to broaden the number of hypotheses considered, there is also always the risk that "group think" will lead to narrowing hypotheses instead. We found that having the collaboration at the end either led to this narrowing or had no effect at all. To optimize the role of collaboration and in light of the fact that our analysts were not experts in the simulated worlds, we moved collaboration to the beginning of the process before they saw the specific questions. This enabled the analysts to expand their understanding of the data and consider each other's viewpoints while not directly narrowing hypotheses since they did not have questions to hypothesize about at that point. Overall, the length and complexity of the RAMPAGE framework is highly adaptive to analysts' needs in different situations.

Complexity within the framework can also be adapted through the flow of information within the process. In our iterations we specifically controlled how many questions an analyst was considering at one time and how much information they had available. In early iterations we restricted the available information to encourage the analysts to do a deeper dive on the available material and address all of the problems for a given simulated world before gaining more information. In later iterations, we shifted to controlling information processing through each analyst focusing on only one problem at a time and varying the order of the questions.

Changes in complexity can cause large changes in cognitive load. The RAMPAGE framework supports adapting the complexity both through length of process and flow of information to enable processes to meet the demands of the particular analysis. When fewer questions are being asked, the framework allows for a deep dive and several cycles through the process to help ensure all possibilities have been considered. When several questions are of interest and the focus is on most likely outcomes, the framework can adapt to focus on a breadth of coverage, helping the analyst to appropriately focus on each problem while not spending too much time on one question at the expense of the overall analysis.

# 5 Conclusion

The RAMPAGE process framework can be used across a variety of intelligence applications. We developed the framework in response to the counter-factual forecasting challenges as part of IARPA's FOCUS program, but it could easily support analysis in a broad range of other domains as well. This adaptive process framework provides a guide for developing processes that employ MPR using combinations of a variety of methods, including combining different intelligence tradecraft approaches.

# References

1. Patterson, E.S., Roth, E.M., Woods, D.D.: Predicting vulnerabilities in computer-supported inferential analysis under data overload. Cogn. Technol. Work 3, 224–237 (2001)
2. Elm, W., Potter, S., Tittle, J., Woods, D., Grossman, J., Patterson, E.: Finding decision support requirements for effective intelligence analysis tools, pp. 297–301. SAGE Publications, Los Angeles (2005)
3. Roth, E.M., et al.: Framing and contextualizing information requests: problem formulation as part of the intelligence analysis process. J. Cogn. Eng. Decis. Making 4, 210–239 (2010)
4. Elstein, A.S., Schwarz, A.: Clinical problem solving and diagnostic decision making: selective review of the cognitive literature. BMJ 324, 729–732 (2002)
5. Trent, S., Voshell, M., Patterson, E. Team cognition in intelligence analysis, pp. 308–312. SAGE Publications, Los Angeles (2007)
6. Asare, S.K., Wright, A.M.: A note on the interdependence between hypothesis generation and information search in conducting analytical procedures. Contemp. Account. Res. 20, 235–251 (2003)
7. Bailey, C.D., Daily, C.M., Phillips, T.J., Jr.: Auditors' levels of dispositional need for closure and effects on hypothesis generation and confidence. Behav. Res. Account. 23, 27–50 (2011)
8. Sprenger, A., Dougherty, M.R.: Generating and evaluating options for decision making: the impact of sequentially presented evidence. J. Exp. Psychol. Learn. Mem. Cogn. 38, 550 (2012)
9. Thomas, R., Dougherty, M.R., Buttaccio, D.R.: Memory constraints on hypothesis generation and decision making. Curr. Dir. Psychol. Sci. 23, 264–270 (2014)
10. Sprenger, A.M., et al.: Implications of cognitive load for hypothesis generation and probability judgment. Front. Psychol. 2, 129 (2011)
11. Dougherty, M.R., Gettys, C.F., Thomas, R.P.: The role of mental simulation in judgments of likelihood. Organ. Behav. Hum. Decis. Process. 70, 135–148 (1997)
12. Lange, N.D., Thomas, R.P., Davelaar, E.J.: Temporal dynamics of hypothesis generation: the influences of data serial order, data consistency, and elicitation timing. Front. Psychol. 3, 215 (2012)
13. Lorenz, J., Rauhut, H., Schweitzer, F., Helbing, D.: How social influence can undermine the wisdom of crowd effect. Proc. Natl. Acad. Sci. 108, 9020–9025 (2011)
14. Klayman, J.: Varieties of confirmation bias. In: Psychology of Learning and Motivation, pp. 385–418. Elsevier (1995)

15. Lehner, P.E., Adelman, L., Cheikes, B.A., Brown, M.J.: Confirmation bias in complex analyses. IEEE Trans. Syst. Man Cybern. Part A Syst. Hum. **38**, 584–592 (2008)
16. Dougherty, M.R., Hunter, J.E.: Hypothesis generation, probability judgment, and individual differences in working memory capacity. Acta Physiol. (Oxf) **113**, 263–282 (2003)
17. Dougherty, M., Thomas, R., Lange, N.: Toward an integrative theory of hypothesis generation, probability judgment, and hypothesis testing. In: Psychology of Learning and Motivation, pp. 299–342. Elsevier (2010)
18. Klein, G., Phillips, J.K., Rall, E.L., Peluso, D.A.: A data-frame theory of sense making, pp. 113–155. Lawrence Erlbaum, New York (2007)
19. Peabody, M., Veinott, E.S.: Focus shift: differences in reasons generated using Premortem and Worst Case Scenario plan evaluation methods. ndm 259 (2017)

# Taxonomy of Physiologically Adaptive Systems and Design Framework

John E. Muñoz[1]([✉]), Luis Quintero[2], Chad L. Stephens[3], and Alan Pope[4]

[1] Department of Systems Design Engineering, University of Waterloo,
Waterloo, ON, Canada
john.munoz.hci@uwaterloo.ca
[2] Department of Computer and Systems Sciences, Stockholm University,
Stockholm, Sweden
luis-eduardo@dsv.su.se
[3] NASA Langley Research Center, Hampton, VA, USA
chad.l.stephens@nasa.gov
[4] Learning Engagement Technologies, Poquoson, VA, USA

**Abstract.** The design of physiologically adaptive systems entails several complex steps from acquiring human body signals to create responsive adaptive behaviors that can be used to enhance conventional communication pathways between human and technological systems. Categorizing and classifying the computing techniques used to create intelligent adaptation via physiological metrics is an important step towards creating a body of knowledge that allows the field to develop and mature accordingly. This paper proposes the creation of a taxonomy that groups several physiologically adaptive (also called biocybernetic) systems that have been previously designed and reported. The taxonomy proposes two subcategories of adaptive techniques: control theoretics and machine learning, which have multiple sub-categories that we illustrate with systems created in the last decades. Based on the proposed taxonomy, we also propose a design framework that considers four fundamental aspects that should be defined when designing physiologically adaptive systems: the medium, the application area, the psychophysiological target state, and the adaptation technique. We conclude the paper by discussing the importance of the proposed taxonomy and design framework as well as suggesting research areas and applications where we envision biocybernetic systems will evolve in the following years.

**Keywords:** Physiological computing · Framework · Adaptive systems · Design · Biocybernetic loop · Machine learning · Control theoretic

# 1 Introduction

The development of physiologically adaptive (also called biocybernetic) systems is a vibrant field of research that has been demonstrating how human body signals can be used to provide an intelligent mechanism for automatic adaptation in

© Springer Nature Switzerland AG 2021
R. A. Sottilare and J. Schwarz (Eds.): HCII 2021, LNCS 12792, pp. 559–576, 2021.
https://doi.org/10.1007/978-3-030-77857-6_40

human-machine interfaces [12]. The field has been named physiological computing, and it refers to the use of human body signals to serve as inputs in technological systems with the goal of improving the systems' functionality. Physiological signals can be sensed from different human phenomena such as cardiovascular (e.g., electrocardiography - ECG), neurophysiological (e.g., electroencephalography - EEG) or electrodermal (e.g., electrodermal activity - EDA) levels [19].

Terms used to describe this type of human-computer interface include non-command computer interfaces [18], implicit or passive brain-computer interfaces [57] and biocybernetic adaptation [12,42]. Biocybernetic adaptation employs the "steering" sense of "cybernetic". For example, in physiologically adaptive automation, biocybernetic adaptation serves the purpose of the system by more fully representing the human operator's overt and covert responses to the system. The focus is on the "biocybernetic loop" – the closed-loop system that is created when a person's physiological information is made available to the person through modulation of the task the person is performing.

Although multiple examples have shown the potential of using adaptation via interpreting bodily signals in real-time for applications such as games and training systems, the design of those systems is still complex and presents multiple challenges such as i) lack of a clear understanding of how to use the detected psychophysiological states to create automatic adaptation [11], ii) absence of a comprehensive set of design elements needed to create novel physiologically adaptive applications [42] and iii) limited availability of software tools to facilitate the prototyping and iteration [30].

In this paper, we propose a taxonomy of biocybernetically adaptive systems that covers two of the most widely used computational techniques for intelligent adaptation: control theoretic and machine learning (see Table 1). Studies have employed control-theoretic approaches to create adaptive biofeedback games aiming at training self-regulation skills [39]. The second category uses more sophisticated machine learning tools to create adaptations based on probabilistic models of the users' psychophysiological reactions.

Additionally, this paper proposes a simplified framework for designing biocybernetic systems which includes four domains that should be defined to streamline the design and development process. The framework proposes four design aspects that we consider as fundamentals in the creation of biocybernetic systems: the Medium, Application area, Psychophysiological state, and Adaptation technique (MAPA).

## 2   Adaptive Techniques for Biocybernetic Systems

Several adaptive techniques have been investigated to empower systems with algorithms capable of modulating their responses based on the pre-processed and interpreted physiological signals. There are two main approaches: control theoretic and machine learning.

## 2.1    Control Theoretic Approaches

Certain neuroadaptive systems may be characterized usefully in feedback control system terms. Biocybernetic adaptation technologies are among these. A closed-loop perspective motivates mapping feedback control systems concepts onto physiological loops. Therefore, one objective of this paper is to demonstrate how systems employing biocybernetic adaptation may be modeled using feedback control principles. For example, controller elements have been used in biocybernetic applications for testing various indices of cognitive engagement [40].

Control theoretic and control systems concepts, for instance, have been exploited in revealing ways to create adaptations using previously identified psychophysiological states. Mulholland and colleagues [28] applied feedback control principles to conceptualize the biofeedback process. They demonstrated a closed-loop procedure for determining stimulus-response relationships in a specific context–that of EEG alpha-blocking with light stimulation [8]. They demonstrated a functional relationship between light stimulation and EEG alpha production. This was accomplished by showing that the temporal patterning of alpha activity, wired to control the light presented to a subject, exhibited the expected behavior for a feedback control system under both positive and negative feedback conditions. An adaptation of this method was employed for making similar determinations in human-system interactions [40]. In the adaptation of the closed-loop method used by Pope and colleagues [40], candidate indices of "engagement" were proposed and tested for their sensitivity to changes in task demand through the mechanism of feedback. This methodology permits researchers to hypothesize about which features of brain signals best modify an automated system to suit human attentional capability and then efficiently test the hypotheses in an experimentally controlled operational analog. This adaptive method is essentially a feedback control process systematically adjusting task demand for operator participation. The method requires the availability of tasks whose demands may be varied in a systematic fashion. Similar indexes have been proposed as "generic" metrics of mental effort, allowing researchers to create an appropriate input to a closed-loop system [10]. Also, an index of Flow (or full involvement) was used in a closed-loop system that captured heart rate and skin conductance (e.g., EDA) and adapt a biocooperative game used in rehabilitation [46].

If there is a functional relationship between a particular candidate index and task mode (and, consequently, task demand), the index exhibits stable short cycle oscillations between modes under negative feedback and longer and more variable periods of oscillation under positive feedback. A negative feedback contingency in this context involves increasing task demand when an index of engagement wanes, while positive feedback reduces demand when the index wanes, thereby exacerbating the disengagement trend. The strength of the functional relationship is reflected in the degree of contrast between the behaviors of the index and the adjustments effected under the two feedback contingencies. The lack of a relationship is indicated by a finding of no difference between the mode switching behaviors of the index under the two feedback contingencies. A strong functional relationship between a candidate index and task operating mode (e.g., manual versus automatic) is reflected in stable operation under negative feedback and unstable operation under positive feedback. Candidate indices are judged on the basis of their relative strength in producing these contrasting feedback control system phenomena. That is, a better index choice causes the index, and consequently task mode, to alternate more regularly and stably under negative feedback than an inferior choice, and a better index also increases the degree of contrast between the behaviors of the index under the two feedback contingencies [22].

This engagement index evaluator [40] is an example of a feedback control system with a bang-bang controller design cycling between automatic and manual control based upon behavior of candidate engagement indices. This closed-loop method may also be characterized as a series of discrete replications of brief open-loop experiments in which task demand variations represent the "independent" variable, the effects of which on the "dependent" variable of EEG response are observed. The EEG response is programmed to, in turn, modulate the changes in task demand, which initiate each brief experiment. The initiation of the events is tied to the state of the experimental subject such that each subject experiences a distinctive chain of small experiments linked together by the decision rules established prior to the start of the overall experiment.

Ros and colleagues [47] prescribe an analogous method of contrasting the functioning of a neurofeedback loop with a control condition. In their case, examples of control conditions are given as "resting-state, sham, or sensory stimulation without control"; in the closed-loop evaluation method presented, the control condition is a reversal of the contingency relationship, to a positive feedback relationship, between task demand and brain activity, resulting in a more pronounced contrast.

In a series of technologies, biocybernetic adaptation, acting over time, has been employed as a biofeedback training method for application in clinical and sports settings [42]. In these technologies, physiological signals modulate some aspects of the training tasks in such a way as to reward trainees for approaching a target cognitive state. These technologies embed biofeedback training in tasks that are engaging – to foster engagement in self-regulation training of cognitive state – and, in the case of sports training, tasks that are relevant to the sports task. Modulated Play Station® games [36] exemplify a feedback control system with a proportional (P) controller design, with desired physiological signal changes driving the speed of cars/characters in video games (positive reinforcement). A "Zeroing Out Negative Effects (ZONE)" golf trainer [44] exemplifies a proportional (P) controller design, with desired physiological signal changes reducing the disrupting behavior of a putting green (negative reinforcement). Exerpong [31] exemplifies a proportional (P) controller design with ball velocity increasing if the heart rate (HR) average is under the target HR and decreasing it otherwise (negative reinforcement). Similar applications used in fitness have been developed wherein Proportional-Integral-Derivative (PID) controllers are implemented to encourage users to exert in desired zones while using fitness equipment (e.g., stationary bikes [53]). Space Connection [29] exemplifies an On-Off controller with a time-freezing power and a telekinesis power turned on or off based upon crossing respiration

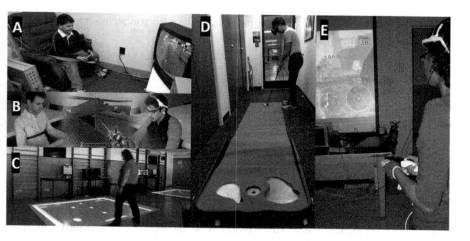

**Fig. 1.** Examples of biocybernetic systems using control theoretic as adaptive mechanism. A: Modulated Play Station® games. B: Space Connection for biofeedback training. C: Exerpong fitness game for older adults. D: Golf trainer system using Zeroing Out Negative Effects (ZONE) technology. E: Mindshift technology using brainwaves combined with motion controllers using the Wii Nintendo® console

relaxation and attention level thresholds, respectively. Wii®-based "MindShift"[1] exemplifies a proportional (P) controller design, with desired physiological signal changes reducing the erratic behavior of a game cursor (negative reinforcement) [41]. Modulated Kinect games [43] exemplify a proportional (P) controller design, with desired physiological signal changes producing rewarding in-game changes (positive reinforcement). Similar concepts have been proposed in modern virtual reality technologies used in police training scenarios (e.g., BioPhys virtual training system [33]) and virtual rehabilitation therapies using fatigue-aware systems with electromyography (EMG) [27].

More recently, intelligent adaptation techniques using control theoretic concepts have been used to create physiologically adaptive tools in digital media applications. In particular, a car simulation used for virtual training applications created by Parnandi and colleagues [39] used a closed-loop system configuration that modulated game variables by feedback control laws using PID controllers. The goal of the control system was to maintain the player's arousal around desired levels, thus the physiologically adaptive game boosted with the PID controller showed effectiveness in reducing the errors and oscillations in the closed-loop system response. Also, dynamic threshold adjustment techniques were used to modulate the game difficulty in the classic Tetris game using EEG signals in a passive Brain-computer interface (BCI) paradigm. Although researchers did not find significant results in a within-subjects experiment, when comparing the physiologically adaptive system against a conventional Tetris used as control con-

---

[1] https://www.nasa.gov/topics/technology/features/mindshift.html.

dition, the research served to demonstrate that more robust control techniques can be used in difficulty adjustment [23].

## 2.2 Machine Learning Approaches

Lately, the use of more sophisticated adaptive algorithms that use machine learning techniques has been proposed (and sometimes implemented). Although the list is not exhaustive and previous research has pointed out the limitations of some of the adaptive techniques [24], the applications can be summarized as follows:

- **Emotional Tetris:** [6]. *Supervised Learning - Classification.* Used discriminant analysis and support vector machines (SVM) to classify three emotional states based on EDA and EEG recorded while playing Tetris game in three different difficulty levels.
- **Upper limb rehabilitation:** [3]. *Supervised Learning - Regression.* Artificial Neural Network to provide subject-specific upper-limb exercises for physiotherapy. This model required a training set where the subject executed an exercise, and based on the initial performance and EMG measure, it calculated a trajectory to be displayed in a virtual environment to enhance the user's performance.
- **Car Simulation:** [35]. *Unsupervised Learning - Clustering.* EMG sensors were used to control a driving video game. Then, clustering methods were used to detect errors from the distribution of the data which might end up in bad control of the virtual car.
- **Robot-assisted rehabilitation:** [51]. *Supervised Learning - Classification.* Movement and physiological values are used to classify whether a participant would prefer more or less difficulty in a robot-assisted rehabilitation task. This work used classifiers like k-nearest neighbors (KNN), neural networks and linear discriminant.
- **Video games:** [13]. *Supervised Learning - Classification.* ECG, respiration, EDA, muscle activity and EMG were captured on more than 200 participants playing multiple sections of a game found to have different level of difficulty. A XGBoost classifier was found to be more accurate on predicting levels of fun from the participants in a three-level scale, and summarizing which features from physiological variables influence the predictive performance more.
- **Aircrew training:** [55] *Supervised Learning - Classification.* Classifier models are trained to recognize the states of 13 trainees during simulated flight scenarios based on patterns of the physiological signals measured during benchmark tasks using EEG, ECG, respiration and EDA [55]. Machine learning models (e.g., random forest, SVM) generate real-time determinations of the cognitive states induced by the scenario tasks that are displayed as gauges embedded in a mosaic of windows that also displays real-time images of the scenario tasks that the trainee is performing (e.g., scene camera, simulator displays, animation of simulator controls), and this mosaic is video recorded.

# 3    Design Frameworks for Physiologically Adaptive Systems

Psychophysiological-based monitoring of the human/operator state permits the use of human bodily signals to describe important psychological states that affect the task's performance (e.g., stress, high workload, or frustration). Design frameworks for intelligent adaptive systems considering the human-in-the-loop observed through the lenses of physiological sensors have been explored by several research groups. A heterogeneous collection of complementary and competing design frameworks have been proposed [17] to which the proposed framework herein is added.

Fairclough and Gilleade [11] proposed a set of criteria and a six-stage design cycle to effectively construct a biocybernetic loop. Additionally, Fairclough and Gilleade presented results from a case study establishing an empirical basis for the capabilities of an effective biocybernetic loop which is a practice modeled by others who have proposed frameworks [14,15,21,54]. Kosunen [21] also created a framework which expanded the temporal limits beyond real-time physiologically adaptive systems. Considerations for the abilities of the user is important to consider, as such adaptation possibilities must be extended to be as inclusive of as many users as possible. The framework proposed by Hardy et al. [16] personalized game-based exercise routines by using, among others, physiological signals.

The previously advanced frameworks are comprehensive and include essential considerations in the design of intelligent systems using physiological computing principles. Several pertinent details specifying the system intelligence, algorithms, and adaptive strategy used to close the loop remain to be explicated. Sufficient maturity of design frameworks has been achieved to permit creation of a taxonomy for discourse about the common elements. Furthermore, fundamental aspects that should be defined when designing physiologically adaptive systems to permit empirical investigation are necessary. The proposed framework includes a taxonomy and methodological considerations intended to enable advances in the evolution of physiological adaptive systems.

# 4    Taxonomy for Adaptive Techniques in Biocybernetic Systems

This section aims to describe a taxonomy that covers the different biocybernetic adaptive techniques used in previously reported articles covering physiologically adaptive systems. As mentioned before, there are two main adaptive approaches that have been widely used in the research community: i) control theoretic and ii) machine learning (as can be seen in Table 1).

The control theoretic category can be divided into two sub-categories called classical and modern. Classical control refers to systems that are well proven and have been around for decades [45]. Examples of such controllers are the On-Off (also called bang-bang) and proportional integrative and derivative controllers

Table 1. Taxonomy for biocybernetic adaptation techniques

|  | Approach | Category | Examples |
|---|---|---|---|
| Control theoretic | Classical | On-Off (Bang-bang) | Space connection [29] Engagement index evaluator [40] |
|  |  | Proportional integrative derivative | [P] Exerpong [31] [P] Wii-based MindShift [41] [P] ZONE golf trainer [44] [P] Modulated kinect games [43] [P] Modulated play station games [36] [PID] BioPhys [32] [PID] Car simulation [39] [PID] Bike exergame [53] |
|  | Modern | Adaptive | Dynamic threshold tetris [23] |
|  |  | Intelligent | Catch biocooperative [46] |
| Machine learning | Supervised learning | Regression | Upper rehabilitation [3] |
|  |  | Classification | DDA theragame [58] Emotional tetris [6] Robot-assisted rehabilitation [51] Aircrew training [55] |
|  | Unsupervised learning | Clustering | Car simulation [35] Driving [49] |
|  |  | Association | *Not found* |
|  | Reinforcement learning | Interactive RL | *Not found* |

(PID or any combination). The Space Connection game, for instance, uses an On-Off controller where super-powers are activated/deactivated when players get In or Out specific targeted physiological zones. Moreover, motion-based games that proportionally modulate considering the player's levels of attention are good examples of classical control theoretic systems using proportional controllers [41]. A second branch in the control theoretic category covers modern systems. Modern control techniques refer to "the sense of appearance of the optimal/digital/adaptive control approaches" [45], which covers more adaptive controllers capable of providing more robust performance to unknown system's behaviors. Robustness can be understood in control systems as entities that can offer certain levels of stability (maximized) and errors (minimized), which are often used to define the system's performance itself. A good illustration of a closed-loop system that used modern approaches of control theoretic adaptation is the game Tetris that used a dynamic threshold adaptation technique [23].

The second category uses machine learning techniques to create adaptations based on automatically recognized psychophysiological states. A main application area in machine learning concerns the analysis of behavioral data to estimate preferences of users and offer personalized recommendations [34], which is closely related to the purpose of biocybernetic loops; hence it is not surprising that some researchers have tried to use these algorithms to create physiology-based adaptation. Machine learning can be divided into three main sub-categories: i) supervised learning, ii) unsupervised learning and iii) reinforcement learning. Supervised learning refers to the process of training a machine learning model that can learn a class from positive and negative examples of a dataset, the output class to be learnt can be either continuous (regression problem) or categorical (classification problem) [1]. For instance, research projects where the adapted variable rely on the estimation of a continuous trajectory [3] or a specific emotion [6] can be solved through supervised learning. Some of the methods commonly applied include random forests, support vector machines, and neural networks. In the case of unsupervised learning, positive and negative examples are not necessary. In fact, these methods rely on unlabeled datasets to find the underlying distribution of the data and create groups with similar characteristics (clustering) or combinations of events that occur jointly and frequently in the dataset (association) [1]. Unsupervised approaches are not as common for physiology-based adaptation, yet a few projects have explored unsupervised learning during long-term acquisition of EMG data; for example, to provide fatigue-based adaptation in video games [35]. Association analysis is more useful on problems that deal with large tabular data; so far, no biocybernetic systems were found using this method and they might not present better results than other available methods. Lastly, machine learning adaptation could also involve reinforcement learning. In contrast to the previous paradigms, reinforcement learning does not intend to create a model from a provided dataset but tries to maximize a reward signal by learning the set of *actions* that needs to undertake for specific observed *situations*. Here, the data is gathered entirely from the interaction with an external environment [56]. In the scenario of biocybernetic adaptation, reinforcement learning could be thought as a way to create artificial entities embedded in the adaptive system. These entities could have a set of possible actions to take (in this case a set of available adaptations), and learn when to trigger a specific adaptation based on the real-time behavior of physiological variables. To the best of our knowledge, real-time adaptation with physiology-based reinforcement learning is still an unexplored research area.

To summarize, this taxonomy can be seen as an initial step towards identifying the types of system's intelligence and techniques that have been used by researchers and technologists, to close the loop using human body signals. We believe this is important for the creation of more intelligent, human-centered and effective adaptive systems since it:

- **Creates a comprehensive and "glanceable" understanding of the state-of-the-art:** From Table 1, researchers can identify that most of the examples of experimental physiologically adaptive systems have implemented classical controllers that use straight-forward and well-proven adaptive techniques. The majority of the examples have used games and digital media applications as medium to create the modulations considering its flexibility and variety of variables to control (e.g., game difficulty). Furthermore, the machine learning side of the table shows how classification algorithms (e.g., support vector machines [24]) have been more popular than regression algorithms to create closed-loop systems.

- **Allows the identification of adaptive techniques, approaches and tools used:** The taxonomy has the advantage of individualizing specific elements of the adaptive systems via deconstructing the core of the intelligence, listing specific techniques (e.g., PID controlling) in a structured manner. The taxonomy, for instance, elucidates that the use of proportional controllers has been popular among the reviewed systems under the control theoretic branch and shows that ECG, EEG and EDA signals are the most popular human body signals used in the closed-loop systems.

- **Unveils research opportunities:** The taxonomy gives insights about possible knowledge gaps that could be covered by the scientific community. For instance, the number of projects that leverage from machine learning is scarce compared to control-based approaches, and techniques such as interactive reinforcement learning could still be exploited for the purpose of physiologically adaptive environments [7]. However, setting up a reinforcement learning scenario requires a lot of data and iterations; which is not always available on experimental research with physiological variables. Simulating data from models that resemble internal dynamics of physiological conditions might help to overcome these limitations.

## 5    Framework for Designing Physiologically Adaptive Systems

The MAPA framework proposes the description of four design aspects that we consider as fundamentals in the creation of biocybernetic systems: the Medium, Application area, Psychophysiological target state, and Adaptation technique:

- **Medium:** Means of communication where the biocybernetic adaptation will take place. The medium can be either physical (e.g., tangible/real objects), virtual (e.g., artificially created elements), or iii) hybrid (e.g., a combination of physical and virtual). The medium plays an important role when providing feedback to the users since it allows the modulation of the self-regulation skills via learning mechanisms widely described in the biofeedback and psychophysiology literature [50]. Trending virtual mediums nowadays include the use of mixed (e.g., augmented and virtual) reality technologies [26,33] whereas internet-of-things devices[2] and socially interactive robots [48] are becoming more and more popular as embodied technologies to be controlled/adapted with the use of bodily signals.

- **Application area:** Context scenario where the biocybernetic system will be used. We have identified four main application areas that have been widely used in the development of physiologically adaptive systems [24]: i) healthcare

---

[2] https://www.weforum.org/reports/the-internet-of-bodies-is-here-tackling-new-challenges-of-technology-governance.

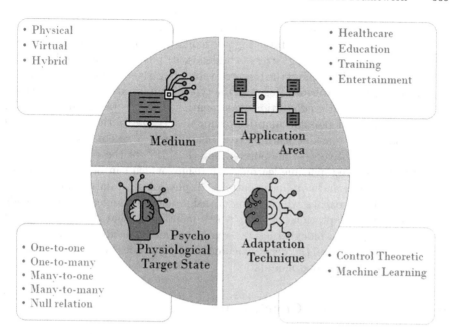

**Fig. 2.** MAPA framework for the design of intelligent physiologically adaptive systems.

(e.g., rehabilitation, psychological treatment), ii) education, iii) training (e.g., skills training), iv) entertainment (e.g., art, videogames). Although most of the biocybernetic systems developed have not been tested in the field [24], there is a growing need and demand to create physiologically adaptive systems that can be ubiquitously used beyond the controlled environments of the research laboratories [2].

– **Psychophysiological target state:** Human physical/mental state used by the biocybernetics system to create the adaptations. A useful construct to explain the potential relationships between psychological states and physiological responses was proposed by Cacioppo [5], who defined that all the elements in a finite set of psychological states are assumed to have an specific physiological response. Therefore, five general categories represent the possible relations within both the psychological and physiological events: i) one-to-one: one element in the psychological set can be associated with only one element in the physiological domain and vice versa (e.g., arousal and electrodermal activity [4]), ii) one-to-many: one element in the psychological set can be associated with a finite subset of elements in the physiological domain (e.g., stress levels can generate both peripheral and central nervous system responses), iii) many-to-one: two or more psychological elements can be associated to one physiological descriptor (e.g., changes in cardiovascular activity can be due to many psychological factors [9]), iv) many-to-many: two or more psychological variables can be associated with a subset of physiological elements (e.g., most recurrent relationship in psychophysiology), and v) null relationship: there is no possible association between both psychological and physiological elements. Thus, important elements to define when designing biocybernetic systems targeting particular psychophysiological states are: i) psychological state (e.g. stress, workload), ii) physiological descriptor(e.g., heart rate variability) and the targeted values (e.g., 90–120 beats per minute).

- **Adaptation technique:** Refers to the type of computational technique used to create automatic adaptations. As mentioned in the taxonomy (Table 1), two are the most popular adaptive techniques: i) control theoretic (e.g., PID controller) and machine learning (e.g., classifiers). A recent review on physiologically adaptive systems pointed out that 41% of the reviewed systems (44 in total) used machine learning algorithms which can be robust in identifying complex and non-linear patterns in physiological data, and 59% used rule-based approaches which focus on using specific ranges and thresholds to create the adaptation [24]. It is worth mentioning that depending on the adaptation goal, a biocybernetic system could have multiple algorithms that can use either control theoretic, machine learning or both types of adaptations to achieve the intended modulation.

## 6     Discussion and Conclusion

We have proposed a novel taxonomy that categorizes the multiple system intelligence that have been popularly used by researchers in the design of biocybernetic systems. Our taxonomy included illustrative systems of two major areas of adaptation techniques: control theoretic and machine learning. The taxonomy intends to better determine and differentiate the computational techniques used when adapting systems in real-time using physiological signals such as cardiovascular or neurophysiological. During the classification, we have taken several examples of adaptive systems that we believe are representative of what has been done during the last two decades. However, our intention is not to have a systematic review of such systems (for a more structured review see [24]) but to create an integrative and comprehensive taxonomy that classifies the algorithms and techniques used to close the loop. The taxonomy also allows the identification of how two very different but yet widely used adaptation techniques (e.g., control theoretic and machine learning) have been integrated to interactive systems in order to maximize the value of sensing and interpreting human body signals. Furthermore, the creation of the taxonomy led to structure a design framework called MAPA, which is presented as a design tool that can be used to better define the elements of a physiologically adaptive systems, including the how (adaptive technique), where (medium) and why (application area) fundamental questions. As a crucial element of the taxonomy, we have included the target psychophysiological state which uses Caciopppo's relationships construct [5] to aid the design process of biocybernetic systems. Without a proper definition of the psychological variables and their physiological descriptors, the design of physiologically adaptive systems cannot be successful since this is the core of the adaptive behavior [11]. Some important implications of the creation of both the taxonomy and the design framework are i) the need of more software tools to facilitate the integration of this technology with interactive (immersive) systems, ii) the emerging trend in using, adapting and validating machine learning models in physiologically adaptive systems, iii) the need for more attention should be paid to the feedback mechanisms and modalities to persuade users to modulate their physiological responses. These implications are discussed as follows:

## 6.1  Software Tools and New Immersive Media

The design of intelligent adaptive systems that uses physiological signals for real-time adaptation covers multiple theoretical and foundational notions these psychophysiological principles have merged with computing paradigms that consider the human-in-the-loop. However, the practical notions that allow moving from the design stage to the development stage, requires more than a solid theoretical knowledge, sensor availability and experience with signal processing; it requires the existence of software tools that can streamline the creation of physiologically adaptive systems. Available software tools such as NeuroPype[3], Neuromore[4] and the Biocybernetic Loop Engine [30] offer interesting options to ease the prototyping stage of physiologically adaptive systems. However, more development is needed to better integrate available consumer-grade and wearable physiological sensors and novel mediums such mixed reality.

Moreover, the combination of more robust adaptive systems (e.g., PID) and novel immersive media (e.g., virtual reality) can bring numerous opportunities to create synergies between industry and academia. For instance, the ultimate goal of the virtual training simulation for police officers previously reported [33] is to help trainees to converge to the desired psychophysiological states. A PID controller could be implemented to optimize the changes of the simulation variables. In this adaptive system, the difference between the trainee's heart rate response and the target or setpoint heart rate is used to drive attributes of the simulation task, e.g., firing range target speed or hindering rain intensity, which, in turn, is expected to drive the trainee's cardiovascular activity. Based on previous work [39] a proportional-integral-derivative (PID) controller element would be expected to improve the accuracy and stability of this type of training system while, novel and immersive simulations deployed in virtual reality can enhance the vividness and realism of the experience [27].

## 6.2  Challenges in Machine Learning and Biocybernetic Adaptation

Machine learning methods usually assume the presence of sufficient samples to learn the underlying distribution of the data, either for modeling or for the creation of reinforcement learning policies. However, psychophysiological variables are user-dependent and can present high variance even for the same individual at two different time points, which make it difficult to create high-quality datasets that encourage the construction of accurate systems for a single task [25].

---

[3] https://www.neuropype.io/.
[4] https://www.neuromore.com/.

Moreover, some papers trying to develop these systems have mentioned challenges regarding the unavailability of ground truth for analysis [49]; as an example, after many years of research it is still unclear what feature combinations of physiological signals are the most relevant for emotion classification [52]. Another complication concerns the training time of machine learning models, specifically in systems where the model is the core of the adaptive controller and it requires to be retrained in real-time for each new user; like in the case of the SVM [35]. Finally, there are few existing projects that use reinforcement learning with physiological data. One of them aimed at designing a controller for a neuroprosthesis that can adapt to the user preferences, their range of possible arm characteristics, and reaching movements [20]. Here, the authors expressed the need of several thousands of iterations before reaching a useful level of accuracy in the controller, which is not a feasible amount of data to collect through empirical experiments. Nevertheless, as a proposal for future work, existing theoretical physiological models could also serve as a basis to generate simulated environments that could train reinforcement learning agents for physiology-based adaptive controllers; ultimately trying to transfer their learning from computer-generated environments to real-life applications. The widespread of wearable and ubiquitous physiological sensing technologies is also a promising source of physiological data that can be used to refine the models needed to create tailored biocybernetic adaptation systems [38].

A potential way to address the unavailability of ground truth data is worth considering. Organizations who capture large volumes of user data (Amazon, Google, Tesla, etc.) could curate centrally located/open source repositories with data continually populated by users around the world. The large volume of data would satisfy the big data need of ML incorporated in biocybernetic adaptation systems. Furthermore, the ML solutions could be periodically redistributed back to biocybernetic adaptation systems after a requisite number of re-adaptation sessions. Further consideration of the appropriate approach to include ML into biocybernetic adaptation systems is necessary to effectively develop and deploy these systems to users.

### 6.3   Feedback and Reactive Ambient

While seeking for effective feedback mechanisms to create adaptive systems, changes in the ambient could be helpful to guide users to reach targeted states. In one such training protocol concept, dubbed "Ariel" for Shakespeare's sprite who summons tempests, trainee pilots experience a flight scenario where environmental conditions are modulated by their self-management of their attentional resources. For example, simulated turbulence or buffet is programmed to be proportional in amplitude to a brain/physiological signature of inattention. Ambient lighting or temperature may be similarly adjusted. In this training system, while dealing with operational challenges in the simulation, subject pilots experience a diminution of adverse environmental conditions as their attention management skill improves. Through this negative reinforcement mechanism,

trainees are rewarded with more-easily or more-quickly achieved flight performance improvement if they maintain effective attention management skill. This
approach is designed to teach trainees to incorporate autonomic or brain physiological self-regulation into simulator training without the need for conscious
attention to such regulation (as opposed to staying attentive to it [37]). Examples
of applications that use different feedback modalities to encourage participants
to reach specific targeted states have been recently developed where smells have
been used to modulate the body responses [2].

# References

1. Alpaydin, E.: Introduction to Machine Learning. Adaptive Computation and
   Machine Learning Series. The MIT Press, Cambridge (2009)
2. Amores, J., Richer, R., Zhao, N., Maes, P., Eskofier, B.M.: Promoting relaxation
   using virtual reality, olfactory interfaces and wearable EEG. In: 2018 IEEE 15th
   International Conference on Wearable and Implantable Body Sensor Networks
   (BSN), pp. 98–101. IEEE (2018)
3. Barzilay, O., Wolf, A.: Adaptive rehabilitation games. J. Electromyogr. Kinesiol.
   **23**(1), 182–189 (2013)
4. Boucsein, W.: Electrodermal Activity. Springer, Boston (2012). https://doi.org/
   10.1007/978-1-4614-1126-0
5. Cacioppo, J.T., Tassinary, L.G., Berntson, G.: Handbook of Psychophysiology.
   Cambridge University Press, Cambridge (2007)
6. Chanel, G., Rebetez, C., Betrancourt, M., Pun, T.: Emotion assessment from physiological signals for adaptation of game difficulty. Syst. Man Cybern. **41**(6), 1052–
   1063 (2011)
7. Dobrovsky, A., Borghoff, U.M., Hofmann, M.: Improving adaptive gameplay in serious games through interactive deep reinforcement learning. In: Klempous, R., Niko-
   dem, J., Baranyi, P.Z. (eds.) Cognitive Infocommunications, Theory and Applications. TIEI, vol. 13, pp. 411–432. Springer, Cham (2019). https://doi.org/10.1007/
   978-3-319-95996-2_19
8. Eberlin, P., Mulholland, T.: Bilateral differences in parietal-occipital EEG induced
   by contingent visual feedback. Psychophysiology **13**(3), 212–218 (1976)
9. Ernst, G.: Heart-rate variability-more than heart beats? Front. Public Health **5**,
   240 (2017)
10. Ewing, K.C., Fairclough, S.H., Gilleade, K.: Evaluation of an adaptive game that
    uses EEG measures validated during the design process as inputs to a biocybernetic
    loop. Front. Hum. Neurosci. **10**, 223 (2016)
11. Fairclough, S., Gilleade, K.: Construction of the biocybernetic loop: a case study.
    In: Proceedings of the 14th ACM International Conference on Multimodal Inter-
    action, pp. 571–578 (2012)
12. Fairclough, S.H.: Physiological computing and intelligent adaptation. In: Emotions
    and Affect in Human Factors and Human-Computer Interaction, pp. 539–556. Else-
    vier, Amsterdam (2017)
13. Fortin-Côté, A., et al.: Predicting video game players' fun from physiological and
    behavioural data. In: Arai, K., Kapoor, S., Bhatia, R. (eds.) FICC 2018. AISC,
    vol. 886, pp. 479–495. Springer, Cham (2019). https://doi.org/10.1007/978-3-030-
    03402-3_33

14. Fuchs, S.: Session overview: adaptation strategies and adaptation management. In: Schmorrow, D.D., Fidopiastis, C.M. (eds.) AC 2018. LNCS (LNAI), vol. 10915, pp. 3–8. Springer, Cham (2018). https://doi.org/10.1007/978-3-319-91470-1_1

15. Fuchs, S., Schwarz, J.: Towards a dynamic selection and configuration of adaptation strategies in augmented cognition. In: Schmorrow, D.D., Fidopiastis, C.M. (eds.) AC 2017. LNCS (LNAI), vol. 10285, pp. 101–115. Springer, Cham (2017). https://doi.org/10.1007/978-3-319-58625-0_7

16. Hardy, S., Dutz, T., Wiemeyer, J., Göbel, S., Steinmetz, R.: Framework for personalized and adaptive game-based training programs in health sport. Multimedia Tools Appl. 74(14), 5289–5311 (2015)

17. Hou, M., Banbury, S., Burns, C.: Intelligent Adaptive Systems: An Interaction-Centered Design Perspective. CRC Press, Boca Raton (2014)

18. Jacob, R.J., Leggett, J.J., Myers, B.A., Pausch, R.: Interaction styles and input/output devices. Behav. Inf. Technol. 12(2), 69–79 (1993)

19. Jacucci, G., Fairclough, S., Solovey, E.T.: Physiological computing. Computer 48(10), 12–16 (2015)

20. Jagodnik, K.M., Thomas, P.S., van den Bogert, A.J., Branicky, M.S., Kirsch, R.F.: Training an actor-critic reinforcement learning controller for arm movement using human-generated rewards. IEEE Trans. Neural Syst. Rehabil. Eng. 25(10), 1892–1905 (2017)

21. Kosunen, I., et al.: Exploring the dynamics of the biocybernetic loop in physiological computing. Series of publications A/Department of Computer Science, University of Helsinki (2018)

22. Kramer, A.F., Weber, T.: Applications of psychophysiology to human factors. In: Handbook of Psychophysiology, vol. 2, pp. 794–814 (2000)

23. Labonte-Lemoyne, E., Courtemanche, F., Louis, V., Fredette, M., Sénécal, S., Léger, P.M.: Dynamic threshold selection for a biocybernetic loop in an adaptive video game context. Front. Hum. Neurosci. 12, 282 (2018)

24. Loewe, N., Nadj, M.: Physio-adaptive systems-a state-of-the-art review and future research directions. In: ECIS (2020)

25. Luong, T., Martin, N., Raison, A., Argelaguet, F., Diverrez, J.M., Lécuyer, A.: Towards real-time recognition of users mental workload using integrated physiological sensors into a VR HMD. In: 2020 IEEE International Symposium on Mixed and Augmented Reality (ISMAR), pp. 425–437 (2020)

26. Marín-Morales, J., et al.: Affective computing in virtual reality: emotion recognition from brain and heartbeat dynamics using wearable sensors. Sci. Rep. 8(1), 1–15 (2018)

27. Montoya, M.F., Muñoz, J.E., Henao, O.A.: Enhancing virtual rehabilitation in upper limbs with biocybernetic adaptation: the effects of virtual reality on perceived muscle fatigue, game performance and user experience. IEEE Trans. Neural Syst. Rehabil. Eng. 28(3), 740–747 (2020)

28. Mulholland, T.: Biofeedback as scientific method. In: Biofeedback: Theory and Research, pp. 9–28 (1977)

29. Muñoz, J., Gonçalves, A., Vieira, T., Cró, D., Chisik, Y., i Badia, S.B.: Space connection-a multiplayer collaborative biofeedback game to promote empathy in teenagers: a feasibility study. In: International Conference on Physiological Computing Systems, vol. 2, pp. 88–97. SciTePress (2016)

30. Muñoz, J., Gouveia, E., Cameirao, M., Bermudez, I., Badia, S.: The biocybernetic loop engine: an integrated tool for creating physiologically adaptive videogames. In: Proceedings of the 4th International Conference on Physiological Computing Systems, pp. 45–54 (2017)

31. Muñoz, J.E., Cameirão, M., Bermúdez i Badia, S., Gouveia, E.R.: Closing the loop in exergaming-health benefits of biocybernetic adaptation in senior adults. In: Proceedings of the 2018 Annual Symposium on Computer-Human Interaction in Play, pp. 329–339 (2018)

32. Muñoz, J.E., Pope, A.T., Velez, L.E.: Integrating biocybernetic adaptation in virtual reality training concentration and calmness in target shooting. In: Holzinger, A., Pope, A., Plácido da Silva, H. (eds.) PhyCS 2016-2018. LNCS, vol. 10057, pp. 218–237. Springer, Cham (2019). https://doi.org/10.1007/978-3-030-27950-9_12

33. Muñoz, J.E., Quintero, L., Stephens, C.L., Pope, A.T.: A psychophysiological model of firearms training in police officers: a virtual reality experiment for biocybernetic adaptation. Front. Psychol. **11**, (2020)

34. Nikzad-Khasmakhi, N., Balafar, M., Reza Feizi-Derakhshi, M.: The state-of-the-art in expert recommendation systems. Eng. Appl. Artif. Intell. **82**, 126–147 (2019)

35. Oskoei, M.A., Hu, H.: Adaptive myoelectric control applied to video game. Biomed. Signal Process. Control **18**, 153–160 (2015)

36. Palsson, O.S., Harris Sr., R.L., Pope, A.T.: Method and apparatus for encouraging physiological self-regulation through modulation of an operator's control input to a video game or training simulator. US Patent 6,450,820, 17 Sep 2002

37. Palsson, O., Pope, A.: Stress counter response training of pilots via instrument functionality feedback. Abstract. In: Proceedings of the 1999 Association for Applied Psychophysiology and Biofeedback Meeting (1999)

38. Parent, M., et al.: PASS: a multimodal database of physical activity and stress for mobile passive body/brain-computer interface research. Front. Neurosci. **14**, 1274 (2020)

39. Parnandi, A., Gutierrez-Osuna, R.: A comparative study of game mechanics and control laws for an adaptive physiological game. J. Multimodal User Interfaces **9**(1), 31–42 (2014). https://doi.org/10.1007/s12193-014-0159-y

40. Pope, A.T., Bogart, E.H., Bartolome, D.S.: Biocybernetic system evaluates indices of operator engagement in automated task. Biol. Psychol. **40**(1–2), 187–195 (1995)

41. Pope, A.T., Stephens, C.L., Blanson, N.M.: Physiologically modulating videogames or simulations which use motion-sensing input devices. US Patent 8,827,717, 9 Sep 2014

42. Pope, A.T., Stephens, C.L., Gilleade, K.: Biocybernetic adaptation as biofeedback training method. In: Fairclough, S.H., Gilleade, K. (eds.) Advances in Physiological Computing. HIS, pp. 91–115. Springer, London (2014). https://doi.org/10.1007/978-1-4471-6392-3_5

43. Pope, A.T., Stephens, C.L., Jones, C.A.: Method and system for physiologically modulating action role-playing open world video games and simulations which use gesture and body image sensing control input devices. US Patent 9,084,933, 21 Jul 2015

44. Prinzel III, L.J., Pope, A.T., Palsson, O.S., Turner, M.J.: Method and apparatus for performance optimization through physical perturbation of task elements. US Patent 8,628,333, 14 Jan 2014

45. Raol, J.R., Ayyagari, R.: Control systems: classical, modern, and AI-based approaches. CRC Press, Boca Raton (2019)

46. Rodriguez-Guerrero, C., Knaepen, K., Fraile-Marinero, J.C., Perez-Turiel, J., Gonzalez-de Garibay, V., Lefeber, D.: Improving challenge/skill ratio in a multimodal interface by simultaneously adapting game difficulty and haptic assistance through psychophysiological and performance feedback. Front. Neurosci. **11**, 242 (2017)

47. Ros, T., J Baars, B., Lanius, R.A., Vuilleumier, P.: Tuning pathological brain oscillations with neurofeedback: a systems neuroscience framework. Front. Hum. Neurosci. **8**, 1008 (2014)
48. Roy, R.N., Drougard, N., Gateau, T., Dehais, F., Chanel, C.P.: How can physiological computing benefit human-robot interaction? Robotics **9**(4), 100 (2020)
49. Saeed, A., Ozcelebi, T., Lukkien, J., van Erp, J.B.F., Trajanovski, S.: Model adaptation and personalization for physiological stress detection. In: 2018 IEEE 5th International Conference on Data Science and Advanced Analytics (DSAA), pp. 209–216 (2018)
50. Schwartz, M.S., Andrasik, F.: Biofeedback: A Practitioner's Guide. Guilford Publications, New York (2017)
51. Shirzad, N., der Loos, H.F.M.V.: Adaptation of task difficulty in rehabilitation exercises based on the user's motor performance and physiological responses. In: 2013 IEEE 13th International Conference on Rehabilitation Robotics (ICORR), vol. 2013, pp. 1–6 (2013)
52. Shu, L., et al.: A review of emotion recognition using physiological signals. Sensors **18**(7), 2074 (2018)
53. Sinclair, J., Hingston, P., Masek, M., Nosaka, K.: Testing an exergame for effectiveness and attractiveness. In: 2010 2nd International IEEE Consumer Electronics Society's Games Innovations Conference, pp. 1–8. IEEE (2010)
54. Stephens, C., et al.: Biocybernetic adaptation strategies: machine awareness of human engagement for improved operational performance. In: Schmorrow, D.D., Fidopiastis, C.M. (eds.) AC 2018. LNCS (LNAI), vol. 10915, pp. 89–98. Springer, Cham (2018). https://doi.org/10.1007/978-3-319-91470-1_9
55. Stephens, C., et al.: Crew state monitoring and line-oriented flight training for attention management. In: 19th International Symposium on Aviation Psychology, p. 196 (2017)
56. Sutton, R.S., Barto, A.G.: Reinforcement Learning: An Introduction, 2nd edn. The MIT Press, Cambridge (2018)
57. Treacy Solovey, E., Afergan, D., Peck, E.M., Hincks, S.W., Jacob, R.J.: Designing implicit interfaces for physiological computing: guidelines and lessons learned using fNIRS. ACM Trans. Comput. Hum. Interact. (TOCHI) **21**(6), 1–27 (2015)
58. Verhulst, A., Yamaguchi, T., Richard, P.: Physiological-based dynamic difficulty adaptation in a theragame for children with cerebral palsy. In: PhyCS, pp. 164–171 (2015)

# Intersectionality and Incremental Value: What Combination(s) of Student Attributes Lead to the Most Effective Adaptations of the Learning Environment?

Jenna Olsen[✉] [ID] and Sydney Shackelford [ID]

Western Governors University, Salt Lake City, UT 84107, USA
jennaanneolsen@gmail.com

**Abstract.** Students can be placed in more than one category at the start, middle, and end of their educational journey. These categories can be based on demographics (age, gender, sex, minority, disability, ethnicity), on behavior (procrastination, struggle, frustrated guessing, pathological re-reading), on individual attributes (help-seeking, locus of control, time management, optimism), on community (internet access, setting, average education and income), and on academic factors (previous grades and degrees). These categories are frequently used by faculty, designers, and leadership to seek a better understanding of students and their needs with the goal to personalize or adapt the learning environment in the hopes of leading to more effective learning and more successful student outcomes. In these analyses we seek to determine the relative value of different student categories – and how these can be combined to result in the most effective educational process. We find ourselves asking what attributes matter the most – and which interact with each other to increase or reduce the amount of relative value. It is worth noting that several of the categories – while they play a large role in our students' holistic selves – are both highly sensitive (frequently protected) and static. If we can approach or match their value (educationally) in other categories which are less sensitive or more changeable, that will be a positive result. Because, while these attributes play a role in who the students *are,* they need not play a role in how the students are *taught.*

**Keywords:** Student attributes · Adaptive learning · Behavior

## 1 Introduction

### 1.1 Potential Student Categories

Students can be placed in more than one category at the beginning – and throughout – their educational journey. These categories can be based on demographics (age, gender, sex, minority, disability, ethnicity), on behavior (procrastination, struggle, frustrated guessing, pathological re-reading), on individual attributes (help-seeking, locus of control, time management, optimism), on community (internet access, setting, average

© Springer Nature Switzerland AG 2021
R. A. Sottilare and J. Schwarz (Eds.): HCII 2021, LNCS 12792, pp. 577–591, 2021.
https://doi.org/10.1007/978-3-030-77857-6_41

education and income), and on academic factors (previous grades and degrees). Students exist in all these categories simultaneously, but the categories are not of equal value to educational adjustments.

These categories are frequently used by faculty, designers, and leadership to seek a better understanding of students and their needs – to personalize or adapt the learning environment in the hopes of leading to more effective learning, and more successful student outcomes.

In these analyses we seek to determine the relative value of different student categories – and how these can be combined to result in the most effective educational process. With this in mind, we find ourselves asking what attributes matter the most – and which interact with each other to increase or reduce the amount of relative value.

It is worth noting that several of the categories – while they play a large role in our students' holistic selves – are both protected and highly sensitive. If we can approach or match their value (educationally) in other categories which are less sensitive, that will be a positive result. It is also worth noting that many of the categories we evaluate are not changeable (or at least extremely difficult to change) including things like community, sex, minority, and disability. Again, these play a large role in who are students are, but they need not play a large role in how we educate them.

## 2    Courses and Student Attributes

### 2.1    Course Selection

Our analysis looks at two different courses – both offered at Western Governors University to different individuals in the student body. There is little, if any, overlap in the student population for the two courses. The data for both courses spans the same time frame – from 2017 through 2020. The criteria for course selection included resource data availability, assessment design, and student size.

Both courses use the same set of learning resources – so the data for student activity were well-matched and accessible. Both courses use an assessment style referred to as an objective assessment. This style uses individual question items where aspects such as validity, reliability, and security are carefully maintained by the psychometric team. This makes it easier to track test outcomes at the item, objective, and competency levels.

Finally, both courses have over 25,000 students in the data set, which allows us to test out various attributes, and attribute groups, for our clustering while maintaining large enough n-counts in the final results to trust our initial findings.

The first of these courses is C785 – Biochemistry (n = 45,445) which is used by students in the College of Health Professions. These students have some amount of nursing training and are attending the university to increase their credentials in order to further their career. This is an extremely difficult course within the program – it is not unheard of for students to retake the course once or twice in order to pass.

The second course is C165 – Integrated Physical Science (n = 26,816). This is a general education course used by students from the other colleges (Health Professions students are – very much – the exception in this student population). This course focuses on chemistry, physics, and earth science.

**WGU Course and Term Structure.** Students at Western Governors University register for academic terms of a six-month duration. A term starts every month (rolling terms) and students may be in two terms over the course of the year. Within these terms, they can be registered for a wide range of courses – counts from 4 to 10 are not uncommon – which they are able to complete at their own pace. It is expected that students will focus on one course at a time during their term, but this is not strongly enforced.

## 2.2  Student Attributes

For this study we focused on three broad categories of attributes related to the students in the courses.

**Student Activity or Behavior.** These attributes include the number of days logged in, number of courses or resources accessed, and assessment attempts. Throughout this study these attributes are measured at various points in time, including 7, 14, and 21 days into a six-month academic term. All measures for these attributes are cumulative from the start of the term through the day of measurement.

**Student Readiness.** These attributes are tied to the individual students' learning styles, technical and reading skills, and individual attributes. The assessment for these attributes has been used by the Health Professions college throughout the duration of our study.

**Student Demographics.** This category, which we frequently called 'Day 0' variables, includes demographic and personal information we collect from students before they start their first term. This includes self-reported ethnicity, pell awards for the first year of study, gender, and student zip code – which we use to connect to census information for the community and state of student residence.

**Student Outcomes.** The student outcome variable of interest is whether they passed the course during that enrollment, which we define as the combination of a student, a term, and a course. This is a binary outcome as students will either pass of rail the course during that enrollment. It is important to note that our analysis specifically excluded those students who were able to effectively 'test out' by passing the final assessment without engaging either with the course materials or with faculty.

# 3  Attribute Selection – C785 Biochemistry

## 3.1  Evaluation of Attributes

One dataset each for activity (measured at day 21), readiness, and demographics was loaded into WEKA explorer. This was done in order to search for the best attributes – those with the highest differentiation in student outcomes - in each dataset which would then be used to create student clusters. Multiple attribute selection methods were used for each dataset to identify commonalities and select attributes that were highly ranked across multiple methods.

For each dataset, two select attribute methods were used. These were BestFirst search with the CFSSubsetEval evaluator and the Ranker search with CorrelationAttributeEval evaluator.

**C785 Activity Attributes.** The selected attributes within the activity category were *days_engaged* and *links_per_day*. The attribute *days_engaged* is defined as the number of days during which the student engaged in *any* course during the first three weeks of the six-month term (through day 21). Links per day is the number of links – again in *any* course – that the student clicked. These links guide students to both required and supplementary resources and to hosted course content (Table 1).

**Table 1.** Activity attribute clusters – C785

| Cluster | Days engaged | Links per day | Description |
|---------|-------------|---------------|-------------|
| Cluster 0 | 15 | 2.2 | Highly engaged students who check in with their coursework often |
| Cluster 1 | 10.3 | 1.8 | Engaged students who may use some, but perhaps not all, of the links |
| Cluster 2 | 7.0 | 1.6 | Average engagement and use of course links |
| Cluster 3 | 1.9 | 0.9 | Very low engagement during the early weeks of the term |
| Cluster 4 | 4.7 | 1.0 | Moderate engagement with low use of links |

**C785 Readiness Attributes.** Three attributes were selected by our methods from the readiness category. These were *personalattpct, readingpct,* and *procrastpct*. The *readingpct* attribute is a measure of the students' relative reading accuracy. The *personalattpct* is an average of all of the personal attributes measured by the survey. Finally, the *procrastpct* is a measure of procrastination tendencies. For all three of these attributes, a higher score is more desirable (Table 2).

**C785 Demographics Attributes.** Three attributes were selected from the demographics category. These were *marital_status, household_income,* and *minority*. The *marital_status* attribute is a self-reported variable and can be one of six possible categories – Married, Divorced, Separated, Widowed, Single, No Response. The *household_income* is also a range of categories, starting with '<$16,000' and ending with '>$65,000'. Finally, the *minority* is a binary status of "yes" or "no" (Table 3).

**Table 2.** Readiness attribute clusters – C785

| Cluster | personalattpct | readingpct | procrastpct | Description |
|---|---|---|---|---|
| Cluster 0 | 88.0% | 79.2% | 95.3% | A student with above average reading accuracy who scores high in all personal attributes but especially well in proactive behavior |
| Cluster 1 | 80.2% | 61.6% | 76.3% | A student with low reading accuracy and room for improvement in proactive behavior while average overall in all personal attributes |
| Cluster 2 | 78.3% | 87.2% | 69.7% | A student who procrastinates but has high reading accuracy and room for improvement all around in personal attributes |
| Cluster 3 | 83.8% | 87.3% | 81.7% | Student who has high reading accuracy and scores quite well in all personal attributes including proactive behavior |
| Cluster 4 | 71.9% | 78.9% | 55.6% | A significant procrastinator who scores well in reading accuracy and has room for improvement in all personal attributes |

**Table 3.** Demographics attribute clusters – C785

| Cluster | marital_status | household_income | Minority | Description |
|---|---|---|---|---|
| Cluster 0 | Married | Not reported | N | Married, non-minority students with unknown income levels |
| Cluster 1 | Married | $45000–$64999 | N | Married, non-minority students with above-average incomes |
| Cluster 2 | Single | $65000+ | N | Single, non-minority students with the highest reported incomes |
| Cluster 3 | Married | $65000+ | N | Married, non-minority students with the highest reported incomes |
| Cluster 4 | Single | $45000–$64999 | Y | Single, minority students with above-average incomes |

# 4   Cluster Creation and Performance – C785 Biochemistry

## 4.1   Clustering Method – C785

The next step was to cluster the students based on the selected attributes in each of the four categories. Each dataset was uploaded to WEKA Explorer and clustered using KMeans method. For the purposes of this study, we used five clusters for each dataset.

For each cluster group the following were recorded; number of clusters, minimum and maximum percent of total student population, spread in percent of total population, minimum and maximum course completion rate, and spread in course completion rate. The binary outcome variable of course completion was averaged into course completion rate across the cluster for the latter two calculations. A greater spread in the course completion rate percentage indicates greater cluster differentiation and goodness of fit.

## 4.2   Clustering Results – Single Attribute Categories C785

**Table 4.** Individual attribute category performance – C785

| Category | Min % of population | Max % of population | Spread in population | Min % completion | Max % completion | Spread in completion |
|---|---|---|---|---|---|---|
| Activity | 8.5% | 38.4% | 29.9% | 56.7% | 92.5% | 35.5% |
| Demographics | 9.5% | 36.4% | 26.9% | 66.9% | 80.4% | 13.5% |
| Readiness | 14.2% | 23.8% | 9.5% | 60.7% | 76.1% | 15.4% |

For individually clustered categories of attributes, the activity category shows the greatest differentiation in both population spread, and outcome spread. The demographics category has the next largest spread in population, while the readiness category has the next largest spread in outcomes (Table 4).

## 4.3   Clustering Results – Two Attribute Categories C785

To evaluate the attribute categories as combinations of two, rather than individually, we cross-matched students to two of their three cluster assignments. Then we repeated the queries from the individual category performance to measure population and outcome spread (Table 5).

By cross-matching the students, we find several pieces of information.

The first is that the combination of activity and any other category of attributes results in a stronger cluster differentiation. It is worth noting that this spread represents a very significant growth in outcome differentiation for the other category (either demographics or readiness) with a much smaller growth for activity outcome performance. Activity improves the outcome differentiation of both the demographic (28.3% gain) and readiness (22.6% gain) categories.

**Table 5.** Mixed attribute category performance (two of the three categories) – C785

| Category | Min % of population | Max % of population | Spread in population | Min % completion | Max % completion | Spread in completion |
|----------|---------------------|---------------------|----------------------|-------------------|-------------------|----------------------|
| Activity & readiness | 1.1% | 9.1% | 7.9% | 57.7% | 95.5% | 37.8% |
| Activity & demographics | 1.0% | 12.1% | 11.2% | 52.2% | 94.0% | 41.8% |
| Readiness & demographics | 1.4% | 9.3% | 7.9% | 64.0% | 86.5% | 22.5% |

The second is that we see that the combination of readiness and demographics clustering is stronger in outcome differentiation than either of the two categories separately, though still not a greater fit than activity either individually or combined with other categories.

## 4.4 Clustering Results – Three Attribute Categories C785

The final step in our evaluation of the different attribute categories for the biochemistry course was to cross-match students to all three of their clusters. By doing so, we are effectively clustering based on all three broad categories at once. We then ran, one additional time, the same analyses to measure both population and outcome differentiation (Table 6).

**Table 6.** Mixed attribute category performance (all categories) – C785

| Category | Min % of population | Max % of population | Spread in population | Min % completion | Max % completion | Spread in completion |
|----------|---------------------|---------------------|----------------------|-------------------|-------------------|----------------------|
| Activity, readiness & demographics | 0.1% | 3.4% | 3.2% | 40.0% | 100.0% | 60.0% |

From these results we see that the combination of all the categories results in the strongest outcome differentiation at a 60% spread. We also see that the individual clusters represent a significantly smaller percentage of the total student population, with the smallest of the new clusters representing a group of less than 50 students, even though we started with a large population.

**Adjustment to Cluster Planning Based on C785 Results.** Our analysis of the biochemistry course provided results which were unexpected, but very intriguing. After evaluating the first of the two courses, we adjusted our planned analysis for the integrated physical science course. Having found activity to be the strongest – by far – of the individual categories of attributes for the biochemistry course, we created additional categories of the activity attributes for the physical science course. We also added an additional question at this point in the analysis – specifically when (measured as number of weeks into the six-month term) did the value of activity data surpass that of demographics in differentiation of both student population and successful outcomes.

# 5   Attribute Selection – C65 – Integrated Physical Science

## 5.1   Evaluation of Attributes

Three separate datasets – all for activity – were built for the C165 course data. Datasets were built for student activity at 7, 14, and 21 days (or 1, 2, and 3 weeks respectively). Data cleansing process again included the removal of data for students who "tested out" of the course. Additionally, for students who took the course multiple times, we focused only on the first enrollment. Each data set was then uploaded to WEKA in order to select the most appropriate attributes. The attribute selection methods were the same across each dataset.

A dataset was also constructed for demographic data. Census data for community information was matched with student's personal data via their zip code. This data was then uploaded to WEKA to select attributes.

Due to the fact that CHP students were not likely to take the physical science course, and the historical readiness assessment data was for CHP students only, we did not create a cluster for readiness.

**C165 Activity Attributes.** For each dataset, two select attribute methods were used. These were BestFirst search with the CFSSubsetEval evaluator and the Ranker search with CorrelationAttributeEval evaluator. For C165, as for the earlier clusters with C785, the selected attributes within each of the activity categories were *days_engaged* and *links_per_day* (Tables 7, 8 and 9).

**Table 7.** Activity attribute clusters – week 1 – C165

| Cluster | Days engaged | Links per day | Description |
|---|---|---|---|
| Cluster 0 | 1.6 | 0.3 | Very low engagement and use of links |
| Cluster 1 | 3.5 | 0.5 | Low engagement |
| Cluster 2 | 7.5 | 1.2 | High engagement, average links |
| Cluster 3 | 6 | 0.9 | High engagement, average links |
| Cluster 4 | 4.9 | 0.7 | Average engagement and links |

**C165 Demographic Attributes.** Two feature selections were run to find the best fit attributes. These were both Ranker search methods with the CorrelationAttributeEval evaluator and the ReliefAttributeEval evaluator. The selected attributes within the

**Table 8.** Activity attribute clusters – week 2 – C165

| Cluster | Days engaged | Links per day | Description |
|---|---|---|---|
| Cluster 0 | 13.3 | 1.2 | Very high engagement and use of links |
| Cluster 1 | 10.0 | 0.8 | High engagement, average links |
| Cluster 2 | 2.9 | 0.3 | Very low engagement and links |
| Cluster 3 | 7.6 | 0.7 | Average engagement and links |
| Cluster 4 | 5.5 | 0.5 | Low engagement and links |

**Table 9.** Activity attribute clusters – week 3 – C165

| Cluster | Days engaged | Links per day | Description |
|---|---|---|---|
| Cluster 0 | 8.5 | 0.5 | Low engagement and links |
| Cluster 1 | 20.1 | 1.3 | Very high engagement and links |
| Cluster 2 | 16.5 | 1.0 | High engagement and links |
| Cluster 3 | 12.3 | 0.8 | Average engagement and links |
| Cluster 4 | 4.4 | 0.3 | Very low engagement and links |

**Table 10.** Demographic attribute clusters – C165

| Cluster | pct_wo_internet | ethnicity | nonresident_alien | Description |
|---|---|---|---|---|
| Cluster 0 | 40.7% | White | 0% | White, very high percent without internet |
| Cluster 1 | 8.7% | White | 0% | White, very low percent without internet |
| Cluster 2 | 19.8% | Black/African American | 1% | Black students, average percent without internet |
| Cluster 3 | 16.7% | White | 0% | White, average percent without internet |
| Cluster 4 | 26.9% | White | 0% | White, high percent without internet |

demographics category were *pct_wo_internet, ethnicity,* and *nonresident_alien.* The *pct_wo_internet* attribute is a community-level descriptor of the percent of those living without internet. It is extracted from census data using the student zip code. Both the *ethnicity* and *nonresident_alien* are self-selected by the student during their initial enrollment process. Ethnicity is categorical - and students are able to select multiple categories as desired. Nonresident alien is a binary condition (Table 10).

# 6  Cluster Creation and Performance – C165 Integrated Physical Science

## 6.1  Clustering Method

Just as we had done for the biochemistry course, each of the physical science datasets was uploaded to WEKA Explorer and clustered using KMeans method into five different clusters.

We again recorded the following data points (number of clusters, minimum and maximum percent of total student population, spread in percent of total population, minimum and maximum course completion rate, and spread in course completion rate), and used these to evaluate the relative value of the different datasets for cluster creation (Table 11).

**Table 11.** Category performance – C165

| Category | Min % of population | Max % of population | Spread in population | Min % completion | Max % completion | Spread in completion |
|---|---|---|---|---|---|---|
| Activity - week 1 | 13.3% | 27.6% | 14.4% | 70.8% | 88.6% | 17.8% |
| Activity - week 2 | 16.3% | 23.1% | 6.7% | 58.3% | 90.7% | 32.5% |
| Activity - week 3 | 11.2% | 25.6% | 14.4% | 57.4% | 93.7% | 36.2% |
| Demographic | 7.1% | 32.2% | 25.1% | 67.0% | 81.5% | 14.5% |

What we see across the activity categories is a sharp increase in goodness of fit from week 1 to week 2 (with the outcome differentiation growing from 17.8% to 32.5%) with a much smaller increase between weeks 2 and 3 (from 32.5% to 36.2%).

The demographic category is slightly behind activity measured at week 1 (14.5% and 17.8% respectively).

As early as seven days into a six-month term – less than 5% of the time of the term – activity data shows more predictive power than demographic data. This is even after using attribute selection to identify the most valuable of the demographic attributes.

## 6.2   Differences by Student College in Outcome Variable – C165

Because the Integrated Physical Science (C165) course fills a general education require-ment, it is taken by students from three of the four colleges (I.T., Business, and Teachers). Health Professions students are extremely rare in this specific course, having their science requirement met by several of the courses in their program. We started by comparing the outcome differentiation (% difference in course completion) across the three clusters.

It is important to note that students need not be in the same number cluster across the three weeks. The clusters are based on student activity through the end of the respective week, and students frequently had different activity patterns week over week throughout the early part of the term. This would be captured in a change for the student cluster assignment (Table 12).

**Table 12.** Cluster outcome differentiation by college and activity cluster

| Category | Week 1 Avg. completion % | Week 2 Avg. completion % | Week 3 Avg. completion % |
|---|---|---|---|
| Business –cluster 0 | 65.2% | 91.4% | 70.9% |
| Business – cluster 1 | 72.1% | 80.2% | 93.2% |
| Business – cluster 2 | 88.9% | 63.9% | 87.8% |
| Business – cluster 3 | 82.5% | 77.2% | 80.0% |
| Business – cluster 4 | 78.3% | 68.9% | 62.7% |
| IT – cluster 0 | 68.4% | 93.9% | 79.1% |
| IT – cluster 1 | 80.5% | 88.9% | 95.8% |
| IT – cluster 2 | 92.5% | 67.7% | 91.0% |
| IT – cluster 3 | 89.2% | 84.1% | 88.0% |
| IT – cluster 4 | 86.8% | 78.4% | 67.7% |
| Teachers – cluster 0 | 58.8% | 89.6% | 63.9% |
| Teachers – cluster 1 | 68.2% | 77.9% | 92.5% |
| Teachers – cluster 2 | 87.4% | 57.4% | 84.4% |
| Teachers – cluster 3 | 79.8% | 70.4% | 76.4% |
| Teachers – cluster 4 | 74.5% | 62.0% | 56.6% |

We see here that the specific cluster-week combination varies for all colleges between the three weeks of interest. As mentioned above, students did not remain in the same number cluster across the three weeks, which accounts for the differences we say in the outcome variable (completing the course) as we moved from week to week in each college-cluster combination.

### 6.3  Differences by Student College in Population Discrimination – C165

Because the Integrated Physical Science (C165) course fills a general education requirement, it is taken by students from three of the four colleges (I.T., Business, and Teachers). Health Professions students are extremely rare in this specific course, having their science requirement met by several of the courses in their program. After comparing the outcome differentiation across the clusters/colleges, we move on to compare the cluster differentiation (% of total population) (Table 13).

**Table 13.**  Cluster Population Differentiation by College and Activity Cluster

| Category | Week 1 Avg. population % | Week 2 Avg. population % | Week 3 Avg. population % | Total Avg. population % |
|---|---|---|---|---|
| Business –cluster 0 | 22.0% | 18.0% | 25.0% | 21.7% |
| Business – cluster 1 | 28.1% | 21.0% | 9.8% | 19.6% |
| Business – cluster 2 | 18.5% | 22.7% | 15.6% | 19.0% |
| Business – cluster 3 | 12.0% | 20.9% | 25.9% | 19.6% |
| Business – cluster 4 | 19.4% | 17.4% | 23.6% | 20.1% |
| IT – cluster 0 | 16.1% | 23.0% | 22.5% | 20.6% |
| IT – cluster 1 | 26.8% | 24.1% | 12.4% | 21.1% |
| IT – cluster 2 | 23.4% | 18.0% | 19.9% | 20.4% |
| IT – cluster 3 | 14.1% | 19.8% | 26.0% | 20.0% |
| IT – cluster 4 | 19.6% | 15.1% | 19.1% | 17.9% |
| Teachers – cluster 0 | 17.8% | 22.9% | 23.2% | 21.3% |
| Teachers – cluster 1 | 27.4% | 24.8% | 12.4% | 21.5% |
| Teachers – cluster 2 | 22.5% | 17.3% | 20.5% | 20.1% |
| Teachers – cluster 3 | 14.4% | 18.7% | 26.5% | 19.9% |
| Teachers – cluster 4 | 18.0% | 16.2% | 17.5% | 17.2% |

Overall, we see fairly consistent population differentiation. At any given week, some clusters will have more or less of the overall college population, but when we average for that cluster-college across all three weeks, our values are between 17.2% and 21.7%

of the total college population. Our smallest individual population proportion is for the Business College students – cluster 1 at week 3 with 9.8% of the total population for that week.

# 7 Discussion of Findings – Recommendations for Adaptive Systems

## 7.1 What Attributes Matter to Student Success?

We are aware that many student attributes – and even the phrase "students like you" – have a heavy connotation, and, in many instances, legal protection. As we started this study, we hoped to find a combination of student attributes with enough differentiating power to outweigh the negative connotations. We intentionally chose difficult courses – so there would be enough variation in student outcomes to make the analysis more meaningful. We quantitatively measured the incremental value of the different categories of attributes to create a framework of selected attributes with data-driven support. We intended to use these to recommend enhancement and meaningful learning guidance for students – to show that it would be worthwhile to include these attributes in adaptive systems because the benefit of the attributes would outweigh the connotation and risk of including them.

We were surprised to find that the attributes with the most value were also those with the least cultural sensitivity. We found behavior to greatly exceed the value of both the readiness assessment and demographic attribute categories (although both readiness and demographic attributes did add to the value of behavior when the categories were combined). Especially when we take into account the spread in population from the individual categories to the combined category, student activity attributes as a standalone category have the greatest value. An increase in discrimination from 35.8% (activity alone) to 37.8% (activity & readiness) or 41.8% (activity and demographics) reduces the population discrimination from 29.9% to 7.9% and 11.2% respectively. The relative cost of adding one of the other categories to activity is to greatly reduce the size of the clusters – to the point that smaller datasets (C785 datasets included over 45,000 students) might not get enough meaningful clusters to proceed.

## 7.2 What Should Designers of Adaptive Learning Resources Do with This?

There are several reasons why these results – though not what we expected – are extremely encouraging to designers, educators, and students alike. We find that the most differentiating characteristics – with the biggest difference in student success – are those with the most potential for change. Student behavior persisted as the best way to identify ultimately successful students – with large gaps in outcomes showing for students alike in all but their behavior.

For designers and developers of learning resources, the value of activity is promising because these are the attributes which are the easiest to gather from learning resource behavior – without relying on systems sharing protected data about students. Organizations that host resources for students can see the activity data without requiring any additional (and protected) data about the students. Adaptive systems can be designed and built based on activity data alone, which is the easiest and safest to collect for these systems.

### 7.3 What Should Instructors and Students Do with This?

For instructors and students this is encouraging because – while changing behavior is no small feat, it is possible, and both resources and instructional plans can be built accordingly. Based on our findings in this study and additional previous research on the Doer Effect [1–4], we recommend designing courses with frequent opportunities for active practice. Additionally, researchers in earlier studies [5] have found that student participation in these practice opportunities is helped by awarding some points for their completion. This gives both students and instructors reasons and ways to motivate changes in activity.

## 8  Next Steps and Research Questions

### 8.1  Exploratory Work

The work we discuss in this paper is very early and exploratory. We did not find what we expected but we are very encouraged by what we did find. As we have discussed activity has the most power in differentiating students and is also the easiest thing to guide and impact.

Possible directions for future analysis include evaluating student outcome not as a binary P/F variable, but instead using the continuous variable of percentage scores – perhaps restricting to individual competencies or learning objectives.

Additionally, we are already planning to include additional variables as part of the day 0 data set – including engineered features from their enrollment timeline, diagnostic data specific to the course content, and others.

We have also discussed evaluation of the clustering attributes as a single dataset used for attribute selection, rather than selecting/clustering attributes for each category individually.

Finally, we find ourselves asking at what point the growth of activity data in value taper off? We have seen a very significant growth between one and two weeks, with continued – though less significant – growth between two and three weeks. At some point, any incremental gain in goodness of fit is likely to be outweighed by the relative cost of waiting that much longer to adapt, something which requires additional analysis or understanding of the value of adaptation at different points in the term. In order to support this discussion with data, an objective for future stages of this research includes understanding where that point is found.

## References

1. Koedinger, K., Kim, J., Jia, J., McLaughlin, E., Bier, N.: Learning is not a spectator sport: doing is better than watching for learning from a MOOC. In: Learning at Scale, pp.111–120, Vancouver, Canada (2015). https://doi.org/10.1145/2724660.2724681
2. Koedinger, K., Kim, J., Jia, J., McLaughlin, E., Bier, N.: Is the doer effect a causal relationship? How can we tell and why it's important. In: Learning Analytics and Knowledge, Edinburgh, United Kingdom (2015). https://doi.org/10.1145/2883851.2883957

3. Koedinger, K.R., Scheines, R., Schaldenbrand, P.: Is the doer effect robust across multiple data sets? In: Proceedings of the 11th International Conference on Educational Data Mining, EDM 2018, pp. 369–375 (2018)
4. Olsen, J., Johnson, B.: Deeper collaborations: a finding that may have gone unnoticed. In: IMS Global Learning Impact Leadership Institute, San Diego, CA (2019)
5. Edgcomb, A., Vahid, F.: How many points should be awarded for interactive textbook reading assignments? In: IEEE Frontiers in Education Conference (FIE), El Paso, TX (2015). https://doi.org/10.1109/FIE.2015.7344350

# The Adaptive Features of an Intelligent Tutoring System for Adult Literacy

Genghu Shi[1(✉)], Lijia Wang[1], Liang Zhang[1], Keith Shubeck[1], Shun Peng[2], Xiangen Hu[1,2], and Arthur C. Graesser[1]

[1] The University of Memphis, Memphis, TN 38152, USA
gshi@memphis.edu
[2] Central China Normal University, Wuhan 430079, Hubei, China

**Abstract.** Adult learners with low literacy skills compose a highly heterogeneous population in terms of demographic variables, educational backgrounds, knowledge and skills in reading, self-efficacy, motivation etc. They also face various difficulties in consistently attending offline literacy programs, such as unstable worktime, transportation difficulties, and childcare issues. AutoTutor for Adult Reading Comprehension (AT-ARC), as an online conversation-based intelligent tutoring system that incorporated a theoretical model of reading comprehension, was developed with great efforts to meet adult learners' needs and be adaptive to their knowledge, skills, self-efficacy, and motivation. In this paper, we introduced the adaptive features of AT-ARC from four aspects: learning material selection, adaptive branching, trialogues, and interface, as well as the rationale behind these designs. In the end, we suggested further research on improving the adaptivity of AT-ARC.

**Keywords:** Adult literacy · Intelligent tutoring system · AutoTutor · Adaptivity

## 1 Introduction

Research shows that literacy proficiency and the ability to use computers are positively related to one's success in finding jobs with relatively higher salary [2, 16]. It also has been documented that literacy proficiency is one of the strongest factors that influence the problem-solving in computer-based environments [17]. Following this logic, literacy should be one's basic skills in modern life. However, one in six adults in the United States have low levels of literacy skills [16]. It has a negative impact on the social health and economic stability of the entire country as well as the personal well-beings [16, 20]. Most literacy programs are not designed to be adaptive to the needs and characteristics of adult learners with low literacy proficiency but for K-12 students because they have a higher priority. And, the existing adult literacy programs, which are often funded by government or non-profit organizations, generally do not reach the level that can accommodate all adults in need. Moreover, it is difficult to teach comprehension strategies at deeper levels because few teachers and tutors in literacy centers are trained to cover these levels of reading difficulty.

© Springer Nature Switzerland AG 2021
R. A. Sottilare and J. Schwarz (Eds.): HCII 2021, LNCS 12792, pp. 592–603, 2021.
https://doi.org/10.1007/978-3-030-77857-6_42

## 1.1 Adult Learners

Adult literacy learners are a highly diverse population [4]. They can be varying not only in demographic variables (age, gender, and race/ethnicity), but also in terms of educational backgrounds, learning disabilities, and their native languages (English or other) as well as their motivation for taking part in adult literacy courses [14]. They also have many difficulties in consistently attending offline literacy programs, such as unstable work time, transportation difficulties, and childcare issues [1, 12, 21]. It is very difficult for a face-to-face literacy program to overcome all these difficulties and adapt to the heterogeneity of the adult learners.

Computer-based instructional systems, especially intelligent tutoring systems, can easily cope with the difficulties the adult learners face in learning. For example, intelligent tutoring systems usually deliver well-fabricated instructions online [9]. Thus, they can be easily accessed by adult learners using digital devices with internet connection anytime and anywhere. Meanwhile, intelligent tutoring systems are generally aligned with theories from cognitive psychology, education, and learning sciences [9]. They also use algorithms to recommend individualized learning contents, strategies, and paths to different learners based on their current knowledge levels, needs, goals, aptitudes, and even personality. We developed a conversation-based intelligent tutoring system, AT-ARC, to help adult learners with low literacy skills to improve their deep levels of reading comprehension in English language. Our system supports adult learners who read at grade levels from 3.0 to 8.0 or equivalent. Massive work has been done by our research group to tailor the instruction and learning materials to meet the various needs and characteristics of the adult learners. Before introducing AT-ARC, we will first learn about prototype of it, AutoTutor.

## 1.2 AutoTutor

AutoTutor is a conversation-based intelligent tutoring system which supports a mixture of vicarious learning and interactive tutoring [15]. Both instruction modes are modeling the behaviors of a typical human teachers when they are giving lectures in class [15]. Vicarious learning is implemented in the Information Delivery mode in which human learners learn from the didactic information provided by the tutor agent as well as the observation of the tutor agent promptly answering deep questions asked by peer agents [2]. During interactive tutoring, human learners answer a main question by interacting with the tutor agent in natural language. The dialogue pattern during this process is called expectation and misconception tailored dialogue (EMT dialogue) which can be commonly observed from the interactions between human tutors and learners [8]. Each main question is associated with a list of expectations (anticipated good answers, steps in a procedure) and a list of anticipated misconceptions (bad answers, incorrect beliefs, errors, bugs). As the learners express their answers over multiple conversational turns by typing, the information they provide is compared with the expectations and misconceptions using both a latent semantic analysis tool and regular expression (Regex). AutoTutor gives positive (e.g., "Great answer"), neutral (e.g., "I see", "Uh huh!"), or negative (e.g., "Not really", "Not quite") feedback to the learner based on the quality of the answers, pumps the learner for more information (e.g., with the question "What else?"), prompts the learner to fill in missing words, gives hints to direct the learner to answer the main question, fills in missing information with assertions, identifies and corrects bad answers, answers learners' questions, and summarizes answers at the end of dialogue turns.

Below is an example of EMT dialogue that illustrates the discourse patterns between the computer tutor and a human student.

(1)  **TUTOR**: Please read the following text. [Request for student to read]
(2)  **STUDENT**: [Student reads the text about the steps to change a blown tire]
(3)  **TUTOR**: Very good. [Positive short feedback] What is the topic of this text? [Prompt]
(4)  **STUDENT**: About changing a tire.
(5)  **TUTOR**: Right. [Positive short feedback] About changing a blown tire. [Prompt completion] What is the first step when you find one your car tire is blown? [Question]
(6)  **STUDENT**: I don't know.
(7)  **TUTOR**: What about this sentence? [Hint]
(8)  **STUDENT**: It says to stop your car.
(9)  **TUTOR**: Not really. [Short negative feedback] Where should you stop your car? [Prompt]
(10) **STUDENT**: Exit the freeway or pull the car over the road.
(11) **TUTOR**: Right. [Short positive feedback] If you drive on freeway, take the next exit to find a safe place. Otherwise, pull your car as far onto the shoulder as possible. [Prompt completion]
(12) **TUTOR**: Now let's recap what the instruction is saying… [Summary]

AutoTutor has been implemented in many domain areas, such as computer literacy, critical thinking, physics, electronics, and adult literacy. Empirical evidence shows that AutoTutor has produced learning gains of approximately 0.80 sigma (standard deviation units) on average when compared to non-interactive learning environments such as reading a textbook [7, 15]. AT-ARC is an instance of AutoTutor implemented in the domain of adult literacy. In the following, we will also describe implementation details and the theoretical model of AT-ARC, as well as the adaptive features of it from four aspects: learning material selection, adaptive branching, trialogues, and interface.

## 2   AT-ARC and Its Theory

AutoTutor for Adult Reading Comprehension (hereafter, AT-ARC) is an online intelligent tutoring system that help adult learners improve their reading comprehension skills. The system was deployed in a learning management system, Moodle (https://adulted.aut otutor.org), as well as a self-made website (https://read.autotutor.org) for public access. The data of AT-ARC is stored in a learning record store (Veracity Learning) which uses a standard (xAPI) to format the data. AT-ARC uses a tutor agent (Cristina) and a peer agent (Jordan) to deliver the 30 lessons. The two computer agents hold conversations with the human learner and with each other, which is called trialogue [8]. Each lesson focus on one or more reading skills in a theoretical model of comprehension [10].

## 2.1  AT-ARC Lessons

Each of the 30 lessons consists of instruction and practice sections. Within each lesson, the adult learners first receive a mini lecture about a reading skill that lesson tapped, then practice the skill by answering multiple choice questions related to words, sentences, texts, or visual information (such as text style and picture images). The number of questions in the AT-ARC lessons ranges from 6 to 30. In most lessons, when an adult learner answers a question incorrectly or does not provide a complete answer, they will receive hints from one of the two computer agents, providing a second chance with somewhat more guidance. It usually takes 20–50 min for an adult learner to complete a lesson.

The 30 curriculum lessons are categorized into 3 groups based on their modalities, that is, the forms of the learning materials. The three groups are *words and sentences*, *stories and texts*, and *computer and internet* (see Fig. 1). The lessons falling in the *words and sentences* category teach knowledge about words (word decoding and identification) and sentences (syntax). The *computer and internet* lessons teach knowledge about using computer and internet to file job applications, send emails, search information, and interact with people on social media sites. The *stories and texts* teach deep reading comprehension strategies related to lengthy entertaining, informative, or persuasive texts. The detailed description of each lesson is included in Table 1.

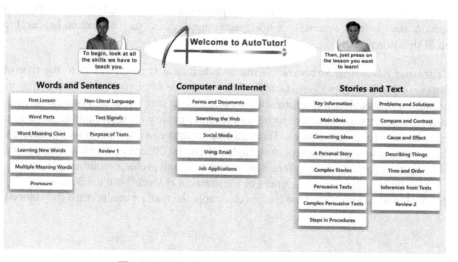

**Fig. 1.** AT-ARC lessons and their categories.

## 2.2  Theoretical Model of Comprehension

The design of AT-ARC curriculum also incorporated a theoretical model of reading comprehension which is proposed by Graesser and McNamara [10]. The theoretical model adopts a multicomponent, multilevel framework. Graesser and McNamara (2011) framework identifies six levels of reading comprehension components: words (W), syntax (S), the explicit textbase (TB), the referential situation model (SM), the discourse genre and rhetorical structure (RS), and the pragmatic communication level (between speaker and listener, or writer and reader). We will specify the meanings and its components of each level. The pragmatic communication level is not tapped in AT-ARC curriculum. Therefore, it will be not introduced.

**Words and Syntax.** Words and syntax are lower levels basic reading comprehension skills. They consist of the reading components of morphology, word decoding and identification, word order, and vocabulary [19].

**Textbase.** The textbase level consists of the basic idea units or explicit meaning of the text but not necessarily the exact wording and syntax. These basic idea units include statements, clauses, or propositions.

**Situation Model.** The situation model (sometimes called the mental model) is the readers' mental representation of the subject matter of the source text. It requires readers to make inferences relying on world knowledge [23]. This situation model varies with the genres of texts. In narrative texts, situation model includes information about characters, settings, actions, and emotions. In informational text, it would contain more technical content (e.g., knowledge and inferences about automobiles when reading a maintenance document on a truck). AT-ARC lessons target on the strategies of using connectives (e.g., because, so that, however), adverbs (finally, previously), transitional phrases (in the next section, later on that evening), or other signaling devices (such as section headers) to build situation models.

**Genre and Rhetorical Structure.** Genre and rhetorical structure refers to the type of discourse and its composition. Genre refers to the type of discourse, such as narration, persuasion, exposition, and information, as well as their subcategories. For example, narrative encompasses folk tales and novels, whereas persuasive texts include newspaper editorials and religious sermons. The rhetorical structure of a text provides the differentiated functional organization of paragraphs. There are different rhetorical frames, such as compare–contrast, cause–effect, claim–evidence, and problem–solution [11].

The Table 1 shows the alignment of the theoretical levels with the 30 lessons. And the labels and description of the lessons can imply the reading components they tapped.

**Table 1.** AT-ARC lessons and alignment of theoretical levels and description. (W = Word; S = Syntax; TB = Textbase; SM = Situation model; RS = Genre and rhetorical structure)

| Lesson name | Theoretical levels | Description |
|---|---|---|
| First lesson | | Learn how to use AutoTutor. |
| Word parts | W | Learn how words are created from parts of words, such as roots, prefixes and suffixes. |
| Word meaning clues | W | Learn how visual and letter clues can help you learn the meaning of a word. |
| Learning new words | W | Learn how the meaning of new words can sometimes be figured out by the words and sentences before and after the word. |
| Multiple meaning words | W, S | Most words have multiple meanings. Learn how to detect the best meaning of a word in a text from the words and sentences before and after the word. |
| Pronouns | TB, W | Learn about pronouns (such as he, she, and it). Figure out what person, place, thing, or idea a pronoun refers to in a text. |
| Non-literal language | SM | Sometimes the author's meaning is different from the literal meaning of the words. Learn how to identify non-literal language and figure out its meaning in texts. |
| Text Signals | SM | Learn about the role of visual information (such as text style and picture images) in helping you understand a text. |
| Purpose of texts | RS | Learn how to identify texts that are stories (narrative), persuasion, versus informational. |
| Review 1 | SM, W | Review the reading strategies learned from the previous lessons in words and sentences. |
| Forms and Documents | SM, TB | Learn how to read documents and fill out forms in real life. |
| Searching the web | SM, W | Learn how to search the Internet for information. |
| Social media | SM, RS, TB | Learn how to use social media, such as Twitter and Facebook. |
| Using email | SM, TB, RS | Learn how to receive, read, write, and send email messages. |
| Job applications | SM, RS, TB | Learn how to write your job resume. |

(continued)

**Table 1.** (*continued*)

| Lesson name | Theoretical levels | Description |
|---|---|---|
| Key information | TB, SM | Learn about the differences between stories (narratives), informational, and persuasive texts. |
| Main Ideas | TB, RS | Learn how to identify the topic and main ideas in a text. |
| Connecting ideas | SM, TB, RS | Learn how to connect the characters, setting, and plot in a story. |
| A personal story | SM, TB, RS | Learn how to make inferences and ask important questions about a personal story. |
| Complex stories | SM, TB | Learn how to make inferences and ask questions about complex stories. |
| Persuasive texts | TB, RS | Learn how to evaluate a persuasive text by identifying the topic, main arguments, and supporting information. |
| Complex persuasive texts | SM, TB | Learn how to understand complex persuasive texts. |
| Steps in procedures | RS, TB, SM | Learn how to read texts that describe steps in a procedure, such as changing a car tire. |
| Problems and solutions | RS, TB, SM | Learn how to identify problems and solutions in texts that solve problems. |
| Compare and contrast | RS, TB, SM | Learn how to identify similarities and differences in texts that make comparisons. |
| Cause and effect | RS, TB, SM | Learn how to identify causes and effects in science texts. |
| Describing things | RS, TB, SM | Learn about texts that describe people, places, things, or events. |
| Time and order | RS, TB, SM | Learn about texts that order events in time or ideas in importance. |
| Inferences from texts | SM, TB | Learn how to make inferences in informational texts. |
| Review 2 | SM, TB, RS | This lesson is a review on previous lessons in stories and texts. |

## 3   Adaptive Features of AT-ARC

Massive work has been done by the AT-ARC research group to tailor the instruction and learning materials to meet the various needs of the adult learners and adapt the interface and interactive features to their characteristics. This section describes the adaptive features of it from four aspects: learning material selection, adaptive branching, trialogues, and interface.

## 3.1 Learning Material Selection

The 30 lessons were carefully scripted to contain learning materials (words, sentences, and texts) that have practical values that are adaptive to the adult learners' needs in their daily life. For example, the learning materials were selected to help adult learners learn knowledge about words (e.g., Word Parts, Multiple Meaning Words, Learning New Words, etc.), read rental agreements, fill job applications (e.g., Forms and Documents), figure out the procedure of recipes or changing a tire (Steps in Procedures), search for health information (e.g., Searching the Web), etc. These materials are expected to interest adults.

The adult learners often read at a grade level of 3 to 7.9. The learning materials in the AT-ARC lessons were selected to be adaptive to the adult learners' zone of proximal development [22]. According to *Goldilocks principle*, the words, sentences, and texts were selected to be at the adult learners' reading level that they can handle (not too hard or too easy), so that they do not become frustrated or get bored. For example, the texts were selected based on their difficulty levels (i.e., grade levels) that were measured by Coh-Metrix, a system that scales texts on difficulty by considering characteristics of words, syntax, discourse cohesion, and text category [6].

## 3.2 Adaptive Branching

Most of the 30 lessons have easy, medium, versus difficult learning materials (words, sentences, and texts) measured by Coh-Metrix [6]. Within the practice section of a lesson, the adult learners start with practice questions pertaining to words, sentences, or a text at the medium level of difficulty. Depending on their accuracy on these questions, the adult learners receive questions pertaining to either easier or harder learning materials. That is, higher accuracy on the questions of medium learning materials leads the adult learners to the more difficult branch of learning materials, whereas lower accuracy leads to the easier branch.

When an adult learner answers a question correctly at the first attempt, he/she gets full credit for answering the question. When the adult learner answers the question incorrectly, AT-ARC adaptively generates a hint with some instructional information based on the incorrect choice the adult picked and gives the adult a second chance; the adult gets partial credit when the answer is correct on the second attempt. The wrong choice selected indicates the adult learner's misconception about the question. If the adult fails at the second try, AT-ARC announces the correct answer and explain why it is correct.

## 3.3 Trialogues

The AT-ARC uses two computer agents to deliver the EMT trialogue. The tutor agent is named *Cristina* and the peer agent's name is *Jordan*. Trialogues can be designed in different ways.

1) ***Vicarious learning with human observation or limited participation.*** The adult learner can observe the tutor agent interacting with the peer agent or have limited

participation. This is known as vicarious learning which has instructional purpose. This form of trialogues particularly benefit the low skilled learners. The occasional participation of the adult learner can promote their engagement. For example, the mini lecture at the beginning of each lesson takes this form of trialogue.

2) *Human interacting with the two computer agents.* The tutor agent interacts with the adult learner and the peer agent with tutorial dialogues. The adult learner contributes and receives feedback. The peer agent adjusts its knowledge and skills according to the learner's skill level. When the adult is a skilled learner, the peer agent usually gives correct answers. When the adult leaner has lower skills, the peer agent takes the criticism by picking the same bad answer as the human learner. This is an approach designed to help adult learners build self-esteem and a sense of self-efficacy. Then two computer agents can also express contradictions, arguments, and different views. These discrepancies stimulate cognitive conflicts, confusion, and potentially deep learning, but this may be beyond the adult learners' zone of proximal development.

3) *Human teaching/helping peer agent with the facilitation of tutor agent.* The adult learner can also teach or help the peer agent with the facilitation of the tutor agent. High skilled learners benefit from this kind of trialogue. For example, Jordan asks for help from Cristina and the adult learner to get familiar with social media use. Cristina always brings up questions for human learner to answer. When the adult learner is correct, the peer agent expresses his appreciation. When the adult learner is wrong, the tutor agent generates hints and gives the adult learner another chance or reveals the correct answer and explain why.

4) *Tutor agent staging a competition between the human and a peer agent.* The tutor agent can guide a competition between a human learner and the peer agent, in which the adult learner and a peer agent takes turn to answer questions that the tutor agent asks. This competitive game may promote the motivation of human learners.

Here is an example trialogue between Cristina, Jordan, and an adult learner. The trialogue happens in the lesson shown in Fig. 2.

(1) **Cristina (tutor agent):** Okay, why might the writer want to go back to school to get a GED, based on what you read in this text? [Main question]

(2) **Adult Learner:** [Pick the first choice] The writer does not know if he wants to get his GED.

(3) **Cristina:** Not quite! [Short feedback] The writer talks about being a poor student in high school. [Hint] With this in mind, which of the following could be true? Try to press a different answer choice below [Provide another chance].

(4) **Adult Learner:** [Pick the third choice] The author did not learn computer in high school.

(5) **Cristina:** Correct! The writer talks about his or her passion for computers, however the text does not mention learning about them.

(6) **Cristina:** Jordan, what was your answer to this question?

(7) **Jordan (peer agent):** I thought the answer was, the writer knows a lot about computers.

(8) **Cristina:** That is incorrect because the writer does not talk about knowing anything about computers, only liking them. This activity can be really tricky! Even I get tripped up sometimes!

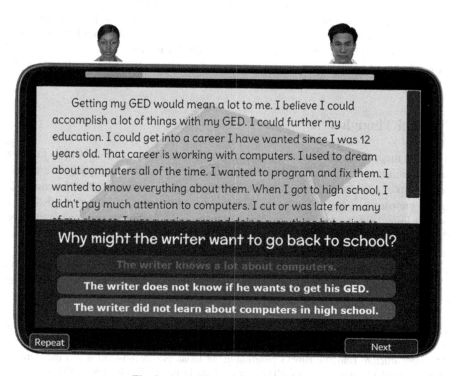

Getting my GED would mean a lot to me. I believe I could accomplish a lot of things with my GED. I could further my education. I could get into a career I have wanted since I was 12 years old. That career is working with computers. I used to dream about computers all of the time. I wanted to program and fix them. I wanted to know everything about them. When I got to high school, I didn't pay much attention to computers. I cut or was late for many

**Why might the writer want to go back to school?**

The writer knows a lot about computers.

The writer does not know if he wants to get his GED.

The writer did not learn about computers in high school.

Repeat                                    Next

**Fig. 2.** Screenshot of a AT-ARC lesson.

To sum up, the trialogues were written to be adaptive to the adult learners' knowledge and skills in reading comprehension. However, these trialogues were not all designed in the same lessons.

### 3.4 Interface

It should be noted that the adult learners have difficulties in writing. So, it is beyond the abilities of most of them to type much verbal information. The best many of them can do is to scroll a webpage, click on multiple choice alternatives, drag and drop information, or toggle on alternatives [18]. In consideration of their limited skills of using computers, AT-ARC does not take the typical form of interaction (by typing answers in a textbox) between computer tutor and human learners. Instead, it tends to rely on point & click interactions, drag & drop functions, multiple choice questions, and limited typing. Therefore, the system does not require much semantic evaluation and regular expression matching of learners' writing contributions to the open-ended main questions, pumps, prompts, and hints.

Several other interface features in AT-ARC were designed to enable self-paced learning. There is a "repeat" button to press whenever the adult learner wants the previous turn of an agent to be repeated. They can press on an option to have text read to them whenever the materials involve a multi-sentence text (but not when a single sentence is presented). They can press the home icon at the bottom whenever they want to start at the beginning of a lesson. In the practice section, after answering a question, the adult learner clicks on the "Next" button to go to the next question. At the end of the lesson, AT-ARC will display an ending page to inform the learners whether they have passed the lesson based on their accuracy on the practice questions. If a learner fails the lesson, AT-ARC suggests they take the lesson again.

## 4    Final Thoughts

Although much work has been done to improve the adaptivity of AT-ARC, it is far from perfect. Future research can explore the deeper levels of human-computer interaction. For example, AT-ARC incorporates all types of trialogues in each lesson. The computer agents choose the type of trialogues adaptive on adult learners' characteristics, such as their knowledge and skills in reading, motivation, self-efficacy, or even personality. Currently, AT-ARC lessons are organized in a linear form. That is to say, the adult learner cannot jump to an activity (e.g., answering a question, reading a text) by skipping over the previous activities. Another strand of research can focus on breaking a lesson into smaller chunks and making each chunk accessible independently when the adult learner would like to review a specific activity.

**Acknowledgment.** This study is supported by the Institute of Education Sciences, US Department of Education, through Grants R305C120001 and R305A200413, the National Science Foundation Data Infrastructure Building Blocks program under Grant No. ACI-1443068 and the National Science Foundation under the award The Learner Data Institute with Grant No. 1934745.

## References

1. Alamprese, J.A., MacArthur, C.A., Price, C., Knight, D.: Effects of a structured decoding curriculum on adult literacy learners' reading development. J. Res. Educ. Effect. **4**, 154–172 (2011)
2. Carnevale, A.P., Smith, N.: Workplace basics: the skills employees need and employers want. Hum. Resour. Dev. Int. **16**, 491–501 (2013)
3. Driscoll, D.M., Craig, S.D., Gholson, B., Ventura, M., Hu, X., Graesser, A.C.: Vicarious learning: effects of overhearing dialog and monologue-like discourse in a virtual tutoring session. J. Educ. Comput. Res. **29**(4), 431–450 (2003). https://doi.org/10.2190/Q8CM-FH7L-6HJU-DT9W
4. Elish-Piper, L.: Defining adult literacy. In: Guzzetti, B.J. (ed.) Literacy for the New Millennium: Vol. 4. Adult Literacy, pp. 3–16. Praeger, Westport, Connecticut (2007)
5. Graesser, A.C., Forsyth, C.M., Lehman, B.A.: Two heads may be better than one: learning from computer agents in conversational trialogues. Grantee Submission **119**, 1–20 (2017)

6. Graesser, A.C., McNamara, D.S., Cai, Z., Conley, M., Li, H., Pennebaker, J.: Coh-Metrix measures text characteristics at multiple levels of language and discourse. Elem. Sch. J. **115**, 210–229 (2014)

7. Graesser, A.C., et al.: Reading comprehension lessons in AutoTutor for the center for the study of adult literacy. In: Crossley, S.A., McNamara, D.S. (eds.) Adaptive Educational Technologies for Literacy Instruction, pp. 288–293. Taylor & Francis Routledge, New York (2016)

8. Graesser, A.C., Cai, Z., Morgan, B., Wang, L.: Assessment with computer agents that engage in conversational dialogues and trialogues with learners. Comput. Hum. Behav. **76**, 607–616 (2017)

9. Graesser, A.C., Conley, M.W., Olney, A.: Intelligent tutoring systems. In: APA Educational Psychology Handbook, Vol. 3: Application to Learning and Teaching, pp. 451–473 (2012)

10. Graesser, A.C., McNamara, D.S.: Computational analyses of multilevel discourse comprehension. Top. Cogn. Sci. **3**, 371–398 (2011)

11. Meyer, B.F., Wijekumar, K., Middlemiss, W., Higley, K., Lei, P., Meier, C., et al.: Web-based tutoring of the structure strategy with or without elaborated feedback or choice for fifth- and seventh-grade readers. Read. Res. Q. **45**(1), 62–92 (2010)

12. Miller, B., Esposito, L., McCardle, P.: A public health approach to improving the lives of adult learners: Introduction to the special issue on adult literacy interventions. J. Res. Educ. Effect. **4**, 87–100 (2011)

13. National Research Council [NRC]. Improving adult literacy instruction: options for practice and research. The National Academies Press, Washington (2011)

14. Newnan, A.: Learning for Life: The Opportunity for Technology to Transform Adult Education (2015). http://tytonpartners.com/library/learning-for-life-the-opportunity-for-tec hnology-to-transform-adult-education/

15. Nye, B.D., Graesser, A.C., Hu, X.: AutoTutor and family: a review of 17 years of natural language tutoring. Int. J. Artif. Intell. Educ. **24**(4), 427–469 (2014)

16. OECD: Time for the U.S. to Reskill?: What the Survey of Adult Skills Says, OECD Skills Studies, OECD Publishing (2013). https://doi.org/10.1787/9789264204904-en

17. OECD: Adults, Computers and Problem Solving: What's the Problem? OECD Publishing (2015). https://doi.org/10.1787/9789264236844-en

18. Olney, A.M., Bakhtiari, D., Greenberg, D., Graesser A.: Assessing computer literacy of adults with low literacy skills. In: Hu, X., Barnes, T., Hershkovitz, A., Paquette, L. (eds.) Proceedings of the 10th International Conference on Educational Data Mining, pp. 128–134. International Educational Data Mining Society, Wuhan (2017)

19. Perfetti, C.: Reading ability: Lexical quality to comprehension. Sci. Stud. Read. **11**(4), 357–383 (2007)

20. Rasu, R.S., Bawa, W.A., Suminski, R., Snella, K., Warady, B.: Health literacy impact on national healthcare utilization and expenditure. Int. J. Health Policy Manag. **4**(11), 747 (2015)

21. Sabatini, J.P., Shore, J., Holtzman, S., Scarborough, H.S.: Relative effectiveness of reading intervention programs for adults with low literacy. J. Res. Educ. Effect. **4**, 118–133 (2011)

22. Wass, R., Golding, C.: Sharpening a tool for teaching: the zone of proximal development. Teach. High. Educ. **19**(6), 671–684 (2014)

23. Zwaan, R.A., Radvansky, G.A.: Situation models in language comprehension and memory. Psychol. Bull. **123**, 162–185 (1998)

# Considerations Towards Culturally-Adaptive Instructional Systems

May Marie P. Talandron-Felipe[1,2(✉)] (iD)

[1] Ateneo de Manila University, Quezon City, Philippines
maymarie.talandron-felipe@ustp.edu.ph
[2] University of Science and Technology of Southern Philippines, Cagayan de Oro, Philippines

**Abstract.** This work proposes a conceptual framework that captures cultural considerations in providing options in the way learners interact with an instructional system. It revisits the longstanding relationship between culture and learning behavior and how cultural background influences the design and implementations of instructional systems. The literature presents some approaches including the use of cultural references embedded into the learning material which draws from the concept of shared meanings and cultural familiarity; and through the development of immersive environments using virtual reality to provide cultural experiences. Aside from domain limitations and technological requirements, these approaches are usually focused on the content or environment rather than the interaction. In order to identify culturally-biased behaviors and preferences, the paper looks at the contextualization of Hofstede's cultural dimensions in educational software linked to interaction concepts in the Cultural Artefacts in Education (CAE) framework. These adaptation rules are then anchored to the Universal Design for Learning (UDL) Guidelines to provide a more cohesive pedagogical structure and as an attempt to make them applicable across disciplines and domains. Future work includes the implementation and validation of the proposed framework.

**Keywords:** Culturally-adaptive instructional system · Cultural artefacts in education · Universal design for learning · Cultural dimensions

## 1 Introduction

The growing research on Adaptive Instructional Systems (AISs) provides more opportunities for global implementation but also poses a challenge for researchers and designers to ensure that AISs are capable to cater culturally-diverse sets of learners especially when there is a cultural gap between where it was developed and tested to where it will be implemented. This aspect is important because cultural background influences perception [19] and cognition [1, 8, 23, 24] as it can offer tools through which one makes sense of its environment and process information being presented [7]; thus, is expected to be considered in user models and embedded in digital learning environments [26]. If pedagogy and technology do not reflect the culture of the learner, it may reduce the learning outcome [15]. This paper capitalizes on this as the motivation in discussing

© Springer Nature Switzerland AG 2021
R. A. Sottilare and J. Schwarz (Eds.): HCII 2021, LNCS 12792, pp. 604–615, 2021.
https://doi.org/10.1007/978-3-030-77857-6_43

the connection of culture with learning behavior and preferences and how this could be realized in AIS designs and implementation. This is also written with the UNESCO's guidelines on intercultural education that the cultural identity of the learner must be respected through the provision of culturally appropriate and responsive quality education and the Global Resources for Online Education vision for personalizing education in the year 2030 [26] as inspiration to promote more personalized education.

This paper aims to derive a conceptual framework on learner's culture-related preferences in terms of interaction with an instructional system by leveraging information from literature.

## 2 Complexities of Culture

Culture is a complex concept and has been defined in many ways over the years but researchers [4, 10, 17, 21] agree that it represents ideas and beliefs of a society which often affect values, assumptions, and perceptions of its members whether consciously and unconsciously. Cultural values serve as standards where people base their behaviors in different situations. These are the bases for social norms which determine what is appropriate or not and how to respond to one's environment or circumstances as they "represent the implicitly or explicitly shared abstract ideas about what is good, right and desirable" [25]. Cultural values are expressed on how the units of society (e.g. family, organizations, government) function, set goals, and operate [21]. For instance, in a culture where importance is given on collective well-being, the community may be more receptive to cooperative and collaborative systems compared to competitive ones. The description of culture in [11] as a "programming of the mind" articulates how culture forms fundamental values and subconsciously controls the society's collective behavior.

With the existing theories and definitions of culture, integrating cultural considerations in systems remains a challenge as these are based on the assumption that there are commonalities in people, which can help to differentiate certain cultural groups characterized by their own concept of identity [19]. Another consideration in understanding culture is distinguishing universalism, group specifics, and individualism. Universalisms are general characteristics of human beings and are shared by a wide cluster of, if not all, cultural groups. Group specifics are characteristics specific to cultural groups in that they are accepted and promoted by a significant portion of insiders [3], while individualism is the concept that people are viewed as autonomous with their own uniqueness and attributes [21]. Literature also points that cultural values of a society can be formed by aggregating the value priorities of individuals [10]. When individuals with different cultures and unique personal experiences come together to form a society, their combined, aggregated cultural values form a shared culture and "the average priorities attributed to different values by societal members reflect the central thrust of their shared enculturation" which are then passed on to the next generation [21]. This is similar to the point of view where people do not only acquire or learn culture, but they are part of its creation and evolution for which through globalization and exposure to foreign cultures, people either adapt or develop resistance to influences which could lead to altering one's cultural identity [20]. In this regard, one can say that an individual may belong to more than one culture although this depends on how the person views how his exposure from one society to another has influenced him which can be either consciously or unconsciously [19]. For instance, people who immigrated to the United States from the Philippines as teenagers may now identify themselves with the American culture or not depending on the extent of adaptation that happened in a span of several years. Their exposure to the environment may have changed their preferences which they have developed growing up in their origin country but this allows them to adjust to both cultures when required by circumstances. With this, it is important to recognize that culture is not limited to race or country of origin but that geography, social class, a nation's status, language, religious affiliations, family history, migration patterns, generation, among others, all have major influences on its development [13]. This dynamic nature of how culture evolves makes it complex to model and understand.

## 3  Culture and Education

In the past, culture was commonly used in language education since being emerged in the corresponding culture has helped students learn the language [23]. It was also common in other areas of humanities including arts, politics, religion and areas of sociology which tackles cultural heritage, history, and social issues. It was, however, uncommon to see culture being used as an environment variable as opposed to other demographics or socio-economic factors such as age, gender, prior knowledge, even financial background, perhaps because these are more tangible and easier to measure. At present, the degree to which we comprehend how culture shapes attitudes and behaviors has remarkable consequences for educators and learners particularly in diverse schools [13]. Studies [1, 8, 23, 24] have established that culture can significantly impact learning as it can affect emotion, comprehension, preference for individual or collaborative tasks, sense of achievement, among other aspects. For instance, in [23], it was found that help-seeking behavior can be culturally biased as respondents from countries like India, Ireland, and China have shown to be more accepting of being left to look after themselves and as such prefers less up-front help while those from Romania and Greece prefer to be given more assistance in tasks. The same is true in terms of the use of educational software as researches [2, 12, 14, 18] have shown that cultural background significantly impacts students' interaction with e-learning systems and the inclusion of culture in user modeling is a key component in personalizing education [26]. This does not come without its difficulties because as emphasized, culture is dynamic and group stereotyping may not represent an individual's preference and cultural identity.

### 3.1  Culture in Instructional Systems

There are several approaches where culture can be integrated into instructional systems. First is through contextual references to localize the content. Cultural contextualization draws from the concept of shared meanings [22] which is the human cognitive process of categorizing observations and experiences. These categories are innately connected to language which conveys cultural knowledge and allows individuals to understand each other's perspectives when communicating [18]. These includes the use of names common in the culture as examples in word problems, referencing prominent local personalities, places, expressions, traditions, etc. so as to give the learner the feeling of familiarity. The learner's comprehension of the reference would be influenced by how familiar the reference is. A tutoring system developed in a western, educated, industrialized, rich and democratic (WEIRD) country to teach a particular domain through cultural contextualization may not translate well when deployed in developing countries in the east, in which case the use of cultural contextualization shall be adaptive in order for it to adjust to the cultural background of the user. An intelligent learning environment for computer programming attempted to implement this by providing culturally adaptive educational content through dynamic cultural contextualization. The system allows students to adjust a cultural density slider which determines the amount of cultural references used in the text and examples. They [18] found that the learners from Trinidad and Tobago preferred content types that featured cultural, semantically congruent references otherwise, they considered the programming tasks to be horrible and boring.

Immersive experience is another approach [3] which can be done through virtual reality (VR) where the integration of culture goes beyond referencing. In this approach, a virtual environment is created leveraging existing technologies to simulate a particular cultural setting. VR has the capability to simulate physical environments which can be tuned to a varying level of multisensory realism to affect users' visual, auditory, tactile, vestibular senses [27]. This requires the underlying immersive reality and interaction method to establish contextual relationship, collaboration, and engagement between users and the virtual environment to enhance the learning experience. For example, [6] adapted a 3D video game for learning Japanese language and culture called Crystallize to be played in virtual reality with the Oculus Rift. Their formative user study showed that that the virtual reality design increased participants' sense of involvement and suggested that an immersive culture-based environment through virtual reality technology provides an opportunity to leverage culturally relevant physical interaction, which can enhance the design of language learning.

## 4 Determining Features with Cultural Biases

Aside from domain limitations and technological requirements, most of the approaches are usually focused on the content or environment rather than the interaction. In order to identify culturally-biased interaction behaviors and preferences, the paper looks at the contextualization of the cultural dimensions in educational software and derives adaptation rules from the Cultural Artefacts in Education (CAE) [23] framework. These adaptation rules are then anchored to the Universal Design for Learning (UDL) Guidelines [5] to provide a more cohesive pedagogical structure and as an attempt to make them applicable across disciplines and domains. The CAE has contextualized Hofstede's cultural dimensions [9]: Power Distance Index (PDI), Uncertainty Avoidance Index (UAI), Individualism versus Collectivism (IDV), Masculinity versus Femininity (MAS), and Long Term versus Short Term Orientation (LTO). The definition of the indices from [9] are given below:

- Power distance index (PDI)

*"The extent to which the less powerful members of organizations and institutions (like the family) accept and expect that power is distributed unequally. This represents inequality (more versus less)."*

- Collectivism vs. individualism index (IDV)

*"On the individualist side we find societies in which the ties between individuals are loose: everyone is expected to look after him/herself and his/her immediate family. On the collectivist side, we find societies in which people from birth onwards are integrated into strong, cohesive in groups, often extended families (with uncles, aunts and grandparents) which continue protecting them in exchange for unquestioning loyalty."*

- Femininity vs. masculinity index (MAS)

*"It refers to the distribution of roles between the genders which is another fundamental issue for any society. The assertive pole has been called 'masculine' and the modest, caring pole 'feminine'. The women in feminine countries have the same modest, caring values as the men; in the masculine countries they are somewhat assertive and competitive, but not as much as the men, so that these countries show a gap between men's values and women's values."*

- Uncertainty Avoidance index (UAI)

*"It deals with a society's tolerance for uncertainty and ambiguity. It indicates to what extent a culture programs its members to feel either uncomfortable or comfortable in unstructured situations. Unstructured situations are novel, unknown, surprising, and different from usual. Uncertainty avoiding cultures try to minimize the possibility of such situations by strict laws and rules, safety and security measures. They are also more emotional, and motivated by inner nervous energy. The opposite type, uncertainty accepting cultures, are more tolerant of opinions different from what they are used to; they try to have as few rules as possible, and on the philosophical and religious level they are relativist and allow many currents to flow side by side. People within these cultures are more phlegmatic and contemplative, and not expected by their environment to express emotions."*

- Long vs. short Term Orientation (LTO)

*"Values associated with Long Term Orientation are thrift and perseverance; values associated with Short Term Orientation are respect for tradition, fulfilling social obligations, and protecting one's 'face'."*

### 4.1 Universal Design for Learning (UDL)

The Universal Design for Learning (UDL) framework [5] aims to provide guidelines to develop expert learners who are resourceful and knowledgeable, strategic and goal-directed, purposeful and motivated. It is organized around three principles for which choices and variations should be provided to bridge the cultural gap between the learning tool and the learner: representation, actions and expressions, and opportunities for engagement. For each principle, there are three (3) guidelines that correspond to three (3) categories of ways to achieve the UDL goals. The "access" category suggests ways to increase access to the learning goal by recruiting interest and by offering options for perception and physical action; "build" includes the guidelines that suggest ways to develop effort and persistence, language and symbols, and expression and communication; and "internalize" provides guidelines that suggest ways to empower learners through self-regulation, comprehension, and executive function (see Fig. 1).

| | Provide multiple means of **Representation** | Provide multiple means of **Action & Expression** | Provide multiple means of **Engagement** |
|---|---|---|---|
| **Access** | Provide options for **Perception** (1)<br>• *Offer ways of customizing the display of information (1.1)*<br>• *Offer alternatives for auditory information (1.2)*<br>• *Offer alternatives for visual information (1.3)* | Provide options for **Physical Action** (4)<br>• *Vary the methods for response and navigation (4.1)*<br>• *Optimize access to tools and assistive technologies (4.2)* | Provide options for **Recruiting Interest** (7)<br>• *Optimize individual choice and autonomy (7.1)*<br>• *Optimize relevance, value, and authenticity (7.2)*<br>• *Minimize threats and distractions (7.3)* |
| **Build** | Provide options for **Language & Symbols** (2)<br>• *Clarify vocabulary & symbols (2.1)*<br>• *Clarify syntax & structure (2.2)*<br>• *Support decoding of text, math notation, and symbols (2.3)*<br>• *Promote understanding across languages (2.4)*<br>• *Illustrate through multiple media (2.5)* | Provide options for **Expression & Communication** (5)<br>• *Use multiple media for communication (5.1)*<br>• *Use multiple tools for construction & composition (5.2)*<br>• *Build fluencies with graduated levels of support for practice & performance (5.3)* | Provide options for **Sustaining Effort & Persistence** (8)<br>• *Heighten salience of goals and objectives (8.1)*<br>• *Vary demands and resources to optimize challenge (8.2)*<br>• *Foster collaboration and community (8.3)*<br>• *Increase mastery-oriented feedback (8.4)* |
| **Internalize** | Provide options for **Comprehension** (3)<br>• *Activate or supply background knowledge (3.1)*<br>• *Highlight patterns, critical features, big ideas, and relationships (3.2)*<br>• *Guide information processing and visualization (3.3)*<br>• *Maximize transfer and generalization (3.4)* | Provide options for **Executive Functions** (6)<br>• *Guide appropriate goal-setting (6.1)*<br>• *Support planning and strategy development (6.2)*<br>• *Facilitate managing information and resources (6.3)*<br>• *Enhance capacity for monitoring progress (6.4)* | Provide options for **Self Regulation** (9)<br>• *Promote expectations and beliefs that optimize motivation (9.1)*<br>• *Facilitate personal coping skills and strategies (9.2)*<br>• *Develop self-assessment and reflection (9.3)* |
| **Goals** | Resourceful & Knowledgeable | Strategic & Goal-Directed | Purposeful & Motivated |

**Fig. 1.** Universal design for learning guidelines 2.2 [5]

These set of guidelines can help educators and designers in making culturally-aware pedagogical decisions. For instance, [7] used checkpoint 3.2 to explain the cultural differences in using relationships in reasoning. Some cultures show a preference for grouping elements or organizing ideas based on membership in a category, while others prefer to use functional relationships and part-whole concepts as an organization tool. If a tutoring system is designed to use only one approach, say to teach reasoning, it would not only present obstacles for culturally varied learners, but would also hinder them from being exposed to different ways of thinking. Another example is checkpoint 8.3 which suggests to foster collaboration and community in the learning experience but it should also be considered that the concept of collaborative work varies from culture to culture. Options for group tasks should be offered so that learners from cultures where individualism is high and who are not comfortable to work in a group should not feel being forced to do so. The framework shows, through its checkpoints, which areas should be adaptive to cater the diversity of learners.

## 4.2 Cultural Artefacts in Education

The CAE [23] was inspired by the work of [16] which contextualized Hofstede's cultural dimensions in global web user-interface designs. CAE was supported by a questionnaire mapped to cultural dimensions indices [10] which has been used to model features for personalized adaptive interfaces for different cultures. The CAE Framework has two ontologies, a full scale ontology, called the CAE-F ontology, and a simplified ontology called the CAE-L ontology. These ontologies detail the human-computer interaction features that need to be integrated into an instructional system for cultural adaptation [23]. CAE has top-level concept indices called Adaptive Education Index (AEI) which measures the value of personalization of the learner and the Cultural Education Index (CEI) which measures learner's acceptance of being taught in another language, presence or availability of access to other languages and cultures. Table 1 shows some of the sub-ontologies of CAE, specific features, and adaptation values.

**Table 1.** Some of the CAE Sub-ontologies and type of adaptation from [23].

| Sub-ontology | Feature concept (Hofstede's Index) | Adaptation values (Index Value: Option Value: *Rule*) | |
|---|---|---|---|
| Authority | Expert (Power distance) | Low: Peers: *learners are open to accept expert teaching from their peers; chat fora could be used* | High: Teachers: *learners only consider their superiors as valid experts* |
| | Help (Power distance) | High: More: *provide more than 1 option for help (scaffolding, hints)* | Low: Less: *at least 1 option for help is enough* |
| Group | Gender separation (Masculinity) | High: Accepted: *references to the opposite gender be avoided if possible* | Low: Rejected: *no need to separate the genders in coursework, groups* |
| Language | Presence (Cultural education) | High: Hide: *ideally, mother tongue should be used in the learning materials* | Low: Show: *materials in non-mother tongue languages may be used* |
| Lesson | Hierarchy (Power distance) | High: Deep: *implementation would take the form of concepts being arranged in a "deep tree" manner, with topics presented in a top down fashion (topics as children)* | Low: Shallow: *topics are presented in a breadth first approach, content trees are shallow in presentation, resulting in more topics presented at the same time (topics as siblings)* |

*(continued)*

| Sub-ontology | Feature concept (Hofstede's Index) | Adaptation values (Index Value: Option Value: *Rule*) | |
|---|---|---|---|
| | Help (Uncertainty avoidance) | High: More: *learners are more likely to desire the presence of additional support functions; not to say that they need it more but that they feel more comfortable with it available, such as links with additional materials, hints, scaffolding* | Low: Less: *while Help should always be available, learners feel that they don't need additional recourse to other Help functionalities aside from the given materials* |
| | Access (Power distance) | High: Limited: *learners are more comfortable with limited access to learning materials, with new materials only becoming available (visible) as they progress through a lesson (as defined by their lesson score or lesson prerequisites)* | Low: Open: *learners prefer to have access to all of the learning materials (under the auspices of the lesson designer) and are encouraged to work through them in any way they wish* |
| | Choice (Uncertainty avoidance) | High: Limited: *the complexity of lesson presentation should be kept to a minimum, with fewer unnecessary choices for the student; a much more highly structured educational methodology, with a less cluttered user interface* | Low: Open: *similar to Open Access features, learners can make their own choices as to the structure and manner of learning allowing complexity in structure* |
| | Ambiguity (Uncertainty avoidance) | High: Less: *learners are presented with multiple redundant cues within each lesson and the interface should give them several ways in which to complete their tasks* | Low: More: *learners do not need the multiple cues and are more comfortable to figure out how to carry on with the tasks* |

In [23], CAE was used to develop stereotypes for various countries and embedded onto an Adaptive Display Environment (ADE) to evaluate its effectiveness and found that a student whose ADE interface was created from a matched CAE stereotype actually performed better than those who had a mismatched stereotype. However, country-based stereotyping is not a guaranteed method as it was also found that respondents from Ireland do not match the CAE stereotype produced. Perhaps, instead of using CAE to create country-based stereotypes, the interaction concepts from the framework could serve as a basis in determining interface options that represents the cultural dimensions.

## 5  Discussion

The literature presented in this paper does not encapsulate all that anthropology has found and written about culture but focus is given on how it was contextualized for educational purposes and an emphasis on the variability of learning preference as an effect of cultural differences. In line with this, it is important that educators are informed which aspects of pedagogy may be affected and may become barriers to learning opportunities if approaches are not adjusted. For instance, the basic implementations of an adaptive instructional design for Mathematics [12] and Physics [14] used a simple rule-based adaptive system which adapts the learning process, particularly providing help, based only on the learner's level of knowledge or performance. However, literature has shown that preference for help-seeking behavior has cultural biases such that those with low UAI prefers less apparent help than those with high UAI who may prefer more scaffolding. In this case, support for low UAI learners must be designed such that the learners do not lose the impression of having autonomy or control. Even the preference of where assistance is given from has some cultural biases as well based on the PDI as those with high index values would prefer help from entities they deem to be on a higher level or authority than themselves such as teachers or tutors but those with low index values would accept help from peers. In this case, those with high PDI may prefer a virtual teacher or tutor as the expert helper while a virtual peer helper may be more acceptable to those with low PDI or a chat fora to seek help from other learners may be more utilized. Designing collaboration may also be gauged by the cultural dimension indices, high IDV learners prefer individual work and access to tasks and may be more aggressive and argumentative in discourse while those with low IDV are more open to engage in collaborative activities. Mixing genders in groups should also be culturally-adapted as those with low MAS index are less concern with gender in relation to tasks while those with high MAS are deemed to have a more masculine perception and are particular in differentiating masculinity and femininity of roles in group activities.

   With these cultural biases, the UDL framework offers a set of guidelines to bridge gaps and enhance teaching and learning for all which resonates with the first principle of UNESCO's Guidelines on Intercultural Education that is to provide culturally appropriate and responsive quality education to cater the cultural identity of all learners. To derive the framework being proposed in this paper, the UDL guidelines are operationalized through interaction features based on the different interaction concepts from the CAE sub-ontologies [23]. For instance, the fourth UDL Guideline states that learners should be provided options for "Physical Actions" which include varying methods for response and navigation and access to tools and assistive technologies. To operationalize these suggestions in the context of culture-based interaction options, they are mapped to the three interaction concepts under the Lesson sub-ontology: Access (limited or open) refers to the level of access to learning materials the learners have whether they can explore tasks and lessons as they wish or be required to achieve a certain score or finish a task before they can proceed; Help (less or more) as described earlier refers to the amount of assistance provided to the learners; and Results (immediate or delayed) refers to the immediacy of feedback. The selection of the appropriate interaction concepts to be mapped to a specific UDL guidelines was based on the checkpoints stipulated for each guideline. Some of these culturally-biased interaction concepts may also overlap with other UDL guidelines such that CAE's 'Access' can also be mapped to UDL's 'Perception' and 'Recruiting Interest', 'Help' is also mapped to UDL's 'Expression' and 'Communication', 'Sustaining Effort and Persistence', 'Comprehension', and 'Self-Regulation'. The CAE's interaction concepts has a many-to-many relationship with UDL guidelines and has a one-to-one mapping with Hofstede's cultural dimensions which results to a many-to-many relationship between the UDL and the cultural dimensions (see Fig. 2).

The conceptual framework leveraged twenty one (21) interaction concepts from CAE which can be used to implement all the UDL Guidelines in an instructional system

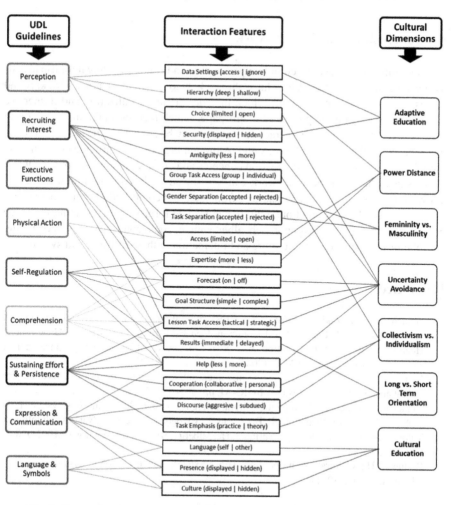

**Fig. 2.** Interaction features mapped to the UDL Guidelines and Cultural Dimensions

614     M. M. P. Talandron-Felipe

in the context of cultural adaptation. Each UDL guideline can be operationalized with multiple interaction concepts which may represent more than one cultural dimension. For example, in "Self-Regulation", its five interaction concepts from CAE are linked to three (3) cultural indices. Each interaction concept has at least two (2) options which could be adapted to the learner's preference based on the approximated value of the cultural dimension index. For 'Goal Structure', if the UAI is high, a simple and concise path towards the goal could be used while for low UAI, a more complex structure may be more effective. The previous application of the CAE framework was done by creating a country stereotype using the nation's cultural index values. It was effective when the learner's index values match that of the country but there were instances when this was not the case which may have caused a negative impact on the learning experience. Measuring individual learner's cultural dimension indices would allow for a more personalized adaptation rather than using country or group-based stereotypes because as we have learned from literature, cultures may also vary within a nation and sub-cultures may have even formed within a culture.

## 6   Conclusion and Future Work

The literature emphasized the complexity of culture and contextualizing it for use in pedagogy. Over the years, researchers have studied how to integrate a learner's background in designing instructional systems which includes content localization and immersive environments. The output presented in this paper which focuses on the interaction is at most a concept on how these interaction features may be adapted to the learner's preferences based on their cultural background. Although literature has provided evidence on the relationship between the interaction concepts and cultural dimensions on a country-based study, the proposed framework can be utilized to develop a cultural model by applying unsupervised machine learning from a dataset composed of individual preferences. As it has been pointed out, culture can also be formed by aggregating the value priorities of individuals. This approach, albeit simple, could contribute in understanding the relationship between one's culture and interaction with an instructional system.

## References

1. Blanchard, E., Razaki, R., Frasson, C.: Cross-cultural adaptation of e-learning contents: a methodology. In: E-Learn: World Conference on E-Learning in Corporate, Government, Healthcare, and Higher Education, pp. 1895–1902. Association for the Advancement of Computing in Education (AACE) (2005)
2. Blanchard, E.G., Frasson, C.: Making intelligent tutoring systems culturally aware: the use of Hofstede's cultural dimensions. In: IC-AI, pp. 644–649 (2005)
3. Blanchard, E.G., Ogan, A.: Infusing cultural awareness into intelligent tutoring systems for a globalized world. In: Nkambou, R., Bourdeau, J., Mizoguchi, R. (eds.) Advances in Intelligent Tutoring Systems, pp. 485–505. Springer, Heidelberg (2010). https://doi.org/10.1007/978-3-642-14363-2_24
4. Bodley, J.H.: Cultural Anthropology: Tribes, States, and the Global System. Rowman Altamira, Lanham (2011)

5. CAST: Universal Design for Learning Guidelines (Version 2.2). https://udlguidelines.cast. org/
6. Cheng, A., Yang, L., Andersen, E.: Teaching language and culture with a virtual reality game. In: Proceedings of the 2017 CHI Conference on Human Factors in Computing Systems, pp. 541–549 (2017)
7. Chita-Tegmark, M., Gravel, J.W., Maria De Lourdes, B.S., Domings, Y., Rose, D.H.: Using the universal design for learning framework to support culturally diverse learners. J. Educ. **192**(1), 17–22 (2012)
8. DiMaggio, P.: Culture and cognition. Ann. Rev. Sociol. **23**(1), 263–287 (1997)
9. Hofstede, G.: Dimensionalizing cultures: the Hofstede model in context. Online Read. Psychol. Culture **2**(1), 2307–2919 (2011)
10. Hofstede, G.: National cultures in four dimensions: a research based theory of cultural differences among nations. Int. Stud. Manag. Organ. **13**(1–2), 46–74 (1983)
11. Hofstede, G.H., Hofstede, G.J., Minkov, M.: Cultures and Organizations: Software of the Mind. Mcgraw-Hill, New York (2005)
12. Holthaus, M., Hirt, F., Bergamin, P.: Simple and Effective: An Adaptive Instructional Design for Mathematics Implemented in a Standard Learning Management System (2018)
13. Howard, T.C.: Why Race and Culture Matter in Schools: Closing the Achievement Gap in America's Classrooms. Teachers College Press, New York (2019)
14. Imhof, C., Bergamin, P., Moser, I., Holthaus, M.: Implementation of an Adaptive Instructional Design for a Physics Module in a Learning Management System. International Association for Development of the Information Society (2018)
15. Islam, N., Beer, M., Slack, F.: E-learning challenges faced by academics in higher education. J. Educ. Train. Stud. **3**(5), 102–112 (2015)
16. Marcus, A., Gould, E.W.: Crosscurrents: cultural dimensions and global web user-interface design. Interactions **7**(4), 32–46 (2000)
17. Markus, H.R., Kitayama, S.: A collective fear of the collective: implications for selves and theories of selves. Pers. Soc. Psychol. Bull. **20**(5), 568–579 (1994)
18. Mohammed, P., Mohan, P.: Dynamic cultural contextualisation of educational content in intelligent learning environments using ICON. Int. J. Artif. Intell. Educ. **25**(2), 249–270 (2014). https://doi.org/10.1007/s40593-014-0033-9
19. Reinecke, K., Bernstein, A., Schenkel, S.: Modeling a user's culture. In: Handbook of Research on Culturally-Aware Information Technology: Perspectives and Models, pp. 242–264. IGI Global (2011)
20. Sahlins, M.: On the anthropology of modernity, or, some triumphs of culture over despondency theory. In: Culture and Sustainable Development in the Pacific, pp. 44–61 (2000)
21. Schwartz, S.H.: A theory of cultural values and some implications for work. Appl. Psychol. Int. Rev. **48**(1), 23–47 (1999)
22. Sharifian, F.: On cultural conceptualisations. J. Cogn. Cult. **3**(3), 187–207 (2003)
23. Stewart, C.: A cultural education model: design and implementation of adaptive multimedia interfaces in eLearning. University of Nottingham (2012)
24. Tomasello, M.: The Cultural Origins of Human Cognition. Harvard University Press, Cambridge (2009)
25. Williams, R.M.: American Society: A Sociological Interpretation. Knopf, New York (1970)
26. Woolf, B.P.: A roadmap for education technology (2010)
27. Zhao, Q.: A survey on virtual reality. Sci. China Series F Inf. Sci. **52**(3), 348–400 (2009)

# Applying Adaptive Intelligent Tutoring Techniques to Physical Fitness Training Programs

Jessica Voge[1(✉)], Alex Negri[1], Paul Woodall[1], Derek Thayer[1], Brent Ruby[2],
Walter Hailes[2], Andrew Reinert[3], James Niehaus[1], and Spencer Lynn[1(✉)]

[1] Charles River Analytics, Cambridge, MA 02138, USA
{jvoge,slynn}@cra.com
[2] Montana Center for Work Physiology and Exercise Metabolism, University of Montana,
Missoula, MT 59812, USA
[3] University of Montana, Missoula, MT 59812, USA

**Abstract.** Adaptive Training Protocols (ATP) is a collection of algorithms and software to apply principals of intelligent tutoring to physical fitness training. To obtain norming data for ATP, we examined exercise performance from 34 participants under an adaptive workout regimen lasting 13 weeks. The goal of the regimen was to train to pass the performance criteria of the US Marine Corps Initial Strength Test (IST; a 1.5-mile run, sits-ups, pull-ups, and push-ups). The weekly regimen comprised an IST, an interval workout, and a maximum workout. Adaptation was accomplished via two algorithms: maximum-day reps were double those accomplished on the prior IST and maximum-day and interval-day runs were performed at specified rates of perceived exertion. Starting capabilities for run, sit-ups, and push-ups negatively correlated with progression rates; participants who exhibited lower performance at the start of the study made steeper gains in performance. Individual logistic curve fitting found decelerating, inflecting, and accelerating progression profiles. Participants showed considerable variation in their profiles both across individuals in each exercise and within individuals across exercises. Progression profiles can be used to forecast the performance that a person can attain in a given timeframe under a given training regimen. This knowledge can be used to adapt the workout to provide more time to reach a goal if needed or to focus on exercises that are in jeopardy of not achieving the goal in time. ATP will help the Marine Corps plan for when intended recruits may be physically ready to ship out to boot camp.

**Keywords:** Adaptive training · Physical fitness progression · Exercise

## 1 Introduction

Physical fitness is a core element of Marine Corps force readiness "toward an end state of a healthy and fit force able to better answer the call in any clime and place" [1]. The Marine Corps has high physical and combat fitness standards, and it invests

© Springer Nature Switzerland AG 2021
R. A. Sottilare and J. Schwarz (Eds.): HCII 2021, LNCS 12792, pp. 616–630, 2021.
https://doi.org/10.1007/978-3-030-77857-6_44

significant time and effort developing and maintaining physical training programs, such as the Marine Corps Martial Arts Program (MCMAP) and the Force Fitness Instructor (FFI) program; workout routines, such as High Intensity Tactical Training (HITT); and facilities. A 2007 study of risk factors associated with discharge from the Marine Corps during basic training found that self-rated poor physical fitness and stress fractures during training were significant predictors of discharge [2]. Other studies have confirmed this finding and indicate that the initial physical fitness of Marine recruits is a strong predictor of musculoskeletal injuries (MSIs) and attrition during basic military training (BMT) [3–16]. Reis et al. [2] observed that 10.4% of 2,137 male participants were discharged from the Marine Corps during their observation period, with more than half (53.4%) of those discharges occurring due to medical reasons such as stress fractures. Attrition rates are particularly high among low-fitness recruits [17] (i.e., recruits who score in the bottom third of physical fitness tests). However, attrition rates can be as high as 30% in some service branches [18].

Pre-conditioning and physical fitness training programs completed prior to BMT, such as the Navy Physical Training Zero Program, Army Fitness Assessment Program, and Army Physical Fitness Enhancement Program, among other similar programs [19], have been demonstrated to lower the risk of attrition and in some cases even the risk of MSIs [7, 10, 18–23]. Knapik et al. [18] found that the Army Physical Fitness Enhancement Program could reduce attrition rates from 25% to 8% for male recruits and from 29% to 19% for female recruits. However, due to logistical necessities, these pre-conditioning fitness programs and current Marine physical training are often applied with a one-size-fits all approach: A 195 cm, 100 kg male Marine seeking to improve his running times may be given the same training routine as a 165 cm, 55 kg female Marine seeking to increase her flexed arm hang score. The current training does not change as a function of the Marine's specific physical fitness goals, nor is it tailored to an individual as they progress toward that goal, meeting and overcoming hurdles along the way. Further, adaptations to workouts in these programs often rely on the recruit to manually adapt sets and reptations of exercises either on paper or in smartphone apps that have been developed for creating and reviewing workout plans and logging progress, leaving the burden of adapting workouts on recruits who may adapt either too aggressively or slowly to meet their fitness goals prior to starting BMT. While the evidence shows that such pre-conditioning training can substantially reduce the rate of attrition and injury during BMT, a substantial number of recruits still attrite and sustain injuries. A physical training program tailored to the needs of individuals may further reduce the risk of attrition and injury.

To provide a tailored approach, we developed Adaptive Training Protocols (ATP), a collection of algorithms and associated software that applies principals of intelligent tutoring to physical fitness training. Intelligent tutoring systems and adaptive training techniques have been applied in a variety of military contexts, including team training and land navigation [24, 25]; however, the application of these techniques to physical fitness has been largely unaddressed. Like intelligent tutoring, the ATP approach is structured by two adaptation loops (Fig. 1). An inner, or within-session, loop provides feedback during each of three weekly workouts. It monitors real-time progress against the goals of the workout and intervenes with feedback. The feedback presents goals and progress, motivates the participant, and cautions against risk of injury. Inner loop adaptation is based on heart rate (HR) from a chest-worn electrocardiogram (ECG) monitor, the rate of perceived exertion (RPE) [26], and current performance is captured in a mobile app. This feedback indicates the effort to maintain by setting HR zone and RPE goals. An outer, between-session, adaptation loop sets the volume and intensity of subsequent workouts. Performance on a workout is used post-workout to initiate or reinforce behavior change. Outer loop adaptation is based on the results from the current workout, self-report elements of post-workout impressions such as between-workout soreness and fatigue, and compliance with the workout schedule.

**Fig. 1.** ATP inner and outer adaptation loops of the intelligent tutoring approach to training

Our initial ATP use case is for Marine Corps Poolees, individuals who have signed up to become Marines but have not begun recruit training at boot camp. Poolees may not have an adequate training program to prepare them for boot camp. Therefore, we created a training regimen aimed at enabling Poolees to pass the Marine Corps Initial Strength Test (IST), a criterion for becoming a Marine Corps recruit. To parameterize the physical fitness progression curves used by the ATP algorithms to adapt inner and outer loop feedback, we conducted a pilot physical fitness study. The goals of the study were to test our automated, ideographically adaptive algorithms for physical fitness progression in the context of our IST regimen, investigate differences in the shape of progression curves across different exercises and within and among participants, and derive a normed sample of progression data for refined adaption algorithms for future fitness training development. Over thirteen weeks, participants engaged in a three-days-per week workout regimen involving four exercises: run, sit-ups, pull-ups, and push-ups.

We hypothesized that individuals who performed better on a given exercise would progress more slowly on that exercise because they are nearer their maximum capacity in the context of a given exercise, workout schedule, physiological state, and psychological motivation. Based on this hypothesis, we made two predictions: (1) across participants, progression slope would negatively correlate with starting performance and (2) individual participants would exhibit a decelerating progression curve (i.e., performance would increase rapidly in early weeks and level off in later weeks). We fit individuals' observed exercise performance data with a four-parameter sigmoid function to capture variability in progression, including stable, accelerating, inflecting, and decelerating progression profiles.

## 2   Methods

### 2.1   Participants and Attrition

Thirty-eight university students (largely undergraduates) participated in the thirteen-week study. Participants gave informed consent according to an Institutional Review Board-approved protocol and were compensated with $200 if they completed 30 of 36 scheduled workout sessions. We excluded four participants from all analyses because they dropped out of the study in the second week. The final sample comprised 34 participants (21 female and 13 male).

We planned to collect physical fitness test data each week, totaling 442 data points for each of four exercises; however, data were missing for several reasons. Three participants started the study late (two in week 2 and one in week 3). One participant began wearing an arm cast after week 7; we excluded subsequent data from this participant from all analyses. The week-8 run was canceled due to cold weather. The week-12 test day fell during a holiday and so was not conducted. Final data were obtained over 11 run tests, and 12 sit-ups, pull-ups, and push-ups tests. Combined with attrition (Fig. 2) and occasional absences, 40% and 34.6% of data points were missing for run and calisthenic data, respectively.

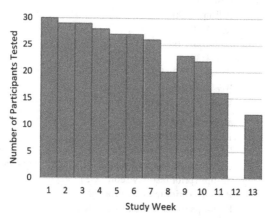

**Fig. 2.** Participant attrition. Tests were canceled on week 12.

## 2.2 Physical Training Regimen

The 13-week physical training program consisted of three weekly workouts, based on [27] (Table 1). On Wednesdays, participants completed a test-day workout, modeled on the IST, which consisted of time to complete a 1.5-mile run, number sit-ups in two minutes, number pull-ups without dropping from the pull-up bar, and number push-ups while continuously supporting body above the deck with hands and feet. On Fridays, participants completed an interval-day workout, which consisted of interval runs and 2–6 sets of a calisthenic circuit of sit-ups, pull-ups, and push-ups (two sets in weeks 1–4,

**Table 1.** ATP training regimen

| Day | Workout |
|---|---|
| Wednesdays "test" | *Initial strength test*<br>1.5-mile run<br>Sit-ups, 2 min<br>Pull-ups<br>Push-ups |
| Fridays "intervals" | *Interval runs*<br>4 min warmup (RPE[‡] 11)<br>2 min (RPE 17–18)<br>2 min (RPE 10–12)<br>2 min (RPE 17–18)<br>2 min (RPE 10–12)<br>2 min (RPE 17–18)<br>3 min (RPE 10–12)<br>*Calisthenics Circuit, as many reps as possible in the time limit*<br>Sit-ups 1:00<br>Rest 1:30<br>Pull-ups 0:30<br>Rest 1:30<br>Push-ups 1:00<br>Rest 1:30<br>*Weeks 1–4: 2 sets*<br>*Weeks 5–8: 4 sets*<br>*Weeks 9–13: 6 sets* |
| Mondays "maximum" | *Moderate run*<br>17 min run (RPE 15)<br>Rest 5 min<br>*Calisthenics, reach target number in any configuration of sets*<br>Sit-ups (prior test-day score × 2)<br>Pull-ups (prior test-day score × 2)<br>Push-ups (prior test-day score × 2) |

[‡] RPE is rate of perceived exertion [26]. On Borg's 20-point RPE scale, 11 is characterized as "Light effort: minimal sweating, can talk easily," 15 as "Hard effort: Sweating, able to push and still maintain proper form," and 17 as "Very hard effort: Can keep a fast pace for a short time period."

four sets in weeks 5–8, and 6 sets in weeks 9–13). On Mondays, participants completed a maximum-day workout, which consisted of a 17 min run and twice as many sit-ups, pull-ups, and push-ups as they completed on their most recent test day workout. Run performance on test days was recorded as time (in seconds) to complete the 1.5-mile distance. Sit-ups, pull-ups, and push-ups performance was recorded as counts.

The workout regimen had two ideographically adaptive elements. In the outer adaptation loop, the maximum-day calisthenic repetitions were double those completed on the prior test day. In the inner adaptation loop, the maximum-day and interval-day runs were performed at specified RPE. Exercise at a given RPE translates to increased work as cardiovascular fitness increases over time, thus adapting the objective intensity of the workout to the increased level of fitness.

## 2.3 Data Analysis

To examine the correlation of starting ability with progression while accounting for missing data, we analyzed the data with a linear mixed-effects model. We ran the model with the lme4 package [28] (version 1.1–26) for the R 4.0.3 statistical computing environment [29]. The random effects were y-intercept (results from the first test day) and linear slope (change in performance over subsequent test days). Prior to analysis, we z-scored the participant data within each exercise, so that variability among intercepts, slopes, and their correlation could be directly compared among the four exercises (i.e., in units of standard deviation rather than counts or duration). Z-scores were computed using composite standard deviations [30]. Run z-scores were inverted (negative to positive and positive to negative values) so that increasing scores corresponded to better performance, to match the directionality of the other exercises. Data missing for all participants (week-8 run, week-12 all exercises) were removed. Data for the three late-starting participants were time-shifted to align start dates with the rest of the sample.

To characterize the shape of individual participants' fitness progression curves for each exercise, we fit a four-parameter logistic function to each participant for each exercise (Eq. 1), where $a$ is the logistic growth rate (i.e., sigmoid slope parameter), $b$ is the position of the sigmoid inflection point on the abscissa, $c$ is the lower asymptote on the ordinate, and $d$ is the difference from the upper to the lower asymptote on the ordinate.

$$y = c + d/(1 + \text{EXP}(-a(x - b))) \tag{1}$$

Prior to curve fitting z-scored data, we filled a participant's missing data with the mean of the immediately neighboring weeks (i.e., effectively assuming a linear progression model over short time periods) and we time-shifted data of the three late-starting participants to align start dates with the rest of the sample. We conducted the sigmoid fitting with the curve_fit function from the SciPy 1.5.2 package for Python 3.81.

# 3 Results

## 3.1 Passing the Initial Strength Test

At the start of the 13-week training program, 26.5% of participants met the Marine Corps IST criteria for all four exercises, and by the end, 67.6% (n = 23) met the IST criteria.

Fewer people met criteria for sit-ups at their first IST than for other exercises, but the run was the most difficult exercise on which to reach criterion for those who started the study below criterion (Table 2, Fig. 3).

**Table 2.** Percentage of sample meeting IST criteria

| Exercise | Criteria | | % Passing 1st IST | | % Passing last IST | |
|---|---|---|---|---|---|---|
| | Male | Female | Male | Female | Male | Female |
| Run 1.5 mi (sec) | 810 | 900 | 46% | 81% | 62% | 86% |
| Sit-ups (in 2 min) | 44 | 44 | 46% | 48% | 85% | 100% |
| Pull-ups | 3 | 1 | 77% | 62% | 92% | 95% |
| Push-ups | 34 | 15 | 54% | 95% | 85% | 100% |

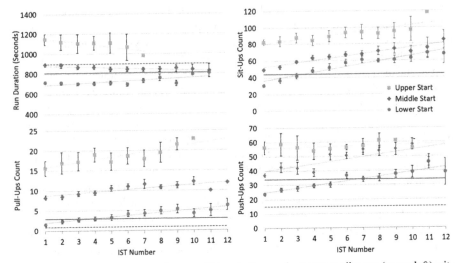

**Fig. 3.** Mean performance at each test, split by starting performance tertile: run (upper left), sit-ups (upper right), pull-ups (lower left), push-ups (lower right). Errors bars indicate ± 1 SE. Least squares lines of best fit are shown. Horizontal red lines indicate performance criteria required to pass the IST (dashed for females where different than for males).

Figure 3 shows mean performance at each test for the four exercises. To visualize a summary of performance over time, in Fig. 3 we separated participants into three groups according to whether starting performance fell in the upper, middle, or lower tertile of overall week 1 scores, by exercise. Standard error bars increase over time due to participant attrition. Lines of best fit suggest differences in rate of progression over time, among performance tertiles, and among exercises. We quantified the relationships suggested in this exploratory visualization with linear mixed-effects statistical analysis.

## 3.2 Statistical Analysis

As predicted, starting performance negatively correlated with progression slope. Participants who started the study at lower performance progressed more rapidly than participants who started the study with higher performance. The linear mixed-effects model showed support for a linear relationship between exercise ability at IST 1 and rate of fitness progression (Table 3). The results also suggested that the relationship differs across exercises: a strong negative correlation for runs, moderate negative correlation for sit-ups and push-ups, and little to no linear relationship for pull-ups. The z-score ranges in Table 3 show that run had the lowest average change in performance across the 13 week study period (0.50 SD), indicating the difficulty participants experienced, as a group, increasing their performance from baseline relative to the other exercises.

**Table 3.** Random effects correlations between performance on the first IST (y-intercept) and linear rate of progression (slope)

| Exercise | Correlation | Z-Score range[‡] |
|---|---|---|
| Run | −0.69 | 0.50 |
| Sit-ups | −0.31 | 1.52 |
| Pull-ups | 0.01 | 0.77 |
| Push-ups | −0.36 | 1.39 |

[‡] Range, across IST 1–13, of mean z-scores computed over participants at each IST.

The patterns shown in Fig. 3 help to interpret the differences in the correlations among the exercises. Pull-ups may have a low linear correlation coefficient either because participants progressed at about the same rate regardless of their initial capability or because the variability of progression in higher performing individuals attenuated discriminability of progression rates among the overall sample. Run appears to have a high correlation coefficient because the relationship between starting ability and progression is fit well by a straight line, suggested by the distinct tertile progression slopes. Sit-ups and push-ups may have moderate correlation coefficients not due to a lack of association (as in pull-ups) but because the association is poorly described by a straight line.

The linear model applied here to analyze the association between starting ability and progression is a useful start, but ultimately unrealistic: physical fitness cannot increase linearly indefinitely due to biological constraints. The negative correlations we found at the sample level indicate that, on average, individual participants should exhibit decelerating progression curves: they should progress rapidly early in the study and the rate of progression should slow as their ability to perform a particular exercise increases. We characterized the non-linearity of individuals' progression with sigmoid curve fitting.

### 3.3  Curve Fitting

As predicted, individual participants exhibited decelerating progression curves. The purpose of the curve fitting was to investigate variability in individual progression curves to characterize differences in fitness progression across different exercises and within and among participants. Prior to characterizing differences, we visually inspected the fits to address cases of overfitting that can arise from use of highly parameterized functions, such as the four-parameter logistic function applied here.

**Artifact Rejection.** For a number of participants, the sigmoid fit placed a reasonable looking inflection point within the 13-week study duration (e.g., Fig. 4, left panel). These participants appeared to exhibit a change from accelerating to decelerating progression partway through the study. However, plotting the $y$-axis to reflect the overall range of the entire sample for a particular exercise suggested that for some of these participants an inflection point within the progression period could be an artifact of over-fitting. Constraining the inflection point to occur prior to the first observation ($b < 1$) produced a more reasonable looking progression curve when viewed within the range of performance exhibited by the sample (Fig. 4, right panel).

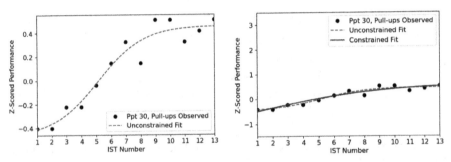

**Fig. 4.** While the inflection point present in unconstrained fits can look reasonable (left), when viewed at a scale reflecting the range exhibited by all participants, the inflection point appears unlikely to be meaningful and progression may be more accurately characterized by constraining it the inflection to be outside the period of study (right). Ppt = participant.

Highly variable progressions were also susceptible to overfitting (e.g., Fig. 5). Understanding progression patterns of such participants also benefitted from constraining the inflection point to occur prior to the first observation.

**Progression Profiles.** From visual inspection, we identified initially overfit progression curves. After refitting under constraint, we found three categories of progression exhibited by participants in the study: accelerating, inflecting, and decelerating. Progression pattern was not strongly associated with particular exercises or starting ability.

Different participants responded differently, and the pattern of progression was not a factor of starting fitness. For example, Fig. 6 shows three participants who all started approximately 1 SD below the mean number of pull-ups and progressed in different ways: decelerating, inflecting, and accelerating.

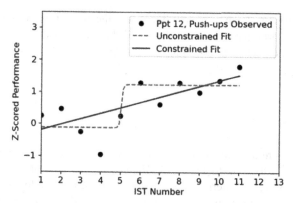

**Fig. 5.** Sigmoid overfitting can manifest as step-like inflections associated with noisy observations.

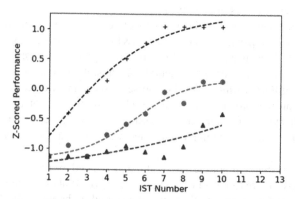

**Fig. 6.** Pull-ups progression curves for three participants who had similar starting ability and exhibited three different progression patterns: + decelerating (participant 34), ● inflecting (participant 31), ▲ accelerating (participant 22).

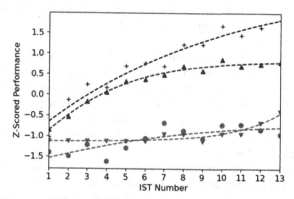

**Fig. 7.** Progression curves for each exercise from a single individual (participant 23): + push-ups, ▲ sit-ups, ▼ pull-ups, ● run). The fit for run was constrained.

The same participant can respond differently to the different exercises. For example, Fig. 7 shows that participant 23 started about 1 SD below the mean for all four exercises. However, the participant progressed much more rapidly on push-ups and sit-ups than on pull-ups and run.

## 4  Discussion

We examined progression of exercise performance under an ideographically adaptive workout regimen lasting up to 13 weeks. The operational goal of the regimen was to train to pass performance criteria on four specific exercises: 1.5-mile run, sits-ups in two minutes, pull-ups, and push-ups. Adaptation was accomplished by two simple algorithms that did not themselves change over the course of the study: maximum-day reps were double those of the prior test day, and timed maximum-day and interval-day runs were performed at specified rates of perceived exertion.

We found that starting capabilities negatively correlated with progression rates in three of four exercises; participants who were less fit made the steepest gains. This decelerating response is consistent with research on the neuromuscular response to exercise (e.g., [31]), which is a function of two neural and physiological processes that dominate the response at different times over the course of days and weeks [32]. A rapid and early recruitment of motor learning, the neural plasticity associated with motor skill acquisition [33], characterizes initial progression. A slower process of muscular hypertrophy, the increase in muscle mass associated with exercise [34], characterizes later progression.

Our data show that is it not the case that inexperienced exercisers make rapid gains because they have "more room" in which to show gains by dint of starting lower. Figure 3 shows that, except for sit-ups, participants who started in the lower third of the performance range for an exercise rarely achieved even the early performance of participants who started at higher levels. Instead, we hypothesize that inexperienced exercisers make relatively more rapid gains because their inexperience affords the opportunity for greater amount of motor learning. In contrast, experienced exercisers may undergo less motor learning, leaving their progression rates to be dominated by the slower process of muscular hypertrophy.

Despite more rapid gains, the 1.5-mile run was the hardest activity on which to reach IST performance criterion those participants who were not already performing well at the first test. Pragmatically, we recommend that future participants use a GPS device for run training if possible. With GPS, participants would be able to pace themselves better and track their overall distance to improve run times. While it may be beneficial to run more frequently (e.g., 4 times per week), risk of shin-splints and lower leg injuries may increase among novice runners.

We found considerable variation in individual patterns of progression both across individuals in each exercise and within individuals across exercises. This variability may arise because different exercises elicit differential molecular and physiological responses, in part because of differential engagement of concentric and eccentric muscle functional modalities [35, 36]. Molecular and physiological mechanisms provide abundant opportunity for individual differences in experience and genetics to influence response to exercise within and among individual participants [37].

The present research had limitations, including: (1) As a pilot study, the sample comprised university students, not Poolees. Therefore, the proportions of participants going on to pass or fail the IST and the proportions of participants exhibiting particular categories of progression profile may not generalize well to a Poolee sample. We anticipate a Poolee study in the future. (2) Attrition likely biased percentages of the sample exhibiting different categories of progression profile and IST pass/fail rates. These measures may be biased by attrition because shorter duration of participation offers less opportunity to progress. (3) Due to attrition, group-level summaries about correlations, progression rates, and curve shapes are biased towards those participants who were motivated to remain in the study. However, our overall results, that progression rate is a function of starting ability and that progression profiles are variable within and among participants, are evident in the curve fitting analysis, which is based on analysis of individuals, not the average over the sample.

This study differs from many other exercise studies because our outcome measure was performance on specific exercises rather than physiological changes in response to exercise. The variation in performance progression we observed was captured by the flexibility of a four-parameter logistic function. The generalized logistic function is widely used to model exponential growth in the context of (eventually) limited resources. We hypothesize that the parameter values that control the shape of the curve are a function of many factors, including differences in exercise or workout regime, the structure and function of particular muscles, and individual differences in physiology, diet, and sleep. Therefore, variation of observations about the curve is not only sampling "noise" per se, but also contains unpartitioned signal variance arising from these factors.

With respect to future directions in adaptive training of physical fitness, our results demonstrate that progression profiles can be used to forecast the performance a person can attain in a given amount of time under a given training regimen. This knowledge can then be used to adapt the workout to provide more time if needed or to focus on exercises that are in jeopardy of not achieving the goal in time. Adaptive algorithms can be designed to modify training based on where a person is on their progression. For example, for someone experiencing a shallow progression profile, training might be adapted to attain an accelerating progression profile by (1) changing the specific motor movements to induce motor learning by isolating or engaging different muscles that are part of the targeted muscle group, or (2) adjusting resistance or modifying the workout schedule to induce increased muscle hypertrophy.

A dynamic, individualized approach to physical fitness adaptative training will require insight into the factors that affect fitness progression in both the inner and outer adaptation loops (Fig. 1). Future areas for research include: (1) understanding individual difference factors that affect the progression profile, which may include, e.g., overall fitness, physiology, motivation, etc. and be influenced by the specific workout regimen; and (2) understanding how changes in exercise can "reset" progression profile parameters, moving the exerciser to a different curve, accelerating training.

Understanding individual variability in progression curves will enable ATP to provide feedback about whether attaining a physical fitness goal (e.g., achieving IST criterion) is attainable in a particular timeframe given the selected workout plan or whether another workout plan or timeframe would be necessary to meet the goal. For our Marine Corps use case, ATP will help Marine Corps Recruiting Command and recruiters plan for when a Poolee may be physically ready to ship out to boot camp. We are developing a mobile application to adaptively guide exercisers through workouts and to use workout results to predict when the exercisers will meet their fitness goals. In forthcoming research with Poolee participants, we will use results of the present study to forecast progression as test-day results accumulate week-to-week and to develop outer loop adaptation algorithms based on individual progression curve shape. The Poolee study will also provide data on additional individual differences, such as age, height, and body weight, which we will combine with gender to refine profile forecasting.

**Acknowledgements.** This material is based upon work supported by the United States Navy Office of Naval Research (ONR) under Contract No. N00014–19-C-2028. Submitted to ONR for Public Release, DCN#43–7669-21. Any opinions, findings and conclusions or recommendations expressed in this material are those of the authors and do not necessarily reflect the views of the US Navy or ONR. We are grateful to Dr. Allie Duffie for discussion of muscle memory and hypertrophy. We are grateful to Peter Squire, Natalie Steinhauser, and Mark White for support and feedback during this research.

# References

1. Neller, R.B.: Changes to the physical fitness test (PFT), combat fitness test (CFT), and body composition program (BCP). ALMAR Announcement R 011230Z JUL 16, ALMAR 022/16 (2016). https://www.fitness.marines.mil/almar/
2. Reis, J.P., Trone, D.W., Macera, C.A., Rauh, M.J.: Factors associated with discharge during marine corps basic training. Mil. Med. **172**(9), 936–941 (2007)
3. Allison, S.C., Cohen, B.S., Zambraski, E.J., Jaffrey, M., Orr, R.: Predictive models to estimate probabilities of injuries, poor physical fitness, and attrition outcomes in Australian Defense force army recruit training. US Army Research Institute of Environmental Medicine, Natick, MA (2015)
4. Allison, S.C., Knapik, J.J., Sharp, M.A.: Preliminary derivation of test item clusters for predicting injuries, poor physical performance, and overall attrition in basic combat training. US Army Research Institute of Environmental Medicine, Natick, MA (2006)
5. Bedno, S.A., Cowan, D.N., Urban, N., Niebuhr, D.W.: Effect of pre-accession physical fitness on training injuries among US Army recruits. Work **44**(4), 509–515 (2013)
6. Canham-Chervak, M., Hauret, K., Hoedebecke, E., Laurin, M.J., Cuthie, J.: Discharges during US Army basic training: injury rates and risk factors. Mil. Med. **166**(7), 641–647 (2001)
7. Dijksma, I., Zimmermann, W.O., Bovens, D., Lucas, C., Stuiver, M.M.: Despite an improved aerobic endurance, still high attrition rates in initially low-fit recruits—results of a randomised controlled trial. Contemp. Clin. Trials Commun. **20**, 100679 (2020)
8. Jones, B.H., Knapik, J.J.: Physical training and exercise-related injuries. Sports Med. **27**(2), 111–125 (1999)
9. Knapik, J.J., Sharp, M.A., Canham, M.L., Hauret, K., Cuthie, J.: Injury incidence and injury risk factors among us army basic trainees at Ft. Jackson SC, 1998 (including fitness training unit personnel, discharges, and newstarts). US Army Center for Health and Promotion and Preventitive Medicine, Aberdeen Proving Ground, MD (1999)

10. Knapik, J.J., Jones, B.H., Hauret, K., Darakjy, S., Piskator, E.: A review of the literature on attrition from the military services: risk factors for attrition and strategies to reduce attrition. US Army Center for Health Promotion and Preventive Medicine, Aberdeen Proving Ground, MD (2004)

11. Niebuhr, D.W., et al.: Assessment of recruit motivation and strength study: preaccession physical fitness assessment predicts early attrition. Mil. Med. **173**(6), 555–562 (2008)

12. O'Neil, P., Hamilton, B.A., Miller, M.: USAF spatial disorientation prevention: a meta-analytical human systems integration perspective. In 19th International Symposium on Aviation Psychology, p. 491 (2017)

13. Orr, R.M., Cohen, B.S., Allison, S.C., Bulathsinhala, L., Zambraski, E.J., Jaffrey, M.: Models to predict injury, physical fitness failure and attrition in recruit training: a retrospective cohort study. Mil. Med. Res. **7**(1), 1 (2020). https://doi.org/10.1186/s40779-020-00260-w

14. Pope, R.P., Herbert, R., Kirwan, J.D., Graham, B.J.: Predicting attrition in basic military training. Mil. Med. **164**(10), 710–714 (1999)

15. Rieger, W.R., Scott, S.J.: Physical fitness in initial entry training. Recruit Med. 111–124 (2006)

16. Swedler, D.I., Knapik, J.J., Williams, K.W., Grier, T.L., Jones, B.H.: Risk factors for medical discharge from United States Army basic combat training. Mil. Med. **176**(10), 1104–1110 (2011)

17. CNA Analysis and Solutions. Assessing how delayed entry program physical fitness is related to in-service attrition, injuries, and physical fitness. CNA Analysis and Solutions, (2014). https://dod.defense.gov

18. Knapik, J.J., Darakjy, S., Hauret, K.G., Jones, B.H., Sharp, M.A.: Evaluation of a program to identify and pre-condition trainees with low physical fitness: attrition and cost analysis. US Army Center for Health and Promotion and Preventitive Medicine, Aberdeen Proving Ground, MD (2004)

19. Kubisiak, U.C., et al.: Review of interventions for reducing enlisted attrition in the US military: an update. US Army Research Institute for the Behavioral and Social Sciences, Arlington, VA (2009)

20. Chai, L.Y., Ong, K.C., Kee, A., Earnest, A., Lim, F.C., Wong, J.C.: A prospective cohort study on the impact of a modified basic military training (mBMT) programme based on pre-enlistment fitness stratification amongst Asian military enlistees. Ann. Acad. Med. Singap. **38**(10), 862 (2009)

21. Knapik, J.J., et al.: Increasing the physical fitness of low-fit recruits before basic combat training: an evaluation of fitness, injuries, and training outcomes. Mil. Med. **171**(1), 45–54 (2006)

22. Knapik, J.J., Darakjy, S., Scott, S., Hauret, K.G.: Evaluation of two Army fitness programs: The TRADOC standardized physical training program for basic combat training and the fitness assessment program. US Army Center for Health and Promotion and Preventitive Medicine, Aberdeen Proving Ground, MD (2004)

23. Lee, L., Kumar, S., Kok, W.L., Lim, C.L.: Effects of a pre-training conditioning programme on basic military training attrition rates. Ann. Acad. Med. Singap. **26**(1), 3–7 (1997)

24. Freeman, J., Zachary, W.: Intelligent tutoring for team training: lessons learned from US military research. Emerald Publishing Limited, In Building Intelligent Tutoring Systems for Teams (2018)

25. Spain, R.D., Priest, H.A., Murphy, J.S.: Current trends in adaptive training with military applications: an introduction. Mil. Psychol. **24**(2), 87–95 (2012)

26. Borg, G.A.: Physical performance and perceived exertion. University of Lund (1962)

27. Cuddy, J.S., Slivka, D.R., Hailes, W.S., Ruby, B.C.: Factors of trainability and predictability associated with military physical fitness test success. J. Strength Conditioning Res. **25**(12), 3486–3494 (2011)

28. Bates, D., Mächler, M., Bolker, B., Walker, S.: Fitting linear mixed-effects models using lme4. arXiv:1406.5823 [Stat] (2014). http://arxiv.org/abs/1406.5823

29. R Core Team. R: The R project for statistical computing. https://www.r-project.org/ (2020). Accessed 27 Jan 2021

30. Burton, D.A.: How to calculate composite standard deviations. http://www.burtonsys.com/climate/composite_standard_deviations.html (2016)

31. Seynnes, O.R., de Boer, M., Narici, M.V.: Early skeletal muscle hypertrophy and architectural changes in response to high-intensity resistance training. J. Appl. Physiol. **102**(1), 368–373 (2007)

32. Moritani, T.: Neural factors versus hypertrophy in the time course of muscle strength gain. Am. J. Phys. Med. **58**(3), 115–130 (1979)

33. Taubert, M., Villringer, A., Lehmann, N.: Endurance exercise as an "endogenous" neuro-enhancement strategy to facilitate motor learning. Front. Hum. Neurosci. **9**, 692 (2015)

34. Travis, S.K., Ishida, A., Taber, C.B., Fry, A.C., Stone, M.H.: Emphasizing task-specific hypertrophy to enhance sequential strength and power performance. J. Funct. Morphol. Kinesiol. **5**(4), 76 (2020)

35. Padulo, J., Laffaye, G., Ardigò, L.P., Chamari, K.: Concentric and eccentric: muscle contraction or exercise? J. Hum. Kinet. **37**(1), 5–6 (2013)

36. Franchi, M.V., et al.: Architectural, functional and molecular responses to concentric and eccentric loading in human skeletal muscle. Acta Physiol. **210**(3), 642–654 (2014)

37. Broderick, T.: Precision high intensity training through epigenetics (PHITE). Office of Naval Research Human Performance, Training, and Education Technical Review: Warrior Resilience. Orlando, Florida, USA (2020)

# Correction to: Teachers' Perspectives on the Adoption of an Adaptive Learning System Based on Multimodal Affect Recognition for Students with Learning Disabilities and Autism

Penny J. Standen⬛, David J. Brown⬛, Gosia M. Kwiatkowska⬛,
Matthew K. Belmonte⬛, Maria J. Galvez Trigo⬛, Helen Boulton⬛,
Andrew Burton⬛, Madeline J. Hallewell⬛, Nicholas Shopland⬛,
Maria A. Blanco Gonzalez⬛, Elena Milli⬛, Stefano Cobello⬛,
Annaleda Mazzucato⬛, and Marco Traversi⬛

Correction to:
Chapter "Teachers' Perspectives on the Adoption
of an Adaptive Learning System Based on Multimodal Affect
Recognition for Students with Learning Disabilities
and Autism" in: R. A. Sottilare and J. Schwarz (Eds.):
*Adaptive Instructional Systems,*
LNCS 12792, https://doi.org/10.1007/978-3-030-77857-6_31

The original version of this book was inadvertently published with some incomplete affiliations in chapter 31. This has now been corrected.

The updated version of this chapter can be found at
https://doi.org/10.1007/978-3-030-77857-6_31

© Springer Nature Switzerland AG 2021
R. A. Sottilare and J. Schwarz (Eds.): HCII 2021, LNCS 12792, p. C1, 2021.
https://doi.org/10.1007/978-3-030-77857-6_45

# Correction to: Personalized Mastery Learning Ecosystems: Using Bloom's Four Objects of Change to Drive Learning in Adaptive Instructional Systems

Anastasia Betts, Khanh-Phuong Thai, and Sunil Gunderia

**Correction to:**
**Chapter "Personalized Mastery Learning Ecosystems:**
**Using Bloom's Four Objects of Change to Drive Learning**
**in Adaptive Instructional Systems" in: R. A. Sottilare**
**and J. Schwarz (Eds.):** *Adaptive Instructional Systems*,
**LNCS 12792, https://doi.org/10.1007/978-3-030-77857-6_3**

Chapter "Personalized Mastery Learning Ecosystems: Using Bloom's Four Objects Change to Drive Learning in Adaptive Instructional Systems" was previously published non-open access. It has now been changed to open access under a CC BY license and the copyright holder updated to 'The Author(s)'. The book has also be updated with this change.

---

The updated original version of this chapter can be found at
https://doi.org/10.1007/978-3-030-77857-6_3

R. A. Sottilare and J. Schwarz (Eds.): HCII 2021, LNCS 12792, p. C2, 2022.
https://doi.org/10.1007/978-3-030-77857-6_46

# Author Index

Printed in the United States
by Baker & Taylor Publisher Services